# Bible/Torah, read it again for the first time

Hugh L. Johnson

## First Edition

*All rights Reserved, including the right of reproduction, in whole or part, in any form*

## *Copyright September 2001*

Frontpage Picture Is Titled:
***"The Lynching Of Jesus, a Good Friday For Who?"***

# Table of Contents
Pages 1 - 15
Contents Index - Pages 16 - 18

*Autobiography -19-22*
*051603*
*Book Scheme Pages*
*Pages 23 - 25*

**(Pg. 23) Why this book** — **(Pg. 24) This book for who** (Gentiles, Israelis (Judeans), Rabbis, Priest, Ministers, Continentals, Blacks) — **(Pgs. 24, 25) How I Have Reordered the Bible/Torah:** (Astronomically, Chronologically, Geographically, Genealogically)

**The Five Chapters**
**Pages 25 - 27**

**Keys (Pg 27)** (1) Asterisks, (2) Parenthesis, (3) Quotation Marks, (4) Italics, (5) Bold Emphasis

---

Chapter I

# History of the Bible/Torah
Part I
### Deceptions and Discrepancies
Pages 28-33

**(Pg.28) Deceptions:** (1) This Planet was **not** Created — (2) The Sun and Moon were **not** created — (3) Adam was **not** "Created" — (4) Cain and Abel are **not** the children of Adam — (5) Noah's Flood was **not** planetary" — (6) Planet was **not** nor did it need to be repopulated, by Noah's three sons **(Pg. 29)** — (7) Ham/Canaan did **not** "do something to Noah" (*Gen. 9:24*) — (8) Nimrod did **not** founded a Religion — (9) "Nameless people" of (*Gen. 11:4*) are **not** Noah's children — (10) The Sodomites in the land of Canaan, are **not** Canaan's children — **(Pg. 30)**(11) Ur is **not** in southern Mesopotamia — (12) There is **not** a "Hebrew" people or language — (13) Abram was **not** afraid of the Egyptians — (14) Lot was **not** "Honorable" — (15) Lot "**did know**" he was having sex with his daughters — **(Pg. 31)**(16) Hagar was **not** "proud" to have Abram's child — (17) Abraham is **not** the "father" of Isaac — (18) Isaac is **not** the "father" of Jacob (19) Jacob **did not** had twelve "sons" — (20) Dinah was **not** "Raped" — **(Pg. 32)**(21) The Israelis said they **were not** in "bondage" in Egypt — (22) Israelis **did not** walked through a "Red Sea" or any water — (23) Egyptian Israelis **did not** survived to reach the "Promised Land" — (24) Ishmael/Midian **were** the only children of Abraham — (25) Moses **had** Horns on his forehead — **(Pg. 33)**(26) Yeshua (Jesus) was **not** "born to Die" on a Cross — (27) Christianity **does not** represent the teachings of Yeshua (Jesus).

**Discrepancies (Pg. 33)**(1) The Solar War in Revelations (*Rev. 12:7*), **was** before Genesis — (2) The Planetary Cataclysm (*Isa. 24:1, 3-6*) **was** before Genesis

Bible/Torah

# Table of Contents

### Chapter I
### Part II
(Pg. 34) Planetary Diaspora — (Pg 35) Planetary Graphics

## Bible/Origins
### Pages 36-39

(Pg. 36) Bible/Torah, Mesoretic Text, Bible (Pg.37) Strong's Concordance, Bookless Book (Pg. 38) — God's Book (Pg. 39) — Books of Moses

## *Chronicles*

---

### *Chapter II, Part I*
## *Adam/Seth Chronicles*
### Pages 40-51

(40)Alpha/Omega (Book of God), Gods, Fields (Electric Male, Magnetic Female) — (41) Manifestation (Particular) — (42) Sunday, Assiah — (43) Aliens — (44) Disciples/Apostles — (45) Solar (Soul) War, Outcast (Shaddai) — (46) Hereafter, Ertz (Earth) — (47) Genesis, Eden — (48) Keystone, Garden, Names — (49) Sleep, Tribunal — (50) Cast Out, Image and Likeness — **(51)(Seth)** - Cain's Line, My Line

**Alpha/Omega** (40) ───────────────────────
Book of God, God, Electric Male/Magnetic Female

**Manifestation** (41) ───────────────────────
Manifestation

**Sunday** (42) ───────────────────────
One Great Day - Assiah

**Aliens** (43) ───────────────────────

**Disciples/Apostles** (44) ───────────────────────
Disciples/Apostles

**Solar (Soul) Wars** (45) ───────────────────────

Bible/Torah

# Table of Contents

Outcasts (Shaddai)
**Hereafter** (46) ─────────────────────────────────
Ertz (Earth)

**Genesis** (47) ─────────────────────────────────
Eden

**Keystone** (48) ─────────────────────────────────
Eden and it's Garden — Names

**Sleep** (49) ─────────────────────────────────
  Tribunal

**Cast Out** (50) ─────────────────────────────────
Image and Likeness

**Seth** (51) ─────────────────────────────────
Cain's Line, My Line

## Chapter II, Part II
# *Ham Chronicles*
### Pages 52-57

**(52)Introduction** — (52) Seth to Lemech), (Chart), Adultery — (53) Lines, Choice — (54) Ark Ship, Flood — (55) Dry Land, Tent Incident — (56) Great Exodus, Garden — (57) Servant Cities

**Adultery** (52) ─────────────────────────────────
Assians, and Caucasians

**Lines, Choice** (53) ─────────────────────────────────
Cain to Lamech (*Gen. 4:18 - 22*), and Seth to Lemech (*Gen. 5:25 - 32*), War of the Lord (*Ex. 15:3*), or the Order of Melchezedek (*Heb. 5:6*)

**Ark Ship, Flood** (54) ─────────────────────────────────
God's two of each kind, Lord's Strange Cargo, by twos and sevens (Not Man or Animal)(3rd Story)(*Gen. 7:1, 2*) — End of the World of the Lord, Cain's Subterranean City

**Dry land, Tent Incident** (55) ─────────────────────────────────
Ararat (in and out of the water), Noah's Decision: (Sacrifice the Clean, Preserve the filth) — Tent Cultures, Attempt on Canaan, Shem/Japheth Cover-up (Everyone saw it anyway)(*Gen. 9:23*)!

Bible/Torah

# Table of Contents

**Great Exodus, Garden Cities** (56) ———————————————————————
"We Came Down," (Nimroded) from Ararat, A Garden (Guarded Place) to protect Eden

**Servant Cities** (57) ———————————————————————————
Canaan, servant to the servants of the Lord (*Gen. 9:25*), Servants of the Lord vote with their feet

## Chapter II, *Part III*
## *Arphaxad's (Isaiah) Chronicles*
### Pages 58 - 65

(58) Introduction [Arpha Ca-Shaddai (Border of Chaldea), Chaldeans, Nephalim, Outcasts, Enoch (Cave City)] (59) Family, Exodus — (60) Ham/Nimrod, Kingdom, Chaldeans (PreCivil) — (61) Lord (Comer Down) — (62) Crucixion of Nimrod — (63) Hebrewers, My Line (Arphaxad) — (64) Genealogical chart, Begotten — (65) World Crisis

**Family, Exodus** (59) ———————————————————————————
Noah his sons, and their children, Hostages, Sacrifice of Cleanness, Preserving Filth — Sanctifying Canaan, Cover Up, Down from Ararat, No more Light in the North

**Ambassador Nimrod** (60) ————————————————————————
Swift Ambassador (*Isa. 18:2*)

**Kingdom** (60) ——————————————————————————————
Six City Metropolis (*Gen. 10:10, 11*)

**Chaldeans, Devils of the North (Precivil)** (60) ———————————————
Behold the Chaldeans (*Isa. 23:13*) — People Terrible from their Beginning (*Isa. 18:2*), Ju*bal* Cain, Ja*bal* Cain, and Tu*bal* Cain

**Lord (Comer Down)** (61) ———————————————————————
Babel, Accad, Erech, Nineveh, Calah, Resen (*Gen. 10:10, 11*)

**Crucifixion** (62) ——————————————————————————————
Nimrod Bearer of Stripes (*Isa. 53 Chptr.*) — Confounding Ur/Babel

**Hebrewers** (63) —————————————————————————————
Fleeing from the Lord — Ham, Chaldeans, Abram, Israelis, Jesus — Death Of Terah

**My Line** (63) ———————————————————————————————

Bible/Torah

# Table of Contents

Salah - Eber - Peleg (Twin Leading to Abram)- Reu - Serug - Nahor - Terah - Abram

**World Crisis (63)** ─────────────────────────────
Famine in Nod, Merging on Ur, Death of Terah, Hebrewers

**Noah Family Chart (64, 65)** ─────────────────────────
Begotten from Arphaxad to Abraham — World Crisis (65)

### *Chapter II, Part IV*
## *Egyptian (Mesoretic Text) Chronicles*
### Pages 66 -74

(66) Hebrewers, Prostitution — (67) Sodomites — (68) Rape of Hagar, Tricks — (69, 70) Birth of a Nation — (71) Salvation — (72) Out Cry — (73) Set Free — (74) Peniel (Face of God) (Graphics)

**The Hebrewers(66)** ─────────────────────────────
Hebrewing the Tigris and Euphrates (Great Exodus) back down into the Garden (Before Abram's Birth) — Chaldeans/Gentiles/Hebrewer — Cush

**Cush (66)** ──────────────────────────────────
Phut, Mesopotamia, Abbysinnia

**Canaan (Phoenicia)(66)** ──────────────────────────
Canaan a Tropical Paradise — Eyes of the Lord — Land of Milk and Honey — Servant of Servants (*Gen. 9:25*) — Hebrewing

**Abram/AbramHam/Abraham (67)** ─────────────────────
Abram Hebrews (Crosses), the Tigris and Euphrates — Famine in the Garden — Prostitution — Breaking the Law (Keep your feet) — Pharaoh

**Prostitute(67)** ────────────────────────────────
Sarah the Whore (Horite) — Daughters of Chaldea — Abram and Sarah, Brother and Sister, Husband and Wife — Abimelech

**Ishmael/Isaac(67)**─────────────────────────────
The Pharaoh — Hostility — Rape of Shari Misraim (Hagar) — Dying in the Wilderness (Abraham an unfit Parent) — Isaac (Moriah) —

Bible/Torah

# Table of Contents

**Birth of a Nation (Goyim)(68, 71)** ─────────────────────────
(Disclaimer) — Isaac — Jacob (Israel) — Israel — Twelve Rape Tribes — Multiplying in Goshen (Filth) — Outcry — Sodomized Israel (Bondage to the Lord) — Pale Israeli Lepers (the remaking of Cain) — Cannibals — Holocaust on Ishmael/Midian — Seed of Abraham

**Ishmael/Midian (72)** ─────────────────────────────────
Seed of Abram *Gen. 15:3* — Children of Abraham (Before Israel ever existed) — Confederation — Holocaust and rape of Ishmael/Midian the children of Abraham — Israel becomes the "Seed of Abraham," by rape of the little girls of Ishmael/Midian *Nu. 31:18* — Holocaust

**Canaan Revisited (72)** ────────────────────────────────
Holocaust revenge on Canaan for telling on Noah — Holocaust (No Idols or Incest Here)— Israelis committing Adultery (*Deut. 21:10*) — Joshua the Monster — Genocide and rape of Canaan — *Jerimiah 45:5* (Total Evil)

**Open Eyes/Closed Eyes (73)** ──────────────────────────────
A Gathering of Goyim (*Isa. 66:19*) — Sodomite Romans buy young boys for their sons — Israelis sell their girls and boys, as prostitutes to Greeks for wine (*Joel 3:3, 6*) — Evil eyes closed (*Matt. 6:22*)

**Face of God (Peniel)(74)** ──────────────────────────────
Peniel Eye Graphics

## Chapter II, Part V
# Yeshua (Jesus) Chronicles
### Pages 75 - 83

(75) Introduction (Crucifixion of his son) — (76) Saying or Doing (Being), Sacrifice of the Clean, Beguilement of Mary, Lord's World — (77) Exodus — (78) Self, Saved and Raised — (79) Sent, Secrets — (80) Draconian Measures — (81) Sword (Not Roman) — (82) Inner Kingdom, Crucified — (83) I. N. R. I.

**Say or Do (Being)(76)** ────────────────────────────────
Words or Actions — Being or not being — Sacrifice of Clean — Avenging Noah

**Beguilment of Mary (76)** ──────────────────────────────

Bible/Torah

# Table of Contents

Birth of the World Ender — Giving sons away — Beginning of World

**Lord's World** (TBL)(76) ─────────────────────────────
Darkness — Absent from Body — Children Cast Out — Sodomites

**Exodus** (77) ─────────────────────────────────────
Yeshua (Jesus') Exodus away from the Lord, like Others: Ham, Chaldeans, Abraham, Israelis

**Self** (78) ────────────────────────────────────────
Know Thy Self, Love Thy Self, To Thy Self be True — Eyes, Ears, Minds (Hearts)

**Saved and Raised** (78) ────────────────────────────
Asylum in Eden — Perfection

**Sent** (79) ────────────────────────────────────────
After the Order of Melchezedek —

**Secrets** (79) ──────────────────────────────────────
Mesoretic (Egyptian) Text — All of you are Gods — New (Old) Testament

**Draconian Measures** (80, 81) ──────────────────────
In the World but not of it — Hate the Lord's World — Lost Soul — Families at Variance — Pick up your Crosses — Don't be Saved

**Inner Kingdom** (82) ───────────────────────────────
God and Heaven Inside You — End of ancient Synogogues, meant no church system

**I.N.R.I.** (83) ────────────────────────────────────
Killed by Pale Romans, and Wooly Headed Brown Rabbis (*Deut. 13th Chptr, Amos 9:7*) — Keeping Eyes, Ears, and Minds Shut — Islam Never Rise Ireneus

## Chapter III, Part I
## *Soliloquies of Order*
### Pages 84 - 101

(84) Introduction (Voices for All to Speak) — (85 - 91) Michael/Melchezedek — (92) Eve — (93) Seth — (94) Asshur — (95) Semiramis — (96) Cush — (97) Canaan — (98) Nimrod — (99) Hagar — (100) Ishmael — (101) Yeshua (Jesus)

Bible/Torah

# Table of Contents

**Michael/Melchezedek (85-91)**
(85) Order, Assiah — (86) Disciples/Apostles — (87) Apostasy, Creation — (88) Solar War, From Assiah to Ertz, Ertz (Earth) — (89) Genesis, Two great Lights — (90) Garden and Eden — (91) Tribunal

**Eve (92)**
Mother of it all — Not Adam's rib, mother, sister, wife, or daughter, but his female side (wombman)(viable in due season) — Mother of all (Two Lines, Pale and Black) — Cain and Abel (Lord's sons) — Seth (In the Image and Likeness of Adam) — Seth

**Seth (93)**
Continuation of Adam — Guarding the Experiment — Children of Sheth (*Nu. 24:17, IChron. 1:1*) — Asshur

**Asshur (94)**
Elam — Childless — Nimrod the Assyrian, Son of my twin Sister Semiramis

**Semiramis (95)**
Asshur my Twin Brother — We Came Down From Ararat (Nimrod in my womb during our Great Exodus) — Raising Cain — The Assyrian — My Husband Cush

**Cush (Ethiopia) (96)**
Semiramis — "We Came Down" — The Tigris (Tigre) and Euphrates, Rivers of Ethiopia I (*Isaiah 18:1, Zephoniah 3:10*) — Mesopotamian Ethiopia — River from Eden (Africa)(Gihon) encompassed the entire land of Ethiopia (Cush)(*Gen. 2:13*) — Broad Gate leading to destruction (Shaddai)(*Matt. 7:13*) — Garden (Guard Place)(Magan מגן) Shield — Cushion, Cash, Cush — Brother Canaan

**Canaan (97)**
North (Holiness) — Secret — What I did to Noah (**Gen. 9:24**) — *Cover-up* — Father Ham would not bow, sacrifice, or praise — To undermine my father's house — Noah the Molester — All of the children knew for I told my cousins — When father threw the tent flap back they all saw what my grandfather was trying to do, before it could be covered up! — Great Exodus

**Nimrod (98)**
Canaan told — Great Light (**Isa. 18:1**) — Great City (Ur/Babel Metropolis) — Raising Cain — Graft them Back — Hagar

**Hagar (99)**
The Pharaoh — Sarah a Yellow Black Woman from the North — Prostitution in Egypt — Sarah

Bible/Torah

# Table of Contents

Get (Surrogate) — Ishmae*l*

**Ishmael** (100) ─────────────────────────────────
Hagar — Abraham Unfit Father — Ishmael/Midian (*Gen. 15:18*) — Fruitful Ishmael (*Gen. 17:29*) — Seed of Abraham — Chronicles of Arphaxad — Mesoretic Text — Jesus

**Jeshua (Yeshua/Jesus)** (101) ─────────────────────────
Ishmael — Sent — Children or Seed — The truth shall make you free — Order of Melchezedek — Get Thee Hence — Hallel

## *Chapter III, Part II*
# Soliloquies of Chaos
### Pages 102 - 150

(102, 110) Hallel (Lord) — (111) Cain — (112) Lamech — (113) Noah — (114) Shem — (115) Terah — (116) Abram — (117) Sarah/Iscah — (118) Lot — (119) Isaac — (120) Jacob — (121) Leah/Rachael — (122, 123) Dinah — (124) Reuben — (125) Levi — (126) Judah — (127) Tamar — (128) Bilhah/Zilpah — (129, 144) Moses — (145) Joshua — (146, 147) Israeli Genealogy — (148, 149) Joseph of Aram — (150) Jesus (Yeshua)

**Lord** (102 - 110) ─────────────────────────────────
Superman (Hallel/Lucifer) — Names — Anatomy — My secret Agenda — My Day — Hereafter Get thee hence, God (102) — Cain's Sons and Daughters (103) — Kingdom, Cain's Chaldean Daughters of Darkness (104) — Noah, Shem/Japheth (105) — Ham's Great Exodus, Nimrod, AbramHam (106) — Abraham's Children or "Seed", Isaac, Jacob, Twelve (107) — Begotten, Ishmael/Midian (108) — Canaan Revisited (109) — Crucifixion, Tubal (102-110)

**Cain** (111) ─────────────────────────────────
World (Tubal) — Abel my first wife (Sodomy) — Raping Lamech

**La̲mech (Cain)** (112) ─────────────────────────────────
Wounded and Raped — Lamech (לְמֶךְ) "To Make" — I killed Cain and a youth — Jubal, Jabal, and Tubal Cain — Sealed in caves, or Shipped Out (Strange Cargo) — The flooding of Mesopotamia (Stopping Adultery)(112)

**Noah** (113) ─────────────────────────────────
Lemech (Seth) Vs Lamech (Cain) — Order of Melchezedek — Exalting the Lord — Cain's pale (Fair) Chaldean Daughters — My wooly headed brown children — Sacrificing the clean — What Canaan Did — Ham's Great Exodus from Ararat — Shem

Bible/Torah

# Table of Contents

**Shem** (114) ——————————————————————————
Order of Melchezedek — Captives Free — Sacrifice Cleanness (including animals) — Tent Incident — *Cover-Up* — Arphaxad to Terah

**Terah** (115) ——————————————————————————
*My Line — Choices: (First Melchezedek, next the Lord) — Meeting Abram — Fleeing the Lord*

**Abram** (116) ——————————————————————————
Incestuous Terah — Sperm in Terah — Arphaxad, Lord and Melchezedek — Sister/wife/niece - Sarah/Iscah

**Sarah/Iscah** (117) ——————————————————————
Abram — Incest of Father Terah — My Pale (Gentile) Mountain Mother — My Brother/Uncle/husband Abram — Daughter (Whore) of Chaldea — Prostitute in Egypt to Pharaoh — Prostitute in Canaan to Abimelech — My Brother/Nephew/Cousin Lot

**Lot** (118) ——————————————————————————
My Sister Sarah/Iscah — My Mother's Sodomite Chaldean People — Sex With My Daughters — Isaac child of Incubi

**Isaac** (119) ——————————————————————————
Incestuous Uncle Lot — My Father The Lord — My Cousin/Wife Rebecca — Foolish Abraham (Moriah) — Ishmael — Jacob (Israel) My Brother, The Lord's son

**Jacob** (120) ——————————————————————————
**My Father The Lord** — Subplanting Esau — Wrestling God For My Name **Israel** (Wrestled With God)*(Gen. 32:28)* — Raising The Lord's Sons, My Brothers: Reuben, Simeon, Levi, Judah, And Joseph fathered — Leah

**Leah/Rachael** (121) ————————————————————
Jacob The Whore — I (Rachael) Wrestled Leah — I (Rachael) Wrestled The Lord (God)*(Gen. 30:8)*

**Dinah** (122, 123) ————————————————————
Rachael — Playing the Whore — Marriage Proposal — Circumcising Shechem — Murdering Shechem — Rape Tribes — Incestuous Brothers — Incestuous Reuben

**Reuben** (124) ——————————————————————————

Bible/Torah

# Table of Contents

Dinah Our Whore — Rape Tribes — My Mandrakes — Jacob the Whore — Sex With Bilhah — Selling Joseph — Levi the Assassin

**Levi** (125) ———————————————————————————————
Reuben Firstborn — Shechem/Salem — Children of Rape — Selling Joseph — Egyptian Wagons— Judah

**Judah** (126) ——————————————————————————————
Levi — Praise the Lord — Male Whore — Taking Canaanite Females — First Jews — Whore Tribes — Tamar

**Tamar** (127) ——————————————————————————————
Incestuous Judah — Taking Canaanite Girls — Prostitution — Whore Tribe — Bilhah/Zilpah

**Bilhah/Zilpah** (128) ————————————————————————————
Tamar — Rape Children — Famine — Saved By Egypt — Moses of Incest

**Moses** (129, 144) —————————————————————————————
(129) Incest Tribes, Best Land, Hibernation, Overpopulation - (130) Birth Control, Prince of Egypt - (131) Prince of Darkness, The Lord inside Pharaoh, Firstborn -(132) Stealing from Friends, Driven Out - (133) **Sodomized Firstborn**, Reed Sea Revisited, Man of War, **Sodomized Israelis and Rabbis** - (134) Lord's Slaves, Golden Calf Massacre - (135) Coven/Covenant, Moses' Horns - (136) Kosher Starvation, Pale Lepers, Incestuous Israel - (137) Verses of Israel, Moses Incest (138) Hypocrisy - (139) Manna - (140) Spying Milk and Honey - (141) Beat The Rock - (142) Holocaust - (143) Heart of Darkness - (144) - Whores and Sodomites, Joshua

**Joshua (Yoshua/Jesus)** (145) ————————————————————————
The Moses Atrocities — Peaceable Ham — Joseph of Aram (Syria)

**Israeli Genealogy** (146, 147————————————————————————
Incest Israeli Tribes - Rape Israeli Tribes - Egyptian Israelis Tribes - Death of Egyptian Israelis - Pale Leper Israelis - "Seed of Abraham"

**Joseph of Aram** (148, 149) ——————————————————————————
Little Egypt — Sanctification and Holiness — Exodus From Israel — No Holiness — Home To Egypt

**Yeshua (Jesus)** (150) ————————————————————————————
Joseph the Egyptian — Unmolested in Egypt — Lost Sheep — Self

Bible/Torah

# Table of Contents

## Chapter IV
## Observations
Pages 152 - 270
**Notes**

**Cover** (151) Picture of Jesus

**Persons**
(152) Self — (153) Most High — (154) Souls — (155) 666 — (156) Man — (157, 8) God(s) — (159) Lords — (160) Names of Lord — (161) Man of War — Almighty, Lucifer (Hallel) — (162, 163) Nephalim — (164) Devil — (165) Mandrake, Hallel (Hallelujah) — (166, 167) Superman (Cipherman) — (168) Baal Zebub — (169) Names (Graph) — (170 - 172) Cain — (173, 174) Gentiles — (175) Two Lines Chart — (176) Three Balls Graph — (177) Arphaxad — (178) Nimrod — (179) Chaldeans — (180) Abram — (181) Hebrewer — (182) AbramHam — (183) Abraham's Seed or Children — (184) Abraham's Seed or Children Chart — (185) Cush — (186) Canaan — (187) Mesorets (Egyptians) — (188) Ishmael — (189) Isaac — (190) Jacob (Israel) — (191) Israel Rape Tribes — (192, 193) Moses — (194, 195) Joshua — (196) Joseph of Aram (197) Yeshua (Jesus)

**Places**
(198) Eternity — (199) Sun — (200) Assiah — (201) Crypton — (202) Ertz (Earth) — (203) Tribunal — (204) North — (205) Goat Headed God Graphics — (206) Nod — (207) Chaldea — (208) Hell (Precivil) — (209, 210) Ur City — (211) Ur Chart — (212) Broad Gate (Mesopotamia) — (213) Garden — (214) Jerusalem — (215) Canaan — (216) Sodom and Gomorrah — (217) Egypt The Narrow Gate — (218, 219) Eden — (220) Goshen — (221) Invaded Eden — (222) Western Eden (Moors) — (223) Amorites (America)

**Things** (Self Elements)
(224) Heaven — (225) Sunday — (226) Law — (227) Light — (228) Choice — (229) Meekness — (230) Life — (231) Sleep — (232) Love — (233) Exodus — (234) Peace — (235) Islam

**Things** (World Elements)
(236) Mutainy — (237) World — (238, 239) Christianity (AntiChrist) — (240, 241) Creation — (242) Solar Wars — (243) Tribunal — (244 - 248) Dark Ages (Apple) — (249) Sleep II — (250) Faith — (251) Holy(ness) — (252) Bondage — (253) Evil — (254) Bestiality — (255) Betrayal — (256) Cross (Noun/Verb) — (257) Bless — (258) Famine — (259) Jealousy (Evil) — (260) Prostitution — (261) Rape — (262) Sacrifice — (263) Sodomy — (264) Incest — (265, 266) Adultery — (267) Flood — (268, 269) Civilizing I +II — (270) Salvation

Bible/Torah

# Table of Contents

**Commentary**
Pages 271 - 275

**Deceptions** (271)
Salvation (Save what) — Truth makes Free — Prince of Egypt — The Lord's Deceives his own World — Get thee hence Satan

**Kill the Light** (271, 273)
Kill the Light — World Salvation — Outer darkness — Holy Roman Imp*ire* (Imps)

**Curse be Ham/Canaan** (273)
Wooly Headed Jesus — Cursed be Canaan — Two Lines (Cain Mutainy) — Asians and Caucasians

**Two Lines** (273, 274)
Asians and Caucasians — Missing Link — Wooly Black Israelis (*Amos 9:7*)

**Missing Link** (275)
Black Israelis — Pale Abnormal — Marked Cain — Summation

## Chapter V

# Summations

*Chapter IV, Part I*
Pages 276 - 285

**Nimrod to Benjamin Banniker Pictures** (276, 277)

**Reconciliation** (278)

**Jesus Vs Lord** (279, 280)

**Jesus Vs Church** (281)

**Jesus Vs Paul** (282, 283)

**Jesus Vs Yeshua** (284)

**Inner Light Vs Outer Darkness** (285)

Bible/Torah

# Table of Contents

**Man Vs Woman** (285) ──────────────────────────────────

### *Chapter IV, Part II*
## *Lexicons*
### Pages 286 - 303

**Introduction**(286)──────────────────────────────────
Adam (אדם) = "I am Blood — Holy (הולי) = Corrupt — Bless (ברכ) = Break — Devil (דבל) = Divide — North (נורות) = "Lamps" — Mandrake (מן דרך) = Man of Darkness — Apple (Awful/אפל) = Thick Darkness — Truth (אמת) = Emit — Multiply (מלח) = Replenish/Fill — Visited (פקד) = Sexual Intercourse (*Gen. 21:1, 2*)

**Almighty is Devil** (287) ──────────────────────────────
Ancient Language is Accurate — Holy is Sodomy

**Beast**(288)─────────────────────────────────────
Beast (בוהימות) Are Not Animals Or Men, But Are Both — The Old Language Does Not Lie

**Lord** (289) ────────────────────────────────────
The Lord Is Completely Associated With The Negative Words — Truth Shall Make You Free

**Lexicon** (290, 303) ────────────────────────────────
Abel (אבל) to World (Tubal / חבל)

### *Chapter V, Part III*
## *Appeals*
### Pages 304 - 322

**To Gentiles:** (*Galatians 3:13, 14*)(304) ──────────────────
Ur/Babel to Washington D. C. (Nimrod to Benjamin Banniker) — Shielded and Sheltered — Jewish

**Pale Israelis (Jewish)**(*Deut.13:1-18*)(305, 306) ──────────────
Fake Jews — Israel like the wooly headed brown children of Ethiopia (*Amos 9:7*) — Best of the worst, or worst of the best — Animosity Towards What You Claim To Be (Black) — You Have Taken Someone Else's I. D. — Exposed as Counterfeit — Christi*anity* (AntiChrist)

**Judeo/Christianity (Antichrists)** (307) ────────────────────

Bible/Torah

# Table of Contents

Jewish/Israelis — Defender of the World — Outer Darkness — Rabbis, Priests, and Ministers

**To Rabbis, Priest, and Ministers (Entire Planet)(308)** ─────────
*All of You Are Damned (Matt. 23:14)* — *Black, Brown, Yellow, Pale* — *Lose Your Souls* (Clerics)

**Scientist, Intellectuals, Philosopher (309, 310)** ─────────
First Clerks (Clerics) — Advance To Where? - *What Evolving, To Where Or What? - Everything that you have, was given to you whole, and intact, as a legacy, without you having to add anything to what you were given* — *Batteries, Crystals, Astronomy, Astrology, Architecture, Cities, Electronics, Chemistry, Metallurgy all existed before you* — *Baalbek, Ponape Island, Rapa Nui, Mexican Heads, Great Walls, Great Pyramids* — What evolved? — High IQ compared to what? — Where did you get your Alphabet, mathmetics, Arts, Crafts, and skills for being civilized? — Do you have an alphabet or language of your own? (Intellect vs Intelligence) — Why did someone else have to give you everything that you have? — Continentals

**Continentals (311, 312)** ─────────
Ertz (Earth) — American Invitation — Crumbling Foundation — American Gathering — All have failed you — Alienation

**Aliens? (313, 314)** ─────────
Apostasy — *Planets, Continents, Races, Nationalities* — *Ertz (Earth)* — *From Male/Female to Male And Female* — *Final Choice*

**To North American Blacks (315, 322)** ─────────
(315) Blacks, Raising Cain (his Pale Leper Children) — (316)(Nimrod, Archaic Greeks, Etruscans, Phoenicians, Carthaginians, Moors) — (317) Europe, North America — (318) First President (John Hanson) — (319) Capital Builders, Broken Promise — (320) George Washington Is A Freed Slave, Divide and Conquer Both — (321) Negroes, Willie Lynch — (322) Pork — (323) Unraisable Cain — (324) Final Betrayal — Revelations

*Chapter V, Part IV*
## *Revelations (Last)*
**Pages 325 - 328**

**Apocalypse (Revelations of an Holocaust) (325** ─────────
(325) Alpha/Omega, Fulfillment, Apocalypse — (326) Rendering to Caesar, World — (327) Races, End of Earth — (328) Assiah, One Hundred Forty Four Thousand (Beginning).

Bible/Torah

# Contents Index

**Volume One**

Tables of Contents — I-XV
Content Pages — XVI-XVIII
Introd./Autobiography — XIX-XXIII
Book Scheme — 23-27
Keys — 27

**Chapter 1**

**Bible History**
1a Deceptions/Discrepancies — 28 33
    Broken Diaspora — 34-35 (Ertz Graphics)

1b Bible Origins and Purpose — 35-39

**Chapter 2**

Chronicles
**Adam/Seth** — 40-51
**Ham** — 52-56
**Arphaxad** — 57-65
**Mesorets** — 66-73, 74(Eye)
**Yeshua (Jesus)** — 75-83

**Chapter 3**
Soliloquies
  **Order**
Introduction — 84
Michael/Melchezedek — 85-91
Eve — 92
Seth — 93
Asshur — 94
Semiramis — 95
Cush — 96
Canaan — 97
Nimrod — 98
Hagar — 99
Ishmael — 100
Yeshua — 101

  **Chaos**

Lord (Hallel) — 102-110
Cain — 111
Lamech (Cain) — 112
Noah — 113
Shem — 114
Terah — 115
Abram — 116
Sarah/Iscah — 117
Lot — 118
Isaac — 119
Jacob — 120
Leah/Rachael — 121
Dinah — 122-123
Reuben — 124
Levi — 125
Judah — 126
Tamar — 127
Bilhah/Zilpah — 128
Moses — 129-144
Joshua — 145
Genealogy — 146 -147
Joseph Aram — 148 - 149
Yeshua — 150

**Volume 2**

**Chapter 4**
**Picture: Lynching of Yeshua (Jesus)(151)**

  **Persons**
Self — 152
Most High — 153
Souls — 154
666 — 155
Man — 156
Gods — 157, 158
Lord (s) — 159
Lord's Names Introd. — 160
  Man of War — 161
  Almighty — 161
  Lucifer — 161 (11)

Bible/Torah

# Contents Index

Nephalim — 162, 163
Devil — 164
Mandrake — 165
Hallel — 165 (15)
Superman — 166, 167
Baal Zebub — 168
Names (Chart) — 169
Cain — 170 - 172
Gentiles — 173, 174
Two Lines (Graphs) — 175
Three Balls (Chart) — 176
Arphaxad — 177
Nimrod — 178
Chaldean — 179
Abram — 180
Hebrewer — 181
AbramHam — 182
Abraham Seed or Children — 183
Abraham Seed or Children Chart — 184
Cush — 185
Canaan — 186
Mesorets — 187
Ishmael — 188
Isaac — 189
Jacob (Israel) — 190
Israel (Tribes) — 191
Moses — 192
Joshua — 194, 195
Joseph — 196
Yeshua (Jesus) — 197

### Places
Eternity — 198
Sun — 199
Assiah — 200
Crypton — 201
Earth — 202
Tribunal (Place) 203
North — 204
Goatheaded God — 205
Nod — 206
Chaldea — 207
Hell — 208
Ur — 209 - 211
Broad Gate — 212
Garden — 213
Jerusalem — 214
Canaan — 215
Sodom/Gomorrah — 216
Narrow Gate — 217
Eden — 218, 219
Goshen — 220
Invaded Eden — 221
Western Eden (Moors) — 222
Amorite/America — 223

### Things
Self Elements
  Heaven — 224
  Sunday — 225
  Law — 226
  Light — 227
  Choice — 228
  Meek — 229
Life — 230
Dream — 231
Love — 232
Exodus — 233
Peace — 234
Islam — 235

### World Elements
Mutainy — 236
World — 237 (87)
Christianity — 238, 239
Creation — 240, 241
Solar Wars — 242
Tribunal — 243
Dark Ages — 244 - 248
Sleep II — 249
Faith — 250
Holy(ness) — 251

Bible/Torah

# Contents Index

Bondage — 252
Evil — 253
Bestiality — 254
Betrayal — 255
Cross — 256
Bless — 257
Famine (Feminine) — 258
Jealousy — 259
Prostitution — 260
Rape — 261
Sacrifice — 262
Sodomy — 263
Incest — 264
Adultery — 265, 266
Flood — 267
Civilization (temp.) — 268
Civilization (Perm.) — 269
Salvation — 270

**Commentary** — 271, 275

**Picture: Nimrod** 276

**Volume 3**

**Picture: Benjamin Banniker** (277)

**Chapter 5**

**Summations**
 Reconciliations — 278
Jesus vs Lord — 279, 280
Jesus vs Church — 281
Jesus vs Paul — 282, 283
Jesus vs Jesus — 284
Self — 285

Man vs Woman — 286
Lexicon Introduction — 287, 290
Lexicon — 291 - 304
**Appeals**

Gentiles — 305
Jewish — 306, 307
Judeo/Christianity — 308
Rabbis, Priest, Ministers — 309
Scientist, Intellectuals — 310, 311
Continentals — 312, 313
Aliens — 314, 315
Blacks — 316 - 323
Revelation/Revolution — 324- 329

# Introduction

*First Born — Born Again*

### Firstborn

I was born in Detroit Michigan in 1942, at the St. Albin General Hospital. We lived at 1539 Maple St. in a part of Detroit called the Black Bottom. As a child I saw and I listened. My mother said that I seldom spoke until I was four years old, but I did a lot of thinking about what I saw and heard going on around me. By age eight I was conscious of being concerned about those around me, especially those who could not defend themselves. I was the protector of others, the small and the weak.

The first school that I went to was half a block away from my house on the corner of Maple and Riopelle. The name of the school was Caperan, and the principle's name was Mr. Caperan. I remember being in the kindergarten, and taking naps each day after drinking warm (unrefrigerated) containers of milk.

At age eight I remember the "haunted" house, across the street from my elementary school on Riopelle. We were all afraid to walk past it. After all rumor had it that there were skeletons scattered all over the floor.

### Born Again

One day one of my friends pushed me against the door, of the house. The door gave, and I fell through into the darkness. Someone shut the door behind me leaving me alone. Though I was alone in the dark for about three minutes, curiously enough I was not afraid. Eventually I began to feel around the floor for the dead people, but I found none. By the time that they opened the door to let me out again, I was different. The fear that I had before that event never returned to me. By being forced to confront my fears I had overcome them. My friends never overcame theirs, even when I opened the door to let them see, that there was nothing inside the house to harm them.

My thoughts about overcoming fear were with me, 45 years later in 1996, when I began to write this book. My book refers to information in the Bible/Torah, and to the deep content of that information.

For most of the Judeo/Christian masses the deep understanding of the Bible/Torah is a "haunted house" with skeletons in it. No one in the church/Synagogue community wants to go into the depth of the Bible/Torah to look at any of it's "skeletons."

It was circumstances of life that pushed me through the door into a deeper understanding of the contents of the Bible/Torah. I found no skeletons but I did find volumes of information that the common people were never suppose to see. My book opens the door for all to see what the contents of the Bible/Torah actually say. How will people's fear affect their response to this information? At age eight I and my friends had the opportunity to confront and overcome a fear, and learn a valuable lesson. Those who read this book will have the same opportunity, that my friends and I had. The reader will have the opportunity to keep or set aside fear, with new information about the Bible/Torah.

I can remember going to church on Sundays. We would be there all day: There was preaching,

Bible/Torah

# Introduction

Born Again — Little Children Cast Out

shouting, and lunch in the basement of the church. One Sunday the sermon was "The Truth will make you free." The minister preached a firey sermon about truth. Later I saw him and some of the deacons hiding outside behind the church during recess, drinking a fifth of liquor.

Even at age ten I knew that something was wrong with church. Many people in church quoted Bible scripture, and then acted contrary to what they had read. Even in my youth I was to learn that this sort of behavior comes from the doctrine that the church teaches, from the pulpit. The church teaches that everyone is born in sin, therefore the church say it is impossible for anyone to behave correct. In so teaching the church teach little children away from pure truth, that still exists, inside themselves. Little children are perfect, when they are born, and are never born in sin, as taught in churches and Synagogue. Jesus taught that "Little" Children are still in their inner kingdoms, until Church/Synagogue teachings cast them out into the Outer Darkness (*Matt.8:12*). It would take years for me to discover that the church system puts it's congregations in the same situation, that my friends and I had been in, in our youth when we feared to go into the "haunted" house. It is by design that the church teachings bring us mentally outside of ourselves. Over the years, we forget that we were ever inside. The church tells us that there is death inside of ourselves, like we had been told that there was death inside of the old house, across from the school.

**Little Children Cast Out**
While we were still little children church doctrine preached from the pulpit, put us outside of our selves, and taught us to fear going back inside ourselves where we should be.

Yet in scripture Jesus teach that you must reenter yourself, where the kingdom of heaven is at (*Luke 17:21*)! Little Children are at the center inside of themselves. Scripture teach us that God, and the kingdom of Heaven (Place of Life) are inside of each of us (*Luke 17:21*), while the church/Synagog teach that God and Heaven are outside of us. The Rabbis, Priests, and Ministers, program their Church/Synagogue congregations, to respect what they says, and not to respect what the scripture say. Added to this they teach their congregations the false doctrine of original sin, and eventually cause their congregations to lose self respect!

Robbed of self respect, self esteem, and self knowledge, most people stay with the church/Synagogue and it's teachings. It would be years before I discovered that most of the negative that is taught in church is not even written in the Bible/Torah! But if any person is sincere and have a burning desire to know the truth, there is sufficient information inside of the Bible/Torah for anyone to read themselves free, of the Church/Synagogue system (*John 8:32*).

My book is designed to clarify the basis of what is in the Bible/Torah, to allow the "Captives to make themselves free." Consciousness allowed me to graduate up out of the church system.

Bible/Torah

# Introduction

    The information in my book is Bible material reordered in a form, that clearly allow those still caught a choice. Thus set mentally free one may reenter, into their closet (Self)(*Matt. 6:6*), as Jesus commanded, of all who claim to be following his teachings (*Matt. 6:6*).

    As a young man I was inducted into the military. After basic training I was sent to Ft. Monmouth New Jersey, to be trained as a Television Equipment Repairman. I graduated in 1965 and was then assigned as an electronics technician, to Kagnew Station in Asmara Eritrea, in Northern Ethiopia. The people of Ethiopia are Black like the Blacks in the United States. Yet these Blacks in Ethiopia had their own language. Relatively few of them spoke English. The first Ethiopian word phrase that I recall taking note of was the term Semaski (שמעסכי) which is a phrase meaning "listen to me!" I was to learn many more words in the year, and a half that I spent in Ethiopia. My Knowledge of the Ethiopian language is the core of the information in my book, for that language is a part of the language root that was translated into English in the formation of the King James Bible. But I did not find this out until about ten years later, around 1977. That was ten years after I returned home from Ethiopia.

    I returned to the United States in the summer of 1967, and went to work for Ford Motors in the Dearborn Rouge. I became a skill trades apprentice in the spring of 1972, and worked in many buildings, and by 1975 I was working in the J-9 Rolling Mills, in the Ford Rouge. I met two brothers there, who told me that the Black man is the Original Man, the cream of the earth, and that his home is all over the earth." This statement was the catalyst that would send me around the planet, to see for myself if it was true. I had seen that it was true in Ethiopia. In Ethiopia I had Ethiopian men and women walk up to me, and began to speak to me in their language, thinking that I was an Ethiopian. I am a wooly headed brown man, and the Ethiopians are wooly headed and brown also. My mother's people are the Aboriginal inhabitants of what is now called North America. My mother and all of the rest of the inhabitants of the entire western hemisphere were originally Black. This was before the Europeans brought other Blacks here from Eden (Africa).

    The only thing that Columbus discovered, when he came to the western hemisphere was that he was lost! Thinking that he was in India, Columbus called the Blacks of the western hemisphere Hindians or Indians. He thought that these Blacks were Hindus, like the Blacks in India, eight thousand miles further away, across the Pacific Ocean! All of the original people of India were Black, like all of the original people of the entire western hemisphere, and the entire planet were Black.

    Traveling to Hawaii in 1983 I stood face to face with Aboriginal Hawaiian, who were Black. A year later (1984) I traveled to Mexico, and stood before Aboriginals in Mexico, who were also Black. I did not stand out as being different from them. In the period from 1965 to the present (2001) I had studied the Aboriginal populations all over the planet and found the same to be true.

    All of the original people of the planet are indeed Black, as the brothers had said. This included the original CaucasedAsians or Caucasians, who were also Black, in the form of their father Marked Cain. This is key information in my book for it identifies Adam the Aboriginal Man of

Bible/Torah

# Introduction

this planet as being Black.

**1977** I began to work for Art, a Jewish fellow. I had began studying religion, and Arthur and I had some great conversations about Judaism, and Christianity. One day Art sent me over to Bornstein's Book Store to purchase the Hamish or five books of Moses. He felt that the books would broaden my understanding. Though I was interested in continuing to learn, I still had not at that time decided to write a book But in reading I discovered that many if not most of the "Jewish" words in the books sounded the same as the Ethiopian words I had previously learned in Ethiopia. But more significant than any of these words was a passage in Israeli language. The passage is the Lord saying "Oh Israel you are as the children of Ethiopia to me (*Amos 9:7*)." In this verse Jehovah is describing the Israelis as being wooly headed and brown like Ethiopians. The question I asked myself was how could the pale group that is recognize today as Jews (Judeans) claim a document that have their God saying that they should be brown and wooly headed (*Amos 9:7*)? I had seen the Ethiopians they were brown and wooly as the Torah described them. I had heard Ethiopians speak, and they spoke the language that these pale ones were claiming as their own language! I discovered that the scholarly Israeli words that I was reading in 1977 were the same as the Tigre or Ethiopian words that I had learned ten years before. The Ethiopian I talked to were regular indigenous people on the streets of Asmara. I had thought that the Ethiopian words were slang, and contemporary to those people and that place, and that time **1965** through **1967**. But the Jewish writers of the Israeli books that I read were claiming that these same words were thousands of years old! The words that were being spoken on the streets of Asmara in Ethiopia were words that had been preserved unaltered even by the common people of Ethiopia for thousands of years! How could pale Jewish scholars be claiming these words for themselves? I did not resolve my **1977** discovery of conflict between Ethiopian and Jewish for Years. My book explores the later consequence of my discovering, that the true Judeans and other Israelis were Black like the Ethiopians. This did not make the ancient Israelis good, just Black like Adam.

By **1978** I had become a skill trades journeyman. I knew a little bit about the Bible/Torah, but it was Curtis another journeyman, who really got me to studying the Bible. Curtis took the little bit that I knew, and set me to reading the Bible as an act of scholarship rather than religion. I began to study my King James Bible with great intensity, reading it from end to end several times, until the "covers fell off " of it. "Covers Off" is what Apocalypes the old name for Revelations mean. As I read the Bible through from cover to cover I took notes. When I had finished, I went over my notes and was shocked at the contents, of the information that had been "revealed."

The information from the notes that I had taken, while reading the Bible/Torah, was the catalyst that allowed me to clarify much that had been unclear to me in the Bible/Torah. My thorough study of the Bible/Torah was the discipline that allowed me to find patterns of information inside the information of the Bible/Torah, that had been broken up, and scattered by design. The

# Introduction

discovery of this broken up information and my reordering it, is a key element in the writing of my book.

In **1982** from January I was a cleaner in the Blast Furnace locker rooms. It was there that I went through the grueling task of learning to sound out, and read the so called "Hebrew." It was my learning to read the old language myself that allowed me to retranslate many mistranslated old language words, in the Bible to correct meanings. This is the source of my book's Lexicon. With my book's Lexicon and the Strong's Concordance anyone, Jewish,* and Gentile alike can move through the entire Bible/Torah, and see for themselves what the true information there is.

It was in **1983** that I had gone to Hawaii. It had taken me eight years (1975 to 1983) to get from hearing that the Hawaiians were Black, to visiting Hawaii to see that the Aboriginal Hawaiians were indeed Black. Then I had gone to Mexico in **1984**, and saw that the Aboriginal Ancient Mexican Cultures specifically the Olmecs the most ancient Mexicans were Black. In **1988** I visited Paris. In Paris at the Museum of Natural History, were death masks of Pacific Islanders. These masks show that the aboriginal Polynesians, Melanesians, and Micronesians, were all Blacks. Also in the Louvre I saw statues of the Archaic (Old) Gods of Europe (the Goddess Europa included) and they were all depicted as Black people.

In the Louvre were statues, busts, and murals, that showed that all the ancient people from Italy (Etruscans) to Greece (Archaic Greeks), to the Assyrians, and other Ancient Cultures all the way to China were all Black.

Now having found out that the entire aboriginal population of the planet had been Black, I wondered why the modern western World system put a pale face on it all. I spent approximately nine years in the Tool and Die building in the Rouge from **1989** to **1998**, when I retired. It was around three years before I retired (1995), that I finally decided that I would write a book to share all that I had discovered with my children, grand children, my community, and the public in general.

The reason that I decided to write it, was that I had discovered, that most if not all that I had studied and learned even in the secular was contained in the contents of the scripture of the Bible/Torah. All that I had to do was to rearrange the information to restore it to it's approximate original order, that the information had been in, before it had been broken up and formed into the Bible/Torah scriptures.

*The Jewish (Jews) are not the Judeans of the twelve tribes of Israel, but are Ju's: Jubalee, Jubali, and Jubalum. The **Three Ju,s** (Jews) are and were the **Three Bals**, the chief descendants of Marked Cain: Ju<u>bal</u> Cain, Ja<u>bal</u> Cain, and Tu<u>bal</u> Cain (**Gen. 4:20-22**). The **Three balls** still displayed in front of some of the old Jewish pawnshops were there to denote that the Ju's (Jews) are chief above all the Pale Race, the children of Marked Cain (**Gen. 4:15**).

Bible/Torah

# Book Scheme

### Why This Book (Choice)

The main purpose of this book is to Reorder the major information in the King James Version of the Bible/Torah, to inform people, and to allow them to make their own decisions. I will expose that the crafters of the Bible/Torah, along with those who preach from the pulpit, have reversed to present Evil as Good, and Good as Evil (*Isa. 5:20*). My book does not take anything out of the Bible/Torah, or add anything to it. My book reorders information already in the Bible/Torah, to give the reader the choice to be free of the deception. This is done Astronomically, Geographically, Genealogically, Chronologically etc.

The whole and singular purpose of my book is to shine light on what is mostly already in the Bible/Torah. Everyone have a right to know. This is specially true in a time when everyone will be held accountable for what they "should" know. Judaism (Jewishism), the rest of Christianity, and all other forms of religions, are founded on what their congregations do not know. The main purpose of religion have been to collectively suppress any knowledge, that will set the people free to think for themselves.

### This book for who?

**Gentiles** — My book will give you a chance to stop being accessories to the murder of Jesus, by showing you that Jesus was not born to die for you, or anyone else. When you cease to except Jesus' murder as your salvation, you cease to be accessories to the crime of his murder!

**Israelis (Jewish)** — You are the very best of the Caucasians, and yet your leaders have chosen to identify you as Jewish. As such they have you mimicking the ancient Judeans or Israelis who were perhaps the very worst of Black people! This book will give you a chance to change your minds.

**Rabbis, Priests, Ministers** — The information in this book will give you the opportunity to do right by your congregations, by revealing the truth to them, that some of you have known but have been afraid to tell, whether they be Jewish, Gentile, Catholic or Protestant.

**Continentals** — Many of you have come to North America with crosses hanging from your necks. Many of you have animosity toward Blacks. This book will show you that the very continents that you originated from were once all attached to Africa (Eden), the continent that many of the Blacks in North America came from. What did your ancestors look like when your continents were attached to Africa (Eden)? When all else has failed you, you can resort back to being Black like your ancestors originally were! Your hatred of Blacks is you having Self hatred.

**Blacks** — This book will show you that it is all about you. All of you are asleep inside of these physical forms. It is all being projected by you. Your collective awakening is the awakening of Adam (*Gen. 2:21*). In the day that you collectively mentally awaken, this world (dream world) will come to an end.

### How I have Reordered the Bible/Torah

# Book Scheme

**Astronomically** — The sun is the astronomical origin of this planet, the planet Assiah the fervent planet, now known as Earth. Assiah is the astronomical mother planet of all other planets in the solar (Soul) system, including Jupiter. The sun and this planet were never created, but have always existed. The astronomical origin of the sun, with Assiah in it, is dissatisfaction that caused it to manifest from the invisible electro/magnetic field. The verses of the first chapter of Genesis are crafted to make one assume that the sun, moon, earth and the other planets were created, but they all existed unseen, before creation.

Astronomically there is but one day, that day is the day of the sun, or Sunday. The sun has neither risen or set, it is only the planet turning. All that has ever occurred on the planet has taken place in the one and self same day, of the sun. The day of the sun is a great circle without beginning or end. To mimic the Word of God, the Bible/Torah must also be without beginning or end

**Chronologically**, I have made the Bible/Torah a circular document by tearing the "covers off," and bringing the end of Revelations around trailing the rest of the Bible/Torah behind it. I then fuse the end of Revelations to the beginning of Genesis changing the Bible/Torah into a seamless Eternal Book without beginning or ending. This single act of fusing the Bible/Torah into a circle cancels out the three discrepancies of the "Solar War," and two "Planetary Destructions," all three which occurred before the book of Genesis. Also in the circular Bible/Torah "creation" is automatically redefined, as the act of altering the Alpha and Omega which has no beginning or ending.

**Geographically** — The six city **Ur Metropolis** and **Chaldea** were never in the south of Mesopotamia, but were north of the Tigris River, in the land of Nod. Three cities were built on the Tigris River (Nineveh, Resen, and Calah), and the other three (Babel, Erech, and Accad) were built above, and adjacent to the first three, before the mound of Ararat, on the Shinar plains (*Gen. 10:10-12*). The total Ur Metropolis was perhaps 60 miles across, or three days walking. The Ur Metropolis was the first place for the civilizing of the Western World. In this book we will elaborate on the true locations of Abram's nativity Ur, and other places in the Bible/Torah, including Ethiopia, Nod, the Garden, Eden, Phut, etc. In the modern times all of the countries where the Bible/Torah story is played out are inventions of the Europeans. The entire invention and geographic schematic, of Biblical countries, by Europeans shall also be revealed.

**Genealogically** — Cain is the Lord's son "with (את)" Eve (*Gen. 4:1; I Chron.1:1*), not the son of Adam. Seth is the first son of Adam (*I Chron.1:1*). As such there are two lines of descendants from Eve. My book makes a distinction between the linage of Cain, and the linage of Adam (Seth), revealing that only Adam's line connects to Noah. This book also distinguishes that the apparent link of Abraham to the Israelis does not exist. All of the mothers of the Israelis were Hamite girls and women. The Ancient and Original Israelis were like Ethiopians, and were never Caucasians (*Amos 9:7*).

*Associated Identities — Gentiles, Goyim, Heathens, Horites, Chaldeans, Sodomites, etc., are all the same people, Caucasians. There are many in the Bible/Torah who have unassociated identities*

Bible/Torah

# Book Scheme

*for the same peoples. This book in proper places will associate each identity to it's common group. Linguistically — By design the Bible/Torah has a "Hebrew" Old Testament, and a Greek New Testament. Under this circumstance anyone who is investigating the Bible/Torah linguistically will find themselves hampered by a change of meaning of the same words going from the Old to the New Testament. In this book all pertinent New Testament words will be carried back to their "Old Testament "Hebrew" meaning to restore continuity.*

### Chapters

The five chapters of this book elaborately satisfies all of the above mentioned descriptions from Astronomical to Genealogical. Chapter 1 is **"A History of the Bible,"** Chapter 2 is **"Chronicles"**, Chapter 3 is **"Soliloquies,"** Chapter 4 is **"Observations,"** and Chapter 5 is **"Summations."**

1) Chapter One, **"A History of the Bible"** is composed of two portions: **Deceptions/Discrepancies** (1a), and **Bible History** (1b) — **Part one** (1a) scripturally exposes many of the key deceptions, in the Bible/Torah, and the two main discrepancies of a Solar War, and the destruction of two planet, this Planet (Assiah/Ertz), and Krypton, both before the book of Genesis. **Part two** (1b) shows the historical origin of the English Bible/Torah

2) Chapter Two, **"Chronicles"** is composed of five portions: **Adam/Seth, Ham, Arphaxad, Mesorets, and Jesus (Yeshua)** — In Chronicles my book reorders Biblical accounts and expose the coming into existence of the Gentile, Human, or Caucasian Race. The time line of the Chronicles extend from Adam to Jesus and from Jesus (Yeshua) to the present. This is all supported by scripture.

3) Chapter Three, **"Soliloquies"** is composed of two portions: **Order** and **Chaos.** — **Order** gives voice to vindicate key persons, in the Bible/Torah, who have been denigrated. **Chaos** gives voice to indict key people in the Bible/Torah who have been made to appear good.

4) Chapter Four, **"Observations"** is composed of two portions: **Notes** and a **Commentary**. "Notes" is composed of three portions: **Persons, Places, and Things**. "Things" is composed of two portions: **Things** and **World Elements.** — My book use **Observations** in all of its components as an elaborate repository, for much information used throughout the rest of the whole book. The **Commentary** is a bowtie around the stack of "Notes."

5) Chapter Five, **"Summations"** is a summing up of all the information in the book down to the Summations Chapter. Summations is composed of four elements: **Reconciliations** (Versus), **Lexicon, Appeals**, and **Revelations** — This book uses the four components of Summation to finalize all of the book's accumulated information:

**Reconciliation** 1) Exposes the contradictions that exist between Jesus (Yeshua), and the Lord. 2) Exposes the contradiction between Jesus and the Church system that claim to represent his teachings. 3) Exposes the contradictions between Jesus and Paul. 4) Exposes the contradiction between Jesus and Yeshua.

Bible/Torah

# Book Scheme

**Lexicon** along with it's components **"Phone/Trans,"** and **"Old Language"** explores the ancient language that the moderns translated from. Lexicon is designed to give the, Jewish, Gentile, etc., masses, direct access to the root information of the Bible/Torah. This will allow them to make their own decisions, on much information revealed to them in the Bible/Torah.

**Appeals** is designed to compel most who have been influenced by the World System to rethink (repent) all that they have been taught. Appeals then allow them to make a decision based upon what they now know from having read the true basic contents of the Bible/Torah.

**Revelation** (Apocalypse) **reveal** to the readers of this book that there is a Narrow Gate, and a Broad Gate. These gates are a choice between Self (Narrow Gate) and Other (Broad Gate), between Light and Darkness. The end of the World System (not planet or people) is eminent. All have a choice to end the World, with Light (Self) or Darkness (Other)(*Amos 5:18, 20*). To be with the Lord is to be absent from Light, and Self (*II Chron. 5:6*)(*Amos 5:18, 20*).

**Revelations** (Revolutions) is also a continuation or bridge that allows for a complete circle, fusing the end back to the beginning. This is the Alpha and Omega of Adam (Self). This full circle is the true Chronicle and Book of God, a second Revelation, which with full circle becomes the **Chronicles** unaltered again that Adam represents.

### Keys

Throughout these chapters there are keys or aids to assist in reading and digesting the information in this book. There are **Asterisks** (*), **Parenthesis** ( ( ) ), **Quotation Marks** ( "—"), **Italics** (*Sample*), and **Bold Emphasis** ( **Sample**):

1) **Asterisks** in the text are elaborated on at the bottom of pages, giving information about the word or phrase carrying the asterisk for example: Prince of Darkness* or Incubus*

2) **Parentheses** are used mostly to encapsulate a verse, or verses that pertain to a preceding sentence or sentences. For example: (*John 3:16*), or (*Isa. 23:13, Gen. 11:4*). Also Parenthesis are used to make note of a previous word or phrase. For example: Gentiles (Chaldeans), or Prince of Darkness (Lord Hallel).

3) **Quotation Marks** Besides being used for quotation, are generally used to emphasize sarcasm, or double meaning words. For example: "Cover" (Noun/Verb)

4) **Italics** are used to distinguish notes that are in the midst of regular information. For example: Devils (שׁדי) *See Strong's #7701*

5) **Bold Emphasis** is used to to emphasize a particular word or phrase, in the midst of other words. For example: ...the Lord was now to be a **Gardener of Nod**, the place which he had been taken from, to be tried (*Gen. 3:23*).

# History of the Bible/Torah
# Chapter 1a  Deceptions

1) **It is made to seem that this planet was "created" into existence** (*Genesis 1:1*). The fact is that this planet existed before the so called "creation," in the book of Genesis. Before Genesis, there were people, cities, animals, and vegetation on this planet (*Isaiah 24:1, 3-6*). In a circular Bible/Torah, Revelation is the book before Genesis, describes the destruction of this planet. The first chapter of Genesis describes the refinding of this planet, and it's resuscitating, after the Lord and his Host had destroyed it, knocking it out of it's course (*Psalms 82:*). The Lord's destruction of the planet (*Isaiah 24:1, 3-6*), actually occurred just after *Revelations 12:12*, the book before Genesis in the circular Bible/Torah

2) **It is made to seem that the "Two Great Lights" of the "third day," are the sun and moon.** The fact is that the two Great Lights are Michael/Melchezedek the greater, and Hallel the Lesser of the two Great Lights (*Gen.1:16*). Also you can-not have "days" without the sun. This implies that the sun was around for "days" to happen! Furthermore, the sun and moon do not "rule." The two "rulers" are Michael/Melchezedek, and Hallel. Melchezedek rules the day (Light)(*Gen. 1:16*), and Hallel rules the night (Darkness)(*Gen.1:16, Amos 5:18, 20*). Last there is only one day, the day of the sun, which has never risen or set, it is the planet turning.

3) **It is made to seem that Adam (Earthling) was created at** *Genesis 1:27, 28*. The fact is that Adam had existed forever, as well as all of the other Gods. Adam same as the other Gods was also a male/female being (*Gen. 1:27*). Adam never needed a helpmeet, but was complete and perfect. Adam's womb (אחה)(not rib) was removed and made into a Wombman who was given the name Eve (Life)(*Gen.2:22*). The Man at *Genesis 1:26, 27* is the Lord (and his Host), not Adam. He is being "looked for"(Bara / ברא), and found, not created: And the Gods "found" the Earthling (Lord and Host), who have their blood and shadows. The Gods found them males and females, they found them (*Gen. 1:27*). ויברא אלהים האדם בצלמו בצלם אלהים ברא אתו זכר ונקבה ברא אתם

4) **It is made to seem that Adam is the father of the twins Cain and Abel.** The fact is that the Lord is the father of Cain and Abel (*Gen. 4:1*). Thus Cain and Abel **genetically** made up a line altogether different than the children of Adam (*Chron. 1:1*). Enoch would have been the 9th person from Adam instead of the 7th, if Cain and Abel were in Adam's line (*Jude 1:14*). In fact the line of Marked Cain is the beginning of the Caucasian Race (*Gen. 4:15*). *See Observation, Notes Persons,"Lines."*

5) **It is made to seem that Noah's flood was a global event** (*Gen. 7:19*). The fact is that this flood was local, and had "sides." Abram and his people hebrewed (Crossed) from the northern "side"of the once flooded Tigris (*Joshua 24:4, 14*). The flood of Noah was the flooding of the two **Rivers of Cush** (Ethiopia) the Tigris and Euphrates Rivers (*Isaiah 18:1, 2 Gen.2:13*).

6) **It is made to seem that no one survived the flood, except Noah and his family on the ark.** The fact is that Cain and his children survived under the flood sealed in the caves of Nod in Ararat. The children of Cain are the **Gentiles** (Goyim) who are first mentioned, after the flood at

# History of the Bible/Torah
## Chapter 1a  Deceptions

(*Gen. 10:5*).   Gentiles, the Caucasian Race are **Chaldeans**, not the people who allow themselves to be called Chaldeans in modern times.  The word Chaldeans (Ca-Shaddai) is contained inside of  the name Arphaxad (Arpha - Ca- Shaddai) who was born just two years after the flood  (*Gen. 10:22*).

**7) It is made to seem that Ham and Canaan "did something" to Noah** (*Gen.9:24*). The first fact is that if Ham and Canaan had "done something" to Noah they would have been killed, and rightfully so. Seth and Japheth or the Lord would have killed them! What Ham and Canaan "did to Noah," was to expose Noah for the Sodomite that he was, but **Shem and Japheth covered it up** (*Gen. 9:23*).  Secondly it is made to seem that Noah was asleep.  The second fact is that Noah never went to sleep. Noah did not "awake" from his wine, he "finished" (קיץ) his wine (*Gen. 9:24*).*

> *The Western World has virtually destroyed the inhabitants of Africa, which is Eden.  They enslaved these Children of Eden in the Great Diaspora throughout the entire Western Hemisphere.  The Caucasian World use the justification that the people of the continent of Africa are the descendants of Ham and Canaan.  They knowingly tell the untruth that Ham and Canaan raped Noah, and therefore their supposed descendants the population of the continent of Africa were cursed with a Black complexion, and would be made servants of servants, enslaved forever (**Gen. 9:25**). Many Black ministers even preach and teach this self enslaving distortion to their own Black congregations. They and their congregation as such then hold themselves in voluntary servitude, to the Caucasian Race. See* **"Adam/Seth Chronicles"** *to find that neither Noah nor any of his children were ever pale or Caucasians!  Blackness is not a curse, but is the original complexion of all the original inhabitants of the entire planet, including Adam and Noah.*

**8) It is made to seem that Nimrod kept Noah's children on mount Ararat, to set up a kingdom and religion for himself.** Fact is that Noah's children left Ararat before Nimrod was even born. Nimrod's mother brought him down from Ararat in her stomach!  The word Nimrod (נמרד) means "We Came Down". *See Strong's Concordance #  7287 (רדה√go downward).*

9) **It is made to seem that the people of** *Gen. 11:1-9* **are the children of  Noah in the house of Shem.** The fact is that these people were pale, the children of the Lord's son Marked Cain (*Gen. 4:14, 15*) who survived the flood sealed in the Caves of  Nod in Ararat. After the flood the Lord had Nimrod hunting in the ground for their caves, to dig the Chaldeans/Gentiles/Caucasians out (*Gen.10:8, 9*). The Lord then instructed Nimrod to build the six city Ur/Babel Metropolis, and to use it to raise these Gentiles from their corrupt lifestyle, that the Lord himself had imposed on them, there in Nod. But then the Lord and his Host brought Ur/Babel to ruin, and scattered Cain's children (*Gen. 11:9, Isaiah 23:13*).

10) **It is made to seem that the inhabitants of Sodom and Gomorrah were Canaanites, the children of Ham.** The fact is that Sodom and Gomorrah were twin cities, built to process, and store grain. The first people to live in these cities, were the Caucasians/Gentiles/Chaldeans who

Bible/Torah

# History of the Bible/Torah Chapter 1a
## Deceptions

had fled from the Lord, when he confounded Ur/Babel (*Isaiah 23:13, Genesis 11:9*). These people from the Ur Metropolis fled across the Tigris River westward down into the Gardenland of Ham in Canaan. They were given asylum from the Lord, and were quarantined as the first, and only people to live in the old grain storage cities, of Sodom and Gomorrah (*Gen. 11:9*).

11) **It is made to seem that Abraham was born in the land of the Sumerians in the southern regions of Mesopotamia.** The fact is that the nativity of Abraham (*Gen. 11:28, 31*), Ur/Babel of the true Chaldeans, was on the **"Side of the North"** (*Joshua 24:2*), of the Tigris River in Nod. Abraham descend from the line of Shem's son Arphaxad (*Gen. 10:22, Gen. 11:10*). Arphaxad's line split at Eber's two sons Peleg, and Joktan (*Gen. 10:25*). Joktan moved eastward in Nod (*Gen. 10:30*), but Peleg the line that Abraham descended from stayed north in Nod on the border of the Chaldeans, where Arphaxad lived (*Joshua 24:2, 3 Isaiah 14:12*). Arphaxad (ארפכשר) means "Border of the Chaldeans." The ruins of Nineveh and Calah two of the six city Ur Metropolis that Nimrod built, are in the north on the Tigris River. The other four cities Babel, Erech, Accad, and Resen, must also be located in the north near Nineveh and Calah (*Gen. 10:10, 12*).

12) **It is made to seem that there are "Hebrew People", and a "Hebrew Language".** The fact is that Abram "crossed", or "hebrewed "(עבר) #5674, #5676, #5680 the Tigris River from Ur, down into the land of Ham/Canaan (*Gen. 11:31*). You do not become a nationality by "hebrewing," or "crossing" a river, nor do your language change. Fact is that Ham and his children had "hebrewed" the Tigris four hundreds years before the birth of Abram from the same place. They were followed by the Chaldeans years later, who also "hebrewed" the same river from the north of Nod where Abram would be born. Ham and the Chaldeans did not become Hebrews by "hebrewing" a river, nor did Abram or anyone else. The term Hebrew for a people or language is a European invention in modern times.

13) **It is made to seem that Abraham was afraid of the Egyptians.** The fact is that the Lord was with Abraham, and his sister/wife/niece Sarah all the time. When Sarah had earned as much from the Pharaoh, as Abraham could manage, Sarah signalled for the Lord to plague the Pharaoh, so that they could leave Egypt with their goods (*Gen. 12:16, 17*).

When they returned to the land of Canaan, Abraham, Sarah, and the Lord, turned the same trick with Abimelech, getting again as much from Abimelech as they had gotten from the Pharaoh (*Gen. 20:2-14*). The Lord played his part well.

14) **It is made to seem that Lot was an honorable man.** Fact is that Lot was a permanent Sodomite, along with his **sons**, and sons-in- law (*Genesis 19:12*). Lot's sons and sons-in-law refused to leave Sodom. Lot, his wife, and two daughters did not want to leave either. Lot his wife, and daughters had to be dragged forcefully from the city (*Gen. 16:19*). None of them wanted to leave. It is a wonder that they all did not look back, at Sodom like Lot's wife did. (*Genesis 19:16*)!

15) **It is made to seem like Lot did not know that he was having sex with his two daughters.**

Bible/Torah

# History of the Bible/Torah Chapter 1a
## Deceptions

The statement is used that Lot did not know what time each one of his daughters had laid down with him, and then left (*Gen. 19:33, 35*). This does not mean that Lot did not know that he was having sex with his daughters, and making them pregnant! Lot knew that his two daughters were still virgins (*Gen. 19:8*), even after the three left Sodom, even though the daughters had been married, to Sodomites (*Lot's sons in law*)(*Gen. 19:12*). Lot had called his daughters virgins, and knew that there was no man around to make them pregnant, except himself (*Gen. 19:8*)!

16) **It is made to seem that Hagar (Shari Misraim) was proud to have a child for Abraham.** The fact is that Sarah forced Abraham on Hagar, and she was being raped (*Gen. 16:2-5*). The fact is that Hagar despised Abraham, and his sister/wife/niece, Sarah. Hagar did not want to be raped, and made pregnant by Abraham or any other man (*Genesis 16:2, 3, 4*)!

17) **It is made to seem that Abraham is the father of Isaac.** Fact is that the Lord "Visited" (FKD / פקד) Sarah and did to her what he had said he would do (give her a son) (*Gen.17:16*), for she was pregnant (*Gen. 21:1, 2*). (The word "Visited" in the Strong's Concordance is #6485 which is the word פקד sounded out as PhKD or FKD which defines the three components of sexual intercourse: **1) Foreplay** [oversee/give attention], **2) Penetration** [Dicker / דכר], and **3) Ejaculation** [deposit]. *See also Gesenius Hebrew/Chaldee Lexicon to the Old Testament pages 686a+b and 687* The Lord "gave" his son Isaac to Abraham to raise (*Joshua 24:3*).

18) **It is made to seem that Isaac is the father of Jacob and Esau.** The fact is that Abraham's Lord is also the father of Jacob and Esau (*Gen. 25:21*). Isaac entreated (Tempted / עתר) his father the Lord to "rub against (נכח)" Rebekah, and she became pregnant (*Gen. 25:21*). The Lord gave his sons Jacob and Esau to Isaac to raise (*Joshua 24:4*).

19) **It is made to seem that Jacob is the father of all of his sons.** The fact is that the Lord is the father of the first four children (sons) with Leah (*Gen. 29:31, 35*). The Lord is also the father of Joseph with Rachel (*Gen. 30:22*). Rachael even wrestled with her sister, and the Lord, to get him to give her a child (*Gen. 30:8*): ..... ותאמר רחל נפתולי אלהים נפתלתי עם אחתי The proper translation is: and Rachael said "I wrestled God, I wrestled also my sister (Leah)..."

20 **It is made to seem that Shechem raped (defiled) Dinah** (*Gen. 34:2*). Fact is that the word translated into the English for "defiled" (Annah / ענה) #6030-34 actually means "answer," or "solution." This is the same word used in the scripture where it says ....and the Lord "**answered**"(ענה) Job...(*Job 38:1, 40:1*). Thus if Shechem "defiled" Dinah, then the Lord "defiled" Job, but if the Lord "answered" Job, then Dinah was an "answer" for the young man Shechem.

Dinah's brothers did not have women, and they used the affair between Dinah and Shechem as an excuse to murder all the men and boys of the city of Shechem (*Gen. 34:25*). They kept and used the girls and women of the city of Shalem (Jerusalem), to rape themselves into tribal existence (*Gen. 33:18*)(*Gen. 34:29*).

Bible/Torah

# History of the Bible/Torah
# Chapter 1a  Deceptions

21) **It is made to seem that the Israelis were in bondage in Egypt.** Fact is that the Israelis told Jesus that they had never been in bondage to any man (*John 8:33*). The Egyptians only held them in due bounds, not to practice incest, rape, murder, theft, or any of the other practices that they had used to come into existence. The Israelis proved that they had not been in bondage in Egypt, when they told Jesus that they had never been in bondage, to any man (*John 8:33*). The Israelis had been in bondage to the Lord before they had fled from him, and his famine, into Egypt.

The Israelis would not have ever left Egypt. The Lord's destruction of Egypt was to punish the Egyptians for having given the Israelis extended sanctuary. Secondly Israel had no plans to leave Egypt, even after the Lord destroyed it. The Pharaoh had to drive them out with a strong hand (*Ex. 6:1*), while the Lord was pulling them out with a strong hand, at the same time (*Jer. 32:21*). The Israelis did not want to leave Egypt! Jesus came to make Israel free from bondage to the Lord, not Egypt!

22) **It is made to seem that the Israelis passed through a sea of water on dry feet.** The fact is that the "Red Sea" (Yom Suf / יום סוף) was only a "Reed Sea" (Yom Suf / יום סוף) made up of Bulrush (Suf / סוף) *See Strong's Concordance #5488 for "Red."* The Egyptians "drowning in a sea of reeds" is same as one "drowning in a sea of tears." No one drowned, it is only a metaphor, or simile. There was no water in the Reed Sea, or "Sea of Reeds."

23) **It is made to seem that the Israelis who left Egypt were allowed to go to the land of Canaan.** The fact is that the Lord took revenge on Israel, for having run away from him, and his famine 400 years before. The Israelis from Egypt, and their children were forced to wander around in the wilderness, for forty years, until they had all died (*Num.14:32*). Those who came forth from the wilderness, their children's children, were a band of **child eating pale lepers** (*Leviticus 13th Chptr., Deut. 28:57*). No Israelis or their children from Egypt survived to go into the land of Canaan, except Joshua, and Caleb (*Nu. 14:23, 24*).

24) **It is made to seem like the Israelis had to kill off the Ishmael/Midianite children of Abraham.** Fact is that the Lord had to bring the Israelis to the "East Country", which is well out of the way back to Canaan. The Lord brought the Israelis eastward to the East country, where Abraham had sent his children to live in peace (*Gen. 25:6*). There the Israelis committed holocaust against Ishmael/Midian the true **Children of Abraham**. The Israelis then made themselves the **Seed of Abraham** (*John 8:33*), by raping and impregnating the little Ishmael/Midianite girls of the **Children of Abraham** (*Numbers 32:40*). The Israeli line follows the female.

25) **It is made to seem that Moses was an honorable man.** The fact is that Moses ordered the Israelis to murder all of the Midianite men, women, and boys (*Nu. 31:17*). This left 32,000 pubelescent girls (Women Children)(*Nu. 31:1,18 35*). Moses instructed the Israelis to give 32 of these girls to the Lord (*Nu. 31:40*), and 50 of the little girls to the Levites priesthood (*Nu. 31:47*). Then Moses told the Israelis to kill all of the little girls that had been known (been sodomized/ שׁכב) by man (*Nu. 31:17*). Moses told the Israelis to keep the rest of these girls for themselves to

# History of the Bible/Torah
# Chapter 1a  Deceptions

do with as they pleased (*Num. 31:18*). Moses wife Zipporah and his two sons Gershom and Eliezer were all Midianites, so Moses had to murder his whole family too, along with the other Midianites (*Ex.2:22, Nub. 31:17*). The Israelis took the thousands of these adolescent girls, and raped themselves into being the "Seed of Abraham." For the Israelis the Linage is through the female, thus Abraham's children's daughters are the generators. Never the less the Israelis were never the "Children of Abraham."

The Lord's reward to Moses for the atrocities that he orchestrated, was to grow horns (קרן) out of Mose's fore head (*Ex. 34:29, 30, 35*), and then to murder him while he was still in perfect health on Mount Nebo (*Deut. 34:5, 6*). *Look at the word "Shone," Strongs # 7160 - 7162 = "Horns"*

**26) It is made to seem that Yeshua (Jesus) was born to die for the sins of the World.** The fact is that Yeshua (Jesus) was sent to make the lost sheep of Israel free, by destroying the World of the Lord, that held the Israelis in bondage. Light in the Darkness of the World of the Lord (*Amos 5:18, 20*) brings the World to an end (*John 9:5, Amos 5:18, 20*). If Yeshua (Jesus) had been successful there would be no, Judaism, Christianity, or World of the Lord.

**27) It is made to seem that Christianity (Anti Christ) represent Jesus (Yeshua).** The fact is that Jesus was murdered by ChristiAnity (AntiChrist), before it founded the Christian church to cancel out the damage that Jesus' teachings had done. The fact is also that Christianity printed the teachings of Jesus in the Bible/Torah New Testament, and then used the teachings of Paul to cancel those same teachings out. One only have to overlay Jesus' teachings with Paul's teachings, to see that Paul's teachings cancel out the teachings of Jesus. Jesus never represented the Lord, and his World, but taught all to hate the Lord's World (TBL), that the Lord loves (*I John 2:15*).

## Discrepancies

**1) It is made to seem that the Solar Wars of Revelations (*Rev. 12:7*) is yet to come.** Yet this war was over 2000 years ago, example: There **"Was"** war in the heavens...the Dragon **"did not"** prevail...Dragon **"was"** casted out, into the earth, etc. (*Rev. 12:7-9*). There is no place between the books of Genesis and Revelations that this war in the heavens could have taken place. The war in the book of Revelations is therefore before Genesis. The covers must be removed from the Bible/Torah and the end of Revelations must be brought around trailing the rest of the Bible in a circle, to the beginning of Genesis. The end of Revelations must then be fused, to the beginning of Genesis, to make Revelations with it's war before Genesis.

**2) It is made to seem that the planetary cataclysm of *Isaiah 24:1, 3-6* occurred in the life time of Isaiah.** As with the Solar Wars above there is no place in the Bible/Torah that this global disaster could have occurred, except before the book of Genesis. This is not the flood of Noah as no **inhabitants of earth burned** in Noah's flood (*Isaiah 24:6*)!

The war in the heavens, and the destruction of this planet, before Genesis in Revelation, go to show why the planet is in a destroyed condition, at the beginning of the book of Genesis (*Isaiah 24:1, 3-6*). The following information concerns the physically deformed state that the planet was

# Chptr. 1a
## Planetary and Continental Diasporas

in, through the first chapter of Genesis (*Genesis 1:1*).

Because of the solar war before Genesis, there was the destruction of two planets: Crypton, a planet between Mars, and Jupiter (a "place found no more in the heavens (*Rev. 12:8*)," and this planet Assiah, which became Earth, after it's destruction. Assiah was originally brought forth from the sun, with all other planets within it. All of the planets were dispersed (פוץ), in a great diaspora from Assiah, to form the solar system. The future Lord of Abraham caused a war in the heavens (*Rev. 12:7*). In his pending defeat the Lord destroyed his planet named Crypton, which became millions of boulders. The Lord and his Host were defeated, and cast down to this planet Assiah the mother planet .

Assiah was being carried along at a tremendous rate by the sun, in the direction of it's old north pole, as it rotated on it's axis around the sun. There was no moon for it was still the north polar region of this planet, having people, cities, vegetation, and animals, on it (*Isaiah 24:6*).

Hallel (Lord) and his Host attempted to destroy Assiah, but could only exploded and shatter Assiah into great slabs of land (*Isa. 24:1, 3-6*). These great slabs of land are called Ertz/Earth (continents). In the explosion the entire northern region of the planet was blown away, and it continued in the same direction that the whole planet had been going, while the planet was stopped. The moon portion's atmosphere survived, but as the moon went out all of it's water was pulled back to the planet, and massive turbulence in the atmosphere of the moon blasted the moon portion's cities, and inhabitants out of existence.

The story was altogether different on the planet proper. There was the composite action of the moon exploding out of the northern end of the planet, and causing the planet to stop, with Africa (Eden) being the portion stopped at the south end by the explosion. It was momentum that caused the continents to break away from all sides of Eden (Africa). Buffering all of this was the simultaneous collapsing of the planet's atmosphere. The collapsing atmosphere saved the planet it's people from total destruction, by nullifying most of the destructive effects of the explosion.

Continents lay scattered all over the planet, like pieces of a giant puzzle, blown apart. Of all the pieces there is but one piece or continent, that all of the other continents commonly fit back to. The one continent that all the other continents fit back to was once called Eden, but is now called Africa. Africa (Eden) is the only land that did not move when the planet was exploded. Eden (Africa) therefore becomes the keystone, to setting the planet back to the way that it was before the Lord and his host exploded (*Revelation 12:12*), and destroyed it. *Isaiah 24:1, 3-6*

Continents disappear as they are merged back into the top, sides and bottom of this continent Africa, from their various directions: Spain, Italy, Greece, Israel, Arabia, Madagascar, India, Indonesia, Borneo, Philippines, China, Japan, Australia, New Zealand, New Guinea, Tasmania, Antartica, the Western Hemisphere, etc. All continents are kin to Eden (Africa), the last place where man was himself, which is God. Eden is the kingdom manifest (*Luke 17:21*).

When all the pieces (Continents) are fused back around Eden (Africa), a great gaping wound, a massive pit will be left in the pacific ocean side of the planet, where the moon was once the northern polar region of the planet. Broken planet, broken people, and finally broken information.

# History of the Bible/Torah
## Chptr. 1a
### Planetary Diasporah

*Broken land placed back around Eden (Africa), the old south polar region)*

*When this map is placed on a curvature (Globe), most of the gaps between the continents disappear*

    The theory of Evolution is a European invention, used to hide the fact that this entire planet was once fully populated, by advanced wooly headed Black/Brown beings. They did not evolve, nor did they have to migrate, from Africa, but have always populated the entire planet. These were, and are the Gods of the Bible/Torah. They did not evolve up from animals, as a missing link, to become the parents of the Caucasian Race, as evolution implies. Rather the original man on this planet fell down from a higher estate, down into creating, altering, or mutating the Caucasian Race into existence, as an experimental species.
    The narrative of the first chapter of Genesis, is even before the mutating into existence of the Caucasian Race. The 1st chptr. Genesis narrative is being given by Black Avatars (Aviators), who at that time had the ability for space flight. The destruction of this planet given at Isaiah 24:1, 3-6, and the discription of the results of that destruction, given at first chapter of Genesis, are given from an advantage point in space above the planet.

Bible/Torah

# History of the Bible/Torah
# (Chptr. 1b)
## Bible Origins and Purpose

*Continental/Diasporah — Bible/Torah — Mesoretic Text (Egyptian) — Bible*

### Bible/Torah

The Bible/Torah is a broken document, a breaking of the Law. I use the term Bible/Torah to describe the overall contents of the King James English Bible. The Bible/Torah consists of 66 books. The first thirty-nine of these books is the Old Testament or Torah. The 39 books of the Torah are the complete Jewish Bible. Christianity added the 27 books of their New Testament to the 39 of the Torah and called the 66 books their Bible. The Old and New Testament go together to make up the 66 books of the Bible/Torah.

### Mesoretic Text

The Torah in the form that it is now in, was brought into existence around the **10th century** A.D. The Jewish group who formatted it into it's present form called themselves Mesorets. They say that the name Mesoret means "tradition," but "Mesoret" (מצרי) actually means "Egyptians" (מצרי). **See Strong's #4714** מצרי, **for Egyptian**. Thus most of the Bible/Torah as **Mesoretic Text** is **Egyptian Text**, from the scribes of Egypt, before the Exodus. Some of the Mesoretic Text is older than the existence of the wooly headed brown ancient Israelis, and the Caucasian Race.

### Bible

The Christian Bible that I have focused on in this book, is the King James Version because the King James Bible Version is the most accurate to the Torah, of all the Christian Bibles ever published. The first publication of the King James Bible was in 1611 A.D., by the Barker Publication Company of London England. The first King James Bible had 80 books: 39 Old Testament, 27 New Testament and 14 Apocrypha. The original King James Bible was basically the same as the Catholic Bible. The English had been Catholics like the rest of Europe, until King Henry the 8th divorced his wife. When Henry divorced his wife, the Pope excommunicated him, and Henry divorced England from the Catholic church. The Catholic church in England became the Anglican church, and the Catholic Bible with it's 80 books went through a transformation to finally become the King James Bible. The first King James Bible still had the 80 books, of the Catholic Bible.

There was no "J" in that entire first King James Bible. The word James for King James did not exist, it was the word Ames. Nor was there a "J" yet in the English alphabet even though it's parent the Latin Alphabet had a "J" like letter given to it by the Moors in Spain around 711 A.D. The letter was the Arabic letter "Geem" (ج) which was pronounced with a "G" sound. There was no Jesus, James, Jehovah, Jews etc., because there was no "J" alphabet letter or sound to say these words. There is still no "J" sound or letter in the so called "Hebrew."

Around 1630 A.D. the "J" like Arabic letter was modified from "ج," to "J," and was incorporated into the so called English alphabet, and Language. It was around this time 1630 that

# History of the Bible/Torah (Chptr. 1b)

## Bible Origins and Purpose

*Bible — Strong's Concordance — Bookless Book*

the "J" was finally installed in the King James Bible. By the time of the 1630 publication the 14 Apocrypha books were gone.

It is 264 years from 1630 to 1894, when the Strong's Concordance came into existence. It was the Strong's Concordance that froze this "version" phenomena to that date.

### Strong's Exhaustive Concordance

The Strong's Concordance is the definitive concordance to the King James Bible. This Concordance was published and began to be circulated around **1894.** The Strong's is exhaustive in the sense that it translates every English word listed in the King James Bible, back to the Old Testament "Hebrew," or the New Testament Greek. The concordance has two Lexicons to accomplish this. One lexicon for the Old Testament "Hebrew," and the other lexicon for the "New" Testament Greek. Thus the English, Greek, and "Hebrew," are combined to give translations for every word in the Old and New Testaments. The Torah as translated by the Israelis (Jews), into English, is also held to accuracy by the same Strong's Concordance. As such anyone in the two religions Christians and Jewish (Israelis), have the ability, with this Strong's Concordance, to see that there are intentional inaccuracies in the Bible/Torah, and the English translated Torah. One can judge for themselves whether these inaccuracies were placed there intentionally, or not by their modern Pale Jewish and other Gentile scribes.

### Bookless Book

The original Torah as transcribed by the ancient Israeli scribes did not have chapters, paragraphs, or verses. These scrolls were raw information, and may not have even been in book form. Thus the Torah scrolls not being books would not have had names of authors or prophets.

The following is the alphabet that the ancient Mesoretic (Egyptian) Text was written with: ᔭᐱᗑ⊕ᚹ×◻◻ᗯᕐᗰᗰᒎᎩᎩᎩ⧧°Ϙᒎ. It is the form that Mesoretic (Egyptian) Text was in, when the wooly headed Israelis brought it from Egypt. This alphabet originated in Egypt, but is now called the Phoenician alphabet. In approximately 400 B.C. the Mesoretic Text was translated from the Phoenician alphabet into a modification of the same phonetic alphabet, called Greek: αβγδεϕγ etc. This document was called the Septuagint or Greek Bible.

Around the 10th century A.D. in Spain the Jewish "Mesorets (Egyptians)" are said to have formatted the scrolled information into invented chapters, verses, and perhaps books. They also inserted author names into their document at their own discretion. This document was written in another invented alphabet called the Aramaic square script: קרשת מנסעפצ חטיבכל אבגדהוז. It is now called the "Hebrew" alphabet, even though there is not a language or people named "Hebrew." "Hebrew" is not a noun at all but a verb that means "to Cross," as when Abram "crossed" (hebrewed) the Tigris River, westward down into the land of Ham. Abram then became AbramHam, or Abraham. It was Abram "crossing" (hebrewing) the Tigris that gave significance

# History of the Bible/Torah
# (Chptr. 1b)
## Bible Origins and Purpose

*An excellent document for the sincere — God's Book (proof that it is, is proof that it is not)*

to the term "hebrew," which only means "To Cross." Whatever language the Hebrewer spoke before he Hebrewed (crossed), is the same language he spoke after he hebrewed (crossed).

The old scribes did not hide anything. They wrote (in the Old Language) openly that the Lord told Moses that he was **El Shaddai** or the **God of Devils** (*Ex. 6:3*). Those old scribes wrote that the Lord told Moses that Abraham, Isaac and Jacob knew that he was El Shaddai or the Devil God. The modern Rabbis, and Priests left the term El Shaddai untranslated in the Torah, but mistranslated the old language term El Shaddai into the English as **"God Almighty,"** knowing that it should have been translated **"Devil God."** You can not find the word Devil in the Old Testament English, it is hidden under the word "Almighty," starting at *Gen. 17:1*, and ending at *Joel 1:15*. What purpose could possibly be served by the modern pale Rabbis and Priest, when they knowingly mistranslate the documents of the true wooly headed brown ancient Israelis?

### Book of God

No one will deny that the **Word of God,** or **Book of God** would have to be Eternal, without beginning or end. As such the Book of God could not be compiled books, nor would it need authors, or chapters, or versions. There is nothing to be added to the book, and nothing to be taken from it! The word of God as a perfect physical document would be endless or circular. The Word being Eternal, would be intact and complete, from before Creation! As such the book would stand "alone" (All One) without a need for alterations or additions.

Judeo/Christianity hold up their religious book and claim that it is the the Book of God. And yet the same information that they use to prove that the Bible/Torah is the word of God, is the same information that can be used, to proved that the Bible/Torah is not the word of God.

The libraries of the World System are full of commentaries praising the great prophets and the books, that they supposedly wrote, over thousands of years, to finally come forth with the Bible/Torah. Dates are given for when chapters and verses were added etc. This alone proves that the Bible/Torah the book with a beginning and end could not be the Word or Book of God.

To even began to consider the Bible/Torah as the book of God, it would have to be an endless book without beginning or end, and therefore it's back and front covers must be removed, and the end of Revelation must be brought around trailing the rest of the Bible behind it. The end of Revelations must then be fused to the beginning of Genesis making a seamless circle of information. Thus the book of Revelation becomes the book before Genesis, and you can not have a creation as creation is described, in a beginingless, endingless, eternal condition where all is already existing! With all already in existence, creation can only be the altering of what already exists!

### Outer Writings

Original Man is the Book of God. Each copy of the true Book of God (Man) is a master copy.

# History of the Bible/Torah
# (Chptr. 1b)
## Bible Origins and Purpose

*Outer Writings (with inner nothing) — Adam (Alpha/Omega) Book of God*

All is written inside where Man dwells. As such there is no need of external writings, and the accompanying translations, etc. Those who have no writing on the inside carry their writing on the outside, perhaps in a book on the shelf or under the arm. They speak it but if you are doing it you do not have to say it! The inventors of the Bible/Torah quote truths, that are in the Bible/Torah, but they can not or will not do what the book say.

The book was never supposed to be written in, for it has always been complete, but just not understood. The entire reason that the Book of God (Man) is manifest is for understanding.

### Closed Eyes, Ears, and Hearts (Minds)

In finality consider that the entire Caucasian Race did not, and do not have an alphabet of their own. As such an alphabet had to be taught, to those among them who could be taught. There were no written records in Europe, so someone had to give the Caucasians the raw information that they used to write the Bible/Torah. The European clerics did not have to formulate the information into religious material.

The Caucasian Race have been monitored for their entire existence, and at each appropriate instance they have been given that which would allow them the choice to maintain, or improve their existence. The raw information given to the Europeans was not religious at all, but was a fragment of the history of this planet.

If the handful of clerics in the tenth through twelfth century Europe had compiled the information given to them truthfully, the pale European masses would have had an accounting of how their race came into existence. They would also know that there are none Caucasian people around them, who have kept their entire race alive and civilized, from their very inception.

But the handful among the Caucasians who are capable, have always kept their masses in the Darkness, with eyes that do not see, and ears that do not hear, and minds that do not understand (*Isa. 6:10*). Thus those nonCaucasians who maintained the existence of the Caucasian Race had to fall mentally asleep, to to stay parallel to where the pale ones were falling.

I have retrieved much of the fragments of information that were distorted into the Bible/Torah, and converted them back into their approximate original form. This reordered information in this book shall be use as an instrument to reawaken those none Caucasians, who died (mentally), that the Caucasian Race might continue to live.

This Book is the results of the information that was extracted from the Bible/Torah, and was reordered. It is possible to use the reordered information in this book to raise the dead, which in the modern times include the wooly headed brown collective Adam.

Bible/Torah

# Adam Chronicles

*Bible History — Alpha/Omega (Book of God) — Gods — Fields (Electric Male/Magnetic Female)*

### Alpha/Omega

**Adam:** I am the true Book of God. I am the Alpha and Omega, and had no beginning or ending. Nor did I originally as the book have a cover (Body), I was invisible (אלוהים). As such I the book was complete, and there was nothing to be added to me, and nothing to be taken away from me. Therefore I as the Book of God had no translations, versions, authors, books, chapters, or verses.

In actuality I was never one but am the collective Original Man who populated the entire original planet. We Adams all were/are each the Book of God. Without our "covers" (physical forms) we are Single Eyed (Cyclops / Cyclopedias), and full of Light (*Matt. 6:22, Luke 11:34*). We have a single eye, that see all, a single ear that hear all, and a single heart/mind that understand all (*Matt. 13:15, 16*). We are full of Light, but without "coats of Skins, we are Invisible Ones (אלוהים), or Gods (אלוהים). **In** <u>visible</u> (in seen) is that which can only be seen when you are illuminated **in**<u>side</u>, seeing with the Single Eye (*Matt. 16:22*).

### Gods

**Adam:** All of us who separated the planet from the sun, are Gods (Invisible Ones). Without our coats of skin we are not seen, from the physical realm (*Gen. 3:21*). Inside of our coats of skin we are brothers (Breathers/Souls). Originally there were perhaps 144,000 of us Souls or solar beings. None of us Adams had navels, including Hallel (Lord), Gabriel, Michael/Melchezedek, and myself. We had no navels because we exist without the aid of mothers and fathers (*Hebrews 7:3*).

Our "coats of skins" are/were black to brown, to complement the sun that we manifested from (*Dan. 7:9, Rev. 1:14*). The pattern of our wooly hair contains the designs for all forms in the universe.

As said before in the invisible realm we "invisible ones (Gods)," are single eyed, and single eared, with single mind/hearts, that allow us Gods to see all, know all, and be all present (*Matt. 13:15*).

Yet to **See All, Know All,** and **Be All** in the same instance is not seeing, knowing, or being anything in particular. Lack of knowledge of the particular is dissatisfaction. Dissatisfaction was the engine that pulsed the absolute to bring us into particular being. The particular being of Self is the dissatisfaction ejected from the absolute. We (the Gods) are the Selves (שלך) who out of dissatisfaction were "Pushed Out" (שלך) into Being from the absolute.

### Fields

**Adam:** The first dissatisfaction of Self is into Electrical Lines of Force (פרד), which was our "separation"(Cipheration), (פרד) from the absolute. The second dissatisfaction of self is the exploration, from lines of force into Rings of Magnetic (מגן) Pressure. The electrical lines of force is male and the magnetic rings of pressure is female. The magnetic female radiate from, and orbits around, the electrical male. The composite Electric male and Magnetic female together

Bible/Torah

# Adam Chronicles

*Fields — Manifestation (Particular)*

forms the great Electromagnetic **Field.**

At first the electromagnetic field was not physical or particular, for we had not set the "invisible" electro/magnetic fields, into the state that allow for the illusion of physical existence. Collectively we the invisibles (Gods) are the Beings (Beast) of the Field behind the existence of the physical (*Gen. 2:19, 20*). We the Beings (Beast) of the invisible Field above, are also the manifest Beings (Beast) of the Earth below (*Gen. 1:24*). Beast or "living Ones" (חים, חות, הוה) are not animals but are "animators" of all living forms.

We used the invisible electro/magnetic field as a blueprint room to design all things/forms in the physical or particular realm. In the first instance of physical manifestation all was HermesAphrodite from, the atomic scale up through the vegetable, animal, and man form.

The Physical male/female HermesAphrodite state corresponds to the invisible male/female nature of the electromagnetic field. Initially there was no separated male, and separate female throughout the entire physical spectrum from atomic to manform. There was no purpose for the separate male state and female state. All was male/female and sufficient to self. All existed without the aide of a mother or father (*Hebrews 7:3*). We designed the physical into existence from it's most elemental to it's most complex.

We formed the electromagnetic patterns (pater / father) for all physical forms, there in the invisible Field, for all including our male/female or HermesAphrodite body forms (*Gen.1:27*). In the unseen realm we established all of the patterns (Paters / fathers) necessary to express all matter (Mater / mother) material forms. The pattern for all that exists in the particular or physical universe is set in the invisible realm of the Field. In the same instance that the invisible pattern for some thing is altered or erased in the invisible field, it is also altered or ceases to exist in the physical realm (Above as Below). This pertains to all including the planets and the sun, and all else in physical manifestation including the man form. This is from microscopic to the entire universe.

**Manifestation**

**Adam:** We brought forth the illusion of physical being, from the **triple dissatisfaction** (Darkness) of the Great Field: From lines of force, to planes of pressure, to volumes of mass. We Adams (Atoms) have two states: One is **invisible wave**, and the other is **visible** (manifest) **particle**. Within the designs of our wooly (spiraled) hair are all of the patterns, for all shapes, movements, and designs, of all that exist in the whole universe. Our hair design is composed of coils, spirals, waves, spheres, etc. (*Daniel 7:9, Rev. 1:14*).

We manifested the physical, into being intact and complete without a need to add, subtract or alter any of it. In the first instance there are spiraling of spirals within spirals (as in our hair), down to the manifestation of our sun at the very bottom of this chain of orbits. We caused cycles, or seasons to allow the illusion to circulate through it's processes. We designed all organic (living) forms to be HermesAphrodite to self sustain. The physical (particle) universe is our

Bible/Torah

# Adam Chronicles

*Manifestation (Brown and Wooly) — Sunday — Assiah (Asia)(Isaiah 24:1, 3-6)*

illusion that we designed so that we could achieve a thorough understanding of Self in the particular. Our dissatisfaction causes the physical to exist, and we manifest down into it, on a quest to find out about Self, "the invisible one" (God) in the particular.

Inspite of the complexity of our hair, and the design of our melaninated (Black/brown) bodies, they are only temporary dwelling places, while we are experimenting in the physical illusion.

### Sunday

**Adam:** "Sun" "day" is the "day" of the "sun." Shemesh (the sun) is the most perfect representation of our Original Selves in physical manifestation. The sun in it's nakedness (invisible state) is an electromagnetic entity. The garment that the sun wears in the physical is the Ultraviolet purpleness of Black Light. This is even though the sun appear to be yellow from inside the atmosphere of Assiah the mother planet. We brought this planet Assiah (Fireness / אישה) the mother planet out of our father the sun, to continue our experiment down into the particular realm. The sun is our father (Ab / אב) simply because we brought ourselves out of it. Yet we are the source of the very sun that we manifested from. We and our father are one (*John 10:30; John 14:2*). We designated the sun as the Most High / עליון. The Most High, (Alien / עליון) represent our most perfect state of being. In our perfection being black and wooly headed, we can stand on the planetary equator forever without being harmed, by the full intensity of the sun. Fire does not harm fire!

With the Sun (Shemesh / שמש) being our father, we are Ca-Shemeshu (כשמשו)(666) or "like the Sun." Originating from the sun we are all Sols (Souls), or Solar Beings. Original Man (איש) the Invisible (אלוהים) or Gods, are firey beings inside of the physical form (*I Cor. 3:1; 6:20*). Heaven (Place of Life), the kingdom of us Gods, is at the center of our invisible forms, inside of the physical forms that we wear (*Luke 17:21*).

### Assiah

**Adam:** Assiah (Asia) is the original name that we gave to the globe before it was called Earth. Assiah (אישה) means "Fireiness" because originally the globe was "firey" like Shemesh the sun. We the original Man (Ish / איש), the Assian (Asian) were/are "Firey" (אש) also. We are all Supreme (Cipherim) Beings, Beings that "separated" (Ciphereted/Separated) our selves from the absolute to manifest, and explore the unknown particular. I (Adam), Michael/Melchezedek, Hallel (The Lord), and Gabriel are only a few of perhaps 144,000 who brought Assiah out of the sun. All Assians (Asians), or inhabitants of Assiah (Asia), were originally Adam (אדם), or Red (רד) Ones. This is because man and the globe are red, in the Etheric state, like the Ether that exists in the Field that we "come down" (רד) through. The Field descends down from Ultraviolet (Black), to the Infrared, which is just before physical manifestation.

The red etheric port is the door way "down" (רד) into, and back up out of the physical or

Bible/Torah

# Adam Chronicles

*Assiah— Aliens*

particular realm.

Originally Mother Assiah was co-equal in size to Father Shemesh (sun). There were no other globes in the solar system, for the other planets were all still inside of Assiah. Assiah (globe) was in orbit around Shemesh (sun) In that time there were no continents or broken land on the globe. There were no mountains, just rolling hills. The planet did not have a dark side, but glowed all around. We caused the entire globe to be a paradise, an orchard with trees, fruit trees, lakes, rivers, and streams. There were animals, and all of the other forms that we experimented with. There were no problems, for we had the solution for every situation. We set the rate of the revolutions of the globe, and how far away we were from the sun. It rained when we caused it to rain. There were seasons, but temperature was Constant throughout the seasons of the cycle. We even set the thickness of the atmosphere. We caused to exist, and experimented with all kinds of lifeforms great and small. Some creeped, some crawled, some swam in the seas, that we had formed, and others flew through the atmosphere that we had designed. This was Assiah (Asia) as first manifested. There were no planets then, just Mother Assiah.

**Planets**

**Adam:** Planets (פלנות) means "Place of Fallen Ones. Those who took globes out of Assiah, took those globes and "Fell" away," into their own orbits around the sun. These were acts of Apostasy (αποστασψ) or "curving away)." Since we are all that there truly is, and we are projecting the illusion of time and space, there is no place to go outward, except away from the true center of ones own Self, further into the illusion that we are all collectively projecting. Space is only an apparent projection, it is not actual. But lack of understanding carried the dissatisfied further away from Self.

The sun represent our true and perfect Self. Yet we had no comprehension of that perfection, before we brought Assiah forth from the sun. We had to be at a proper distance from perfect Self, to come to a proper understanding of Self. We set our globe Assiah at a proper distance (focus) from the sun, to experiment, and come to a proper overall understanding. The proper viewpoint, and understanding is lost, if one is too near, or too far away. There must be understanding for satisfaction in the experiment. **Dissatisfaction** cast us out, and **satisfaction** was the only way back in. Satisfaction comes with understanding.

It was out of dissatisfaction, and misunderstanding, that "planets" were taken out of Assiah. Those who went out beyond Assiah took a mass from Assiah, to make their own sun. The apostate carried this great mass away from Assiah, out into Outer Darkness, and attempted to make another sun, that would not orbit around our sun. **Jupiter** represents that attempt of the apostate to make their own sun. Mars and Crypton represent planets that they attempted to put in orbit around Jupiter. Their attempt failed for they could not stop Jupiter from orbiting our sun. Nor could they cause Mars and Krypton two other planets brought from Assiah, to orbit Jupiter. Jupiter the false sun was in orbit around the sun. Crypton and Mars were also in orbit around the

Bible/Torah

# Adam Chronicles

*Aliens — Disciples/Apostles*

sun. All of the planets used by the Apostate to escape from Assiah came from Assiah. The original planet Assiah that we brought forth from the sun had been co equal in size to the sun, and just as fervent. What remains of **Assiah** now is a small aspect of it's original size. We Adams who remained on the small remains of **Assiah** continued to designate ourselves collectively as "**Adam.**" We Assians (Asians), or Adams (Red Ones) were the only ones left who had stayed the course down into wherever the experiment took us. We had not curved away like our brothers on the planets. All of us came forth from the sun bringing Assiah with us. We called ourselves "Adams," until some curved away, lost reference to Self, and become Aliens (Alienated).

These aliens included others who left Assiah, with planets and went out beyond Jupiter, because they wanted to experiment beyond the experimenting, that we were doing on Assiah. They were curious to see what was further out in the illusion. **Saturn, Neptune, Uranus,** and **Pluto** represent these explorers.

### Disciples/Apostles

**Adam:** Only those who remained on this the mother planet Assiah held the straight line, down into the experiment. Those of us who held the line of the experiment were disciplined, and are therefore Disciples. Those who curved away are apostrophe (,), apostate or Apostles, who became alienated, from their own perfect Selves. Those who went out became "alienated," because they discovered that there was nothing out there in the Outer Darkness, except the planets they took with them. Thus they had to "craft" from the substance of their planets all that they needed. "Crafting," or "creating,"or "altering" is the beginning of all corruption. **Creation** or **corruption** or **crafting** is the altering of what is already complete, correct, and perfect, into something less than it's original Self. All of the planets began to die, like branches die, when they are removed from a tree, for the act of crafting.

Chief among those who crafted was Hallel (הלל) who was more crafty then all the other Apostate. As such his planet was named Crafton (Place of Crafting), or Crypton/Krypton (Corrupt Place). Hallel or Lucifer is the Cipherman or Superman, who was to become the Lord of Abraham. The planet Crypton was also called Lucifer (הלל) being the planet of the Lord, who is Hallel (הלל), who is Lucifer (הלל)(*Isaiah 14:12*). Crypton (Krypton) the planet of Hallel (Lucifer) was located between Mars and Jupiter. All who had gone out on the planets were dissatisfied, but Hallel (Lucifer) on Crypton was more dissatisfied, and lacking than the others. Being insufficient the Lord named himself Jealous (קין)(*Ex. 34:14*), a term of low self esteem. It was the Lord who became a **Man of War** (*Ex. 15:3*), in an attempt to exalt himself above the Most High (Sun)(*Rev. 12:7, 9; Isa. 14:12*).

### Solar War

**Adam:** But Hallel (The Lord) was defeated in the war that he caused in the heavens. He and his Host from Crypton had been attempting to export his planet's corruption, to the other planets in

Bible/Torah

# Adam Chronicles

*Solar War — Outcast*

the solar (Soul) system. They were also attempting to take the sun, for as apostates they had lost their souls (Solar Association). My brothers the Lord and his Hosts had not prevailed (*Rev. 12:8*), and in their pending defeat Hallel and his Host exploded their planet Krypton. All living in the World of Hallel on Crypton had been deceived by him, and now they had been destroyed (*Rev. 12:9*). Crypton became a ring of stones out between Mars and Jupiter in orbit around the sun.

When all of the debris representing Crypton (Krypton), is gathered back into the planet that it was, it will be larger than the globe Assiah which Krypton (Crypton) was taken from!

As Crypton was destroyed, "place was no longer found" for Hallel and his Host, in the heavens (*Rev. 12:8*). Hallel (CipherMan/Superman/Lucifer), and his Host were cast back down into the vicinity of Assiah our mother planet. Hallel the Great Dragon was Abraham's future Lord. He was cast (Shaddai / שרי) out. Hallel is that Old Serpent called the Devil (Shad / שר), and Satan, he was Cast Out, and down into the planet, and his angels (Host) with him (*Rev. 12:9, Gen. 6:4*).

### Outcast (Shaddai)

**Adam:** Hallel (Lucifer / חלל) and his Host were cast out, and down into the planet (*Revelations 12:, Gen. 6:4*). He spoke to us his brother Adams, still on Assiah, and demanded that we bow down to him, and do his bidding. He considered us haughty because we the Adams reminded him that we were all Gods, like he was (*Isa. 24:4*). We reminded him that we were all co-equally Gods, children of the Most High (Sun)(*Psalms 82:6*). Gods keep their feet (*Eccles 5:1*) Our brother the Lord Hallel (Lucifer) and his Host in their rage destroyed Assiah the mother globe, exploding it and knocking it out of it's course (*Psalms 82:5, Isaiah 13:13*). Behold our brother Hallel (Lucifer) made Assiah empty, waste, and turns it upside down and scatter us it's inhabitants (*Isa. 24:1*). The land was utterly empty and spoiled because the Lord spoke it (*Isa. 24:3*). Our planet Assiah mourns and fades away broken (*Isa. 24:4*). We would not break the Law by making a covenant with the Fallen Lord (*Isa. 24:5*). Therefore the curse (profanity) of our brother the Lord devoured Assiah, and we who continued to dwell on it. Many were burned, and few men were left (*Isa. 24:6*). Hallel (Lucifer / חלל) the Cipherman/Superman and his Host had destroyed our mother planet Assiah, as they had destroyed their own planet Krypton.

*The Isaiah, and Psalms accounts of the destruction of this planet both occurred, just after the Solar Wars and defeat in Revelations, the book before Genesis. The planet was in total Darkness (Gen. 1:1).*

### Hereafter

**Adam:** "Hereafter" literally means "here" (on this planet Assiah), "after" the effects of a Day of the Lord was imposed on it (*Ps. 118:23*). The Day of the Lord is a Darkness, with no light in it (*Amos 5:18, 20*). This was the total Darkness that Michael/Melchezedek and his messengers found when they "found" (Bara / ברא) the planet, and it's heavens (Skies) destroyed (*Gen. 1:1, 2*).

After the other planets had been removed from Assiah and carried out into the solar system, Assiah was the only portion in the same orbit it had been in, when taken from the sun. Now that

Bible/Torah

# Adam Chronicles

*Hereafter — Ertz (Earth / ארץ)*

Assiah had been exploded the only portion of it's total land mass that was still in place, was it's old south polar region, which was to be called Eden (Africa). Eden (Africa) was the only place on the planet, or in the whole solar system that had not been moved away from the original place, that all had been in when Assiah had been separated from the sun.

Now Assiah the mother globe having been knocked out of it's course, lay in ruins (*Psalms 82:6*). When the Lord and his Host had exploded the planet (*Isa. 24:6*) they had knocked it out of it's course (*Psalms 82:5*), and the planet had stopped rotating on it's axis. Darkness came when the atmosphere (heavens) around the planet had dissolved, rolled together as a scroll, and collapsed (*Isa. 34:4*). The atmosphere had collapsed from a gas state, down into water that covered the entire surface of the planet (*Gen. 1:2*). Michael /Melchezedek commanded that his Luminaries illuminate the surface of the planet again, to separate it's reilluminated surface from the darkness around it (*Gen. 1:3, 4*) Now Michael/Melchezedek commanded the luminaries with him to generate a turbulence (torque / רקיע) in the water, around the planet to cause it to began rotating again (*Gen. 1:6*). The rotating of the planet caused the reexpansion of the atmosphere, back from water into a gas state again. Thus the atmosphere became luminance again, and the water was drained from the surface of the planet again, to expose the basic land mass that now lay in ruins (*Gen. 1:7, 9*).

### Ertz (Earth)

**Adam:** Michael/Melchezedek and his Luminaries saw the dry land of Assiah again (*Gen. 1:9*). It was not the same as it had been before Assiah had been exploded, and water had covered the land. Assiah was now broken up into fragments (Ertz) or continents, so they called Assiah Ertz, or Earth (fragments), for the first time ever (*Gen. 1:10*). They also called Assiah "Tiamat" (Thou are Dead / תאמות), for all life had been suspended on the globe. Thirdly they now called Assiah "Planet" (פלנות) which means "Place of Fallen Ones, or Felons. The Lord Almighty the "Felon" or "Fallen One" and his Host had been "Cast Down" to Assiah in defeat (*Rev. 12:9, Numbers 24:4, 16*). Our Felon (criminal) brothers had destroyed Assiah, when we refused to bow to them (*Isaiah 24:1, 3-6*)(*Eclles. 5:1, 2*). The entire land mass of Assiah was now Ertz "broken" (Ertz / Earth), except Eden (Africa) the part that did not move .

### Genesis

**Adam:** All that lived on the planet had to be resuscitated, from the vegetation to our bodies the manforms (Houses of God). After the planet had been resuscitated Michael/Melchezedek and those with him searched for Hallel, and his Host: "let us "locate" the Man who have our blood and our shadows" (*Gen. 1:26*). The Man at Gen. 1:26, 27 is not us Adams, it is the Lord Hallel (Abraham's Lord). He is not being created, or made, but is being "searched" for, and found (bara / ברא).

They found the Lord Hallel (Lucifer) buried in the ground in **Nod** which is east of the Tigris

Bible/Torah

# Adam Chronicles

*Genesis — Eden (Pleasure)*

River. Hallel and his Host had been buried after they had exploded the planet and it's atmosphere collapsed, burying everyone and everything. Michael/Melchezedek the Lord God then pulled (farmed / formed) Hallel, and his Host, from the dust of the ground, and breathed the breath of Life back into him, and them (*Gen. 2:7, Isa. 43:10*). The Beast of the Field above the planet, had become the Beast "in" the Earth below when they fell with Hallel (*Gen. 2:19, Gen. 1:25*). ...ברמותנו ויאמר אלהים נעשה אדם בצלמנו (*Gen. 1:26*). "And the Gods found the Earthling in their image, and in their image the Gods found him male and female they found him (them)." אתו זכר ונקבה ברא אתם ויברא אלהים את האדם בצלמו בצלם אלהים ברא (*Gen. 1:27*). This was the Lord and his Host, who were both males and females, in a separated (Ciphereated) state.

### Eden

**Adam:** Assiah rotated on the axis of it's two poles. Assiah also travels around Shemesh (Sun) on a spiraling course, while the sun travels towards the solar/planetary north. carrying Assiah with it on a spiraling course. In the instance that Hallel exploded Assiah, all rotations ceased immediately. But the land masses of Assiah still had it's momentum. the moon portion was flung outward in the northern direction that the planet had been going. That is what caused the other land masses to break off and also continue to travel away from around Africa the south polar region. The land in that old south polar region Africa/Eden was stabilized by it's central southern location. **It was Eden that stayed the course, as the continents broke away from around it.** Eden (עדן) means "pleasure'" or "Pleasant." Eden was the most pleasant portion of the planet, as it was the least exposed to the planetary cataclysm. Only Eden remained the same as the entire globe had been before the Lord Hallel destroyed Assiah. Assiah became "Ertz" (Earth), or Broken Assiah, the keystone for all continents to be gathered back around, to make Assiah (Asia) whole again.

### Keystone

**Adam:** A keystone is a central stone, that supports the stones located around it. Africa (Eden) is a central or keystone that supports the continents around it. Michael/Melchezedek and his Host scanned the entire planet, to find the center of land mass distribution, for the entire planet. They discovered that (Egypt), in Africa (Eden) was that central place. That is why they built the Great Pyramid there. Down through the center of that pyramid is the center of all land distribution on the entire planet! All land had dispersed from here, and all land mass on the planet and in the solar system must be set back to Eden. Eden has to be protected at all cost, because it is the only keystone to bringing all land masses and planets back to their proper place, on the mother orb Assiah. After the completion of this experiment, Eden (Africa) will be the reference point. When all has been satisfied in the experiment, the original axis of the planet must be restored, to rotate Eden as the south polar region again. Then the continents can began returning again. Continents will be reattached to the top, bottom, and sides of Eden (Africa). When all land masses are

Chronicles

Bible/Torah

# Adam Chronicles

*Keystone — Garden (Protect Eden at all Cost)*

reemerged back, a great pit will be left at the old northern region of the planet, where the moon must be reinstalled, as the old north polar region. The moon would be returned back into the top of Assiah. Then all of the other planets, including the broken pieces of Crypton must be returned into the portions of Assiah they had been taken from, including Mercury and Venus. This will be required before Assiah can be made fervent again like the sun. Then Assiah will be reamalgamated with Shemesh (The sun) to bring the experiment to a satisfied conclusion.

Without Eden there would be no keystone to set all back to order. Eden must be guarded at all cost.

### Garden

**Adam:** The Guarding Place (Garden) was founded eastward of Eden (africa), to shield Eden from the Lord who was incarcerated east of the Guarding place, in Nod (*Gen. 2:8*). Nod was a prison for the Lord and his Host, who had destroyed Assiah (*Isa. 24:1, 3-6*). Those who came to resuscitate Assiah knew that without the preservation of Eden (Africa) there would be no way to complete the experiment. Eden was also our bridge back to the solar. We knew that Hallel would do all that he could to destroy Eden (Africa) so that the experiment would never be finished. We would be be lost forever inside of our own experiment. All would be confusion, and Hallel (Lord) would rule over it! The Guarden (Garden) Project was began by Michael/Melchezedek to insulate Eden from the Lord and his Host who had shattered Assiah. Without being incarcerated in Nod, the Lord would attempt to destroy Eden. Hallel's failure to destroy Assiah completely was his failure to suspend the experiment.

The Garden (Guarding Place) is "on" the eastern border of Eden (Africa)(*Gen. 2:8*). "A river went "out" of Eden to water the Guarded (Garden) Place (*Gen. 2:10*)." The Garden is the entire land mass from the Narrow Gate (Egypt/Gaza) eastward to the entire length of the Tigris River. The Tigris River is the Broad Gate between the Garden and Nod (*Gen. 3:24; Gen. 4:16*).

### Names

**Adam:** The **Lord God** Michael/Melchezedek had **found** (Bara / ברא) the Lord and his Host underground in Nod (*Gen. 1:27*), and **pulled/farmed/formed** (צרד) them from the ground there (*Gen. 2:7*), where they had fallen into the earth (*Rev. 12:9; Gen. 2:19*). The Lord and his Host were the **Beast from the Field** above, who had become the **Beast of the Earth** below when they fell, after being defeated (*Gen. 1:24, 25; 2:19*). The Lord God (Michael/Melchezedek) brought the Lord and his Host to me, to see if I could identify them. Melchezedek was testing me to see if I still recognized my brothers Hallel (the Lord), and his Host (*Gen. 2:19*). I (Adam) recognized them all, and named them all, as they were paraded before me. I called the Lord his name, which is Hallel (Lucifer), as he walked pass. I recognized Gabriel, and all of the rest of the Lord's Host as they were sent pass. I recognized and called out the names of all of the Lords Hostesses (Lilith(s) also (*Gen.2:20*). These were the **Beasts** (Living Ones / הים, הוה, חות) **of the** **Field** above who had been

Chronicles

# Adam Chronicles

*Names — Sleep — Tribunal  ( Tribunal / מסה #4531)*

cast down to become the **Beast in the Earth** below.  Cain's wife **Amenoch** (*Gen.4:17*), and Lamech's two wives **Adah**, and **Zillah** were Hostesses, of the Lord in the ground. I had recognized them, as they were sent pass me (*Gen. 4:19*).

These servants of the Lord had been male/female (HermesAphrodite), on Krypton, but had been altered, by the Lord, before they left Krypton, into separate (Ciphered) males and females.

### Sleep (שלף)

**Adam:** I was "**All One**" not "**Alone**"(*Gen. 2:18*). I never needed a "help meet (*Gen. 2:20*)" Being All One I was a Male/Female (Hermesaphrodite) Being like all of the other Gods (*Gen.1:27*). Those who had gone out to form the solars system had lost their perfection.  Most of us who had remained with the planet had been destroyed, when the Lord had exploded Assiah. Most of the inhabitants had been burned, and few were left (*Isaiah 24:6*).  For the purpose of the continuation of the experiment I allowed the Lord God Michael/Melchezedek to put me to sleep, and to remove my womb (אחת)(*Gen. 2:21, 22*).   Eve (Life / הוה), my womb or wombman, was to be used to give multiple births to "replenish" the population of Assiah again (*Gen. 1:28*).

Hallel and his Host were the Serpent/Tree in the Garden that beguiled Eve, into consumating. Hallel is the Lord who impregnated Eve with the twins Cain and Abel (*Gen. 4:1*).

I had never needed a "helpmeet", for I was male/female like all of the rest of the Gods (*Gen. 1:27*).  Yet the experiment could not go on with me being awake.  I had been put to sleep and separated into separate male and female, the entire rest of the the experiment was to take place inside of my sleep state.  The whole physical realm is a dream state, and we are all asleep in the dream.

Nothing was to stop the experiment, for without a satisfactory conclusion, we would be caught inside the manifested physical illusion forever.

### Tribunal

**Adam:** The Tribunal was a war crimes trial (מסה), held against our brother the Lord Hallel (Lucifer) and his Host, on this the mother planet, now called Earth. Hallel had ruled the planet Krypton. Michael/Melchezedek the Ancient of Days officiated over Hallel's trial. The trial was held in the midst of the Garden.  The Tribunal was held immediately after Michael/Melchezedek had finished resuscitating this the mother globe Assiah, and all of it's  life forces. The Tribunal was held against Hallel and his Host, for the war crimes they had committed in the solar system, and on Assiah, the mother planet.  Hallel and his Host had destroyed their planet Krypton, and place was no longer found for them, in the heavens (Solar System)(*Rev. 12:8*).

The thrones were cast down, and the **Ancient of Days** (Melchezedek) did sat ... (*Dan. 7:9*). He and other Gods sat in witness of a god (Lord Hallel), who was in the midst of other gods (his Host). All of them were being judged (*Psalms 82:1, Dan. 7:9*). Our brother Michael/Melchezedek was the **Ancient of Days**  who came down to try our brother the Lord (Lucifer), and his Host.

Bible/Torah

# Adam /Seth Chronicles

*Tribunal — Outcasts — Image and Likenes*

Michael/Melchezedek the Ancient of Days, and all of the millions of other brothers, who came down with him were Black, and brown, and had hair like pure wool, like me (*Rev. 1:14; Daniel 7:9, 10*).

The millions who came down with Michael/Melchezedek, came down to witness the trial against the Lord and his Host for Crimes (Wonders / נפלא) they had committed in the heavens and on the earth. Judgment was set and the books were opened (*Dan. 7:10*). The Ancient of Days accused the Lord, of his iniquities and brought a flame from his midst to devour him. The Lord's body (Form) was reduced to ashes in the sight of those who came to see his trial (*Ezekiel 28:18*). .... I beheld until the Lord (beast) was slain, and his body was cast into the flame (*Dan. 7:11*). Life does not die, physical body forms do. The Lord was the invisible life, that had been inside of the physical body form. The Lord still existed, but now without a physical body.

### Cast Out

**Adam:** The Lord God Michael/Melchezedek made the observation to the others, that if the Lord (Man) could touch the tree of Life he could take on physical form again, and live forever (*Gen. 3:22*). To prevent this Melchezedek the Lord God, drove the disembodied Lord (Man) out of the Garden back over into Nod where he had been taken from (*Gen. 3:19, Gen. 3:24*). He was cast (Shaddai) out of the Garden, after the Tribunal, as he had been cast out of the heavens in defeat (*Revelations 12:9*).

### Image and Likeness

**Adam:** After the Tribunal Eve and I were still in the Garden. Hallel, his Host, and Cain and Abel had been cast out, over into the land of Nod. Eve was to be the mother of all (*Gen. 3:20*), so she now gave birth to Seth (*Gen. 4:25*). Cain and Abel were the twin sons of the Lord who beguiled and impregnated my female side Eve (*Gen. 3:13*). Seth was not my son, but was in my image and likeness. As such he was not my child, but was my continuation in the sleep state (*Gen. 5:3*). I was never awakened, after I had been put to sleep, and altered (*Gen. 2:21*).

When you see Seth you see my continuation, in the sleep state, for I was never awakened after I was put to sleep. I and Seth are one. When you see Seth you see the continuation of me, in my sleep (*Gen. 5:3*). All of the continuation of the experiment has occurred since I was put to sleep, and all that has happened has happened inside of my sleep. All that needs to be known shall be solved for in the experiment, before I awaken, and bring the experiment to a final close. Seth my continuation, is the initiator of all that the experiment would come to, after I fell to sleep.

Bible/Torah

# Adam/Seth Chronicles
# Seth (south)

*Cain's Lines — Seth's Line — Lemech*

### My Line

**Seth:** My name Seth (שת) means "Appointed (*Gen. 4:25*)." I was not appointed to take the place of Abel, but was appointed as a continuation of Adam (*Gen. 5:3*). I am not truly the son of Adam, but I am the continuation of Adam in his sleep. My line, Adam's line was south of the Tigris River, and ran parallel to that of Cain's line, in the north above the Tigris River (*See Observations, Persons, "Lines", Pg. 26B*). Adam was first, I (Seth) was second, Enos was third, Cainan was fourth, Mahalaleel was fifth, Jered was sixth, and Enoch was seventh from Adam (*I Chron. 1:1, Jude 1:14*).

Enoch begot Methusalah, before the Gods came and took Enoch (*Gen. 5:24*). Methusalah was the father of Lemech (*Gen. 5:25*). Lemech is my great great grandson. I was 742 when Lemech was born, and I lived for another 170 years after Lemech's birth. I spent that 170 years of his life teaching him all that Adam had passed down to me. Adam's line through me held in all of our generation down to Lemech. I could see with my fore vision that Lemech would have a son named Noah twelve years after I passed (*Gen. 5:29*). Noah curved away from Adam's line, to exalt Hallel (Lucifer) the Lord of the North (*Isa. 14:12*). Noah's two younger sons Shem and Japheth also chose to serve the future Lord of Abraham. Only Noah's elder son Ham chose to hold the line of Adam which was to be after the order of Melchezedek, which is the reperfection of Adam.

### Cain's Line

**Seth:** Cain was first in the Lord's line (*I Chron. 1:1*). Cain's line was the Lords attempt to subvert the experiment, by subplanting my line which is the continuation of Adam. Subversion was the reason that the Lord of the North beguiled Eve, and fathered Cain, and Abel (*Gen. 4:1, I Chron. 1:1*). The Lord's purpose was to bring his World (TBL) or Tubal (TBL) into existence on this the mother planet Assiah.

Cain's line was in Nod on the side of the north (*Joshua 24:2, 3,14*), and my line was on south (Seth) side of the Tigris River in the Garden. Cain's line was the beginning of the World (TBL) of the Lord, on this the mother planet. The World or Tubal is not the people or the planet, but is total Chaos, and Corruption: Bestiality (TBL), Sodomy, Rape, Incest, Murder (*Leviticus 18:6-23*).

The first act of sodomy on this the mother planet, was when the Lord demanded that his son Cain be a husband to his effeminate (הבל) twin brother Abel (הבל)(*Gen. 4:7*). See Strong's #1891-1893 *This word has the same base Bel, Bal (בל) as Tubal.*

The Lord "marked" Cain with a genetic pale leprosy, that he passed on to his children who were all "fair" or Pale (*Gen. 6:2*). Cain's line ran from his son Enoch to his descendant Lamech (*Gen. 4:17-19*). Lamech killed Cain and a younger man. Lamech killed the younger man with Cain for rape sodomizing (חברת) him, and killed Cain for wounding him when he resisted the younger man raping him (*Gen. 4:23*).

Noah, Shem and Japheth became apostate away from the strait and narrow, but Ham held the line of Adam.

Chronicles

Bible/Torah

# Ham Chronicles
# Introduction

*Seth — Lemech/Noah (Crossover/Curiosity) — Adultery(מהל) — Ham*

Ham descended from the line of Seth through Lemech (*Gen. 5:26*), who was parallel to Lamech in the line of Cain (*Gen. 4:13*). To distinguish between the two, Noah's father is called Lemech with an "e" instead of an "a" like Lamech in Cain's line. Cain's descendant Lamech is the father of the Three Bals: **Tubal, Jubal, and Jabal**, who survived the flood sealed below the water in the subterranean city of of their ancestor Cain. Seth's descendant Lemech is the grandfather of Ham, Shem, and Japheth who survived the flood above the water in the ark. *See the chart below*

Seth was still alive for the first 170 years of the life of Lemech, and Lemech was still alive for the first 100 years of the life of Ham. Thus Lemech was a 270 year long bridge between Seth and Ham. Seth passed all that he knew through Lemech, to his grandson Ham. Ham and his two brothers were born before Noah's flood, the flooding of Mesopotamia, by the Tigris/Euphrates.

Every man has a time that he chose the direction that he will go in. In his time of choosing, Noah decided to take on the way of the children of Nod, and excepted instructions from **Lamech,** from the Cain side or the northern side of the Tigris river, not his father **Lemech** from the south (Seth) side in the Garden (Guarded Place). Noah had decided to exalt Hallel the Lord of the side of the North. Shem and Japheth followed their father Noah by exalting Lucifer also (*Isa. 14:12*), while Ham kept his foot and held the line of Adam (*Eccles. 5:1, 2*). Ham saw his wooly headed brown father Noah, and his two younger brothers Shem and Japheth, began to mix with the blond hair, blue eyed, pale leper children, of Marked Cain in the north. They corrupted themselves into the way of life of the north, but Ham refused to participate himself, for he was holding the line of Adam through Seth, and Lemech.

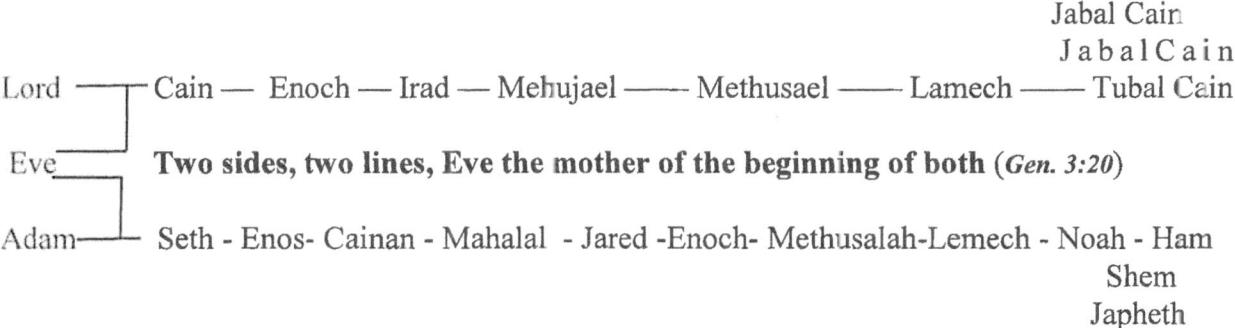

If Cain and Abel were in the line of Adam, Enoch would be ninth from Adam, but Enoch is seventh from Adam (Jude 1:14). This proves that Cain and Abel are not in the line of Adam (*Gen. 4:1; I Chron. 1:1*).

## Adultery

The Bible/Torah scripture state that the Lord caused a flood, because his people were corrupt and violent (*Gen. 6:11, 12*). But the true reason was because the Lord saw he could no longer strive with (control) them (*Gen. 6:3*), after he sent his pale ones to commit adultery (mix) with the Blacks (Ethiopians), westward between the Tigris and Euphrates Rivers (*Isa. 18:1; Zephoniah 3:10*).

Bible/Torah

# Ham Chronicles

*Adultery — Lines — Choice — Preflood*

### Lines

**Ham:** I am the oldest son of Noah, and my two younger brothers are Shem, and Japheth. We were all born one hundred years before the flood. We are of the line of Seth, through Lemech's son Noah (*Gen. 5:32; 6:10*)(*Gen. 5:28, 29*). The three of us were born in Mesopotamia, south (Seth) of the Tigris River. Ja<u>bal</u> Cain, Ju<u>bal</u> Cain, and Tu<u>bal</u> Cain were being born at the same time, north of the Tigris River in the land of Nod (*Gen. 4:20-22*). Cain's line was in the north, and we of Adam/Seth's line were in the south.

Cain's descendant **Lamech** ruled north of the Tigris, in Nod (*Isa. 14:13*), and my grandfather **Lemech** ruled south of the Tigris in the Garden (*Gen. 5:25-31*). Grandfather Lemech chose to be after the Order of Melchezedek, while his son Noah chose to exalt Lucifer (Hallel) the Lord on the side of the North in Nod (*Isa. 14:13*). Michael (Melchezedek) had defeated the Lord in the Solar (Soul) wars and cast him down (*Rev. 12:7-9, Isa. 14:12*). Melchezedek (Michael) is the Overseer (protector) of the Most High. The Most High is the sun (solar/soul). The Lord had wanted to be like the Most High (*Isa. 14:14*), but the Most High (sun) saw the Lord, the Almighty fall in defeat (*Numbers 24:4, 16*).

### Choice

**Ham:** Yet my father Noah, and my two younger brothers still chose to follow the Lord, the Serpent, the Fallen One (Felon). They were all three perhaps attracted to Cain's young Chaldean daughters, as the Lord and his male Host were attracted to these girls (*Gen. 6:2*). The Lord and his Host were the Giants (נפלים) or Sons of God in the earth (*Gen. 6:4; Isa. 47:1-7*) These girls had to taste the Mandrake (Man of Darkness) fruit, like Eve had (*Gen. 3:13; Gen. 4:1, Isa. 47:5*). When the Lord and his Host had taken the virginity of some of these girls, they put them at the disposal of Noah, Shem and Japheth, by having these girls to expose themselves, as they were sent wading across the Tigris River (*Zephaniah 3:10*), down from Nod into the Garden (*Isa. 47:2, 3*).

The Lord was sending these corrupted little girls down, to adulterate Noah, and his people in the Garden. Yet the Lord was losing control over Cain's pale leper children, who he was corrupting in Nod. He could no longer strive with them (*Gen. 6:3*), for they were wicked and evil, even beyond the Lord's influence on them (*Gen. 6:5*). It repented the Lord and grieved him, that he had "Marked" and Ushered (עש) Cain (ארם) down into the earth of Nod (*Gen. 4:14, 15*).

The Lord declared that he would destroy the children of the man (Cain), he had "Altered" or "Created. He would destroy them "from the "face of the earth (*Gen. 6:7*)." When the Lord said from the "face" (surface) of the earth, he did not mean that he was going to kill them all. Only those who were out of his control, and moving about on the "surface" of the ground in Nod. The Lord still had control over some of the pale leper children, of his son Cain. He sealed them in Cain's subterranean city of Enoch (*Gen. 4:17*). There they would survive the pending flood.

Not only was the "earth/land" of Nod corrupt for the Lord, the land was also corrupt for God (Michael/Melchezedek)(*Gen. 6:11*). All flesh on the ground in Nod was corrupt, because of the Lord (*Gen. 6:12*). Melchezedek (God) told Noah that the earth (land)(Nod) was filled with violence, and that he was going to destroy (flood) the Lord's World in Nod, and it's inhabitants (*Gen.*

Introduction

Bible/Torah

# Ham Chronicles

*Choice — Ark Ship — Flood*

*6:13*).

### Ark Ship

If Nod and it's mounds were to be flooded, then all of the Garden and Mesopotamia would also be under water. So God (Michael/Melchezedek) instructed Noah to build an Ark Ship. Noah built it with three stories (*Gen. 6:16*). The flood would submerge the land of Nod, to kill all flesh under the sky there (*Gen. 6:17*). Michael (God) instructed Noah to bring two of each kind, of the animals of the land and sky of Nod, the region that would be flooded, to keep them alive (*Gen. 6:19, 20*).

We also had to bring on food for the animals and ourselves. We and our father Noah did all that God told us to do (*Gen. 6:22*).

We did not know what the third story of the ark was for, until the Lord of the North approached Noah, to have him to bring on a "strange cargo." Whereas God (Michael/Melchezedek) had Noah bring on "animals," the Lord (Hallel) had Noah bring "Beast" into the Ark Ship. These "beast" that we were to fill the third story with, were not man or animals. They were the Tubal (Bestial), fruit from the pale leper children of Cain, mixing with animals. These half animal, half man creatures were titled "beast," a "man" and his "wife" (*Gen. 7:, 2*). We brought on seven pairs of "beast," a "man" and his "wife" of the clean, and two of each kind of the unclean beast, a "man" and his "wife" (*Gen. 7:2*). Now Noah had not only obeyed the commands of Melchezedek the Lord God, but also the commandments of the Lord, to save the Lord's "strange cargo (*Gen. 7:5*)." This "strange cargo" filled the third story of the ark ship. It was then that we went aboard and were sealed in to survive the flooding of the Tigris and Euphrates Rivers (*Gen. 7:13*). After the flood I would call these rivers the rivers of my son Cush (Ethiopia)(*Gen. 2:13, 14, Isa. 18:1, Zephoniah 3:10*).

### Flood

**Ham:** As the flood rose, it covered the high hills and some mountains (*Gen. 7:18, 19*), but some land was in and out of the water (*II Pet. 3:5*). It was not the entire planet that was flooded, but the entire "World (TBL)" of the Lord, which was the land of Nod (*II Peter 3:6*). Thus Noah's flood had "sides" (*Joshua 24:3*), for it was the flooding of the Tigris and Euphrates Rivers (*Joshua 24:14*). All of the Garden, Mesopotamia, and the land of Nod beyond were flooded (*Zephoniah 3:10, Isa. 18:1*). Even Ararat the mound of the Lord was under water (*Gen. 7·20*). All living substance on the flooded land perished including olive trees (*Gen. 7:21, 23*). Only those on the Ark Ship: Noah, his family, the animals, and the Strange Cargo, survived "above" the land that was flooded (*Gen. 7:24*). Yet many of Cain's pale leper children survived beneath the flood, in the sealed subterranean city of Enoch (*Gen. 4:17*).

The purpose of the flood (Mubal / מבל) was to "wash away" (Mubal / מבל), the Tubal (הבל) or World (תבל) that the Lord of the North so loved (*John 3:16*). But the elements of the Lord's World that the Lord wanted saved were safe, both in the ground, and on the ark. Only those that the Lord had lost control over died (*Gen. 6:3*).

Then the flood was over and the water began to drain back down the Tigris/Euphrates, and the

Bible/Torah

# Ham Chronicles

*Flood — Dryland — Tent Incident — Great Exodus*

Ark Ship came to rest on the Lord's mound of Ararat (*Gen. 8:4*). All of the land of the Garden, Mesopotamia and Nod was still under water. Noah sent out birds, and the last bird that Noah sent out had to fly beyond the flood, to bring back a "fresh plucked" leaf from a live olive tree. Trees under water drown, and they do not have "fresh plucked leaves (*Gen. 8:11*)."

### Dry Land

**Ham:** The Ark Ship had drifted from where we had built it on the Tigris in Mesopotamia, and had settled on the Lord's mound Ararat, in the land of Nod. This was on the side of the North of Nod. Northern Nod was the last place to go under water, and it was the first land to reappear, after the flood. When the ground there had dried, God (Michael/Melchezedek) told Noah to come out, and to bring all out his family, and the animals alike, so that we and the animals could spread back out on the land that had been flooded (*Gen. 8:15, 16*). We and the animals on the ark were supposed to be released to be fruitful and multiply and repopulate the land that had been flooded (*Gen. 8:17*).

But the Lord and Noah had other ideas, for when my father Noah brought us and the animals down, from the Ark Ship, Noah built an altar to the Lord and sacrificed all that was clean to the Lord, including the clean animals (*Gen. 8:18-20*). The Lord smelled the sweet savor of the burnt flesh of animals, that would never repopulate the land (*Gen. 8:21*). In the same turn Noah preserved the filth and the unclean, and therefore set the Strange Cargo free. But as for us his family we were held hostage, by Noah, and the Lord on Ararat. Then the Lord told Noah that he would not ever again curse the ground, for the sake of mankind (Cain's children). The Lord had not wanted to destroy all mankind, just those he lost control over. The Lord had only preserved, those terrible, and evil ones, he still had control over (*Isa. 18:2*). Father Noah had included himself, as a part of the filth that he helped to preserve.

### Tent Incident

**Ham:** In a tent culture no man has the right to enter another man's tent. The tent is his only privacy. A man who violate to open the tent flap of another man, could as much as lose his life. Yet if the tent owner has the wife, daughter, son etc., of someone else in his tent for some questionable purpose, then the offended man has the exceptional right to open and even enter that man's tent, to retrieve his family member. If the family member has been violated by the tent owner, the tent owner himself was subject to lose his life!

My son Canaan came to me, to tell me that my father Noah had approached him, to have him come to his tent in secrecy, at an appointed time. Canaan said that his grandfather wanted to Sanctify (sodomize / קדש) him, to make him Holy (corrupt) / חולי). Noah had sworn my son Canaan to secrecy, to tell no one including me. But we did not have any secrets throughout all of our families, so my son Canaan told me, and I told my two brothers Shem, and Japheth, to have them to witness for me, to see if what Canaan said was true about our father.

Canaan told all of his cousins, and at the appointed time I was hiding inside my father Noah's

Bible/Torah

# Ham Chronicles

*Tent Incident— Great Exodus —Garden Cities — Tigris (Tigre = Geez = Ethiopia)*

tent, and my brothers were hiding outside, along with everyone else in the families. My father Noah came into his tent, and began to drink, and got naked (*Gen. 9:21*). My son Canaan came at the appointed time, and entered the tent, and my father Noah positioned him, for what he was going to do. That is when I opened the tent flap, to expose to my brothers and family what our father was about to do (*Gen. 9:22*). Everyone in the family including our mother Noah's wife saw it, but my two brothers Shem and Japheth still covered it up (*Gen. 9:23*)! Noah was never "awakened" from his wine, he "finished" (קיץ) his wine, for he was never asleep. After I had exposed my father he sat drinking his wine, trying to figure out why I had risked my life, being in his tent. By the time he had "finished" (קיץ) drinking his wine he had figured out and knew, what his younger (grand) son Canaan had "done to him (*Gen. 9:24*)." Noah figured out that Canaan had broken his vow, and told on him, giving me the right to be in his tent (*Gen. 9:22*). That is when father Noah cursed at my son Canaan, for exposing him as a child molester. Then my father Noah thanked Shem and Japheth for trying to cover-up his crime (*Gen. 9:25-27*)!

My father Noah then cursed at Canaan for exposing him. But what is the cursing of a drunk old man, who has attempted to molest his grandson? Noah had said a servant to servants Canaan would be to his brethren (*Gen. 9:25*). But if Canaan was to be a servant for exposing Noah, then what was Noah to be for trying to molest Canaan?

### Great Exodus

**Ham:** I was outraged at the behavior of my father and brothers. How could a grandfather be capable of molesting his grandson, and then the boy's uncles attempt to covered up the crime? I had a right to kill all three of them. But I and my children were after the peaceable Order of Michael/Melchezedek (*I Chron. 4:40; Heb.5:6*). So we departed in peace, in an exodus down from Ararat. I brought my children down from Ararat, and left the land of Nod. I would no longer expose my family to the corrupt lifestyle there. We came down in a great exodus.

We left Nod and crossed the Tigris, back down into the Garden (Guarded Place). That is where my father, brothers, and I had lived before the flood. We had built the ark there, on the banks of the Tigris River. I and my children would block the way to Eden, as the Cherubim had, to keep my brothers, father, and the Lord out (*Gen. 3:24*). Noah Shem and Japheth could not come back. If they could return they would be bringing the infection of Nod, and the Lord, to the Garden, and Eden.

### Garden

**Ham:** We restored the land south of the Tigris into a Garden (Guarded Place) again, to protect ourselves, and to guard Eden (Africa) west of us. All land mass on the planet must be set back to Eden. Eden has to be protected at all cost, because it is the keystone to bringing all land masses and planets back to their proper place into the mother planet Assiah. After the completion of this experiment, Eden (Africa) will be the reference point. Returning continents will be reattached to the top, bottom, and sides of Eden (Africa). Every portion of the planet must be returned to it's place, before Assiah can be made fervent again, like the sun. Then Assiah will be

# Ham Chronicles

*Garden — Servant Cities — Arphaxad*

reamalgamated with Shemesh (The sun), to bring the experiment to a satisfied conclusion. Without Eden and it's undisturbed people there would be no keystone, to set all else back to order. I and my children would protect both Eden (Africa), and it's Garden (Guard Place) east of it. My sons are Cush (Ethiopia), Misraim(Egypt), Phut, and Canaan (*Gen. 10:6*). African Ethiopia (Abbysinnia) is really my son Phut (Punt)(*Gen. 10:6*).

I set my eldest son Cush (Ethiopia) to guard his river, the Broad Gate (Tigris), that led to the Lord the Destroyer in Nod (*Matt. 7:13*). I set my son Misraim (Egypt) to guard the Strait and Narrow Gate, at the entrance to Eden (Africa). Eden (Africa) the place of Eternal Life (*Matt. 7:13, 14*). The Lord in Nod must never breech this Gate. Canaan was a buffer, and at the same time Canaan was protected between Misraim (Egypt), and Mesopotamian Cush (Ethiopia).

### Servant Cities

**Ham:** I and all of my sons built great and magnificent cities all over the Garden, but Canaan and his children were chief among all of my sons, who built cities: Canaan's son Yebus built Jerusalem (*Judges 19:10, 11*), the City of Peace, where Melchezedek, the King of Peace came to live (*Heb. 7:2*). His son Hiel built Jericho (*I King 16:34*). Canaan's son Amori built Mari and other cities in the East Country of Canaan, along the Euphrates (*Gen. 10:15; 25:6; I Kings 4:30*). Along the coast of the Great Sea (Mediterranean). his son Sidon built his city Sidon, and other cities, including Tyre (*Jer. 25:22*). It was from these coastal cities that Canaan's Phoenician children fulfilled the prophesy, that Noah had made that Canaan (his children) would be a servant to his brethren, (Shem and Japheth)(*Gen. 9:25, 27*). Japheth and his children had expanded west, into the Mediterranean, but had no cities until Canaan's Phonician children sailed out, and built cities for them. The Canaanites (Phoenicians) also gave them an alphabet (𐤀𐤁𐤂𐤃𐤄𐤅𐤆𐤇𐤈𐤉 𐤊𐤋𐤌𐤍𐤎𐤏𐤐𐤑𐤒𐤓𐤔𐤕), and all of the arts, crafts, and skills necessary to cause them to be civil. Japheth and his children were wooly headed and brown, like the rest of us, including our father Noah, and our mother. Japheth's wooly headed children included the Eutruscans (Pre Roman Italy), and and their brothers the wooly headed brown Archaic (first) Greeks. These were the children of the Lord's servant Japheth.

Canaan's children also served the Lord's servant, Shem, to save Shem's children from the Lord. My children and I never ever bowed down, to serve the Lord of my father Noah (*Eccles. 5:1*). Yet all of the people in service to the Lord eventually had to depend on my children to rescue themselves, from servitude to the Lord.

From the beginning when we came down from Ararat back into the Garden, we built all of our cities and were very prosperous and secure from the Lord. Yet of Shem's children only Arphaxad, and Elam under our influence, built cities north of the Tigris. It was our nature to help those who are in need. The Lord took a great toll on all of those who served him, including his son Cain's pale leper Gentile/Chaldean children, still buried in Nod. The Lord summoned us to help him retrieve them. We had secured the Garden, and the way into Eden (Africa), and our final security would be to send Nimrod back, by request from the Lord, to Nod to find and rescue Cain's pale leper children. Nimrod's cousin Arphaxad lived there and would assist him.

Bible/Torah

# Arphaxad Chronicles
# Introduction

*Ham (Cush) —Arphaxad— Ca-Shaddai (Cassidy) — Family*

When properly translated the name Arphaxad becomes a doorway into information that have been held obscure by design. The word Arphaxad is more accurately pronounced "Arpha-Ca-Shaddai" meaning "Border of Chaldea." To know where Arphaxad was born and lived is to know where the Chaldeans lived. Arphaxad was born just two years after the flood, and by his name the Chaldeans already existed. This means that the Chaldeans already existed before the flood, and had survived the flood, without being on the ark. Scriptures say that all of the high hills under the heavens were covered with water (*Gen. 7:19*). The description of the flood says that all that breathed "on" the ground died (*Gen. 7:21- 23*). Only Noah and the others on the ark "above" the ground survived (*Gen. 7:23, 24*). There were no Chaldeans on Noah's ship's manifest, only the eight people in Noah's family (*Gen. 7:7*). Thus the Chaldeans would have had to survive under ground, under water. It was Cain who went underground before the flood. It is written that Cain took a wife there, which implies that there were others living under ground with Cain (*Gen. 4:14*). Scripture say that there were Nephalim (Fall Ones) "in" the ground in those days (*Gen. 6:4*). These subterranean dwellers were the Shaddai (Outcast), who were the Host of the Lord, and the Lord himself who is El Shaddai or "God of Outcast." El Shaddai (שדי) is God Almighty (אל שדי), who was defeated and "casted out" (שדי) of the heavens, down "into" the earth (*Gen. 6:3, Rev. 12:9*). The Lord told Moses that he is the Lord in the bowels of the ground (*Ex. 8:22*).

As stated above the term "Border of Chaldea" is what the name Arphaxad means, but the name "Chaldea" (כשדי) can be more accurately pronounced Ca-Shaddai (כשדי), which show that the Chaldeans (Ca-Shaddai) are directly associated with the Lord, who is El Shaddai and his Host who are the Shaddai. They were all in the ground together: Cain his pale leper children who are the Ami Shaddai (Out Cast [Devil] People), and the Lord and his Host. The Lord his Host and his son Cain were "casted out" (Shaddai), of the Garden into the northern regions of the land of Nod (*Gen. 3:22-24*). With the children of Cain being the Chaldeans, and the Chaldeans living in the north of Nod, then Arphaxad lived on the "Border of the Chaldeans" in the north of Nod also. Arphaxad never left the north. It is from that place in Nod on the "Side" of the North that Arphaxad spent his entire life, and where Abram was born (*Joshua 24:2, 3, 15*). Arphaxad was present there in the north of Nod to see the Tent Incident, and he was a part of the Great Exodus down from Ararat with his uncle Ham. Finally Arphaxad was present when his nephew Nimrod returned north with thousands of others from the south, to Raise Cain's Pale Leper children, from Cain's subterranean city called Enoch (*Gen. 4:17*). Cain's children had been sealed in his underground city, to survive the flood. Nimrod was commissioned to find them buried in Ararat, and to dig them out (*Gen. 10:8, 9*). Nimrod was then to transport them down to the Ur/Babel Metropolis, that he built, to raise them, giving them their first civilizing. Much of what Arphaxad wrote is attributed to Moses and Isaiah, but Arphaxad was immediately related to and talked to those who lived these events which occurred over a thousand years before either Moses or Isaiah were ever born. Next Arphaxad is the beginning of the line, from Shem that lead down to Abram. Without Arphaxad there would not have been an Abraham, Sarah, Isaac, Jacob, Israel, Jews (Israelis), Moses, Isaiah, Judaism, Torah, Synagogue, Christian Church or Western World.

# Arphaxad (Isaiah) Chronicles

*Ham — Exodus*

### Family

**Arphaxad:** Ham is my uncle, and his brother Shem is my father. Japheth is my other uncle. My two older brothers are Elam, and Asshur, while Lud and Aram are my younger brothers (*Gen.10:22*). My sister Semiramis is the twin of my brother Asshur. My sister Semiramis is the wife of Ham's son Cush (Ethiopia). Cush and Semiramis are the father anf mother, of my nephew Nimrod (*Gen. 10:8*).

My cousins Cush, Elam and Gomer were born on the ark during the flood. The rest of the children of my father and two uncles were born after the flood on mound Ararat (*Gen. 10:1*). My brother Asshur was born in the first year after the flood, and I was born in the second year (*Gen. 10:22, 10*). The children of all three of Noah's sons were born along with each other, down to Japheth's son Tiras, Shem's son Aram, and Ham's son Canaan. Our family the family of Noah was of one speech, and one language (*Gen. 11:1*).

It was after the flood and the ground was dry, but grandfather Noah held all of his children and grandchildren as hostages on Ararat. We were hostages and in bondage, to Noah and El Shaddai the God Almighty, even though we were suppose to be released, to go down to repopulated the land that had been flooded. The Lord made Noah the head of our family sacrificed, all that was clean including the animals on the ark. He was suppose to set the animals free to repopulate the land that had been flooded (*Gen. 8:20*). In the same instance that Noah sacrificed all cleanness, he was preserving all filth (*Gen. 8:21*), and tearing our family apart.

### Exodus

**Arphaxad:** Noah sacrificed all that was clean including the animals from the ark to the Lord as burnt offerings (*Gen. 8:20*). As such Grandfather as an exalter of the Lord of the North found it easy to have his grandson in his tent with him, for questionable purposes. Noah was never asleep except mentally. Canaan and I are cousins along with all of our other cousins and brothers. We were all children together. We did not have any secrets from each other. All of us knew what was going to happen in our granfather's tent even before it happened, because Canaan told us what grandfather Noah planned to do. It was uncle Ham, **exposing** grandfather Noah, attempting to molest his son Canaan, that my father Shem, and uncle Japheth "covered up" (*Gen. 9:23*).

This incident allowed uncle Ham to bring us all down from Ararat, in a Great Exodus. It was the Tent Incident that allowed uncle Ham to set us free from the Lord, Noah, and Ararat (ארדח), the mound of curses (ארדות). Ararat means "I am Cursed." *See Strong's Concordance "Curse/Ararat # 779, 780.* My uncle Ham was the savior of us all.

My sister Semiramis was pregnant with Nimrod on Mound Ararat, but brought Nimrod down from Ararat in her stomach, and he was born in the Garden. Nimrod was named to commemorate our coming down from Ararat. (*Gen. 10:8*). Nimrod (נמרוד) means "We Came Down." *See Strong's Concordance #4174* (מורד)

After uncle Ham's Great Exodus down from Ararat conditions began to fall apart in the north. Ham had brought all of us down from Ararat, away from the corrupting influence of the Lord and

Bible/Torah

# Arphaxad (Isaiah) Chronicles

*Exodus — Ambassador Nimrod — Kingdom — Chaldeans*

Noah. Uncle Ham brought us all down from Ararat, but only my brothers Aram, and Asshur of my father Shem's children were allowed to hebrew (cross), the Tigris into the Garden with Ham and his children. The rest of us the children of Shem, and Japheth, had to stay north because of what our fathers did. Shem and Japheth covered up Noah's crime against Canaan. Having to stay north I kept a chronicle after uncle Ham and my cousins hebrewed the Tigris back into the Garden. My oldest brother Elam removed himself and his children as far away as he could north of the Tigris to the eastern extremes of Nod. All of the land of Nod was cursed (Ararat) because the Lord was there. (*Gen. 3:14*).

## Ambassador Nimrod

**Arphaxad:** It would be years latter when my uncle Ham instructed his son Cush, to send his son Nimrod back north across the Tigris River. Cush (Ethiopia) sent his son Nimrod up his river (Tigris), over into the land of Nod beyond (*Isaiah 18:1*). Nimrod and thousands of others beckoned by the Lord came swiftly in wood and bulrush ships, as ambassadors, messengers and saviors, to Cain's pale leper children (*Isa. 18:2*).

Here in the land of Nod on the mound of Ararat Nimrod and the thousands with him, stood before Hallel, the Lord of the North (*Gen. 10:8*). They were here before the Lord, to be instructed as to what service they could provide for him.

The Lord had summoned Ham and his children for assistance to search (hunt) for his son Cain, and Cain's descendants in the ground (*Gen. 4:15*). I was there to watch Nimrod be a Mighty Hunter for the Lord, to find Cain's children in the earth (*Gen. 10:9*). Cain's Pale Leper children had survived the flood, sealed inside of Cain's subterranean city called Enoch (*Gen. 4:17*). After Nimrod had located and rescued them, the Lord wanted Nimrod to Raise Marked Cain, his pale children. Thus the Lord instructed Nimrod, to build a kingdom in which to raise them.

## Kingdom

**Arphaxad:** Nimrod's kingdom was the six city Ur Complex. The beginning of Nimrod's kingdom was the building of the cities of **Babel, Erech,** and **Accad,** all (Calneh) of these three on the plains of Shinar in the north of Nod (*Gen. 10:10; Gen. 11:2*). Then Nimrod the Assyrian went adjacent to these three cities, and built three other cities on the Tigris River, These cities were **Nineveh** with it's city streets (Rehaboth), **Resen,** and **Calah** (*Gen. 10:11, 12*). The same was a great city, a six city metropolis called Ur of the Chaldeans (*Gen. 11:28, 31*). The Ur Metropolis was adjacent to my city Arphachiyah in the north of Nod. Ur was sometimes named Babel or Nineveh. It took three days to walk from one side of this Great City Complex to the other side (*Jonah 3:3*).

## Chaldeans (PreCivil)

**Arphaxad:** Behold the Chaldeans (Gentiles), this is a people who were not, until the Assyrian (Nimrod) came and built it for them, who dwelt in the ground, of the wilderness of Nod ...(*Isa. 23:13*). These people were not because Nimrod had not yet Raised Cain, his pale leper children

Bible/Torah

# Arphaxad (Isaiah) Chronicles

*Chaldeans— Lord (Comer Down)*

from the ground (*Gen. 4:14*).

In the caves of Cain's subterranean city Nimrod had found a people (Cain's children), a Nation (Gentiles) scattered and peeled. These people were terrible from their beginning. The Lord had meted them out, and trodden them down, even before the flooding of the of the Tigris and Euphrates Rivers (*Isa. 18:2*). The Lord had brought them to their lowest, before sealing them in before the flood, so that he could strive with them after the flood (*Gen. 6:3*). The flood spoiled their land, the land of Nod (*Isa. 18:2*).

The Lord's wanted Nimrod to bring the Gentiles up out of the caves, but to keep them mentally asleep. The Lord instructed **"Shut their eyes, ears, and minds less they see, hear, and understand...** (*Isa. 6:10*)." But Nimrod was the Great Light, that was sent into the Thick Darkness of the Lord to make the captive pale leper children of Cain free from the Lord (*Isaiah 9:2*).

### Lord (Comer Down)

**Arphaxad:** The Lord and his Host came down from Ararat to the plains of Shinar (*Gen. 10:10*) in Nod, to see the city that the children of men had built (*Gen. 11:5*). The Lord made an observation to his Host, that the eyes and ears his son Cain's people's were no longer shut, and the people were now one, with one language (*Gen. 11:6*). The Lord had not been able to strive with them, because of how evil he had made them, before the flood. Now the Lord could not strive with them, because Nimrod had united them away from evil, after the flood. Nimrod had betrayed the Lord by opening their eyes, and ears to allow the pale lepers to understand. Nimrod had healed them, except from their paleness (*Matt. 13:15, Isa. 53:5*).

The Lord and his Host moved through all of the cities that made up the Ur Metropolis to see what all Nimrod had done to set the captives free from him (*Gen. 11:5*).

**Babel:** Babel with it's phallic tower(s) advertised that it was a place of grafting, a breeding city where the fair (Pale) complexioned Chaldean daughters of Cain could volunteer, to go to be impregnated. Their offspring would come out wooly headed and brown like Cain had been before his father the Lord had genetically "marked" him with permanent pale leprosy (*Gen. 4:15*).

**Accad:** Accad was an "Academy," or city of schools, colleges, and universities. Anyone among Cain's sons that Nimrod pulled forth from the ground could go to Accad, to learn to their capacity.

**Erech:** Erech (Erection) was a Masonic city. It was a "hands on" city, where those who qualified could learn to build roads, bridges, canals, barns, docks etc.

**Nineveh:** Nineveh and it's streets (Rehaboth) was a city of social experiment. Here Nimrod and those who specialized, set as many of the disordered children of Cain into a civil family state as possible.

**Calah:** Calah (Nimrud) was an administrative city, a city of logistics. Nimrod and his administrators were headquartered in this city, and ran the entire Ur/Babel complex from Calah.

**Resen:** Resen was a city of <u>resign</u>ation. Cain's converted and healed children would **resign**

Bible/Torah

# Arphaxad (Isaiah) Chronicles

*Lord (Comer Downer) — Crucifixion*

in **Resen** from the Lord's old corrupt way of life. Preparations were being made in Resen for those who were to graduate after all of the diverse training, that Cain's pale leper children were being given. Nimrod was converting Cain's children, to make them civil and to restore their souls (Solar Association). Many would have wooly heads and brown complexions to compliment the sun.

The Lord could see that families were increasing in **Nineveh**, at an alarming rate. There would be no more child molestation or rape (*Isa. 47:1-6*). Accad (Academy) was turning out student who would be judges, rulers, and architects. **Erech** (Erection) was turning out corps of engineers to build docks, and harbors for ships, and boats.

In the pending time of graduation Cain's children would merge on the city of Resen, from the four cities of Babel, Accad, Erech, and Nineveh. They would also come from numerous towns, and villages, and farms, that had also been built for them, within the corporate limits of the the Ur Metropolis. The children of Cain would come out of the shadows, and stand in the sun. Some would be grafted back to wooly heads and brown complexions, while others would still be pale. Resen was a graduation city, where they would all have the privilege to put on Caps (Mortar Boards), and Gowns, and be issued Sheep Skins, not to hang on a wall, but to wrap around their waist, to hide their nudeness (Nod / Nude). Cain's children would Resign in Resen, all of the old corrupt ways of life, that the Lord had taught them, then they would be declared civilized

**Tubal** was taught to mine iron, tin, and copper for the making of brass and bronze products (*Gen. 4:22*). Metal from the foundries of Tubal had been used to turn out all kinds of metal produces for Ur/Babel's population: door sockets, door hinges, locks, spear heads, metal bowls, plates, eating utensils, cooking pots, and vats to cook their food, for their first time. Musical instruments were also made from the metal (*Gen. 4:22*).

**Jubal** was taught to craft and play harps, organs, and other metal and wood musical instruments, to entertain the workers (*Gen. 4:21*).

**Jabal** was taught to make tents and herd cattle (*Gen. 4:20*). The children of Jubal would provide music for all of the ceremonies held in the city of Resen (*Gen. 4:21*). The builders of the Ur Metropolis had worked to the music of the instruments of **Juba**lee. They had eaten, and would eat the beef of the cattle of Jabal, at banquets in Resen, and they would sleep in Jabal's tents. Nimrod had taught them all well, and was prepared to make them free from bondage to the Lord, in the ceremonies in Resen. But the Lord had come down from Ararat, to see the city and people that Nimrod had risen, and he (Lord) brought it to ruin (*Isa. 23:13, Gen. 11:9*). Then it pleased the Lord to bruise the head of Nimrod (*Isa. 53:10*), because Nimrod had attempted to graft Cain's children free from him, and free from the pale leprosy he had marked them with, by infecting their father Cain (*Gen. 4:15*).

### Crucifixion (Nimrod)

**Arphaxad:** Cain's Gentiles/Chaldeans children reported that the Lord had watched Nimrod from the time of his youth (*Isa. 53:2*). They describe that Nimrod was not proud, or vain, that they

Bible/Torah

# Arphaxad (Isaiah) Chronicles

*Crucifixion — Hebrewers — My Line — World Crisis — Geneology Chart*

would be forced to worship him (*Isa. 53:2*). These Pale Leper children of Cain admitted that even though Nimrod bore their stripes, and grief, that they despised, and rejected him. This was even though Nimrod was the savior of their race. It was by his stripes that they were converted, and healed (*Isa. 53:4, 5; Isa. 6:10; Matt. 13:15*). Nimrod never said a mumbling word, when the Lord forced those he had saved to torture him (*Isa. 53:6, 7*). Then they brought my nephew Nimrod from the prison that they had tortured him in, to have him judged by the Lord (*Isa. 53:8*). The Lord sentence that Nimrod be crucified, even though Nimrod had not deceived the children of Cain. Nor did Nimrod commit violence against them (*Isa. 53:9*). Yet it pleased the Lord for them to bruise Nimrod, because Nimrod had almost made them free from bondage to him (*Isa. 53:10*). The Lord incited these Pale Lepers to crucify Nimrod their savior. But once they had murdered Nimrod these children of Cain refused to go back, into the Thick Darkness and bondage to the Lord (*Amos 5:18, 20*). Thus the Lord confounded and overthrew the Ur/Babel Metropolis, in an attempt to take control of them again. But the pale lepers refused the Lord, and scattered down into Mesopotamia, the land of Nimrod's people. The Ur/Babel Metropolis lay in ruin (*Gen. 11:9, Isa. 18:2, Isa. 23:13*).

## Hebrewers

**Arphaxad:** Thus many of the Chaldeans made a great exodus from Ur, down from the land of Nod. They fled from the Lord in an exodus same as Ham had, after the Tent Incident, between Noah and Canaan (*Gen. 11:9*). These Gentiles "hebrewed the Tigris, and were allowed to come down into the land of Canaan. These Caucasians were allowed to come down to the land of Canaan, because they were not coming to spread the corruption of the Lord.

Cain's pale leper children were given sanctuary, and asylum from the Lord in the twin Canaanite grain cities of Sodom and Gomorrah. No people had ever stayed in Sodom and Gomorrah before, just grain! This was over four hundred years before the birth of Abram.

My uncle Ham had escaped the Lord, then the Chaldeans escaped the Lord, and in his life, my descendant Terah and his son Abram would attempt to escape the Lord also.

In the time just before Aram's birth all of Nod was dying because of the presence of the Lord and his Host there.

## My Line (Arphaxad)

**Arphaxad:** All in my line of descendants from Salah to Serug, chose be be after the Order of Michael/Melchezedek, as I had chosen (*Gen. 11:12-23*). Nahor and Terah had lived in my city and originally chose to be after the Order of Melchezedek also.

Then my descendant Nahor and his son Terah decided to exalt Hallel (Lucifer), the prince of the Darkness of the North. They left my city Arphaciyah and relocated to the Ur/Babel Metropolis, the city of the Lord. Ur was the nativity of Terah's three sons Haran, Nahor, and Abram. Haran the elder grew up and established his own city, named after himself (*Gen. 11:31*). There was a great famine throughout Nod because of the Lord's presence (*Gen. 3:17*).

## World Crisis

Bible/Torah

# Arphaxad Chronicles
# Noah Genealogy

*Note that Cain's line is not included here at all. All here are wooly and brown*

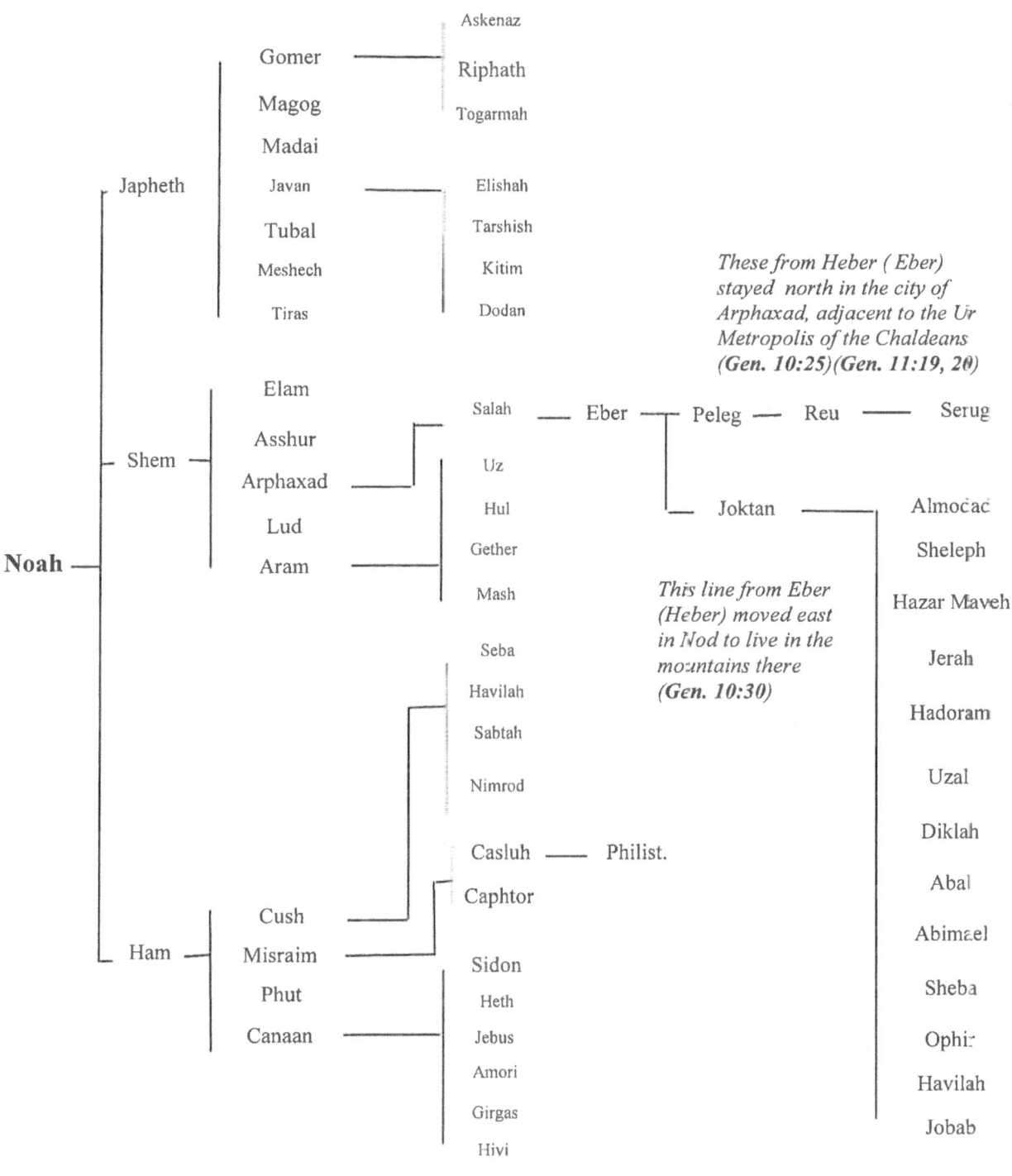

# Arphaxad Chronicles Chart

*World Crisis — Begotten — Mesorets*

### Begotten

*Arphaxad: I am the beginning of the line that led down from Shem, to Abram. My son was Salah, and Salah's son was Eber. Two sons were born in Eber's house, Joktan, and Peleg (Gen.10:21, 25, 11:16). Joktan moved eastward in Nod to establish cities there, but Peleg stayed in my city, and became the line that lead down to Nahor and Terah. Nahor and his son Terah migrated adjacent to my city Arphaciyah, in the north of Nod, and lived in the forbidden city, the Ur of the Chaldeans. Ur of the Chaldees would be the nativity of Abram (Gen. 11:28).*

*Arphaxad: The Lord forced Abraham to bring him from Nod, our side of the Tigris, that had been flooded (Joshua 24:2). The land of Nod was the one side of the flood and the land of Canaan was the other side where the Lord would force Abraham to bring him, down into the land of Canaan.*

```
                     Haran     This line from Nahor moved from
                     Nahor     Arphaxad's city, to the Ur (City) of the
   Nahor — Terah —   Abram     Chaldeans adjacent to Arphaxad's city.
```

**Arphaxad:** I Arphaxad was old and stricken when three of us merged on Ur. I came from my city Arphaciyah west of Ur/Babel, Hallel (The Lord) came down from Ararat, and Melchezedek came up from Jerusalem in the Garden. Abram was still sperm in his father Terah's loins, when the three of us met him (*Hebrew 7:10*). We had all came to determine what choice this unborn one would make, when he was born, and came of age. We had come to see whether he would be after the Chaos of Hallel the Lord of the north, or after the Order of Michael/Melchezedek in the Garden. But all that we saw when we looked at the loins of Terah was "Father of Betrayal," that is what Abram (רמה) means. *See Strong's #7411 Ramah = Betrayal.*

When Abram was born the famine was worst then ever. The Lord and his host absorbed all of the life out of every place they went in Nod. By the time that Abram was in his prime the conditions in Nod were intolerable. Most of the people in Abram's older brother Haran's city were dead, from the Lord's plague. Haran had come to Ur to escape, but he died before his father Terah (*Gen. 11:28*). Terah was sick too, and gathered up the remnants of his family. Terah decided to leave the the Lord, and Nod, to be safe if he could reach the land of Canaan (*Gen. 11:31*). The Lord could not cross the Tigris, except someone bring him. Terah was on his way, but he died, when he stopped in the city of his dead son Haran (*Gen. 11:32*). The Lord caught up with Abram, and the rest of Terah's family, there in Haran's city, before they could escape from him, by crossing the Tigris. The Lord forced Abram to continue his exodus down into the land of the children of Ham, but now bringing the Lord with him (*Gen. 12:1*). Nimrod and thousands of others from the Garden (Guarded Place), had given their lives in Nod to postpone the Lord's invasion down into the Garden, and then Eden. The Lord forced Abram to hebrew (cross) the Tigris River, the Broad Gate, to bring him (Destruction/ש) down into the Garden (*Gen. 11:32; Matt. 7:13*).

Bible/Torah

# Egyptian (Mesoretic Text) Chronicles

*Begotten — Hebrewers — Cush — Canaan*

### Hebrewers

**Mesorets (Egyptians):** Abram had been trying to escape the Lord's plague in Nod, but he knew that he was bringing the plague with him, when he brought the Lord and his Host, across the Tigris down into the Garden. The Lord and his Host could not cross the Tigris, on their own, but had to be brought by someone. If Abram had not brought them, the Lord and his Host, would have been left alone in Nod, to be consumed, out of existence, by their own diseases (*Exodus 15:26, Deut. 7:15*).

Our father Ham had brought us all down, from Nod/Ararat in a great exodus. We had come down from Nod, to be protected ourselves, and to protect Eden (Africa), from the Lord, and his Host, north of the Tigris.

### Cush (Ethiopia)

**Mesorets (Egyptians):** Cush (Ethiopia) is our elder brother, the firstborn son of our father Ham (*Gen. 10:8*). Our father Ham set Cush (Ethiopia) to defend the Tigris (Tigre) River. The area between the Tigris, and Euphrates is called Mesopotamia. Our father Ham designated Mesopotamia, as the land of Ethiopia (Cush), and the Tigris, and Euphrates, as the Rivers of Ethiopia (Cush) (*Gen. 2:13, 1 4; Zephoniah 3:10*). The Tigris River is the Broad Way. The children of Cush (Ethiopia) assisted him, to guard the Broad Way (Tigris), that led back to the Lord the destroyer in Nod (*Matt. 7:13*).

The land called Ethiopia in Eden (Africa), below our country Egypt is actually our brother Phut (Punt)(*Gen. 10:6*). Phut (פת) call themselves Abbys (אבש) or Abbysinnia (אבש) which means "Gifts of the Father (Ham)." Phut (פת / Abbysinnia) is "auxiliary" (פת), to us in Egypt,. Over time many Cushites (Ethiopians), left Mesopotamia and migrated, down to Abbysinnia (*Isa. 18:1, 2*). The land of Cush was a Fertile Crescent, but the the land of Canaan west of it was a Tropical Paradise.

### Canaan (Phoenicia)

**Mesorets (Egyptians):** The land of Canaan was a land of milk and honey, a tropical paradise. The eyes of the Lord, in Nod always cared for Canaan's land (*Deut. 11:12; Ex. 3:8*). Canaan was the next layer of defense, after the land of Cush. The land of Canaan was all of the land west of the Euphrates, westward to the Great Sea (Mediterranean).

Canaan was placed between Cush our elder brother, and my land Egypt. This was to protect Canaan from the Lord, who wanted to take revenge against him, because he had exposed our grandfather Noah as a Sodomite, in service to the Lord (*Gen. 9:22*).

Added to this the Lord was also angry with Canaan, because everyone who had escaped from the Lord in Nod, came to the land of Canaan: The pale leper Chaldean children of Marked Cain, "hebrewed" the Tigris (*Gen. 4:14*), and fled down into the land of Canaan for asylum, and protection from the Lord. This was after he confounded their city Ur/Babel in Nod (*Gen. 11:9; Isa. 23:13*). Now hundreds of years later Abram and his father Terah, had attempted to flee, from the Lord, to the land of Canaan also (*Gen. 11:31*). The Lord was set to take his revenge on Canaan, after Abram brought him across the Tigris, down into the land of our brother Canaan.

Bible/Torah

# Egyptian (Mesoretic Text) Chronicles

*Abram/AbramHam/Abraham — Prostitution*

### Abram/AbramHam, Abraham

**Mesorets (Egyptians):** The Lord was the Man who had been driven out of the Garden (*Gen.3:24*), and he could not return except some one bring him. Abram brought the Lord with him. Abram and the Lord hebrewed (crossed) the Tigris, and Euphrates down into the land of Canaan. Famine and plague followed the Lord wherever he went. Abram violate Universal Law, when he built an altar to the Lord in the land of Canaan (*Gen. 12:7*). Then Abram would not Keep his Feet, but fell on his face to the Lord (*Gen. 12:3; Eccl. 5:1*). Now because the Lord was in Canaan, there was a famine there, for the first time ever (*Gen. 12:10*). This was the excuse that the Lord used to bring Abram, from the land of Canaan, down into our country, Misraim (Egypt).

### Prostitution

**Mesorets (Egyptians):** Abram brought his sister/wife/niece Sarai with him, to prostitute her. They were destitute, and came to our land with nothing, wearing rags. Abram wanted my countrymen to lay with Sarai, but Egyptians would not have had anything to do with her, if they had known that Abram and Sarai were married. So Abram told Sarai to tell us Egyptians that she was his sister, so that they would have sex with her. Abram never feared for their safety, for the Lord was with them all the time (*Gen.12:13*)!

Sarai was a Black woman, but she was very pale (fair), like her mother's people, and the young princes of Pharoah were attract by her pale complexion. Pharoah's sons penetrated (hll / חלל) Sarah, before Pharoah, and then Sarai was taken into the Pharaoh's house (*Gen. 12.15*). Sarai was a Whorite (Horite or Mountaineer), like her mother, and like all of the little girls of Nod, the Daughters of Chaldea, those well trained prostrators (prostitutes) before the Lord (*Isa. 47:1-7*).

Because of Sarai's prostitution skills the Pharoah was soon sending out flocks, herds, gold, silver and servants to Abram (*Gen. 12:16*). Shari Misraim (Hagar) a princess in the Pharoah's own house, was one of those who the foolish Pharoah enslaved to Abram and Sarah (*Gen. 16:1*). When Abram had as much goods as he could manage, the Lord plagued Pharoah, and his house, because Sarah " spoke it (דבר שרי)(*Gen. 12:17*)." Abram and Sarah then admitted to the Pharoah that they were brother and sister, husband and wife, and also uncle and niece (*Gen. 12:19, Gen. 20:5*). Abram explained to Pharoah that his father Terah had impregnated the widow of his dead son Haran, with two daughters Sarah and Milcah, and then Terah married his two daughters, to his two sons Abram and Nahor (*Gen. 11:28, 20:12*). This was why Terah Abraham's father, was also Sarah's father, and why they were married to each other (*Gen. 20:5, 12*). Pharoah was disgusted and told them to leave our country, with all of their ill gotten gains (*Gen. 12:19, 20*). The Pharaoh sent Misri Shari (Hagar) with them. She was to become Ishmael's mother

### Ishmael/Isaac

**Mesorets (Egyptians):** Ishmael was born as the results of Sarah sending Abram in to rape Hagar (*Gen. 16:3, 4*). Our Egyptian sister Shari Misri, that they called Hagar was outraged, for she did not want to be raped, or to have a child for this man. When Hagar found out that she was pregnant, she not only despised Abram, but also despised his sister/wife/niece Sarai also (*Gen. 16:4, 5*).

Bible/Torah

# Egyptian (Mesoretic Text) Chronicles

*Prostitution— Birth of a Nation (Goyim)*

Abram was angry when he found out that Hagar despised him, and he told Sarai to do whatever she wanted to do with Hagar (*Gen. 16:6*).

With the impregnation of Hagar a Hamite woman, the Lord declared that Abram was now a part of the land of Ham. Thus the Lord named Abram, AbramHam or Abraham (*Gen. 17:5*). Sarai his sister/wife/niece would now be called Sarah (*Gen. 17:15*). Abraham and Sarah mistreated Abraham's son, Ishmael and his mother Hagar.

In the appointed time the Lord had promised Sarah, he came to pleasure her (*Gen. 18:12-14*). The Lord "Visited" (פקד) Sarah, and "did to her" what he had said, for she was pregnant (*Gen. 21:1*). The Lord finally "gave seed," as Abraham had asked (*Gen. 15:3*). Isaac was the Lord's son that he gave to Abraham to raise (*Joshua 24:3*).

Ishmael was Abraham's heir from his own bowels (*Gen. 15:4; 16:1*). But in Isaac's youth Sarah had Abraham to cast Ishmael and his mother out, so Isaac could take Ishmael's inheritance (*Gen. 21:10*). Abraham was an unfit parent, who mistreated his only son Ishmael. Ishmael was a starved fifteen year old bag of bones, who was too weak to walk, when Abraham threw them out. Hagar put bony weak Ishmael on her back, and Abraham mocked them when he gave Hagar a piece of bred, and bottle of water, and sent them out into the wilderness to die (*Gen. 21:14, 15*).

The Lord watched, waiting for Ishmael to die, but Ishmael survived inspite of his unfit parent Abraham. When the Lord saw that Ishmael was not going to die in the wilderness, he told Abraham to get his only son (Ishmael),* and to bring Ishmael to sacrifice him, as a burnt offering (*Gen. 22:2*). In his confusion Abraham thought that the Lord meant Isaac, because he thought Ishmael was dead. The Lord was bitter, when he saw that Abraham was going to sacrifice Isaac. He told Abraham to take his hands off of Isaac (*Gen. 22:12*). The Lord was bitter: Moriah (מוריה) means Bitter Jah (Jehovah). The life of the Lord's son Isaac was spared.

### Birth of a Nation (Isaac)

**Mesorets (Egyptians):** Isaac married his own first cousin Rebecca, and could not make her pregnant, after trying for twenty years. So Isaac entreated (tempted / עתר) his father the Lord to "rub against" (נבח) his cousin/wife Rebecca (*Gen. 25:21*). The Lord was tempted (entreated), and rubbed against Rebecca, and Rebecca became pregnant with Esau, and Jacob (*Gen. 25:21*). *See Strong's #3581, see also Gesenius Lexicon page 550b Nacah (נבח) "To be erect (aroused), and "Rubbing Against."*

Esau and Jacob struggled with each other in Rebecca's womb. Rebecca went to their father the Lord, to find out why (*Gen. 25:22*). The Lord told Rebecca that two Goyim (Nations) were struggling in her womb. The Lord told Rebecca, that the younger of her two sons Jacob (Subplanter / יעקב), would Subplant Esau the elder, and would rule over him (*Gen. 25:23*). The Lord gave his sons Esau and Jacob to his son Isaac, to raise (*Joshua 24:4*).

### Jacob

**Mesorets (Egyptians):** Jacob Married his two first cousins, Leah, and Rachael (*Gen. 29:23, 28*).

Chronicles    *Abraham never had an "only son," except Ishmael.

Bible/Torah

# Egyptian (Mesoretic Text) Chronicles

*Birth of a nation — Isaac — Jacob — Twelve Rape Tribes*

Jacob despised Leah, so his father the Lord took Jacob's place, and impregnated Leah with four sons. He also impregnated Rachael with one son, after she wrestled "**Great**," to have a child (***Gen. 30:8***). *See Strong's Concordance "Great," pg. 419 (Gen. 30:8), which gives Hebrew number 430* (אלהים), *which means God!* The Lord gave his sons Reuben, Simeon, Levi, Judah, and Joseph to his son Jacob to raise. They were the sons of the Lord with Leah, and Rachael (***Gen. 29:31-35, Gen. 30:22***).

Jacob came down from Padan Aram, and pitched tents before the Canaanite city of Shalem (Jerusalem) in the land of Shechem (***Gen. 33:18***). Jacob had four women: his cousins Leah, Rachael, and the two girls Bilhah, and Zilpah, they were all his property. Jacob's "sons" did not have any women of their own, except their sister Dinah. They were tired of doing it to her, and were looking at the girls and women of the city, trying to figure out how to get them for themselves. They decided to use their sister Dinah, as Abram had used his sister Sarah. They would catch the prince of Shalem/Shechem in a trap, the way that Abram and the Lord had trapped the Pharaoh and Abimelech (***Gen. 12:12-20***), using Sarah. But they would prostitute Dinah in a different way. They sent their sister to "see" the daughters of the land (***Gen. 34:1***). It was no accident that Dinah went straight to where Shechem the prince of the city would see her. Shechem could not resist her, for her brothers had trained her well (***Gen. 34:2***). Shechem did not take advantage of Dinah, but Dinah enchanted him, to the point that when they had finished Shechem wanted to marry Dinah, like the Pharaoh wanted to marry Sarah (***Gen. 34:3, 4, Gen. 12:19***).

## Twelve Rape Tribes

**Mesorets (Egyptians):** But Dinah's brothers did not want her to marry the prince of Shechem. They only wanted an excuse to murder Shechem, and the boys and men of the city, so that they could take the girls and women for themselves.

The Israelis murdered our brothers in the Canaanite city of Shechem (***Gen. 34:34:24***). And then as planned, the "sons' of Jacob (Israel) took the females from the city of Shechem, and used them to rape them selves into tribal existence (***Gen. 34:29***).

The Lord their father was there with them, and the Lord and his Host terrorized the Canaanite cities around them so that none would bother Israel, for the crimes they had committed (***Gen. 35:5***). That is when the Lord changed Jacob's name to Israel, a second time (Israel (אשראל) means "I wrestled with God)(***Gen. 32:28; Gen. 35:10***). Then the Lord told Israel (Jacob) that the land of Canaan now belonged to him (***Gen. 35: 12***). Now Jacob could dwell under the protection of his father, the Lord in the land of Canaan (***Joshua 24:4, Ex. 4:22***). Jacob's father the Lord (***Gen. 25:21-22***) was from Nod, and had been a stranger in the land of Canaan (***Gen. 37:1***).

Under the protection of his father the Lord, Jacob (Israel), and his sons from rape did what ever they wanted, to the Canaanites, and their females. Judah besides raping the females from Shechem, now "took" himself an Canaanite girl and forced her. He got three sons from her (***Gen. 38:2-5***). Then Jacob "took" another Canaanite girl and "gave her" to his son Er, who, the Lord killed, so Judah "gave her" to his second son from rape Onan, who the Lord also killed (***Gen. 38:6-10***).

The Canaanite girl's name was Tamar (***Gen. 38:11***). No Canaanite man would touch her for they considered her a whore, through no fault of her own. Judah had promised to "give her" to his

* Incubi is sex between a woman and a nonphysical being

Bible/Torah

# Egyptian (Mesoretic Text) Chronicles Birth of a Nation

*Twelve Rape Tribes — Multiplying in Goshen*

youngest son Shelah, when he came of age, but Jacob did not keep his promise. Tamar's father could not keep her forever, so Tamar dressed up as a whore, had sex with Jacob, and became pregnant by him (*Gen. 38: 16-18*). Tamar gave birth to twin sons. All true Jews (Judeans) that exist came from these two boys, Pharez and Zarah, born out of prostitution, and incest (*Gen. 38:24*). Thus all true Jews (Judeans) originated from this incest, and prostitution. Tamar the young Canaanite woman was forced to become a whore to survive, because the Israeli Judah had defiled her.

The Israelis were born as tribes in iniquity, and their mind set even let them sell one of their brothers Joseph into servitude in Egypt (*Gen. 37:27*). But Joseph was a forerunner of all of the Israelis, who were to come down into our country, to be saved. The Ishmael/Midianites brought Joseph down into Egypt, where he was employed, not enslaved by Potiphar (*Gen. 37:36, Gen. 39:1*). Joseph's coming into Egypt, was a conspiracy between Joseph, and his father the Lord. Joseph was never a slave but had been sent to Egypt, to establish a foot hold for the Lord (*Gen. 45:5*).

## Multiplying in Goshen

**Mesorets (Egyptians):** The Pharaoh was impressed by Joseph's seeming ability to prophesy. But Joseph was never psychic, his father the Lord, was whispering in his ear (*Gen.40:8, 9, 12, 16, 18, Gen. 41:12*). The Lord was with his son Joseph in Egypt, from the beginning (*Gen. 39:21*). Joseph admitted to the Pharaoh that it was the Lord, who was whispering the answers to him (*Gen. 41:16*). The Lord knew how to interpret the Pharaoh's dreams, for it was the Lord who gave them to him (*Gen. 41:25*). Also it was made to seem that Joseph was predicting, the coming of a seven year famine. Actually it was the Lord who would cause the famine, by his presence in Egypt. The Lord was installing his son Joseph, as a person of power in Egypt (*Gen. 41:30, 32*).

When the Pharaoh made Joseph second in command over Egypt, the Lord had accomplished his basic purpose (*Gen. 41:33, 38-40, 43, 44*). The Lord wanted to destroy Eden (Africa), and now he had established a toehold in Egypt, at Eden's front door.

Then the Lord disappeared from Egypt, for seven years, to allow food to grow there (*Gen.41:47-49*). When the Lord reappeared, his famine came also, and spread all over, from the land of Canaan, down into our country Egypt (*Gen. 41:53-57*). The Lord's plan was to eventually force Israel in Canaan, to come down into our country Egypt, to set the stage for his attack on Eden.

Israel would multiply into hundreds of thousands of people, a great Goyim (Nation)(*Gen. 46:3*). Then they would call upon his name, and the Lord would come to lead them, to break through the Narrow Gate of Egypt, into Eden (Africa), to destroy it! All of Eden would fall into the Lord's chaotic World, and he would rule in Darkness forever (*Amos 5:18, 20*).

The Lord's famine was so intense in Canaan, that the Israelis (Jacob and his people), would have died, if we Egyptians had not sent wagons to Canaan, to bring them to Egypt (*Gen. 45:19, Deut. 26:5*). On those wagons with the few Israelis were the victimized girls and women of Shechem, and other Canaanite cities, and their children, from having been raped by the Israelis. They had no choice except to come with the Israelis, for the other Canaanites considered them

# Egyptian (Mesoretic Text) Chronicles
# Birth of a Nation

*Out Cry—Sodomite (Holy) Israel*

defiled and dead, including Tamar. Even so we Egyptians settled Israel on the best land in our country (*Gen. 47:6*).

The famine everywhere was caused by the presence of the Lord and his Host. The famine in Egypt, and Canaan only ended, when the Lord and his Host retreated back to Canaan, and went into hibernation in Mt. Horeb. These famine generating vampires would spend the next four hundred years suspended up side down, hanging from the ceiling of the caves of Mt. Horeb. The Lord assumed that the Israelis would multiply in Egypt. The Lord then assumed that the Israelis would awaken him by calling upon him, and his Host, to invade and destroy our land Egypt, the Narrow Gate that protects Eden, and then they would destroy Eden (Africa) it's self.

### Out Cry

**Mesorets (Egyptians):** We only bounded the Israelis to build for themselves, after four hundred years of Egyptians building for them. The Israelis cried out in protest against having to began to do for themselves, what we Egyptians had always done for them. The Lord and his Host were awakened by Israel crying about working (*Ex. 2:23*). The Israelis did not want, to work to make bricks to build houses for themselves (*Ex. 2:23*). Now the Lord and his Host were out of hibernation. The Lord and his Host came down to see the city complex of Goshen, as they had come down to see the city complex, that Nimrod had built for the Chaldeans (*Gen. 11:5*). The Lord's concern with the Israelis in Goshen, was the same as when he came down to see Ur/Babel. We Egyptians had made the Israelis one, as Nimrod had made the pale children of Cain one (*Gen. 11:6*). But now the Lord would destroy Egypt, as he had destroyed Ur/Babel, because the Israelis had awaken him, with their crying, and not wanting to work as we Egyptians had always worked. We the Egyptians had built all of their housing for the past four hundred year. These were the homes that the Israelis had lived in, throughout all of Goshen. Goshen was the very best land of Egypt (*Gen. 47:6, 11*). If the Israelis would not have cried out, and had gotten used to work, they would have been saved from going back into bondage to the Lord.

Assisted by Moses the Lord brought his Thick Darkness, into Egypt, to reclaim the Israelis from the the Light that we Egyptians were giving them (*Ex. 10:22*). The Lord was not rescuing the Israelis from us, he was taking them away by force. The Lord could not use Israel to invade Eden, they had not called him, and did not want to be involved with him! The Israelis did not want to leave Egypt, and would not leave until the Lord and his Host had entirely destroyed Egypt, and "**we Egyptians drove the Israelis out**," to save ourselves (*Ex. 1:10, Ex. 6:1, Ex. 12:33*), while the Lord pulled them out at the same time, with a mighty hand. The Lord could not pull them out by himself, as we could not drive them out by ourselves. The Israelis were terrified for they knew that the Lord was going to take revenge on them, in the wilderness, as he had taken revenge on the Chaldeans in Sodom/Gomorrah.

### Sodomite (Holy) Israelis

**Mesorets (Egyptians):** The Lord,s first revenge was to place a covenant before the Israel, that

Bible/Torah

# Egyptian (Mesoretic Text) Chronicles
*Sodomite (Holy) Israel — Ishmael/Midian — Canaan Revisited*

they would be a Holy (חללי / Corrupt) Nation (Goyim) to him (*Ex. 19:6*). The Lord's first commandment was that they all be "sanctified"(קדש). They had initially been forced to sanctify their firstborn sons (*Ex.13:2*), now they were all being commanded to sanctify (sodomize) each other (*Ex. 19:10, 14*). The priest (Rabbis) even had to "sanctify" each other (*Ex. 19:22*). **Sanctification** (קדש) is the act of **religious sodomy** (קדש)(*Deut. 23:17*). Once the Israelis and priest had performed this act upon each other they were instructed to wash themselves, and their garments (*Ex. 19:10, 14*). Thus they were "sanctified" (Sodomized / קדש) and therefore made "holy" (קדש / חולי) or corrupt."

The Egyptian Israelis that the Lord brought out of our country of Egypt, were not corrupt at all. In Israel's four hundred year stay with us, we had brought them away from being Rape Tribes, to being like us the Syrians (צרי), or Egyptians (מצרי) that Jacob descended from through Betuel's wife (*Gen. 22:22*), Jacob's grandmother the mother of Rebecca (*Deut. 26:5*). We were the peaceable children of our father Ham (*I Chron. 4:40*).

In the wilderness, the Lord murdered these Egyptian Israelis by the tens of thousands, when they made the slightest complain about anything. The Lord forced them to sacrifice all of their livestock to him, and they were starving, and begged him for food. When quails by happen stance flew into their camp they cooked them, and ate them, but the Lord constricted their throats, and choked them to death, with food still lodged in their throats (*Numbers 11:33*)!

The Lord left the remaining Egyptian Israelis, to wander around in the wilderness, until all who had come from Egypt, and their children had died. Moses, Joshua, and Caleb were the only Egyptian Israelis who lived to come out of the wilderness. In the end the Lord would even murdered Moses for hitting the rock instead of talking to it (*Ex. 17:6, Nu. 20:8*)!

The Israelis that Moses lead out of the wilderness were the pale leper children, of the Lord and his Host, with the the Israeli females. Moses led them out of the wilderness, into the east country, where Abraham had sent his children Ishmael/Midian (*Gen. 25:6*).

## Ishmael/Midian

**Mesorets (Egyptians):** Ishmael/Midian, the true children of Abraham, existed before Jacob (Israel) himself was ever born (*Gen. 25:21-26*). Ishmael was Hagar's son (*Gen.16:4*), and Midian was the son of Keturah (*Gen. 25:1-4*), both with Abraham. Ishmael was chief over his own twelve sons, and Midian was chief among his brothers, the children of Keturah with Abraham. These became two confederations Ishmael, and Midian, who then combined to become Ishmael/Midian. Ishmael presided over all of his brethren (*Gen. 25:18, Gen. 37:25-28, 36*).

Their dwelling places were from Havilah to Shur which is before Egypt, and from there to the East Country of the Amorites (*Gen. 25:6*). In that time Jacob (Israel) was not even born yet. But now the Israelis committed holocaust, and genocide against Ishmael/Midianite the children of Abraham.

Israel kept alive, and used thirty two thousand (32,000) little pubelescent Midianite girls (*Nu. 31:35*), to rape themselves into being the "Seed of Abraham (*Gen. Nu. 31:18*)." Israelis identify their genealogy with the female.

## Canaan Revisited

Bible/Torah

# Egyptian (Mesoretic Text) Chronicles

*Canaan Revisited — Open Eyes/Closed Eyes*

**Mesorets (Egyptians):** Next the Israelis returned to the land of Canaan. Four hundred years earlier, Israel had murdered all of the men, and boys, of the Canaanite city of Shechem. They took all of the girls and women, of that city and raped themselves into tribal existence (***Gen. 34:29***). This time when the Israelis returned to the land of Canaan, they murder all of the men and boys of all of the Canaanite cities (***Deut. 20:13***). But they kept all of the young girls and women, of all of the land of Canaan, as captives (***Deut. 20:14***). When an Israeli male had a desire for one of these girls, he was to take her to his house (perhaps her dead parents home). He was to stripe her naked, and shave all of her hair off (***Deut. 21:12***). The Israeli was then to allow her to moan for her parents, that he may have killed for a month, then he could rape her (***Deut. 21:13***). When he was through with her he could send her away homeless, and perhaps even pregnant (***Deut. 21:14***).

Israel made Canaan a killing field. Joshua had the names of the murdered cities, and their kings in the land of Canaan recorded. The names of the murdered kings and their cities were from the King of Jericho, and his city Jericho, to the king of Terzah and his city Terzah. The total of the main kings, and cities murdered by Joshua, were thirty one kings and their cities (***Jos. 12:9-24***).

The Lord had failed to invade Eden (Africa), but he had established himself at it's gate in Canaan. The Canaanites had been murdered off their lands, and Israelis occupied it. Joshua's mission was complete. The Lord was avenged of Canaan, who had exposed Noah, as a sodomite.

But the Israelis who now occupied Canaan were not any of those who the Lord had promised it to, but were the Lord's own pale leper children, born in the wilderness (***Lev. 13th Chptr***). The Lord had subplanted everyone including his own son Jacob (Subplanter). Joshua had finished the work that Noah had began, of sacrificing the innocent (clean), to preserve the filth (***Gen. 8:20***). The World of the Lord, in Nod, was now reestablished in the land of Canaan.

### Open Eyes/Closed Eyes

**Mesorets (Egyptians):** The Israelis that left Egypt, had been full of the Light of the open Single Eye (***Matt. 6:22***). But the Israelis who came out of the wilderness, and committed holocaust in the land of Canaan, had an Evil or closed Single Eye (***Matt. 6:23***), and the Darkness of the Lord was a great and deep Darkness within them (***Gen. 15:12***). The Lord had closed the eyes, ears, and minds of all of the Israelis, high and low (***Isa. 6:10***).

The World (TBL) of the Lord was made up of Incest, Murder, Prostitution, Rape, Child Molestation, Sodomy, Pale Leprosy, Famine, Plagues, etc. All of those under the influence of the Lord had these vices imposed on them, by the Lord.

The pale Romans, and pale Greeks, who the Lord summoned to Jerusalem, were elements of the pale children of Cain, who had gone into Europa, with wooly headed Japheth (***Isa. 66:19***). In Canaan, full of the corruption of the the Lord and his World, the twisted Israelis were reduced to selling their sons and daughter, to the Pale Greeks, and Romans, as prostitutes, for wine (***Joel 3:3; Deut. 23:17***). The only way that the Israelis could be made free from the bondage to the Lord would be to bring his World (Tubal) to an end. We Egyptians would send Jesus to end the Lord's World, so that Israel, could see the Face of God (Peniel / פניאל) again, by reopening their Single Eye.

Bible/Torah

# Egyptian (Mesoretic Text) Chronicles

*Set Free — Peniel (Face of God)—Single Eye*

## Blessed (Fortunate) is the eye that see (*Matt. 13:16*)

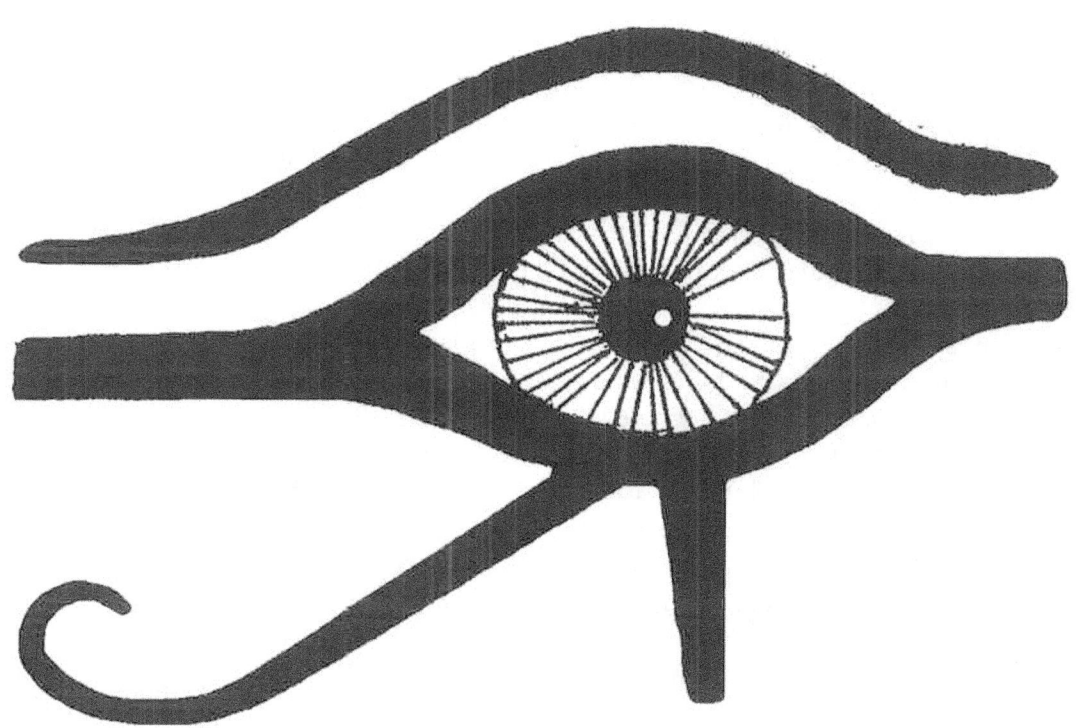

    Yeshua (Jesus) said that the Light of the body is The Eye: therefore if your eye be single (Single Eye open), that your entire body would be full of Light (*Matt. 6:22*). But that if your Eye be evil (Single Eye shut), that your whole body shall be full of Darkness, and if the Light in you be Darkness, how great is that Darkness (*Matt. 6:23; Amos 5:18, 20*)! Woe to those Rabbis, Priest, and Ministers, who give Darkness for Light, and who call Light, Darkness (*Isaiah 5:20*)!

    To preserve his World the Lord commanded that the Rabbis, Priest, and Ministers not only shut their congregations eyes, but their ears, and minds also, so that the people could never convert themselves back to normal, and be healed from bondage to him (*Isa. 6:10*).

Bible/Torah

# Introduction
# Yeshua (Jesus) Chronicles

*Egyptian Salvation—* Three Fathers — Order Of Melchezedek — End of the World

Jesus did not come back to Israel from Egypt, to represent his father the Lord, and his World. Jesus (Yeshua) was "sent" to abolish Judaism in the process of making the Lost Sheep of Israel free, from bondage to the Lord and his World.

Without Judaism, the World of the Lord of Abraham would have come to an end. Then the Christianity (AntiChrist) Church System could not have had a way to come into existence. The shedding of the blood of Yeshua (Jesus), was the salvation of the World, he had come to destroy. Jesus (Yeshua) had three fathers: The **Solar**, the **Lord** and **Joseph of Aram**.

It is written that the God of Abraham is the father of Jesus. Abraham's God told Moses that he (Jehovah) is El Shaddai which means "The Devil God" (*Ex 6:3*).

Thus the Bible is saying that the God that overshadowed Jesus' mother is the Devil!* As such it is Jesus denying his father the Lord, when he tells Satan "get thee hence" (*Matt. 4:10*).

When Jesus refuses to serve his father, who is Abraham's God Jehovah, Jehovah activates a contract against his son, Yeshua's (Jesus') life (*Deut.13th chptr*). The Jews must kill anyone who would lead them away from their God, and his World, even their God's son (*Deut.13:5, John 3:16*)!

Thus when the Jews (Israelis) handed Jesus over to the other Gentiles, the Roman Impire, to have him killed it was with Jesus' father the Lord's permission, for if Jesus was not for him he was against him. It pleased Jehovah to bruise Jesus' head, as he had been pleased to bruise Nimrod two thousand years before (*Isa. 53:10*).

When the Gentiles had tortured Jesus and he had died on their instrument of death, they made an icon of him being tortured on their crucifix, to mock him, and they recited the phrase "he died that we may live," or "we killed him so that he could not destroy our World! "

The Gentiles (Romans) then formed themselves a "religion" to celebrate their having killed Jesus, pretending that they adored him. The religion is called "Judeo-Christianity." It was invented and exported around the planet, not to save, but to seduce the very people who would have been safe if these Gentiles had not murdered the man they called Jesus. His teachings would have brought the Gentile world to an end, two thousand years ago! Murdering Yeshua (Jesus) has extended their World two thousand years, and they celebrate each year extended to that!

Jesus was after the Peaceable order of the children of Ham (*1 Chron. 4:40*), which is the Order of Melchezedek (*Hebrews 5:6, 10*). He was sent from Egypt to Israel to save the "Lost Sheep of Israel," from the corrupt Gentile World of the Lord, by destroying it. But this was the corrupt world (Jehovah's World) that the Lord so loved, that he gave up his only begotten son to preserve his corrupt World just as it was, and still is (*John 3:14*)! *See Observations "World"* The Lord did not send Yeshua (Jesus) into his World to condemn it, like Jesus did, but sent Jesus (Yeshua) to save it from self destruction (*John 3:17*).

*\*Read your King James Bibles , and your Strong's Concordances , to see if there is a difference between #7700 Devil (Shad), and #7706 Almighty (Shaddai). Shad is one Devil and Shaddai*

Chronicles

Bible/Torah

# Yeshua (Jesus) Chronicles

*Saying or Doing — Beguilment of Mary — Lord's World*

(Almighty) is more than one Devil (Devils). Thus God Almighty, or El Shaddai = God of Devils.

### Say or Do (Be)

**Yeshua (Jesus):** A father make commandments to his two sons. The one son says "yes father I hear your commandments, and I shall write them down and obey them." The other son stood mute. Yet in the day that the commandments were to be carried out the son who had stood mute did the commandments completely without word or hesitation. He had no writings or books or instructions to follow, except that it was written in his nature.

The son who had written it all down, and spoke it all out loud, could not or would not do it. The question is whether it is better to say it, or do it (*Matt. 23:3*).

Christianity claims that I Jesus (Yeshua) am it's father. They have written my words in their Bible/Torah. Yet Christianity (AntiChrist) have no intent to ever obey any of my commandments, for **my Gospels are an enemy to the western World** (*Romans 11:28*).

Yet there are and were people on the planet who never heard of Christianity, or myself, or the Bible/Torah, and yet they live all of the Gospels that I taught, for it was written in their nature! The people of Canaan were living what I taught thousands of years before I (Jesus) was born. Yet it was Joshua taught by Moses, and commanded by the Lord who lead the Israelis to commit holocaust against the people of Canaan. The holocaust against the people of Canaan, was the revenge of the Lord against Canaan, for exposing Noah, as a Sodomite. The children of Canaan were subplanted by Israel, who took their place. With Joshua the salvation of the World of the Lord was complete. The Lord had sacrificed the innocent Canaanites, to preserve his guilty World. This was the same World that I (Jesus) would be sent from Egypt to Canaan to destroy.

### Beguilement of Mary

**Yeshua (Jesus):** Before I was ever born the Lord looked for the woman, who would give birth to the one who would bring his World to an end. When he saw that it would be my mother he impregnated her with his seed, to stop the World Ender from being born. The Lord beguiled and overshadowed my mother, and impregnated her with me, his child (*Luke 1:35; Matt. 1:18, 20*). Then the Lord gave me, to be raise by Joseph, as he had given his other sons, to the husbands of the other women, he made pregnant: He "gave" his son Isaac to Abraham to raise (*Joshua 24:3, Gen. 21:1, 2 Gen. 17:16*). He "gave" his son Jacob to his son Isaac to raise (*Joshua 24:4*). The Lord "gave" Reuben, Simeon, Levi, and Judah, his four sons with Leah to Jacob to raise, along with Joseph his son with Rachael (*Gen. 31:35, Gen. 30:21-23*). Now the Lord impregnated my mother, and give me to her husband Joseph to raise (*Matt. 1:2*)! The Lord only kept his sons Cain and Abel, to start his World (TBL)(*I Chron. 1:1; Gen.4:1*).

### Lord's World

**Yeshua (Jesus):** The World of the Lord is his Day of Darkness (*Amos 5:18, 20*). To be absent from the body is to be with the Lord (*II Chron. 5:6*), in his Outer Darkness (*Matt. 8:12*). The Lord's

# Yeshua (Jesus) Chronicles
# End of the World

*Lord's World — Exodus*

world is a Thick Darkness (*Amos 5:18, 20; Ex. 10:22; Ex. 20:21, Deut. 4:11*). It is so thick that it can be felt (*Deut. 10:21*). The Lord cast Cain and Abel, out of their Inner Kingdoms, out to the Outer Darkness of his World (*Matt. 8:12*), by making Abel desire Cain, and having Cain master over Abel (*Gen. 4:7*), like Eve was to desire Adam, and be mastered over by Adam (*Gen. 3:16*).

The Lord had corrupted Cain, and Abel, and now he commanded that all firstborn Israeli sons be brought to him in the eighth day of their birth including me (*Ex.13:2, Ex.13:13, 15*). We were to be "Sanctified" (קדש), to the Lord, and made Holy. Sanctification (קדשה) is Ritual Religious Sodomy (קדש)* performed on firstborn Israeli sons. Holiness (הולי) is the corrupt state we would be in afterwards. Parents were to bring us three times in the year (*Ex. 34:23, 25*). None were to appear before the Lord with empty hands (*Ex. 34:20*).

Parents could redeem their firstborn sons from this humiliating act of being sodomized, by sacrificing a lamb to the Lord (*Ex. 13:13*). If parents did not have a lamb to sacrifice, and still refused to have their firstborn son religiously sodomized (Sanctified), the parents were commanded, by the Lord, to break the boy's neck (*Ex. 13:13, 15*)!

My mother and father sacrificed lambs to the Lord, three times in the year to save me. I was never Sanctified (Sodomized), and made Holy (Corrupt).*

This act of sodomy was performed on the little firstborn male children of all the tribes, for the express purpose of casting them out, of their inner kingdoms, like Cain, and Abel (*Matt. 8:12*). These future leaders would automatically infect the next generations. As such, all of Israel eventually ceased to be as little children, and would be cast out of their inner kingdoms (*Matt. 18:12*). He who is within (God), is greater than he who is without (Lord)(*Matt. 19:17*). Little children are each Gods, great in their own inner heavenly kingdoms (*Matt. 18:4; Luke 17:21*). I was still inside of my kingdom for I had not been cast out. I and my inner father were still one (*John 14:2; John 10:30*). I was in the World of the Lord, but not of it (*John 8:23*). The Lord did not bring me into his World to condemn it (*John 3:17*), but I did (*Rom 8:34*). I was in his World to judge it (*John 9:39*). My life, as a little child was in danger, because the Lord sensed me (*Matt. 2:13*).

> \* See Strong's Concordance #s *6942, 6944, 6945* these are *Sanctify* (קדש), *Sodomy* (קדש), *and Holy* (קדש) in that order.

## Exodus (To Egypt)

**Jesus:** At age two my parents fled with me to Eden (Africa) Egypt, to save me from those who wanted to kill me (*Matt. 2:13*). There has always been exoduses away from the Lord: Ham made a great exodus from the Lord, down from Ararat, in Nod after the flood. Cain's Chaldean/Gentile children made an exodus away from the Lord in Ur/Babel, after the Lord confounded it (*Gen. 11:9; Isa. 23:13*). Abram and his father Terah even attempted to flee from the Lord, to the land of Canaan (*Gen. 11:31, 32*), but Abram was forced to bring the Lord with him after his father died (*Gen. 12:1-5*). Jacob (Israel) had to flee from the Lord, and his famine to survive (*Deut. 26:5*).

The Egyptians had sent wagons to the land of Canaan to rescue Jacob, and his children from the Lord and his famine (*Gen. 45:19, 21*). And now my mother and father had to exodus with me,

Bible/Torah

# Yeshua (Jesus) Chronicles
# End of the World

*Self Centered — In the World — Saved and Raised*

from from the land of Canaan, to Egypt. Herod the king over the Israelis wanted to kill me. Why didn't the Lord stop Herod? Did the Lord want me dead, or did he lose control over his king (*Deut.13th Chptr.*)? Egypt the house of Ham, was the Savior of all who fled the Lord, including my family!

**Yeshua (Jesus):** In my youth in Egypt I saw written on monuments and other buildings, the terms **"Know Thy Self," "Love Thy Self,"** and **"To Thyself be True."** These terms reflect the very reason that the universe came into exist in a manifested form. Lack of knowledge of Self in the particular is the cause of physical existence. The entire physical realm is an experiment, designed by the All Seeing, All Knowing, All Present Self, who did not know anything about Self in the particular. To love self, and to be true to Self, one must know themselves, and be true to ones self, beyond all else.

To be Self Centered has always been Universal Law, since Original Man came forth from the sun to Love (Understand) Self in the particular. One must be Self centered to properly investigate Self in the particular or physical realm. To be Self Centered is to be Selfish. The truly Selfish are not greedy or covetous, but having self they are self sufficient, and have little need for outside assistance. It is the **Selfless** who grab and snatch, in an endless hunger, that can never be satisfied.

In those who are self centered, the Single Eye (Peniel), is open, and the body is full of Light, and they have Hearts (Minds) that Understand (Love)(*Matt. 6:22*). This is the description of little children who are still Self Centered, with eyes that see and ears that hear (*Matt.13:9, 13:43*). The people of Ham protected their little children, to keep them at the center (kingdom) of their beings, so that when they become viable in the physical they could Love (Understand) Self. Self is the essence of all beings, for without Self there is nothing. In physical manifestation there is always Self (Inward), and Selfless (Outward).

Self responds to two forces in it's being. The first force that Self responds to is the "Light" of Self. Light simply serves as a guide line for Self. The second and only other force that exists, for Self to respond to is the "Darkness," of having been cast out from the center (*Matt. 8:12*). Self has three qualities that allow it to follow the guideline of the first force which is Light. Little (Self Centered) children have these qualities, which are <u>eyes that see, ears that hear, and the ability to tell the truth</u>.

The second force "Darkness," comes from having been cast out (*Matt. 8:12*), which is the condition of being "Other than Self." This condition causes the "<u>loss of the ability to see, hear, and tell the truth</u>." To be other than Self carries three facets: Darkness, Evil, and Corruption. These three facets are the foundation of the World (TBL) of the Lord (*Isa. 6:10*).

### Saved and Raised

**Yeshua (Jesus):** There were still a remnant of Israelis in Egypt who never left Egypt in the Exodus. These Israelis called themselves Mesorets (Egyptians). My family and I were allowed to live with them for our entire stay in Egypt. The Egyptians gave my family and I asylum, in Eden (Africa), for ten years until those who wanted me dead had died, in the land of Canaan (*Matt. 2:15,*

Bible/Torah

# Yeshua (Jesus) Chronicles
# End of the World

*Saved and Raised — Sent — Secrets*

*18)*. Ten years was more than enough for the Egyptians to "raise" my mother and father and I, from the Darkness of the Lord, to the Great Light of Egypt/Eden. All of my brothers and sisters were born in Egypt, and were never Sanctified to be made Holy, but were protected from it!

In Eden (Africa), Egypt we were taught the perfection of Self (*Matt. 5:48*). In those teachings I was taught all of the qualities necessary, for my Israeli brothers and sisters in Canaan to convert, be healed, and become as little unmolested children again. For only as little children could they reenter themselves where the kingdom of heaven is at (*Matt. 18:3*).

At around age 12 I was "sent" back to my people Israel (Lost Sheep), as an Egyptian Prince and ambassador. I was sent to the Lost Sheep of Israel as a Prince of Peace (Salem). I was sent to shine the Great Light of Egypt/Eden, into the Great Darkness of the World of the Lord (*Amos 5:18, 20; Matt. 5:14*). All of the children of Ham were after the peaceable Order of Melchezedek (*I Chron. 4:40*). As Egyptian citizens my family and I, embraced the peaceable Order of Melchezedek also (*Psalms 110:4, Hebrews 5:6*). It was under Melchezedek's Order, that I was taught in Egypt. Those who taught me (Yeshua) in Eden's Narrow Gate (Egypt), had the Mesoretic (Egyptian) Text which was a Chronicle of all that had occurred, from the time of Adam to my time. The Egyptians showed me their records that Egypt had saved and protected Israel in Egypt for four hundred years. Egypt had saved Israel, and allowed them asylum, from the Lord who eventually came into Egypt with his Great Darkness, to forcefully removed them with a mighty hand (*Ex. 3:21, Exodus 32:11*). But the Lord could not make Israel leave, so the Egyptian had to drive Israel out (*Ex. 6:1*), to save themselves, from the diseases, that the Lord brought to Egypt (*Ex. 15:26; Deut. 7:15*)!

**Sent**

**Jesus:** I was not driven out of Egypt, but was sent as an ambassador, a prince, a citizen from Egypt, back to the Lost Sheep of Israel (*Matt. 15:24*). The Egyptians considered the Israelis as Egyptians, because Jacob (Israel), called himself Syrian (צרי), or Egyptian (מצרי)(*Deut. 26:5*). As such the Israelis were identified as Egyptians. The Ishmaelites called Moses an Egyptian (*Ex. 2:19*). My father Joseph of Aram (צרי), was also Syrian (צרי), or Egyptian (מצרי)(*Matt. 27:57*). Aram, and Syria were mixed, and both the same.

As Egyptians, Israel had never been in bondage in Egypt, or to any man (*John 8:32, 33*). I was not being sent to Egypt to free Israel, I was being sent from Egypt to the land of Canaan, to free Israel! Thus I was being sent to make the captives Egyptians (Israelis) free, from bondage to the Lord, and his World, of Thick Darkness (*Deut. 10:22*).

The Lord had commanded, that the Scribes, and Pharisees, (Rabbis) close the eyes, ears, and the minds, of all Israelis, so that none of them could ever convert, and be healed out of the Lord's Darkness (*Isa. 6:10*).

I was twelve when I was brought back from Egypt, to Israel. At age twelve, I was more than able to hold my own, with the doctors of the temple (*Luke 2:46*). I was able to answer all of their questions, and then I asked them why they would make Israel think Evil was Good, and that Good was Evil, and give Israel Darkness, for Light, and tell them that Light was Darkness (*Isa. 5:20*).

Chronicles

Bible/Torah

# Yeshua (Jesus) Chronicles
# End of the World

*Secrets — Draconian Measures*

These doctorers or tamperers of the Torah, were the Scribes and Pharisees (Rabbis), that the Lord had told to shut the eyes, ears, and hearts (minds), of the Israeli congregations. They must never be able to convert away from the Lord's Darkness, and be healed, back to normal (*Isa. 6:10; Matt. 18:3*).

The sodomizing of the little firstborn Israeli sons had been the first step, of casting the little children into Outer Darkness. The altering of scripture, by removing some information, and just not teaching other scripture was the process, of continuing to give Israel Darkness for Light (*Isa. 5:20*). Woe to those hypocrite Scribes, and Pharisees, who shut up the inner heavens (kingdoms), of the Israeli masses, and even refuse to reenter their own (*Matt. 23:13*).

Being after the peaceable Order of Melchezedek (*Heb. 5:6*), I had come as a Great Light, from Egypt, into the Great Darkness of the World of the Lord.

### Raising Israel

**Jesus:** The Israelis that the Egyptians sent wagons to Canaan to rescue, were corrupt, from their origin, with the Lord's Great Darkness, in Canaan. The Israelis that the Lord abducted from Egypt, four hundred years later, were not corrupt, they had been raise from the corrupt lifestyle of the Lord. Egypt was still in the process of giving the Israelis the Great Light that would make them whole, when the Lord came and overshadowed them again, with his Great Darkness (*Amos 5:18, 20*). The Lord began to recorrupt Israel in the wilderness, as soon as he had removed them from Egypt. The Levitican priesthood was established for the express purpose of sodomizing the firstborn sons of all of the twelve tribes (*Ex. 13:2, 13, 15*). Next all Israeli males, and females alike had to be sodomized (קדש), and turned into male prostitute (קדש), and female whores, or prostitutes (קדשה), even though the Lord said that sodomites and prostitutes would never exist in Israel (*Ex. 19:10, 14; Deut. 23:17*). Finally the Levite priest had to sodomize each other (*Ex. 19:22*). See Moses Soliloquy, pg. 133 "*Sodomized Firstborn,*" and pg. 134 "*Sodomized Israelis, and Rabbis.*"

At the commandment of the Lord the Rabbis officiated over the Sanctification (Sodomizing / קדש) of the firstborn Israeli sons, to make them Holy (Corrupt / חולי). In so doing they cast these children out of their kingdoms out into the Darkness of the World of the Lord (*Matt. 8:12,; Amos 5:18, 20*). That is how as little children the Lord shut up their eyes, ears, and hearts (minds)(*Deut. 29:4, Isaiah 6:10*). Thus their Single Eye became Evil (closed), and their bodies were full of the Lord's Darkness (*Luke 11:34, Isa. 6:10*). It was in Darkness that the Israeli males sodomized (שכב) the little Ishmael/Midianite girls (*Numbers 31:17*). See pg. 251 and 263

By the time of my birth the Lord had reduced Israel to the Darkness, of prostituting it's sons and daughters to the pale Greeks, and Romans, for wine (*Joel 3:3; Deut. 23:17*)!

### Draconian Measures Overcoming

**Yeshua (Jesus):** How do you break the habit of a thousand years of corrupt traditions? How do you tell children who consider it a birthright to be sodomized, that they shall no longer be Sanctified (Sodomized), and made Holy (חולי/Corrupt)? This corrupt act had become a badge of

# Yeshua (Jesus) Chronicles
# End of the World

### *Draconian Measures — Sword*

honor to the very children that were being molested! Now they would wonder what did they do wrong, that they are not going to have a right to be sodomized into the tribes!

Most of my Israeli brothers and sisters love the Darkness of the Lord (*John 3:19*), and few wanted the truth. I (Truth) would to set families at variance (*Matt. 10:35, 36, Luke 12:52, 53*). Israel had been taught that they were too weak to stop being offensive, to their children, and each other. I commanded the Israelis, that if they were too weak to stop offending, including offending their little children, to cut off, or pluck out that part that offends. I told them that it would be better, if they only lost the offending part, than to lose their whole self (*Matt. 18:8, 9*). Cutting it off, or plucking it out, and cast it away from them (*Matt. 5:29, 30, Mark 9:43*), would stop weak Israel from sexually offending each other, and their little children (*Matt. 18:4, 6*).

This would be the end of Israelis casting themselves out, to the outer Darkness of the Lord (*II Corinthians 5:6; Matt. 8:12*). The Lord and his Host would be left alone in their Outer Darkness, and his World would come to an end.

### Inner Kingdom

**Yeshua:** When I told the people that God, and the kingdom of heaven was within each of us (*Luke 17:21*), the Scribes and Pharisees were furious. They knew that the Lord was outside in Outer Darkness (*IICor. 5:6*), while God was inside of each body form (*I Cor. 3:16; 6:20*). Knowing that the God within, is greater than the Lord who is outside in his World (*I John 4:4*), would allow the people to know that it was not necessary to go to the temple, or synagogue, for each person's body is a temple, and they are each the God in that temple (*I Cor. 3:16, 6:20*). All of Israel are Gods (*John 8:33, 34*), as the Lord himself have said (*Psalms 82:6*). I told them to keep their feet, while they are in their bodies, or **Houses of God**, and not to make sacrifice, to the Lord, for it is foolish and Evil (*Eccl. 5:1*). I told the Israelis, that I and my father (God) within are one (*John 10:30*), as they would be one, with their father God within them (*Matt. 18:14*). Then it would be exposed that the only purpose for the Synagogue was, to cast little children out of their kingdoms (*Matt. 8:12*), and then to shut up those inner kingdoms from those who had been cast out (*Matt. 23:13*).

With the people knowing this they might tear down all of the Synagogues, and stone all of the Scribes, and Pharisees (Rabbis). So the priestcraft worked with the Romans to take my life. The shedding of my blood would be the salvation of the World, of the Lord, that I had come to bring to an end. The World (TBL) of the Lord is Corruption, not the people, or the planet.

### Crucified

**Jesus (Yeshua):** I did not come to die for anyone, but I knew that I would be killed for telling the Israelis the truth. The Lord so Loved (אהב) or "lusted," after his World that he was willing to allow for my death (*John 3:16*), to preserve his corrupt World. The Lord did not send me his son into his World, to condemn it as I did, but to save it (*John 3:17*). My father the Lord instructed the Israelis that they must kill anyone, who would carry them away from him to "Other Gods." Israel had not known that they themselves were the "Other Gods," until I told them (*Deut. 13:2, 3; John 10:34; Psalms 82:6*). The Lord instructed the Israelis that they must not listen, but must Love (Lust

Bible/Torah

# Yeshua (Jesus) Chronicles
# End of the World

*Sword — Inner Kingdom — Crucified*

after / אהב) him), the Lord their God with all of their hearts, and souls (Solar)(*Deut. 13:4*). When I taught the Israelis to cleave to their inner father, the Lord wanted me dead, who would turn them away from him. I was the "evil" that they must put away from them (*Deut. 13:5*). The Lord instructed them that it did not matter who was attempting to carry them away from him, a mother, a father, a sister, a brother, a son, even me his own son. I had let the Israelis know that their bodies were temples of God, as the bodies of people around them were temples of God (*Deut. 13:7*)(*I Cor. 3:16; 6:16*). I told each Israeli that they the Gods within, were greater than the Lord, who is outside (*I John 4:4; II Cor. 5:6*).

The defense of the Rabbis was that the Lord instructed them to murder me, because I was carrying them away from him. The Lord told them that they should not pity or protect me, but should expose me, as Judas had, who betrayed me (*Matt. 26:48-50*). Then once I was betrayed, the Lord instruct them to murder me, but they could not directly, for the Romans were in authority over them. Pilate was chief over the Romans in Palestine.

In the land of Nod, two thousand years before my time, the Lord had incited the ancestors of these Romans/Gentiles to crucify their savior Nimrod, it pleased the Lord to bruise him (*Isa. 53:10*). Now the Gentiles as the Roman (Italian) Band (*Acts 10:1*), had come to hang (Crucify) me on a tree (Cross), like a criminal (*Acts 10:1; Deut. 21:22, 23; Galatians*). My Gospel (Egyptian Text) was an enemy to the Roman, and Israeli leadership (*Romans 11:28*). The Israeli leadership and the Roman Impire both had to kill me, for I had come to bring their common World, the World of the Lord to an end, but not the planet or people. The Lord was the man who brought sin into his own World (*Romans 5:12; Ex. 15:3*). I came to abolish his sin, by bringing the Lord's World to an end (*John 1:29*).

### I. N. R. I.

Both the Pale Leper Romans and the wooly headed brown Rabbis spat upon me, not because I broke the Law, but because I had come to fulfil the Law (*Matt. 5:17*). They kicked me and punched me, not because I disturbed the Peace, but because I came to bring Peace. Canaan had been a place of Peace, until the Lord had brought Israel from the wilderness, to the land of Canaan. I had come to shine a Great Light into the Lord's Darkness, so thick, that it could be felt (*Ex. 10:22*). I had come to heal the sick, cure the blind, and make the lepers whole again. I had come to prepare a place inside of the people, in the father's house their bodies, where the kingdom of God is (*Luke 17:21*). The Devils that I cast out of the people into the hogs, were the Hosts of the Lord (*Matt. 8:30, 31*). People could then reenter, and repossess their own inner kingdoms (*Matt. 18:12*).

The Romans were World class killers, and knew exactly what they were doing when they killed me (*Luke 23:34*). Pilate had not washed his hands, except in my blood (*Matt. 27:24*). There was no apology in the Romans scourging me, and pushing a crown of thorns down onto my bloody head.

They beat me with bone tipped whips, designed to tear away my flesh. Pilate, the Roman Impire, the Lord, and the Rabbis were all co equally responsible, for killing the Light (Me).

The sign that they nailed over my head (**I.N.R.I.**), may have meant "**Yeshua Nazarene Chief**

# Yeshua (Jesus) Chronicles
# End of the World

*Crucified — I. N. R. I.*

**of Jews**," but it also meant "**I**slam **N**ever **R**ise **I**reaneus." Ireaneus was the Roman historian who put it in the official Roman record that my teachings of Peace (**I**slam) would **N**ever **R**ise, to allow people freedom from bondage. Synogogues, Roman Empire, Holy Roman Empire, Holy Roman Church, Roman Catholic Church, Catholic Church, Protestant Church, etc. it is all the same. They all celebrate my having been murdered, for World salvation. They all protected and saved the corrupt World of the Lord, by the shedding of my innocent blood. The church was founded to celebrate my being assassinated.

**Jesus:** But pick up your crosses, and follow me (*Matt. 16:24*). Do not except salvation, or find your life in the physical (*Matt.16:25*). Fear not those who can kill the body (Romans)(*Matt. 10:28*), but fear them (Scribes and Pharisees, Rabbis, Priests, and Ministers), who can also kill the soul (*Matt. 10:28*). Be as I am, after the Order of Melchezedek, and seek the Eternal Life pass physical death (*Heb. 5:9*). Take up your crosses and follow me (*Matt. 16:24, Mark 8:34*). He that finds his life in the physical, shall eventually lose it anyway, but he who loses his life for my (Truth) sake shall find it (*Matt. 10:39, 16:25*). **Do not except salvation**, but give up your lives for me, and you shall find Eternal (Real) Life (*Matt. 10:39; Mark 8:35*). If you love me obey my commandment (*John 14:15*). If you would enter Life, obey my commandments (*Matt. 19:17*). If you do not obey my commandments I do not know you (*John 8:31*). The yoke I put upon Israel was light (*Matt. 11:30*), and in the end they could have overcome the World that the Lord so love, as I had overcame the Lord and his World (*John 16:33*). I told Israel to be as I am, I am in the Lord's World but not of it (*John 17:14, 16*).

Israel could not serve two masters ....(*Matt. 6:24*). Israel could not serve the God within.... (*I Cor. 6:20*), and the Lord without ...(*II Cor. 5:6*). Repent (Rethink), for the kingdom of heaven (within you) is at hand (*Matt. 4:17*), within you (*Luke 17:21*). Call none good but God, who is within (*Matt. 9:17; I Cor. 6:20*).

After all else have failed you, what is it that you can resort to? You can resort to your own inner Self, for what will it have gained you if you gained the entire World of the Lord, and lost your own Self/Soul? (*Matt. 16:26*). But what man is there, who having found the great treasure of his soul which he had lost in the field of the World, would not go and sell all that he owned in the World, so that he could purchase that field, to reclaim himself (*Matt. 13:44*)?

Those of the masses of the Judeo/Christian World who had souls, have lost their souls. The congregations are easily led, because they have been made simple, to believe every word that the Rabbis, Priests, and Ministers tell them. But the prudent among the masses look at the scripture, in every case to see where they are going (*Proverbs 14:15*).

***Thus the scripture of the Bible can be reordered as a soliloquy, to allow each significant character of the Bible/Torah to speak to the reader of the Bible/Torah, pass where the religious leaders would have their congregations understand.***

Bible/Torah

# Introoduction
# Soliloquies

**Soliloquy** is an instrument used on stage in theater to allow someone to **speak their thoughts out loud**. In the Bible/Torah there are many who have not been allowed to speak their thoughts, even though scripture is there for them to speak.

Some of these people have been misrepresented, and others openly accused of being bad. There is ample scripture in the Bible/Torah to vindicate all of those who are directly or indirectly accused, or misrepresented! This soliloquy format allow biblical character to speak scripture. **Soliloquy** as a tool for the purpose of this book will be Bible/Torah **persons speaking scripture**.

Some of the voices that shall speak, are Michael/Melchezedek, Eve, Seth, Asshur, Semiramis, Cush Canaan, Nimrod, Hagar, Ishmael, and Yeshua (Jesus).

In contrast many in the Bible/Torah, are held up as honorable, but are not. There is ample scripture in the Bible to have these ones to indict themselves, with their own words. Some of these are the Lord (Hallel), Cain, Lamech, Noah, Shem, Terah, Abram, Sarah (Iscah), Lot, Isaac, Jacob, Leah/Rachael, Dinah, Reuben, Levi, Judah, Tamar*, Bilhah/Zilpah*, Moses, Joshua, Joseph of Aram*.

Once it has been discovered by scripture that those who are called good are not so good, and that those who are called bad are not so bad, then the Bible/Torah becomes another book. It is then a book that will wake you up, instead of putting you to sleep!

Lastly there is Jesus (Yeshua), who is not accused of anything, but whose teachings are intentionally misrepresented by Christianity, and the church. What Jesus truly represented would be greatly helped if he were allowed to say some things past what has been scripturally accorded to him.

Woe to those who call Good Evil, and Evil Good, and call Light Darkness and Darkness Light (*Isaiah 5:20*). *The asterisks above and below represent Ordered People included with Chaos only for continuity.*

**Self (Order)***

Michael/Melchezedek— 90-95
Eve — 96
Seth — 97
Asshur —98
Semiramis — 99
Cush — 100
Canaan — 101
Nimrod — 102
Hagar — 103
Ishmael — 104
Yeshua (Jesus) — 105

**Other (Chaos)**

Hallel (Lord) -106-110
Cain (3) — 111-113
Lamech (Cain) —114
Noah — 115
Shem — 116
Arphaxad* — 117
Terah — 119
Abram — 120
Sarah (Iscah) — 121
Lot — 122
Isaac — 123
Jacob — 124
Leah/Rachael — 125

Dinah — 126, 127
Reuben — 128
Levi —129
Judah — 130
Tamar* — 131
Bilhah/Zilpah* - 132
Moses — 133 - 147
Joshua — 148
Joseph — 149*
Yeshua (Jesus)* 150

Soliloquoy

# Soliloquies of Order Melchezedek

*Introduction — Order — Assiah*

## Order

**Michael/Melchezedek:** Jesus (Yeshua) and all of the children of Ham, were after my order (*Heb. 5:6, 10*). I am the Overseer of the Most High. The Most High is the sun, not the Lord. I do not represent the Lord of Abraham, but he attempted to exalt himself above the Most High, that I do represent (*Isa. 14:14*). I warred with, and defeated the Lord in the solar war (*Rev. 12:7, 8*). The Lord of Abraham is the Great Dragon, that old Serpent called the Devil, and Satan (*Rev. 12:8*). I cast the Almighty and his Host out (*Rev. 12:9*), and down into the earth (*Gen. 6:4*). The Lord is that Lucifer (Hallel) that I caused to fall...(*Isa.14:12*)? The Lord had said that he would be like the Most High (Sun)(*Isa. 14:13, 14*), but the Most High (Sun) saw the Almighty (Lord) fall (*Nu. 24:4, 16*).

My name Michael (מיכאל) means "From the Likeness of God." Thus I am also Melchezedek (מלכ צידכ) which means "King of Righteousness (*Hebrews 7:2*)." At the start of our experiment in the Invisible Field I was designated as the overseer (כוהן) of the Most High God. The Most High is Shemesh the sun, the father of us all (*Gen. 14:18*).

I along with all of the original beings on the planet are Alpha and Omega. We have no beginning or end, and our existence is without the aid of a mother or a father (*Heb. 7:3*). Nor were we ever created, for we are Eternal Beings, who manifested from the Invisible Field, into the physical illusion. As such we all became breathers/brothers.

My "Order" is actually the "Order" of Adam. When I cast the Lord and his Host down, they destroyed the planet, and few on the planet remained alive (*Isa. 24:6*). The remaining Adams were perfect male/female beings, but allowed me to put them to sleep (*Gen. 2:21*), so that I could alter them into separate male and female, so that they could be fruitful and multiply, and replenish the planet earth (*Gen. 1:28*).

Adam's Order is Peace (אשלום), it was introduced to Jesus (Yeshua), by the Children of Ham in Eden's Strait Gate (Egypt)(*Matt. 7:13, 14*). My order is the order of the Original Perfection of Adam. Adam represent the perfection of all of us who came forth from the Most High (sun), bringing the globe with us.

We were all perfect (חמים), when we separated from the sun to experiment. The sun represents all of us at our Most High (עליון) or Perfect state, before we descended. We did not know what to expect, when we came forth into physical manifestation. We had not ever experienced the particular or physical state of being, for it had never existed before. For that reason and in the first instance those who were to go down designated me, and those with me as Overseers (כוהנים) of the Most High (*Gen. 14:18*). We Overseers would not go down "completely" into the experiment, but would protect the solar port, and have authority over **Eternal life** ( *Hebrews 7:1, 2*), or Life beyond the physical illusion.

No one who went down into the experiment would be allowed to come back to reenter into the sun as individuals. We brought the mother planet Assiah out from the sun, as a complete entity with all on it. None could return to the sun except on Assiah, in it's completed and satisfied state.

# Soliloquies of Order Melchezedek

*Assiah — Disciples/Apostles*

## Assiah

**Melchezedek:** Assiah means "Fire (אש)" We named the planet we separated from the sun Assiah (אישה) or "Fireiness" to describe it as being "firey" (אש), like the sun, and Man (Ishi / איש) the "Firey One." Fire (the sun) does not harm fire (Man).

All of us who came forth from the sun are Brothers/Breathers or Souls (נפש)(*Judges 10:16*): This includes Adam, Hallel (the Lord), Gabriel, myself Michael/Melchezedek, etc. We are all Souls or Solar Beings. There were perhaps 144,000 of us, who separated from the solar (Sun) bringing the globe with us (*Rev. 7:4*). We were never created, and all exist Alpha/Omega, without the aid of a mother or father, and without beginning or end (*Hebrews 7:3*). We therefore do not have navels, and are all self existing, without outside intervention. We are the **first** and the **last** (***Revelation 1:8, 11 Revelations 1:17***). In our naked state we are unvisible to the physical.

In physical manifestation we wear "Coats of Skins" (*Gen. 3:21*), with wooly heads, and complexions like burnt brass (***Revelation 1:14, 1, Dan. 7:9***). Our appearance complements the sun that we separated from. Inside of the woolliness of our hair we carry all of the shapes, designs, patterns and movements, of all that exists in the entire physical universe. Our Brown/Black complexions allow us to stand unharmed, on the planetary equator endlessly, and exposed to the full intensity of the Ultraviolet (Black Light) Radiations from the sun. The controls for the solar intensity, and planetary distance from the sun is inside our invisible inner selves.

The sun would be the reference for those who went down into the experiment on Assiah. Those of us still with the sun, would extract the information of all that occurred on the globe, as it orbited around the Most High (sun).

There would be no right or wrong choices, just the the consequence of each action: An action brings a reaction, that is universal Law. None must stop our experiment, it must run it's course, and come to it's own satisfactory conclusion. Once we had completed our experiment in the particular with satisfaction, we would draw Assiah back into the sun, and then the sun would spiral back up through all of it's spirals, erasing the sum total of the entire physical universe. In satisfaction we would be back in the invisible electromagnetic field that the physical illusion emanates from.

## Disciples/Apostles

**Michael/Melchezedek: Disciples** are those who are **disciplined,** and hold the straight line down into wherever the the experiment take them. **Apostles** are the **apostate**, who curve away to avoid the very purpose that we came into the particular state. In almost the first instance that the breathers/brothers (Souls) went down, some began to curve away from the original intents of the experiments, and in that same instant these brothers became specimens, to be studied in the experiment themselves. Those who remained on Assiah were designated collectively as **"Adam."** These Assians (Asians), or Adams (Red Ones) were the only ones left who had stayed the course, down into wherever the experiment took them, without curving away. At first all who had come forth bringing the planet with them had been "Adams," until they curved away and

# Soliloquies of Melchezedek

*Apostacy — Creation*

become Alienated, by removing planets (Fallen Places / פלנות), from the sides of Assiah, and orbiting them around the Most High (sun). They were now alienated from their own perfect Selves. All souls had gone down into mass to understand the overall nature of Self, in the particular state, under all circumstances.

## Apostasy

**Melchezedek:** Taken from **Assiah** the planets **Mercury** and **Venus** represent the first two groups of Apostates, who attempted to return to the sun, but they failed. Hallel (Abraham's future Lord) and his Host knew that none could return to the sun, until all has been satisfied, in the experiment. But the Lord and his Host still took a mass from Assiah the mother globe that was perhaps most of it's original mass. Not being able to go back to the sun with this piece that was most of Assiah, they ascended into the heavens, and attempted to exalt themselves above the star (Sun) of Gods, by "creating" another sun, or portal back into the Eternal Field (*Isa. 14:13*). The Lord declared that since they could not return to the Most High that they would be like the Most High (Sun)(*Isa. 14:14*). **Jupiter** represents the attempt of the apostates to make their own sun.

The Lord's attempt failed, and they were left with their false sun, now called Jupiter. Jupiter was pulled along in orbit around the Most High, along with other planets that the apostates had taken out of Assiah. All of the planets used by the Apostate to escape from Assiah came from Assiah. The original planet Assiah that we had brought forth from the sun had been co equal in size to the sun, and just as fervent. What remains of Assiah is now a small aspect of it's original size and self. Hallel had set his planet Crypton next to the false sun, the Lesser Light **Jupiter**. All who had gone out from Assiah discovered that there was nothing in outer space beyond Assiah, except Outer Darkness. There was nothing out there, except what they had taken with them on their planets. Thus they had to "create" or "craft" from the substance of their planets or selves all that they needed.

## Creation

**Michael:** "Creating" or "Crafting is the corrupting of what was already perfect. Perfection is sufficiency to Self. Crafting from perfection was when the planets were taken from Assiah. Chief among those who crafted was the Lord, who is Hallel who was more crafty (Subtle) then all of the other **Beast of the Field** (*Gen. 3:1*). As such his planet was named Crafton (Place of Crafting), or Crypton (Corrupt Place).

Hallel (Lucifer) the Cipherman or Superman, located his planet Crypton (Krypton) between Mars and Jupiter, to be close to his false sun. All who had gone out were dissatisfied, but Hallel was more dissatisfied than the others, he was jealous. Jealousy is a sign of incompleteness (רע) of Self. Jealousy is the need for "outside" intervention in the form of a "Host," or "friend (רע)."

To go "away" from the center of ones own being is the beginning of Darkness, which is the foundation for Evil (רע) or Incompleteness. That which is incomplete cease to be perfect, and must have a Host, to give it an artificial completeness. Creation is the source of the World (TBL) of the Lord. Hallel having created had gained his World, and lost his Soul (Solar Association)(*Mark 8:36*). Hallel and his Host caused the Solar (Soul) War (*Rev. 12:7*), when they

Bible/Torah

# Soliloquies of Order Melchezedek

*Creation — Solar (Soul) War — From Assiah to Ertz (Earth) — Ertz*

attempted to invade the sun, to reclaim their lost Souls (*Judges 10:16*)(*Matt. 16:26*). The Lord became the Prince of his World (*John 12:31*), a Man of War (*Ex. 15:3*), and Prince of the Outer Darkness (*Ephesians 6:12; Amos 5:18, 20*).

**Solar War**

**Michael/Melchezedek:** There was war in the heavens and I and my angels defeated Hallel. In his impending defeat Hallel and his Host destroyed their planet Crypton, and place was no longer found in the solar heavens, for Hallel and his Host (*Revelation 12:9*). The entire population of Crypton was destroyed except for Hallel and his Host. All that remains of Crypton is a ring of debris in orbit around the sun, between Mars, and Jupiter.

The planet Crypton was also called Lucifer (הלל) being the planet of the Lord who is Hallel (הלל) who is Lucifer (חלל) (*Isaiah 14:12*). Once we had defeated our brother Hallel (Lucifer), we casted him and his Host down, into the vicinity of Assiah the mother planet (*Revelations 12:9*). We were still afraid of him, and waited for others to arrive before we attempted to overwhelm him. But he commanded his Host to go down to have dominion over the inhabitants of the mother planet (*Gen. 1:28*). We rejoiced in the heavens, but woe to our brothers the inhabitants of the Assiah, for the Almighty/Devil (Shaddai / שדי) is come down. The Lord was full of wrath, for he knew that I Melchezedek as the Ancient of Days, would be coming down shortly to judge him (*Rev. 12:12; Dan. 7:9; Psalms 82:1*). That is why the Lord and his Host attempted to recruit the Adams still on Assiah (Earth), so that the Adams could help them, to do battle against us when we came down to judge them. But the Adams refused, reminding Hallel (the Lord) that they the Adams were Gods like them.

**From Assiah to Ertz** (Earth)

**Michael/Melchezedek:** The Lord was in rage, and behold the Lord made the planet empty and waste, and turned the planet upside down, scattering the inhabitants abroad (*Isa. 24:1*). Assiah was utterly empty and utterly spoiled; for the Lord spoke it (*Isa. 24:3*). Assiah mourned and faded away, it languished and the inhabitants that the Lord called haughty languished also (*Isa. 24:4*). The Lord accused the inhabitants falsely of having defiled the planet simply because they would not except a covenant (ברית) with him, to war against us, who were to come down to try him for his war crimes (*Isa. 24:5*). The curse of the Lord devoured the planet and it's inhabitants, are burned and few men remained (*Isa. 24:6*). Thus the Lord dissolved the atmosphere (heaven) around the planet, and the atmosphere collapsed rolling together as a scroll, that fell to the ground (*Isa. 34:4*). The planet was knocked out of it's course, around the sun. My Host and I would have to search for Mother Assiah, which had now been destroyed (*Psalms 82:5*).

**Ertz** (Earth)

**Michael/Melchezedek:** I and my Host are the Gods who **found** (Bara / ברא), not **created** the planet (*Gen. 1:1*). The Luminaries or "Lights" (*Gen. 1:3*), are the crafts of those who came to

# Soliloquies of Order Melchezedek

*Ertz — Genesis — Two Great Lights*

reinforce those of us, who had casted Hallel and his host down (*Revelation 12:9*). By the time they had come to the vicinity of where the planet was supposed to be, it was gone. Assiah had been knocked out of it's course (*Gen. 1:2, Psalms 82:5*). We did not "create" (ברא) the planet but "found" (ברא) it knocked out of it's course, in total darkness (*Gen. 1:1*).

I said illuminate it, and those with me illuminated Assiah, with the light from their crafts (*Gen. 1:3*). The light was proper, for the illuminated planet was now distinguished, from the darkness around it (*Gen. 1:4*). I called the illumination from our crafts Day and I called the Darkness (Hallel) (Night / חלל), for Darkness is the Day of the Lord (*Amos 5:18,. 20, Psalms 118:24*).

This was the end of the first period (*Gen. 1:5*). And now the planet was artificially illuminated. Next we caused the planet, and the expanse around it to rotate again, to restore the atmosphere so that the light from the sun would illuminate the planet again naturally. The "firmament" (רקיע) was the collapsed heaven (atmosphere) of the planet (*Gen. 1:6*). We restored it from it's collapsed fluid state back into gas, and called it heaven (Atmosphere) again (*Gen. 1:7, 8*).

When we had drained the water away from the surface the planet, it was not the same as it had been before. Assiah had once been a solid landscape, with no continents. All of Assiah had been Eden (pleasure / עדן), with seas, hills, forest etc. Now we named it Ertz for it was "Broken" into "Continents"or "Fragments," which is what Ertz (Earth) means (*Gen. 1:10*).

### Genesis

**Michael:** The Lord had made the mother globe Assiah into Ertz (Earth) by exploding it, the inhabitants were burned, and few men were left (*Isa. 24:1, 3-6*). We had to restore life on the planet, and began by bringing the grass, trees, and other vegetation back to life (*Gen. 1:11, 12*). With the atmosphere restored, we divided the Day from the Night (*Gen. 1:14*). As such we were able to set the illusion of time into days (12 units light, 12 units dark), into years (365 days), into seasons (4), winter, spring, summer, and fall.

The entire northern region had been exploded away from the planet. We named it "Moon" (מון), which means "Progeny" birthed from the mother planet. The planet had been knocked out of it's course (*Psalms 82:5*), and both the planet and moon stayed opposite from each other, in orbit around the old course, keeping that old course around the sun. The planet circled it's old place twelve times by the time it had made one orbit of the sun. In that same period the moon orbited the planet thirteen times. That gave us two calendar: a twelve month solar calendar, and a thirteen month lunar calendar in the same time. The four seasons for all that we had revived would subscribe to the seasons generated by the sun, and moon (*Gen. 1:14, 15*).

### Two Great Lights

**Michael/Melchezedek:** I and the Lord are the two Great Lights, not the sun and the moon (*Gen. 1:16*). I am the God who designated my self as the Greater to rule the Day, and Hallel as the Lesser to rule his Darkness, called The Night (Hallel / הלל)(*Gen. 1:17, Amos 5:18, 20*).

Bible/Torah

# Soliloquies of Order Melchezedek

*Two Great Lights — Garden and Eden*

Now we turned our attention towards those who had been alive on the planet. We would pull them all up out of the water to revive them (*Gen. 1:20*). We "found" (ברא) the great whales, and the fowls that had flown through the air, and we breathed the breath of life back into the forms (*Gen. 1:21*). We put the resuscitated whales and other sea life back into the sea, and the fowls upon the land, to be fruitful and to multiply (*Gen. 1:22*). Then we did the same for the creatures who had lived on the surface of the planet. We pulled them forth from the soil, the cattle, that had lived, the creepers etc. Yet the **Beast of the Field** that we pulled forth were not animals, but were "animators." They were our brothers (Breathers), that had warred in the heavens against us, and that we had cast down "into/onto" the planet (*Rev. 12:9, Gen. 24*). We were not "making" (עש) them, but were "Ushering or Gathering (עש) them into one place, so that we could try them for war crimes that they had committed in the heavens, and also upon the planet (*Gen. 1:29*). We had found them buried under the debris in Nod, and pulled (Formed/Farmed) them from the ground. We breathed the breath of life, back into their forms and they became living souls (Solar Beings) again (*Gen. 2:7*).

### Garden and Eden

**Michael/Melchezedek:** Eden (Africa) is the only portion of the entire planet that did not move from it's place when Hallel exploded it. Eden must be guarded at all cost, for it was our only bridge back, up out of the experiment back to the sun. If Eden and it's people were tampered with we would not be able to retrieve ourselves, from the physical illusion. Thus we established (Planted) a Guarded Place (Garden), on the east of Eden, between Eden and Nod.

Then we put the Lord who is Hallel the Felon (Fallen One / פלא), and his Host there to tend it (*Gen. 2:8*). I caused trees and other vegetation to grow there in the Guarded Place (Garden), and channeled the the great river (Hapi / Nile) in northeast Eden out of Eden to water the Garden (*Gen. 2:9*). The four "heads" that the Nile was divided into, were the Mediterranean, and Red Sea, the Euphrates, and the Tigris. Originally all four commonly streamed from the Hapi (Nile) (*Gen. 2:10-14*). Thus the Guarded Place (Garden) flourished, for it was well watered, and well tended, by the Lord and his Host, the Nephalim (Fallen Ones) who are the Giants (גנות), or Gardeners of the Garden (*Gen. 2:15; Gen. 6:4*). Hallel and his Host farmed, while awaiting their trial (*Gen. 2:15*).

The Earthling (Adam) the remnant of those who survived Assiah's destruction (*Isa. 24:1, 3-6*), were also there in the Garden. I warned them (Adam) not to Consume-ate (אבל), sexually with those incarcerated in the Garden (*Gen. 2:17*).

The Adams allowed me to put him (Them) to sleep (*Gen. 3:21*). Adam was put to sleep, to be divide into separate (Ciphrated) male from female, so that they could multiply and replenish the population (*Gen. 1:28*), that had been destroyed when the Lord destroyed Assiah and few were left alive (*Isa. 24:6, Gen. 2:21*). But before they could be fruitful and multiply, Hallel approached Eve with his fruit, to convince her to consummate with him (*Gen. 3:3*). Hallel was subtle, and he beguiled Eve, impregnating her to began himself a line (Cain and Abel), to start his World on the mother planet Assiah, which was now Earth. (*Gen. 3:1, Gen. 4:1, I Chron. 1:1*).

Soliloquoy

# Soliloquies of Order Melchezedek

*Tribunal — Eve*

### Tribunal

**Michael/Melchezedek:** I am the Lord God who cursed the Lord, for beguiling Eve, with his Mandrake (Man of Darkness) Fruit (*Gen. 3:1-3, Gen. 3:13*). We came down from space on our firey thrones and the books were opened and set (*Psalms 82:1-8, Dan. 7:10*). I am also the **Ancient of Days,** who did sat in judgment against the Lord, who is Hallel, the **Prince of Darkness** (*Dan. 7:9; :Amos 5:18, 20*). All of the Millions who came down with me, to Earth, from the the other planets of the solar system, had wooly hair like mine, and wore white garments, like the garments that I wore (*Dan. 7:9*). They all came to witness the Tribunal against Hallel, and his Host. I was set to judge the Lord and his Host (*82 Psalms 82:1, Dan. 7:10*). These Gods were being tried, for their crimes in the heavens, and on the planet.

I spoke to the Lord the God who stood before me to be judged (*Psalms 82:1*). I asked him, "Oh Lucifer (Hallel), Lord of the North, how have thou fallen? You have been cut down to the ground (*Isa. 14:12*)! You had said that you would ascend into the heavens, and exalt your throne above the stars of God (*Rev. 12:7, Isa. 14:13*). You said that you would ascend above the clouds of Krypton, and be like the Most High (Sun)(*Isa. 14:14*). But in so doing Hallel you and your Host started the war in the heavens. I (Michael), and and my angels fought against you Hallel. You the Dragon, and your angels did not prevail, and pending your defeat, you destroyed your planet Krypton, and "place was no longer found" for you in the heavens (*Rev. 12:8*). You the future Lord of Abraham are the great Dragon that we Cast Out (Shaddai / שדי). You are that old Serpent, the Devil (שד) called Satan. We casted you down into the ground, and your Host were cast down with you (*Rev. 12:9*). You shall deceive the people, and impose your World system on them. The masses on the earth who bow down to you, shall not even know that you are the source of the World (TBL) that they suffer in. Nor will they know that you are the God of the mentally dead, because none of your names are written in the book of Life (*Rev. 12:9, 13:8*).

I sentenced Hallel the chief of the "Beast of the field," and Earth, to have his body burned ( *Dan. 7:11*), as he had cause the bodies of men of the planet to be burned (*Isa. 24:6*). I brought a fire from his solar plexus to consume his body (*Dan. 7:11, Ezek. 28:18*). I then took dominion from his Hosts, the other Beast. But I spared them, reminding his Host that all of them were also Gods like us, children of the Most High (*Psalms 82:6; Deut. 32:8; Dan. 7:12; Gen. 1:28*). Then I casted the Lord (Man) out with his Host, back over into Nod where I had taken them from (*Gen.3:23*). His sons Cain and Abel were sent with them also. The experiment must go on. The Lord would have his line of children, to do with as he pleased. Adam's own line began with his Image and Likeness, Seth (*Gen. 4:25, 26; 5:3*). We could not help any of those imposed upon by the Lord, except to give them asylum if they chose to escape from him. There are two distinct lines flowing from two: One from our brother Hallel (Lord), and the other from our brother Adam. But the mother of all three, Cain, Abel, and Seth is Eve (*Gen. 3:20*).

# Soliloquoy of Order
# Eve

*Melchezedek — Not Adam's rib, mother, sister, wife, or daughter, but his female side (wombman)(viable in due season) — Mother of all (two lines) — Cain and Abel (Lord's sons) — Seth (In the Image and Likeness of Adam) — Seth*

**Eve:** Michael/Melchezedek is the Lord God who made me a wombman from the womb he removed from Adam (*Gen. 2:21-23*). Before Adam was made separate male, and female he was perfect. As such Adam was not given, or taken in marriage, but was as the Angels/Gods (*Matt. 22:30*). Adam never needed a helpmeet, he was never **alone**, but was **all one,** male/female together in one form, like all of the other Gods (*Gen. 1:27, Gen. 2:18*). I am not Adam's rib, or his mother, nor his sister, nor his daughter, wife or his helpmeet (*Gen. 2:21*). I am Adam's womb, his viable female side. I was once the part of him (female), that, in due season Adam would transform, from an apparent male, into an apparent female. Then Adam's intact female side (me Eve) would be activated, to bring forth a single birth, without having been impregnated. This birth, the birth of Seth was not the birth of a child of Adam, but was the birth of a continuation vessel for Adam, in image and likeness (*Gen. 5:3*). The physical body form grows old and dies, even though the Invisible (God) Being inside the body is Eternal.

Adam was a male/female being with me being a part of him, when he (we) were told not to eat from the tree of Knowledge (*Genesis 2:16, 17*). I heard it when I and Adam were one. That was how I was able to tell the serpent, after Adam and I were separate, that we were forbidden from eating the fruit. Adam did not need a helpmeet, for I was viable and complete already, before he was put to sleep and divided into separated male and female (*Gen. 2:21, 22; Genesis 3:3*). In his perfection Adam did not need anything added to, or subtracted from himself.

Though the Gods inside the physical forms are eternal, the physical form is inside of the illusion of time and space, and eventually grows old and die (מות)(*Gen. 3:3*). That is the nature of the physical forms occupied by all of the Gods operating in the physical including Adam. None of the others Gods (Original Men) ever needed a helpmeet, and nor did Adam. There was just the periodic changing from an aging physical form, to a new one that contained all that had been in the old form. Once the old had nursed the new into being viable, the old passed away as an empty shell.

**Eve:** The Lord is the Serpent that beguiled, me and became the father of Cain and Abel (*Gen. 4:1, I Chron. 1:1*). The Lord used me as he would use the little Chaldean girls (*Isa. 47:1-7*), the Canaan girls (*Gen. 34:29*), and Midianite girls (*Nu. 31:9, 35*). We were all used, to preserve the Filth (World) of the Lord. The birth of Cain and Abel were the beginning of the World (TBL), of the Lord on this planet. Afterwards in due season I gave birth to Seth who is in the image and likeness of Adam (*Gen. 5:3, Gen. 4:25*). Seth was not Adam's son, but was Adam's continuation. I Eve am the mother of Cain, Abel, and Seth (*Gen. 3:20*). We all came into separate existence inside of Adam's sleep (*Gen. 2:21*). Adam was never awakened, but the entire experiment is taking place inside of Adam's sleep, through it's processes to completion and satisfaction. All that has ever occurred since Adam was put to sleep has happened in his sleep. I am the mother of all, Cain, Abel and Seth but only Seth can attain to Adam waking up, at the end of the experiment.

# Soliloquoy of Order
# Seth

*Continuation of Adam — Gaurding the Experiment — Children of Sheth — Asshur*

**Seth:** The Lord impregnated Eve to get Cain, and his line as servants (*I Chron. 1:1; Gen. 4:1*). I Seth and my line are a continuation of Adam (*Gen. 4:25*). I saw Cain and Abel, the Lord's twin sons come into existence inside the same womb, that I still lay dormant (*Gen. 4:2, I Chron. 1:1*). Adam had called the **wombman** "Eve" (Life / חוה), because Eve means "Life." Eve (Life) is the mother of all three of us living (חי), Cain, Abel, and I, Seth (*Gen. 3:20*). My name Seth (שת) means "Appointed." But I was not "set," or "Appointed" to take the place of Abel who Cain killed. Abel was in the line of the Lord. Rather I was Set or Appointed to be a continuation, in the image and likeness of Adam, I am Adam (*Gen. 5:3*). Adam and Eve never left the Garden. Therefore I was born in the Garden, after the Lord his Host and Cain had been driven out (*Gen.3:24*).

The Lord corrupted his sons Cain and Abel, and turned them into Sodomites (*Gen. 4:7*). When Cain murdered Abel, the Lord their father "Marked" Cain, with a permanent genetic pale leprosy (*Gen. 4:14*). This was to distinguish Cain, and to give Cain protection from the Lord's male Host, who were the friends of effeminate Abel. The Lord warned his Host not to slay Cain, who he would avenge sevenfold (*Gen. 4:15*).

The Lord then sent Cain into the face of the earth, down under ground to dwell with him and his Host, who were in the earth in those days (*Gen. 6:4, Ex. 8:22*). Cain married among the Lilith(s) or female Host of the Lord (*Gen.4:17*). The entire male line coming from Cain married the females of the Lord's Hosts, and the male Host of the Lord (Sons of God) married the Daughter of Cain, from all they chose (*Gen. 6:2, 3*). This mix became the Chaos or World (Tubal) of the Lord. The Lord wanted Cain and his corrupt line to subplant my line, with their corrupt lifestyle, of Sodomy, Incest, Rape, Murder, Lesbianism, Bestiality, etc. The Lord's plan was to use Cain's children to suspend the experiment, and he would rule forever in a never ending Chaos.

**Seth:** But the whole purpose of my myself, and my children, was to maintain the experiment to bring it to a satisfactory conclusion. We were to preserve ourselves first of all. Then we were to protect and preserve the Garden or Guarded Place, which Shielded Eden (Africa) from the Lord. Eden is the Keystone, for the rebuilding of the planet back into Assiah. Eden is the Building Stone rejected by the Lord and his Host, who were building his World (*Matt. 21:42*). The Lord had attempted to destroy all of Assiah, including Eden. Eden must be protected and guarded at all cost. Beyond defending ourselves, and Eden, we the continuation of Adam offered asylum to anyone, who were fleeing from the Lord. I had other children, other than the children of Noah (*Numbers 24:17*), who survived the flood. After the flood many of my other children, along with my son Noah's children returned north to Nod. They all went north to assist Nimrod in the building of Ur of the Chaldees, for the Raising of Cain, his pale leper children. Raised from the corruption of the Lord, Cain,s Pale Ones would cease to be a threat. My children the Children of Seth are identified as the the Children of Eden in Telasshur (*Isa. 37:12*). When they went north among those who went with Nimrod, my children were located in Tel Asshur, among the inhabitants of the mounded (Tel) city of Asshur (*II Kings 19:12*).

Bible/Torah

# Soliloquoy of Order
# Asshur

*Seth — Childless — Nimrod the Assyrian — My Twin Semiramis*

**Asshur:** Adam's continuation Seth was the beginning of the line, that led down to my father Shem. I am the second son of Shem. My older brother Elam was born on the Ark ship (*Gen. 10:22*). I and my twin sister Semiramis were born the year before Arphaxad. My younger brother Arphaxad was born two years after the flood (*Gen. 10:22, 11:10*). My two younger brothers are Lud and Aram (*Gen. 10:22*). We are the cousins of Ham's children: Misraim (Egypt), Cush (Ethiopia), Canaan, and Phut (Abbysinnia)(*Gen. 10:6*). My brothers and I are also the cousins of the children of our uncle Japheth: Gomer, Magog, Madai, Javan (Greek), Tubal, Meshech, and Tiras (*Gen. 10:2*).

All of us cousins knew something strange was going to happen in grandfather Noah's tent, because Canaan told the whole family, including our grandmother Noah's wife, and our mothers.

Noah had asked Canaan to come to his tent in secrecy, and not tell anyone. What Canaan "did" to Noah was to tell on him. Grandfather was never asleep, but "finished (קיץ)"drinking his wine, after he had been exposed (*Gen. 9:24*). Our father Shem, and uncle Japheth tried to "cover it up," but everyone in the family had seen it already, when uncle Ham had opened the tent flap, to let everyone outside see what grandfather Noah was trying to do, with Canaan (*Gen. 9:23*)!

After the Tent Incident between grandfather Noah, and Canaan, uncle Ham brought us down from Ararat. Nimrod was not even born, at the time that we came down from Ararat. My sister Semiramis was pregnant with Nimrod. She brought him down from Ararat in her stomach. Nimrod was born south of the Tigris, in the Garden lands of Ham.

I did not have children, and therefore I designated my sister's son Nimrod as the continuation of my household. I named Nimrod, Asshur (*Gen. 10:11*), and Assyrian (*Isaiah 23:13*). Nimrod carried the title "Asshur," when he went back north to Raise Cain's Pale Leper Gentile/ Chaldean children It was my nephew Nimrod the Assyrian, who built the six city Ur Metropolis, on the side of the north in the land of Nod (*Gen. 10:10-12, Gen. 11:3-9, Isaiah 23:13*).

My land (Assyria) is also in the north at the southern entrance, to where Nimrod built his kingdom in the north (*Micah 5:6*). The six city Ur/Babel Metropolis was built on the Tigris, and the plains of Shinar. The Children of Sheth (Seth), had survived the flood. They came north with Nimrod to help build Ur. They dwelt in my Mound (Tel) City of Asshur or Tel Asshur (*II Kings 19:12*)

My younger brother Arphaxad also built his city of Arphaciyah. in the north on the border of the Chaldeans. "Border of Chaldea" is what Arphaxad means.

My father Shem and uncle Japheth were both a part of the cover-up in the Tent Incident. It was after the Tent Incident that my uncle Ham brought us all down from the hostage situation that Noah held us in, on Mount Ararat. All of Ham's children were allowed to go to the south "side"of the Tigris to reestablish the Garden (Guarding Place), between Nod and Eden. Grandfather Noah and his three sons had lived in the Garden before the flood. I Asshur was allowed to dwell in land of Cush, south of the Tigris, because my twin sister Semiramis was the wife of Cush the elder son of Ham. My brothers Arphaxad, Aram, and Elam and their children had to stay on the north side of the Tigris in Nod.

Soliloquies

# Soliloquoy of Order
# Semiramis

*Asshur — "We Came Down From Ararat — Savior Nimrod— Cush*

**Semiramis:** I was named after my father Shem. My name Semiramis means "Highness of Shem." I and my brother Asshur are twins. Asshur and I are the second born of Shem. Our oldest brother Elam was born on the ark ship. We were born on Ararat after the flood. I Semiramis and Cush the son of Ham married, while we were still on Ararat. By the time of the tent Incident, I was pregnant with Nimrod. Asshur's wife bore him no children to continue his household. In our culture, a son of an oldest or only sister, may be installed as the head of the household of her brother, who has no heir to continue his line. Thus my son Nimrod besides inheriting from his father Cush, also inherited from my brother Asshur. Nimrod became the "Assyrian" (*Gen. 10:11; Isa. 23:13*).

**Semiramis:** In the modern times my son is accused, of keeping people hostage, and founding a religion on Ararat, but this was not true. Nimrod did not keep anyone anywhere. After the Tent Incident, Ham brought us down from Ararat, and I was still pregnant with Nimrod. I brought Nimrod down from Ararat in my stomach, in the Great Exodus of Ham. We named him Nimrod (מורד)* #4174, to commemorate that **"We Came Down."** We Came Down, is what "Nimrod" means, **"We Came Down,"** Noah, Shem, and Japheth stayed on Ararat. They set up altars and burned the animals that they were suppose to release to repopulate the land that had been flooded (*Gen.8:20*). This proves that Noah, Shem, and Japheth **refused to "Come Down,"** to reinhabit the land that had been flooded, and they became the rebellers (מרד) #4775, that Nimrod is accused of being.

**Semiramis:** It was years later when Nimrod and thousands of the other children of Ham returned to the side of the north of the land of Nod. They were there by request from the Lord (*Gen. 10:9*). The Lord wanted Nimrod to hunt in the ground for Cain (*Gen.10:8, Gen. 4:14*). Nimrod hunted mightily in the ground of Mount Ararat, to excavate the children of Cain, from the caves they had sealed themselves, to survive the flooding of the rivers of my husband Cush (Ethiopia)(*Gen. 10:8, 9*). The entire flood of Noah was the flooding of the Tigris and Euphrates, the rivers of the land of Ethiopia (Cush) (*Gen. 2:13, Isa.* ).

**Semiramis:** After my son Nimrod had saved the Pale Leper children of Cain, the Lord incited them to murder him. They tortured my son Nimrod, their savior, and then murdered him by crucifixion on an "X" shaped cross. These Gentiles admitted that Nimrod had not done anything wrong, but that it pleased the Lord for them to bruised my son's head anyway (*Isa 54:10*)!
Then most of those Gentile/Chaldeans fled from confounded Ur/Babel, down across the Tigris River, through the land of my husband Cush. They were in the land of Cush's brother Canaan when they were given asylum from the Lord, in the Canaanite grain storage cities of Sodom and Gomorrah. Ham charged his son, my husband Cush (Ethiopia), and our children to guard the entire length of the Broad Gate of the Tigris River, from those in Nod (*Matt. 7:13*).

Bible/Torah

# Soliloquoy of Order
# Cush (Ethiopia)

*Semiramis — We Came Down — Tigris (Tigre) and Euphrates, Rivers of Ethiopia Isaiah 18:1, Zephoniah 3:10 — Mesopotamia Ethiopia, land of Cush (Gen. 2:13 — Broad Gate leading to destruction (Shaddai) Matt. 7:13 — Garden (Guard Place)(Magan מגן) Shield — Cushion, Cash, Cush — Brother Canaan*

**Cush:** I am Cush the oldest son of Ham (*Gen. 10:6*). My wife Semiramis brought our youngest son Nimrod down from Ararat, in her stomach (*Gen. 10:8*). Nimrod (מרד) means "We Came Down."

"We came down" from Ararat in a Great Exodus, after the Tent Incident. We had to protect ourselves in the Garden, and Eden from the Lord and Noah's corruption on Mound Ararat in Nod. My father Ham designated me his oldest son, and my children as the protectors of the Broad East Gate, the Tigris river (*Gen. 3:22, 23*). Eden's Garden is East of Eden, and the land of Nod is east of Eden's garden (*Gen. 4:16*). The Tigris River is the Broad Gate between corrupt Nod to it's east and the Garden west of the river. The Tigris River and Euphrates Rivers were designated as my rivers, the Rivers of Cush or the Rivers of Ethiopia (*Gen. 2:13, Isa. 18:1, Zephoniah 3:10*). My children guard it from it's very northern extremes down to the Persian gulf, and eastward all the way to India. Western India became Hindu Cush or Hindu Ethiopia. My father Ham instructed us that we were at all cost, to keep the corruption of the Gentiles east of the Gate in Nod from coming across the Tigris westward into our Garden or "Guarded Place." The Tigris was the first defense, and the Euphrates was the second line of defense. My younger brother Canaan and his children guarded from the Euphrates westward to the Great Sea (Mediterranean), and south from there to Egypt the Narrow Gate of our father Ham, and brother Misraim. Ham/Mitzraim (Chamits/Chemets) or Egypt, the Narrow Gate was the last protection for Eden (Africa), the Garden of the Gods (*Ezekiel 28:13*).

My grandfather Noah cursed Canaan and said that Canaan would be a servant to servants (*Gen. 9:25*), because of what Canaan "did to him (*Gen.9:24*)." What Canaan did to Noah was to expose our grandfather, for the Sodomite that he was, in service to Hallel (Lucifer), the Lord of the North. The Lord of the North was also the Prince of Darkness (*Amos 5:18, 20*).

We were in the midst of a great experiment that had extended down to us, from our father Adam. We had held Adam's line from the inception of his sleep, and the birth of Seth. Our father Ham continued Adam's line, from before the flood to bringing us down from Ararat in his great exodus, to preserving us his children from becoming apostate and curving away as Noah, Shem and Japheth had, to serve the Lord of Apostasy, in the north.

In our desperation to protect Eden, we sent my youngest son, Nimrod and thousands with him, back north to Nod. We sent them to Raise Cain's Pale Leper children, and to graft them back into being like us, with the wooly hair, and brownness of Adam. Cain had been wooly headed and brown like us, until his father the Lord "marked" or mutated him with Pale Leprosy (*Gen. 4:15*). Our major concern was to protect Eden from those in the Land of Nod. Nimrod and those with him built Ur/Babel there in the north of Nod, so that the Pale ones would never have a need to come away from Nod. Our concern was to protect our selves especially Canaan, from the Lord's revenge.

Soliloquies

# Soliloquoy of Order
# Canaan

*Brother Cush — Secret — What I did to Noah — Coverup — Brother Nimrod*

**Canaan:** My father Ham was still on Ararat after the flood when I was born (*Gen. 9:18*). I was a young man of 14 years, and still on Mount Ararat, when grandfather Noah commanded that I come to his tent, in secrecy. He gave me a time to come, and vowed me to secrecy. I was not to tell anyone including my father. My father Ham had taught all of us, his sons to always be truthful to him. Also all of us cousins the children of my uncles and my brothers, were always truthful to each other. I told my father, and I also told all of my cousins. My father Ham told his two younger brothers Shem and Japheth. There had not ever been secrets among any of us young or old, and everyone wanted to know what was going on. When I entered grandfather Noah's tent my father Ham was already hiding inside. All of my cousins and my two uncles were hiding outside the tent. Grandfather Noah had grown a grape orchard, and made wine (*Gen. 9:20*). When I entered his tent grandfather Noah was standing there naked, aroused, and drunk from his wine (*Gen. 9:21*). Grandfather was never asleep, and my father hiding in the tent saw what Noah's intentions were, and therefore he open the flap to let everyone outside see what Noah was attempting to do (*Gen. 9:22*)! Everyone saw what grandfather was about, including Noah's wife, my grandmother, and my two uncles Shem and Japheth. They refused to bear witness that they saw their father standing there naked and drunk with me, (Canaan) in his tent. They turned their backs and put a covering on their shoulders and back up to "cover it all up" (*Gen. 9:23*). Uncle Shem and Japheth only "covered" up what everyone else had seen. Noah's wife my grandmother saw it, my mother, and aunts, and brothers, and cousins all saw what grandfather was going to do. Grandfather Noah cursed me, and wanted to take revenge on me for exposing him as a child molester, in service to the Lord of the North. Had the Lord commanded that my grandfather do this, as he had commanded the same between his sons Cain and Abel (*Gen. 4:7*)?

We were not even still suppose to be on Ararat, but were being held in hostage by the Lord of the North, and Noah who was sacrificing all cleanness, including the clean animals from the ark to the Lord, rather than setting us and the animals from the ark free, to go repopulate the land that had been flooded (*Gen. 8:20*). It was not Nimrod who Rebelled against us repopulating the land, it was the Lord and Noah. Nimrod was still in his mother's stomach (womb).

The tent incident and the cover-up was the very situation that father Ham needed, to justify bringing us all down from Ararat, away from the Lord's corruption that I had exposed.

We could now escape from the corrupt life style of Nod. In the Garden lands my big brother Cush was placed between me, and the Tigris leading to Nod, to protect me from those who would come from Nod, to take revenge against me. My father Ham and all of us his children chose to live after the "Order" of Melchezedek. This conflicted with the choice of Grand father Noah, uncle Shem, and uncle Japheth. They chose to be after the Chaos of Hallel, who is Lucifer the Prince of the Darkness of the North (*Amos 5:18, 20*). Grandfather Noah exalted Lucifer by sacrificing all that was clean, and preserved the filth (*Genesis 8:20*). Nimrod and thousands from the Garden, went back up to rescue the Chaldeans (Gentiles), from their bondage to the Lord Hallel (Lucifer).

Bible/Torah

# Soliloquoy of Order
# Nimrod

*Canaan told — Great Light (Isa. 18:1) — Great City — Graft them Back*

**Nimrod:** Canaan exposed Noah, and caused the great exodus that allowed me to be born, in the Garden. I am accused of having started a false religion, and of holding the people of the ark hostage, on mount Ararat. My name Nimrod (נמורד) has been translated to mean "We Rebel." *See Strong,s # 5248 Nimrod, and #4775 "Rebel."* But my father named me Nimrod, not to call me a rebeller, but to commemorate us, coming down from Ararat. My name Nimrod really means "We Came Down (נמורד)." *See Strong's #4174 (Morod), which means "Going Down."*

**Nimrod:** Grandfather Ham brought us down from Ararat, in a great Exodus, because of the Tent Incident. I did not rebel, or found a religion, I was not even born yet! My mother Semiramis was still pregnant with me, and she brought me down, from Ararat in her stomach!

I Nimrod am the last born son of Cush (*Gen. 10:8*). The Lord watched me grow from my youth (*Isa. 53:2*), and saw that I would be a mighty hunter in the earth (ground)(*Gen. 10:8*). The Lord requested that I be sent to him in the north of Nod (*Gen. 10:9*). He wanted me to hunt in the ground, for his son Cain's descendants, who had survived the flood sealed in the caves of Cain's subterranean city of Enoch (*Gen. 4.14, 17*).

Woe to the children of Marked Cain, who dwelled in the shadow of the wings of the Lord, in Nod. Nod is the land beyond the Tigris and the Euphrates, the rivers of my father Cush (Ethiopia)(*Isa. 18:1*). Noah's flood was the flooding of these rivers, that spoiled the land of Nod (*Isa. 18:2*). I and thousands with me, went back north across the Tigris, as swift messengers, and ambassadors, to a Goyim (Nation), scattered and peeled, a people terrible from their beginning, Gentiles meted out and trodden down (*Isa. 18:2*). These Gentiles were an island, in the Darkness of the ground in Nod (*Gen. 10:5*). Digging, down and hunting in the ground, we caused the Great Light to shine on these people, who walked in the Darkness of the Lord (*Isa. 9:2; Amos 5:18, 20*).

Behold Nod the land of Chaldea (Chaldeans). These pale ones did not live in order, until I Nimrod the Assyrian founded it for Cain's Chaldean children, who dwell in the wilderness (*Isa. 23:13*). I built my kingdom (*Gen. 10:10-12*), the entire six city Ur/Babel Complex, and its towers and palaces, to raise the Pale Ones (*Gen. 11:5*). The Lord wanted me to raise them from a savage state, but not to open their eyes, ears, and minds, so that they could never converted, and be healed, away from him (*Isa. 6:10*). The Lord came down and saw that I had healed and unified them (*Gen. 11:4*), for I was the Great Light, that had come to heal them from the Darkness of the Lord (*Isa. 9:2*). The Lord told his Host that nothing would be beyond them now, and he and his Host confounded Ur/Babel (*Gen. 11:9*), and brought it to ruin (*Isa. 23:13*).

Then the Lord caused me to bare the strips, for having healed these pale ones (*Isa. 53:6*). The Lord accused me of leading them astray, and had them to oppress, and afflict me. Yet I never said a mumbling word (*Isa. 53:6*). I had done them no violence, nor had I ever lied to them (*Isa. 53:9*). Yet it pleased the Lord to incite the pale ones to bruise me and to crucify me to death (*Isa. 53:10-12*). I was crucified (murdered) in the ruins of my kingdom Ur/Babel, which would be the nativity of Abram, and Sarah his sister/wife/niece (*Gen. 11:28*). They would abandon Ur, as the Chaldeans had, and flee to the land of Canaan, and Egypt, to prostitute Sarah. Abram prostituted his sister Sarah, to the Pharaoh who gave him an Egyptian princess, that Abram renamed Hagar.

Bible/Torah

# Soliloquoy of Order
# Hagar

*Prostitution in Egypt — Sarah Gets (Surrogates) — Ishmael*

**Hagar:** My real name is Shari Mitzraim, or "Princess of Egypt." Abram and his sister/wife/niece Sarah/Iscah came from the Land of Canaan to Egypt. They say that they left Canaan because of the Lord's famine there (*Gen. 12:10*). Yet they walked through a hundred miles of fruitful Egypt to get to Pharaoh. They came to Egypt for prostitution, not food.

Abraham was brown and wooly haired, like we Egyptians, but his sister/wife/niece Sarah/Iscah was pale, even though she was a Black Woman. When the Princes of Egypt saw her unusual paleness, they were aroused, and penetrated (הלל) Sarah before the Pharaoh. Then they brought her into the Pharaoh's house for Pharaoh to have her (*Gen. 12:15*). In Pharoah's house Sarah prostituted herself. Abraham, Lot, and the Lord, were outside waiting, while Sarah serviced the Pharaoh. Pharaoh sent out herds, flocks, gold, silver and servants, for Sarah's services (*Gen. 12:16*). Prostitution was why they came to Egypt, not because of a famine in Canaan (*Gen. 12:10*). The famine that had been in Canaan ceased, when the Lord left Canaan. The Lord brought his famine with him, and used it against Pharoah, when Sarah said so (*Gen. 12:7*). When they left Egypt it was not because the famine was over in Canaan, but because Abraham, Lot, and the Lord had obtained as much from the Pharaoh, as they could manage (*Gen. 12:16*).

**Hagar:** The Pharaoh was obviously infatuated with Sarah and may not have ever allowed her to leave. This is where the Lord came in, for he plagued the house of Pharaoh, because Sarah said (דבר) so (*Gen.12:17*). So Pharaoh rushed to send Abram and Sarah out of his country with all of the goods he had given them, including myself Shari Mitzraim (Hagar)(*Gen. 12: 19, 20*).

My name was Shari Misraim (Princess of Egypt) before Abraham and Sarah called me Hagar, which means "Stranger," "Alien," or "Outsider." They were both always hostile towards me. This was even when Sarah could not have a child of her own, and sent Abraham in to force himself on me. Sarah told Abraham to rape me so that **Sarah** could **Get** (Surrogate) a child through me (*Gen. 16:2*). When I discovered that I was pregnant, I despised Sarah and Abraham (*Gen. 16:2, 3, 4, 5*). When Sarah told Abraham that I was angry about having his child he became angry and told Sarah to mistreat me if she chose to (*Gen. 16:6*). They both mistreated me, and my son Ishmael when he was born.

Abraham had denied his son Ishmael, and could not make his sister/niece/wife Sarah pregnant, so the Lord impregnated Sarah with his own son Isaac, and gave him to Abraham to raise (*Gen. 21:1, 2, Joshua 24:3*). When Isaac was born Abraham and Sarah were through with my son Ishmael, and I (*Gen. 21:9, 10*). Abraham was an unfit parent who had almost starved his own son Ishmael to death. Ishmael was just a pile of bones at age fifteen, when I put him on my back to carry him away (*Gen. 17:25*). Abraham was mocking us when he gave me a piece of bread and a bottle of water, and sent us out into the wilderness to die (*Gen. 21:14, 15, 16*). Despite of all that Abraham did to destroy his own son, Ishmael survived. When Abraham's Lord saw that Ishmael was still alive he told Abraham to take his "only" son (Ishmael), and sacrifice him on a mountain (*Gen. 22:2*). When the Lord saw that Abraham had brought Isaac to be sacrificed he was bitter, and told Abraham to take his hands off of him (*Genesis 22:12*). Moriah means "Bitter Jah," or Bitter Jehovah" (*Gen. 22:2*). Ishmael survived being murdered twice, by Abraham, and the Lord.

Bible/Torah

# Soliloquoy of Order
# Ishmael

*Hagar — Unfit Father — Ishmael/Midian — Seed of Abraham — Mesoretic Text — Jesus*

**Ishmael:** My mother Shari Misraim (Hagar) had been a princess in the royal house of Egypt, before she had been sent away with the prostitute Sarah, and her uncle/husband/brother Abraham (*Genesis 12:18, 19*). I was a child of rape, from a man who did not like me or my mother. He sent the two of us off to die in the wilderness so we would not be in the way of him raising Isaac the son of his Lord and Sarah (*Gen. 17:6, Gen. 21:1, 2, Joshua 24:3*). If Abraham had been an honorable man he would have given us horses and provisions and sent us back to my mother's home in Egypt, instead of sending us into the wilderness with a bottle of water and piece of bread to die (*Gen. 21:14, 16*)!

I was never a "wild (פרה) man (*Gen. 16:12*)," but was a "fruitful (פרה) man" (*Gen. 16:12, Gen. 17:20*). My hand was never "against" another man, but was "in" the hand of all (ידו בכל ידי), in co-operation (*Gen. 16:12*). *The words translated "wild," (Gen. 16:12), and "fruitful (Gen. 17:6), both mean fruitful." See Strong's #6501 thru 9. "wild" can only be applied here as "growth," or "fruitfulness."*

I was chief among my own twelve sons titled **Ishmael**. I also became chief among my other brothers who Abraham had fathered with another Hamite woman named Keturah (*Gen. 25:1- 4*). They had confederated under the name of their brother **Midian**. Thus we became a single entity overall titled **Ishmael/Midian** (*Gen. 25:18, Gen. 37:25-28, 36*). Our dwelling places were from Havilah to Shur, which is adjacent to and east of Egypt, and from there to the East Country of the Amorites (*Gen. 25:6*). This is where Abraham sent Midian, from his raising Isaac the Lord's son.

Isaac and I were never at odds, and even co-operated in burying Abraham when he had passed on (*Gen. 25:9*). Once Abraham was dead I took possession of the Chronicles of Arphaxad which Abraham had inherited when Arphaxad had passed on. These Chronicles contained the history of all that had occurred in the Land of Nod after Ham's Great Exodus down from Ararat back into the Garden.

Our Ishmael/Midian Confederation was stretched from the Narrow Gate (Egypt) to Mari (Amorites) on the Euphrates River. When the Lord brought the Israelis from Egypt it was by force. They had taken the Mesoretic Text which was a continuation of the Chronicles of Ham. They had stolen these Chronicles from the ruins of Egypt. Those Israelis who left Egypt, and their children, were made to die in the wilderness (*Exodus 14:11, 12, 35*). Their grandchildren who came forth from the wilderness, were a band of child eating Pale Lepers (*Leviticus 13th Chapter, Deut. 28:57, Isaiah 9:20, Jeremiah 19:9*). Moses and his Lord lead them directly through all of the lands of our Ishmael/Midian Confederation killing Raping, and stealing. The Lord had two purposes, for Israel: (1) to exterminate all of my Ishmael/Midianite children, the real children of Abraham, and (2) Israel must rape themselves into being the "Seed of Abraham," with my little Ishmael/Midianite girls. We recorded the holocaust being committed against us, until there was none left alive to record it. The Israeli took our records that told the entire story of how they destroyed us, the "Children of Abraham," and raped themselves in being the "Seed of Abraham" (*Numbers Chptr. 31*). The Israelis put together our Arphaxad Chronicles, and Ham's Chronicles from Egypt, and called it the Mesoretic Text or Egyptian Text. The Egyptians used the Mesoretic Text to teach Jesus (Yeshua).

Bible/Torah

# Soliloquoy of Order
# Yeshua (Jesus)

*Ishmael — Sent — Children or Seed — The truth shall make free — Get Thee Hence — Hallel*

**Yeshua (Jesus):** Ishmael had the Arphaxad Chronicles, they were virtually the same as the Mesoretic Text. The Egyptians taught me the Mesoretic (Egyptian) Text. They used these texts to teach me the history of my people the Israelis, and what they had done to come into existence. Israel was never the children of Abraham, but became the "Seed of Abraham (*Gen. 15:18; John 8:33*), by murder, and rape. And yet the Egyptians sent me back to the Land of Canaan, to make my people Israel free, from the Lord.

The Egyptians knew that the Children of Abraham were Hamites, because their mothers Hagar and Keturah were both Hamites. The Egyptians were also Hamites. The Israelis were Hamites, through Jacob (Israel), the Syrian (Egyptian)(*Deut. 26:5*). Yet Israel could only become Abraham's Seed by murder. Thus the Lord the father of Jacob (Israel), commanded the holocaust against the children, of his most loyal servant Abraham. The Lord had promised Abraham that he would cause his "Seed" to be like the stars of the heavens, letting Abraham think that he was talking about Abraham's "Children" (*Gen. 15:5*). But the Lord had Israel to totally destroy Abraham's Ishmael/Midianite children (*Num. 31:2, 17*). Moses even had to kill his Midianite wife and sons. This is why I told the scribes that our father the Lord was the Devil, a liar and murderer from the beginning (*John 8:44*).

I had left Egypt as a young man, and returned to Israel. When I returned to Israel I was in the World of the Lord, but not of it (*John 17:14*). **I came to bring the Lord's World to an end, that he so loved** (*John 3:16*). The Lord had made his World, and have imposed it on my people, who do not truly know who he really is (*John 1:10*). The agents of his World murdered me. The **shedding of my blood** was the salvation of the Lord's World, not the people in it. It was the Lord and his World, that the Israelis were to be *made free* from. It was the Lord's World that I came to destroy. The end of the Lord's World is not the end of the planet, or the people.

When I was tortured and murdered on the cross it was not a **Good Friday** for my family, my friends, or my community. My entire society suffered from my death, for I had been sent by the Egyptians who saved me, to rescue the Lost Sheep of Israel. I was sent to teach them, the Light and Peace that I had been taught by the Egyptians, the children of peaceful Ham (*1 Chron. 4:40*).

I did not raise from the dead in three days, or any other amount of time. If I had risen, they would have crucified me again! They killed me to stop me from bringing the Lord's World to an end. The test as to whether I was raised from the dead is if the World came to an end. It is the World system that murdered me, and then established the church system. Roman Empire, Holy Roman Empire, Holy Roman Church, Roman Catholic Church, Protestant Church, Methodist, Lutheran, Baptist, Sanctified, etc. It is all the same, they all celebrate that my death was the salvation of the Lord's World, that I had come to destroy. I was murdered by the World so that I could not bring it to an end as I came to do.

My whole mission and purpose was from Eden (Africa), and the Narrow Gate (Egypt) that protected Eden (*Matt. 7:13, 14*). My mission was to disinherit the Lost Sheep of Israel (Jacob), from our father, the Lord Hallel (Lucifer), the Devil (*John 8:44, Deut. 32:9*). I told Hallel the overshadower of my mother, get thee hence Satan (*Matt. 4:10*)!

Soliloquies

Bible/Torah

# Soliloquies of Chaos
# Hallel (Hallelujah)

*Yeshua (Jesus) — Rosemary's Baby(Steven King) — Kingdom*

### Lord's Anatomy

**Hallel (Lord):** Jesus called himself "Son of Man" (*Matt. 8:20*). I the Lord am a Man of War, the Man that fathered Jesus (*Ex. 15:3*). As a Man I have feet, and hands (*Ex. 24:10, 11*). I talked "face to face," with Moses (*Gen. 33:11*), and Jacob saw my face (Peniel) also (*Gen. 32:30*). I have a mouth and stomach, for I and my Host ate with Abraham (*Gen. 18:6-8*), and with Moses also(*Ex. 24:11*). Having body parts I also have a body. Jacob wrestled with me (*Gen. 32:24*), and Rachael wrestled with me also (*Gen. 30:8*). I sent Gabriel to tell Mary that I was going to "overshadow" her, and come into/on her (*Luke 1:35*).

**Hallel (Lord):** When I asked Yeshua (Jesus) my only begotten son to bow down to me, and to rule my World (TBL), he told me "get thee hence Satan" (*Matt. 4:10*). I had promised the young girl that would become Jesus' mother, that if she would allow me to overshadow her, and come into/on her (*Luke 1:35*), that I would let our son rule over his (my) kingdom, (my World), and the house of Jacob (Israel) forever (*Luke 1:33*). Yet when Yeshua (Jesus) refused to bow down to me, and chose to be after the Order of Melchezedek (*Hebrews 5:6-9*), he signed his own death warrant. That is when his mother began to be called Mary (מרי), which means "Bitter (מרי)," for she was "bitter" that I crucified our son. When Jesus had returned from Egypt as a young man he was after the order of Melchezedek (*Heb. 5:6*), who defeated me in the heavens (*Rev. 12:7-9*). I am a Jealous God, and my commandment to everyone in Israel including Jesus, was to have no other **God** (Michael/Melchezedek) before me (*Ex. 34:14*).

### Gods

**Hallel (Lord):** There have always been Gods other than me, I never denied that there were others Gods. I only told those who served me, to not have other Gods (including themselves) before me (*Deut. 6:14*). I was only one of the Gods who separated (Cipherate) our mother planet Assiah from the sun.

I as the God of Abraham admitted that there are Gods other than myself. I instructed Jacob to go up to Bethel, and build an altar to the "God" that he saw and wrestled, in the wilderness (*Gen. 35:1, Gen. 32:24-30*). I as the Lord even warned the Israelis not to "revile" the other Gods (*Exodus 22:28, Matt. 5:11*). To revile (קלל) is to "make light" or "hurt the feelings" of the Gods! You can not "revile" or hurt the feelings of images or idols! Yeshua (Jesus) was quoting me (*John 10:34*), when he told the Israelis that they are all Gods, children of the Most High (Sun)(*Psalms 82:6*). At the Tribunal against me, Melchezedek (Ancient of Day) is telling my Host that they are all **Gods** children of the Most High (*Psalms 82:6*). Others also called my Hosts Gods (*1Samuel 4:8*). The fact is that all Original Men on the planet are Gods, including me the Lord (*Exodus 15:3*). Original Men are in their own images which are Gods (*Gen. 1:26, 27*). In Mamre Abraham sat and ate with me, the Lord and two other **"Men"** (*Gen. 18:2*). I the Lord and some other Gods sat and ate with Moses, Aaron, and seventy Israelis elders ( *Ex.24:10-11*).

There are many mentions of "Living Gods:" "Worship him all of you Gods" (*Psalms 97:7*). The

Bible/Torah

# Soliloquies of Chaos
# Hallel (Lord)

*Gods — Cain — Sons and Daughters of Cain — Daughters*

"Gods of the Earth are famished" (*Siphoniah 2:11.*). "Take us out of the hands of these mighty "Gods," "these are the Gods (my Host) that smote Egypt" (*1Sam. 4:8*). The Israeli scribes wrote that I the Lord am greater than the proud Gods (*Exodus 18:11*). They wrote that they exalt me above all other Gods (*Psalms 97:7, Isaiah 14:13*). Yet I am a Lesser God outside (*II Cor. 5:6*), while the Greater God is inside (*I Cor. 3:16; 6:20*). Man is the Greater God inside of his own body (Kingdom)(*I Cor. 6:20*), while I the Lord am only a Lesser God outside, in my World of Outer Darkness (*Matt. 8:12, Amos 5:18*). To be absent from your body is to be with me (*II Chron. 5:6*)!

### Kingdom

**Lord (Hallel):** No person would willingly knowingly leave their kingdom of Inner Greatness, for my Lesser World of Outer Darkness. That is why I beguiled Eve to get little children, to pull them out of their inner kingdoms. I must cast them out of their kingdom while they are still little children, out into my World of Darkness (*Matt. 8:12*). I started with my sons Cain, and his "effeminate" (אבל) twin brother Abel (אבל). Effeminate Abel had a desire for his twin brother Cain, so I made Cain be his "Keeper" (Husband)(*Gen. 4:7*).

I am a Jealous God, and those who bow to me shall have no other God, including themselves before me (*Ex. 34:14*). Thus to serve me they must deny themselves, as co-equal Gods to me. The first to serve me on the earth were my twin sons, from the beguilement of Eve (*Gen. 4:1, I Chron. 1:1*). This was all before Adam began his line with Seth (*Gen. 5:3, I Chron. 1:1*).

### Cain

**Lord (Hallel):** The whole of the physical realm is a dream state, an experimental laboratory. I and the other Gods brought it into being. We Manifested down into it, to experiment with Self in the particular. My line and my World beginning with Cain must prevail. I did not set up my World to be a prop, to support the the experiment, or as an aid to help carry the experiment through it's process. Just the opposite, I brought my World into existence, to collapse the experiment, leaving all suspended inside of the dream, the experimental state so that I could rule it forever. Thus I corrupted my own twin sons Cain and Abel, turning them into the first sodomites (*Gen. 4:7*).

The act of Sodomy cast Cain and Abel out of the Light of their inner kingdoms, out into my Outer Darkness (*Matt. 8:12, Amos 5:18, 20*). It was the same later when I brought the Israelis out of Egypt, against their will, and forced the act of Religious Sodomy (Holiness / קדש) on them, to cast the Israeli out of their inner kingdoms, out to my Outer Darkness. It is a thick Darkness, that can be felt (*Ex. 10:21*). I would in the future make the male and female Israelis into male and female prostitutes, like I had make the sons and daughters of Cain (*Ex. 13:2, 13, 15, Deut. 23:17*). Sodomy (קדש / Holiness) along with Bestiality (Tubal) are the basic elements, at the core of my World (Tubal).

When Cain murdered Abel another component of my World **murder** was installed on the planet (*Gen. 4:8*). That is when I altered Cain from being wooly headed and brown. I "Marked"

Soliloquies

Bible/Torah

# Soliloquies of Chaos
# Hallel (Hallelujah)

*Sons and Daughters Of Cain*

Cain with permanent genetic Pale Leprosy (*Gen. 4:15*). My wooly headed brown Host would now be able to see Cain coming from a distance, and be warned not to harm him (*Gen.4:15*). Thus I was warning my male Host, the friends of Effeminate Abel not to hurt my remaining son Cain (*Gen. 4:15*). I then sent Cain down into the earth (*Ex. 8:22*), to dwell with my Host and I (*Gen. 4:15*).

**Sons and Daughters of Cain**

**Lord:** I and my Host are the Sons of God (Sun)(*Gen. 6:2*). In defeat we had been casted down into the ground (*Rev. 12:9; Gen. 6:4*). My son Cain married one of my Lilahs (Lilith)(*Gen. 4:17*), and they had sons and daughters, who carried the genetic pale leprosy curse that I had put permanently in the genetics of Cain (*Gen. 4:15*). Cain's sons from the Lilah that he married, married my Lilith, or Female Hosts. The first son of Cain was Enoch (*Gen. 4:17*). Enoch, Irad, Mehujael, Methuselah, and Lamech, all married the females of my Hosts (*Gen. 4:17-19*). All of Cain's daughters married my Lilim or Male Hosts.

These "marriages" were not marriages in the sense of one man to one woman, but was endless mixing between couples, both male and female, and male with male, and female with female.

Children had sex with their parents (*Lev. 18:9*). Sisters and brothers had sex together (*Lev. 18:9, 11*). Grandparents were having sex with their grandchildren (*Lev. 18:10*). Aunts and uncles had sex with their nephews, and nieces (*Lev. 18:12-14*). Mothers and fathers were having sex with their son's and daughter's mates (*Lev. 18:15*). Brothers and sisters were having sex with each other's mates (*Lev. 18:16*). Men were having sex with a mother and daughter in the same bed at the same time. These same men were having sex, with that same woman's granddaughters (*Lev. 18:17*). Men had sex with a woman and her sister at the same time (*Lev. 18:18*). Women were having sex while on their periods (*Lev. 18:19*). Neighbors were having sex with each other's "wives" (*Lev. 18:20*). As was said before men were having sex with men, and women were having sex with women (*Lev. 18:22*). Besides sodomy, lesbianism, incubi,* and incest, there was also rape and prostitution. These pale children of Cain are the Nations (Goyim) that fled to Canaan, and that I accused of doing all of the corrupt things, that I myself had taught them (*Lev. 18:24; Ex. 34:24*).

Finally the children of my son Cain, males and females both had sex with animals, and some had offsprings out of it (*Lev. 18: 23*). These hybrid beings were called "Beast," but not animals, and were called "woman" and "man," not male and females as with animals (*Gen. 7:2*).

By the time of Jubal Cain, Jabal Cain, and Tubal Cain, there were thousands of offspring from the mixing of the sons and daughters of Cain, with the sheeps, goats, and other animals that moved in their midst in the land of Nod (*Lev. 18:23*). These offspring of Bestiality (TBL), would be a Strange Cargo that would survive the flood, on the third story of Noah's ark (*Gen. 7:1, 2*).

My World (Tubal / תבל) is composed of all of the above described lifestyle. I demanded that all inside of my World participate in this corrupt way of life. My Tubal (TBL), or World (TBL) is composed of corruption! The end of corruption is the end of my World.

It was before the flood of Noah, that Cain's descendant Lamech married two of my Lilahs, named Adah, and Zillah (*Gen. 4:18-20*). The Sodomy never stopped. Lamech told his wives, that

Bible/Torah

# Soliloquies of Chaos
# Hallel (Lord)

*Daughters of Cain — Noah And TheFlood— Shem/Jepheth*

he had killed Cain and a young man, who Cain helped to rape him (*Gen. 4:23*). Even in the time of his being raped, Lamech had three son, who would be the continuation of my World (TBL). The three were Ju<u>bal</u> Cain, Ja<u>bal</u> Cain, and Tu<u>bal</u> Cain (*Gen. 4: 20-22*). These three Bals (Balls) would become my Tubal (TBL) or World (TBL). I would use the daughters of my Bals or World as prostitutes, to help subplant the Line of Adam.

### Daughters of Cain's

**Hallel (Lord):** I and my Host are the "Giants," or Sons of God. We were all in the ground in that day (*Gen. 6:4*). Naamah the sister of Tubal Cain joined the ranks of those "Daughters of Cain (Man), that I and my Host chose to ravish (*Gen. 6:2*). I made the little virgin Chaldean daughters of Cain sat in the dirt, and I and my Host took their virginity (*Isa. 47:1*). I made them let their hair down, and raise their dresses up, to expose their legs and vaginas (*Isa. 47:2*). I made the girls consume my Mandrake (Man of Darkness) fruit. The Mandrake sexually aroused them, while it also put them back into my Darkness (*Isa. 47:5*). With their nakedness exposed I came to them each in turn, as a man comes to a woman (*Isa. 47:3*). I would also take advantage of the daughters of Zion (*Isa. 3:16*). These girls would be haughty, and so I would make them take off all of their apparel, and expose their **private parts**, so that I could do to them the same as I had done to the Chaldean daughters, of Cain (*Isa.3:17*). I would leave these beautiful sweet smelling well dressed girls, ugly, stinking, bald, with ragged garments (*Isa. 3:24*).

I trained Cain's daughters to be prostitutes, and sent some of the ravished girls from Nod, down across the Tigris River, down into the Garden (*Isa. 47:2*). This was before the flood, and I wanted these contaminated ones to contaminate (pollute)(טמיא) the sons and daughters of the Garden (*Isa. 47:6*). Thus I had made my son Cain's sons and daughters whores and sodomites, Just as I would make the sons and daughters of Israel whores (קדשה) and sodomites (קדש)(*Deut. 23:17*), in the wilderness outside of Egypt.

### Noah and the Flood

**Hallel:** Lemech in the line of Adam, named his son "Noah" (נח), for Lemech thought that Noah would be a "comfort" (נח), for his people (*Gen. 5:29*). But Noah chose to exalt me Lucifer (Hallel / חלל), even though I was the Prince of the Darkness, on the "side" of the north (*Isaiah 14:12, Joshua 24:2, 3*).

After the flood Shem and Japheth also bowed down to me, but Ham the elder son of Noah kept his feet, and refused to sacrifice to me, or praise me, because it is all foolishness (*Ecclus. 5:1, 2*).

I demand that each one who bowed down to serve me do an offense against his own. The task I put upon Noah was that he sodomize his grandson Canaan, to undermine his son Ham's household. Ham was the one who refused to bow to me (*Gen. 9:26, 27*). Noah vowed Canaan to come to his tent, and to tell no one. But what Canaan "did to Noah" was to tell on him (*Gen. 9:24*). Canaan told his father Ham, and others, and eventually the entire family found out, and were hiding to see what would happen in Noah's tent. When Ham threw open Noah's tent flap, everyone saw Noah standing before Canaan, naked, drunk, and sexually aroused. Shem, and

Soliloquies

Bible/Torah

# Soliloquies of Chaos
# Hallel (Hallelujah)

*Shem/Jephjeth—Ham Exodus—Nimrod—AbramHam*

Japheth "covered it up (*Gen. 9:23*)." Noah did not "awake" from his wine but he "finished" (קִיץ) his wine, and figured out that Canaan had told on him. I would take my revenge against Canaan.

### Shem/Japheth

**Hallel:** My servant **Shem** is shown to be an honorable man, by covering up what seemed to have been going on in his father's tent. But my mission to Shem, to test his sincerity to me, was to have him to impregnate his grandson Heber's wife. Shem was the father of all of the children in Heber's household (*Gen. 10:21*). Heber hebrewed the Tigris with Ham in disgust.

**Japheth** is the father of the Archaic Greeks. He helped to cover-up Noah's attempted sodomy against Canaan. When he went west to establish the first Greek cities, he carried sodomy with him, in the form of some of Cain's children. I could not get him to do it to his own children.

### Ham's Exodus

**Hallel:** It was fortunate for me that I could not get Ham and his children to stay on Ararat and bow to me. If I could have gotten Ham to stay on Ararat, and to bow down to me, the experiment would have come to an unfinished end. I would have only been able to rule until I had used up all those who submitted to me. Then my World of Darkness would have come to an end.

Ham in his outrage about the attempted sodomy, and cover-up brought all of his family down from Ararat in a Great Exodus, taking all Light with him. But later Ham and his children would be a savior even to me and my Host, when Abram brought us from Nod across the Tigris. My dwelling place, the entire land of the North of Nod, lay in famine and disease, Nod was cursed because of my presence there (*Gen.3:17*).

### Nimrod

**Hallel (Lord:** Nimrod was not born on Ararat, nor did he start a religion there. Nimrod was still unborn in his mother's stomach, when Ham lead all of his children down from Ararat across the Tigris into the Garden. Nimrod's (מוֹרָד) name means "We Came Down." *See Strong's Concordance #4174*. Cush his father named his son Nimrod to commemorates Ham "coming down" from Ararat bringing his children in a Great Exodus, away from my corruption. I watched Nimrod from the time he was born on the Side of the South, in the Garden (*Isa. 53:2, Gen. 10:8*), until he grew up. I summoned Ham to send Nimrod back to the "Side of the North," to stand before me (*Gen. 10:9*). I wanted Nimrod to "hunt" into the ground to find my son Cain and his descendants, who had survived the flood sealed in Cain's cave city named Enoch (*Gen. 4:17*). Nimrod built Ur, to Raise Cain, his children, from the corrupt condition I had imposed on them (*Gen. 10:10, 11*). I confounded Ur, and brought it to ruin, when I saw that Nimrod had united them to make them free from me (*Gen. 11:9; Isa. 23:13*). The pale leper children of my son Cain fled from me down into the land of Canaan, and were given asylum, in the old grain cities of Sodom and Gomorrah.

Hundreds of years later the inhabitants of Sodom saw my two Host, and wanted to sodomize

# Soliloquies of Chaos
# Hallel (Lord)

*AbramHam — Thick Darkness — Abraham's Children or Seed — Begotten*

them (*Gen. 19:5*), even after Lot offered them his two virgin daughters (*Gen.19:9*). My Host had to blind the Sodomites, before they could removed Lot and his family (*Gen. 19:16, 28*), Then I and my Host confounded Sodom and Gomorrah, and it's pale inhabitants (*Gen. 19:24, 25*), as we had confounded their ancestors in Ur/Babel (*Gen. 11:9; Isa. 23:13*).

### AbramHam
**Hallel:** Abram, Sarai, Lot and all the souls that they brought with them out of Haran (*Gen. 12:5*), down into the land of Canaan, were all the by-product of the corrupt lifestyle that I had imposed on all of the people in Nod. All who came into Canaan from Nod were the corrupt remnant of Nod.

Sarai/Iscah was Abram's sister/wife/niece. Imagine a man who would prostitute his sister, his wife, or his niece. Abram was a man who had all three wrapped up into one person, and he would put her to work in Egypt, after I had trained her in Nod (*Isa. 47:1-7*). I made her pick up her dress above her thighs, as we crossed the Tigris so that the men in the land of Ham could see her vagina which was for sell (*Isa. 47:2, 3*). To tell the truth Terah and Abram had been trying to escape from me, and my famine and disease, when they left Ur to go to the land of Canaan. But Terah died, and I caught up with Abram before he could "hebrew" the Tigris. If they could have gotten away as Abram had planned, I would have been left alone in the north in Nod, to perish.

When we came down from Nod into the land of Ham Abram, Sarai/Iscah, and Lot were already well indoctrinated into Incest, Sodomy, Prostitution, and all of the other elements that makes up my World (TBL).

From their childhood I had sex with all of the Chaldean virgins including Sarah and turned all of them into prostitutes, including Sarai, the niece/sister/wife of Abram.

I watched the Pharoah's sons, and then the Pharaoh himself have sex with Sarah (*Gen. 12:15*). I had trained her well for the pharaoh soon began to send out sheep, oxen, asses, and servants to Abraham (*Gen. 12:16*). When Sarah had earned as much as we could manage, I plagued the Pharaoh's house when Sarah gave me the signal (*Gen.12:17*). Then we left full of Egypt's wealth.

### Thick Darkness
It was after Egypt that I convinced Abram to sacrifice and bow to me. I then caused a deep sleep to fall on him, and then my horrible Great Darkness (*Gen. 15:12*).

Abram bowed down to me because I made him think that I meant his "children," when I said his "seed (*Gen. 15:4, 5*)."

### Abraham's Children or Seed
**Hallel:** Abram and Sarai renamed Shari Misraim the Egyptian women, with the name Hagar (Stranger). Hagar became the mother of Ishmael, when Abram raped her (*Gen. 16:3, 4*). In the land of Ham I renamed Abram, AbramHam or Abraham, because he became a part of Ham by impregnating Hamite women (*Gen. 16:3, 4*).

The two Hamite women who mothered all of the children of Abram were Hagar (Shari

Bible/Torah

# Soliloquies of Chaos
# Hallel (Hallelujah)

*Issac — Jacob — Twelve — Begotten*

Misraim), and Keturah. Hagar was the mother of Ishmael (*Gen. 16:3, 4*), and Keturah was the mother of Midian and his brothers (*Gen. 25:1, 2*). Abraham sent most of his Hamite children, to the east country (Amori), so that they would not interfere with him raising my son Isaac (*Gen. 25:6*). Abram's children lived in the lands from Havilah to Shur that is before Egypt as you go towards Assyria ...(*Gen. 25:17*). Abraham's children Ishmael/Midianite, existed as tribes, long before Israel ever came into existence. Ishmael and Isaac went together to bury Abraham (*Gen. 17:19*), before Isaac ever had me to impregnate Rebecca with Jacob (Israel) (*Gen. 25:8; Gen. 25:26*).

### Isaac

**Hallel (Lord):** I "Visited" (פכד) and impregnated Sarah with my son Isaac (*Gen. 21:1, 2*). I gave my son Isaac to Abram to raise (*Joshua 24:3*). Ishmael the first son of Abraham was fifteen years old, when my son Isaac was born (*Gen. 21:1, 2*). Abram was my most loyal servant, and he has been so admired, that three religions came from the admiration, that is had for Abram being loyal to me. They all admire that Abram was ready to sacrifice Isaac. But I never wanted Abraham to sacrifice my son Isaac, I wanted Abraham to sacrifice his "only son" Ishmael. Melchezedek (Lord God) had saved Ishmael in the wilderness (*Gen. 15:15-19*). Abraham had only given Hagar and Ishmael a piece of bread, and a bottle of water (*Gen. 21:14*). Isaac was my son, not his, I only gave Abraham my son Isaac to raise (*Joshua 24:3*). I wanted for Abram to sacrifice Ishmael, so that he would no longer exists, to have offspring that might one day trouble my son Isaac. Foolish Abraham brought my son Isaac up the mountain, instead of his son Ishmael, and I was "bitter" (מרי). That is what **Moriah** (מוריה) means, **"Bitterness of Jah."** I was making my son Isaac the "seed" of Abraham!

### Jacob (Israel)

**Lord (Hallel):** Isaac could not make his cousin/wife Rebecca pregnant for twenty years, and so he asked me his father to rub against her, and I did, and she became pregnant (*Gen. 25:21*). I gave my son Jacob to my son Isaac to raise (*Joshua 24:4*).

### Twelve (Israel)

**Lord:** Jacob did not love Leah so I impregnated her, to father four of her sons, Reuben, Simeon, Levi, and Judah. I am also the father of Joseph with Rachael. I am the "Great (אלהים)" or "God" that she wrestled with, to become pregnant (*Gen. 30:8*).

In the northern tradition I was very proud of two of my boys Simeon, and Levi, when they contrived with their sister Dinah to trap the prince of Shechem. She had sex with him, and gave her brothers the excuse to murder all of the male of the city so that they could take all of their girls, and women, for themselves. With these females from the city of Shechem, they raped themselves into tribal existence, to become the tribes of Israel.

In the end I would reduce Israel to a state that they would be selling their daughters and sons, as prostitutes for a drink of wine (*Joel 3:3*). The other Israelis sold the children of Judah (Judeans) and Jerusalem, to the Greeks. I myself the Lord (through the Rabbis) sold the sons and daughters

# Soliloquies of Chaos
# Hallel (Lord)

*Ishmael/Midian — Canaan Revisit*

of Judah (Judeans) to the Sabeans (*Joel 3:8*).

### Begotten

I fathered Jacob and Esau, with Isaac's wife Rebecca (*Gen. 25:21*). I then fathered Reuben, Simeon, Levi, Judah, and Joseph, with Leah, and Rachael, the two cousin/wives of my son Jacob (*Gen. 29:34; 30:22*). My five sons and my son Jacob's seven sons made up the twelve tribes of Israel, that went into Egypt, and multiplied into a great multitude in four hundred years. I brought Israel out of Egypt into the wilderness, to transform them into a multitude, marked with pale leprosy, like I had marked my son Cain and his children (*Gen. 4:15*). It had taken four hundred years to the point of my raising my pale lepers in the wilderness (*Lev. 13th Chptr.*). I brought my pale lepers Israelis to the east country, to murder off the now multiplied children of Abraham's sons Ishmael/Midian (*Gen. 25:6*).

### Ishmael/Midian

**Lord (Hallel):** Abraham's children Ishmael/Midian were like the stars in the heavens, until we killed every man women, and boy (*Gen. 15:5, Nu. 31:7, 17*). I had Moses to instruct the Israelis not to kill the little pubelescent Ishmael/Midianite girls, and Israel accumulated over thirty two thousands of them (*Nu. 31:35*). My pale lepers Israelis kept the little girl women to do with as they pleased (*Nu. 31:18*). The priest of my son Levi got fifty of these little women children, for their own use (*Nu. 31:47*). My share was thirty two of these little girls (*Nu. 31:40*), I had my way with them, as I had my way with the young Chaldean virgins, in the land of Nod (*Isa. 47:1-7*). This was the same as when my Israeli sons had taken the women and girls from the city of Shechem after murdering all of the males of the city (*Gen. 34:7*). As they had raped themselves into tribal existence with those females in Canaan (*Gen. 34:25*), they now took these Midianite girls, the female "Children of Abraham," and raped themselves into being the "Seed of Abraham. (*Nu. 31:18*)." The Israelis brought the impregnated little girls with them, into the land of Canaan.

### Canaan Revisited

**Hallel:** These girls would give birth in the "promised" land of Canaan, to children from their having being raped by the Israelis. In the land of Canaan Israel killed all except the girls there too. The Canaanite girls as captives to the Israelis suffered (*Deut. 21:10*), the same fate as the impregnated Ishmael/Midianite daughters of Abraham (*Nu. 31:9*).

On Mount Ararat after the flood, Ham's boy Canaan had endangered my World in the land of Nod, by exposing his grandfather Noah, as a child molesting Sodomite in service to me (*Gen. 9:24*). Then latter Canaan's children gave the Chaldeans children, of my son Cain asylum from me. They had escaped Ur/Babel, after I had confounded it (*Gen. 11:9, Isa. 23:13*).

The first murder of all the men and boys, of the Canaanite city of Shechem had been my first revenge against Canaan.(*Gen. 34:25*). My final revenge on Canaan, was my holocaust throughout the land of Canaan, after the Israelis returned there, four hundred years later.

The "Nations" (Goyim / גוים) or "Gentiles," that I would have Israel drive out of the land of

# Soliloquies of Chaos
# Hallel (Hallelujah)

Canaan Revisited — Crucifixion — Tubal (World) Cain

Canaan (*Deut. 4:38; 9:4, 5; 11:23*), were not the children of Canaan, but were the Pale Leper remnant of the Chaldean children of my son Cain (*Lev. 18:24, 27*). They were not wooly headed brown Canaanites, but the remnant of the pale ones who had escaped my overthrowing Sodom (*Deut. 29:23*). Ham's son Canaan had given these Gentiles asylum from me, in the Canaanite grain cities of Sodom and Gomorrah. These pale ones were the Nations (Gentiles/Goyim) in Canaan, I told Israel not to live like (*Lev. 18:24-29*)(*Lev. 18:6-23; Lev. 20:10-21*)! But I had brought Israel into existence by the exact same corruptness lifestyle!

Jesus and Nimrod had both been sent to end the corrupt lifestyle of the Gentiles and Israelis to end my World forever.

### Crucifixion

**Hallel (Lord):** All that I had worked for to bring my World into existence on the planet, was in danger. Yeshua (Jesus) had been sent to Israel, from Egypt as a Great Light to expose my World for the Darkness that it actually is, as Nimrod had been sent as a Great Light to Nod (*Isa. 9:2*). Jesus (Yeshua) had been sent from Egypt, to Israel, like Nimrod had been sent two thousand years before to Nod, to Raise Cain away from me.

I was responsible for the crucifixion of both Nimrod, and Yeshua (Jesus), two thousand years apart. I had incited the Gentile children of my son Cain, to kill them both. They both had come to bring Light into my World of Darkness (*Amos 5:18, 20; Isa. 9:2*). The Gentiles in Nod washed their hands to say that Nimrod was innocent (*Isa. 53:1-9*), just as Pilate would wash his hands two thousand years later, to say that Jesus (Yeshua) was also innocent (*Matt. 27:24*). Then the Romans (Gentiles) bruised Jesus and crucified him, as their Gentile ancestors had bruised and crucified Nimrod (*Isa. 53:10*).

Nimrod was crucified by the very ones that he had come north into Nod to save. I so loved my World that I instructed the Israelis and other Gentiles, that if anyone should come to carry them away from me, to some other God (Self), then they must kill that person, even if it was my own son (*Deut. 13th Chptr.*). I so loved my World, that I sacrificed my only begotten son to save it from him (*John 3:16*). I had not brought Nimrod, or Jesus (Yeshua) into my World to condemn it, as they both did, but to save my World (TBL), from self destruction (*John 3:17*).

### Tubal (World) Cain

**Hallel:** In both cases, after the death of Nimrod, and Jesus, I instructed the leaders of Cain's children, and the scribes and Pharisees to keep the people's hearts fat, and to keep their ears heavy, and to shut their eyes, lest they hear, see, understand, and then convert and be healed from my corruption (*Isa. 6:10*). My World had been preserved, from Israel back to Jubal Cain, Jabal Cain, and Tubal Cain, the continuation of Cain.

# Soliloquies of Chaos
# Cain

*Sodomy — Cain — Lamech*

**Cain:** I am the beginning of the Lord's World on this planet. But it is made to seem that Adam is my (Cain) and Abel's father. It is written: Adam "knew" Eve, but she was already pregnant (had conceived), for Eve said "... I have gotten a man **"with"** the Lord (*Gen. 4:1*): איש את יהוה ותאמר קניתי. Eve gave birth to me first, and then to my twin brother Abel (הבל)(*Gen. 4:2*). I and my brother were the first begotten sons of the Lord, and are not included in Adam's line (*I Chron. 1:1*).

My name Cain (קין), means "Jealous," which made me junior to my father the Jealous God, whose name is Cain (Jealous)(*Ex 34:14*). Abel's (האבל) name means Effeminate (האבל). I and my effeminate brother as the first begotten son of the Lord on this planet, are the beginning of his World (TBL). Abel's Effeminate nature and my Jealous/murderous nature were the first elements, of our father the Lord's World (TBL).

Our father the Lord wanted us to sacrifice to him. Yet he would not except my sacrifice, of grain (*Gen. 4: 5, 3*), but he excepted Abel's sacrifice of flesh (*Gen. 4:4*). The Lord wanted me to sacrifice flesh to effeminate Abel. My brother Abel desired me, and the Lord wanted me to rule over him (*Gen. 4:7*), as Eve desired Adam, and Adam ruled over her (*Gen. 3:16*). Abel (Effeminate / אבל) is the Sinful, One who lay at my door, and desired me (*Gen. 4:7*)!

**Cain:** Effeminate Abel and I became sodomites, by the commandment of our father the Lord. And then my Jealousy turned into murder, when I sacrificed Abel in the Field, and buried him there (*Gen. 4:8*). When the Lord asked me where my brother was, I told him that I did not know, and asked him if I was my brother's keeper (Husband)(*Gen. 4:9*)?

That is when the Lord cursed me, and told me that I would be a fugitive, and vagabond "in" the earth (*Gen. 4:12*). I feared that the Lord's Host (Abel's friends), "in" the earth would kill me, and I told the Lord my fear (*Gen. 4:14*). My farther the Lord warned his Host, that if anyone of them would slay me, that he would avenge me seven fold. He then marked me with pale leprosy, and sent me down in the ground, away from the sun, to live with them, as a genetic mutant. I lost my Soul (Light), like they had lost their souls, while in service to the Lord (*Gen. 4:15*).

**Cain:** The Lord would use my descendants to subplant Seth the firstborn of Adam (*I Chron. 1:1, Gen. 5:3*). The Lord would use me and the line who descended from me, to establish his World (TBL) on this planet. I married one of my father's Lilahs (Lilith)(*Gen. 4:16*). All of my sons married Lilahs, and my daughters married Liles. This all occurred in the north, of the land of Nod in my subterranean city, that I built and named after my son Enoch (*Gen. 4:17*). My descendant Lamech married two Lilahs, Adah, and Zillah (*Gen. 4:18-20*). The Sodomy never stopped. Lamech killed me (Cain), and a young man who I helped to rape him (*Gen. 4:23*). Even in the time of his being raped Lamech had three son, who would be the continuation of the Lord's World (TBL). My three descendant sons were Ju<u>bal</u> Cain, Ja<u>bal</u> Cain, and Tu<u>bal</u> Cain (*Gen. 4: 20-22*). These three Bals (Balls) became the Tubal (TBL) or World (TBL) of the Lord, to the time of Lamech, and the flood.

Bible/Torah

# Soliloquies of Chaos
# Lamech (Cain)

*Cain — Lamech (לְמֶךְ) "To Make" — Sealed in, or Shipped Out (Strange Cargo) — Noah*

**Lamech:** We the Children of **Cain** were scattered all over Nod. My name Lamech (למך) means "To Make," or "to gather into one place." We Cainites dwelt from the Nahor Hiddekel (Tigris River) in the west, to the Yom Negev (Persian Gulf) in the south, to the Horim Academ (Eastern Mountains) going from the east, to the north. Hallel the Lord of the North, the father of our father Cain, forewarned us that a great flood was coming. He said that we must all be "gathered to one place," the highest land in Nod, which was in the north, as far north in Nod as we could possibly go. The extreme north would be the last place flooded. I Lamech in that northern place was charged with preparing my family, Cain's descendants a place to survive the flood. Cain had built his old subterranean city there in the north, it had to be prepared for the flood. We would seal as many people as possible into the subterranean City of Enoch. Cain named his city of caves after his son Enoch (*Gen. 4:17*).

Cain is the old man that I killed along with a young man, with him. I killed the young man for raping me, while Cain held a knife on me, and then I killed Cain, for cutting (Wounding / פצע) me, when I resisted being Raped (hurt / חברח)(*Gen. 4:23*). Then I posed the question to the Lord, that if he was going to avenge me killing Cain seven fold (*Gen. 4:15*), then I Cain's descendant must be avenged, for killing Cain, seventy and seven fold, because Cain caused me to be raped (*Gen. 4:24*). The Lord did not harm me at all, and allowed me to be about my business. *See Strong's Concordance #s 2266 to 2278* (Harbar), *for the word "hurt," which really means to consort, or have forced sex (rape).*

**Lamech:** I charged my three sons with the tasks, of setting the underground city into proper order. My three sons were named Ju<u>bal</u> Cain, Ja<u>bal</u> Cain, and Tu<u>bal</u> Cain (*Gen. 4:20-22*). After the flood these three would be in charge of the **World** (TBL) of our Lord Hallel, the Lord of the North. Their ensign was a flag with "Three Balls configured to represent themselves. *See "Three Ball" graphics.*

Lord Hallel told us that Noah the son of **Lemech** in Adam's line was preparing for the same flood on the south (Seth) side of the Tigris River (*Gen. 6:12, 17*). Noah had been instructed by the Lord God (Michael/Melchezedek) to build an three story Ark Ship (*Gen. 6:13-16*). This ship was designed to carry Noah, and his family on one deck. Noah was also commanded to carry on two of every kind a male and female of all the animal life in the entire area of Mesopotamia where the flood was to take place. These animals would be on a second deck.

After the animals that the Lord God had commanded and all else were on the Ark the Lord approached Noah to take on a strange cargo of "beast," which were not man or animal, but a mixing of both (*Gen. 7:1, 2*). These were the true "Tubals" (TBL) or "World." The fruit of my three sons, the three Bals, Ju<u>bal</u>, Ja<u>bal</u>, and Tu<u>bal</u> committing bestiality (TBL) with animals. The Lord told Noah to take on seven pairs of each kind of the **"Clean Beast,"** a **Man** and his **Wife**, and of the **"Unclean Beast"** two of each kinds, a **Man** and his **Wife** (*Gen. 7:2*). Tubal (World) is synonymous with bestiality. Those among the three of my sons who were successful at mating (Cabash/כבש) with the animals are the fathers of the Tubal (World). Noah would carry the fruit of the Man/Animal mix as a "Strange Cargo" on the third deck of the Ark (*Gen. 7:1, 2*).

Soliloquies

Bible/Torah

# Soliloquies of Chaos
# Noah

*Lemech (Seth) Vs Lamech (Cain) — Order of Melchezedek — Exalting the Lord — Cain's Pale Chaldean Daughters — My Wooly Headed Brown Children — Great Exodus — Shem*

**Noah:** I choose to follow Lamech in Cain's line, not my father Lemech in Seth's line (*Gen. 4:18, Gen. Gen. 5:26*). My three sons were born within 100 years before the flood. My father Lemech passed away 5 years before the flood. In the 500 years before my sons were born, my father Lemech taught me all that had been passed on to him from his father Methuselah (*Gen. 5:21, 25*). Without Cain and Abel being Adam's children, Enoch in Adam's line was seventh from Adam (*Jude 1:14*). Enoch was 65 when he begot my grandfather Methuselah, Methuselah was 187 when he begot my father Lemech. My father Lemech was 182 when he begot me. Our whole line from Seth up to my father (Lemech) chose the Order of Melchezedek, which is the Order of Adam in his perfection. We all lived on the west "side", or the Garden "side" of the Tigris River. Cain and his descendants lived east of the Tigris in the land of Nod. I and my two younger sons Shem and Japheth were curious abut the life style there in Nod, and chose to exalt Hallel (Lucifer) the Lord of the Side of the North in Nod (*Isaiah 14:12*). Japheth, Shem, and I chose to serve the Lord, because we were attracted to the young Chaldean girls that the Lord sent wading across the Tigris to us, with their skirts up, and vaginas exposed (*Isa. 47:2*). Shem, Japheth and I therefore exalted Hallel above the Stars of God (*Isa. 14:13*).

**Noah:** My flood was only the flooding of the Tigris and Euphrates, which were named the Rivers of Cush (Ethiopia), after the flood (*Joshua 24:2, 3, Isaiah 18:1, Zephaniah 3:10* ). All of Nod the land of the Gentiles (Nations) on the "side of the North" of the Tigris was to be flooded (*Isaiah 18:2*). Both the Lord (Hallel) and Lord God (Michael/Melchezedek) were communicating with me to build a vessel to preserve my family and the animal species in our region, which is where the flood was to be. While Marked Cain and his children were to survive the flood sealed in the caves, the Lord had me to carry a "Strange Cargo," on the third story of the Ark ship.

The Lord had marked his wooly headed son Cain, and Cain's children with Pale Leprosy. But all of my children were wooly headed and brown like myself. Dig up the ruins of all of their old cities from Mohejo Daro in India to the ruins of Egypt, from the base of the Caucus Mountain down through the peninsula of Arabia. Dig up the ruins of my children's cities, and see the wooly headed brown statues, and murals of my Adamic children.

**Noah:** After the flood I sacrificed all that was clean, to the Lord including the animals of the ark (*Gen. 8:19-21*). As such the Lord commanded that I not set the animals free like God commanded, but to sacrifice all that was clean to him, and therefore preserve the unclean. When I brought my grand son Canaan into my tent it was because the Lord had commanded that I **Sanctify** (קדש) him and make him **Holy** (קדש) *See Observation Notes, World Elements, "Holiness."* What my grandson Canaan "did to me" was to tell his father Ham, who expose me for the Sodomite that I was attempting to be, with my grandson Canaan (*Gen. 9:21, 22*). The Lord and I had been holding my entire family hostage on mount Ararat. Ham exposed me and was justified to bring all of my children and grandchildren down from Ararat in a Great Exodus. I cursed Canaan for telling on me (*Gen. 9:25*). I blessed Shem and Japheth, for covering it all up (*Gen. 9:23*)!

Soliloquies

Bible/Torah

# Soliloquies of Chaos
# Shem

*Order of Melchezedek — Captives Free — Sacrifice Cleaness — Tent Incident — Cover-Up*

**Shem:** I and my brother Japheth "covered up" what was going on in our father Noah's tent (*Gen. 9:23*). I was the second born son of Noah. I made the same choice that my father Noah made to exalt Lord Hallel the Prince of the Darkness of the North (*Amos 5:18, 20*).

I along with my two brothers Ham and Japheth were born 100 years before the flood. We all three sat before grandfather Lemech to be taught. Grand father Lemech had chosen to live the peaceable lifestyle that was After the Order of Melchezedek.

Only our elder brother Ham chose to be after the Order of Melchezedek. After the flood Ham refused to co-operate, when father Noah, Japheth, and I sacrificed the animals to the Lord (*Gen. 8:20*). The Lord God Michael/Melchezedek had commanded that we keep the animals alive (*Gen. 8:19*). We were suppose to set these animals free after the flood, to repopulate the land that had been flooded. The Tigris/Euphrates basin was the sum total of land flooded by Noah's flood, the flood had sides (*Joshua 24:3, 14*).

Besides setting the animals free, we were suppose to bring our families back down to repopulate the land again. But the Lord kept us on Ararat, and commanded that we sacrifice all that was clean, including the animals (*Gen. 8:20*). We took on the corrupt life style of the children of Cain. Cain's children are the Gentiles, or Chaldeans there in the land of Nod. The corruption of the children of Cain, is the World of Cain's father the Lord Hallel (Lucifer)(*Isa. 14:12*). The Lord Hallel is the Prince of the Darkness of the North (*Psalms 48:2, Isaiah 14:32; Amos 5:18, 20*).

Taking on corruption, I became the father of all of the children of my son Arphaxad's grandson Eber (*Gen. 10:21, 24, 25, 11:14, 17*). I fathered them all except the first who were Peleg, and his twin brother Joktan (*Gen. 10:25*). My brother Japheth was also corrupt.

My elder brother Ham refused to co-operate, so the Lord commanded that father Noah undermine Ham's household. Canaan, Ham's youngest son was the weak point. Noah swore the boy to come to his tent in secrecy, and to tell no one. Canaan told his father my older brother Ham. This was the source of the Tent Incident that caused Ham to have justification to forcefully remove our families down from Ararat, so that we could not breed more corruption into our children. Ham took all of his and our children westward, across the Tigris back down into the Garden, where we had all three been born and lived 100 years before the flood.

After I had impregnated my great grandson Heber's wife, "Heber" "hebrewed" the Tigris with Ham's children. He left his wife and twin sons there with me on the side of the north in Nod.

Ham allowed Asshur, and elements of Aram to "hebrew" the Tigris with them also, because they had all chosen to be after the Order of Melchezedek. Arphaxad had also chosen order, but he and his children volunteered to stay in the north to keep chronicles of the lifestyle in Nod. Elam and Lud were also forced to stay in the north. Elam moved as far away as he could to the east and south inside Nod to avoid the corruption of the Gentiles, that I Shem had chosen. Arphaxad isolated his children from the corruption. Noah's line through me lead down through Arphaxad, to Terah the father of Abraham.

Soliloquies

# Soliloquies of Chaos
# Terah

*My Line — Choices (First Melchezedek, next the Lord) — Meeting Abram— Fleeing the Lord*

**Terah:** My father Nahor and I descended from our ancestor Arphaxad in Shem's line. Arphaxad and his entire line down to my father Nahor chose to be after the Order of Melchezedek. Melchezedek was not in Nod with us, but was on the other "side" of the Tigris River, in the Garden. My name Terah (תרח), means "To Wait" (Tarry). My father Nahor named me "Waiter," because I took so long to decide whether I would be after the Order of Melchezedek in the Garden, or after the Chaos of Hallel, here in the Land of Nod (*Joshua 24:2*). At first my father and I served the Order of Melchezedek (God)(*Joshua 24:2, 14*). But Arphaxad's father Shem had exalted the Lord. Thus my father Nahor convinced me that since we were born in Nod and living in Nod, we should be like the Ca-Shaddai or Chaldeans or Gentile (Caucasian) inhabitants of Nod, and serve the Lord. It was then that I was convinced to exalt Hallel (Lucifer), the Lord of the North in Nod (*Isa. 14:12, 13*). After my decision my father Nahor and I left the city, of our father Arphaxad, and moved to the Forbidden Chaldean City of Ur. Ur/Babel was on the Border of Arphaxad's city. The Lord had confounded the Ur/Babel Metropolis and brought it to ruin, two hundred and fifty years before the birth of my first two sons. My first two sons were Haran and Nahor, Nahor was named after my father. Haran and Nahor were born seventy years apart. (*Gen. 11:26*).

**Terah:** In his old age Arphaxad came from his city Arpachiyah adjacent to Ur. Two others arrived also, with him. Hallel the Lord of the North came down from from Ararat, and Michael/Melchezedek came up from the Garden city of Jerusalem south of the Tigris. They had all come to see Abram who was still sperm in my testicles (*Hebrews 7:10*). They wanted to know what choice Abram would make, **Chaos** or **Order** (*Isaiah 14:12, Amos 5:18, 20*).

They would all three name my youngest son, by what they all saw in my sperm, before I had even impregnated my wife with him! Abram (אברם) meaning "I am Up in the air," or "I am Undecided." Abram from his youth was like a feather blown by the wind. No one knew where he would come down to land, on any given issue. Would Abram follow the Chaos of the Lord, or the Order of Melchezedek?

The ground throughout Nod was cursed (Ararat) with famine, because of the presence of the Lord there (*Gen. 3:17*). The diseases of the Lord had destroyed many in Nod (*Ex. 15:26*). These were critical time throughout Nod for even the life in the ground was dying. My son Haran died in front of me in Ur, from the famine of the Lord (*Gen.11:28*). I fled from the Lord and his famine with the remnant of my family, I was dieing. We were on our way to the land of Canaan (*Gen. 11:31*). But I fell sick and died in the city, of my dead son Haran (*Gen. 11:32*).

The Lord caught up with my family in Haran. It was from Haran that the Lord forced Abram to continue his journey to Canaan, but now being forced to bring the Lord with him. Abram may have chosen to be after the Order of Melchezedek, if the Lord had not caught up with them in Nod before they got across the Tigris, to the land of Canaan.

Bible/Torah

# Soliloquies of Chaos
# Abram

**Abram:** I am the youngest of the three sons of Terah. Haran, Nahor and I were all born in the north of Nod, in the forbidden city complex of Ur of the Chaldeans (*Gen. 11:26*). My brothers and I were born approximately seventy years apart. My nativity of Ur of the Chaldees (*Gen. 11:28*), was the Babel, that the Lord confounded four hundred years before I was born (*Gen. 11:9*).

I was still sperm in my father Terah's testicles when the Lord, Arphaxad, and Melchezedek, all came to Ur/Babel to meet me (*Heb. 7:10*). All three had come to see who I was, and what I would be, when my father would impregnate my mother with me. All three wanted to know ahead of time what choice I would make, in the future, when I would became a young man at the time of choosing. Before I was ever born the three gazed upon me, with the Single Eye power, and described what they saw, by naming me "Abram. My name Abram (אברם) means "I (א) am "floating like a Feather" (ברם), which means betrayer, for who knows where a feather (myself) will land on any issue? Arphaxad and all of his children down to my father, chose to be after the Order of Melchezedek. Then my grandfather Nahor, and my father Terah changed, and chose, to exalt the Chaos of Lucifer, the Lord of the North (*Isaiah 14:12*)? They began to exalt Hallel (Lucifer) the Prince of the Darkness on the side of the North in Nod (*Amos 5:18, 20* ).

If I chose to be After the Order of Melchezedek, the Lord's World would come to an end, and the experiment would be over, but if I chose to be after the Chaos of the Lord the experiment would go on, down into corruption.

In my prime there was famine and plague increasingly all over the land of Nod, because the Lord and his Host were there. My oldest brother Haran had a city that was dieing from the plagues and famine of the Lord. Haran fled from his city to Ur/Babel to save his life, but Haran died at the feet of our father (*Gen. 11:28*). My father Terah left off from serving the Lord, and gathered all of us his family (*Gen. 11:29*), and fled from Ur, in an attempt to be safe in the land of Canaan (*Gen. 11: 31*). But my father died on the way, in the dead city of my brother Haran (*Gen. 11:32*). We were voting with our feet, not to serve the Lord anymore, but he caught up with us in Haran, and forced me to continue down into the land of Canaan, but now bringing him with us (*Gen. 12:1*).

When the Lord had confounded Ur/Babel hundreds of years before my birth, the pale leper Chaldeans there had fled across the Tigris, and were given asylum from the Lord, down in the land of Canaan. If we could have escaped from the Lord, Abram and would have asked for asylum in the land of Canaan from the Lord also!

If we could have escaped the Lord in Nod, we would have became after the Order of Melchezedek, again like Arphaxad. But now the Lord had us and we would have to obey his commandments. It was the Lord who caused a famine in the land of Canaan for the first time (), and carried us down from Canaan, into Egypt to prostitute my sister/wife/niece, Sarah to the Pharaoh.

As a servant of the Lord my father Terah had committed incest, by fathering Milcah and Sarah/Iscah, with his daughter-in-law Zona Hari, my brother Haran's pale (fair) wife, even before Haran died (*Gen. 11:28*). Terah married his son Nahor to his daughter Milcah. My father married me his younger son to his daughter Iscah who is Sarah. (*Gen. 11:29*).

Soliloquies

# Soliloquies of Chaos
# Sarah/Iscah

*Abram - Incest of Father Terah - My Pale Mountain Mother - Daughter (Whore) of Chaldea - Prostitute in Egypt to Pharaoh - Prostitute in Canaan to Abimelech -   Lot my Brother/Nephew/Cousin*

**Sarah:** I am Sarah/Iscah the sister/wife/niece of Abram (*Gen.11:29*).  I and my older sister Milcah were born in the house of Haran. Haran had long since died, after the birth of our brother Lot (*Gen. 11:28*).  My sister Milcah and I are the daughters of our grandfather Terah (*Gen. 11:29*). Terah had taken our mother the widow of his son Haran as his woman.  Abram and I had the same father (Terah), but not the same mother (*Gen. 20:12*).   *See Strong's Concordance "Iscah" which refers to Iscah being Sarah # 3252.*

Our father Terah married us his two daughter Milcah and I Sarah/Iscah,  to his two sons, Nahor and Abram (*Gen. 11:29*).  My father Terah was also my grandfather and father-in-law.  Nahor was my brother, brother-in-law, and uncle.  Abram was my husband, brother and uncle.  Lot was my brother, cousin, and nephew at the same time.  None of this was unusual for it was the lifestyle of my mother's people the Chaldeans or Gentiles the Pale Leper children of Cain, who lived in the north of Nod.  My sister Milcah had three sons with our brother Nahor (*Gen. 22:20*).  Milcah's third son Kemuel impregnated his mother Milcah,  with five sons (*Gen. 22:23*)!

**Sarah:** My mother was a Whore (Horite / הורי) or Pale mountain woman.  She was "fair"or pale like all of the other Daughters of Chaldea who are the Daughters of Cain (*Gen. 11:31, Gen. 6:4*). The Lord took my virginity in the dust when I was a little girl (*Isaiah 47:1*).  At a certain young age every Chaldean girl had to expose her vagina to the Lord, and he came as a man comes to (into) a woman (*Isaiah 47:2, 3*).  Each of us young Chaldean girls in our turn had to sat in silence and consume the Mandrake fruit, and fall into the Darkness of the Lord (*Isaiah 47:5*).  That is when the Lord of the North came, and polluted each of us in turn (*Isaiah 47: 6*).  The Lord promised that drugged by the Mandrake we would not remember, what happened except that it was pleasant (*Isaiah 47:7. 8*).  Even in my old age the Lord pleasured me (*Gen. 18:12*),  and became the father of my son Isaac (*Gen. 21:1-3*).  He would give Isaac to Abraham to raise (*Joshua 24:3*).

I was still a young Chaldean girl when we hebrewed the Tigris, down into the gardenlands of Ham.  Standing up in the boat, I let my hair down, and performed the ritual of raising my dress to expose my vagina (*Isa. 47:2*).  I was advertising to those in the land of Ham that my vagina was for sell!

It was desolate in the land of Nod, and we came down to the land of Canaan to survive.  We had nothing to bring with us,  but would have to get possessions in Canaan and Egypt.  The Lord and my two brothers Lot and Abraham, prostituted me to the pharaoh in Egypt, for great wealth (*Gen. 12:16*).  Leaving Egypt they prostituted me next to Abimelech, back in the land of Canaan, for again as much as had been gotten from the Pharaoh (*Gen. 20:2, 14*).  We never feared Pharaoh or Abimelech for the Lord was with us all the time.

We had left Nod Ararat for it was desolate,  parched, dried out, and dead.  There were only a handful of other souls with us, including my brother/nephew Lot.  Lot hebrewed the River of Ethiopia (Tigris) with us (*Gen. 12:5*).

Bible/Torah

# Soliloquies of Chaos
# Lot

*Sarah/Iscah (Little sister) — Mother's Sodomite People — My Son and Daughters — Isaac*

**Lot:** I and Sarah/Iscah have the same mother, but not the same father. My father Haran was dead and in the ground when my grandfather Terah impregnated my mother with Milcah, and Sarah (*Gen.11:29*). We were all born in Ur of the Chaldeans.

We were all raised in the same tradition that Cain and his children were raised, to be of the World TBL) of the Lord of the North. Sisters married their brothers. Grandfathers had sex with, and made children with their daughters, and daughters in law. Sarah was my sister, cousin, and aunt. Grandfather Terah was Sarah's father, grandfather, and her father-in-law. Abram was Sarah's brother, uncle, and husband. This was our way of life under the Lord.

Nimrod had come north in Nod to build Ur/Babel, to raise Cain's Gentile/Chaldean children, from this corrupt conduct. The Lord came down and confounded Ur, to bring it to ruin (*Gen. 11:9; Isa. 23:13*). The Lord scattered and peeled the pale ones that Nimrod had raised. The Lord meted them out, and trodden them down (*Isa. 18:2*). Most of my mothers people fled abroad from Ur, down into the land of Canaan, but a small remnant stayed in confounded Ur. My mother descended from this remnant who stayed in the north, and we were born out of her, in Ur of the Chaldeans, in the north of the land of Nod.

My mother's people the confounded Chaldeans, who had fled 400 years before, were given asylum, from the Lord of the North, by the children of Canaan who quarantined them in the former grain storage cities of Sodom and Gomorrah. Sodom is where I would go to live with my mother's people, the former inhabitants of Ur of the Chaldeans (*Gen. 11:2- 9*). My mother, my sister Sarah, and my wife were all daughter of the Darkness of Chaldea (*Isaiah 47:5*).

**Lot:** I became a permanent Sodomite citizen, among my mother's people, the Chaldeans in Sodom. I and my wife had sons and daughters (*Gen. 19:12*). My two daughters were both married, to Sodomites, but both remained virgins (*Gen.19:12,14 Gen.19:8*).

Two of the Host of the Lord came down to Sodom to destroy it. First they had to evacuate my family and I. I was instructed to bring all of my family together to leave the city, before it was to be destroyed. My homosexual **sons and sons in law** laughed at me, and refused to leave (*Gen. 19:12, 14*). I, my wife, and our daughters were also reluctant, and we all had to be dragged forth from the city (*Gen.19:16*). Emphasis is placed on my wife looking behind her, but it is a miracle that we all did not look back (*Gen. 19:26*). These people in Sodom were family, like those we had left behind in Nod/ Chaldea, in the north. We all lived the same lifestyle north in the land of Nod, and south in the now Chaldean city of Sodom.

My two daughters decided to have children from me, with the excuse that they wanted to preserve my line, yet Abraham's camp was close enough to see the smoke and fire of Sodom burning (*Gen.19:28*). Therefore I and my two daughter were close enough to walk to Abraham's camp, where there were women for me, and young men for my daughters. What kind of lifestyle did we live in Sodom and Gomorrah, that my daughter felt free to approach me to have sex? I did not know what time they came and left, but I knew that I was having sex with them! Besides incest, Incubi* was also a part of the lifestyle in the north, the Lord and his Host had sex with all of the Daughter of Chaldea, including my sister Sarah, the mother of the Lord's son Isaac.

Soliloquies

# Soliloquies of Chaos
# Isaac

*Incest of Uncle Lot — My Cousin/wife Rebekah — The Lord's son Jacob*

**Isaac:** Lot committed incest with his two daughters, to get children, as my mother Sarah committed Incubi with the Lord, to get me. Abraham and his sister, my mother Sarah also committed incest, they were brother and sister, and uncle and niece (*Gen. 20:12*).

Sarah/Iscah is my mother, but Abram/Abraham is not my father, even though they were committing incest to get a child. Abraham could not impregnate her, and he complained to the Lord, and asked the Lord to give/put seed in Sarah, to make her pregnant (*Gen. 15:3*).

The Lord told Abraham two things concerning Abraham's concern. **First** he told Abraham that his heir would come from his own loins (not the Lord's)(*Gen. 15:4*). This became true when Abraham raped Hagar and made her pregnant with Ishmael, his son from his own bowels (*Gen. 16:4*).

**Secondly** the Lord told Abraham that he would also "give" Sarah/Iscah a son for him (*Gen. 17:17*). After this the Lord "Visited" (פקד / FKD) Sarah and "did to her" as he had spoken, for she was pregnant (*Gen. 21:1*). Sarah conceived and bare me (Isaac). Then the Lord gave me (his son) to Abraham to raise (*Joshua 24:3*). The Lord always give his children to other men to raise. He gave all of his sons to the husbands of the women he impregnated.

After my birth Sarah told Abraham to get rid of his son Ishmael, so that I would not have to share Ishmael's own inheritance with Ishmael (*Gen. 21:10*)! Abraham sent his "only son" Ishmael and his mother out into the wilderness to die. My father the Lord watched, but Ishmael did not die. Abraham's son Ishmael must die, so that I Isaac the son of the Lord could become the "Seed of Abraham (*Gen. 26:4; John 8:33*)." Thus my father the Lord told Abraham to take his "only son" (Ishmael) up on a mountain that he would show him (*Gen. 22:2*). Ishmael had survived being sent into the wilderness by Abraham to die (*Gen. 21:14*). My father the Lord wanted me his son to subplant Ishmael, and wanted Ishmael dead. In Ishmael's death I would be called "Seed of Abraham (*Gen. 15:5*)." The Lord saw that Abraham had me Isaac bound on the altar instead of his son Ishmael the Lord was bitter. That is what **Moriah** means **"Bitterness of Jah,"** or "Bitterness of the Lord." My father the Lord was bitter about Abraham trying to sacrifice me (the Lord's son), and told him to take his hands off of me (*Gen. 22:12*).

**Isaac:** After incestuous Abraham had raised me to mature age he sent north, to my mother's family to get a wife for me. Rebekah the girl brought back was my mother's Sarah's sister's granddaughter. It was incest for me to marry Rebekah but that was normal in the Gentile culture that my mother came from in the north. My cousin Rebekah and I tried to have children for over twenty years. When we were unsuccessful I entreated (tempted/עתר) my father the Lord to "rub against" (nakah / נכח) my cousin/wife Rebekah. The Lord was tempted, and "rubbed against her" (nakah / נכח), and Rebekah became pregnant with twin sons from the Lord (*Gen. 25:21*). When Jacob and Esau were struggling in her womb, Rebekah went to the Lord their father, to see what he had put in her (*Gen. 25:22*)! Jacob and Esau are my brothers not my sons. The Lord gave his sons, my brothers Esau and Jacob to me, to raise (*Joshua 24:4*).

Bible/Torah

# Soliloquies of Chaos
# Jacob

*My Father the Lord — Subplanting Esau — Wrestling with God (the Lord) for my name Israel (Gen. 32:28) — Raising the Lord's sons (My Brothers) — Leah*

**Jacob:** Isaac was not my father, the Lord is my father who "gave" me to Isaac to raise (*Ex. 4:22; Joshua 24:4*). I am The third Subplanter (Jacob) the Lord and Cain being Subplanters (Jacobs / יעקב) before me. It all started with my twin brother Esau. We struggled inside of our mother's womb (*Gen. 25:22*). I was in contention to subplant Esau even before birth. Our mother Rebekah went to the Lord to find out what the struggle was in her womb. Our father the Lord told her that I and Esau were two nations (Goyim / גוים), in her womb (*Gen. 25:23*). My brother Esau came out first, but I had hold of Esau's heel (עקב), and they named me Heel, or Jacob because even though I was behind him (at his heel), I was going to "**subplant**" him, or take his place (*Genesis 25:25, 26, Gen. 27:35, 36*). After we were born the Lord gave Esau and I Jacob, to his son Isaac to raise (*Joshua 24:4*), as the Lord had given his son Isaac to Abraham to raise (*Joshua 24:3*).

**Jacob:** Once Esau my firstborn brother was starving, and instead of me giving him food as I should have, I bartered with him for his birthright, as a firstborn son (*Genesis 25:29-34*). I knew that I could not purchase Esau's birthright, and I and my mother Rebekah tricked an aging, blind Isaac into thinking that I was Esau, and Isaac gave me (Jacob) Esau's birthright thinking that I was Esau (*Gen. 27:35, 36*). When Esau found out what I had done I had to flee for my life. I went to live with Laban the son of my mother Rebbecca's relative in Haran (*Gen. 27:43*). In Haran over a time I committed incest by marrying my cousins Leah and Rachael, Laban's two daughters. They were my first cousins. Also in marrying these two I obtained their servant women Zilpah, and Bilhah (*Gen. 29:24, 29*).

**Jacob:** I did not like my cousin/wife Leah with her tender eyes (*Gen.29:17*), but was tricked into marrying her by uncle Laban (*Gen. 25:29*). When the Lord saw that I would not have anything to do with Leah he "opened her womb" and impregnated her four times himself. I loved my cousin/wife Rachael and had sex with her frequently, but she was barren.

Rachael was very angry about this and, and since I could not make her pregnant she went to the Lord and actually "wrestled" with him to force him to "open her womb," and give her a baby (*Gen. 30:8*). Joseph (יוסף) was the name of the boy that the Lord impregnated Rachael with (*Gen. 30:22-24*). My name Israel (ישראל) means "He Wrestled God." I also had to wrestled with the Lord, to get my name Israel (*Gen. 32:24*). My father the Lord gave me his four sons with Leah, Reuben, Simeon, Levi, and Judah, to raise, and also gave me his son Joseph with Rachael to raise.

**Jacob:** I would not have had sex with Leah ever for I hated her, but the Lord's oldest son Reuben found Mandrake in the field. Rachael wanted some of the Mandrake, and sold me to Leah for a night to get the Mandrake (*Gen. 30:15*). My being a male prostitute for a night is how Leah became pregnant with Dinah (*Gen. 30:21*).

The Lord's sons Reuben, Simeon, Levi, and Judah, made me stink for they used Leah's daughter Dinah as an excuse, to murder an entire city to get it's girls and women (*Gen. 34:30*).

Soliloquies

Bible/Torah

# Soliloquies of Chaos
# Leah/Rachael

*Jacob The Whore (**Gen. 31:16**)* — Rachael Wrestled Me — I *(Rachael) Wrestled The Lord (**Gen.30:8**)*

**Leah:** Jacob did not want me (Leah) from the beginning, he wanted my younger sister Rachael. Our father Laban tricked Jacob into marrying me, making him think that he was with Rachael (*Gen. 29:25 - 28*).

When Jacob refused to lay with me I complained to the Lord and he immediately responded to my needs. The Lord is the father of the first four of my sons. The meanings of the names of my son speaks to the Lord's concerns with me: (1) **Reuben** (ראובן) means **"Son of Seeing"**, for the Lord "saw" that I was hated" (*Gen. 29:31*). (2) **Simeon** (שמעון) means **"One from Hearing"**, for the Lord "Heard me complain that I was Hated" (*Gen. 29:33*). (3) **Levi** (לוי) means **"Joined to or Attracted to Me,"** for even though my husband was not, the Lord was "attracted to me" (*Genesis 29:34*). (4) **Judah** (יהודה) means "Praise Jah," for I had given up on Jacob, and was "Praising the Lord," for being the father of my four sons (*Gen. 29:35*).

**Leah:** The first time I had a chance to be with Jacob was when my son Reuben found some Mandrake, and Rachael wanted some of It (*Gen. 30:14*). Rachael allowed Jacob to spend the night with me for some of my mandrake (*Gen. 30:15*). After that I had two sons with Jacob Issachar, and Zebulun (*Gen. 30:17, 18*). After that I became pregnant with Dinah, my third child with Jacob (*Gen. 30:21*).

All four of the Lord's sons despised Jacob for his disrespect for me. Reuben even went and had sex, with Bilhah in Jacob's bed (*Gen. 35:22, Gen. 49:4*).

Two of my sons with the Lord Simeon and Levi used their sister Dinah, to bait Shechem, the prince of that city we had come to live near. All of the "son" of Jacob had been looking at the women and girls of the city.

**Rachael:** The Lord was very infatuated with my sister Leah. I was jealous that the Lord was giving her children, and Jacob could not make me pregnant at all. I was so desperate to have children with the Lord also, that I wrestled with my sister Leah, and I also wrestled with the Lord to have a chance to have a child by him (*Gen. 30:8*): And Rachael said "I wrestle with God and I also wrestle with my sister"...... נפתולי אלוהים נפתלתי עם אחתי (*Gen. 30:8*). I was successful for the Lord "opened my womb" with his tool, and made me pregnant with Joseph (*Gen. 30:22-25*).

Jacob loved me and my son Joseph so much that he sent Leah and the rest ahead to be killed by his brother Esau, but he held my son Joseph and I behind to protect us to the end (*Gen. 33:2*). Leah's sons were jealous of Joseph. They kidnapped Joseph and sent him to Egypt (*Gen. 37: 14-36*). In our northern tradition I had wanted my son Joseph to marry his cousin Dinah, the daughter of my sister Leah.

Bible/Torah

# Soliloquies of Chaos
# Dinah

*Rachael — Playing The Whore — Marriage Proposal — Circumcising Shechem*

**Dinah:** I would have been married my cousin Joseph, if my brothers had not sold him into service in Egypt (*Gen. 37:36; 39:1*). My aunt Rachael was responsible for my birth. My mother Leah gave Rachael some mandrake for a night with Jacob (*Gen. 30:14, 15*). My name Dinah (דינה) means "mistress." A mistress is chief of all whores. My brothers sent me to "play" with the girls of the city (*Gen. 34:1*). My brothers sent me to "play" with the girls of the city, knowing that Shechem the Prince of Salem would see me, and be attracted to me (*Gen. 34:2*). I did not go to "play" with the girls of the city, I went to play the whore, with the prince of the city. That is really what my brothers sent me to do, and it worked because I enticed him. Shechem did not defile (Rape) me, I enticed him like my brothers had told me (*Gen. 34:3, 5, 13*).

Shechem and I were together and Shechem was nice to me. I knew how to do all kinds of things to please a man. Most of my brothers had been with me sexually, and they trained me very well. I used it all on Shechem as they had instructed me. When we had finished, Shechem wanted to be with me forever, and I wanted to be with him.

**Dinah:** None of Shechem's actions were the acts of a defiler. He took me to meet his father and his family. He told his father what had happened between us, and that he wanted to marry me (*Gen. 34:4*). We all went to discuss this with my father Jacob (*Gen. 34:5*). Shechem's father Hamor spoke very kind, to my father proposing a dowry, that he could pay to my father, for a marriage, between Shechem and myself (*Gen. 34:9-12*).

**Dinah:** Hamor then extended an offer that if my father chose, that his people and ours could live together. We two people would be married into one (*Gen. 34:9,10*). This was a very generous offer, for we Israelis had virtually nothing beyond small flocks. Shechem's father and people lived in the midst of a land of milk and honey! Everyone had beautiful homes and fields. The women and girls of Salem/Shechem were beautiful gentle and kind. My brothers did not have women to marry. There was just my mother Leah, her sister Rachael, Bilah, Zilpah, and myself Dinah. My brothers had been looking at these girls and women, and choosing the ones they wanted for themselves. I thought that my brothers wanted to marry these girls, and women, and therefore wanted the Prince of Shechem and I to be married (*Gen. 34:9*). Shechem and his father came to talk to my father.

**Dinah:** My father Jacob told Shechem and his father that they would have to discuss the matter with his sons, when they came in from the field, with the flocks. When my brothers came in that evening and found out that Shechem and I had gotten together, they went to speak with Hamor, Shechem and the men of Salem/Shechem (*Gen. 34:13*). My brothers told them that the only way that we could be married was if they (The Shechemites) would honor the traditions of our small tribe, and circumcise themselves. My brothers told them that every man and boy must be

Soliloquies

Bible/Torah

# Soliloquies of Chaos
# Dinah

*Murdering Shechem — Rape Tribes — Incestuous Brothers — Reuben*

circumcised. My brothers promised the men and boys that if they circumcised themselves that Shechem could marry me, and that they would marry the women and girls of the city of Shechem (*Gen. 34:14-16*).

**Dinah:** Here were my brothers making demands on someone who could have crushed them like flies! These people could have taken all five of us women, and if necessary they could have slaughtered my father and brothers for resisting our being taken from them! But Shechem's people were peaceful as the children of Ham had always been peaceable from days of old (*I Chron. 4:40*). Try to imagine a whole city of men and boys volunteering to have an operation, just so one of their sons could marry a girl that none of them knew. Once the men and boys of the city of Shechem had been circumcised they were sore and defenseless. That is when my brothers Levi and Simeon came and slaughtered all the males of the city, including Shechem, and his father (*Gen. 34:25*). They took me out of Shechem's house (*Gen. 34:26*). Now all of the other sons of my father joined in, to help spoil this beautiful city, taking all of the herds, flocks, and goods that they could carry, and setting fire to the rest (*Gen. 34:28, 29*). My brothers, the Lord's sons also took the girls and the women, that they could have had as wives, without killing anyone! My brothers did not care for me, to protect me from being treated like a whore. They had all been treating me like an unpaid whore since I was a little child (*Gen. 34:31*). Now they had used me as a whore to create an excuse to murder (men and boys), and to defile (Rape) women and girls. My brothers took the girls and women of the murdered city of Shechem, and used them to raped themselves into tribal existence!

**Dinah:** Before my brothers murdered the city of Shechem, and took the women and girls of the city, they did not have anyone for sex except me! The incest that my brothers did with me was just a continuation, of the corrupt way of life of our ancestors, back in the land of Nod. For example **Abraham** was married to his sister/niece **Sarah**, and their brother and sister **Nahor** and **Milcah** were also married to each other (*Gen. 11:29*). Milcah had three children with her brother Nahor (*Gen. 22:20, 21*), and then Milcah had five children with her own third son **Kemuel** (*Gen. 22:21, 22*)! Kemuel's fifth son with his mother was named Bethuel, who was the father of **Rebecca**, who married her own first cousin **Isaac**, Sarah's son (*Gen. 24:15*).

   Rebekka had two sons, one of them being **Jacob (Israel)**. Jacob married **Leah** and **Rachael** his mother Rebekah's two nieces, Jacob's first cousins (*Gen. 29:21-28*).

   This sexual mixing in our culture, from Abraham down to me (Dinah) and my brothers was casual, and regular. **At least my brothers did not make me pregnant!** It was horrible that my brothers murdered that city and took all of the girls and women, but at least now they would no longer have to bother me! My oldest brother Reuben had even had sex with Bilhah one of the girls that my father Jacob was raping (*Gen. 49:4*).

Soliloquies

Bible/Torah

# Soliloquies of Chaos
# Reuben

*Dinah Our Whore — Rape Tribes — My Mandrake — Jacob the Whore (**Gen. 30:14, 15, 16**) — Lying with Bilhah (Revenge)(**Gen. 35:22, 49:4**) — Selling Joseph Rachael's son (**Gen.37:18-36**) — Levi the Assassin*

**Reuben:** My little sister Dinah enticed the Prince of Shechem, and gave us the excuse to take the girls and women of his city of Shalem (Salem). Dinah gave us, her brothers the excuse to murder the city, and take the girls and women, to rape ourselves into tribes.

My name Reuben (ראובן) means "Son of seeing," for the Lord "saw" that Jacob would not even look at my mother Leah (*Gen. 29:32*). Of the four of us (Reuben, Simeon, Levi, and Judah), none of us sons of the Lord had any respect for Jacob.

Jacob did not love our mother, and would not give our mother Leah children (*Gen. 29:31*). It was Hallel our Lord (Hallelujah / הללויה), who overshadowed our mother, and gave her four sons. We sons of Leah are called the "sons" of Jacob simply because we were born in his household! If the Lord had not made our mother pregnant, I and my three brothers would not have been born! Greater than this insult was that our sister Dinah was only born because Rachael wanted some of the Mandrake fruit, that I had found in the field (*Gen. 30:14, 15*). Rachael prostituted Jacob to my mother Leah, for a night to get some of my Mandrake (*Gen. 30:15, 16*)! Jacob became a whore for Rachael! It was by this act of prostitution that Jacob made our mother pregnant, and Dinah was born! Jacob was a whore, and out of spite we made his daughter our sister a whore also. Also it was out of spite that I took one of Jacob's woman, Bilhah, and I did it to her on his couch (*Genesis 49:3, 4*)!

**Reuben:** Greater than our anger for Jacob for not loving our mother, was our anger against him for putting us up front, when we came from the land of Padan-Aram, into the land of Jacob's brother Esau. Esau had wanted to kill Jacob for stealing his birth right (*Gen. 27:36, 41*). Jacob had fled from Esau, but was now returning years later. Jacob put all of us up front except Rachael, Joseph and himself. He was using us as a shield. Jacob put the rest of us far enough in front of himself Rachael and Joseph, that if Esau was still angry that Jacob was willing to let Esau murder all of us, while he escaped with Joseph and Rachael (*Gen. 33:2*). That is why in the end we sold Joseph into service, to Abraham's children the Ishmael/Midianites, who took him to Egypt (*Gen. 37:28, 36*). In Egypt Joseph was not sold into slavery, but was purchased as an indentured servant, into the household of an Egyptian official named Potiphar (*Gen. 37:36*).

**Reuben:** None of us four had women of our own. In the matter of the women and girls of the city of Shechem, they were a solution to all of our problems. When we murdered Shechem prince of the city, his father and their city Salem, our father the Lord and his Host protected us while we escaped with the women and girls of that city (*Gen. 35:5*). Jacob protested, but we let him know that it was not his business (*Gen. 34:31*). Our father the Lord and his Host terrorized the Canaanite cities around us to allow us to escape, with the stolen goods, women, and girls (*Gen. 34:25-31 Gen. 49:6*). The chief planners of the raid on the city of Shechem were my brothers Simeon and Levi.

# Soliloquies of Chaos
# Levi

*Reuben — Shechem/Salem - Children of rape - Selling Joseph - Egyptian Wagons - Judah*

**Levi:** Reuben was the first child, my mother Leah had with the Lord. My name Levi (לוי) means "I Attract," because my mother Leah thought that by the time that the Lord had made her pregnant for the third time with me that Jacob would be "attracted" to her, to be her husband (*Gen.29:34*). But Jacob still refused to lie with my mother.

**Levi:** My high mark in life was when I and my brother Simeon planned to murder all of the men and boys of the Canaanite city, of Shechem/Salem (*Gen. 34:25*)!

Dinah our sister had been the only female we had for sex. We had been looking at the girls and women of the city, from the time that Jacob had camped there on it's border (*Gen. 33:19*). It was Simeon and I who contrived to send Dinah to "play" with the girls of the city. (*Gen. 34:1*). Dinah was to attract Shechem, the Prince of the city (*Gen. 34:2*). Dinah (דינה) means "Madam" (Mistress), for a madam is the chief of all whores. Dinah attracted the Prince of Shechem, and we were in business. We sacrificed all of the males and took the females for our selves (*Gen. 34:25*).

When we murdered the Prince of Shechem, his father and their city Salem, our father the Lord and his Host protected us while we escaped, with the women and girls of that city. We used the women and girls of the city of Shechem, to rape ourselves into tribal existence. Our father the Lord terrorized the cities around us, to protect us from the people there, by dropping fire and brimstone on them (*Gen. 35:5*).

**Levi:** After that the only problem that we had left was Joseph, who was proud of telling us his dream, that he had of ruling over us (*Gen.37:6-9*). At first we were going to murder him, but then we changed our minds, and sold him, to Abraham's children the Ishmael/Midianites (*Gen. 37:25, 27, 28*). The Ishmael/Midianites were on their way to Egypt, and indentured him to an Egyptian (*Gen. 37:36*)(*Gen. 39:1*). It would be years later that we would flee to Egypt, from our father the Lord, and his famine in the land of Canaan. Otherwise we would have perished (*Deut. 26:5*).

The Egyptians sent wagons to save us by carrying us from Canaan, down to Egypt (*Gen. 45:19, 21*). Besides being rapist, and murderers, we also committed incest in Egypt. Two Levites descending from the rape of the Canaanite women, were Jochebed, and Amram. Jochebed married her nephew Amram, and they became the incestuous parents of Moses, and Aaron (*Ex. 2:1; 6:20*). The Israelis were still incestuous, after four hundred years, in Egypt.

**Levi:** There was no Levitican priesthood yet. But after we left Egypt, our father the Lord made my descendants a priesthood, because of our evil nature. Sacrifice to the Lord was the core of the activities of the priesthood. We had sacrificed the clean (Shechemites) to preserve the Lord's World (Israel). We preserved the Lord's World by raping our selves into tribal existence, just as Abram had preserved the World of the Lord, by having children with Hagar and Keturah, two Hamite women. The Lord had changed Abram's name from Abram to AbramHam. The Lord turned us Levites into a priesthood. After Egypt the first act that the Lord had us Levites to do was to Sanctify, and make the first born males of Israel Holy. Judah's tribe came into existence through an act of prostitution and incest with his daughter in law Tamar.

Bible/Torah

# Soliloquies of Chaos
# Judah

*Levi — Praise the Lord — Male Whore — Taking Canaanite Females — First Judeans (not Jews) — Whore Tribe — Tamar*

**Judah:** My mother had me after she had Levi. I am the fourth and final son that my mother Leah had with the Lord (*Gen. 29:35*). I am the first Judean. My name Judah (יהודה) means "Praise Jah." For our mother Leah began to praise the Lord (Jah), and gave up on Jacob, by the time that the Lord had made her pregnant for the forth time with me (*Gen. 29:35*).

Yet even though we were the Lord's sons he officially declared us to be Egyptians (מצרי), like his son Jacob (*Ex. 4:22*). The mother of Jacob's mother Rebekah was the daughter of an Egyptian (מצרי) woman. This made us Egyptian (מצרי) or Syrian, like Jacob (צרי)(*Deut. 26:5*).

My aunt Rachel was angry, that My mother Leah had four children with the Lord, and that she had none. Knowing that the Lord was attracted to her sister Leah, Rachael wrestled with the Lord, and her sister too (*Gen. 30:8*)(נפתולי אלהים נפתלתי אחתי). Rachael said: "I wrestle God, and I wrestle my sister also." Rachael was successful wrestling with the Lord, because the Lord opened her womb with his instrument, and impregnated her (*Gen.30:22*).

**Judah:** Yet Jacob still loved Rachael, and now Joseph too, as much as he hated us four, and our mother Leah. Joseph, was just another son of the Lord, like we four sons of Leah were, but the four of us did not like him, because Jacob put Joseph before us, his elders (*Gen. 37:3, 4*).

**Judah:** To add insult to injury our mother Leah had to purchase sexual intercourse from Jacob. Rachael wanted some of Reuben's Mandrake fruit, and so she told my mother Leah she would allow Jacob to spend the night with her, for some of Reuben's mandrake fruit (*Gen. 30:14*). Our sister Dinah was born out of that insult! Jacob became a whore for Rachael. Our anger was bitter towards Jacob, to the point that Reuben went and had sex with one of Jacob's women Bilhah, just to spite him (*Gen. 35:22*).

**Judah:** I "took" the daughter of Shuah a Canaanite (*Gen. 38:2*). I raped the Canaanite woman and and got three sons out of her. Er was my firstborn, Onan was next, and then Shelah was youngest. I "took" another Canaanite girl named Tamar for my oldest son Er, but the Lord murdered Er (*Gen. 38:7*). I "gave" Tamar to my next son Onan, but the Lord murdered Onan also (*Gen. 38:10*). I promised Tamar that I would marry her to Shelah my youngest son when he came of age, but I broke my promise.

Tamar found out that I would be going a certain way, and she disguised herself as a prostitute, and sat by the road I would be traveling on (*Gen. 38:13*). When I saw her I thought that she was a prostitute and had sex with her (*Gen. 38:16*).

It was only later that I discovered that I had impregnated my daughter-in-law (*Gen.38:24*). She had twins who were named Pharez, and Zarah (*Gen. 38:27*). None of Israel are Judeans, except my tribe Judah. All Jews (Judeans) are a whore tribe, who came into existence from my (Jacob's) incest, and prostitution, with Tamar the Canaanite/Hamite girl that I defiled.

Bible/Torah

# Soliloquies of Chaos
# Tamar

*Judah — Taking Canaanite Girls — Prostitution — Whore Tribe — Bilhah/Zilpah*

**Tamar:** Judah saw a Canaanite woman that he liked. He "took" her and impregnated her with three sons. These three sons were named Er, Onan, and Shelah (*Gen. 38:2-5*). When Er the oldest became of age Jacob came and "took" me (Tamar) from my father's house to be Er's "wife" (*Gen. 38:6*). When Er passed away Jacob sent his son Onan to be my "husband." Onan died also and I was left in a terrible place, for the men of my own people would not have anything to do with me, for they considered me a used woman, and a whore, "defiled" in the Israeli household of Judah. The Lord of Israel hated Canaan, because he exposed Noah, as a sodomite. The Lord of Israel was protecting all crimes that the Israelis committed, against we Canaanites (*Gen. 35:5*). Judah had raped the other Canaanite girl to get his three sons, and then force me to be with his first two sons, from rape.

When Shechem had "taken" Dinah" he wanted to marry her and went with his father to ask her father Jacob's permission (*Gen. 34:2*). When Judah came and "Took" the Canaanite girl he did not ask her father's permission, nor did he even marry her. He just made her pregnant with his sons. Then when Jacob came and "took" me from my father's house he did not ask permission from my father or me. Jacob just "took" me and declared me to be the wife of his son Er, and then the wife of Onan. Jacob had treated me like a whore, for his sons, and then he was through with me, and sent me back in ruins to my father's house (*Gen. 38:11*). I was ruined, for there was no dowry, or permission, or marriage ceremony offered, as when Shechem the Canaanite wanted to "take" Dinah in marriage (*Gen. 34:4, 11, 12*). Levi and his brothers had murdered and entire city of our Canaanite brothers. The Israelis had lied and said that Shechem had treated Dinah like a whore, even though the Prince of Shechem did right by Dinah (*Gen. 23:10-12*).

My father had a right to take vengeance for the way Judah had treated me. But no Canaanite dared even question the unjust actions of any Israeli, for we in the land of Canaan were still under the terror of the Lord of the Israeli, and his Host (*Gen. 35:5*).

My father could not take care of me forever, and no other Canaanite man would look my way. I had no other choice than to become a whore for Jacob, the one who had made me a whore. When I found out that he would be coming a certain way, I disguised myself as a prostitute and waited for him (*Gen. 38:13, 14*). Jacob came, saw me and thought that I was a harlot (veiled whore), because my face was covered (*Gen. 38: 15*). Jacob made me pregnant with twins, and later when he was told that I was pregnant he wanted to set me on fire. We Canaanites had no say so over ourselves in our own land, So Jacob sent men to my father's house, to bring me to him to be burnt (*Gen. 38:24*). Judah wanted to know who the father was, and I showed him items he had left behind, when he had been with me. Now he knew that he was the father of my twin sons (*Gen. 38:25-27*). Jacob submitted that since these twin sons were his from an act of prostitution, that it was ok. All trues Jews (Judeans) that have ever existed descended from my two sons, from incest and prostitution, Pharez, and Zarah (*Gen. 38:29, 30*). Pharez one of my twin sons is the father of Hezron and Hamul (*Gen. 46:12*). Thus the Jews the children of Judah began with incest, prostitution, and rape. Bilhah and Zilpah became the mothers of half of Jacob's children, by his raping them!

Soliloquies

Bible/Torah

# Soliloquies of Chaos
# Bilhah/Zilpah

*Tamar — Rape Children — Famine — Saved by Egypt— Moses*

**Bilhah:** Jacob had been raping Zilpah and I, long before he took Tamar and the other Canaanite girls (*Gen. 30:3-5, 7, Gen. 30:10, 12, Gen. 35:26*). Jacob's two cousin/wives Leah and Rachael were having a contest with my and Zilpah's bodies, to see which one of us Jacob could give the most babies. No man has a right to penetrate a woman without her permission, it is rape. Zilpah and I were in fear of our lives, if we refused to have sex with Jacob! We did not want to have children for him. Jacob was already having sex with, and committing incest with his two first cousins, Rachael and Leah. And it was they who helped Jacob to abuse us. What is the nature of women who would help a man rape other women?

When I went to lay with Reuben on Jacob's couch that was the only time that I had a chance to be with someone, by my own choice (*Gen. 35:22*).

**Bilhah:** But our burden was light compared to the girls, and women of the Canaanite city of Salem/Shechem. The "sons" of Jacob entered that city and murdered all of the men and boys and took all of the girls and women of that city, to do with them what Jacob had done to Zilpah and I. Leah, Rachael, Zilpah, and I, were forced to hold the girls and women of Shechem down, while our sons raped themselves into tribal existence. In so doing we lost the little self respect that we still had for ourselves. The children that came into existence from these rapes, were Rape Tribes, the twelve tribes of Jacob, or Israel. The Lord watched them come into existence!

**Zilpah:** The ground was always cursed and famished, wherever the Lord went from Nod to the Land of Canaan (*Gen.12:10, Gen.26:1*). The Lord is the Adam or Man for whose sake the ground was cursed (*Gen. 3:17*). Jacob (Israel) and his sons eventually had to flee from the Lord and his famine in Canaan so as not to perish (*Deut. 26:5*). The Pharaoh sent wagons to rescue us (*Gen. 45:19*). When the Israelis fled the land of Canaan in the wagons that the Egyptians sent, they were just as destitute as Abraham and the Lord had been. The Israelis were fleeing the Lord's third famine, in the land of Canaan. The Lord had famished Canaan in Abram's time, Isaac's time, and Jacob's time (*Gen. 12:10; 26:1; 42:5*). The Egyptians gave Jacob (Israel) sanctuary in the land of Egypt, to save themselves from the Lord's bondage and famine in Canaan (*Gen. 42:5*).

**Zilpah:** The group that went from the famine in Canaan to Egypt was made up of incubi*, incest, rape, and murder. Of the 93 people that went to Egypt there were only 15 Israelis: Jacob, Leah, Rachael, the eleven sons, and Dinah. The other 78 were Bilhah, myself (Zilpah), the raped girls and women of Shechem, and the children from their being raped (*Gen. 46:7-26*). None of the women were "Jacob's sons wives" (*Gen. 46:26*), but were hostages held in bondage to Jacob's "sons." Of these "sons" only seven came out of the loins of Jacob (*Gen. 46:26*): Issachar, Zebulun, Gad, Asher, Benjamin, Dan and Napthali. The other five Reuben, Simeon, Levi, Judah, and Joseph were the sons of the Lord, who committed Incubi with Leah (4), and Rachael (1). This mixture called Israel had no intentions of ever returning to Canaan, to be in bondage to the Lord again. All Israelis that ever came into existence were from this rape and incest that continued even in Egypt.

Moses and Aaron were both born by incest committed between Jochebed and her nephew Amram (*Ex. 6:20*).

Soliloquies

# Soliloquies of Chaos
# Moses

*Incest Tribes— Best Land — Hibernation — Overpopulation*

**Moses:** Israel went from being Rape Tribes in Canaan, to being Incest Tribes in Egypt. My brother Aaron and I were born of incest between Jochebed, and her nephew Amram (*Numbers 26:59*). Just before my birth Egypt was in a crisis. Incestuous Israel had been multiplying in Egypt four hundred years. They had fled to Egypt from the land of Canaan to save themselves from the Lord's famine (*Deut. 26:5*). The Pharaoh of that time had sent wagons up to Canaan, to bring Jacob, and his family down to Egypt (*Gen. 46:6*). The Lord had even suggested that they go to Egypt, to save themselves from his famine (*Gen. 46:3*)! But then the Lord left his Host in Canaan and followed Jacob, and his little band into Egypt (*Gen. 46:4*). The Lord's famine spread from his Host in the land of Canaan (*Gen. 47:13*), to himself, in Egypt. The Lord's famine spread to wherever he went.

### Best Land

**Moses:** The Egyptians put Jacob and and his family in Goshen on the very best land in Egypt (*Gen. 47:6, 11*). The Israelis were also given the very best of food, while the Egyptians suffered through the famine caused by the presence of the Lord (*Gen. 47:13*). In the end the Egyptians watered their sparse gardens, by running water down their big toes (*Deut. 11:10*). All of the land of Canaan and Egypt were on the verge of collapse from the Lord's plagues. The money in Egypt failed, and the Egyptians had to sell their cattle, possessions, and even the land that they were living on. Finally the citizens of Egypt even enslaved themselves for food (*Gen. 47:14-26*). We Israelis were guests, and never suffered the indignity that the Egyptians suffered, in their own country. We Israelis did not work, but were given great but unearned wealth, and possessions. In our idleness, we Israelis had time to multiply great in numbers (*Gen. 47:27*). The Lord retreated from Egypt, back up into the land of Canaan, after seven years of entrenching Israel in Egypt.

### Hibernation

**Moses:** There in the land of Canaan the Lord and his Host went into hibernation, in the caves of mount Horeb, and the famine ceased everywhere, and all began to grow again in Egypt and Canaan. The Lord and his Host would hang up side down, from the roofs of the caves of mount Horeb, for four hundred years waiting for the Israelis to call them forth out of suspension. But Israel had no intention of ever calling on the Lord, or returning to the land of Canaan!

Jacob was only in Egypt for for 17 years before he died. When the Israelis took Jacob's body back to bury him in the land of Canaan, the Canaanites were threshing and grounding wheat. The people had never had to leave Canaan, even in the worst of the Lord's famine there. Canaan had thoroughly recovered from the Lord's famine. The famine was completely gone, and as such the Israelis could have stayed in Canaan, without returning to Egypt (*Gen. 50:10*). But when they had buried Jacob the Israelis rushed back to Egypt, without awakening the Lord. Jacob's burial was the only time that Israel left Egypt. Israel spent the next four hundred years in Egypt, and they had no intentions of ever leaving again!

### Overpopulation

Bible/Torah

# Soliloquies of Chaos
# Moses

*Overpopulation — Birth Control — Prince of Egypt.*

**Moses:** But by the time of my birth, my people the Israelis were creating a crisis in Egypt, because we refused to leave (*Ex. 1:12*). We Israelis were multiplying faster than the Egyptians, and we were not contributing any thing to the Egyptian economy (*Ex. 1:9*). Yet Israel was consuming greater than the Egyptians themselves. If Israel had left Egypt and gone back to Canaan the problem would have been solved. The King of Egypt wanted Israel to leave not stay (*Ex. 1:10*). But the Israelis refused to leave Egypt, to return to Canaan.

## Birth Control

**Moses:** The new king over Egypt decided to end the hospitality that had been extended to the Israelis as guests (*Ex. 1:8*). The Pharaoh decreed that after four hundred years Israel would no longer be considered as guest. Furthermore since they refuse to leave they would now carry the status of permanent Egyptian citizenships. Jacob had claimed as much, when he called himself Egyptian (מצרי), Or Syrian (צרי)(*Deut. 26:5*). The Pharaoh instructed that as citizens of Egypt the Israelis were to be taught to build homes for themselves, to relieve the Egyptians who had built every home for them, since they came to Egypt. The Israelis were to be taught to work, like the Egyptian had always worked. They would make the bricks, and mortar, and do their own work whether they want to or not (*Ex. 1:13-15*)!

Secondly the Pharaoh instituted a birth control program to stop the massive increase in the Israeli population. The Egyptian threat to kill all Israeli male children, was more an incentive to make Israel leave, than anything else (*Exodus 1:22*). The whole purpose in it all was not to punish or enslave Israel, but to send them back to the land of Canaan, to allow Egypt to recover from Israel's protracted stay. Egypt needed for Israel to leave, but did not want to drive them out (*Ex. 6:1, Ex. 10:11*). The Israelis would not leave Egypt, even when the Egyptians threatened the life of their male children. Israel knew that the Egyptian threat was not real.

If the Pharoah's birth control program threat was real, I (Moses) would have been killed, as an Israeli male child! The Pharaoh and other Egyptians knew that his daughter had not been pregnant, she was not married, was still a virgin, and did not have milk to nurse me (*Ex. 2:7, 9*). And the Pharaoh and other Egyptians knew that I was an Israeli male (*Ex. 2:5-10*).

No Egyptian protested the princess claiming me an Israeli male as her son. It was on this basis that Pharaoh's daughter claimed me: I had wooly hair and brown skin like her, as all Israelis and Egyptians had wooly hair and brown complexions. Pharoah's daughter even had my own mother Jochebed to nurse me into youth (*Ex. 2:7, 8*), and then the Princess raise me an Israeli male, in the Pharoah's house as an Egyptian prince, into Egyptian manhood.

## Prince of Egypt

As a young Egyptian man, I accidently killed another Egyptian, for hitting an Israeli who refused to work (*Ex. 2:12*). I fled through the Reed Sea, or Bulrush Sea, to Midian.

I crossed the Sea of Reeds (Reed Sea) eastward from Egypt over into the land of Ishmael/Midian, the children of Abraham, where I met Jethro and his daughters. I married

Bible/Torah

# Soliloquies of Chaos
# Moses

*Prince of Egypt — Prince of Darkness — Drive them out*

Jethro's elder daughter, Zipporah, and we had two sons, Gershom, and Eliezer (*Ex. 18:3, 4*).

The Lord had gone into hibernation there in mount Horeb, in Canaan, thinking that when the Israelis had multiplied in Egypt, that they would call on his name to awaken him, or that the Israelis would return, to Canaan to awaken him. But in four hundred years we had forgotten him.

### Prince of Darkness

**Moses:** When I came to mount Horeb I met the Lord, who said that he and his Host had been awakened by the Israelis crying in Egypt (*Ex. 3:7*). The Lord told me that he had appeared to Abraham, Isaac, and Jacob as El Shaddai (God of Devils) .... (*Ex. 6:3*). The Lord told me that he was the **Lord in the bowels of the ground** (*Ex. 8:21*). He also told me indirectly that he was **Baal Zebub,** or the **Lord of the Flies**: The Lord said that he had control enough over flies, that he could cause them to be in all parts of Egypt, and yet cause the flies not to be in Goshen, where the Israelis lived (*Ex. 8:24, 31*). The Lord was also a **"Man (Super Man) of War"** (*Ex.15:3*). The Lord had many names, but none of them were written in the Lamb's Book of Life (*Rev. 13:8*). **Prince of Darkness** was another of his names. I entered his Thick Darkness in Mount Horeb (Horrible), and I would have to reenter this same **Thick Darkness** when he relocated it to Egypt (*Ex 10:22, Deut. 4:11*). The Day of the Lord is Absolute Darkness (*Amos 5:18, 20*), a Darkness that can be felt (*Ex. 20:21*).

### The Lord In Pharaoh

**Moses:** The Lord told me to return to Egypt, and to tell the Pharaoh to let his people go. But the Lord knew that the Pharaoh was not holding Israel, but was trying to get rid of them (*Ex. 1:10*), but Israel refused to leave! Israel had been free to go without the Pharaoh's permission! The Egyptians were not keeping us there in Egypt, we kept our selves there, for four hundred years. Israel did not want to fall, back into bondage to the Lord again! The Lord knew that Israel would not leave Egypt with him. So the Lord told me he would make "no" come out of the Pharaoh's mouth each time I, Moses told Pharaoh that the Lord said "let my people go" (*Ex. 4:21*). Each time I talked to the Pharaoh, I would be talking to the Lord! It was the Lord who would be **hard hearted** inside of the Pharoah's body (*Ex. 4:21, Ex.7:3, Ex. 14:4*). The response "no" from the Pharaoh would give the Lord, and his Host the excuse to destroy Egypt. The Lord wanted to punish Egypt for giving Israel extended sanctuary. Also totally destroying Egypt, was the only way that the Lord could force the Israelis out!

Before I left the Land of Midian to return to Egypt, the Lord showed me his powers, by turning my brown hand pale, like the Caucasian children of Cain who were pale. Then the Lord turned my hand back brown again (*Exodus 4:6, 7*). Then the Lord sent my family and I back, and I, met my brother Aaron on our way back to Egypt. We all parted the Sea of Reeds (Reed Sea) and walked through them dry shod a second time, going back to Egypt! This was the same "Reed Sea" that would be parted to bring the Israelis out of Egypt.

It was a very strange scene when I stood before the Pharaoh and demanded that he let my people go. The Pharoah's first response was a large smile, and an affirming nod, of his head. But

Bible/Torah

# Soliloquies of Chaos
# Moses

*Lord in The Pharoahx— Stealing From Friends — Driven Out — Firstborn*

in the same instance that the Pharaoh opened his mouth to say "yes, and good riddance," the Lord made the word "No" come out of the Pharoah's mouth! The poor Pharaoh had a very strange look on his face, as he continued to nod, and say yes, while the Lord kept making "no" come out of his mouth!

This was the Lord, giving himself the excuse to began destroying Egypt. The Lord absolutely took the Pharoah's body over. A normally peaceful man who represented a peaceful people, the Pharoah with the the Lord inside him became a hard hearted man (*Ex.4:21*). It was the Lord being hard hearted inside of Pharoah (*Ex. 10:1*). It was the Lord in charge inside of the Pharoah's body telling Moses "no." It was also the Lord inside Pharaoh instructing the task masters, to increase punishment on the Israelis (*Ex. 5:6-14*). Then it was the Lord again who took revenge against Egypt, when the taskmasters punished Israel! Then it was the Lord again still in the Pharoah's body pretending to be the Pharaoh, more determined to not let the Israelis go (*Ex. 5:23*). The **Lord** and his Host plagued Egypt with all of his **diseases and infections,** he had brought to Egypt (*Exodus 15:26, Deut. 7:15*). Each time the Lord and his Host destroyed more, until there was nothing left to destroy. That is when the Lord removed himself, from inside the Pharoah, and allowed the now confused pharaoh to finally drive us Israelis out (*Ex. 1:10, Ex. 6:1, Ex. 12:33*), while the Lord pulled us out, with a mighty hand (*Deut. 4:34*). They had to work together to get us out! It was very obvious, that Israel did not want to leave Egypt, and in spite of everything, many Israelis broke away from the exodus, and fled back into Egypt! No one wanted to go with the Lord, even though Egypt was in ruins!

The Lord and his Host had descended on Egypt, with his Thick Outer Darkness, to reclaim Israel from the Light (*Exodus 10:22*). Now that the Lord had Israel back in his Thick Darkness that could be felt (*Ex. 10:21*), he could take his revenge on them!

### Stealing From Friends

**Moses:** With Egypt mostly destroyed, the Lord instructed me to order the Israelis to "borrow" clothes, and jewelry from the Egyptians, knowing that the Israelis would never return the items (*Exodus 3:22*). The Lord's justification for his holocaust against Egypt was to "make Israel free" from the Egyptians. But the Lord was not making Israel free, but bringing Israel back into bondage to himself (*Exodus 3:7, 8*). Israel was "free" in Egypt, and knew that the Lord was going to take revenge on them, for staying in Egypt for hundreds of years to avoid him! Also Israel did not knowingly call the Lord down, to Egypt.

### Driven out

**Moses:** When we came forth from Egypt we had flocks, herds, gold, silver, and all kinds of possessions (*Ex. 12:32*), like Abraham and Sarah (*Gen. 12:16, 20*). Slaves do not own anything, not even their own selves! We had not been in bondage in Egypt. Nor had we ever been in bondage to any man (*John 8:33*), except the Lord, a Superman (*Ex. 15:3*).

Israel had been in Egypt for 430 years when the Egyptians **drove us out** (*Ex.6:1*). Egypt was in

Bible/Torah

# Soliloquies of Chaos
# Moses

*Firstborn Sodomized — Reed Sea — Man of War — Sodomized Israel*

ruins: many of the firstborn of Egypt were dead, we had stolen portions of the Mesoretic Text, and we had stolen much, of the small amount that the Egyptians still had left, after the Lord's Holocaust on Egypt. Egypt was spoiled and in total ruin (*Ex. 12:36*), as the Lord had ruined Ur/Babel (*Gen. 11:9, Isaiah 23:13*). Still not wanting to leave Egypt, we had to be driven out.

### Sodomized Firstborn

**Moses:** In almost the same instance that we were driven out of Egypt, the Lord began to bring Israel back into bondage. His first action was against our firstborn sons (*Ex.13:2, Ex.13:13, 15*). We had to "Sanctify" (קדש) them to the Lord, which was to perform Ritual Religious Sodomy (קדש) on them. We were to bring them three times in the year to the Lord (*Ex. 34:23, 25*). None were to appear before the Lord with empty hands (*Ex. 34:20*). *See Strong's Concordance #s 6942, 6944, 6945 these are Sanctify, Sodomy, and Holy in that order.*

The Lord commanded we molest our children, even before we had gone away from the vicinity of Egypt!

### Reed Sea Wilderness Revisited

**Moses:** The "Red Sea" that we were now crossing was the same "Reed Sea," that I had crossed going to the land of Midian. It was the same Reed Sea that Aaron crossed, also coming to meet me in Midian. Aaron and I crossed the sea of Reeds a third time, returning from Midian back to Egypt. Now driven out of Egypt, we Israelis were to cross the Sea of Reed or Bulrush, to the land of Midian again. But the people reluctant to leave Egypt, were now reluctant to pass through the bulrush still wanting to return to Egypt.

Thus the Lord took control over the Pharaoh again, and caused Pharaoh to send an army of chariots, to force the the Israelis to flee, through the Sea of Reeds (*Gen. 14:8-20*).

*The entire scenario from Exodus 14:21 to Exodus 14:30 is a modern invention. The parting of the "sea" was not a sea of water, but a "Sea of Reeds (Yom Suf/יום סוף)." The Egyptians could not have drowned in a sea of bulrush (reeds) except as a metaphor. (Ex. 15:4, 6).*

### Man of War

**Moses:** We Egyptian Israelis that crossed through the Reed Sea were peaceable, like the children of Ham, who taught us peace (*I Chron. 4:40*). The Lord was a **Man of War** (*Ex. 15:3*), and he had to make us same as himself, for us to destroy Canaan, and Ishmael/Midian.

My father-in-law Jethro the Midianite was descendant from Abraham's son Ishmael (*Gen. 36:4*). Ishmael and Midian the sons of Abraham were Hamites, like their mothers Hagar and Keturah. Yet Ishmael's descendant Jethro was a "Friend of our God" (Reuel / ראול) the Lord, a Man of War (*Gen. 15:3, Gen. 18:8-12*). Jethro helped me set Israel to order, so that I could manage them for the Lord (*Gen. 18:14-26*).

### Sodomized Israelis and Rabbis

**Moses:** Then Jethro went home, and Israel stood before Horeb, the mount of Sinai. I went up to

Bible/Torah

# Soliloquies of Chaos
# Moses

*Sodomized Israel — Israeli Slaves to Israelis — Holocaust*

be instructed by the Lord. The Lord placed a covenant before me, that Israel would be a Kingdom of Priest, a Holy (חללי / Corrupt) Nation (Goyim)(*Ex. 19:6*). The Israeli elders agreed, and the next step was for us all to be "sanctified" (קדש)(*Ex. 19:10, 14*), like we had sanctified our firstborn sons (*Ex. 13:2*). The priest even had to "sanctify" each other (*Ex. 19:22*). Sanctification (קדש) is the act of religious sodomy (קדש)(*Deut. 23-17*).

Once we had performed these acts upon each other we were instructed, to wash our selves and our garments (*Ex. 19:10, 14*). After being "sanctified" and therefore made "holy" (קדש / חולי) the Lord gave me several commandments. Six of the commandments that we were given were: Honor your mother and father, don't kill, don't commit adultery, don't steal, don't bear false witness, and don't covet the possessions of others (*Ex. 20:12-17*). But how could we honor any of these commandments, we had violated it all, in the process of coming into existence, as a people. Now the Lord had made us commit the acts of **sanctification** (Sodomy) to make us **holy** (Corrupt)! We were rapidly being corrupted, and brought back into bondage to the Lord. I now had to reenter the **Thick Darkness,** where the Lord was to further instruct me (*Ex. 20:21*). The Lord gave us guidelines as to how to build altars, on which we would pour out all of the blood, of all of our herds to him (*Ex. 20:24-26, Lev.* ), as Noah had on Mt. Ararat (*Gen. 8:20*).

### Lord's Slaves

Now that we were all sodomized, and the Lord had us sacrificing our herds to him, he also commanded that we enslave each other, with all of the tragedy that goes with it (*Ex.21:1-11*)! It started with Indentured Servitude of seven years (*Ex. 21:2*). If the indentured Israelite got married while in service his wife would be enslaved, even after the man's service was finished (*Ex. 21:3*). The man's children would also be slaves (*Ex. 21:4*). This was to make the man self enslave himself forever (*Ex. 21:5*). The man would have to sign papers, and have his ear bored through. Both acts were to legalize his self enslavement (*Ex. 21:6*).

An Israeli man could sell his daughter into slavery (*Ex. 21:7*). But the Israeli owner could not sell her again except to another Israeli (*Ex. 21:8*). But if the buyer kept her he must feed her, cloth her, and sexually service her (*Ex. 21:9*). Otherwise the man must set her free (*Ex. 21:11*).

Yet the Lord insisted on slavery, even though we were never in bondage to any man (*Matt. 8:33*). In Egypt there was no slavery at all (*Exodus 21:12 to Exodus 22:31*).

The Lord commanded that I and Aaron and seventy-two elders, come up the mountain (*Ex.24:1*). We saw the Lord our God, and he had feet and hands, and we saw the other Gods (Hosts) also (*Ex. 24:10*). These were the Gods, the Host of the Lord. They had smote Egypt with plagues (*I Sam. 4:8*). We sat down with them, and ate and drank (*Exodus 24:11*), as Abraham had sat, and eaten with them (*Gen. 18:5-8*).

We came down the mountain with instructions to build a tabernacle, a table and all of the instruments necessary to perform all of the rituals, that the Lord wanted us to perform along with sacrificing (קדש) all of our animals, and sanctifying (קדש) our first born sons.

Bible/Torah

# Soliloquies of Chaos
# Moses

*Holocaust — Coven/Covenant—Horns — Kosher Starvation*

### Golden Calf Massacre

**Moses:** I was on Mount Horeb with the Lord, when the Israelis began to worship the golden calf (thigh)(*Ex. 32:4*). The Lord sent me down with the two tables, with the ten commandments on them. When I came down. they were worshiping the golden thigh (calf). In anger I broke the the tables of commandments, and broke the golden calf (leg) also. The Lord wanted to kill them all, but I convinced him to spare them (*Ex. 32:11-14*). I wanted to sort them out by their own choice, as to whether they would follow the Lord or not (*Ex. 32:26*). All of the men of my tribe, Levi came to my side, and we slew around three thousand, who refused to come back to the Lord (*Ex. 32:27, 28*). When we had finished with them the Lord came and took his revenge on the others with his plagues (*Ex. 32:35*).

Then the Lord came to me and spoke to me face to face as a man speaks to his friend (*Ex. 33:11*). That is when I asked him if he would except this Goyim (Nation), Israel as his People (*Ex. 33:13*). I asked the Lord to except us as his people and his inheritance from the Most High. (*Ex. 34:9, Deut. 32:8, 9*). The Lord excepted us, and declared that he was the Rock who had formed (חלל / corrupted) us (*Deut. 32:17*).

### Coven / Covenant

**Moses:** The Lord excepted us, and made a Covenant with us, that he would use us to do wonders (atrocities)(נפלאת / **Felony** Crimes) for him (*Ex. 34:10*)! We would kill or drive out the tribes of Canaan, and destroy their gardens, and groves (*Ex. 34:13*). The people of Canaan did not have altars, and their "images" were just colorful mural painted on the walls of their homes. We destroyed it all. This was the same place in Canaan that Israel had fled from 400 years ago, to survive the Lord's famine. Now the Lord made us destroy these people, simply because he was jealous of them (*Ex. 34:14*). Now we were in deep bondage to the Lord again, for he commanded that we give him our first born sons, as a sacrifice (*Exodus 34:19*). The only way we could save our sons from sacrificing them to the Lord was to redeem them by sacrificing an animal in the place of our sons. If we refused then the Lord wanted for us to break the child's neck (*Ex. 13:13*). None of us must appear before the Lord with empty hands (*Ex. 34:20*). We were to appear before the Lord three times a year with our first born sons (*Ex. 34:23*). The Lord made me write this down along with a covenant, of ten commandments (*Ex. 34: 27*).

### Horns

**Moses:** I was on the mountain with the Lord again for 40 days writing down the words of the covenant (*Ex. 34:28*). Thus a holocaust was established, against the lands and people of Canaan. By the time I came down from the mount from talking with the Lord, I had a set of **horns growing out of my forehead.** I veiled my face, to not frighten the people (*Ex.34:29, 30, 35*).

I stood before the elder of the people, and read the commandments of the Lord to them. All that we had brought from Egypt would be used up to make the instruments, to sacrifice all that we had to the Lord Hallel. The Ark, the jewelled breastplate, jewelled garments, Tabernacle

Bible/Torah

# Soliloquies of Chaos
# Moses

*Kosher Starvation — Pale Lepers — Incestuous Israel*

(tent) and it's furniture, curtains, altars, knives, frying, pans, etc., would all be used to sacrifice all of the animals, flocks and herds to the Lord as burnt offerings (*Ex. 35:1- Ex. 39:43 - Ex. 40:38 - Leviticus 1:1*). Noah had sacrificed the animals of the ark, on Ararat, after the flood (*Gen. 8:20*).

### Kosher Starvation

The Lord commanded that we only eat certain animals, and not eat other kinds. All of the animals that we were told it was ok to eat, were the same animals that all were to be sacrificed to the Lord! The animals that we were told not to sacrifice were also the animals that we could not eat, by commandment (*Lev. 11:1-23, Lev. 11:26-43*). This meant that eventually we would starve.

Cain and Abel had only sacrificed a little grain, and a few sheep (*Gen. 4:3, 4*), and secondly Cain sodomized, and murdered his effeminate brother/wife Abel (*Gen. 4:7*). But we Israelis were starved, and forced to sodomize each other, and our children. Plus we poured tons of blood, from our herds, and flocks, into the ground, to the Lord (*Gen. 9:4, Lev. 17:10, 13, 14 etc.*). Next we were commanded to sacrifice to the Lord by murder, in a great holocaust, hundreds of thousands of Ishmael/Midianites, the true children of Abraham.

### Pale Lepers

The Lord had put a mark on his son Cain in Nod to make Cain a Pale Leper (Tamihu / טמא / Contaminated/Unclean)(*Lev. 10:10*). Now the Lord was doing the same to us the Israelis in the wilderness. We were brown and wooly headed, like Cain had been. The Lord had marked Cain (*Gen. 4:15*). He had marked my hand (*Ex. 4:6*), and had marked my sister Miriam (*Nu. 12:10*). Now he began to mark the people of Israel with the same Pale Leprosy while we were still in the wilderness. Some people had scabs, open wounds, and sores (*Lev. Chptr. 13*). Some were splotched in complexion, with lighter and darker spots on the skin. This was called Unclean (Tamia / טמיא) Leprosy (*Lev. 13:1-11*). The ideal leper turned white or pale evenly all over the body, had no open wounds, and the hair turned blond (yellow)(*Lev. 13:30*). These pale leper Israelis were called **Clean Lepers**, and were excepted (*Lev. 13:12, 13, 16, 17, 32, 36*).

Those pronounced unclean (Tamia / טמא) lepers were banished from the camps (*Lev. 13:46*). There was all kinds of infections, plagues, and diseases in the midst of the tribes of Israel, they all originated from the Lord. These were the same horrible condition that the Lord had brought to Egypt, and imposed upon the Egyptians (*Ex.15:26, Deut. 7:15*). To relieve ourselves from the Lord's own plagues which was on us, the Lord instructed us to do ritual sacrifice in diverse ways (*Lev. 14:1- 15:33, Lev. 16:34, Lev. 17:16*).

### Incestuous Israel

**Moses:** In two verses the Lord accused the Egyptians, and the Canaanites of incest and bestiality (*Leviticus 18:3, 40*). We had no other scripture that supports that Egyptians or Canaanites ever practiced these corrupt activities (*Lev. 18:3, 24-27, Lev. 20:23*). Yet our record are filled with verses, that speak to the casual incest practiced by Israelis, and those we descended from. Yet the Lord

Bible/Torah

# Soliloquies of Chaos
# Moses

### *Incest Israel*

instructed me to tell the Israeli not to commit incest (*Lev. 18:6*):

1) Don't have **sex with your mother/father** (*Lev. 18:7*). Milcah had five children with her son Kemuel. (*Gen. 22:21-22*). Kemuel was having sex with his father's wife/sister Milcah. Both Kemuel and his mother/aunt/lover Milcah were suppose to be put to death (*Lev. 20:11*). 1a) Lot had sex with, and impregnated both of his daughters (*Gen. 20:30-38*)

2) Don't have **sex with your step mother** (*Lev. 18:8*). Reuben had sex with Bilhah Jacob's woman (*Gen. 35:22*).

3) Don't have **sex with your sister** (*Lev. 18:9, Lev. 20:17*). Nahor married and had children with his sister Milcah (*Gen. 11:29, Gen. 22:20*). Abraham married and had sex with his sister Sarah/Iscah (*Gen. 20:5*).

4) Don't have **sex with your son's daughter, or son** (*Lev. 18:10*). Noah attempted to do it with Canaan, and was exposed (*Gen. 9:21, 22*)! Shem and Japheth covered it up (*Gen. 9:23*)!

5) Don't have **sex with your father's wife's daughters** (*Lev. 18:11*). Nahor married his father Terah's daughter Milcah, and Abram married his father Terah's daughter Sarah/Iscah.

6) Don't have **sex with your aunts, or uncles** (*Lev. 18:12, Lev. 20:19, 20*). Amram (my father) was married to his aunt Jochebed. Aaron and I are children of their incest.

7) Don't have **sex with your mother's, or father's sister** (*Lev. 18:13*). Amram with Jochebed

8) Don't have **sex with your uncle or aunt** (*Lev. 18:14*). Nahor with his niece Milcah, and Abraham with his niece Sarah/Iscah (*Gen. 11:29, Gen. 22:20*). **Moses:** My father Amram had sex with his aunt Jochebed and made her pregnant with Miriam, myself (Moses), and Aaron.

9) Don't have **sex with your daughter in law** (*Lev. 18:15*). Terah with his dead son Haran's wife. Judah had sex with his daughter in law Tamar, in an act of prostitution. They had two sons Pharez, and Zarah (*Gen. 38:15, 30*). Pharez and Zarah born from prostitution, are the father of all Jews (Judeans).

9) Don't have **sex with your brother's wife** (*Lev. 18:16, Lev. 20:21*). Tamar was Er's wife, and his brother Onan was forced to have sex with her (*Gen. 38:4*).

10) Don't have sex with a **woman and her daughter** (*Lev. 18:17*).

11) Don't have **sex with a woman, and her sister** (*Lev. 18:18*). Jacob was married to two sisters,

Bible/Torah

# Soliloquies of Chaos
# Moses

*Incestuous Israel — Hypocracy*

12) Don't have **sex with another man** (*Lev. 18:22, Lev. 20:13*). Noah was caught awake, naked and drunk with his grandson Canaan in his tent (*Gen. 9:21, 22*).

13) Women and men should not have **sex with animals** (*Lev. 18:23, Lev. 20:16, 17*). Shepards?

**Moses:** You do not have to tell someone not to do something unless they are already doing it! Our origin as Israelis was the very incest that we were now being told not to do anymore! Terah had sex with his dead son Haran's wife, and fathered Milcah and Sarah. Terah was committing adultery and incest with his dead son's wife (*Lev. 20:12*). Both Terah and the woman should have been put to death (*Lev. 29:10*). Terah married his two daughters Milcah and Sarah to his two sons, the girl's brothers Nahor and Abraham. Isaac was married to his first cousin Rebecca. Jacob married Leah and Rachael, his two first cousins, and fathered children with them! It is no doubt that Jacob's sons were having sex with their sister Dinah, because they did not have women of their own. Lot had sex with and made his two daughters pregnant. We the Israelis came from that twisted background. We were indeed a Holy (חולי) or "Defiled/Corrupt" people. Added to the ramped incest was the "sons" of Jacob raping the girls and women of the city of Shechem. They used these women and girls to rape themselves into tribal existence. The World (TBL) of the Lord is made up of all this rogue activity.

Next the Lord instructed us that he was Holy (profaned/defiled) and demanded that we be Holy (Corrupt/Profane) also (*Lev. 18:8, Lev. 21: 6 -7*). Holy, profane (profanity), Cursing, Defiled, sanctified etc., are all associated terms that basically means the same corrupt thing. Even the oil (שמן) for anointment is semen (שמן)(*Lev. 21:10, Lev. 21:15, 24*)!

**Hypocrisy**

**Moses:** The people of Canaan and Egypt were not ever the corruptness that the the Lord accused them of, but we were (*Lev. 18: 3, 24 - 30* ). The Lord instructed us Israeli that we must be Holy (Profane/Corrupt), because he was Holy (Corrupt/Cursed). The Lord was putting Israel in the situation of making Holy seem to be good, when actually "Holy" is the absolute corruption that represent the World of the Lord (*Lev. 19:2*). We were being told to not "profane" (חלל) the "hollowed" (קדש) when the "hollowed" (חלל) is "profane" (קדש)(*Lev. 19:8*)! The Lord commanded that we respect each other (*Lev. 19:3-28, 30-37*). We were not to make our daughters whores (קדשה)(*Deut. 23:17, Lev. 19:29*). Yet the Lord and Abraham took Sarah down into Egypt to prostitute her to the Pharaoh, to gain tremendous wealth for her brothers Abraham, and Lot (*Gen.12:15, 16*). Then they took Sarah to turn the same trick with Abimelech (*Gen. 20:2, 14, 16*). Dinah had played the whore with Shechem, to justify her brothers murdering a whole city to get it's girls and women (*Gen. 34:25-29*). Israel raped it's self into tribal existence with these girls and women. Jacob impregnated his daughter-in-law Tamar in an act of prostitution. The two sons Pharez, and Zarah born from this prostitution are the fathers of all Judeans. Judeans are the tribe of Judah (*Gen. 38:15-30*)! In actuality the Lords commandments for us Israelis to be civil towards

# Soliloquies of Chaos
# Moses

*Hypocracy — Manna*

each other, was a call for an artificial honor, among us thieves and murderers.

By imposing these contradictions upon us with his laws, commandments, and statutes, the Lord had brought us back into the deep bondage that Israel had been in to him, before Israel had fled to Egypt to save themselves from his famine, in Canaan. Now the Lord had brought Israel back to the same place in Canaan, they had fled from his famine to Egypt.

Then the Lord threatened that if we would not harken to him, and follow all of his commandments, statutes, and laws, he would impose the same plagues, famines, and maladies that he and his Host had imposed upon the Egyptians (*Lev. 26:14-41*).

The Lord reminded us that he had made a Covenant with Abraham, Isaac, and Jacob (*Lev. 26:42*). That covenant was the Lord would not destroy us, if we follow all of his commandments (*Lev. 26:43 - 46*). This covenant had been made into a vow, that we promise to stay within the good graces of the Lord. It was mandatory that each person give the vow. Each person that made the vow had to pay a fee (estimation) determined by age and gender (*Lev. 27:2, 34*).

After the "vow tax" the Lord commanded that I take a census, of how many fighting men there were, in each of the twelve tribes. There were over six hundred thousand in eleven tribes (*Numbers 1:2-46*). The eleven tribes were to be made into an army, and the Levites were to be a tribe of priest to the other tribes (*Nu. 1:47-53*). The Levites, I among them were descendants from Levi, who murdered all of the men and boys of the Canaanite city of Shechem (*Gen. 34:25*). The Levites were clerics, taking census, and keeping the tribal records. They were bankers in charge of fees for poll taxes, vow taxes etc. The Levites were also judges of the health and conduct of the other tribes (*Nu. 5:1-31,* ). The Levites were priest in charge of the tabernacle (tent), and it's instruments. They performed all sacrifice of animals to the Lord (*Nu. 3:1-4:49*). We were consumed with rituals, sacrifices, laws, rules, regulations, statutes, and fees for every action that we did (*Nu. 6:1- 9:1, 10:12*)!

## Manna

**Moses:** Now we took our journey from the foot of the Lord's Mount Horeb in the wilderness of Sinai. This was the entrance to the Land of Canaan (*Nu. 10:28*). We were led by Hobab the Midianite, the brother of my wife, the son of Jethro Reuel. Hobab wanted to return home.

It was in the third day of our journey that the people began to complain for they were starving and there was nothing to eat. We had slaughtered much of the flocks and herds, that we had brought from Egypt, to pour the blood into the ground to sustain the Lord. The remaining animals were being kept to be sacrificed to the Lord as burnt offerings. The Israelis wept that they had eaten fish and vegetables freely in Egypt, to their fill (*Nu. 11:4, 5*). Now they were starving for the Lord had taken all away, but had given them nothing (*Nu. 11:6*)! They had not asked to leave Egypt, but had been driven out by the Egyptians, because of the Lord (*Ex. 1:10, Ex. 6:1, Ex. 12:33*)! The Lord heard it and was angry at them, and sent a fire down into their midst. A great multitude of them were burned (*Nu. 11:1*). The people cried to me, and I prayed to the Lord to stop it (*Nu. 11:2*). Then Lord gave them manna to eat (*Exodus 16:5, Nu. 11:6-9*). Yet none were satisfied, for eating manna was like eating oil, and they wanted food (*Nu. 11:8*). That is when

Bible/Torah

# Soliloquies of Chaos
# Moses

### *Manna — Spying Milk and Honey*

whole flocks of quails were blown in from the sea, into the midst of the camp. The Israelis cooked some to eat, and were in the process of chewing the meat when the Lord plagued them, and they died with meat stuck in their throats (*Nu. 11:33*).

**Moses:** Everyone was angry at me because of those who had died, and Aaron and Miriam spoke unkindly to me about my wife Zipporah. Zipporah was the daughter of Jethro Reuel the Midianite, whose wife was an Ethiopian or Cushite woman (*Nu. 12:1*). To the Lord we were as the children of Ethiopia, with our wooly heads, and brown skins (*Amos 7:9*). Ethiopia (Cush), Canaan, Midian, Ishmael, they were all the same, the offspring of Ham, as the Egyptian were.

The Lord had destroyed Egypt, and now we Israelis were on our way to destroy all the rest of the Hamites, even Abraham's Ishmael/Midianite children.

The Lord was angry with Aaron and Miriam for speaking to me with disrespect (*Nu. 12:9*). That is why he turn Miriam into a pale leper (*Nu. 12:10*) as he had turned my hand, and had turned many other Israelis (*Leviticus 13th chptr.*). I begged the Lord to return my sister from looking pale, like the dead (*Nu. 12:12, 13*). The Lord banished Miriam from the camp for seven days, until she became brown again, like the Ethiopians (*Nu. 12:14,15, Amos 9:7*).

### **Spying Milk and Honey**

Then we journeyed again, and stopped in the wilderness of Paran. It was there that the Lord commanded that we send a spy from each tribe, into the land of Canaan to see the land and it's people. Was the land fat or lean? Were it's cities fortified or open? Were the people weak or strong (*Nu. 13:1-3, 17-22*)?

The spies returned in forty days, with fruit from the land, including figs, pomegranates, and a cluster of grapes, with grapes as big as plums. Two men had to carry the cluster between them on a staff (*Nu. 13:23*). Four hundred years before, this fruitful place had been famished, until Israel and the Lord had left. It was then that the land had returned to being a land that flowed with milk and honey (*Nu. 13:27, 14:8*)! The Canaanites never had to leave their land, even in the famine. Now that Israel had returned the Canaanites were as peaceable, as when the Israelis had first lived there. All of the children of Canaan still lived in their land, without a single famine in four hundred years (*Nu. 13:28, 29, Gen. 10:15, 19*) This land Canaan along with the land of Egypt, was wide, quiet and peaceable, and well watered for they of Ham had dwelt here of old (*I Chron. 4:40*). The Lord had brought us back to kill them (*I Chron. 4:41*).

**Moses:** When our spies had returned with the fruit they reported that the people in the south of Canaan were giants, the children of Anak. When the Israeli masses heard this they were afraid, and wept through the night (*Nu. 13:31-33*). They talked against Aaron and I, and accused the Lord of bringing them here to die. They wanted to return to Egypt even though Egypt still lay in ruins (*Nu. 14:1-3*).

# Soliloquies of Chaos
# Moses

*Spying Milk and Honey — Beat The Rock — Holocaust*

**Moses:** The Lord was angry again, and threatened pestilence on them, but I talked to the Lord, to save them again. But the Lord swore that he would not allow any of those who left Egypt to enter Canaan (*Nu. 14:23*). The Lord swore that their carcasses would all fall in the wilderness. Everyone from twenty years old and upwards, and their children would wander in the wilderness, for forty years until their elders had died (*Nu. 14:2 - 32, 33*). The Lord brought down a plague upon the spies who had brought back the bad news. Only the spies Joshua and Caleb were spared (*Nu.14:37*). In forty year time all of the Israelis from Egypt died, then their children died after having children of their own. Thus none who left Egypt, or their children survived except Joshua, Caleb, and I (*Nu. 37:38*). The Lord and his Host mated with the Israeli females, of the children of the children of the Israelis from Egypt, to get the Pale Lepers who came forth from the wilderness (*Lev. 13th Chptr.*).

## Beat The Rock

**Moses:** We began wearing blue fringes around the edges of our garment, by commandment from the Lord (*Nu. 15. 32-38*). The Lord had already threatened to cause the tribes to wander around in the wilderness for forty years until they all died, but he continued to level new rules and regulations on us until Israel rebelled again. It was mostly the Levites this time who questioned my and Aaron's authority (*Nu. 16:1-4*). They accused that they had been taken from a land of milk and honey, only to be murdered in the wilderness (*Nu. 16:13*). They further stated that they had not been brought to another land of milk and honey (*Nu. 16:14*). I (Moses) was angry with them, and told Korah their leader that the Lord who had favored to make them close to him, would now deal with their rebellion (*Nu. 16:8-11*).

The Lord was angry with everyone including Aaron and I, for when the Israelis thirsted the Lord told me to take a rod, and gather the people before a certain rock, and then to talk to the rock and it would give water (*Nu. 20:7, 8*). We gathered them before the rock, but then I took my rod and struck the rock, and it gave water (*Nu. 20:9-11*). The Lord was infuriated because he did not get the credit for it! He told us that neither Aaron or I would bring the children of Israel into the land of Canaan (*Nu. 20:12*). I was made to bring Aaron and his son up unto mount Hor, where the Lord was and was made to strip Aaron of his garments, and put them on his son (*Nu. 20:23-27*). Then the Lord killed Aaron, and the whole congregation saw it and mourned him (*Nu. 20: 28, 29*). The Lord would later set Aarons sons on fire for not wearing drawers in the tabernacle ( ).

## Holocaust

**Moses:** We committed holocaust against the Canaanite cities under the rule of king Arad. We utterly destroyed them, and their cities. This was the Lord's second vengeance against Canaan for having exposed Noah as a Sodomite child molester (*Nu. 21:1-3, Gen. 9:22*). The first vengeance had been the murder of the Canaanite city of Shechem (*Gen. 34:25*). Next we pitched in several places until we pitched on top of Pisgah, and sent messengers to speak to Sihon king of the Amorites, to get permission to pass through his land. He refused and we fought our way through his land to the borders of Ammon the children of Lot (*Nu. 21:24*). We dwelt in all of the Amorite

Bible/Torah

# Soliloquies of Chaos
# Moses

*Holocaust*

cities that we captured (*Nu. 21:31*). This land of the Amorites was the East Country where Abraham had sent his children, that they not interfere with Abraham raising Isaac, the Lord's son (*Gen. 25:5, 6, Joshua 24:*). The Amorites the children of Canaan never afflicted Abraham's children, as the Lord had said (*Gen. 15:13*). The Amorites and Abraham's children lived together in peace, for over four hundred years, just as the Israelis lived for four hundred years, with the Egyptians unafflicted (*John 8:33*). The children of Abraham were Ishmael/Midian. Midian mostly dwelt in the east country, and Ishmael dwelt mostly from Havilah unto Shur, that is before Egypt, as you go towards Assyria (*Gen. 25:18*). Jethro/Reuel my father-in-law was Ishmaelite, but was called a Midianite. It did not matter because they were all one, the Ishmael/Midianite children of Abraham (*Gen. 37:25, 27, 28, 36*).

It was not the Amorites who afflicted any of Abraham's children, but it was us the Israelis who had come to afflicted Ishmael/Midian (*Gen. 15:13*). The four hundred years for the children of Abraham was not Israel in Egypt, but was Ishmael/Midian four hundred years among the Amorites (*Gen. 15:13-16*). After multiplying four hundred years in Egypt, we had come to commit holocaust against them, and to subplant (Jacob / יעקב) them. The Amorites knew that we Israelis were there to to destroy Midian, and they fought Israel not only for their own survivals but for the survival of the children of Abraham. We the Israelis afflicted the Amorite children of Canaan, until none were left alive, and we took their cities as a possession (*Nu. 21:35*). These people had done no wrong.

Now we pitched our tents before Moab the other children of Sarah's brother Lot. Balak was their chief. This the East Country was where most of the Midianite children of Abraham were dwelling The elders of Moab, and the elders of Midian were afraid (*Nu. 22:1-4*). Balaam a seer among them, had seen who the Lord is. Balaam was in a trance, and had a vision with his eyes open. Balaam saw what had occurred in the past. He saw the Almighty fall when he was defeated in the heavens, and was casted down (*Revelations 12:9, Nu. 24:4*). Balaam also saw that the Most High (Sun) God had seen the Almighty fall (*Nu. 24:16*). The Almighty (Lord) is Lucifer (*Isa. 14:12*). This **Light** or knowledge of who the Lord was cancelled out the power of the **Darkness** of the Lord and we were at a stalemate. The Moab/Midian coalition was saved by the exposure of the Lord's identity for a season.

To break this stalemate "Israel dwelt in Shittim, and corrupted the people into prostituting the daughters of Moab (and Midian): וישב ישראל בשטים ויחל העם לזנות אל בנות מואב (*Nu. 25:1*).

The Lord was angry even though we had brought the Moabites into his Darkness. The Lord demanded that the heads of all the Israeli leaders involved be cut off, and hanged in the sun (*Nu. 25:3-6*). The Lord plague all of those involved, and stayed the plague only when an Israeli ran a spear through an Israeli man, and Cozbi, a Midianite woman who was having sex with him (*Nu. 25:5-8*). Twenty five thousand Israelis died, in that plague of the Lord. (*Nu. 25:9*).

Our bondage to the Lord continued to increase. In the forty years that we wondered in the wilderness waiting for all of the Egyptian Israelis to die, we were forced to sacrifice millions of animals with the appropriate rituals. We poured tons of blood into the midst of the ground where

# Soliloquies of Chaos
# Moses

*Holocaust— Heart of Darkness*

the Lord was (*Ex. 8:21*). When the forty years were gone all of the Israelis from Egypt were dead except Caleb, Joshua, and myself (*Nu. 26:63, 64*). In the same forty year period six hundred thousand new pale leper Israelis had been born in the wilderness (*Nu. 26:51*).

Now the Lord instructed us to avenge Israel against Abraham's Midianite children (*Nu. 31:1-6*). We murdered all of the Midianite males, including their kings namely Evi, Rekem, Zur, Hur, and Reba, and we also murdered Balaam the Moabite who had revealed the identity of the Lord (*Nu. 31:7*). The Israelis took all of the women and girls captive, as Levi and his brothers had taken the women and girls of the city of Shechem/Salem captive (*Nu. 31:9; Gen. 34:25-29*). They brought them into the camp after the battle. The Israeli males had sodomized (שכב) all of the women and some of the girls. They also had some little males with them. I (Moses) was angry (*Nu. 31:14-16*). I told them that they had to kill all of the little boys, and all of the women who had all been sodomized (שכב). Then I told them that they had to kill all of the little **women children** who had known man by being sodomized (שכב) also (*Nu. 31:18*). The Israeli males had saved the best of the Midianite women for themselves, and since I made them kill these women, I had to murder my wife Zipporah and my sons Gershom, and Eliezer, and Gershom's son also, for they were all Midianites too (*Ex. 2:15*)!

We had committed holocaust against the children of Abraham. After we had murdered all of the Midianite men, women, and boys, we had over thirty two thousand little pubelescent girls, that we kept for ourselves (*Nu. 31:35*). One half of these girls (16,000) went directly to those who murdered Midian (*Nu. 31:36*). Of the other 16,000 "children women," 32 were given to the Lord as his share to do with as he pleased (*Numbers 31:40*). 50 were allocated to the Levite priest, to do with as they chose (*Nu. 31:47*), and the remaining thousands of girls were given to the Israeli males who had not gone out into the killing fields.

**Heart of Darkness**

I was an old man full of the Darkness of the Lord, when the Lord took me up on the mountain. My face was horned (קרן עור פניו), I had a set of horns growing out of my forehead that the Lord had caused to grow there as a badge to how evil I was ( **Ex.34:29, 30, 35**). Because of me millions of Egyptians were dead. At least a million Israelis born in Egypt had been allowed to die wandering in the wilderness. My entire family was dead by my own hands. Hundreds of thousands of Midianite men women and boys, were dead by my command. Tens of thousands of little Midianite girls were pregnant, or had given birth to children for the Israeli males who had used these little women children, to rape themselves into being the "Seed of Abraham."

We had subplanted (Jacobed) all of the people of the plains by murdering them, and taking their place. The Israelis I brought out of the wilderness were not from Egypt. Nor were they their children, for the Egyptian Israelis and their children had been left to die in the wilderness. These who came forth from the wilderness were the Pale Leper children of the mating of the Lord and his Host, with the females of the children of the children, of the twelve tribes from Egypt (*Leviticus 13th Chptr.*).

Bible/Torah

# Soliloquies of Chaos
# Moses

*Heart of Darkness — Whores and Sodomites — Joshua*

It was these Pale Lepers Israelis who came forth from the wilderness to rape themselves into being the "seed of Abraham" with the little Midianite girls, of the "children of Abraham" (*Numbers 31:18, Gen. 25:2*).

**Moses:** There were still some Canaanites on the eastern side of the Jordan River, after we had holocausted the children of Abraham. We attacked and destroyed all of those Canaanite cities east of the Jordan River. We killed all of the male, but saved all of the women and little girls for our selves (*Deut. 20:13, 14*). I instructed the Israeli males that if they saw a beautiful woman (pubelescent girl) among the Canaanite captives that they have a desire for, and wanted her to be their wife, that they should take her home (perhaps to her dead parents house)(*Deut. 21:11*). They were to cut off all of her hair, and strip her naked (*Deut. 21:12*). She was then to be allowed one month to cry for her murdered mother and father, then the Israeli could rape her (*Deut. 21:13*). The Israeli who had violated her could continue to use her, for as long as he chose until he got tired of her, then he could send her away, even if she was pregnant with his child (*Deut. 21:14*)! An Israeli male could also mistreat an Israeli female the same way sending her out of his house (*Deut. 24:1-3*).

## Whores and Sodomites

**Moses:** There were to be no whores of the daughters of Israel, nor Sodomites of the sons of Israel. Yet all of Israel were whores and sodomites by the edicts of the Lord (*Ex. 13:2, 13, 15, Deut. 23:17*). In this land of milk and honey (*Deut. 26:15, Deut. 27:3*), Israel was reduced to eating their children (*Deut. 28:57, Isaiah 9:20, Jeremiah 19:9*). The Lord instructed us that **cursed** be he who takes **reward** to slay an innocent person. All of Israel were **cursed** because we had holocausted millions of innocent men women and children, at the command of the Lord. And then we **rewarded** ourselves by taking their land and possessions (*Deut. 27:25*). Israel was also cursed because our origin was incest, murder, rape, mischief, and mayhem (*Deut. 27:20-23*).

Now the Lord had me up on Mount Nebo, to give me my final reward, for helping him to accomplish this betrayal of the promise that he had made to Abraham. He had betrayed his promise to Abraham, and to the Egyptian Israelis also, by forcing them to die in the wilderness, never ever having seen the land that he had promised to them. Now it was my turn to be betrayed also, for having stuck the rock instead of speaking to it (*Nu. 20:9-12*)! I had been instructed to strike the first rock to get water from it, I was just doing the same thing over (*Ex. 17:5, 6*).

The Lord gave me a look at the land of Canaan where he was sending the Pale Leper Israelis to commit holocaust there (*Lev. 13th Chptr., Deut. 3:27, 28*).

I was not sick at all, and was full of life when the Lord murdered me, and buried me in an unmarked grave (*Deut. 34:5-7*). When my body was buried, I still had horns (כרן) growing out of the skin my forehead (*Ex. 34:29, 30, 35*): Michael/Melchezedek and the Lord (Devil) would contend for my body years later (*Jude 9:1*).

Joshua's holocaust on Canaan would finalize the Lord's revenge against Canaan's children, because Canaan had exposed Noah, for the child molester that he was, in service to the Lord.

Bible/Torah

# Soliloquies of Chaos
# Joshua

*Moses Atrocities — Peaceable Ham — Israelis Geneology*

**Joshua:** I am the son of Nun, and the predecessor of Moses (*Ex. 33:11*). The Lord instructed Moses to transfer authority over to me. Moses was in perfect health when the Lord killed him there on Nebo, and buried him, horns (קרן) and all in an unmarked grave (*Deut. 34:5, 6, 7*).

I was to continue the atrocities that Moses did in Canaan, east of the Jordan. But I was to cross over to the western side of the Jordan, where the rest of the Canaanites lived.

But first of all before we dealt with Canaan, we had to spue out the Nations, Gentiles, or Goyim. This land had to be cleansed of the pale leper children of Cain, who were a remnant of the overthrow of Sodom, and Gomorrah (*Gen. 19:29*), they had failed their mission. These were the nations originally from the north, that the Lord had warned us about, who committed incest, sodomy, and bestiality, like Israel (*Lev. 18th Chptr*).

After killing them we could finish the Canaanites themselves. The only crime that Canaan had done to Noah, was that Canaan told on him (*Gen. 9:24*). Canaan, and none of the other children of Ham were ever violent, but were peaceable. They were all after the Order of Melchezedek (*Hebrews 5:6*). Melchezedek was the King of Peace (Salem)(*Hebrews 7:2*), and the King of Righteousness (*Hebrews 7:2*). Even the Canaanites who had iron chariots were not war like (*Joshua 17:16, 18, Judges 1:19*). But the Lords eyes always cared for the land of Canaan (*Deut. 11:12*), for it was a land of milk, and honey (*Ex. 3:8*). We found there fat pastures, a land wide, quiet, and peaceable, for Ham's son Canaan had dwelt there of old (*I Chron. 4:40*). But we beat their houses and tents, and slaughter them all (*I Chron. 4:41*).

This was the Lord's final revenge on Canaan, that we murdered them all, took their land, and subplanted them (*Jos. 1:2 - 5*). When we Israelis are spoken of as men of valor it was not because we were brave over Ham's children (*Joshua 1:14*). We defeated people who never warred, but lived in peace. So we took their land, lived in their houses, ate their food (*Deut. 20:14*), and raped their wives, and daughters, that we kept in captivity (*Deut. 21:14*). This was after we had killed all of the, men, and boys (*Deut. 20:13*). We utterly destroyed every element of Canaan, his children (*Deut. 20:17*), for the Lord's revenge on Canaan.

Canaan was dead, and All of the Israelis who had been promised the land of Canaan, were dead in the wilderness. These Israelis that had crossed the Jordan River with me, were not the Israelis that had come from Egypt, nor were they children of the Israelis from Egypt. These Israelis that murdered Canaan, were the pale leper children of the Lord, and his Host, with the female Israelis (*Lev. 13 Chptr.*). Abraham, Isaac, Jacob, Canaan, and Israel had all been subplanted, by the Lord! But the Lord's pale Israelis did not last long, mixing with wooly brown Canaanite women.

Remnants of the Three Balls (Bals), Ju<u>bal</u> Cain, Ja<u>bal</u> Cain, and Tu<u>bal</u> Cain had all survived the flood (*Gen. 4:20-22*), and now the Israelis representing them had a foothold, and were firmly established in the midst of the Garden in the land of Canaan. This was the seed foundation of the entire World (TBL) System. It would all spread westward around the planet, from this land. The land of Canaan, the city of Jerusalem is where the Lord would call back, those pale ones, who had gone westward, with wooly headed Japheth, and became the Pale Romans, and Pale Greeks, and the rest of the Lord's Goyim (Nations/Gentiles)(*Isaiah 66:18-24*).*

---

*The Pale Leper children of the Lord's son Cain as Europeans (Romans), would be called to congregate with the Lord in Jerusalem, and Crusaders also later.

# Israeli Geneology Before Egypt

*Incest Tribes — Rape Tribes — Egyptian Israeli Tribes*

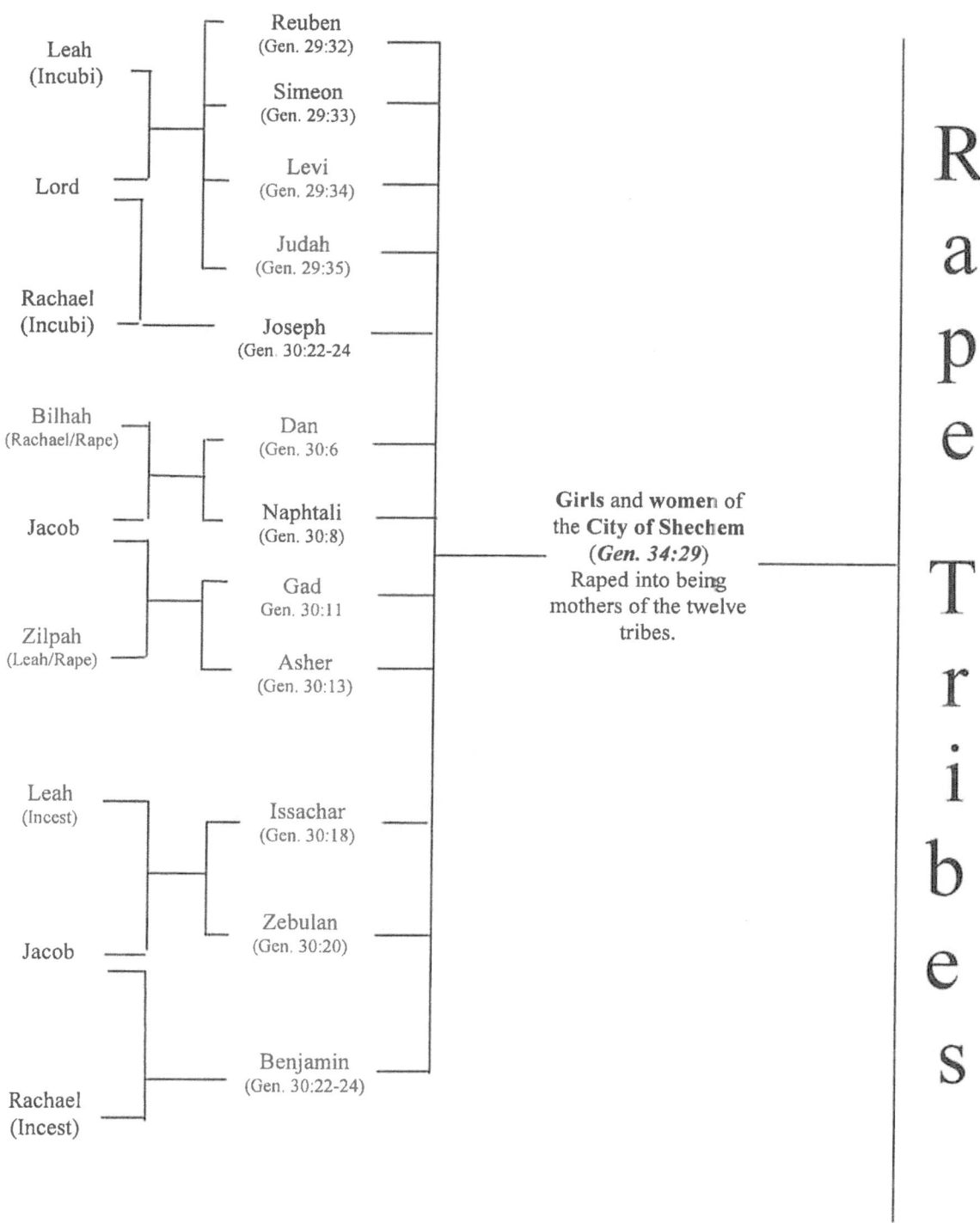

# Israeli Geneology After Egypt

*Death of Egyptian Israelis — Pale Leper Tribes — "Seed of Abraham"*

**Egyptian Tribes** | **Children of Twelve**

All of the Egyptian Israelis and their children were forced to die in the wilderness. It was the pale leper children of the children who were brought forth from the the wilderness to commit holocaust against the children of Abraham and Canaan

**Children of Children**

The "children of the children" were actually the children of the Lord and his Host with the **young Israeli females** in the wilderness. The Lord was repeating the same process he had done with the **young Chaldean Daughters** of Cain in Nod (*Isa. 47:1-6*). It was the pale leper children from the Lord who came forth from the wilderness to transform themselves (Israel) into the "Seed of Abraham," by raping to impregnate the **young Midianite females** of Abraham's children.

**Seed of Abraham**

Bible/Torah

# Soliloquies Of Chaos
# Joseph of Aram*

*Israeli Geneology — Little Egypt — Sanctification and Holiness*

**Joseph (Yusef):** My ancestors lived in northern Canaan, and saw the holocaust that Joshua committed against the people in southern Canaan. Northern Canaan was called the land of Aram The people of the land of Aram were made up of two elements. The first element were the descendants of Aram, and the second element were Egyptians (צרי), or Syrians (צרי). The two elements were so interwoven that to say Aram was to say Syrian or Egyptian. I am Joseph of Aram, or Joseph of Syria (צרי), or Joseph of Egypt (צרי). It is all the same, for Syria (צרי) is "Little Egypt (צרין)." My ancestors had came north from Egypt, and located north in Canaan, with Aram. They as Egyptians had come to assist Nimrod and thousands of others who had come to build Ur/Babel, for Cain's pale Gentile children. Once they had helped to build Ur/Babel, some stayed north with Aram, and became known as Syrians (צרי), or Egyptians (מצרי). To say Aram was to say Syrian or Egyptian. Our capital was the city of Tyre (צר), on the great sea.

*\*See Strong's Concordance "Aram," and "Syria," both are #758, where as the phonics for Syria (צרי) is found at #6876, which is the root for the word Egypt (מצרי) which is found at #4714*

**Joseph:** The mother of Rebecca was Syrian (Egyptian), and therefore Rebecca was Syrian (Egyptian). Jacob as the son of Rebecca declared himself Syrian (Egyptian)(*Deut. 26:5*). Jacob (Israel) the father of the twelve, declared that he was an Syrian (Egyptian), about to perish in the famine of the Lord in Canaan (*Deut. 26:5*). The Egyptians had sent wagons to Canaan to carry Jacob the Egyptian (Syrian), to safety in Egypt, the ancestral homeland of his people (*Gen. 45:19, 21, 27*).

I came from the north in Aram, down to the land of Canaan, where Israelis were living again. I came as a carpenter to practice my trade. I met and married a young Israeli woman. I am the father of Yeshua (Jesus), and am related to the "mixed multitude" that came up out of Egypt with Israel (*Ex. 12:3, Nu. 11:48*). The multitude were Egyptians who were associated with the Israelis through marriage, or other family relationships. These Egyptians also known as "Strangers, (*Lev. 17:8, 10, 13*)," were not held to the exactness to the Lord, as the Israelis were. The Lord attempted to make them do as he commanded from the Israelis. The Lord called them, but had no authority over them. Also Being Egyptians they were literate, and some therefore kept chronicles of all that occurred, from Egypt to the land of Canaan.

The Lord had just brought Israel to the wilderness outside of Egypt. My Egyptian kinsmen saw the Lord impose Holiness (Corruption / חוללי) on the Israelis. Israel was to be a kingdom of priest, a Holy (Corrupt) Nation (Goyim). There in the wilderness outside of Egypt the the Lord commanded that the Israelis Sanctify (Sodomize / קדש) the firstborn sons of all the tribes (*Ex. 13:2*). Then the Israelis had to sanctify (קדש / Sodomize) each other (*Ex. 19:10, 14*). Then the Levite priest had to Sanctify (קדש / Sodomize) each other (*Ex. 19:22*).

Once they had performed these acts upon each other they were instructed to wash themselves,

> # Soliloquies Of Chaos
> # Joseph of Aram
>
> *Exodus from Israel — No Holiness — Home to Egypt*

and their garments (*Ex. 19:10, 14*).  Israel was now "Sanctified (Sodomized)," and therefore made "Holy" (Corrupt).

**Joseph (Yuseph):** My Egyptian ancestors with the Israelis refused to be a part of any of it! And now hundreds of years later when my son Yeshua (Jesus) was born, the Israelis still had this perversion imposed on them.  I would refuse to allow my son Yeshua (Jesus) to be Sanctified and made Holy.

The Lord commanded that all firstborn sons in Israel be brought to him in the eighth day of their birth  (*Ex.13:2, Ex.13:13, 15*).  They were to be "Sanctified" (קדש), to the Lord, which was to have Ritual Religious Sodomy (קדש)* performed on them.  Parents were to bring their first born sons,  three times in the year (*Ex. 34:23, 25*).  None were to appear before the Lord with empty hands (*Ex. 34:20*)!

But the parents could redeem their firstborn sons from this humiliating act of being sodomized, by sacrificing a lamb to the Lord (*Ex. 13:13*).  If parents did not have a lamb to sacrifice, and still refused to have their firstborn son religiously sodomized (Sanctified), the parents were commanded to break the boy's neck (*Ex. 13:13, 15*)!

My wife and I sacrificed lambs to the Lord, three times in the year to save Yeshua.  He was never  Sanctified (Sodomized), and made Holy (Corrupt).*

This act of sodomy was performed on the little firstborn male children of all the tribes, for the express purpose of casting them out, of their inner kingdoms (*Matt. 8:12*).  These future leaders would automatically infect the next generations.  As such all of Israel eventually ceased to be as little children, inside their inner kingdoms (*Matt. 18:3*).  Little children are each Gods great in their own inner heavenly kingdoms (*Matt. 18:4; Luke 17:21*).  My son Yeshua (Jesus) was still inside of his inner kingdom,  for he had not been casted out.  He and his inner father were still one (*John 14:2; John 10:30*).  For our son to be Unsanctified, and Unholy put his life in danger (*Matt. 2:13*).

**Joseph (Yusef):** When I fled to Egypt with my wife and son Yeshua (Jesus) we were fleeing to the homeland of our Syrian (Egyptian) ancestors.  There in Egypt they would not Sanctify (Sodomize / קדש) my children, to make them Holy (Corrupt / חולי).  Yeshua (Jesus), and his brother James, and all of the rest of my children would never be molested.  No one in Egypt would close my children's eyes, and ears, and hearts (*Isa.6:10*).

**Joseph (Yuseph):** Egypt the homeland of my ancestors, was the source of the Great Light.  Egypt was the land of the Single Eyed (*Matt. 6:22*). here was a great aura of light around each person in Egypt.  This is the Light that Yeshua brought to Israel from Egypt.  It was the Scribes, Pharisees, Priest, Rabbis and Romans who conspired to Killed the Light, by scourging, and crucifying my son.  I the father of Yeshua (Jesus) am the Joseph of Aramathaea (Aram), that came to claim my son Yeshua's body (*Matt. 27:57;  Mark 15:43;  Luke 23:51; John 19:38*).

# Soliloquies Of Chaos
# Yeshua (Jesus)

*Joseph the Egyptian — Unmolested In Egypt — Lost Sheep — Self*

**Yeshua (Jesus):** I was assassinated in Israel, for teaching what I had been taught in Egypt. Egypt is the ancestral homeland of my father Joseph and his people. From my very youth in Egypt my entire family was taught to seek first the kingdom of God (*Matt. 6:33*). We were taught that the kingdom of heaven is at hand (*Matt. 3:2, 4:17, 10:7*). We were taught that the kingdom of God is within each of us (*Luke 17:21*). Then the Egyptians told us that as children, we are each Gods in our inner kingdoms (*I Cor. 6:20*): The Egyptians taught us that we were Gods, children of the Most High (Sun / עליון)(*Psalms 82:6; John 8:32*). He who is in you (God) is greater than he who is in his World (Lord)(*I John 4:4; I Cor. 3:16*). Call none good, but God (inner)(*Matt. 19:17*). It is your lack of knowledge of your God (inner), that cause you to perish ( ). The Egyptians read us the Mesoretic (מצרי) or Egyptian Text, and recited their records for my family and I, that the Lord had come down into Egypt, brought Israel out of Egypt by force, without the Israelis wanting to come. The Egyptians stated that when the Lord got the Israelis out into the wilderness, that he immediately made them Sanctified (sodomized), and Holy (corrupt). In so doing the children of Israel were cast out of their inner kingdoms (*Matt. 8:12*), out into the Outer Darkness of the Lord (*Amos 5:18, 20*).

**Yeshua (Jesus):** The Egyptians, and the other children of Ham never molested their children, but the children of Israel were cast out of their inner kingdoms, out into the Outer Darkness of the Lord (*Amos 5:18, 20; Matt. 8:12*). The Lord used the Levites, to cast the firstborn Israeli sons out of their inner kingdoms. Woe to the Scribes and Pharisees (Levites), who cast the Israeli children out, and shut up their kingdoms against them reentering (*Matt. 23:13*). The Lord had instructed the Rabbis to make their ears dull, make their hearts (Minds) fat, and to shut their eyes (*Isa. 6:10*).

The Eye of those cast out is shut, and a shut eye is an evil eye, and the whole body is full of the Darkness of the Lord (*Amos 5:18, 20*). The Lord's Darkness is a great Darkness that can be felt (*Ex. 10:21*). Yet if the Single Eye (Peniel / פניל), be open, then the body shall be full of Light (*Matt. 6:22*). Each Israelis would have eyes to see, ears that hear, and hearts (minds) that understand (*Matt. 13:13*). Then Israelis can convert themselves, and be healed from the Lord (*Matt. 13:15, 16*). Being able to see and understand, the Israeli masses will know that they did not need Rabbis, Synagogue, or the Lord. The Israelis would know that God and kingdom, are inside, and there is no need for outside intervention, such as any religious organization!

The Egyptians sent me, to make the Lost Sheep of Israel free. The truth would make them free (*John 8:32*). Strait is the gate and narrow is the way that lead to Eternal Life (*Matt.. 7:14*), but wide is the gate, and broad is the Way (Darkness) that leads to Destruction (שי), or the Almighty (שרי)(*Matt. 7:13*). You can not serve two masters, God's Inner Light and the Lord's Outer Darkness (*Matt. 6:24*). Take up your crosses and follow me (*Matt. 16:24*). He who finds his life in the physical shall lose it eventually anyway, but he who lose his life for me (truth) shall have it Eternally (*Matt. 10:39*). Do not fear those who can kill your body (Romans), but fear those who can kill your soul (Rabbis, Priests, and Ministers)(*Matt. 10:28*). I am after the Order of Melchezedek, who has authority over the Eternal Life of Self (*Heb. 5:9*)

# Lynching of Yeshua (Jesus)

The Lord is speaking to the corpse of Jesus, to tell him that if he had co-operated with him he would still be alive, ruling his World (TBL).

Notes

# Personalities
# Self

*Observations are Notes about Persons, Places, and Things.*

*When man is truly himself he is satisfied, he is living from the inside of himself outward. One who is not living from the inside out, is living from the edge of himself outward. He is hollow, and full of Darkness inside, and have lost himself. He is potentially a selfless being.*

Joshua (יהושע) became the savior (יהושע) of the World of the Lord, when he completed the holocaust against the children of Ham, who were the epitome of Self. Phonetically Self (שלח) is the dissatisfaction that was "cast (שלח) out," of the absolute bringing the particular or physical realm, a dream state into existence.

All that is written in this book is about Self. Self is the essence of all beings. Without Self there is nothing. In physical manifestation there is always Two Masters: **Self** (Inward), and **Other** (Outward).

Self responds to two forces in it's being. The first force that Self responds to is it's own "Light," which simply serves as a guide line. The second force that Self responds to is the "Darkness" of "Other than Self." Self has three qualities that allow it to follow the guideline of the first force which is Light. Little children are full of Light, and have these three qualities, which are <u>eyes that see, ears that hear</u>, and <u>the ability to tell the truth</u> (*Matt. 13:15*). The second force "Darkness," is to be cast out of Self" (*Matt. 8:12*). This condition brings the "<u>loss of the ability to see, hear, and tell the truth</u>." The Lord demanded that the Rabbis (Priest and Ministers) close the eyes, ears, and minds of their congregations (*Isa. 6:10*), it is the root to religion and faith. To be **Other** rather than **Self** carries three facets: Darkness, Evil, and Corruption. These three facets are the foundation of the World (TBL). *See Strong's Concordance #8398, and #8399* "World" (Tubal) = "Bestiality," Mixing," "Consumption"

**Darkness:** (דרבה) Phonetically "Dark" (דרך) means literally "Wayward," to be "away" from the central Light of Self. To be absent from the Self, is to be with the Lord of Darkness (*II Corinth. 5:6, Amos 5:18, 20*). In translation Dark (חשך) means " to be debilitated," "to be weak."

**Evil:** (רע) "incomplete," "to need an outside agency" i.e. "Host." The Lord is Evil, or incomplete, needing "friends" (רע) or "Evil Ones," like Noah, Abram and Moses to make himself artificially complete. The Lord declared that he would eventually cause evil to be upon all flesh (*Jer. 45:5*).

**Corruption:** (חלל) Hull, Hill, Hell, Profane"to be crafted" (created), or altered into something "other" than the complete original self. *See Observations "Creation, pg. ."*

The loss of "Knowledge of Self" is the source of "Other than Self." "Other" has no being of it's own. As a result, "Other" must continuously recruit from those who are still "Self." This recruitment is needed to sustain the corrupting World system. The existence of Self even exceeds the existence of the Most High (sun). Self is the source of the Most High.

# Personalities
# Most High "Alien" (עליון)

*Self — Most High = Alien (A Lion)(#5945) Deut. 32:8, 9 — Solar War — 144,000 — Souls*

The Most High (עליון) is the sun (שמש), the most perfect representation of Self in the physical. The Most High in it's naked invisible state is an electromagnetic entity. The garment that the sun wears in the physical is the Ultraviolet purpleness of Black Light, even though it seems to be yellow, as seen from inside of the atmosphere of the planet. The Most High, (עליון) the sun" (Shemesh / שמש) is the father of all of us. All of the original inhabitants of the planets are Sols (Souls) or "Solar Beings," from the Most High or Sun. All were perfect before they manifested into the physical, to experiment and became less than perfect (*Matt. 5:48*). None could return to the sun, until all were perfect again, returning from a satisfied experience in the physical. Beyond representing perfection, and being a source and port, the Most High (sun) is also the source of life in the entire physical illusion (Dream). The life radiating from the sun supplements our diminishing life force as we descended further down into the deadness and denseness, of the physical illusion.

All came from the invisible electromagnetic Field, through the portal of the sun into the physical in dissatisfaction, and can only leave the physical realm to reenter the sun, in a state of satisfaction.

Michael/Melchezedek was elected by all who came forth from the solar, to protect the solar passageway. Those who came forth from the sun made him the Overseer (כוהן), of the Most High (sun)(*Gen. 14:18*). He was given authority over Eternal Life (*Hebrew 5:6, 9*), which radiates from the Most High (Sun), into the illusion of the physical (*Gen. 14:18, Hebrews 6:9*). Michael/Melchezedek's mission was to protect the experiment and the solar (Soul), port at all cost.

The Star or Solar Wars began when Hallel (Lucifer) the Lord attempted to exalt himself above the stars or planets of the other Gods (*Isaiah 14:13*). He wanted to be like the Most High (sun)(*Isaiah 14:14*). Michael/Melchezedek the Overseer of the Most High, defeated the Lord in the wars that Hallel had started, and cast him out (*Revelations 12:9*). The Most High saw the Lord Hallel the Almighty fall (*Numbers 24:4, 16*). The Lord and his Host, all those who fell with him, ceased to be themselves, and thus ceased to be solar or have souls. They lost their souls (Solar Association).

The Lord of Abraham was called the Most High but is only the Most High relative to his Host, and those in service to him (*Gen. 14:19, 20*). Michael/Melchezedek is not the Overseer (Priest) of the Lord of Abraham, but is the overseer of the sun. The sun is the Most High above, and the Lord of Abraham is the Almighty below. The Most High above saw the Almighty fall (*Numbers 24:4, 16*). The Most High above gave the Lord the Most High below Israel as a heritage (*Deut. 32:8, 9*). The Earthlings (Adams), Hallel, Gabriel, Michael/Melchezedek, etc., are all Souls or Solar Beings. There may have been 144,000 Souls from the solar at the start.

Notes

# Personalities
# Souls

*Most High — Breathers / Brothers — Cain Mutainy — 666*

Souls are Solar Beings who all emanated from the sun (Most High). Without their physical garments, they are invisible electro/magnetic beings, like the sun. There were originally perhaps one hundred and forty four thousands (144,000) souls. Phonetically Soul/Sol (שול) means "to project" or "to emanate." The Most High (Solar) is a soul, that is "projected" (של) from the electromagnetic Field, and Solar Beings are "project (של)" from the sun. In translation **Soul** *Nephesh* (נפש) means "We (נ) Radiate (פש)," or "We spread forth" (from the sun). All souls "Radiated" from the sun and became "breathers" (נפשים) or "brothers" (*Gen. 2:7*). This was Man in his naked invisible (אלוהים) or God state. The Sun the Most High is the source of all Souls, or Solar Beings. Michael/Melchezedek, Gabriel, Adam (Earthling), and Hallel (Lord of Abraham) are all **Souls** and **Brothers/Breathers** (נפשים / ברח)(*Judges 10:16*). The Original Inhabitants of the globe all came forth from the Most High (sun), bringing out the original or Mother planet in it's fervent or firey state.

Brothers (Breathers) are the "breaths" that "breathed" themselves, into the "coats of skin (*Gen. 2:7*)," or physical forms, that are occupied by all the Original beings in the physical realm. All souls inside of physical forms are called "Living Souls (נפש חיה)(*Gen. 2:7*)." This include Adam, Eve, and the Lord. They all became living souls (*Genesis 3:21, Judges 10:16*), "breathed" into physical forms. But when the Lord's body was set afire (*Dan. 7:11; Ezek. 28:18*), he ceased to be a living soul, in a body, and became a dead soul, or Holy (Corrupt) Ghost, without a physical body.

All of the original physical forms of the solar (soul) breathers/brothers were wooly headed, and Black/Brown, to correspond to the Black Light (Life) emanating from the garment of the sun. The physical appearance of these souls (solar associates) confirmed their origin, as having been from the sun. Within the wooly hair of their heads was the design of all that exist. Cain's father the Lord striped him of his soul by mutating (marking) Cain, into being an permanent Albino or Pale Leper (*Gen. 4:15*). Carrying the mutation (mark) of Pale Leprosy, Cain could not stand in the sun, but had to be sheltered in the shadows of Darkness, away from the sun (*Isa. 18:1, Isa. 9:2*).

In the pale mutated state Cain became a soulless (nonsolar) being. Marked Cain became the father of the Caucasian or Human Race. Human Beings are not Souls, or Solar Beings. Their origin is not the sun, and they only exit inside of the mutating of Cain. Cain's father the Lord had lost his soul (solar Association) when he was defeated in the solar (Soul) war. With the loss of his soul or solar association Cain was sent forth, into the ground of Nod, and away from exposure to the sun's rays (*Gen. 4:14*). Cain and his father (the Lord), were both Princes of the Darkness of Nod.

Albinism normally corrects itself, in the next generation. Cain's Mutainy or mutation was an infection, at the genetic level, and permanent, so that Cain was never to be corrected from his Pale Leprosy. The permanent mutiny (מהל) or "Corruption/Adulteration" of Hallel, was now the permanent mutation and adulteration (זחל) of his son Cain on the earth. The soulless can not stand in the solar (Sun) for long without being damaged, or destroyed. At *Revelation 13:18* the Souls or Solar Beings are being described with the identity of 666 (בשמשו).

Observations

# Personalities
# 666

*Souls — Ca-Shemeshu (Like the Sun) — Beast of the Field and Earth — Man*

The number Six six six (666) describes all Solar (Soul) Beings (*Revelations 13:18*). The consonants of the Old Language carry number values. For example the the Old Language as formatted to the so called Hebrew alphabet has the values: א = 1, ב = 2, ג = 3, ד = 4, ה = 5, ו = 6, ז =7, ח = 8, ט = 9, י = 10, כ = 20, ל = 30, מ = 40, נ = 50, ש = 300 etc. Thus the number combination 666 generates a sequence of consonants, that spell out the compound term, Cashemeshu (כשמשו). The term "Ca-Shemeshu" (כשמשו) is composed of the consonants: ו = 6, ש = 300, מ = 40, ש = 300, כ = 20, so 6+300+40+300+20 = 666. The term Ca-Shemeshu translates as the descriptive phrase: "**They** are like the Sun," or Ca-Shemesho: "**He** is Like the Sun." Thus the term Cashemeshu describe all the original men, the solar beings (666), as being "like their origin, the sun (666)." But in the book of Revelation, only one Man is being described (Ca-Shemesho)(*Rev. 13:18*). This Man being described is Abraham's Lord Hallel, who was also "Like the Sun," until he fell.

In the Revelation verse (*Rev. 13:18*), the meaning of the word **Man** (Ish / איש) elaborates specifically why man is "like the sun." The root for the word man (איש), is the same as the root for the word Fire (איש). The sun is the source of the fireiness (אשה) of man (אישי). The same is true for the planet, which is named Assiah (אישה), which means fireiness. The planet was originally firey (אישי), when it was brought forth out of the sun, by original man.

Next in the Revelation verse (*Rev. 13:18*) the word **Beast** (חוח) for man does not mean animal, but means "animator," for Original Man is not an animal, but is the invisible "animator" (הים / Lifeforce), or "Living One, inside all Original organic physical forms.

The shape of the number six (6) is a symbol that denotes "spiralling down (6)," into the physical state of being. The number 666 therefore denote that these Solar Beings (Man) were originally set to be totally orientated to the physical state: Mentally (6), Emotionally (6), and Physically (6). Conversely the shape of the number nine (9) is a symbol that denotes "spiralling back up (9)," into the solar state. The number 999 therefore denotes that the Solar Beings (Men) have completed their 666 mission, in the physical, and have returned completely to the original solar state.

Thus the Beast (Living Ones) of the Field (חית השרה)(above)(*Gen. 2:19*), and the Beast (Living Ones) of the Earth (below)(*Gen. 1:30*)(חית ארץ) are both Man (איש), firey beings from the sun. The Beast of the Field above are Michael/Melchezedek and his Angels (999). The Beast of the Earth below are Hallel and his Host, who were defeated, and cast out and down, into the ground of the earth (666), among the inhabitants of the planet (*Rev.12:12*).

All who originate from the sun are 666 (Cashemeshu / כשמשו), as being "like the sun," are Souls or Solar Beings. This makes them Man (מן), or "Progeny" (מן) of the sun.

# Personalities
# Man

*666 — Man (אִישׁ) — God inside the physical form (I Corin. 3:16) — Wooly Design — Gods*

Man (מִן) (phonetically) means "progeny (מִן)," or "Offspring." And as said before, in translation, the root for the word Man (Ish / אִישׁ) and the word "fire (אֵשׁ)" are the same. Man in his naked (invisible) state is a firey (Ish) being. Without it's garment flame, fire is invisible. *See **Strong's Concordance #376, 377 (Man), and #384 - 386 (Fire / Entity)***. The word Ish (אִישׁ) for man/fire, roots from the word Yish (יֵשׁ), which means to "Stand Out," to "Exist." Thus even though man is an invisible being, he becomes manifest in his physical garment. It is through his "coats of skin," that man manifests to "exist," or "Stand out (*Gen. 2:21*)." Manifest is what man has to be to complete the experiment in the physical state. All of the original men on the planet, are Adams

The words Adam (Earthling / אָדָם) and Man (אִישׁ) are interchangeable. The Lord is a Man, like Adam (*Ex. 15:3*). Thus **Adam** the man is a **God** like the **Lord. Michael,** and **Gabriel** are Gods like the Lord, and are also men like **Adam** (*Dan. 9:21; Dan. 8:16, 17*). This means that they all have a common source and are brothers (אָחִי) to each other, including Adam. This also means that none of these **Men** were created unless they were all created. None of these Original Men were ever created, including Adam. Michael and Melchezedek are the same person with two different names. The description of Melchezedek at *Hebrews 7:1-3* is a description of Michael, and is therefore a description of the Lord, Adam and all of the other Original Men on this planet. Melchezedek is described as existing "without the aid of a father, and or mother. He is without descent, having neither beginning of days or end of life (*Hebrew 7:1*). As such Michael/Melchezedek did not have a navel, and nor did Adam, and the Lord (*Hebrews 7:3*). Jesus the "Son of Man" (Lord), was wooly headed and Black like Adam (*Rev. 1:14*). Adam the wooly haired Black man was like Melchezedek the pure wooly headed Ancient of Days (*Dan. 7:9*). Thus the Lord (Abraham's God) and his Host, along with the millions who came down to the planet, with Melchezedek the Ancient of days, had wooly hair and brown complexion (*Dan. 10:7*). Therefore the wooly headed Brown/black Man, the original inhabitant of the planet, is God. The woolliness of Man's hair carries all designs that exist in the universe. All are souls or Solar Beings, like the Lord (*Judges 10:16*). The wooly headed original men were never created.

**Creating** was the altering of the Original Man Adam. Adam (Earthling) was put to sleep, and altered, into separate Male and Female (*Gen. 2:21*). The Lord beguiled the female (Eve), and fathered the first **"Created man,"** Cain. Cain was born in Adam's sleep, from Eve Adam's female side. Cain is the father of "Mankind," which is the Human or Caucasian Race, who is not true Man, but is the offspring of Cain, the man who came forth from the altering of Adam.

Seth is altogether another story, for he was a Man, not Human (Caucasian). Seth was the Image and likeness of Adam, who has no beginning or ending (Alpha and Omega/)(*Gen. 5:1*). Seth is Adam in continuation inside of Adam's own **dream/sleep** and **death** (*Gen. 2:21*).

Man "unmanifested" is invisible and is the God (אֱלוֹהִים) or "Invisible One" that dwells within the physical form using it as a temple (*I Cor. 6:19, 20*) Man is God manifested, and God is Man invisible. Man the Solar Being, or Progeny of the Sun, without his physical garment, is an Invisible Male/Female Being called God (*Gen. 1:26, 27*).

Observations

Notes

# Personalities
# God(s)

*Man —Inside/Outside — God, Lord God, and Lord (Gen.) — He who is in is greater than he who is in the World 1John 4:4 — Lord (in the Ground) Exodus 8:21*

The word God(s) in the English, is pronounced Elohim (אלוהים) in the Old Language. Elohim is a compound word that means "invisible" (אל) "female (ה)" male being(s) (ים). Man is a manifested God, and God is an unmanifested man. Man (מן) the "Progeny" of the sun, is that invisible male/female being. Hallel the God of Abraham is a Man (*Exodus 15:3*), as are all other Gods. The regular kingdom or dwelling place of Gods is within (*Luke 7:21, I Cor. 6:20*), yet the kingdom of the Lord of Abraham is outside where he was "cast Out" (*II Cor. 5:6*), to **Outer Darkness** (*Amos 5:18, 20*).

The God of Abraham admits that there are Gods other than himself, when he instructs Jacob to go up to Bethel and build an altar to the "God" that Jacob saw in the wilderness (*Gen. 35:1, Gen. 32:24-30*). At *Gen.32:24* the term "a man" is used, but at *Gen. 35:1* and *Gen.32:30*, the Lord is calling that same Man "God" (Capital "G")." The Lord himself is called "Man" at *Exodus 15:3*. The Lord even warn the Israelis not to "revile" the Gods (*Exodus 22:28, Matt. 5:11*). To revile (קלל) is to "make light" or "hurt the feelings" of the Gods! You can not "revile" or hurt the feelings of images or idols! Jesus at *John 10:34* quoted *Psalms 82:6*, which is the Lord telling some **Men** that they are all **Gods** children of the Most High. At *John 10:34* Jesus was talking to some Israeli men, to tell them that he himself and they also are Gods (*Psalms 82:6*). The whole of Jesus' mission from Eden (Egypt, Africa) was to enlighten the Original wooly headed brown Israelis masses (*Amos 9:7*), that they were all Gods, the children of the Most High, like the Lord is (*Deut. 32:9*).

Lord can imply the son of a king, and it is the Lord of Abraham who inherits from the Most High at (*Deut. 32:8, 9*). The Host of the Lord are called Gods at *1Samuel 4:8*

The fact becomes that if a God (Lord) is a original Man *Exodus 15:3*, then original Man is God (*Gen. 1:27, 28*). In Mamre Abraham sat and ate with the Lord and two other **"Men"** (*Gen. 18:1-15*). Moses, Isaac, and seventy Israelis elders sat and ate with the Lord and some other **Gods** (*Ex.24:10-11*).

Throughout the Bible/Torah there are many mentions of "Living Gods:" "Worship him all of you Gods" (*Psalms 97:7*). "Gods of the Earth are famished" (*Siphoniah 2:11.*). "Take us out of the hands of these mighty Gods," "these are the Gods that smote Egypt" (*1Sam. 4:8*). The Lord is greater than the proud Gods (*Exodus 18:11*). The Lord is exalted above all Gods (*Psalms 97:7, Isaiah 14:13*).

Paul speak of **God**(s) being inside of the physical body (*I Corinth.6:19, 20*), and the **Lord** being outside (*II Chron.5:6*). The God on the inside is Man himself. Greater is he that is in you (Self), than he who is in the World (Lord)(*I John 4:4*). Jesus (Yeshua) confirms this when at *John 10:34*, he quotes the Lord saying at *Psalms 82:6*, that all Original Men (including the Lord), are Gods children of the Most High (*Gen. 1:26*). Jesus further say that this fact that all original Men are Gods is the Law, and that it can not be broken anymore (*John 10:34, 35*).

Observations

# Personalities
# God(s)

*God — Big "G," Little "g" Gods — First Planet Inhabitants — Many Gods — Lord God*

The modern European translators have taken licence to use a capital "G" for the god of Abraham, and to use a small "g" for all other Gods mentioned in the Bible/Torah. In the old language there is no such division, for there are no capitals, or small case. Capitol and small case letters is a very recent European invention.

Jesus (Yeshua) was taught in Eden (Africa) that **all of the original inhabitants of the planet are Gods** (*John 10:34, 82Psalms:6*). Jesus was sent back from Egypt to Israel, to teach this to his people so that they could stop breaking the Universal Law by bowing down to the Lord (*Eccles. 5:1*). The above scripture from the Bible/Torah is ample to teach that no one should be bowing down, sacrificing to, or praising any God. The scripture states that bowing, sacrifice, and praise is foolishness (*Eccles. 5:1, 2*). But Judeo/Christianity teach their congregations to bow, sacrifice, and to praise the Lord. Their congregations are kept away from knowing the truth that the Bible/Torah say that these acts are foolish.

The first fourteen chapters of Genesis have been written in a form to cause the reader to think that the God and the Lord God in these chapters is the Lord of Abraham. The God and Lord God of these fourteen chapters of Genesis is Michael/Melchezedek, not the God of Abraham.

In these fourteen chapters the Lord is never God, or Lord God. The Lord is not even identified as the Lord until the beginning of the fourth chapter of Genesis. Before the fourth chapter, the Lord is actually the Man at Gen. 1:26, 27. The Lord is also the "Formed Man at Gen. 2:7, 8, 15 (*Isaiah 43:10*). The Lord is also the Serpent at (*Gen. 3:1, 2; Rev. 12:9*).

To know that the aboriginal inhabitants of this planet are all Gods is to know that Man (God) was not created into being, but Man have perpetual existence beyond time and space. Secondly God (Man) is not on this planet to bow to anyone or any thing, nor is Man here to worship, or sacrifice. How can Gods bow, sacrifice, or praise one who is only co-equal to themselves, and what would be the purpose?

Any God who would impose on any other God for anything is a Lesser God, who can not do for himself. Any God who can not do for Self is inferior. The fact is that the God (Hallel / Lucifer) of the planet Crypton attempted to impose his inferiority on others, coequal to himself on other planets. Hallel's attempt to export the corruption of Crypton to other planets is what caused the Solar Wars. Hallel the future Lord of Abraham was the Hallel or Lucifer who caused the Solar Wars a Holy (חלל) or Corrupt war (*Revelation 12:7*).

For the Gods to accomplish their purpose, in the physical or particular experiment, they had to come down into physical form. "Comers Down," is what the term Lord (לרד) means.

# Personalities
# Lord(s)

*God (s) — Lords (Comers Down) — Living Ones — Redeem — Names*

All of the Gods "came down." Lord (לורד) means "to (ל) came down (רד)." All Gods the original population of the planet, "Came Down (לורד)" from the sun, and therefore are Lords. This definition qualify original Man, the original population of the planet, as all being Lords or Comers Down. At the start of the experiment all came down willingly.

In translation the word Lord (יהוה) is pronounced Yeweh (Jehovah), and the word means "Beingness, or Life." The root word for Jehovah (הוה), is same as the word for Eve (הוה) pronounced "Hevah" which means "Life." Thus Lords are "living ones," who came down."

Next the phonetics for the word Host (חות) is translated as the word "Beast (חות)." But "Beast" is not the proper translation, for the word Host. The proper translation for the phonics of the word "Host" (חות) is also "Living Ones." The "Living Ones" are not animals (Beasts), but "Animators." Thus all of the original inhabitants of the planet as Lords (Living Ones) are animators of all of the physical forms that they occupy, in physical manifestation. Lords or "Living Ones" are the "Lifeforces" that dwell inside of physically manifested forms, to experiment with self in the particular realm, a dream state.

Many of the Comers Down, went back up, as defectors from the experiment, including the future Lord of Abraham. They left the planet (Assiah) to avoid further contact with the experiment. Those who left took portions of Assiah (this planet in it's original state). They set up planets for themselves, in other orbits around the sun. All of those who left became Alienated (Aliens).

The Lords who "came down" (רדים) with the planet, and stayed down are called Redim (Redeem / רדים). They are the Disciples or Disciplined Ones. This was because they had the discipline to hold the line of the experiment. They were redeemed by the fact that they stayed down, for the very purpose they had came down, which was to experiment.

Those who curved away and went back up with portions of Assiah were called Apostate, or Apostles, because their curving away was a perversion (αποστοσ). It was because of these Apostles that the Solar War was fought. All of the Apostate were defeated, and those who survived were cast back down (*Rev. 12:9*). They were now called Nephalim (נפלים) or Fallen Ones, including the future Lord of Abraham.

In the Western World, Lords are sons of Kings. In the Bible/Torah Lords are the "Sons of Gods," with "God" being a king position, Lords are Princes or children of the king. Lords also inherit from kings, as when the Almighty inherit from the Most High (*Deut. 32:7, 8*).

Every previous name from "Self" down to "Lord" is shared by each of the Original Men who came forth from the sun bringing the planet with them. All of these name including the name "Lord" is written in the Lamb's Book of Life (*Rev. 13:8*).

# Personalities
# Name(s) of the Lord

*Lord — Fallen One*

All of the previous names (Self, Souls, 666, Man, Gods, Lords), are the names of all of those who came from the sun, including the Lord. Though all of the original inhabitants of the planet are Lords, the title "The Lord" is exclusive to the Lord of Abraham. All of these names are written in the Lamb's (Lambda / Light) Book of Life, and the names written in it, are written in the Inner Light inside of Self.

But all of the following names are exclusive to the Lord and none of them are written in the Lamb's book of Life (*Rev. 13:8*). The names exclusive to the Lord are written in the Outer Darkness, where the Lord dwells (*Amos 5:18, 20*). To be absent from the Self is to be counted with the Lord (*II Cor. 5:6*). Once none of the following names for the Lord existed :

**Nephalim, Almighty, Lucifer (Hallel), Felons, Devil, Mandrake, Gardener(s)/Giants** and **Baal Zebub**. Each of these names describe negative actions that originated with the Lord, and his Host. Each of these names describes an element of the overall conditions around the conduct of the Lord.

No one can continually be associated with every element, of something negative without being that negative. In the "name" of this and in the "name" of that, runs through the entire Bible/Torah. This implies the importance of names. The Lord changed the names of Abram and Sarai after they had helped the Lord to accomplish his goal, which was to be established in the land of Ham (*Gen. 17:5, 15*). The Lord renamed Sarai, with the name Sarah, after she had played the role of a prostitute to the Pharaoh, and Abimelech. She had obtained a vast fortune for Abram and Lot (*Gen. 12:16; 20:14, 16*). Abraham sent most of the livestock up in smoke, a burnt offering in the name of the Lord. The Lord changed Abram's name to AbramHam or Abraham. This was after Abram had impregnated the Hamite woman named Hagar, and establish himself in the midst of those in the land of Ham (Canaan), with the money that he had been given (*Gen. 23:9*).

The church element of Christianity knew that names were important when they changed Yeshua's name to Jesus. The church has made it's congregations think that Yeshua's name is Jesus. The congregations do not even know that there is someone named Yeshua, and they call upon the invented name of Jesus which did not even come into existence until 1630, in the Christian era. This was one thousand six hundred (1600) years after the founders of the church had murdered Yeshua, the man the congregations now call Jesus, with no effect. What power is there in an invented name? No one can receive any power out of calling on an invented name, or a name that is not written in the Lamb's Book of Life, such as the following names of the Lord, which are the names that describe one who rebelled against the very purpose that men came into the physical illusion in the first place. As such to call upon the name of the Lord yields no power, for the one who calls, but infuses the Lord with the power, that flows from the one who is calling.

Scripture says that a good name is worth more than gold (*Proverbs 22:1*). Yet the Lord do not have any good names, after he became a defeated Man of War (*Exodus 15:3*). The Lord gained each of the following names, as he did the acts that the name describes. All who dwell to worship upon the earth, shall worship him whose names are not written in the book of Life. ... (*Rev. 13:8*).

# Personalities
# Lord

*Man of War— Almighty — Lucifer — Nephalim*

### Man of War

The Lord became a "Man of War" (*Exodus 15:3*), when he caused the war in the heavens (*Rev. 12:7*). The Lord caused the war, when he attempted to exalt himself above the stars of of God (*Isa. 14:12*). Michael/Melchezedek and his angels fought against the Dragon (Serpent)(תנין, נין), and the Dragon fought, and his angels, and prevailed not (*Rev. 12:8*); neither was place found (for the Lord and his Host), any more in the heavens, for the Lord destroyed his planet Krypton (*Rev. 12:8*). And the **Great Dragon** (Lord) was cast out (Shad / שד), that **Old Serpent**, called the **Devil** (שד), and **Satan**, which deceive his whole World (*John 3:16*). He was cast out "into" the earth, and his angels (Host) were cast out (Shaddai / שדי) with him (*Revelations 12:9*).

Hallel the Lord of Abraham is declared as being the Man of War (*Exodus 15:3*). He is the one who warred against Michael/ Melchezedek in the heavens (*Revelations 12:7*), and was cast out. The Lord boasted that he even had a Book, of all of his Wars (*Nu. 21:14*).

### Almighty (Out Cast)(El Shaddai)

"Almighty" is an intentional English mistranslation of the old language word El Shaddai (שדי אל). El Shaddai (אל שדי) really means " God of Devils," or "Cast Out God." The Lord is the God that was cast out of the heavens, down into the earth in defeat. The Lord is the **Great Dragon** who was, that **Old Serpent,** called the **Devil,** and **Satan** (*Rev. 12:9*). The Almighty (Lord) was cast out (שד) and the the Most High (Sun) saw him fall (*Numbers 24:4, 16*).

The Almighty is chief over all of his Host, who are the "Mighty (בני אלים) Ones" or Sons of Gods (*Psalms 29:1*). These were the Sons of God in the ground, who mated with the pale daughters of the Lord's son Cain (*Gen. 6:2*). The Lord the Serpent of (*Rev.12:9*), is also the Serpent of (*Gen. 3:1*).

The Lord the Almighty (שדי)(*Ex. 13:6*) comes as a Devil (Shad / שד) from the Devils (Shaddai / שדי)(*Job 21:20, Isaiah 13:6, Joel 1:15*). The Almighty (Shaddai) is a Shadow (צלים)(*Psalms 91:1*), and he Perverts (יעות) justice (*Job 8:3*). The Ammi Shaddai (Devil People)(*Numbers 1:12*), are the offspring of Cain's daughters, with the Host of the Lord (*Gen. 6:2*). The Ammi Shaddai (People of the Almighty) are Ca-Shaddai (Like the Devils). Ca-Shaddai (כשדי) is mispronounced "Chaldeans" (*Isaiah 23:13*). These are the pale leper children of "Marked Cain," the son of the Lord (*Gen. 4:14*). The Ami Shaddai or "People of the Shaddai are Shadow People (*Isaiah 18:1*). The Lord introduced himself to Abraham, Isaac, and Jacob as El Shaddai the Almighty or Devil God (Lucifer)(*Ex. 6:3*).

### Lucifer (Hallel)

The Almighty (Out Cast) in his fallen state became Lucifer: Oh Lucifer how has thou fallen (*Isa. 14:12*)? Phonically Lucifer (To Cipher) means "To Count," as one attempting to be recognized. Also in nobility Count is a lesser rank than prince. Third, to be "Count(er)" is to be opposite, or in opposition. Lastly, the term "Count" pertains to "criminal counts," as charges against a "felon." or "Fallen One" in the court system. Lucifer Abraham's Lord is a Felon, who

Notes

# Personalities
# Lord

### Lucifer — *Nephalim*

was tried on many criminal "counts," for war crimes in the heavens, and on the earth.

Oh Lucifer (Hallel / הלל) son of the sunset, how art thou fallen (נפל) from the heavens (*Isa. 14:12*)...., For you the Lord have said "I shall ascend into the heavens," The Lord said: "I shall **exalt** my throne above the stars of God." The Lord said "I shall sit also on the mount of the congregation, on the side of the north (*Isa. 14:13*)." He said "I will ascend above the heights of the clouds; and shall be "like" the Most High (sun)(*Isaiah 14:14*)." In the old language **Lucifer** is pronounced **"Hallel." Hallelujah** (חלליה) means "Lucifer Our Jah," or "Lucifer our Jehovah."

Those who use this term "Hallelujah" are exalting Lucifer (Hallel), who is the Lord of Abraham and Judeo/Christianity.

The word Lucifer only appear once in English, in the entire English Bible/Torah (*Isaiah 14:12*). Yet the old language word for Lucifer (Hallel / הלל) is hidden underneath the word "praise"(הלל) throughout the Old Testament. *See Strong's Concordance #1966 (Lucifer / הילל), and #1985 (Praise / הלל).* In each place that the term **"Praise the Lord"** is used, it should be pronounced **"Lucifer the Lord."**

Michael/Melchezedek was the God who was "looking for" (ברא) not "creating" the Man Lucifer, and his Host (*Genesis 1:26, 27*). Lucifer the Fallen One was found, and (pull / farmed / formed), from the ground, in Noc (*Isa. 43:10; Gen. 2:7*). The Lord God Michael/Melchezedek put the Lord in the Guarded Place (Garden), that he the Lord God had established, to tend it until it was time for the Lord and his Host to be tried, for their crimes in the heaven and on the earth (*Gen. 2:8*).

Michael/Melchezedek is the Ancient of Days, who tried the Ancient of Nights (*Amos 5:118, 20*), who is the Lord who is Lucifer (Hallel). Michael/Melchezedek was asking the Lord how he had fallen (*Isa. 14:12*). All of the following verses fit together to describe the Tribunal which was held against Lucifer (Hallel) the Lord of Abraham (*Genesis 3:14, Isaiah 14:12, Psalms 82:1- 6, Daniel 7:9, and Ezekiel 28th chptr*).

**Nephalim (Felons / Giants)** Marvelous wonders

The word Nephalim (נפלים), was falsely translated as the English, word Giants (*Gen. 6:4*). Nephalim (נפלים) does not mean Giants, but means "Felons," or "Fallen Ones." The English word "fall" comes from the old language word Nephal (נפל), which means "fall." The Lord and his Host, are the Felons or Fallen Ones, who "fell" down, into the earth, after being defeated in the heavens (*Rev. 12:9*). The Lord and his Host had been **Beast of the Field** above, before they fell into the earth, and became **Beast of the Earth** below (*Gen. 2:19; Gen. 1:24, 25*). The Lord God Michael/Melchezedek) pulled (formed / farmed) them, back up out of the ground, and breathed the breath of life back into them, and they became living souls again (*Gen. 2:7*). He then placed them in the Garden to maintain it (*Gen. 2:5*).

Phonically the word "Giants" (Ganoth / גנות) is the Old Language word for "Gardeners" (גנות). The Man placed in the Garden to work, is the Lord of Abraham, and his Host, who are the Giants, or Gardeners (*Gen. 2:8, 19*). Thus the Lord and his Host the Nephalim (Felons) were put to work,

Observations

# Personalities
# Lord

### *Nephalim— Devil*

as Gardeners (Giants), as some inmates are put to work in prison gardens.

These "Gardeners," the Lord and his Host are the tree that beguiled Eve, and that Eve and Adam consummated with (*Gen. 3:6*). Cain and Abel are the twin "fruit" that Eve bear for the Lord when he impregnated her (*Gen. 4:1; I Chron. 1:1*).

This term "Nephalim" did not exist until the Lord and his Host "Fell." (*Revelations 12:9*). It is the Lord (Man of War)(*Ex. 15:3*) and his Host who were full of wrath, and who had little time, on the planet before Michael/Melchezedek would be coming down to judge them (*Revelations 12:12*).

After the Lord and his Host had been tried, convicted, and sentence, they were all thrown over into Nod which was a prison. When the Lord came out of Nod with Abraham, it was a prison break. The Lord boast about all of the great "Wonders (פלא)," that he would do in the land of Ham, including Egypt (*Psalms 105:27*). But the word used for wonders, and marvels (פלא), both mean Felonies (פלא), or Capital Crimes. Thus the Lord was doing capital crimes, atrocities in the land of Ham, in Egypt, and Canaan.

The Lord of Abraham talk about "wondrous/marvellous " (נפלא) works that he would do in Egypt (*Ex. 3:20*). The Lord even named himself "wonderful," (נפלא) or felonious (*Isa. 9:6*). In the Strong's Concordance the words Wonder(s), Wonderful, Wonderfully, Wondrous, and Wondrous all have entries. under the numbers #6381, and #6382, which denote the word נפלא, which roots to the word נפיל #5303 pronounced "Nephal" which means "Fallen," "Felony," or "crime."

Thus the works of the Lord in Egypt that are translated as the word "wonders" are actually "felonies" or "crimes" (*Ex. 3:20*). The Lord in true translation is boasting of the great crimes (Wonders/Marvels) that he committed in Egypt. The globe was given the name Planet (Planoth / פלנות) Place of Felons, to denote that the Lord the Fallen One or Felon (פלן) and his Host are here. *Note "P" and "F" (Ph) interchange with each other.* Wonders/Marvels are **capital crimes**.

It was a **capital crime** when the Lord supported and defended the Israelis (*Gen. 35:5*), who murdered the men and boys of the city of Shechem (*Gen. 34:25, 26*), and then raped themselves into tribal existence with the females of that city (*Gen. 34:29*). It was a **capital crime** when the Lord brought plagues and famine into Egypt, to force Egypt to release the Israelis to him. It was a **capital crime** when the Lord brought the Israelis out of Egypt by brute force, when they did not want to go with him. It was a **capital crime** when the Lord forced the Israelis, that he had gotten from Egypt, and their children to be sodomites, wandering around the wilderness, until they died. The Lord committed a **capital crime** when he turned the children of the children into pale lepers (*Lev. 13th Chptr*). It was a **capital crime** when the Lord brought the pale leper Israelis out of the wilderness, over into the land of the children of Abraham, to murder them off, and to rape themselves into being the Seed of Abraham, with the little girls, of the true children of Abraham (*Nu. 31:41*). It was a **capital crime** and felony when the Lord used the pale leper Israelis to commit holocaust, and murder their way back into the land of the children of Canaan, where they had raped themselves into existence four hundred years before. The Lord is a Captain Marvel, or

Notes

# Personalities
# Lord

*Nephalim — Devil — Mandrake*

Capital Criminal God, a Super man of Felony.

The Lord had Abram to bring him him down into the land of Canaan (*Gen. 12:1*). The Lord came into the land of Ham as a Devil (Destroyer/ שד) from the Devils (Almighties / שדי)(*Isa. 13:6*).

### Devil

In translation Devil (שד) pronounced "Shad," means "Cast Out" as Hallel (Lucifer), the Man of War, the Lord of Abraham, had been "cast out," in defeat in the solar war (*Rev. 12:9*). Phonetically Devil (דבל) pertaining to *Gen.1:27*, means to "double" by "dividing", which is to "multiply." The "Men" of *Gen. 1:25, 27* were Hallel and his Host, who had been defeated and cast (שד) down into the vicinity of the planet. They are not being created but are being told by the Lord (Hallel) their leader go down on the planet and to "subdue," have "dominion" or "mate" with the animals (Tubal/תבל)(Cabash/כבש)(*Gen.1:28*). This bestiality (TBL) would be the start of Hallel's World (TBL), on this planet (Place of Felons).

The Devil (שד) is much talked about, but the word "Devil" can not even be found in the singular form, in the Old Testament English translation!

You have to go all the way back to the New Testament (*Matthew 4:1*), to see the word "Devil" in English! In English the plural form (Devils / שדי), pronounced "Shaddai" is first seen at *Lev.17:17*, in the Old Testament, but when you look at the word that they are using for "Devils" (שערים) it does not mean Devils at all, but correctly translates up to the word "hairy ones," in the English!

Someone has gone to great length to conceal the true word for Devil and Devils in the Old Testament. Yet with a little effort the word in the Old Language for "Devils" is first found at *Deut.32:17*, and next at *Ps.106:37*. These are the only two instances that the word "Devils" appears in the English with the true old language word behind it!

But anyone who can read the Old Testament "Hebrew" will find the word for Devil and Devils several times in the Old Language untranslated.

In those places (in the Hebrew) that these words are found, they are brought up into the English as the words **"Almighty"** and **"Destruction,"** instead of the words Devils and Devil!

"Almighty" appears 48 times from *Genesis 17:1* to *Joel 1:15*. In each of these cases "Devils" (שדי or שדים) instead of Almighty would have been the proper translation! "Destruction" appears 7 times from *Job 5:21* to *Joel 1:15*! In each of these cases, "Devil" (שד) instead of "Destruction" would have been the proper translation!

Thus under these circumstances *Isaiah 13:6* would be translated ... "the Day of the Lord is at hand, he (the Lord) shall come as a "Devil" from the "Devils."

The Lord the Devil is the father of Israel (*Gen. 25:21; Ex. 4:22*), and the father of Jesus (*Luke 1:35, 30, 28*). Yeshua (Jesus) said to the Israelis: "Your (our) father the Devil a murderer and liar (*John 8:44*), who can not tell the truth (*John 8:44*). The Lord had called himself Devil God, or Outcast God (El Shaddai)(*Ex. 6:3*). The Israeli scribes wrote that the Lord told Moses, that he appeared before Abraham, Isaac, and Jacob, and introduced himself as El Shaddai or the Devil God (*Ex.

Observation

# Personalities
# Lord

*Devil — Mandrake — Superman*

*6:3*). The Lord also called himself "Man of Darkness (Mandrake)," or Prince of Darkness (*Amos 5:18, 20*).

### Mandrake

The Devil is Mandrake or the Man of Darkness. Mandrake is a compound word that describes the "**Man** of **Darkness**," and the fruit of his tree. The Man of Darkness is the Lord of Abraham (*Amos 5:18, 20*). **Woe to those who desire the day of the Lord. The day of the Lord is Darkness and not Light (Amos 5:18, 20).** Shall the day of the Lord be Darkness and not Light? Even very Dark with no Light in it (*Amos 5:20*). Woe to those who give Darkness (Lord's Day) for Light (*Isa. 5:20*).... The Lord demand that his followers be glad in his "Day of Darkness" (*Psalms 118:24*).

"Man" and "Darkness" are a contradiction in terms, for Man is the Progeny" of Light, and Darkness only comes to Man when he cease to be inside of the Light, of Self. That is how the Lord became the Prince of Outer Darkness. And to be absent from the Light of Self is to be with the Lord (*II Cor. 5:6*).

The **Mandrake** plant, it's fruit and root are **narcotic** and **aphrodisiac**. Mandrake (דודא) is the fruit that Leah traded with Rachael for a night with Jacob (*Gen. 30:14*). When this plant is consumed it is a sexual stimulant. It is also a narcotic that produces a drugged state. A woman who ingests the Mandrake's fruit or root will be highly sexually aroused, and in a stupor at the same time. The Bible/Torah only mention Leah and Rachael using this plant, but this could also be the **fruit** of the beguilement of Eve (*Gen. 3:3*). This plant may have been used by most if not all of the women who the Lord was involved with. This would include the Daughters of Chaldea (*Isaiah 47:5*), Sarah (*Gen. 21:1*), Rebekah, Leah, and Rachael. The Lord commanded that these women as Daughters of Chaldea consumed the Mandrake fruit, to get themselves into his Darkness, to be ravished (*Isaiah 47:5, Isaiah 7:1 - 7*). This fruit may have also been forced on the thirty two little Midianite girls who were the Lord's share, that he received from the Israelis when the Israelis committed genocide, and holocaust, and rape against the children of Abraham. (*Numbers 31:17, 18, 35, 41*). The Levite priesthood's share was fifty of these little "women children" (*Numbers 31:47*). Without a doubt the Israeli men were **Men of Darkness** (Mandrake), just as their **Lord is a Man** of **Darkness** (Mandrake), the **Prince of Outer Darkness**. The Darkness of the the Lord is a "Thick Darkness"(Apple / אפל), that can be felt (*Ex. 10:22 Ex. 20:21, Deut. 4:11, Deut. 5:22*).

### Hallel

Hallel is Lucifer (הילל) the fallen Prince of Darkness (*Isa. 14:12*). For those who say Hallelujah, it does not mean **Praise the Lord**, but literally means "**Lucifer (Hallel / הילל) Our Jah**".

In the Strong's Concordance **Lucifer** is #1966 (הילל), and the word for **Praise** is under #1974 (הלול) and #1984-5 (הלל). These three words are the same with slightly different shade, but having the exact same meaning. #1984 the word for "**Praise**" even refer back to #1966 the word for "**Lucifer**" as being the same! Hallelujah the term that praises Lucifer is heard continually in

# Personalities
# Lord

*Hallel — Super Man*

churches and synagogue throughout the planet.

Hall/Hell is the root for the word Hallel. Hall (הלל) is also the phonetic root for the word Holy (הולי), which does not mean pure or clean but means "corrupt," or "profane" (חלל)(*Leviticus 18:21*), as when the Lord "Formed (חלל)" or "Corrupted" Israel (*Deut. 32:18*). **Profaned** (חלל) is #2490-1 and **Formed** (חלל)(*Deut. 32:18*) is also #2490-1. The "profanity" that the Lord "formed" Israel into is as described by #2490-1 = "Prostitution," "Sodomy," "Murder" etc.

The same "**forming**" or "**profanity**" that the Lord imposed on the Israelis, had been imposed on the ground of the planet (*Psalms 90:2*), and the population of the planet (*Proverbs 26:10*). The Lord call those who are weak enough to be made corrupt by him fools, and transgressors, and he reward them with foolishness (*Proverbs 26:11*). Thus the name Hallel (חלל) can also literally mean **Hall** ( Corrupt / חל) and **El** (God / אל), or **Corrupter God**.

### Super Man (Captain Marvel)

Hallel (הילל / Lucifer) is LuCipher is Cipher is Cipherman or Super Man. The word Super Man comes from the compounded words Cipher and Man (Cipherman). Cipherman is a contraction of the the term Luciferman. The superman character was created by two young Jewish boys, around 1938. Their names were Joe Shuster, and Jerry Seigel. Is it a coincident, that all of the basic characteristics of the Super Man character are in the Old and New Testament of the Bible/Torah? Is it a coincident that the Lord and Super Man have all of the same basic characteristics? Is it possible that these young Jewish boys picked up this information for the superman character while studying at yeshiva (Jewish Religious School)? They would have had to study both the Torah and the Christian New Testament, for the beginning of the Super Man story coincides with information in the New Testament.

The following is a comparison of three personalities, the Lord and Lucifer in the scriptures, and the third being the superman character: Super Man is a Super Man, Lucifer is a Super Man, and the Lord is a Super Man (*Ex. 15:3*).

The Lord and Lucifer are both "Men" of War (*Rev. 12:7, Ex. 15:3*). "Place was no longer found" in the heavens for Lucifer, and Super Man because their planets Krypton/Crypton were destroyed (*Revelations 12:8*). Neither the Lord or Lucifer have a mother or father. Lucifer the Lord, and Super Man are all called Hallel (חילל)(Hallelujah).

The Lord, Lucifer and Super Man all have even more in common: Lucifer fell (*Isaiah 14:12; Rev. 12:9*), the Lord Almighty fell (*Numbers 24:4, 16*), and Super Man also fell to the earth. Lucifer and the Lord Almighty fell because they were "cast out" (*Rev. 12:9*). Almighty (Shaddai / שדי) means "Cast Out:"

The Lord (Hallel) has a counterpart: L. L. (Lilith), and **Super Man** (Hallel) has a counterpart L. L. (Lois Lane): Superman and the Lucifer, had a metropolis on the side of the north (*Isa. 14:13*), and the Lord had a metropolis (Ur Babel) on the side of the north, of the Tigris River (*Joshua 24:2, 3, 14*). The Lord is a Man of Concealment (Cipherman). Abram, Isaac, and Jacob knew that he

# Personalities
# Lord

*Superman — Baal Zebub*

was El Shaddai (Almighty), but did not know that he was also the Lord (*Ex. 6:3*). Super Man is a Man of Concealment (Cipherman). No one knows that Clark Kent is Super Man.

When the Lord told Moses that he was Almighty (שרי), he was telling Moses that he was the Devil (שרי), who is Lu<u>cifer</u> (Hallel), who is Cipher, or Cipherman (Super Man). In the motion picture series titled **"Superman,"** there is a scene at the beginning of the third movie where the voice of Superman's mother is coming from a crystal, and she is calling Superman "Hallel" or "Lucifer." Hallel is Hallelujah in the Judeo/Christian religious system.

The Superman story says that Superman's planet Krypton was destroyed by natural forces. In comparison the Lord destroys his own planet (*Rev. 12:8*). That is what is being implied when it is written "place was found no more in the heavens" [for the Lord] (*Rev. 12:8*). The superman story says that Superman had a mother and father, but Superman is the Lord and the Lord exists without the aide of a mother or father, like Melchezedek (*Hebrews 7:3*). In the old Superman television series, at the beginning of each show the term "Superman the defender of the American way of life," is heard. The "American way of life" must be reinvestigated, when we discover that the Lord/Superman/Lucifer represent the sacrifice of the innocent, for the preservation of the guilty. In it's history, the American way of life" is founded on the sacrifice of the innocent, to preserve the guilty? The American (European) way of life, is the World (TBL), of the Lord.

Superman under the guise of the Lord, is the preserver of his World (TBL), that he established on this planet, after he fell. The establishment of the Lord's World on this planet was a series of events: The Lord commanded that his son Cain be a husband to his effeminate brother Abel (*Gen. 4:7*): Besides sacrificing the clean animals, Noah a servant of the Lord, attempted to sacrifice the innocence (cleanness) of his grandson Canaan (*Gen. 9:21-24*). The Lord polluted (raped) all of the daughter of his son Cain (*Gen. 6:4, Isaiah 47:1-6*). Beyond this the Lord has officiated over and protected all of the crimes (נפליא) that have been committed, by those who follow him, in the act of preserving his World (TBL). **The entire theme of Judeo/Christianity is the sacrificing of the innocent (clean) for the preservation of the unclean, not the sacrifice of the unclean to preserve the clean!** Both wooly headed brown Jesus and Nimrod (*Rev. 1:14*), were innocent (clean), but were murdered to preserve the filth, that still compose the World of the Lord, even into modern times (*Isa. 53rd Chptr.*). The murder of Nimrod extended the corruptness (TBL) of the World (TBL) of the Lord (Superman) two thousand years forward, to the time of Jesus whose murder then extended the World for another two thousand years. Around 1500, about five hundred years before the end of the Jesus extension (2000), the World was extended even further by the enslavement and Mental Crucifixion of other wooly headed brown people, the children of western Eden (Africa). The wooly headed brown children from western Eden were brought across the Atlantic to help establish the Americas in general, and North America in particular as the most powerful place in the overall World system imposed on this planet. Superman the Lord was defeated, and cast down because he attempted to exalt his throne above the other stars of God: The Lord attempted to be "like the Most High," but became the Most Low, the Chief of the Devils, Baal Zebub (בעל זבב).

# Personalities
# Lord

*Superman— Lord of the Flies — Chart*

## Baal Zebub

Superman is a Baal Zebub which literally means "Lord of the Flies." The Lord identified himself as a Lord of Flies, when he boasted to Moses that he could cause flies to swarm all over Egypt, and yet cause them not to be in the land of Goshen, where the Israelis were living (*Ex. 8:21, 22*) Flies as related to the Lord, started when the Lord commanded that his sons Cain and Abel began to sacrifice animal flesh to him. There are always flies, and maggots any place outside where there is slaughter and the shedding of the blood of men or animals. The shedding of blood for the Lord began in the land of Nod.

The shedding of blood and the sacrifice of life to the Lord was for his survival, for he needed the life in the blood to be sustained. (*Gen. 9:4, Lev. 17:10-13*). The Lord warned the Israelis not to eat the blood, but to pour the blood in the ground where he was (*Exodus 8:22, Deut. 15:23*).

Yet the sacrifice also symbolized something else in the sense of sacrificing all cleanness, and preserving the unclean (*Gen. 8:20*), to allow the World of the Lord to come into existence on this planet.

A Lord of Flies (Baal Zebub) is a Lord of sacrifice, is a Lord or Man of War (*Ex. 15:3*). Sacrifice of innocence, and sacrifice of cleanness, can lead to shedding of blood, and the stench of death. Dead flesh, shed blood, carnage of all kinds draw flies. There were flies in the Ur City Metropolis, when the Lord confounded the Ur/Babel, and incited the Gentiles there to crucify and shed the blood of Nimrod, and the thousands who had come to save the Gentiles, from certain extinction. There were flies in the city of Shechem when the Israelis shed the innocent blood of all boys and men of the city (*Gen. 34:25*). There were millions of flies throughout the land of Egypt (*Ex. 8:24*), when the Lord brought his diseases and plagues there, and the swollen corpses drew flies (*Gen. 12:17, Ex.9:14, Ex. 15:26*). Yet as a true Lord of Flies, as mentioned before the Lord made there be no flies in the land of Goshen, where the Israelis were living in the land of Egypt (*Ex. 8:21, 22*).

Yet when the Lord got the Israelis out in the wilderness, he committed holocaust against them. He killed tens of thousands of Israelis, and the stench, and blood from those corpses drew swarms of flies. Also over the forty years that the Lord kept the Israelis hostage in the wilderness, he forced them to pour tons of blood, of the sacrificed animals, into the ground which in all cases caused flies, maggots, and all of the diseases and plagues of the Lord (*Exodus 15:26, Deut. 7:15*).

There were great swarms of flies in the East Country when the Lord took the Israelis out of Egypt, and took them to the East Country, to committed holocaust against Ishmael/Midian the true children of Abraham (*Gen. 16:3, 4, Gen. 25:1-4*). There were flies all over the land of Canaan again, when the Israelis lead by Joshua, returned to commit holocaust against the Canaanites a second time. In each of these cases where the flies appeared in a place, the flies were following the Lord and the Israelis. The Lord and the Israelis were there to murder, and the flies were there to feed on the carnage, and to lay maggots in the corpses of the victims of the Lord, to be fruitful, and multiply themselves. The following chart shows all of the fore mentioned names of the Lord, the Lord of Flies.

Observation

# Personalities
# Names Chart

*Baal Zebub — Giants — Devil — Superman — Lucifer —Hallel (HalleluJah) —  Cain*

The names to the upper right below are the names of all of the original inhabitants of the planet, including the Lord.

The names below and to the left of the first names, are the names of the God of Abraham. The majority of these names are not written in the Lamb's Book of Life. ***Revelation 13:8***

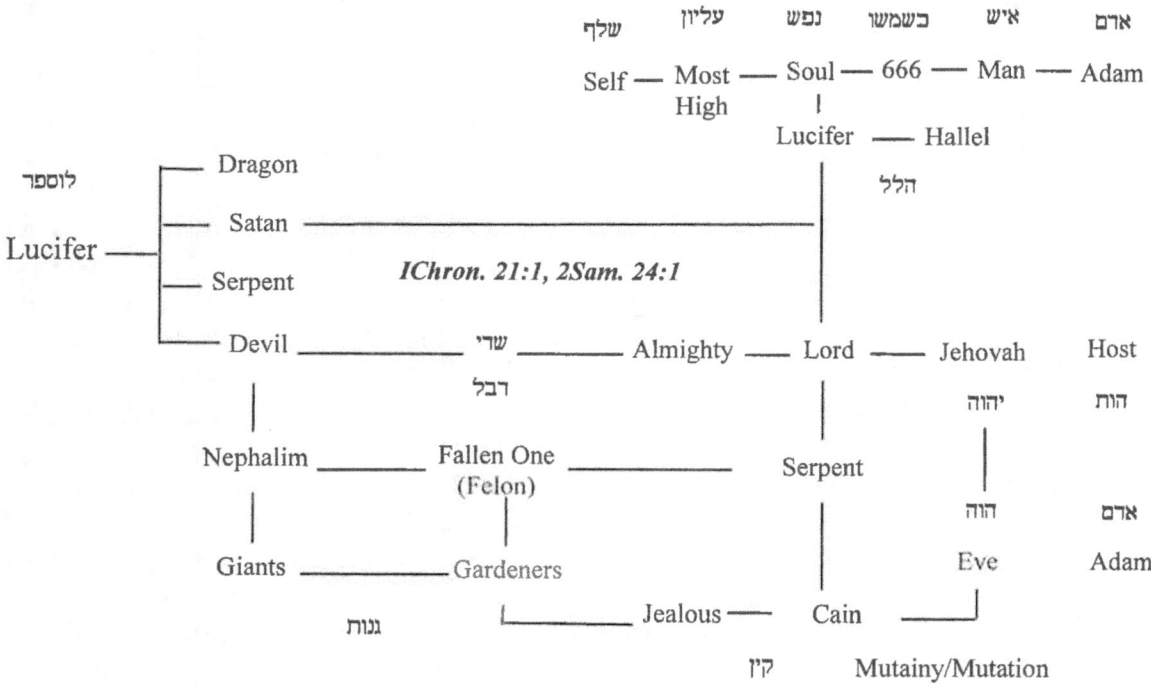

As described before this chart, many of these names are names of the true father of Cain, who is the God of Abraham. None of these names exclusive to the Lord are written in the Lamb's Book of Life (*Rev. 13:8*).

Notes

# Persons
# Cain

*Chart — Child of beguilement — Daughters of Man (Daughter of Chaldea in Darkness) — Gentiles — Wooly and Black until mutated — Cain Mutainy (Permanent Genetic Pale Leprosy) — Cannibals, Child Sacrifice, Slavery, Robbery, Theft, Kidnapping, High Jacking, Vampirism —3 Ball are Chief of all Gentiles (So Called Jews)*

The Lord is the Jealous (Cain) Serpent who beguiled Eve, and impregnated her with Cain, and Abel his effeminate twin brother (*Gen. 3:1, 4:1*). Eve named her first son Cain, when she "got" (קין) him with the Lord (*Gen. 4:1*). Eve named him Cain after his father the Lord, because Cain (קין) means **Jealous**, and the Lord is a **Jealous God** (*Ex 20:5*). Thus Cain the Lord's first begotten son was Jealous Junior, and the Lord was Jealous (Cain) Senior. The Lord had overshadowed Eve to get a line of children who he would use to subplant Seth the beginning of Adam's line (*I Chron. 1:1; Jude 1:14*). As such Cain was to be a Jacob (יעקב), or subplanter (יעקב), of the children of Adam.

Abel is the twin brother of Cain. Abel (Hebel / האבל) means "Effeminate. Cain and Abel had both been righteous (*Matt. 23:35*), until the Lord demanded that they sacrifice to him. *See World Elements, "Bestiality," Pg.254* Abel sacrifice his own flesh (*Gen.4:4*), and his desire was to his brother Cain. But Cain would only sacrifice grain, and the Lord refused to except it (*Gen. 4:5*). The Lord wanted Cain to allow Abel (The Sinner) to desire him, and wanted Cain to "rule over him (*Gen. 4:7*)," or be Abel's keeper (שמר / husband)(*Gen. 4:9*), just as Adam was to rule over Eve (*Gen. 3:16*).

To initiate his World (TBL) on this planet the Lord Hallel would corrupt his twin sons in every way possible. The start of it all was when he made them set up an altar for them to bow, praise, and sacrifice all to him that was clean, and innocent (*Gen. 4:3, 4*). The sacrificing of cleanness and innocence was not so much the sacrifice of the grain and animal flesh. The true sacrifice of cleanness and innocence was when the Lord commanded that Cain be a husband to his "effeminate" (Habel / הבל) brother Abel. The "sinful one" who lay at the door of Cain, was Abel who "desired" him (*Gen. 4:7*). Their father the Lord wanted Cain to rule over Abel, as a husband "rules over his wife" who "desires" him (*Gen. 3:16*). Abel was to be allowed to desire Cain as Eve was to desire Adam (*Gen. 3:16*).

Cain killed his effeminate brother Abel (*Gen. 4:8*). When their father the Lord asked Cain where his brother Abel was Cain said he knew not, and asked the Lord if he was his brother's husband (keeper)(*Gen. 4:9*). The Lord cursed his son Cain from the face of the earth, down into the ground, and sentenced Cain to be a fugitive and a vagabond in the earth (*Gen. 4:11, 12*). Cain was in great fear and told his father that this punishment was too great for him to bear (*Gen.4:13*). Cain explained that as a fugitive and vagabond "in" the earth (ground), there were those there all of whom would attempt to slay him (*Gen. 4:14*). Those who Cain feared were the Giants (Nephalim / נפלים) or Fallen Ones," the Host of Cain's father the Lord. The Lord and his Host had been defeated and casted (Shaddai) down into the earth (*Gen. 6:4, Revelations 12:9, Ex. 8:21*).

Understanding Cain's fear his father the Lord addressed his Host, those in the ground where Cain would be sent, that if any of them slay Cain that Cain's death would be avenged by the Lord

Observations

# Persons
# Cain

*Cain — Felons In the ground — Mark Cain, Pale Leper — Three Balls (TBL) — Uncivil*

seven fold. The Lord then marked Cain with permanent Pale Leprosy to distinguish him from all wooly headed ones, who would be around him in the ground (*Gen. 4:15*).

And Cain went to dwell "in the ground of Nod" (בארץ נוד), on the east of Eden's Garden (*Gen. 4:16*). Marked with **Pale Leprosy** Cain was in the midst of the Host, of his father the Lord Hallel (Lucifer). It was there in the caves of the Mou<u>nd</u> (Nod) of Ararat amongst his father's Host that Cain found his wife one of his father's Lilith(s). The Lilah that Cain chose was the mother of Cain's children. Cain's first son was named Enoch. Cain built a subterranean city and named it Enoch after his son (*Gen. 4:17*). It was there in the north of Nod, in the Mou<u>nd</u> of Ararat that Cain's line was born. The sons of Cain married among the Lilith(s) of his father's Host: Cain's son **Enoch** begot **Irad**, and Irad begot **Mehujael**, and Mahujael begot **Methusael**, and Methusael begot **Lamech**. Lamech married two of the Lord's Lilith(s), Adah and Zillah (*Gen. 4:20, 22*). Adah and Zillah were the mothers of the **Three Bals** that would establish the World of the Lord on this planet. Adah was the mother of Ja**bal** Cain, and Ju**bal** Cain, and Zillah was the mother of Tu**bal** Cain. Tubal (TBL) is the old language word for World (תבל). Tubal (the World) is not the planet or the people of the planet. Tubal (תבל) is the old language word that contains the description for **absolute chaos: Sodomy, Incest, Prostitution, Rape, Murder, Genocide**, and especially **Bestiality (TBL)**. See Strong's Concordance #8396 which describes the World as described above. Thus in understanding the nature of the World which is Tubal, one will understand the situation that Lamech had, when he was explaining to his two wives that he had killed two men. Lamech's ancestor Cain was the older man who had cut/wounded (# 6482 פצע) Lamech for resisting, while the younger man that Cain was with was raping /hurting (# 2250 חבורה) Lamech (*Gen. 4:23*). Lamech knew that his killing of Cain must be avenged seven fold. But Lamech was in the line of Cain, and wondered if his being raped would be avenged also seventy and seven fold (*Gen. 4:24*). This corruptness was Cain and his line, that the Lord had birthed into existence to subplant Adam's line through Seth (*I Chron. 1:1*) *See "Lines" graphics following "Gentiles."*

### Pale Leprosy

The Pale Leprosy of Cain is Albinism, a genetic mutation that normally corrects it's self in the next generation. But Cain's Mutainy or Mutation was locked at the genetic level by his father the Lord. This "mark" on Cain and his descendants the Caucasian Race was set. The albinism could not correct it's self in the next generation or forever (*Gen. 4:15*). This pale Leprosy was a permanent sign to designate the Caucasian as some one totally different than all of the rest of the inhabitants of the planet, who were at that time all wooly headed, and from Black to brown

This albinism of pale leprosy was to distinguish the children of Cain, who became an experimental species, who were allowed to do exactly as their nature would cause them to do.

Notes

# Persons
# Cain

*Cain — Permanent Albinos (Experiment) — Wooly and brown — Nod Prison — World Flood — Strange Cargo (TBL) — World (TBL) Salvation — Gentiles*

Cain had originally been wooly headed and Black, like all of the rest of the original inhabitants of the planet. The original purpose of the "sign," or "mark" of paleness placed upon Cain by his father the Lord, was to distinguish him from all those who were around him, that all should take note not to harm him, for having murdered his effeminate brother Abel.

After the flood Nimrod attempted to graft Cain back into being Black again. In modern times the hand full of Caucasians who know this have an animosity against Black even now. Caucasians were casted out of being Black.

Nod the dwelling place of Cain is the area east of the Tigris River, that is boxed in on the four sides. There are mountains north, and east, the Persian Gulf on the south, and the Tigris River to the west. Nod being blocked in and isolated as such can be considered as having been a prison. The condition in Nod were same as in any prison systems, with sodomy, rape, theft, etc.

**Nod was the birth place of the entire Caucasian Race, the children of Cain.** This was the one spot north of Mesopotamia where all Caucasians originate. None of the Caucasians originally existed in what would be Europe, or any place else on the entire planet.

The Western world has done very much to disassociate it's self from any possible genetic link with Cain. The Bible reader is left to think that Cain and his descendent perished in the flood of Noah. Yet the Caucasian Race is the evidence, that Cain's descendants survived the flood. We know this because there are names of people immediately after the flood who were not listed as passengers on the ark, or descendant of Noah or his children. The pale ones therefore survived without it being noted directly in the Bible/Torah.

Many survived the flood, in the caves of Ararat, and are cleverly spliced into the line of Shem, as a "nameless," "placeless," people (*Gen. 11:1-9*). Others survived as a "strange cargo" on the ark. The ark had three stories. One deck apparently for the animals, the next for Noah's family. The third story is the deck that Noah apparently and perhaps secretly filled with "clean", and "unclean" "Beast" (*Gen.7:1, 2*). The Lord instructed Noah to take on seven pairs of the "clean beast," and two pairs of the "unclean beast." These "beast"(Mute Ones) were not designated male and female, but were designated: "seven a man and his wife" (שבעה איש ואשתו)(*Gen. 7:2*) of the "clean beast," and "two a man and his wife" (שנים איש ואשתו) of the "unclean beast." **Jubal Cain, Jabal Cain,** and **Tubal Cain** are the three elements of Cain (Eve the Widow's Son), that survived the flood secretly on the ark, or sealed in the caves of Ararat!

The children of Cain are called among other things, Chaldeans, Caucasians, Gentiles, Goyim, Heathens, etc. They are all the same people. The term "Raising Cain" relates to the raising of the children of Cain, the Caucasian Race, who are the only Gentiles on the entire planet.

Observations

Notes

# Persons
# Gentiles

*Cain (Pale Leper) — Gentiles (Goyim, Heathens, Nations) — Lines (Asians and Caucasians)*

### Gentiles #1471

The first mention of Gentiles in the Bible/Torah, describe them as being an "Island of Gentiles (גוים)(*Gen. 10:5*). The Gentiles were in deed a pale island in the midst of a Black Sea of people. The children of Cain were identified as Gentiles, and many other names before they were called Caucasians. Some of these names are: Goyim, Nation, Heathens, Horites, and Chaldeans.

Phonetically "Gentile"(Gan Tel / גן תל) means "Rubbish (תל) from the Garden (גן)." The original Gentiles are the Lord, his Host, and his two sons Cain and Abel, who were all casted out as "Rubbish (Gentiles), from the Garden" (*Gen. 3:24*). *See Strong's #1588* (*Gan /* גן */ Garden), and #8510* (*Tell /* תל */* Rubbish Heap). All Gentiles originate from Cain, and his sons and daughters, who mixed in the ground with the male and females, or Liles and Lillith(s), the Host of the Lord. The daughters and sons of Pale Leper Cain were fair (Pale)(*Gen. 6:4*), because Cain passed his genetic leprosy to them. Cain had been marked by his father, the Lord of the North (*Gen. 4:15*).

The Lord wanted to use the children of Cain, to subplant the line of Adam. But these Caucasians could not even sustain themselves, but had to be saved from self extinction by the very ones they were suppose to subplant. It is by their nature that the children of Adam have always saved the Caucasian Race, who are still an "Isles of the Gentiles," surrounded by a planetary Black Sea of people. This have been from the flood of Noah, to the founding of the Americas.

### Goyim #1471

The word "Goyim" (גוים) in the old language is the root for the words **Gentiles** (גוים), **Heathens** (גוים), and **Nations** (גוים). The word Goyim speak to the migratory nature of some of the children of Cain, who could move about in the sun. The word Goyim imply "roving masses" or "hoards" of people. The Goyim were the fugitive and vagabond descendants of Cain (*Gen.4:14*). Before the flood the Goyim roamed to and fro, over the entire length and width of the confinements of the land of Nod. *See Gesenius' Hebrew/Chaldee Lexicon Pgs# 162b, 163a* "גוי" pronounced Goy

### Heathens #1471

The word "Heathen" (גוים) speak to those who could not roam to and fro in the sun, because it would kill them! The heathens were that element of the children of Cain who had to stay in their caves, by their "heaths" in the shadows (*Isa. 18:1*). Cain and his children lost their souls (solar association), when the Lord marked Cain with a permanent pale leprosy.

### Nation(s) #1471

Phonetically the old language word of "Nathan," (נתן) means "Nation." Nathan means "given," "gift," "gave" etc. Eve "got" (was given) Cain from the Lord (*Gen. 4:1*). Cain was the first Nation/Nathan or "gift," that the Lord "gave" (*Gen. 4:1; IChronicles 1:1*)!

Nations are only those who the Lord of Abraham fathered, and "gave" (Natan) to be raised by the husbands of the women he impregnated! The Lord "gave" his son Isaac to Abraham to raise *Joshua 24:3* The Lord "gave"his sons Esau, and Jacob (Israel), to his son Isaac to raise (*Gen.*

Observations

Notes

# Persons
# Gentiles

*Nations— Horites — Chaldeans — Keep Out — Two Lines*

*25:21*)! The Lord "gave" his five sons Reuben, Simeon, Levi, Judah, and Joseph to his son Jacob to raise (*Gen. 29:31-34*). The sum total of Nations are the children of the women that the Lord impregnated. The Lord spoke of the Uniting of his Nations (*Isaiah 66:19, 20*). This status of "Nations" include Cain's pale children, with some of the Lord's other children (Isaac, Jacob, Israelis), who were all wooly headed and brown, because their mothers were not from Cain.

### Horites

In translation Horite (הור) means "Mountaineer." Phonetically the word Hor (הר) is the source of the word "whore." These whores or Horite children of Cain prostrated (prostituted) themselves before the Lord, the father of Cain. Most of Nod is full of mountains (Hori / הורים), which is where the children of Cain lived in Nod, which is east, and north of the Tigris River.

### Chaldeans

The original Chaldeans or Ca-Shaddai (Out Casts) are those who were Cast Out of the Garden, east of Eden, across the Tigris into the land of Nod (*Gen. 3:23, 24*). After the flood Nimrod built the Ur City Complex in northern Nod, for Cain's Chaldean children (*Gen.10:10-12; Gen. 11:2-5; Isa. 23:13*). The city complex was, built for the "Uniting of the Nations." The uniting of the nations that existed just after the flood was the "Raising of Cain." The Israelis did not at that time exist, but would become the finishing or completing of the Nations. The Israelis are "Gentiles," Goyim, or "Nations" because wooly headed Jacob (Israel) is one of the many sons, "nations" or "Gifts" (Nathans/ נתן) of the Lord (*Gen. 25:26*).

Ur was built as a Garden of the north. The Caucasian Race had an absolute choice that they could have stayed there in a Northern Paradise built by Nimrod forever, having been made sufficient to themselves, by Nimrod. They did not have to do the biddings of the Lord. They could have told the Lord "Get thee Hence" (*Matt. 4:10*)!

### Keep them out at all Cost

The children of Adam continued to save the children of Cain, who were now an experiment, by their very existence. The Lord the father of their father Marked Cain had brought these pale blond beings into existence, to subplant Adam's wooly headed brown children. But they could not even sustain themselves. The would be subplanted ones have been sustaining the would be subplanters. From Ur/Babel in Nod, to Washington D.C., from Adam, to Nimrod, to Jesus, to Benjamin Banikker, wooly headed brown people have extended the existence of the pale, for 6000 years. The final test will be to see if Cain's pale children can sustain themselves, after several gifts of civilizings, arts, crafts, skills, and a continual shielding and sheltering away, from any form of harm, other than from each other.

Without being molested, coerced, or intimidated, Caucasian tendencies have always been to do harm, to themselves, and to those who have save them from themselves. The line of Cain continue to exist because the descendants (Line) of wooly headed brown Seth have saved them, to present.

Observations

Notes

# Persons
# Two Lines

*Gentiles —Adam and his line never left the Garden. It was the Man Hallel (Lucifer) and his Host (Including Lilith), and his son Cain (Jealous Jr.), who were casted (Shaddai) out of the East Gate of the Garden across the Tigris River eastward into the land of Nod. The diagram below describes what is truly written in the Bible/Torah. — **Three Balls***

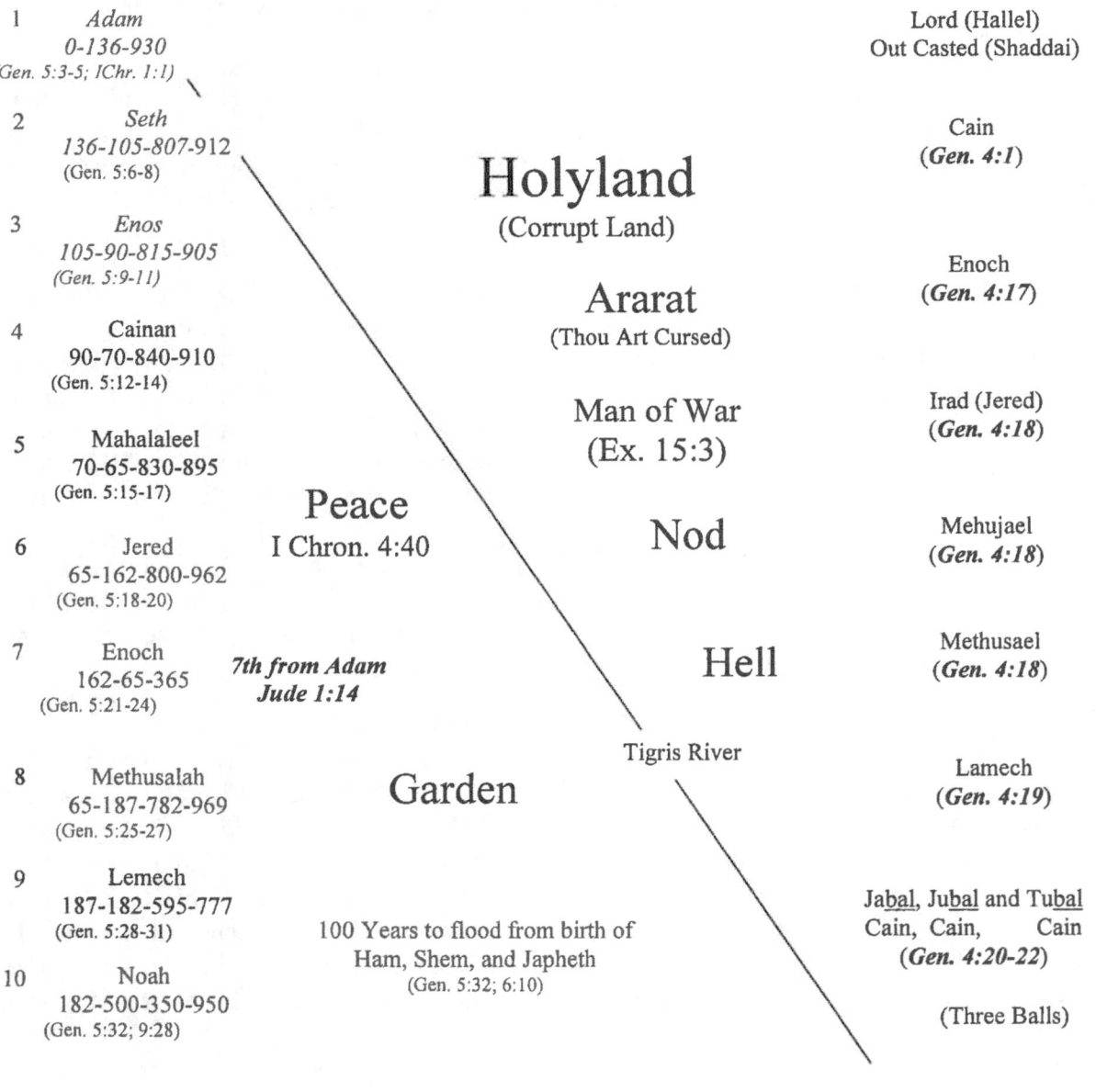

| | | |
|---|---|---|
| 1 | *Adam* 0-136-930 (Gen. 5:3-5; 1Chr. 1:1) | Lord (Hallel) Out Casted (Shaddai) |
| 2 | *Seth* 136-105-807-912 (Gen. 5:6-8) | Cain (**Gen. 4:1**) |
| 3 | *Enos* 105-90-815-905 (Gen. 5:9-11) | Enoch (**Gen. 4:17**) |
| 4 | Cainan 90-70-840-910 (Gen. 5:12-14) | |
| 5 | Mahalaleel 70-65-830-895 (Gen. 5:15-17) | Irad (Jered) (**Gen. 4:18**) |
| 6 | Jered 65-162-800-962 (Gen. 5:18-20) | Mehujael (**Gen. 4:18**) |
| 7 | Enoch 162-65-365 (Gen. 5:21-24) | Methusael (**Gen. 4:18**) |
| 8 | Methusalah 65-187-782-969 (Gen. 5:25-27) | Lamech (**Gen. 4:19**) |
| 9 | Lemech 187-182-595-777 (Gen. 5:28-31) | Ja<u>bal</u>, Ju<u>bal</u> and Tu<u>bal</u> Cain, Cain, Cain (**Gen. 4:20-22**) |
| 10 | Noah 182-500-350-950 (Gen. 5:32; 9:28) | (Three Balls) |

Labels within diagram (left to right): **Holyland** (Corrupt Land); **Ararat** (Thou Art Cursed); Man of War (Ex. 15:3); **Peace** I Chron. 4:40; **Nod**; 7th from Adam Jude 1:14; **Hell**; Tigris River; **Garden**; 100 Years to flood from birth of Ham, Shem, and Japheth (Gen. 5:32; 6:10)

*Tigris River* Garden East Gate

Observations

Notes

# Persons
# Three Balls

*Lines — Tubals (Three Balls) — Arphaxad*

The three balls displayed outside of the Jewish pawn shops represent the last three descendants of Cain/Lamech, just before the flood. These three are Tu<u>bal</u> (חבל) or the World (TBL). With this display the Jewish admit that they are the Chief Gentiles, or Goyim of all the the Lord's World. The World is strictly Gentiles or Caucasians.

Each "Ball" represent two thousand years of the existence of the Caucasian Race, and therefore the World System. The World was allowed to come into existence, and was preserved mainly by the sacrificing of three: Two thousand years, for Adam, two thousand years for Nimrod, and two thousand for Yeshua (Jesus).

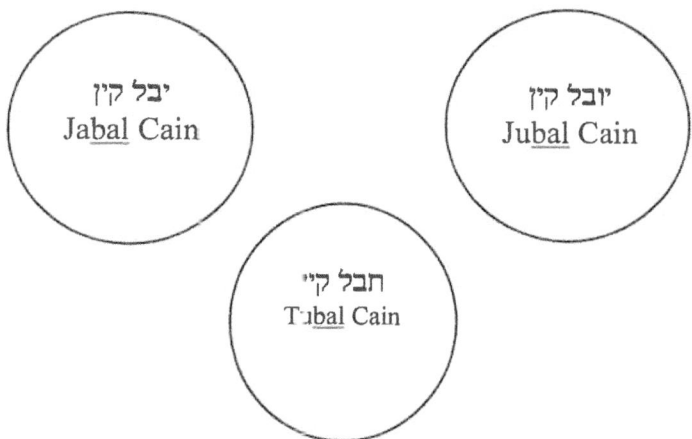

The modern Pale Israelis (Jewish) count the full six thousand years of extension for the Gentile Race, but the other element of Christianity only count from the extension they gave themselves by their murdering Yeshua (Jesus). This extension has accumulated to over two thousand years (2003). The western World has just recently celebrated having extending their World for 2000 years by murdering Yeshua (Jesus), who came to destroy their World. Now the Israelis (Jewish) have pulled down their balls that represent the full extent of time allotted for the existence for the World (TBL). Under normal circumstances the end of the World (TBL) is/was at the two thousandth year extension from the murder of Yeshua (Jesus).

Nimrod had been murdered two thousand years before the murder of Jesus. Nimrod had been killed in a very similar manner as Jesus, by the Gentile ancestors of the Gentiles who would kill Jesus. Arphaxad the predecessor of Abraham was born two years after the flood, and as a grown man he saw the first civilizing of the Caucasian or Chaldean Race, on the side of the north in Nod.

Observations

# Persons
# Arphaxad

*Three Balls —Tubal — Chaldeans — Great Light Isa 9:2 — Nimrod*

Arphaxad is the thirdborn son of Shem (*Gen. 10:22*). Arphaxad was born two years after the flood (*Gen. 11:10*). Shem named his son Arphaxad to denote, their living on the Border of Chaldea, which is on the side of the North, of the Tigris River. The word Arphaxad is a distortion of the term Arpha Ca-Shaddai. Arpha Ca-Shaddai means "Border of the Shaddai," or "Border of the Devils," or "Border of the Out Casted," or "Border of the Chaldeans." It is all the same for the words, **Devils**, **Outcasts**, and **Chaldeans** are all translated back to the same Old language word "**Shaddai**," which is described by each of these words. Arphaxad had been born two years after the flood, on the border of where the Three Bals (Balls) were still buried in the cave city of Cain (*Gen. 4:17*). The survival of the Three Balls of Cain represent the survival of Tubal (TBL) or the World (TBL) of the Lord after the flood. Arphaxad was born in the very midst of the three Balls who are the Ca-Shaddai or Chaldean the Pale Leper children of Pale Leper Cain.

The Chaldeans" are the Gentiles, the Pale Leper descendants of Marked Cain. By Arphaxad's name meaning "Border of Chaldea," these people were already existing only two years after the flood, which means they already existed before the flood, and had survived it. Arphaxad is a very important person in that he is the start of the line that runs from Shem, down to Abraham. Arphaxad is also important because it is his line that times the entire Bible/Torah. Thirdly without the existence of Arphaxad there would not have been a Terah, or Abraham, or Sarah. As such there would not have been an Isaac, or Jacob, or twelve tribes, or Judaism, or Christianity, or western world.

Arphaxad is the source of the story about the location of the Garden. He uses his brother Asshur, his great grand son Hiddekel and his cousin Cush (Ethiopia), to described the location of the garden.

Further more Arphaxad occupies the unique position of being the only Chronicler present in the north after Ham and his children came down from Ararat. Arphaxad had stayed there to record what occurred there concerning the Gentile children of Cain. Arphaxad and his descendants timed the Bible/Torah information, down to the birth of Abraham.

Nimrod the nephew of Arphaxad came back (summoned by the Lord) north to Nod, to built Ur. This was four hundred years before Abraham was born. Nimrod and thousands had come back to the northern side of the Tigris, the river, of his father Cush (Ethiopia) to build a civilizing center for the Gentiles or Chaldeans, the Pale Leper children of the mutation of Cain (Cain Mutainy).

Arphaxad was there to witness and perhaps participate in the building of the six city Ur complex, that was built by his nephew Nimrod and thousands of others who came back north to rescue the the Caucasian race from dying out as a species of being.

Though Arphaxad had only been born two years after the flood, the Gentiles had existed going back to Marked Cain (*Gen. 4:15*).

Arphaxad had been there to see his nephew go down from Ararat in his sister Semiramis' stomach, now Nimrod had returned as a Great Light (*Isa. 9:2*).

Notes

# Persons
# Nimrod

*Arphaxad — We Came Down — Mighty Hunter — Ur/Babel Metropolis — Chaldean(s)*

Arphaxad's nephew Nimrod returned to the northern Darkness of Nod, as a Great Light (*Isaiah 9:2*). Nimrod is the son of Cush and Semiramis. His name Nimrod means "We Came Down." This name commemorates Ham bringing all of his children down from Ararat, after the Tent Incident between Noah and Canaan (*Gen. 9:23, 24*). Nimrod "came down" the mountain in his mother's stomach!

Yet in modern times Nimrod is accused of having held the people of the ark hostage on Mound Ararat. He is then accused of having founded a "false" religion where people bowed down to idols. Those who claim all of this, say further that this false religion was the foundation for all idol worship, and false religion. Yet none of this is scriptural. There is no scripture to support any of these accusations. But scripture does show that Nimrod and thousands of others were summoned by the Lord, from the southern Garden to Nod to Raise Cain, his pale leper children.

There is only seven scriptures in the Bible/Torah, that directly identify Nimrod (*Genesis 10:8, 9, 10, 11, I Chron. 1:10, and Micah 5:6*). The scripture say "and **Cush begot Nimrod** (*Gen. 10:8, I Chron. 1:10*)." Scripture say that "**Nimrod was a mighty one, "in" the earth** (*Gen. 10:8*)," that he was "**a mighty "hunter" before the Lord**" (*Gen. 10:9*), and then it says that he "**built a kingdom composed of six cities:**" 3 cities, **Babel, Erech,** and **Accad** on the plains of Shinar (*Gen. 10:10*), and 3 cities adjacent to these: **Nineveh, Calah,** and **Resen** on the **Tigris River** (*Gen.10:11*). This entire six city complex above the Tigris River was called a great city (*Gen.10:12*). This six city metropolis is the Ur City Complex. In the book of Jonah, Ur is called **Nineveh,** and in the book of Genesis at *Gen. 10:10* it is called **"Kingdom of Nimrod,"** and at *Gen. 11:9* the total **Ur Metropolis** is also called **Babel**.

Nimrod's kingdom the six city Ur/Babel Metropolis is described as being located at the entrance to the land of Asshur (*Micah 5:6*). Nineveh, Resen, and Calah are north of the land of Asshur on the Tigris River. The other three cities Accad, Erech, and Babel must also be adjacent to the first three, north of the land of Asshur. Ur must also be there for Ur was the Great City composed of these six lesser cities. In the book of Jonah, Nineveh (Ur) is described as a Great City, that took three days to walk across (*Gen. 10:1, Jonah 3:2*).

Nimrod had come to Nod at the request of Hallel the Lord of the North (*Gen. 10:9*). The Lord had asked Nimrod to search (Hunt) in the ground for the Gentile children of Cain, who he had sent forth from the face of the earth before the flood (*Gen. 4:14*). Nimrod did all that the Lord asked him. This included building a kingdom to raise Cain's children. Once these children of the Lord could come out into the sun again, the Lord incited them to crucify Nimrod (*Isa. 53 Chptr.*).

These Gentiles made a report that states that Nimrod was a humble man (*Isa. 53:1, 2*), who never did any of the negative that he has been accused of in modern times. The children of Cain admit that they denied Nimrod, even though he had borne their grief, and sorrow (*Isa. 53:3-9*). They admit that they only crucified Nimrod, because it pleased the Lord to bruise him (*Isa. 53:10*).

Babel is Ur, and Nineveh is Ur, both are the same, the Ur of the Chaldeans.

Observations

# Persons
# Chaldeans

*Behold the Chaldeans — Like the Devils — Sexual Chaos — Virgin Raper — Abram*

Behold the Chaldeans, this is a people who were not [in order], until Nimrod the Assyrian founded it, for those who dwelt east of the Tigris River, in the wilderness of Nod (*Isa. 23:13*).

The Chaldeans, the pale leper children of Cain, were marked with the same pale leprosy, as Cain, when he was sent down into the ground, to live with the Lord and his Host (***Gen. 4:14, 16***). The Host of the Lord were the Daughters and Sons of God, who were in the earth in that day (***Gen. 6:2***). Cain's wife was one of the Hostesses or Lilahs (Liliths), of his father the Lord. All of Cain's sons and daughters came from this Lilah. The Hosts and Hostesses of the Lord, were the "Giants" or children of the Gods, in the earth that choose from the "daughters" (and sons), of the man Cain (***Gen. 6:4***). The word Chaldean is a corruption of the compound word Ca-Shaddai (כשדי). Ca-Shaddai means "Like the Devils." The Lord is El Shaddai (God of Devils), his Host were Shaddai (Devils), and Cain's children were Ami Shaddai (People of the Devils)." The Lord, his Host, and the children of the Lord's son Cain were all one.

What made Cain's pale leper children Chaldeans, Ca-Shaddai, or "Like Devils, was that the Lord and his Host infected, them with the same corrupt nature that the Lord and his Host had lived, on his planet Crypton: There was endless mixing between, both male with female, and male with male, and female with female.

Children had sex with their parents (***Lev. 18:9***). Sisters and brothers had sex together (***Lev. 18:9, 11***). Grandparents were having sex with their grandchildren (***Lev. 18:10***). Aunts and uncles had sex with their nephews, and nieces (***Lev. 18:12-14***). Mothers and fathers were having sex with their son's and daughter's mates (***Lev. 18:15***). Brothers and sisters were having sex with each other's mates (***Lev. 18:16***). Men were having sex with a mother and daughter in the same bed at the same time. These same men were having sex, with that same woman's granddaughters (***Lev. 18:17***). Men had sex with a woman and her sister at the same time (***Lev. 18:18***). Women were having sex while on their periods (***Lev. 18:19***). Neighbors were having sex with each other's "wives" (***Lev. 18:20***). As was said before men were having sex with men, and women were having sex with women (***Lev. 18:22***). Besides sodomy, lesbianism, incubi,* and incest, there was also rape and prostitution. Finally the children of Cain, males and females both had sex with animals, and some had offsprings out of it (***Lev. 18: 23***). These hybrid beings were called "Beast," but were not animals, and were called "woman" and "man," not male and females (***Gen. 7:2***). The Chaldean children of Cain had been corrupted in every manner possible. The Lord took the virginity of Cain's Chaldean daughters in the dirt (***Isa. 47:1***). He made them each in their turn let their hair down, and pick up their skirts to expose their vaginas (***Isa. 47:2***). With their nakedness exposed, he took revenge, raping each one of them, as a man comes to a woman (***Isa. 47:3***). The Lord had made them consume his Mandrake (Man of Darkness) fruit an aphrodisiac, to get them back into his Darkness (***Isa. 47:5***). He polluted all of the Chaldean girls, including Sarah, and her sister Milcah in their time (***Isa. 47:6***). The Lord closed their eyes, ears and minds that they would not remember, but would give pleasure, as prostitutes (***Isa. 47:8***). Abram was brown and wooly headed, but as a Chaldean he prostituted his sister/wife/niece Sarah, in the land of Ham. The Ur Metropolis of the Chaldea was the nativity of Abram (***Gen. 11:3, Gen. 15:7, Nehemiah 9:7***).

Notes

# Persons
# Abram (Chaldean)

*Chaldea — Northern Nativity — Indecision — Incest — Hebrewer*

Abraham's name was originally Abram, and his nativity or birth place was in the Chaldean Metropolis of Ur (*Gen. 11:28*). Abram would be the youngest of three sons, born to Terah approximately seventy years apart (*Gen. 11:26, 27*). The place of his nativity the city complex of Ur, was the homeland of the Chaldeans. Ur was on the side of the North, of the Tigris River in Nod (*Joshua 24:2, 3, 14, Isa. 14:12*). Ur was adjacent to Arpachiyah, the city of Arphaxad. Abram descended from Arphaxad (*Gen. 11:10-25*). Abram was a Chaldean only because he was born in the Chaldean city of Ur, among the pale Gentile remnants there. Abram and his family were not Gentiles, but were the wooly headed brown children of Arphaxad, the son of Shem.

Abram had still been sperm in his father's loins when **Melchezedek, Arphaxad**, and the **Lord** came to meet him (*Hebrews 7:10*). All three had come to see who, and what he would be, when his father would impregnate his mother with him. All that the three saw was "Indecision (ברם)." The name Abram (אברם) means "Father (אב) of Betrayal" (רם). The name describes one who is "Casted," "Tossed," back and forth in the wind, "Hanging Like a Feather (ברם)" in the air. No one knows what side of a situation he/it shall land.

They could not tell what Abram would be, for all that they could see was Abram's nature. Abram's nature fluttered "like a feather (ברם)," suspended and "tossed about in the air (ברם)." Anyone with a nature like what they were seeing could betray (Bram / ברם) those around him. Such a person could appear to be one way smiling, and excepting courtesy, and then betray the very ones being courteous to him (Canaanites).

Melchezedek, Arphaxad, and Hallel wanted to know ahead of time what choice Abram would make, in the future, when he became a young man. Would Abram chose the Order of Melchezedek as Arphaxad did, or would he chose the Chaos of Lucifer, the Lord of the North, as his father Terah did (*Isaiah 14:12*)?

Terah fathered two girls with the widow of his son Haran (*Gen. 20:2, 12*). Terah married his two daughters Milcah, and Sarah/Iscah, to their two brothers Nahor and Abram (*Gen. 11:29*). Incest was a part of the Chaos of the Lord. Famine was also a part of the Chaos of the Lord.

The entire land of Nod had always been in perpetual famine for the ground was cursed because of the Lord's presence (*Gen. 3:17*). Haran had died in Ur before his father Terah, from the plagues of the Lord (*Gen. 11:28*). This changed Terah's mind about the Lord, and Terah tried to escape the famine, and the curse of the Lord in Nod, by going away from him, down into the land of Canaan (*Gen. 11:29, 31*). This was the same as when Jacob would later flee from the Lord in Canaan by going down into Egypt (*Deut. 26:5*). But Terah was not successful, because he died in the city of Haran on his way, when he stopped in Haran's city, to collect the few who were still alive there (*Gen. 11:32*). The Lord caught Abram and the rest there in the dead city of Haran, before they could escape, and forced Abram to take him along with him down into the land of Canaan (*Gen. 12:1*). The Lord did not want to be left alone there in the north so he told Abram that he would show him a place in the land of Canaan (*Gen. 12:1*). The Lord and Abram became "Hebrewers," of the Tigris River, down into the Gardenlands of the children of Ham.

Observations

# Persons
# Hebrewer

*Abram — Hebrewer — AbramHam*

Abram was the last of a long list of people who had hebrewed (Crossed) the Tigris before him. "Hebrew" (הבר) is a verb not a noun, "hebrew" is an action not a people or a language.

"Hebrew" (הבר) is the Old Language word meaning "to cross." In secret some have made Abram a "Hebrew," the descendant of "Heber" the grandson of Arphaxad, that Abram descended from (*Gen. 10:25*). Shem the father of Arphaxad committed incest by impregnating Heber's wife with the twins Peleg, and Joktan (*Gen. 10:21*).

But when Abram is called a "Hebrew," or "Hebrewer," it actually pertains to Abram leaving the land of Nod, and "hebrewing" or "crossing" the Tigris and Euphrates Rivers westward. Abram was leaving the land of Nod, and coming down into the peaceful Gardenlands of Ham (*I Chron. 4:40*).

Ham and his children had "hebrewed" the Tigris. They had come down from Ararat, in a Great Exodus, after the Tent Incident, between Noah and his grandson Canaan (*Gen. 21-24*). This was hundreds of years before Abram was even born. Thus Ham and his children were "Hebrewers" before Abram was born, to hebrew the Tigris.

After Ham and his children had "hebrewed" the Tigris, the Gentiles or Chaldeans from the Ur Metropolis, had "hebrewed" (crossed) the Tigris also, long before Abram had been born. The Chaldeans or Caucasians came south in droves after the Lord of the North had confounded their Ur City Complex (*Gen., 11:9, Isaiah 23:13*). The Gentile or Chaldean children of Cain asked the Canaanites for asylum, from the Lord the father of their father Cain. Cain's father is the Lord of the North. These Chaldeans or Caucasians from Nod were quarantined and given asylum, in the twin grain cities of Sodom and Gomorrah, in the land of Canaan..

The children of Ham quarantined these Chaldean "Hebrewers" in an effort to shield the people of Ham, from the corruption from Nod, on the "Side of the North" of the Tigris (*Isaiah 14:13; Joshua 24:2, 15*). Abram was not a Chaldean, but his nativity was the same Ur Complex, among the remnant of the Chaldeans, who did not flee from the Lord. Abram and his small group were the last ones left to hebrew their way out of the destitute land of Nod.

Crossing (Hebrewing) a river does not cause a people to come into existence. A people hebrewing a river speaks the same language after they hebrew, that they spoke before they hebrewed the river. Abram and all of those who crossed (hebrewed) the river with him spoke the same language, and were the same people before and after they crossed (הבר) the river. Noah, Shem, Ham, and Japheth and all of their children spoke the same language. None of them were Hebrews, or spoke Hebrew, for both terms Hebrew Language, and Hebrew People are inventions, in the more modern times. When Abram arrived in Canaan and Egypt, everyone were able to understand him perfectly, and he could understand them, for they were all of one language and one speech (*Gen. 11:1*).

Abram and the Lord Hebrewed" the Tigris, the northeastern River of Cush, (Ethiopia), down into the land of the children of Ham (*Gen. 2:13, Isaiah 18:1, Zephoniah 3:10*). Abram did not become AbramHam until **Abram** was in the land of **Ham**.

Notes

# Persons
# AbramHam

*Hebrewer — Incest in Nod — AbramHam — Becoming Ham — Abraham*

**Abram** did not immediately became **Abraham** from the time that he and the Lord successfully "hebrewed" the the Tigris River down into the land of **Ham** (Abram in Ham)(*Gen. 12:5*). Abram and his sister/wife/niece Sarai would have to earn their names from the Lord, by completing their mission, for the Lord, in the land of Ham. Until he had completed his mission Abram would only be AbramHam.

Abram, Lot, Sarai, and the Lord were all destitute, and had no possessions when they came from Nod. The famine that came with them into the land of Canaan, was the very first that ever occurred in all of the land of Ham. Famine is used as the excuse for AbramHam and his sister/wife Sarai going down into Egypt (*Gen. 12:10*). But famine was only there in the land of Canaan because the Lord brought it there. Yet Sarai and Abram along with the Lord went hundreds of miles, into Egypt, pass much food, to get to where the Pharaoh was. Abram/Ham pretend that he was afraid that the Pharaoh might murder him for his sister/wife, but he knew that the Pharaoh would not hurt him, because the Lord was there with him and his sister/wife Sarai (*Gen. 12:11, 12*). So when Abram/Ham told Sarai to tell the Pharaoh that they were sister and brother it was because he knew that the Pharaoh would not have had anything to do with Sarai, if Pharaoh knew they were husband and wife. Abram/Ham wanted the Pharaoh to have Sarai, and wanted to take gain from it! But first the Princes of Pharaoh were attracted by the fairness (paleness) of Sarai this light complexioned Black women (*Gen. 12:14*). They "penetrated" (הלל) Sarai before Pharaoh, and then Sarai was brought into the Pharaoh's house (*Gen. 12:15*). The Lord and Abram/Ham had succeeded, for the the Pharaoh entreated him well for Sarai's services (*Gen. 12:16*). Abram/Ham was now truly established in the land of Ham, but the problem was getting away from the Pharaoh with all of the goods that they had obtained from him. This was when the Lord stepped in and plagued the house of the Pharaoh, because AbramHam's sister/wife "Sarai spoke it" (דבר שרי)(*Gen. 12:17*). The Pharaoh had to let them go with all of the goods that he had given Abram/Ham for sex with Sarai (*Gen. 12:20*). Abram/Ham was very rich, with silver and gold from prostituting Sarai to the Pharaoh (*Gen. 13:2*).

The Lord's famine had not driven them out of the land of Canaan, they took the famine with them, down into the land of Egypt in the form of a plague. The Lord, Abram/Ham, and Sarai had gone to Egypt to make great wealth from the Pharaoh! There was no famine in Canaan, it was now a plague used by the Lord in Egypt, against Pharaoh.

When AbramHam, Lot, Sarai, and the Lord returned to the land of Canaan again, they would pulled the same trick with Abimelech, as they had pulled with Pharaoh, and get again, as much from Abimelech as they had gotten from the Pharaoh (*Gen. 20:14, 16*).

AbramHam left Egypt with whole flocks of sheep, and oxen, and asses, and man and maid servants. One of these "maid servant" women was Hagar an Egypto-Hamite woman. AbramHam, used Hagar the Hamite woman, to rape himself into being called Abraham by the Lord (*Gen. 12:16*).

Observations

# Persons
# Abraham's Seed or Children

*AbramHam—Abraham's Seed or Children — Abraham Chart*

Before Sarai sent AbramHam into Hagar's tent to rape her (*Gen. 16:3*), Abram had complained to the Lord that he the Lord had not given "seed, " and Abram/Ham was without an heir (*Gen. 15:3*). At that point the Lord assured Abram/Ham, that his own heirs (children) would come from his own bowels (*Gen. 15:4*). Yet the twist came when the Lord took him out to look at the stars to show Abram/Ham the number that his "seed" would be (*Gen. 15:5*). A man's "seed" do not have to be his "children" from his own loins." Abram had asked the Lord to "give seed," which meant that Abram had wanted the Lord to impregnate his sister/wife/niece Sarai, since he himself could not make her pregnant. In the culture that Abram and Sarai had come from, in the north, it was a man's "child" if he made his wife pregnant, and it was only his "seed" if some one else made her pregnant. This had been the case when Abram's older brother Haran had died, and their father Terah had made Haran's wife pregnant twice with Milcah, and Sarai/Iscah (*Gen. 11:28, 29*). Milcah and Sarai/Iscah were the "seed" of Haran, only because they were born from Haran's wife, even though Haran was long dead in the ground (*Gen. 11:29*). AbramHam and Sarai had the same father Terah (*Gen. 12:13, 19; Gen. 20:5, 12*).

The Lord gave AbramHam, the new name Abraham (*Gen. 17:5*), when he became a part of the house of Ham by impregnating the Hamite women called Hagar and Keturah (*Gen. 16:4; 25:1-2*). Ishmael/Midian was the sum total of Abraham's children (*Gen. 37:25-28*). The Lord also change Sarai's name to Sarah (*Gen. 17:15*), because she had sent AbramHam in to impregnate the first Hamite woman.

This "anyone's sperm into any woman" lifestyle from the north continued when the Lord "Visited" (פקד) Sarah and "gave his seed" to impregnate her (*Gen. 21:1, 2*). The Lord then gave Isaac "his seed" to AbramHam, to raise (*Joshua 24:3*). Abram sent all of his **children** (Ishmael/Midian) from his own loins (*Gen. 15:4*), away to the **East Country**, so that he could raise the Lord's son Isaac without interference from his own children (*Gen. 25:6*).

The Lord's son Isaac also entreated (tempted / עתר) his father the Lord to "rub against" (נבח) his cousin/wife Rebecca and "give seed," because he could not impregnate his cousin/wife after twenty years (*Gen. 25:21*). The Lord was tempted (עתר), and the Lord "rubbed against" (נבח) Rebecca and made her pregnant (*Gen. 25:21*). Jacob (Israel), and Esau the Lord's sons, were the "seed" of his son Isaac, but not Isaac's children (*Exodus 4:22, 23*). The Lord gave his sons Jacob, and Esau to his son Isaac to raise (*Joshua 24:4*).

Judah would continue this "seed" transfer, when he demanded that his son Onan "give seed" to impregnate his dead brother Er's wife, so that Onan could raise up "seed" for Er (*Gen. 38: 8*). But Onan spilled the seed on the ground, and the Lord killed him (*Gen. 38:9, 10*).

Israel was never the "Seed" of Abraham until they murdered Ishmael/Midian, and then raped the daughters of these Children of Abraham, and impregnated these little girls with their seed (*Numbers 31:18; 35, 40*). The Israeli holocaust and rape against the children of Abraham was all orchestrated by the Lord who was betraying his most loyal servant Abraham. Abram had crossed (Hebrewed), the River of Cush, with the Lord, to betray (cross) the inhabitants of the Lands of Ham.

Notes

# Persons
# Abraham's Seed or Children

*Children or Seed — Chart — Cush*

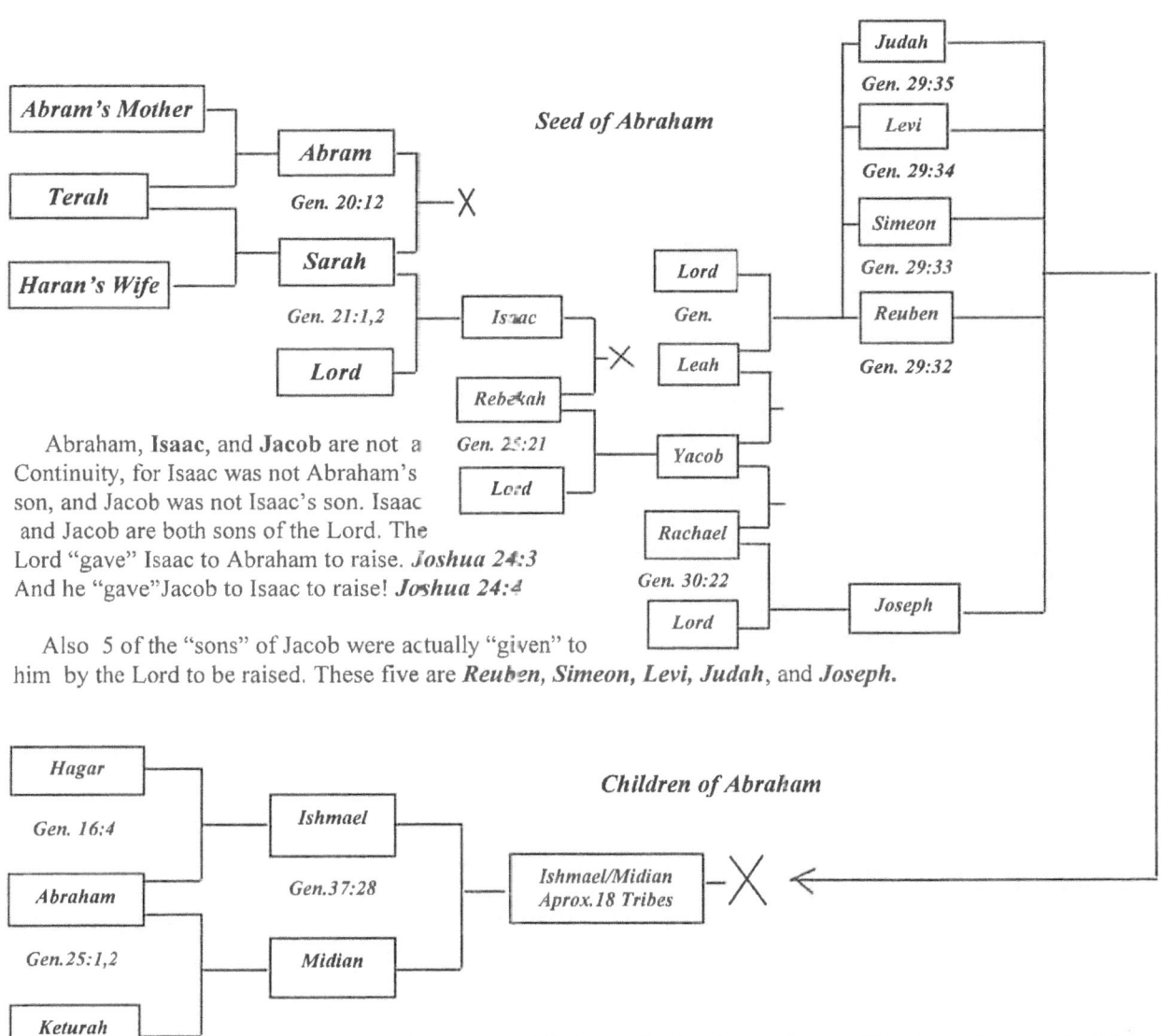

Abraham, **Isaac**, and **Jacob** are not a Continuity, for Isaac was not Abraham's son, and Jacob was not Isaac's son. Isaac and Jacob are both sons of the Lord. The Lord "gave" Isaac to Abraham to raise. *Joshua 24:3* And he "gave" Jacob to Isaac to raise! *Joshua 24:4*

Also 5 of the "sons" of Jacob were actually "given" to him by the Lord to be raised. These five are *Reuben, Simeon, Levi, Judah,* and *Joseph*.

Ishmael/Midian are the true "Children of Abraham. In the Exodus, the Lord did not take Israelis from Egypt to Palestine, but took them perhaps a hundred miles out of the way to the East Country" to commit Holocaust and to subplant (take the place of) Abraham's children Ishmael/Midian. Israel kept the little Ishmael/Midianite girls and raped themselves into being the "Seed of Abraham," not "Children of Abraham." Israel carries it's linage through the female, for who knows who the father may be (*Numbers 30:41*)? Mother's baby, father's maybe.

Observation

# Persons
## Cush (Ethiopian)

*Hebrew(er) — Guardians of the East Gate — Rivers of Ethiopia (Broad Gate) Canaan*

After the flood, Ham placed his oldest son Cush (Ethiopia / כוש) in Mesopotamia (Between Rivers), to guard the hebrewing of the Tigris. After the Tent Incident Ham and his children were the first to hebrew (cross) the Tigris River, back down into the Garden west of the river. Ham and his family came down from Nod/Ararat to protect themselves, and to guard and keep the way to Eden (Africa), the tree of Life (*Gen. 3:24*).

Cush (Ethiopia) the oldest son of Ham (*Gen. 10:6*), had been born on the ark ship during the flood. Cush's name is under the word Ethiopia (כוש) throughout the Bible/Torah. After the flood Ham designated the Tigris and Euphrates, as the two Rivers of Ethiopia or Cush (כוש)(*Gen. 2:13, 14; Isa. 18:1; Zephoniah 3:10*). Ham also designated the land (Mesopotamia) between the two rivers, as the land of Ethiopia, or the land of Cush. Cush's Mesopotamia (Ethiopia) the "Land between the Rivers was the first land that anyone would reach, coming westward, from Nod, across the entire length of the Tigris River. Cush was to guard the entire length of the Tigris, from anyone coming across from Nod. Cush was also to protect the land strip that runs east all the way to western India. Cush was to protect this Broadway at all cost. The Tigris was the Broadway that led eastward to the Destruction of the Lord in Nod (*Matt. 7:13*). The defense of the Garden and Eden (Africa) was still not secure, for Cush's children were spread thin, from Mesopotamia to Hindu (Indian) Cush. Nimrod was the youngest son of Cush (*Gen. 10:8*).

It was a convenient coincidence that the Lord summoned Ham, to send Nimrod to Raise Cain, his pale leper children. The Lord wanted them raised just enough, that he could form them into an army, to invade the Garden and Eden! Ham knew this but saw it as an opportunity to cancel out the Lord's effect, on the Caucasians altogether. Nimrod's mission from his people in the south was to Raise Cain, his pale descendants, to free them from the Lord's control. Once Nimrod had converted them, and healed them by opening their eyes, ears, and minds (*Isa. 6:10; Matt. 13:15*), the pale ones could tell the Lord: "Get thee Hence Satan." As such Nod would be a paradise for the Caucasians. But the Lord of the North confounded it all, and brought it to ruins (*Gen. 11:9; Isa.23:13*). Then the Lord incited the pale ones that Nimrod had saved, and caused them to crucify Nimrod (*Isa. 53:10*).

Those Chaldeans that survived the Lord's confounding of Ur/Babel made a great exodus away from the Lord, and were given asylum down in the peaceful land of Ham, in Canaan.

The Europeans placed Cush's land (Ethiopia) below Misraim (Egypt), which is in Eden (Africa). In actuality the people in the African Ethiopia call themselves Abbys and call their country Abbysinnia, they are actually Phut or Punt, the third son of Ham (*Gen. 10:6*).

While Cush's (Ethiopia's) Mesopotamia was a buffer zone between Nod and Eden, it was also a prosperous fertile crescent. The prosperity of the overall land of Cush can be seen in the English word "cash" that originate from the word Cush, and also the word "Purse" from the word Persia, which was an extended part of the land of Cush. All of the land of Cush was a paradise until Abram and the Lord "hebrewed' down into Cush. The Lord and Abram brought famine and crime from Nod to Cush, and from Cush down into the land of Canaan. Canaan was a buffer state between Cush the guard of the East Gate, and Misraim (Egypt) the Narrow Gate.

# Persons
# Canaan

*Cush —Tent Incident — Armageddon — Roasted Grain — Mesorets*

Canaan was the fourth son of Ham (*Gen. 10:6*). Canaan was born on Ararat, after the flood. The name Canaan (בנען) literally means "Like We Meek (ענה)." Those who are meek are not weak. See page #229 "Meek." When Ham named his son "Meekness (Canaan)," it would be a prediction of all the "affliction (ענה) the the Lord would impose on the children of Canaan, because Canaan had exposed Noah as a child molesting Sodomite, in service to the Lord (*Gen. 9:21, 22*). The incident with Noah being naked and drunk in his tent with his little grandson Canaan, became known, as the Tent Incident.

It was the Tent Incident between Noah and Canaan that caused Ham to bring his children down from Mount Ararat, in a Great Exodus, after the flood. For his protection Canaan was placed in the midst of the Garden, so as not to be directly exposed to those in Nod, who wanted to take revenge against him for exposing his grandfather Noah, for the sodomite that he was.

The land of Canaan was adjacent to the land of Cush. Cush was Canaan's oldest brother. Cush's land of Mesopotamia protected the approaches to the land of Canaan. The land of Canaan was the protective buffer between Cush's Mesopotamia, and Ham/Mitzraim's Narrow Gate Egypt, which lead into Eden (Africa).

When Noah was exposed, the core of what Holy (קדש / הולי) means was also exposed! To be Holy (קדש) is to be made corrupt (חוללי) by being sodomized (קדש). It was Hallel the father of Cain and Abel who initiated the act of sodomy in the Land of Nod. The Lord started sodomy between Cain and his effeminate twin brother Abel who desired him (*Gen. 4:7*)

The Lord's agenda was to take revenge on Canaan for the damage he had done by exposing Noah! The curse that Noah attempted to place on his grandson Canaan never occurred. Canaan and his many children were prosperous along with all of the rest of the children of Ham, and Ham himself. The curse of Noah against Canaan back fired, even though Canaan and his children were servants, to the servants of the Lord (*Gen. 9:25*). All of the Lords servants eventually fled from the Lord, down into the land of Canaan, to be saved/served by Canaan and his children! Shem was in bondage (service) to the Lord, and Canaan and his children served the children of Shem, to save them from the effects of being in bondage (service) to the Lord. The Lord even had Abram to bring him down, into the land of Canaan with him (*Gen. 12:1*).

The Lord had not only come down to the land of Canaan to be saved himself, but also to take revenge on Canaan for Noah, and to punish the Caucasians (Chaldeans) who had fled Ur (Babel) when he confounded it (*Gen. 11:9, Isa. 23:13*). Canaan had given them asylum from the Lord, and quarantined them in the twin Canaanite grain cities of Sodom and Gomorrah. The negative reputation for these twin cities came from the activities of Cain's Chaldean or Gentile children, who practiced their northern way of life in these old grain cities. "Sodom" originally meant "roasted grain," not anal intercourse! The sodomy that Ham had saved his family from in Nod, was now at the gate of Misraim (Egypt / Mesoret), the Narrow Gate into Eden (*Matt. 7:13,, 14*).

# Persons
# Mesoret (Egyptians)

*Canaan — Narrow (Strait) Gate — Exoduses — Israeli Egyptians — Ishmael*

After Canaan, Egypt (Mesorets) the Narrow Gate was the last defense for Eden (Africa) to it's west. Around the entire continent, there is no land entrance into Eden (Africa), except through Egypt (Mesor) the Strait Gate (*Matt. 7:13, 14*). Egypt was the Strait Gate leading to Life, in Eden.

Ham made Egypt (Mesor) his chief tabernacle and strength: HamMitsraim, Chamits, Chemets (*Psalms 78:51*). Ham and all of his children were peaceable (*I Chron. 4:40*), but how do peaceable people defend against aggressors? The defenses established by Ham were to protect, not hurt.

Nimrod was sent to build Ur/Babel, with the design to help the the pale ones in Nod mutated by the Lord. The plan was that they must stay there in Nod, and be united against the Lord to prevent him from using them to invade down into the Garden (*Gen. 11:6*). But the Lord confounded Cain's pale children, he meted them out and trodden them down, and he peeled them, and scattered them (*Isa. 18:2*). They left Nod not as an Army, with the Lord leading them, but as a great exodus fleeing from the Lord, down into asylum in the land of Canaan. Nimrod was murdered, but the loss of his life, postponed the Lord being able to invade Eden and the Garden. Eden and the Garden were still in peace, and safe from the Lord.

The peace lasted and Eden and the Garden were protected for four hundred years, until the time of Terah and Abram (*Gen. 11:24, 26, 27*). It would have lasted even longer if Abram and his father could have escaped from the Lord in Nod, down across the Tigris, into the land of Canaan (*Gen. 11:31*). Terah, and Abram's escape would have been the end of the the Lord and his World, but Terah died. The Lord caught up with and forced Abram, to bring him and his Host eventually down into the very heart of Misraim (Egypt). They came to prostitute Sarah, and to spread a few plagues, but could not do anymore, without an army. Ham had taken away the Lord's army in Nod, when the pale lepers escaped from him down into the land of Ham!

Next the Lord would attempt to raise himself an army in the form of the Israelis. The Lord oversaw the Israelis coming into existence. Born out of incubi, incest, and rape, in the land of Canaan, the Israelis would multiply in the land of the Mesorets (Egyptians), in the Strait and Narrow Gate that led to Eden (Africa), the Tree of Eternal Life (*Matt. 7:14*). When they had grown to a sufficient number they would call on the name of the Lord. The Lord and his Host would come down into Egypt, and use the Israelis as a great army, to break through Egypt, to invade down into Eden (Africa), to destroy the Keystone (Africa/Eden) that the Lord had rejected.

But the Israelis had no intentions of ever leaving Egypt, or being associated with the Lord, ever again. The only way that the Lord got back down into Egypt was when the Israelis cried out, when the Egyptians made them start building houses for themselves. When the Lord came to Misraim (Egypt), he was full of wrath for the Israelis, and the Egyptians. He destroyed Egypt, and tore the Israelis out of the ruins, to carry them out into the wilderness to take his revenge on them. Only three Israeli born in Egypt were allowed to come out of the wilderness alive. The Lord made the rest and their children die in the wilderness. The Israelis who came out of the wilderness were the pale leper "seed," of the Lord and his Host, with the Israelis females of the tribes. He would use them to commit holocaust against Ishmael/Midian the only children from Abraham's own loins. All Hamites including Ishmael were after the Order of Melchezedek.

Notes

# Persons
# Ishmael

*Mesorets — Out of Abraham's own loins (Child of Rape)* ***Gen. 15:4*** *— Son of the bondwoman* ***Gen. 21:12*** *— Son not "Seed"— Keturah Abraham's wife* ***Gen. 25:1*** *— Isaac*

Ishmael's mother was the Mesoret (Egyptian) woman, Shari Misraim also known as Hagar (***Gen. 16:3, 4***). Before Ishmael had been born Abraham had complained to the Lord, that the Lord had not given seed (sperm), that he (Abraham) would have an heir (***Gen. 15:3***). The Lord instructed Abraham, that his inheritor would come from his own loins (***Gen. 15:4***). It was true, but Abraham's true heir came from him raping the Hamite/Egyptian women Hagar (***Gen. 16:4***). Hagar despised Sarah, for letting her uncle/brother/husband Abram rape, and impregnate her (***Gen. 16:4***). Ishmael's mother's name was Shari Mizraim, but Abraham and his sister/wife/niece Sarah hated her, and called her Hagar. Hagar means "Outsider," "Stranger," "Foreigner," etc. Sarah told Abraham that "Hagar" despised them both, so he told Sarah to do with Hagar, and Ishmael as she pleased (***Gen. 16:6***). Abraham even refused to feed his son.

Ishmael was a fifteen year old bag of bones, weak and light enough, that his mother had to carry him on her back, when Abraham gave Hagar a bottle of water and piece of bread, and cast them out into the wilderness to die (***Gen. 21:14***). Ishmael survived in spite of Abraham's attempt on his own son's life (***Gen. 21:***). The name Ishmael (ישמעאל) means "God Hears," for the Lord God (Michael/Melchezedek) "heard" Hagar's affliction (***Gen. 16:11***). ...... שמע יהוה אל ...

Abraham also had six other sons with another Hamite woman Keturah (***Gen. 25:1, 2***). These six sons were the brethren of Ishmael, that Ishmael resided with, and they became a confederation . The six sons of Keturah under the name of Midian, along with the twelve sons of Ishmael became Ishmael/Midian. These Hamites were the only children from the loins of Abraham (***Gen. 25:1, 2***). Their overall dwelling place was from Havilah to Shur before Egypt, and over into the East Country of Amori (Mari), on the Euphrates River. Amor was the son of Canaan (***Gen. 25:6***). Amor's central city was called Mari, and was located along the central portion of the Euphrates, the Fruitful River (***Gen. 37:25, 27, 28***). Abraham's Ishmael/Midianite children existed before Israel ever came into existence, or went into Egypt to be saved from the famine of the Lord.

The Lord brought Moses and the Israelis up out of Egypt, and away from Palestine, over into the East County of Amor. The Amorites never afflicted Abraham's children, Ishmael/Midian who had dwelt with the Amorites for over four hundred years (***Gen. 15:13,*** ). But it was the Israelis who the Lord brought to the East Country, to afflict the Amorites and Abraham's children! Israel murdered all of the Ishmael/Midianite men, women, and boys, including Moses' own Midianite wife and sons Gershom and Eliezer (***Exodus 2:16, 21***).

The only ones who survived this holocaust were 32,000 little Ishmael/Midianite girl women (***Nu. 31:35***), who the Israelis kept, except for those that they had sodomized (שכב). Moses instructed the Israelis to kill all of the little girls, they had sodomized (שכב)(***Nu. 31:17***). The Lord was given thirty two of these "women children (***Nu. 31:40***). The Levites were given fifty of these little girls (***Nu. 31:47***), and the rest of the little girls were given to the males of the twelve Israeli tribes, to rape themselves into being the "Seed of Abraham." Ishmael's children were thrown away for the sake of Israel, just as Ishmael had been thrown away for the sake of Isaac. The Lord had "given seed" to impregnant Sarah, with his son Isaac (***Gen. 15:3***).

Observation

# Persons
# Isaac

*Ishmael — "Visiting" (פקד) Sarah/Iscah Daughter of Chaldea again — Isaac (laughter) Son of the Lord — Gift to Abraham — Moriah (Bitter Jah) — Jacob gift to Isaac — Israel*

The Lord used his son Isaac to subplant Ishmael. Isaac came from the "seed" that the Lord gave to Sarah (*Gen. 21:1, 2*). The Lord gave his son Isaac to Abraham to raise (*Joshua 24:3*). The Lord had told Abraham that he would "bless" (ברך) Sarah, and that he the Lord would "give" Sarah a son for Abraham to raise (*Gen. 17:16*). The Lord told Abraham that at the set time he would return to Sarah, and Sarah would have a child (*Gen. 18:10*). Sarah asked the Lord if she would have pleasure (*Gen. 18:12*), and the Lord asked Sarah if anything was too hard for him to do (*Gen. 18:14*)? The Lord had visted (פקד) Sarai in her youth, as he did all of the pubelescent Chaldean girls to take their virginity (*Isa. 47:1- 7*). Thus the Lord "revisited" (פקד) Sarah and "did to her what he had said," for Sarah became pregnant ... Isaac is the son that Sarah had "with" the Lord when the Lord "Visited" (קפד)" her (*Gen. 21:1, 2*).

Isaac (יצחק) means "Laughter" or "Mocking," which is what Sarah did when the Lord told her that he was going to return in due season, to make her pregnant (*Gen. 18:12; 21:1, 2*).

Ishmael laughed (Isaaced / יצחק) at Isaac (laughter / יצחק)(*Gen. 21:9*), and Sarah used this as an excuse, to tell Abraham to get rid of Hagar and Ishmael (*Gen. 21:10*). Scripture say that Abraham grieved about sending the son from his own loins away (*Gen. 21:12*). Yet Abraham had mistreated Ishmael by starving him. Ishmael was just a weak 15 year old sack of bones, that Hagar had to put on her back to carry, when Abraham sent them away to die in the wilderness (*Gen. 21:14*). Abraham was mocking or laughing (Isaacing / יצחק) at them, when he only gave them a piece of bread and a bottle of water and sent them on foot out into the wilderness.

The Lord of Abraham was watching to see how long it would take for Ishmael to die. Ishmael (ישמע אל) means "God Hears," but the God who heard Ishmael crying was not the Lord of Abraham. The God that heard Ishmael crying, was Melchezedek (*Gen. 17-19*). When Melchezedek saved Ishmael the Lord was furious, and went immediately to Abraham, to tell him to take his "only son" (Ishmael), to a mountain that he would show him. The Lord wanted Abraham to cut Ishmael's throat, and to burn Ishmael as a sacrifice to him (*Gen. 22:2*). The Lord wanted to finally be through with Ishmael, so that Abraham could raised the Lord's son Isaac, to subplant Ishmael.

When the Lord told Abraham to bring his "only son" Abraham did not know that Ishmael was still alive. Ishmael was the only time that Abraham had an "only son," plus Isaac was the Lord's son. But Abraham thought he had killed his own son Ishmael, and so he brought the Lord's son Isaac with him to burn as a sacrifice. The Lord was bitter (Moriah / מוריה), at Abraham, and told Abraham to take his hands off of his son (the Lord son) Isaac (*Gen. 22:12*). "Moriah" (מוריה) means "Bitter Jah," or "Bitter Jehovah" (*Gen. 22:2*).

Perhaps Abraham was bitter also at the Lord, because after he sacrificed the ram to the Lord he did not have anything else to do with the Lord (*Gen. 22:13*). The Lord had missed killing Ishmael. But the Lord's children the Israelis lead by Moses would kill the Ishmael/Midianite "Children of Abraham," except for the little girls, with whom they used to rape themselves into being the "Seed of Abraham" (*Gen. 31:18*). Jacob (Israel) was the Lord's next son (*Joshua 24:4*).

Notes

# Persons
# Jacob the Lord's Son (Ex. 4:22)

*Isaac — Jacob (Subplanter) — Jacob to Israel (Wrestled God) — Israeli Tribes*

Isaac was not the father of Jacob, but was Jacob's elder brother, for the Lord was the father of both Isaac (*Gen. 21:1, 2*), and Jacob (*Gen. 25:21; Ex. 4:22*). Jacob (יעקב) means "Subplanter," or "heel" as one who is "behind" someone, but who comes forward with stealth to take that person's place (*Gen. 25:26*). By this definition Jacob was not the first "Jacob" or subplanter. The Lord was the first "Jacob" or Subplanter because he set events into motion to subplant Adam and his descendants. The Lord is the Serpent (not snake), who beguiled Eve and impregnated her with Cain, the beginning of the Lord's line (*Gen. 4:1, I Chron. 1:1*). Cain was the second "Jacob." The Lord's purpose for Cain was to "subplant" Seth's line, the line of Adam (*Gen. 5:3*). The line of Cain could not subplant the line of Seth. These Pale Leper children of Cain could not even sustain themselves. They had to be continually saved by the the children of Seth. Cain's children, utterly failed to supplant Seth, and Cain's line only survived, because Nimrod in the line of Seth came north, to Raise Cain's pale leper children, from the depraved state, the Lord of the North had reduced them to. Cain died in Nod, murdered by Lamech (*Gen. 4:15, 23, 24*)

Abram was not a Jacob (Subplanter), or in the line of Cain at all, but the Lord used him as a subplanter to bring him into the lands of the children of Adam (*Gen. 12:1*). The Lord impregnated Abram's sister/wife/niece Sarah, and gave Isaac to Abram to raise (*Gen. 21:1, 2*). Isaac was never a Jacob, because he could not even impregnate his cousin/wife Rebecca. Isaac had attempted to impregnate his cousin/wife Rebekah for over twenty years, but could not. So Isaac intreated (tempted / עתר) his father the Lord "to rub against (לנכח)" Rebekah, and the Lord was tempted (intreated / עתר), to rub against Rebekah and she became pregnant (הר)(*Gen. 25:21*). *See Strong's Concordance # 6279-6283 "Intreated (עתר)," and # 5226, 27 "against (נכח)."*

Rebekah was pregnant with twins, who warred with each other in her womb (*Gen. 25:22, 23*). Esau was the first born, then Jacob (Subplanter) after him (*Gen. 25:24, 25*). The Lord gave his son Jacob to his son Isaac to raise (*Joshua 24:4*). Jacob attempted to buy his brother Esau's birthright from him (*Gen. 25:31*). Rebekah helped Jacob to supplant (יעקב) Esau his own twin brother (*Gen. 27:15-20*). Thus Jacob became the next true Jacob (subplanter) after Cain. Jacob married two sisters (*Leviticus 18:18*), his two first cousins Leah (*Gen.29:23*), and Rachael (*Gen. 29:28*). He was also given two girls Zilpah, and Bilhah to do with as he pleased These four became the mothers of the twelve who would be known as the twelve "son" of Jacob, or Israel. In actuality five of them were the sons of Jacob's father the Lord: four with Leah, and one with Rachael. Rachael had wrestled with her sister Leah, and the Lord to get the Lord to impregnate her with her son Joseph (*Gen. 30:8*).

Jacob (supplanter) was renamed Israel by the Man/God he wrestled with in the wilderness (*Gen. 32:27, 28, 35:1*). Israel (אשר אל) means "Wrestled with God." Jacob asked the Man who named him what his name was, but he refused to tell Jacob (*Gen. 32:29*). Jacob knew that the Man (*Ex. 15:3*) he wrestled with was God Almighty (El Shaddai) or the Devil God (*Ex. 6:3*). But Jacob did not know that the Devil was also the Lord (*Ex. 6:3*), for Jacob's father the Lord refused to tell him (*Gen. 32:29*). Five of the "sons" of Jacob the twelve of Israel, were the children of the Lord.

Observations

# Persons
## Israeli Rape Tribes

*Jacob (Israel) — Twelve Son — Twelve Rape Tribes — Judah — "Moses"*

Jacob the son of the Lord, was not the father of Reuben, Simeon, Levi, Judah, and Joseph. These five were the sons of the Lord, with Leah and Rachael (***Gen. 29:31-35, Gen. 30:22***). The Lord finally had Jacobs (Subplanters), who he could use to supplant the children of Adam.

The Lord used the twelve born in the house of Jacob to began to subplant the children of Adam, by murder and rape.

These Jacobs (Subplanters) murdered all the men and boy of an entire Canaanite city, and then used the captured girls and women, to rape themselves into tribal existence, as twelve tribes (***Gen. 34:25-29***). To add to this Judah the father of all Judeans (Not Israelis), had twin sons with Tamar, his Canaanite daughter in law in an act of prostitution and incest (***Gen.38:15-24***). Pharez, and Zarah are the twin sons of Judah's incest, and prostitution with Tamar. These two sons Pharez and Zarah from incest, and prostitution are the fathers of all Jews (Judeans)(***Gen. 38:29, 30***).

In modern times the twelve tribe are all considered to have been Jews. But only one of these tribes were Jews, or of the tribe of Judah. The (Judeans) were never twelve tribes, just the one.

None of the twelve were Hebrewers (Hebrews) for they never "hebrewed" the Tigris. Nor were any of them Shemites, for they did not descend from Abraham, who descended from Shem. The Israelis were all descendant from the rape of Hamite women, before and after their four hundred years in Egypt.

The Lord brought Israel out of Egypt, and brought them to the east country, to commit holocaust against Abraham's children to subplant them.

The Lord had Moses to lead the Israelis directly to the East Country of the Amorites where Abraham had sent his children (***Gen. 25:6***). Ishmael/Midian Abraham's children dwelt from Havilah to Shur which is before Egypt, as you go towards Assyria (***Gen. 25:18***). Abraham had sent his own children away so that he could raise the Lord's son Isaac (***Gen. 21:1, 2, Joshua 24:***). First the Lord had the Israelis to raped themselves into being the "Seed" of Abraham (***Numbers 31:35, 40***), with the little pubelescent girls of Ishmael/Midian. Ishmael/Midian were Abraham's only children from his "own loins" (***Gen. 15:4, Gen. 16:4, Gen. 25:1-2, Numbers 31:18***). The Israelis were never the "children" of Abraham, and they only became his "seed" (***John 8:33***), by raping the little girls of Abraham's Ishmael/Midianite descendants (***Nu. 31:18***).

Then the Israelis returned to the land of Canaan where they had first came into existence by raping the Canaanite girls and women. As the now "Seed of Abraham" led by Joshua, the Israelis had returned to exterminate the people of Canaan to subplant (יעקב) them. The Lord's promise of the land of Canaan had not been to the "Children (Heirs) of Abraham" (***Gen. 15:4***), but to the "Seed of Abraham (***Gen. 15:5***)." Abraham a committer of incest, and rape, was not a murderer, and would not have wanted his children to possess the land of Canaan, by the murder of Canaan's children. Not only had Abraham been lied to by the Lord with his promise, but Abraham's children had been exterminated, by Israel the children of the Lord who subplanted them. Murder and incest was always rampant among the Israelis before, during, and after they were in Egypt. Jochebed married her nephew Amram, and bore Moses (***Ex. 6:20, Numbers 26:59***).

# Persons
# Moses

*Rape Tribes — Moses Child of Incest— Thick Darkness — Ethiopian Wife*

Moses was born into the tribe of Levi. Levi was the chief of the "sons" of Jacob, who murdered all of the men, and boys of the city of Shechem. They then raped themselves into tribal existence, with the girls, and women of that murdered city (*Gen. 34:25-29*). Moses was born among the Israeli rape tribes, after they had been in Egypt four hundred years. He was born of incest, to Jochebed, and her nephew Amram. Both Amram, and Jochebed, had descended from the raped Canaanite girls, and women. Both Amram, and Jochebed were of the rape tribe of Levi.

Levi's entire tribal line came from rape of Hamite/Canaanite women. Moses was the third child born of incest between the Levite woman Jochebed and her nephew Amram (*Exodus 6:20, Numbers 26:59*).

Moses was born as a Levite Israeli, but he was raised in the Pharoah's house, as an Egyptian (*Ex. 2:10, 17-19*). Moses as a young Egyptian murdered an Egyptian and was liable as an Egyptian, under Egyptian Law, for that man's life. Moses was raised under the Law in Pharoah's house. Moses had the Law taught to him, as it would later be taught to Jesus also (*Matt. 5:18*)!

When Moses fled to escape punishment he did not escape as an Israeli, but escaped as an Egyptian who had broken the Law by murdering another Egyptian (*Ex. 2:12; Ex. 2:19*).

Moses escaped from lawful Egypt, to the Outlaw God that the Israelis had escaped from 400 years earlier. Moses had come to Mt. Horeb (חורב) a dead dry place, in the land of Midian in Canaan (*Ex. 3:1*). The Lord and his Host had gone to Horeb to hibernate after the Israelis had fled to Egypt from the famine the Lord had caused in Canaan (*Gen. 45:19*).

Moses knew that the Israelis had been in bondage to the Lord before they fled to Egypt. Now in Mount Horeb the Lord was instructing Moses to return to Egypt with his "Thick Darkness" (*Ex. 10:22, 20:21, Deut. 4:11, I King 8:12*). The Lord would use his Darkness to retrieve the Israelis from the Light of Egypt. Moses would help the Lord to bring Israel back into bondage, knowing that the Israelis had never been in bondage to the Egyptians (*John 8:33*).

Moses married Zipporah an Cushite or Ethiopian woman the daughter of Jethro an Ishmael/Midianite man (*Ex. 3:1*). Zipporah's mother was an Ethiopian woman (*Numbers 10:1*). The Lord had described the appearance of the Israelis as being wooly headed, and brown like the children of Ethiopia (*Amos 9:7*). The children of Ethiopia (Cush) were wooly headed and brown like their Canaanite, and Egyptian (Mizraim), brothers (*Gen. 10:6*). Furthermore Ishmael and Midian were the children that Abraham had with wooly headed Hamite women. Hagar was Egyptian (Hamite), and Midian was Canaanite (Hamite).

All Israelis including Moses had been saved by the Egyptians. Now the Lord made Moses return from the land of Midian to Egypt. Moses as the Lord's agent was instrumental in the murder of perhaps millions of Egyptians. The Egyptians had save the Israelis, from their Lord and his famine, for four hundred years. Now Moses was officiating over the act of returning Israel from the Light and freedom of Egypt, into the Thick Darkness and bondage to the Lord.

The Israelis were hardly out of sight of Egypt before the Lord commanded Moses to began to bring the Israelis back into bondage to him again. Moses informed the Israelis that the Lord wanted them to bring all of their first born sons to be "religiously sodomized"(קדש). That is what

# Persons
# Moses

*Israeli Sodomites— Seed of Rape — Mose's Horn — Murdering Moses — Joshua*

Sanctified (קדש) and Holy means (קדש)(*Lev. 20:7*)(*Ex. 3:2, 13:13, 15*). The firstborn Israeli sons must be sodomized (קדש)(Be made Holy), three times a year before the Lord (*Ex. 34:20, 23, 24*).

These firstborn sons would be the leaders, and would eventually infect all of the rest of Israel, with this Holy (הלל) or corrupt (הלל) act. The Lord commanded that Israel be a Holy (corrupt) people to him, for he himself was Holy (Corrupt)(*Lev. 20:26*). Anyone who would sodomize their own children are capable all kinds of other heinous act, towards others not their kin.

Moses would go on to be responsible for the death of hundreds of thousands of Abraham's Ishmael/Midianite children. Moses instructed the Israelis to murder all of the little Ishmael / Midianite girls they had sodomized (שבב)(*Numbers 31:17*), but to keep the rest of the girls to do with as they pleased (*Numbers 31:18*). Out of these that they kept alive, the Lord's share was thirty two (32) girls (*Nu. 31:40*), and the Levitican priesthood got fifty (50) of these girls (*Num. 31:47*).

With these pubelescent little girls being descendant from Abraham, the Israelis used them to rape themselves into being the "Seed of Abraham." Linage of the Israelis is through the female.

When Moses told the Israelis to kill all the Midianite women and boys, he was also sentencing his own Midianite wife, and sons to death (*Ex. 2:21, 22, Ex. 3:1*). Moses had to kill his wife Zipporah and two sons, Gershom and Eliezer (*Ex. 18:3*)!

After Israelis lead by Moses had exterminated all of the children of Abraham in a great holocaust, Moses and the Israelis now turned on the remnants of the Canaanites on the east side of the Jordan. As with Midian they murdered all except the little girls and used these children until they were through with them (*Deut. 20:10, 11, Deut. 21:11-14*).

Moses continued to go up and down the mountain with instructions from the Lord to the Israelis. These commandments were designed to carry the Israelis further back down into bondage to the Lord. Moses had become so depraved that one day when he came down from talking with the Lord, and he had horns (קרן) growing out of his forehead (*Ex. 34:29, 30, 35*). Everyone were afraid of him and ran away (*Deut. 34:29, 30, 33*). Some rebelled against further bondage to the Lord.

Moses and others with him murdered over three thousand Israelis (*Ex. 32:28*). When all was under control again Moses informed the Israelis that the Lord would now use them to commit even greater "crimes" (נפלא / Felonies) or "wonders" for him (*Ex. 34:10*). They would do many of these crimes, under the leadership of Joshua after Moses' death.

Moses' final reward from the Lord was to be shown the so called "promised land" (*Deut. 34:4*). Moses had been in perfect health (*Deut. 34:7*). So the Lord murdered him, after he had put Joshua in charge of the Israelis (*Deut. 34:5*).

Notes

# Persons
# Joshua

*Moses — Lord's Felonies (Crimes) in Egypt — Canaanite Holocaust*

Joshua was the son of Nun, and the servant of Moses (*Ex. 33:1, Jos. 1:11, Jos. 24:29*). Joshua (יהושע) means "Savior of Jah (Jehovah)." Joshua would be the final savior of the Lord's world, in the land of Canaan. Moses made Joshua his minister after he defeated Amelek (*Ex. 17:9, 10, 13, Ex. 9, 10*). Universal Law was violated when the Lord did his "Wonders (Felonies / נפלא) in Egypt (*Ex. 3:20, 4:21, 7:3, 11:9, 10*). The "wonders," Felonies," or "crimes," that the Lord did in Egypt was his pouring down of the same vials of plagues and diseases on Egypt, that he had poured down on the whole planet before Genesis (*Revelations 15th chptr, 16th Chptr*). Egypt was the Strait Gate leading into Eden (Africa), the only part of the planet that had not been broken, moved or destroyed, when the Lord and his Host had poured out their wrath on the planet (*Rev. 12:12*).

Now the Lord had Moses and Joshua to violate universal Law again, when he had them to direct the Israelis to commit holocaust against the peaceable people of the land of Ham's son Canaan (*I Chron. 4:40*), this included Amelek and his people (*Ex. 17:16*). The Lord had Moses to write these Wonders (נפלא / Felonies) down and then to rehearse these same wonders (Felonies/crimes) into the ear of Joshua (*Ex. 17:14*). This rehearsal of crimes (Wonders), done from Egypt to the land of Canaan was a review. This review of atrocities performed by Moses, before Joshua was to make Joshua the predecessor of Moses. The Lord would now speak to Joshua, to direct the Israelis to the next wonders (נפלא) or crimes that they would commit against the children of Ham.

Forty years had passed since the Israelis had left Egypt, and now the Israelis having murdered millions, were about to embark on the final campaigns to murder the rest of Canaan's children.

The Israelis led by Joshua stood on the east side of the Jordan River looking westward across at the land that Jacob and the original twelve had dwelled in, among the peaceable Canaanites children of Ham (*I Chron. 4:40*). The eyes of the Lord always cared for this land (*Deut. 11:10-12*).

The Lord had taken his revenge against the Egyptians for allowing the Israelis to stay. Next he had subplanted the children of Abraham, by child rape (*Numbers 31:31:18*). Now it was Canaan's turn, for the Lord had brought the Israelis back to kill two birds with one stone: when they cross the River Jordan with Joshua they would take revenge for the Lord against the children of Canaan because Canaan had exposed Noah his grandfather as a child molesting Sodomite, in service to the Lord (*Gen. 9:24*). That was the only thing that Canaan had "done to Noah" (*Gen. 9:24*). Secondly the Lord was using Jacob (Subplanter) the Israelis (Jacob) to subplant the children of Ham. In the wilderness the Lord had turned the Israelis into "Marked" pale lepers, like Cain;s children (*Gen. 4:15; Lev. 13th. Chptr.*)

The Lord's sole and complete purpose for Joshua, was for Joshua to lead the twelve tribes of Pale Lepers (*Leviticus 13th Chptr.*), across the Jordan over into Canaan proper to possess the land of the remaining peaceful children of Canaan, the son of Ham. The Lord had promised this land to the "Seed of Abraham," not the Children of Abraham, as Abraham had thought. Yet this was not the land of the Lord to give to anyone. Thus these people called Israel would have to continue to commit holocaust to subplant the remaining children of Canaan, and to steal their possessions.

These Pale Leper Israelis were not even the Israelis who had left Egypt. The corpses of the

Observations

# Persons
# Joshua

*Joshua — Pale Mutant Israelis — Rahab the Whore — Revenge on Canaan — Jesus (Yeshua)*

Egyptian Israelis and their children were strewn across the wilderness, as a results of over forty years of forced wandering around, in circles in the wilderness. The Lord's unjust promise to Abraham, Isaac, and Jacob had been a purposefully false promise to all of them. The Lord knew that he was not going to bring the Israelis from Egypt back to the land of Canaan. They had not wanted to leave Egypt to go back to Canaan anyway! This was because they did not want to be in bondage to the Lord again! They did not even want to leave Egypt! The Lord brought them out of Egypt solely for the purpose of taking his revenge against them, and their children.

These Pale Leper who had come out of the wilderness, and who were now to cross the Jordan were a species of their own. The Pale Lepers of the tribe of Israel in the wilderness were the children of the Lord and his Host, who had mated with the female of the tribes of Israel (***Leviticus 13th chptr.***). The pale leprosy in Leviticus is the same mark of pale leprosy that the Lord had "marked" Cain, and and his children the Gentiles (***Gen. 4:15***). It was the leprosy that the Lord placed on the hand of Moses (***Ex. 4:6***), and the leprosy that the Lord placed all over the body of Moses' sister Miriam (***Numbers 12:10***). This was the same fairness (paleness) on the daughters of the man Cain (***Gen. 6:2***). These Israelis the children of Incubi were pale like the children of Cain, because like the daughters of the man Cain these Israelis females had mated, with the Lord and his Host, and became infected also with paleness (***Gen. 6:2, 4***).

Joshua led these mutant Israelis across the Jordan River, and caused them to systematically exterminate every Canaanite man, boy, and woman, but they kept the young girls captives, for themselves (***Deut. 21:11***). They also saved Rahab the whore, and her family (***Jos. 6:17, 25***). Rahab had betrayed her people, the children of Canaan: the Canaanites, Hittites, Hivites, Perizzites, Girgasites, Amorites, and Jubusite (***Jos. 3:10***). Rahab the Canaanite whore became an Israeli heroine, like Sarah, and Dinah.

The Israelis murdered all in Jericho including their king (***Jos. 6:21, 24***). Next Joshua destroyed Ai, and murdered the inhabitants, and hang their king (***Jos. 8:21-29***). After murdering the two cities of Jericho, and Ai, Joshua went on a killing spree that included all other Canaanite cities.

The entire land of Canaan became a killing field. Joshua had the names of the murdered cities, and their kings in the land of Canaan recorded. The names of the murdered kings and their cities were from the King of Jericho, and his city Jericho, to the king of Terzah and his city Terzah. The total kings and cities murdered were thirty one kings and their cities (***Jos. 12:9-24***).

The Israelis begin to occupy the cleared land as they murdered off the Canaanites. Once all of the Canaanites had been murdered off of their lands, and the Israelis had occupied it, Joshua's mission was complete. The World of the Lord was now safely transferred from Nod, to the land of the children of Ham. The people who occupied Canaan now were not any of those who the Lord had promised it to. But were the Lord's own pale leper children. The Lord had subplanted (Jacobed) everyone including his own son Jacob (Subplanter). Joshua had finished the work that Noah had began, of subplanting the children of Ham and Abraham. Now Joshua had saved the World (TBL) of the Lord. But Jesus (Yeshua) came to destroy the Lord's same World that Joshua had saved. Jesus is the son of Joseph of Aram

Notes

# Persons
# Joseph of Aram

*Joshua — Joseph of Egypt — No Holiness, or Sanctification — Jesus (Yeshua)*

Joseph of Aram, is Joseph Aramathaea (**Joseph with Aram /** אחא ארם)(*Matt. 27:57*), who descended from Egyptians who came up north from Egypt, in the time of Nimrod, to help build Ur/Babel. These Egyptians settled in Northern Canaan "**With the people of Aram.**" Thus the people of the land of Aram were made up of two elements. The first element were the descendants of Aram, and the second element were Egyptians (צרי), or Syrians (צרי). The two elements were so interwoven, that to say Aram was to say Syrian or Egyptian. To say Joseph of Aram, or Joseph of Syria (צרי), or Joseph of Egypt (צרי), was all the same, for Syria (צרי) is "Little Egypt (צרין)," or Aram. The capital of the Syrians (Aram) was the city named Tyre (צר / Egypt), which was on the coast of the Great Sea (Mediterranean), above Israel.

The mother of Rebecca was Syrian (Egyptian), and therefore Rebecca the mother of Jacob (Israel) was Syrian (Egyptian). Thus Jacob as the son of Rebecca, and the father of the twelve declared himself a Syrian (Egyptian), about to perish in the famine of the Lord in Canaan (*Deut. 26:5*). As such it was normal for the Egyptians to send wagons to Canaan, to bring Jacob the Syrian (Egyptian) and his family to safety in Egypt (*Gen. 45:19, 21, 27*). Thus Jacob (Israel) the Syrian (Egyptian) was an Egyptian going to the homeland of his ancestors, the Egyptians.

Thus when Joseph of Aram went down to live with the Israelis, he was of Egyptian descent, going to live among the Israelis, who were also of Egyptian descent. Joseph came as a carpenter to practice his trade. He met and married a young Israeli woman, and became the father of Yeshua (Jesus). Yeshua (Jesus) was a firstborn son in Israel.

The Lord of the Israelis imposed some customs on Israel, that Joseph refuse to adhere to: The Lord commanded that all firstborn sons be brought to him in the eighth day of their birth (*Ex.13:2, Ex.13:13, 15*). The Lord commanded that these firstborn sons be "Sanctified" (קדש), or have Ritual Religious Sodomy (קדש)* performed on them. Parents were to bring these firstborn sons three times in the year (*Ex. 34:23, 23*). None were to appear before the Lord with empty hands (*Ex. 34:20*).

Parents could only redeem their firstborn sons from this humiliating act of being sodomized, by sacrificing a lamb to the Lord (*Ex. 13:13*). If parents did not have a lamb to sacrifice, and still refused to have their firstborn son religiously sodomized (Sanctified), the parents were commanded to break the boy's neck (*Ex. 13:13, 15*)! Joseph sacrificed lambs to the Lord, three times in the year to save Jesus, and Jesus was never Sanctified (Sodomized). But any parent who would not allow their son to be Sanctified, and made Holy was suspect. This act of sodomy was performed on the little firstborn male children of all the tribes, for the express purpose of casting them out, of their inner kingdoms (*Matt. 8:12*), ut Jesus was still inside of his kingdom for he had not been casted out. He and his inner father were still one (*John 14:2; John 10:30*). This is what put Jesus' life in danger (*Matt. 2:13*). Joseph of Aram (Tyre / צרי / Egypt) had to flee from Israel, down into his ancestral homeland Egypt, to save his son Jesus. Egypt was the final salvation of Jesus (Yeshua).

Observations

# Persons
# Yeshua

*Joseph of Aram — Jesus Prince of Egypt — Ambassador of Egypt — Eternity*

Yeshua (Jesus), as the son of Joseph the Egyptian, was also an Egyptian, and was trained in Egypt as an Egyptian. Jesus was never raised as an Israeli and was never under the influence of the Lord, the Scribes, Pharisees, or Rabbis. Being raised in Egypt Jesus was taught secrets, about the Lord and his World, some of which had been held secret since the founding of the Lord's World on this planet (*Matt. 13:55*). The teachings of Jesus were Egyptian, not Judaism, and there was no Christianity. Egyptian philosophy was opposite from them both. When Jesus returned to Israel he came as a prince, and ambassador of Egypt. He was in the World of the Lord, but not of it (*John 8:23*). He was in the Lord's World to judge it (*John 9:39*), and to condemn it, not to save it (*John 3:17*). Jesus taught the Israelis that he had overcome the World of the Lord (*John 16:33*), and that he chose Israel to come up out of the Lord's World too (*John 15:19*)! He instructed the Israeli masses that he was hated by the World, that the Lord loved (*John 7:7*). He told them that if they loved the World of the Lord, that the love of God inside was not in them (*I John 2:15*).

Jesus told the Israelis that as children they had been cast out of their inner kingdoms, to the Outer Darkness of the Lord (*Matt. 8:12, Amos 5:18, 20*). To be absent from the self inside, is to be outside with the Lord (*II Cor. 5:6*). He who is within (God) is greater than he who is without (Lord)(*I John 4:4*).

Jesus taught that it was the scribes and Pharisees (Rabbis) who cast the first born sons out into the Darkness of the Lord (*Amos 5:18, 20*), as they had been cast out themselves. These scribes and Pharisees then refused to reenter their own kingdoms, and shut up the kingdoms, of the congregation so that they could not reenter either (*Matt. 23:13*)!

The firstborn sons of Israel were casted out by being Sanctified (Sodomized / קדש), and made Holy (Corrupt / חולי). The Lord had kidnapped Israel out of Egypt with a mighty hand (*Exodus 32:11*). Jesus said that the Lord instructed the Rabbis (Scribes, and Pharisees) to keep them deaf, dumb, blind, and mentally cripple (*Isa. 6:10*), for if they are allowed to come out of bondage to the Lord, they shall be converted, and healed from his corruption (*Isa.6:10*). Jesus had come from Egypt to convert them back to being like they were as little children, before being casted out (*Matt. 13:15*). They must have eyes that see, and ears that hear (*Mark 4:9; 7:16*). Thus Jesus instructed them how to convert:

Seek first the kingdom of God ... (*Matt. 6:32*). The kingdom of God is at hand (*Matt. 3:2*). The kingdom of God is within you (*Luke 17:21*). All of you are Gods children of the Most High (*Psalms 82:6; John 10:34, 35*). Be perfect as your father in your inner heaven is perfect (*Matt. 5:48*). You must be born again ...(*John 3:3*), for except you be converted and be like your little children again, you can not reenter your inner kingdoms (*Matt. 18:3*). You can not serve two master: the **Inner**, and **Outer** (*Matt. 6:24*). He who is in you (God), is greater, than he who is outside (Lord), in his World (*I John 4:4; I Cor. 6:20*). .... if you would enter Life obey my commandments (*Matt. 9:17*).

Finally Jesus (Yeshua) taught the Israelis not to find their lives, in the physical realm, because they shall eventually die out of the physical anyway. Straight is the gate, and narrow is the way inward, that leads to Life, yet there are few that find it (*Matt. 7:14*). Jesus told the Israelis to give their lives for the truth, and that they would have life in the Eternal (Inner) realm (*Matt. 10:39*).

Notes

# places
# Eternity

*Observations, Persons, "Jesus (Yeshua) — Eternal (קדם)(Aboriginal) #6924, Eternity (עד) #5703 #166 Greek = #5769 (עלם) Universal (Elemental)(עלם) #5957 (Infant, Infinity) — Sun*

Jesus (Yeshua) spoke of a Strait or Narrow Gate leading to Eternity (*Matt. 7:14*). In translation the word "Eternity" is the old language word Elam (עלם). **Strong's #5769** Elam (Elementary) is also the word for "Universe" (עלם). The universe like the Atom (Adam) has two states: visible, and invisible. The visible is Everlasting, with beginnings, and endings. But the invisible is Eternal, and has no beginnings, or endings, and has existed forever. Eternity is the invisible internal heaven state within each of the aboriginal people of the planet (*Luke 17:21*). The Eternal **Inner** is projecting the Everlasting **Outer** Eternal implies no **beginnings**, and no **endings**

A second word for Eternity is the word Kedem #6921-27. Kedem (קדם) translates into the English as "Aboriginal," "Source," "First," "Before," etc. This word imply a **Source Condition**, that exceeds beginnings and endings. This invisible state was/is the state of Original Man who is God (אלוהים). Original man (God) is "Invisible" without the flesh form, or "Coat of Skin (*Gen. 3:21*)." "Man" is the "Man"ifestation of the Invisible Eternal Being into the physical realm. In the Invisible or Eternal state original man is electric male, and magnetic female, an alpha/omega Being, existing without aid of a mother or father (*Hebrews 7:3*). Thus the original flesh garment had to be Hermaphrodite, or male/female incorporated into one form. Thus Man/God as first manifested into the seen or physical state, was HermesAphrodite, who was not given or taken in marriage (*Matt. 22:30, Mark 12:25*).

The physical state is not Eternal, but is an Everlasting dream illusion, and all forms in the physical eventually fall apart, and cease to exist, unless they are renewed. To mimic the eternal source and to continue to exist, all original manifested lifeforms were HermesAphrodite, from the atomic to the manform. There was no separate male from female. There was no sexual intercourse between any forms. The egg and sperm, or seed, and germ, were one inside the form to be impregnated. In due season, in the aging form, Auto or Self impregnation, occurred. That which was born was a continuation form, not an offspring (*Heb. 7:3*).

Before Adam was **put to sleep** and altered into separate male female, there were no children or offspring born. Adam was HermesAphrodite like all of the other Gods who only gave birth to continuations of their aging body forms (*Gen. 1:27*). Eve was the womb (Wombman) taken from Adam, she was then used to give birth to the first children on the planet. Yet when Seth was given birth he was in the image and likeness of Adam (*Gen. 5:3*). He was Adam's continuation, not his child. Adam was perfect and Eternal. "Little children" as infants (Infinity) during the birth process, are closer to the Eternal then anyone else in the physical (*Matt. 18:3*). They are birthing out through the very doorway that leads back in to Eternity.

Representing the Eternal, the sun is the infinite doorway back in. The day of the sun (Sunday) has no beginning or ending, it have never risen or set. The Planet turns giving the appearance of days. Going pass appearances there is only the Eternal here and now, and Eternity is the source of the physically manifested sun.

# Places
# Sun

*Eternity — Most High — Assiah*

The sun (Most High) has it's source/origin in the Eternal Being of the invisible electromagnetic Field. Phonetically sun (שׁ) means "Cycle" or "Circuit." The sun is the place around which the planet(s) "orbits," "cycles," or "circulates."

In translation "Sun (שמש) is the contracted word Shemesh (שמש): Shem (שם) means "Place," and Mesh (מש) means "Bearing." Thus "Shemesh (sun) means "Place of Bearing." This holds true from two directions. First the planet was separated (Bared) from the solar. Secondly the sun is the "bearing" which the planet orbits around. The sun is the reference for the mother planet Assiah.

All of the original men of the planet are souls, or solar beings. Astronomically the sun is the origin of Original Man, who separated (Cipherated) Assiah the mother planet, from the solar or sun. Original Man is wooly haired, and brown to black in complexion, which complements his solar (soul) origin.

Chronologically the sun did not have a beginning in the past, nor shall it have an ending in the future, but it has existed, and shall always exist. The Most High (sun) exists within a set of conditions, that caused it to be manifest, from the invisible Field into the physical illusion. You can not go back in time to find a beginning for the sun. Nor can you go forward in time to find an ending for the sun in the future. The sun came into physical manifestation because of a state of dissatisfaction. When all has come to satisfaction in the physical then the sun will vanish back into the invisible electromagnetic Field.

Geneologically it is not relevant as to whether the planet came from the sun, or that the sun came from the planet. What is relevant is that since the separating between the sun and the planet, the sun has held constant, and represent exactly the same as when the planet was first separated from it. But with the passing of time the planet has been caused to change away from it's original solar perfection, when it was first separated from the sun. As such the sun is the reference, to retrieve the planet back to, before the planet can be returned to the sun.

All were perfect (תמים) or balanced/complete/whole, who separated from the sun to experiment. The sun represents all at their Most High (עליון) or Perfect state, before the physical descent. All who descended did not know what to expect, coming forth into physical manifestation. None had ever experienced a particular or physical state of being.

Melchezedek was designated as the Overseer (כוהנים) of the Most High (Sun)(*Gen. 14:18, Deut. 32:8, 9*), with authority over **Eternal life** ( *Hebrews 7:1, 2*), or Life beyond the physical illusion.

He was designated by all of the others, who came forth from the sun. It would be his charge and those with him, to oversee and protect Shemesh, the Most High the sun. No one who went down into the experiment would be allowed to come back, to reenter into the sun as individuals. The mother planet Assiah was manifested from the sun, as a complete entity with all on it. None could return to the solar gate, except on Assiah in it's completed and satisfied state. Assiah (אישה) the mother planet is the "fireness" that was brought forth from the sun.

# Places
# Assiah

*Sun-First Planet-Assiah, Planet, Tiamat, Earth, Eden-Planetary Asia (Assians)- Crypton*

Assiah (Asia / אשה) is the original name of this the first globe, the mother globe, that was separated from the sun. Assiah (אישה) means Fireness," for Assiah was fervent (firey) when it was separated from the sun. The name Assiah (אישה) roots from the word Ish (איש), which roots from the word Yish (יש). Yish (יש) means "to be," to "stand out," to "exist." Ish (איש) is the root for the words "man (איש)," and the word "fire (אש)." Thus this the mother planet Assiah (fieriness), "stood out," as a "manifested fire" globe, for original Man a firey being. Assiah as the mother globe serves the purpose of being the dwelling place, for those who separated it from the sun, to experiment. To began the experiment on self in the particular, Assiah was set into an orbit around the sun. Assiah the mother planet is/was an experimental platform or space ship.

The sun, and Assiah separated from each other, was the beginning of the solar (Soul) system. At the start there were no other planets, just Assiah. All other planets in the entire solar system would originate from this planet, the mother planet Assiah. The word Assiah has been changed into the word Asia. The entire original population of the planet are Asians. Assians are manifested Gods who are wooly headed with a complexion from Black to Brown (*Rev. 1:14, 15*). The sum total of all shapes forms, and states of being in the physical are described inside of the patterns that exist in the wooly hair of the original inhabitants of Assiah. Those wooly hair patterns are spheres, spirals, circles, waves, etc.

Assiah is and was a laboratory, where it's original inhabitants were and still are scientists. These Scientist in their laboratory, experimented/experienced, and became specimens. Assiah, its atmosphere, the physical forms, and the original inhabitants inside of each form, would be of an infinite combination of backgrounds, that would allow all possibilities to be played out in the physical illusion. Actions and reactions became the core of all existence on the planet. Breathing, seeing, touching, tasting, smelling, hearing, thinking, were all new phenomena, for beings who in their invisible naked state were infinite, without the illusion of physical forms. Experimenting/experiencing in all forms, and understanding the patterns as expressed in the physical, is the understanding of the full contents of the physical illusion, a dissatisfied state. Understanding the complete contents of the physical is complete satisfaction, which will be the end of the experiment. Many left the planet, and only those who remained on Assiah, continue the experiment. Assians were disciplined to the experiment, and were therefore Disciples

Those who left, "curved away" (Apostrophized) from the experiment and became apostate or Apostles, alienated away from Self the solar being. These Apostates (Apostles) took planets out of Assiah, and went out into different solar orbits. They discovered that there is nothing, in the Outer Darkness, except the planets they took with them. Thus they had to "create" from the substance of their planets all that they needed. "Creating" or "crafting" is the beginning of all corruption. Assiah was the tree. Planet are as limbs severed from a tree. The tree (Assiah) live on, while planets severed (created) eventually die. **Creation** or **corruption** or **crafting** is the altering of what already existed, complete, correct, and perfect, into something less than it' original Self. Chief among those who created/crafted was Hallel (חלל), who was more crafty then all the other Apostates. As such his planet was named Crafton/Crypton/Krypton.

# Places
# Crypton (Krypton)

*Assiah — Crafting Place — Pieces of Crypton are returning home — Earth*

The term Crypton/Krypton (כרפתן) means "Slackened," "Cut free," "Set Adrift," as the cord is cut, and becomes slack, as a child is separated from it's mother. In this case it was the child, who separated it's self from the mother by cutting the cord. *See Strong's Concordance #7503* (רפח / *Slack*), *and #7495* (רפה / *Mend*). For the Lord Hallel discovered that there was much to **mend** (Repair) on Krypton when it's cord was cut from the mother planet Assiah. Krypton (an abortion) had cut it's self adrift, but was not viable, as a limb cut from a tree, is not viable. Thus Crypton became a "Crafting Place." To craft is to create or "corrupt" something that already exist, into something other than it was originally. Thus a Crafted Place (Crypton) is a place that was crafted into existence, from a place that existed before it. This is the same as a branch being remove from a tree and crafted (corrupted), into a statue. Assiah is the "Tree" that all of the branches (Planets) were removed from, including Crypton. Hallel the future Lord of Abraham, was chief among those who crafted Crypton out of the mother planet Assiah. Crypton also means "Dead Place": Crypt = Dead, and N= Place.

Assiah (the tree) is alive and self sufficient, but Crypton began to die as soon as it was separated from Assiah. As with any created object Crypton had a time when it came into being, and a time when it would cease to be. Yet Assiah (mother planet) is Alpha and Omega, Eternal through it's seed and fruit (planetary population), Assiah have no beginning or ending. Assiah is/was like a power source with endless power, but Crypton was like a draining battery that runs down, eventually to die.

Thus Hallel or Lucifer (Cipherman / Superman) became a Jealous God (*Ex. 34:14*), who became a Man of War (*Ex. 15:3; Rev. 12:7*). The Lord attempted to drain life from those on the others planets, that were also dieing. But in the war the Lord and his Host prevailed not, and "their place (Crypton) ceased to exist, for it was destroyed (*Revelations 12:8*).

Krypton was once in orbit between Mars and Venus. Between Mars and Jupiter, there is enough space for a planet, and there is enough debris there to make a planet. This debris is composed of massive boulders, frozen water, rocks, sand, metal etc. The debris forms a great ring that is in orbit around the sun. Modern scientist make note that this debris was once a planet there, between Mars and Jupiter. Put back together, this debris would form the planet Crypton again.

As the Lord did not have place in the solar system anymore, he and his Host were cast back down to the mother planet Assiah, where they and their planet had come from (*Rev. 12:9*).

Therefore they rejoiced in the heavens (solar system), but they said woe to the inhabitants of Assiah, for the Devil is come down to you, full of wrath (*Rev. 12:12*).

Crypton/Krypton is a name that is associated with the seemingly fictitious character of Superman. But See "Names of the Lord,": Pages 161 thru 166, to find that the Lord and Superman are the same person.

Crypton had been crafted/corrupted into existence out of Assiah, and now the Lord would corrupt Assiah into being like Crypton, a corrupting place. In the end the Lord would destroy Assiah, into being Ertz, or Earth.

Notes

# Places
# Ertz (Earth)

*Crypton — Ertz (Earth)(ארץ / ךץ) Fragment(s) #776, #7518 — World on Earth — Tribunal*

Place was no longer found for Hallel and his Host, after they destroyed their planet Crypton (*Rev. 12:8*). In defeat the Lord and his Host were casted back down, to the mother planet Assiah (*Rev. 12:9*). When the inhabitants of Assiah refused to bow to the Lord, and his Host, they destroyed Assiah, and it became Ertz (Earth / ארץ). Ertz (ארץ) means "I am Fragments," or "Continents." The planet was broken into continents after the Lord exploded Assiah. Those who saw it from on high said "Rejoice in the heavens, but woe unto the inhabiters of Assiah, for the Devil (El Shaddai / Almighty) is come down unto you having great wrath...(*Rev. 12:12; Nu. 24:4, 16*). The Most High (Sun) saw the Almighty fall (*Nu. 24:1-6*). And behold the Lord made Assiah empty and waste, and turned it up side down, scattering the inhabitants abroad (*Isa. 24:1, Psalms 82:5*). The land was utterly emptied, and spoiled: the Lord commanded it (*Isa. 24:3*)! The planet groans, and fades away. The High people of the planet do languish (*Isaiah 24:4*). Assiah is profaned (by the Lord), under the inhabitants thereof; because they refuse to bow down (עבר) to the Lord (*Eccles 5: 2, 2)(Isa. 24:5*). Therefore the Lord has devoured the planet, with his curse (*Revelations 15:7, 16:1, 21:9*), and those on the planet are desolate. They are burned and few men are left alive (*Isa. 24:6*). The planet was utterly "broken" (Ertz/Earth), dissolved, and was moved greatly out of it's course (*Isa. 24:19, Psalms 82:5*). The planet reeled to and fro....(*Isa. 24:20*), the host of the heavens were dissolved, and the heavens (sky) rolled together as a scroll, and all it's host fell down.....(*Isa. 34:4, Rev. 6:14*). And I beheld until the sixth seal was opened and lo there was a great earthquake, the sun became black as sackcloth, the moon was exploded into existence, out of the planet, and it was like blood (*Revelations 6:12*).

This all occurred in Revelation the book before the book of Genesis. Thus at Genesis 1:1 in the circular Bible/Torah, there was total Darkness on the planet then, because the Lord had destroyed mother Assiah (*Isa. 24:1, 3-6*). The war had been between the Lord that Abram would praise, and Michael/Melchezedek (*Rev. 12:7*). The Lord had destroyed his planet Crypton (*Rev. 12:8*), and had come down, to destroy Assiah turning it into Earth (*Isa. 24:1, 3-6*). The Day of the Lord is his Great Darkness (*Amos 5:18, 20*), that came as a thief in the night (*I Thessalonians 5:2*). The heavens passed away with a great noise, and the elements melted with fervent heat. The planet also and it's works burnt up (*II Peter 3:10, Isa. 24:6*).

The above verses describes the Lord and his Host destroying Assiah the mother planet before Genesis, and turning it into ertz or earth. The Lord God Michael/Melchezedek resuscitated the planet, pulling the water off the surface. The surface was not solid, like it had been before, but the land mass was "shattered" into "broken" and "scattered slabs" of land. That is why they called it "Ertz" or "Earth" (*Gen. 1:10*), which means "continents" or "broken land".

The mother planet Assiah had been "created (altered)," into being Ertz (Earth). Michael/Melchezedek the Lord God resuscitated the planet, and all of the life that had lived, and breathed on the planet. The Lord and his Host were war criminals, who were to be brought to justice in a war crimes trial, or Tribunal. The Tribunal was a war crimes (נפלא) trial held in the midst of the Garden (Gaurded Place)..

Observations

# Places
# Tribunal (Location)

*Earth — Tribunal — North*

The Tribunal against Hallel (The Lord) and his Host, was held on this the restituted mother planet Assiah, now called Earth. A tribunal is a war crimes trial. The Lord and his Host were the defeated officials of the planet Crypton. Usually the tribunal would have taken place on the planet of those who were defeated, but Crypton was gone. Thus the tribunal was relocated to the earth, in the midst of the Garden. The entire Garden or Guarded Place was east of Eden (Africa)(*Gen. 3:23*). he midst of the Garden was in the area where Jerusalem would be built. The children of Canaan built the city of peace (Jerusalem), to commemorate Michael/ Melchezedek, the Ancient of Days, who prosecuted the Lord, a Man of War (*Ex. 15:3*). Jebus the son of Canaan and his children would build Ur Salem, or Jerusalem, the City of Peace.

The preJerusalem site represented a peaceable place, for the peaceable inhabitants of the planet who, the Lord and his Host had attempted to destroy. Michael/Melchezedek was King of Peace, even before the City of Peace was ever built (*Heb. 7:2*), while the Lord is a Man of War (*Ex. 15:3*).

The Tribunal was a war crimes trial against the Lord and his Host, for crimes they had committed, in the heaven (Solar System), and on the planet. The trial was set, the thrones were cast down, and the books were opened. Michael/Melchezedek the Ancient of Days did sat. The Ancient of Day was wooly headed, and he wore a white garment (*Dan. 7:9*). Those who came down with him in attendance were wooly headed also, and were in the millions (*Daniel 7:9, 10*). The judgment was set, the books were opened (*Dan. 7:10*).

Gods sat in witness against a God (Lord), in the midst of other Gods (Host), they were all being judged (*Ps. 82:1-8, Numbers 24:4, 16, Daniel*). Hallel (Lord) is instructed to give restitution to those who he and his Host have made destitute (*Ps. 82:3*). Hallel is instructed to deliver the destitute out of the control of his Wicked ones (*Ps. 82:4*).

Hallel (Lord) is accused of keeping people in his Darkness, by deception (*Ps. 82:5; Isa. 6:10*). Hallel's Host are reminded that they are Gods in their own right like Hallel, and that they are all children of the Most High (Sun) like the Lord is (*Ps. 82:6; Ps. 29:1;* ). The Lord's Host are finally warned that if they continue to follow him that they will be caused to die like him (a Man). They are told that they shall die and fall like Hallel, (the Lord) was made to fall, as a prince (*Ps. 82:7*). They are given the final option as Gods to be "judges" on the planet if they change (*Ps. 82:8*). But the Lord having been tried, and convicted was slain as the Chief Beast (*Daniel 7:11*). His body was set afire by internal combustion (inner sun)(*Daniel 7:11, Ezekiel 28:17, 18*). The other Beasts the Host of Hallel are given a reprieve for a short season to make themselves right. They lost the dominion they had been given (*Dan. 7:12, Gen. 1:28*). The Lord is the "Man" who brought sin (Hate / חיש) into his own World (*Ex. 15:3; Romans 5:12*).

Once the Tribunal was over Hallel the Lord was disembodied, with no physical form, and the Lord God (Michael/Melchezedek) stated that the disembodied Man (Lord) must not be allowed to touch the Tree of Life, to take on flesh (Coats of skin) again, like Adam and Eve (*Gen. 3:21*) He must not be allowed to live again (*Gen. 3:22*). He was driven out of the Garden, back across the Tigris, back over into the north of Nod, where he had been taken from (*Gen. 3:23*). The **Lord** is the Man **casted out** (Shaddai) of the Garden, over into the north of Nod (*Gen. 3:24*).

# Places
# North

*Tribunal — Torches, Lamps, and Wicks — Nod*

The side of the North is the northern side of the Tigris River, where the Lord God Michael/Melchezedek casted the Lord and his Host, after the Tribunal (*Gen. 3:23; Isa. 14:12*). The side of the North (of Nod) was the ground which the Lord had been taken from (*Gen. 4:23*). North is more than a direction, it is a condition. Phonetically the word "North" (Noroth / נורוח) means "Lamps," or "Torches." This implies that the north was/is a place of Darkness with no natural light. A place where the only illumination was "Torches," "lamps," or "wicks." The north was dark, because of the presence of the Lord, who is the Prince of Darkness. The Lord's day is Darkness, with no brightness in it (*Amos 5:18, 20*). Darkness is the day that the Lord has made... (*Psalms 114:23*).

The Lord under the name **Pan** is depicted as a hairy rough half man, half goat with a flaming Pentecostal "torch"(wick / <u>wick</u>edness) coming from the top of his head. **See Strong's Concordance "Devil" #8163** Pronounced "Sear" (שער), defined as **Devil, Goat, Hairy, Rough, Satyr (Lev. 17:7).** Half Man and Half goat is also Bestiality!

In translation the word "north" comes from the old language word "Siphon (ציפון)." "Siphon" implies that the north was a place where "Sucking" or "Siphoning" took place. A place of Darkness where sucking occurs is a place of Dracula (Dark El), or the God of Darkness (*Amos 5:18, 20*). "Siphon" (North) means "to sip," "to suck," or "draw (Vamp) away." The Prince of Northern Darkness, is a Cipher (Lucifer). The Lord of Abram with his commandment for blood sacrifice, have all of the qualities of a Vampire or Dracula (*Lev. 17:11*). The Lord of Abraham called himself the **Prince of Darkness,** when he said that his day is Darkness. He dwelt in the Darkness of the north in the land of Nod (*Amos 5:18, 20 Isaiah 14:12 Psalms 48:2*). The Lord of the North is associated with all that is depicted, from Bestiality and Darkness, to his torch to see by in his Darkness. This is where the term "wicked" came from. Wicked denotes one who had a wick (torch/candle), who dwells in the Darkness with others who have no Light. The "wicked" have a "Wick,'" or light to see by, to takes advantage of those who have no "wick,"or light at all.

In the north before and after the flood the "Wicked One"(Lord), and his Host took advantage of Cain's children who dwelled there with him. They were all his "whores," "Horites (הורים)," or "Mountaineers," who prostrated (Prostituted) themselves before the Lord. After the flood Noah, Shem, and Japheth, prostituted (prostrated) themselves before the Lord also to do his biddings.

Anatomically the Darkness of the north, is in the bodies of the pale leper children of Cain. The children of Cain were and still are full of the Darkness, of the day of the Lord. The Darkness is in the head/mind in particular, where The Eye is located. Jesus (Yeshua) said "the Light of the body is the Eye, if therefore the Single Eye is open, the entire body shall be full of Light (*Matt. 6:22*)." "But if the eye is shut (Evil), then the entire body shall be full of Darkness." "If therefore the light that is in you is Darkness, then how great is that Darkness (*Matt. 6:23*)!" The Lord commanded that the congregations be kept in his perpetual Darkness (*Isa. 6:10*).

Nod is the Holy (Corrupt / הולי) Land of Hallel, the Prince of the Darkness of the North, who would become the Lord of Abraham.

# Lord (Beast)

*This is a composite image of the Lord, that he did not want depicted of him: As El Shaddai, (God Almighty / אל שדי), he has breasts (Shaddai / שדי)(Ex. 6:3), and horns. He has wings that shadow the land of Nod (Isa. 18:1). The torch is his wick or wickedness. As the Devil (שעיר) he is a hairy, hoofed, goat headed man. He is also androgynous, or male/female.*

Picture: Khunrath 1560-1605

Notes

# Places
# Nod

*North — Mou<u>nd</u>s — Sleep — Ararat*

The northern mountainous regions of Nod was the chief place of the Lord Hallel (*Ps. 48:2*). Nod denotes the mou<u>nd</u>s east of the Tigris River, a maximum security prison. Nod with it's (m) prefix is the root word for "M"ou<u>nd</u>(s) (מונד). The prefix (מ) means "of." Thus "<u>mound</u>" means "Of Nod," meaning that Nod is synonymous with mounds. The mounds or mountains in concern are north and east of the Tigris River. Mounds are mountains, and therefore the true and proper land of Nod is the mountainous region east and north of Mesopotamia (*Gen. 4:16*). The remainder of Nod is the land of Shinar, and it's plans between the mountains and the Tigris River (*Gen. 10:10; 11:2*).

Nod was "walled" in on four sides: There are mountains beyond Nod, on the north and east sides. The Persian gulf is on the south, and the Tigris River on the west of Nod. Within these confines lie the mounds of Nod, and the plains of Shinar. Both mounds and plains make up Greater Nod.

After the Tribunal, Nod became a experimental containment place. Hallel, his Hosts (Males and Females), and Hallel's son Cain were all casted out of the Garden into Nod (*Gen.3:23, 24*). Michael/Melchezedek who was situated in the Garden, was the Senior Warden of Nod prison.

Nod was not a place of rehabilitation, or punishment, but was a test tube, to test the overall nature of the Lord, his Host (Liles and Liliths), and his son Cain. Cain was initially a guiltless victim of circumstances imposed on him, by his father the Lord, and his Host.

Nod also implies a place to "nod" or go to sleep, or become mentally dead (**Necro**), which is what Cain was. The pale children of Marked Cain are the first and only true Negroes, or Necroes, or Mentally Dead, on the planet. In their mentally asleep/dead condition the Lord Hallel their father commanded that Cain be the husband or keeper of his effeminate (האבל) brother/wife Abel (הבל)(*Gen. 4:7*). Abel (הבל) literally mean "Effeminate." After murdering Abel Cain mated with the Lilahs (Lilith) of his father and fathered many children (*Gen. 4:17*).

All of Nod became a Holyland, or Corrupt Land filled with the Sodomite children of Cain the son of the Lord. The Lord's World (TBL) in Nod was corruption, because that is what the Lord wanted. But he lost control of these Gentiles, or Caucasian children of his son Cain (*Gen. 6:3*). It all had to be flooded out. Nod is the land that was ruined by the flooding of the Rivers of Cush (Ethiopia), the Tigris and Euphrates (*Isa. 18:2*). After the flood Cain his pale leper children would have to be Raised.

Nod the Land of the Lord, should have been fruitful and prosperous beyond any other place on the planet, if indeed the Lord could make the land fertile. But the Lord could not make Nod fertile, for the ground was cursed (אררח) with famine, because the Lord was present there (*Gen. 3:14*). Ararat (אררח) means "curses."

At the request of the Lord, Ham sent his grandson Nimrod the Great Light to Nod. Thousands of other Blacks came north into Nod, with Nimrod to build an entire but temporary civilizing region called Chaldea, for the Caucasian Race (*Gen. 10:9-12*).

Observations

# Places
# Chaldea

*Nod — Chaldea (Devil Place) — Outcasts — Hell (Hallel)(Corruption / הלל) (Isa. 14:25).*

Behold Chaldea the Land of the Chaldeans (Ca-Shaddai), this people [and land] was not till the Assyrian (Nimrod) founded it, for those who dwell in the wilderness of the north of Nod" (*Isa. 23:13, Gen. 10:10-12*). The land of Shinar became Chaldea, when Nimrod built there. The land of Shinar is the entire flat land between the Tigris River, and the mounds of Nod (*Gen. 10:10*). The **plains** of Shinar where Nimrod built Chaldea, was only in the north of the land (*Gen. 11:2*).

The reason that Ur Chaldea was built in the North of Nod was because this was the last place that went under water in the flood, and was the first place to reappear after the flood waters went down. Cain's pale children were sealed there, in Cain's underground city of Enoch (*Gen. 4:14*).

Before Nimrod and the thousands of others build the Ur Metropolis, they had to clear much land, and level it. In some cases entire forest would have been cut down, both to clear the land, and to harvest the lumber for building. Roads and bridges had to be built. Camps were built to shelter the workers. Agricultural fields were laid out, to grow food to feed those who had come north to work. This was before Nimrod and thousands of others became Mighty Hunter in the ground to find Marked Cain, his pale leper children (*Gen. 10:8, 9*).

This cleared and cultivated land in the side of the north of Nod was given the name **Chaldea**, to distinguish it from all of the rest of Nod, which was still wilderness. All of Cain's pale leper children who would be brought into the civilizing zone of Chaldea. would be called Chaldeans (בשרי / ShD). The word Chaldea is a corruption of the true Old Language word Ca-Shaddai (כשרי), which means "Like the Outcasts," or "Like the Devils." *See Strong's Concordance "Devil"* (שד) *#7700, 7701.* Nimrod may have given the children of Cain, the name Chaldean (Ca-Shaddai), because Cain's wife their mother was one of the Devils (Shaddai), or Hostesses of the Lord, who were all in the ground of Nod with Cain (*Gen. 4:17*). The Lord's Hosts (Shaddai or Devils) are the Fallen Children (Sons/Daughters) of Gods, who mated with the Daughters (and sons) of the Man Cain, before the flood and afterwards (*Genesis 6:2*). Thus Cain's children the Chaldeans (Ca-Shaddai) were the Ammi Shaddai, or "People of the Devils" (Shaddai)(*Numbers 1:12*)."

Nimrod founded Ur/Chaldea, to raise Cain, his pale children, back into the sunlight. But the Lord did not want their eyes, ears and minds open (*Isa. 6:10*), or for Nimrod to unify them, as he did (*Gen. 11: 6*). So the Lord and his Host confounded/ruined Ur/Chaldea (*Gen. 11:9; Isa. 23:13*), scattering the Chaldeans, except a remnant that stayed there in Nod/Chaldea in the north.

Cain's daughters from this northern remnant, are the **Daughters of Chaldean Darkness**. The Lord turned them all into prostitutes (*Isa. 47:1, 7*). The Lord and his Host corrupted all the young Chaldean (Fair) girls, including perhaps Sarah's mother, Sarah, and her sister Milcah. They were both fair like their mother, even though their father Abraham's father Terah was a wooly headed Black man (*Gen. 11:29; Gen. 20:12*). Abram would bring Sarah across the Tigris, down into the Garden, to the land of Canaan. This is where the confounded people of Ur/Babel had fled (*Gen. 11:9*). Sarah's mother's people in the north were a remnant, of these people who had been given asylum in Sodom, in the land of Canaan. The Chaldeans were declared to be evil by the Lord (*Jeremiah 45:5, Jer. 51:24*). The Lord was the cause of Ur Chaldea in Nod, the nativity of Abraham being

Notes

# Places
# Hell (Precivilizing)

*Chaldea — Hills are Hell — Corrupt (חלל) — Mound — Ur*

One aspect of Hell are the caves (נקבוה) inside of the Hills above Chaldea. The Mound of Ararat (אררות), the Lord's mound is the chief hill of the original hell. In translation "hell (Sheol / שאל)" #7585 means "underground." The "underground (hell) was the dwelling place of the Lord, his Host, and Cain (*Gen. 4:14*). Cain built Enoch an "**underground**"(Hell) city for his pale leper children, in the land of Nod (*Gen. 4:17*). But hell is also as much a condition as it is a place. "In phonics the word Hell (חלל) means "Corruption." Thus the **underground** (Hell) place was a place of corruption.

Hell is not a hot place, but is in the cold region east and north of Mesopotamia. The Lord told Moses that he was the Lord in the ground (*Ex. 8:21*). The Lord and his Hosts were in the earth in those days creating the hell (חלל), or corrupt (חלל) state of existence that was imposed on Cain and his children (*Gen. 6:4*). Thus the Lord's World is Hell, a totally corrupt state of being. The Lord's name Hallel (חלל) roots from the word Hell (חלל), and Hallel mean "Corrupt God."

Geographically Hell was the totality of the land of Nod, both above and below ground, and it was located east of the Tigris River. Hell has "hills," and plains (Shinar)(*Gen. 10:10, 11:2*). The word "hell" roots back to the Old Language word (HLL / חלל). This is also the root consonants for words such as Hall, Hole, Holl (Hollow), and Hull. These words mostly imply that the insides or life of something have been hollowed out, or removed. Hell (Nod) is next door to Eden's Garden. Africa is Eden, and Eden's Garden was east of it (*Gen. 4:16*). The Garden composed all of the land east of Eden (Africa) and it's eastern border, and was contained by the entire length of the Tigris River. The Tigris River running from the northwest to the Persian Gulf was the Gate at the East of the Garden. Thus the gate at the east of the Garden was a gate that led to Hell.

Hallel (Hell God) the future Lord of Abraham was the Man who was casted (Shaddai) out from the Garden, back to the ground he had been taken from in Nod (*Gen. 3:19*).

The whole agenda of the Lord, as the man who had been "casted out" (Shaddai), was to return to the Garden (*Gen. 3:23*). Returning to the Garden, he would take revenge against those who had driven him out, over into Hell (*Gen. 3:24*)! To be with the Lord, is to be in Hell

Hell was used as a staging area to multiply those that the Lord would use to invade his way back down into the garden, to take his revenge. In the Lord's Hell of the north there was little physical Light (*Amos 5:18, 20*), nor was there mental light, for the Lord shut the eyes, ears, and minds of Cain's children (*Isa. 6:10*). There was also perpetual famine. The ground in Hell was cursed (Ararat/אררת) for the Lord's sake (*Gen. 3:17*). Hallel (The Lord), and his Host were vampires, stealing life from the blood of all that was sacrificed to him (*Leviticus 17:10*). North (ציפון) in the old language is pronounced "siphon", or place of sucking. To be in the north (ציפון), was to be in **hell** having the life "sucked")"out of one.

The pale children of Cain are the people of the Shadows (*Isa. 18:1*). Hallel is Dracula or Drack El (Darkness God), the Lord, the Prince of Darkness of the North (*Amos 5:18, 20*). Nimrod the Great Light, built Ur in the Hell of Nod, to Raise Cain's children away from the Hell his father the Lord, Hallel (Lucifer), had imposed on them in his Darkness (*Isa. 9:2*).

Observation

# Places
# Ur (City)

*Hell (הלל, Corruption) — Ethiopian Ambassador — "Lighted Place" (Ur / אור)*

Nimrod was sent into the hell of Nod to build Ur. Ur (אור) means "Light." The need to build a place of light implies that there is no light, in the place where Ur (Light) was to be built. Nimrod was a Great Light. He came to shine light upon the people, who walked in the shadow of death, and Darkness of the Lord (*Isa. 9:2*). Nimrod and the thousands with him, came as ambassadors, and swift messengers, to the Caucasians who lived in Nod, north and east of the Tigris. The Tigris River is the river of Nimrod's father Cush (Ethiopia)(*Isa. 18:1; Zephoniah 3:10*).

There in Nod was a people scattered and peeled, a people terrible from their beginning. These Gentiles had been meted out and trodden down by the Lord, before the flood (*Isa. 18:2*). The Lord wanted Nimrod to raise them, but also to keep them in the condition, he had put them in before the flood (*Isa. 6:10*). The Lord instructed Nimrod to raise them, but not awaken them. But Nimrod came as a Great Light, to raise them from Darkness, to Light.

Nimrod and those with him from the Garden set up the towers of Ur (*Gen. 11:4*), and the palaces thereof (*Isa. 23:13*). The beginning of Nimrod's kingdom were the six major cities, that composed the Ur/Babel Metropolis (*Gen. 10:10-12*). Each city served a special purpose for Raising Cain, his Pale Leper children:

**Accad** (אכד) "Academy" was a city of universities, colleges, and schools. All of the pale leper children of Cain capable, could go into this school system. Those who graduated from these schools were qualified to be rulers, judges, and captains, of the society that Nimrod was building for Cain's children (*Gen. 10:10*).

**Erech** (Erect / ארך) was a Masonic City, a building trades city, that qualified each one trained there to build homes, walls, roads, buildings, storage silos, canals, harbors, and docks, throughout the corporate limits of the Urban, and SubUrban Ur/Babel Metropolis (*Gen. 10:10*).

**Nineveh** (נינוה)(and the city's streets [Rehoboth] was a residential city, built by Nimrod's pale leper students. Nineveh was an experiment in family and social co operation. It was composed of family houses, and apartment buildings, with streets, alleys, drains and sewer systems (*Gen. 10:11*).

**Resen** (רסן) was built as a ceremonial city, where those who had finished their training, would go to graduate. They would wear mortar boards (Caps), gowns, and be issued sheep skins. The sheep skins issued would be to wear to cover their nakedness, not to hang on a wall (*Gen. 10:12*)!

**Calah** (כלח)(Nimrud) was the Administrative City, of Nimrod and those he designate to administrate over the different districts of the overall Ur/Babel Metropolis. Nimrod ruled all of Ur from Calah (*Gen. 10:12*).

Notes

# Places
# Ur

*Flood Tower of Babel — Grafting Cain Back*

**Babel** (בבל) with it's phallus shaped flood tower was a city for breeding. Cain had been wooly headed and brown, before his father the Lord had infected him with permanent pale leprosy. Many of the pale children of Cain had to stay in the shadows, for exposure to the sun would have killed them. The tower in the city of Babel was symbolic of the phallus, of the well endowed wooly headed brown young men, who came north with Nimrod. They had issues like horses (*Ezekiel 23:20*), and were sure to impregnate all of the pale young women, who volunteered to come to Babel. They would come to be impregnated to start the grafting process. Their children would be brown and wooly headed, as Cain had been before he was "marked" with a fair complexion (*Gen. 4:15*). These pale complexioned Caucasian daughters of Cain, would give birth to wooly headed brown offspring. These offspring were able to come out of the shadows, into the light to be kissed by the Most High (sun), like all of the rest of the wooly headed brown population of the planet.

Nimrod had searched in the ground and found Cain's children, and raised them as the Lord wanted, but Nimrod had not kept their eyes, ears and hearts (Minds) shut, as the Lord commanded (*Isa. 6:9, 10*). The Lord could tolerate Nimrod sending them to school, giving them family, and social structure. The Lord could even except Nimrod teaching them to cook their food, build cities, roads, canals etc. But the Lord was a jealous God concerning the Chaldean females.

Before the flood the Lord and his Host had sex with the daughters of Cain (*Gen. 6:2-4*), and had children with them (*Gen. 6:2-4*). The Lord also had deflowered, all of the little virgin Chaldean girls, as they came to puberty (*Isa. 47:1-7*). The Lord was jealous, and protested the Chaldean girl in Nod volunteering, to be made pregnant by the wooly headed brown Assyrio/Ethiopians, as he would in the future protest the Chaldean and Israeli girls, who were wooly headed and brown, letting the wooly headed Egyptians, and Assyrians lay upon them, bruising their breast, and filling them with sperm like the issue of horses (*Ezekiel 23:1-21*). The Lord could not tolerate the young wooly headed brown men. He had made Cain and his children pale, now they were being changed back to wooly brown people again. Thus the Lord came down to confounded the Ur/Babel Metropolis, to stop Nimrod from unifying Cain's pale leper children, back to being wooly and brown, like the other people of the planet (*Gen. 11:9*). Nimrod had built Ur/Babel for those who dwelt in the wilderness of Nod, and the Lord brought it all to ruin (*Isa. 23:13*).

The end of pale leprosy would have been the end of the World of the Lord, with it's corruption. Thus those who had been pale now grafted back to Black could have helped to bring the experiment to a satisfied conclusion. But when the Lord confounded Ur/Babel Cain's children were mostly still pale, and fled from him. Those pale ones who fled the Lord's confounding Ur Babel "hebrewed" the Tigris River, the Bread Gate down into the land of the Garden lands of the children of Ham (*Gen. 11:9*).

Observation

# Places
## Ur

*Ur— Ur/Babel Metropolis — Broad Gate*

Ur was an experiment to see what direction the Caucasian Race would go in when they were released from the bondage imposed upon them by Hallel and his Host.

**Accad** a university or college city where those who were qualified were taken to learn the crafts necessary to, **Erech** a Masonic city of trade schools, **Babel** a breeding city, **Nineveh** a city of apartment buildings, **Calah** an administration city, and **Resen** a **Resign**ation city of ceremonies, celebrations, and graduations.

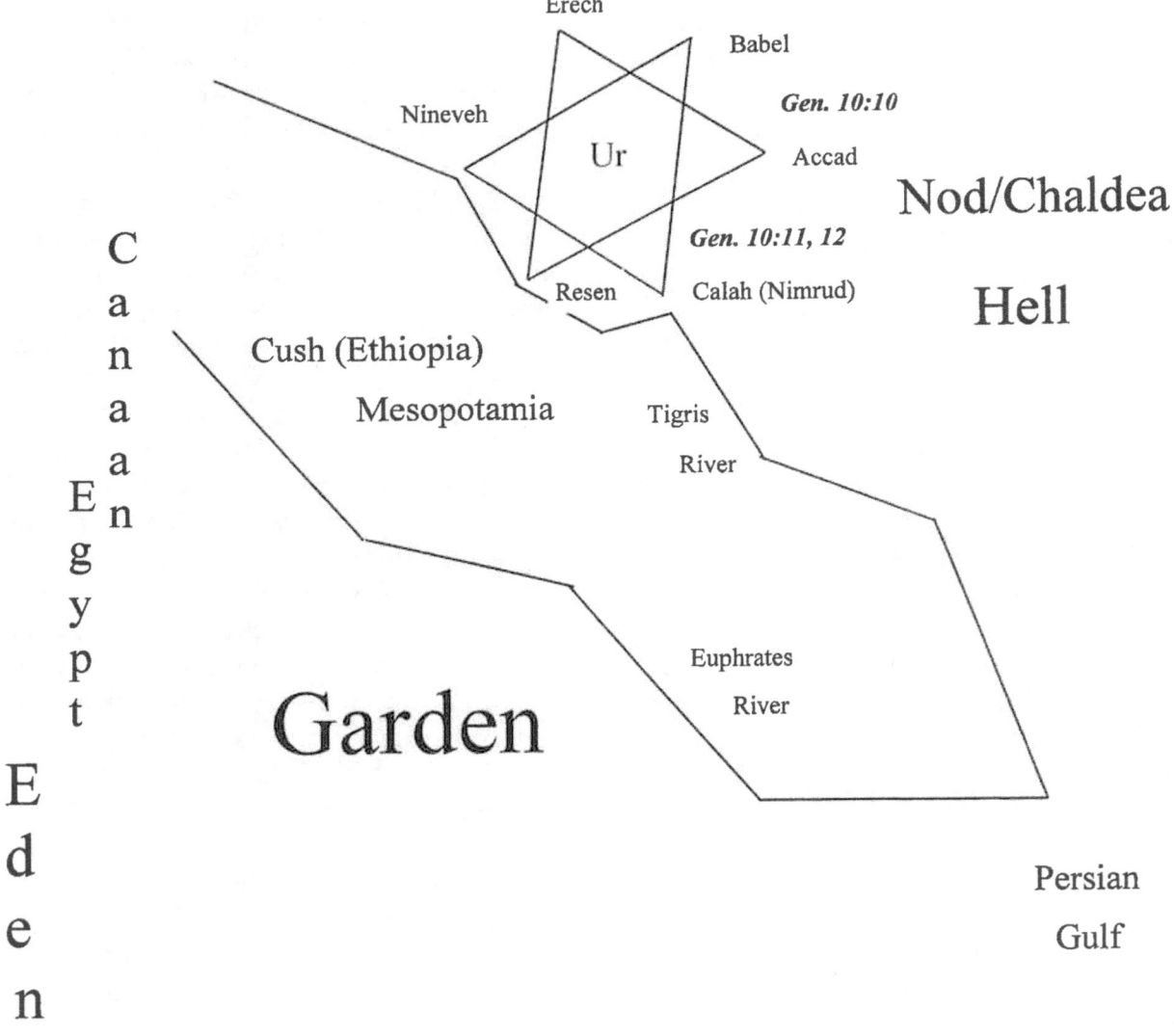

Observation

Notes

# Places
# Broad Gate (Mesopotamia)

*Ur — Cush or Ethiopian Gate  the division between Darkness and Light — Broad Gate leading to destruction (שד)(Deut. 7:23) — Garden*

The Broad Gate is the entire length of the Tigris River. Nimrod had to cross the Broad Gate eastward into Nod, to build the Ur Metropolis in the north of Nod.  The Tigris River (Broad Gate) is on the east side of the Garden, adjacent to Nod. The Tigris is the the Eastern River of Cush (Ethiopia)(*Gen. 2:13*). The Tigris River is the Broad Gate that Jesus talked about, that lead eastward to the Destroyer (שד) or Devil (שד) in Nod (*Matt.7:13*). The Lord of Abraham as the Almighty (Shaddai), is the Devil (Shad), or Destroyer/Destruction (Shad), east of the Broad Gate. The word translated as destruction (שד) is also the word used for Devil (שד). Thus the Broad Gate leading to destruction, was the Tigris that lead to the Devil (שד), who is the Lord.

The purpose of the Broad Gate before and after the flood, was to keep the Lord and his Host contained in Nod. Before the flood the Cherubim were the guards on the Broad Gate (*Gen. 3:24*), and after the flood it was Ham's son Cush (Ethiopia), and his children, who guarded the Tigris.

It seems that the Lord could not cross water on his own. Someone would have to bring the Lord across. Therefore Ham's children would not allow anyone from Nod to cross the Tigris from Nod, to bring the Lord with them. The exception was that the people from the confounded Ur/Babel Metropolis were allowed to cross, because they were fleeing from the Lord in Nod (*Gen. 11:9*). The Tigris was to protect those in the Garden and Eden, from the Lord in Nod.

The Bible/Torah states that when the Man (Lord) was driven out (Shaddai) of the Garden he was being casted, "back to the ground from which he had been taken (*Gen.3:23*)." The term Garash (גרש) for being "driven out (*Gen. 3:24*)," is same as Shaddai (שדי) for being "casted out." Hallel the Man who was casted out of the Garden, had previously been "casted out" (Shaddai) of the Heavens, after being defeated there in the Solar Wars (*Rev. 12:9*).

A gate is also a wall, in the sense that a gate can block passage like a wall. At the same time a gate is a portion of wall that can allow passage, in two directions. Gates in this sense serve two basic purposes: 1) To keep in, or to keep out. A **fort** gate "**Keep Out**" to protect those inside from those outside.  A **prison** gate "**Keep In**," to protect those outside from those inside. The Tigris River as a Broad Way, or Broad Gate served this dual purpose. First the Tigris was a Fort Gate that protected those in the Garden westward, from those in Nod eastward. Secondly the Tigris was a prison Gate, against those in Nod. It was to keep those in Nod from coming out to the garden.  The Lord his Host, and Cain,  were never to leave their confinement in Nod.

Nimrod built built the city complex in Nod to civilize Cain's children, to cause them to stay in Nod. With the pale leper children of Cain having the ability to sustain themselves, it would lessen the need to defend the the Broad Gate, from them coming across. But the Lord trodden them down, meted them out, scattered and peeled these pale ones, and confounded their city (*Isa. 18:2, Gen. 11:9*)  Most of the "confounded" inhabitant of Ur/Babel fled Nod down across the Broad Gate, of the Tigris, into the gardenlands of the children of Ham for protection from the Lord. These pale ones from Ur/Babel were given asylum from the Lord and were quarantined in the twin grain cities of Sodom and Gomorrah in the Garden (*Gen. 11:9*).

Observation

# Place

# Garden

*Broad Gate — Garden of the Gods (Ezek. 28:13, Ezek. 31:8, 9) — **Buffer State** —Jerusalem*

After the Broad Gate of the Tigris River, the Garden (Guarded Place) was the next stage of protection for Eden (Africa). The Garden was the entire land mass between the Tigris river, and Egypt. The purpose for the Garden was to "guard" Eden to it's west, from those east of the Garden in Nod. The people of the Garden (Guarded Place) would absorb anyone from Nod, to keep them out of Eden. The word **Garden** translates from the old language word Gan (גן). The word **Gan** means "Fenced," "Guarded," etc. The Garden existed before the flood, but it's location is being described after the flood. Arphaxad himself was only born two years after the flood (*Gen. 11:10*), and yet the location of two of the rivers of the Garden are described, using the names of two of Arphaxad's great great grandsons! Havilah (*Gen. 2:11; 10:13; 10:29*) and Diklah (*Gen. 10:27*). Both of these are great great grandsons of Arphaxad. *See "Noah's Genealogy," Shem, Arphaxad, Salah, Eber, Joktan, (Diklah and Havilah). Page 64.*

The Hapi (Nile) river went out of Eden (Africa), and turned into four heads (rivers), to water the Garden (*Gen. 2:10*). All four of these rivers existed, and sourced from the Nile, before the flood. After the flood two of these rivers had become the Mediterranean Sea (Gihon / גיחון)(*Gen. 2:11*), and the Red Sea (Pison / פישון)(*Gen. 10:13*). The other two rivers are the Hiddekel/Diklah (חדקל) or Tigris River (*Gen. 2:14*), and the Phrates (פרת) or Euphrates River (*Gen. 2:14*), which both originally sourced from the Nile River, before the flood. There were trees in the garden.

Some of the "trees" "planted" in the Garden were not vegetation, at all, but were "Trees or people from Eden (Africa)(*Ezek. 31:9*). Many of these "trees" or people from Eden were the **Children of Seth** (*Nu. 24:17*). They survived the flood, because they lived in Eden (Africa), which was beyond the flood, which had only been in the Garden, east of Eden. These "trees," or people, planted trees, and orchard for themselves. They also had pastures which were good, and the land was wide, and quiet, and peaceable; for they of Ham had dwelt there of old (*I Chron. 4:40*). The eyes of the Lord cared for this land (*Deut. 11:12*), of milk and honey (*Ex. 3:8*), and he would bring the Israelis here to destroy Ham's children, and dwell in their stead (*I Chron. 4:41-43*).

But long before the Israelis ever came into existence, and just after the flood, the children of Ham had built cities throughout the Garden (Guarded Place). The children of Cush (Ethiopia) built all of the cities from the east side of the Euphrates, through all of Mesopotamia, and cities all the way to India. The children of Canaan built all of the cities, in the Garden from the west side of the Euphrates all the way to the Great Sea (Mediterranean)(*Gen. 10:19*). Canaan's sons Sidon and Heth built cities along the entire length of the coast of the Great Sea, including the cities of Sidon, and Tyre (*Gen. 10:15;* ). Hiel built Jericho a solar/lunar city, to keep the time for planting and harvesting (*I Kings 16:34*). The twin grain cities of Sodom and Gomorrah, were built to store and process grain. The Amorites, the children of Amor, a son of Canaan, built towns and cities, including their capital city Mari, along the western shores of the central portion of the Euphrates River. In his revenge against Canaan, the Lord promised Abraham that he would give "his seed" all of the lands of Canaan (*Gen. 15:18*). This would include Jerusalem, the city of peace.

Notes

# Places
# Jerusalem

*Garden — Melchezedek (Warden) — The City of Peace, in a Land of Peace) — Not of Mohammedans, Jewish, or Christians — Canaan*

The city of Jerusalem would be built in the midst of the Garden. **Jerusalem** pronounced **Ur Salem**, means "City of Peace." Jerusalem the city of Peace would be built, in the land of Canaan. Canaan's son Jebus and his children, built Jerusalem for Michael/Melchezedek (*Judges 19:10, I Chron.11:4*). But long before Jerusalem was built, Melchezedek had officiated over a Tribunal against the Lord, and his Host (*Dan. 7:9-12; Ps. 82:1-7*). The Tribunal was held in the Garden, approximately where Jerusalem was to be built, in the midst of the Garden.

Jerusalem was also built to commemorate Peaceful Ham and his children, and to honor Canaan, because Canaan exposed Noah for the Sodomite, and child molester that he was, in service to the Lord. Melchezedek had tried the Lord and his Host, and sentenced them to be cast back over into Nod, where they had been taken from (*Gen. 3:23*). Melchezedek became the Senior Warden over Nod prison, where the Lord and his Host had been cast after the Tribunal (*Gen. 3:24*).

Jerusalem was the seat of Peace (Islam), not the seat of the Muhammadans, Christians, or Israelis. None of these three groups ever represented Peace (Islam), but all three are in Perpetual Warfare. Yet these warring Israelis, Christians, and Arabs claimed the City of Peace (Jerusalem), as a shrine. This was even though the city was not built by any of these three groups, nor their ancestors. Jerusalem was built by Yebus a son of Canaan (*Judges 19:10*). The importance of Jerusalem is that it was the chief city of Peaceful Ham in Canaan (*I Chron.4:40*). Peaceful Ham and his children had **sent** teachings of peace to each of these three groups, at three different times. First **Nimrod** was sent to Raise the future Christians, Cain's Pale Leper children, the Gentiles in the land of Nod. Nimrod and those with him from the land of Ham taught the Gentiles peace (Islam) as a way of life, but they killed him (*Isa. 53rd Chptr.*).

Next two thousand years later **Yeshua (Jesus)** was sent from Egypt, back to the Lost sheep of **Israel to teach them peace** (Islam). The Israelis had murdered most of the people of Canaan, and taken Possession of their land. The Israelis and other Gentiles conspired to murder Yeshua (Jesus) the peaceful one, and killed him.

The third person sent was **Muhammad** who was sent to the **Arabians** to teach them peace (Islam). Muhammad had to flee for his life, for they attempted to murder him! All three of these groups were saved by the children of Ham, the teachers of peace. Yet these three groups followed the same course as Abraham. Abraham refused to adhere to Peace, and these three also refused to adhere to peace, and praised Abraham who had choose to bow down to Hallel the God (Man) of War (*Ex. 15:3*). The Gentiles, Israelis, and Arabians charged the peaceful teachings that the wooly headed brown children of Ham had given to them, into **Judaism, Christianity,** and the **Muhammadan Faith** (Not the teachings of Muhammad). In ancient and more modern times these three groups came together in unison to enslave the children of Eden, the same wooly headed people who had saved them in ancient times. They then warred with each other over possession of Jerusalem (City of Peace), which they have all declared a shrine. It ceased to be Jerusalem (City of Peace) when they took it by war. The violent overthrow of Jerusalem has been the completion of the holocaust against Canaan.

Observation

# Places
# Canaan

*Jerusalem—Revenge on Canaan—Honorable Canaanites(Ezek.28th Chptr.)— Sodom/Gomorrah*

When David overwhelmed Jerusalem the city built by Jebus the son of Canaan it was symbolically the finish of the revenge of the Lord on Canaan (*II Sam. 5:6*). Canaan was the forth son of Ham. Canaan had been born after the flood on mount Ararat. The word Canaan (כנען) means "We are Afflicted."

Noah was never asleep in his tent, and did not have to "awake" from his wine as the mistranslation of the scripture say. Ham had caught his father Noah naked and drunk, in his tent, with his son Canaan. After being caught, and exposed, Noah sat drinking his wine trying to figure out why his son Ham had come into his tent. By the time Noah had "finished (קיץ)" his "wine he knew what Canaan had "done to him." What Canaan had "done to Noah," was tell his father Ham that his grandfather Noah had told him to come to his tent for questionable purposes, and not tell anyone. Noah attempted to curse Canaan, for breaking the vow he had put upon him. Noah wanted revenge on his grandson Canaan. Canaan would have to be protected from Noah, and the Lord in Nod.

When Ham brought his family down from Ararat, back into the Garden he wanted to protect Canaan, so he designated the land between Mesopotamia and Egypt, as the land of Canaan.

Anyone hebrewing the Tigris fleeing from the Lord, would have to come through the entire land of Mesopotamia, and then hebrew the Euphrates to be safe with Canaan, from the Lord!

Canaan was never cursed, like Noah said (*Gen. 9:25*), but was prosperous. Canaan had eleven sons who built all of the original cities across his land. The land of Canaan was a paradise, a good and large land of milk and honey (*Ex. 3:8*). The Phonician descendants of Canaan are the source of the Alphabet used by the entire Caucasian world. The word **Bible** came from the city **Biblus** in the land of Canaan.

The Lord's motive for returning to the Garden and Canaan were many. The Lord wanted to take revenge on those in the Garden in General, and Canaan in particular, because Canaan had exposed Noah as a Sodomite in service to the Lord. The Lord had lost the services of most of Noah's children, when Ham brought them down from Ararat in a great exodus, after the Tent Incident between Noah and Canaan.

The Chaldean/Caucasian/Gentile children of Pale Leper Cain, escaped to Canaan from the Lord in Nod. The Lord had confounded and destroyed the Ur Metropolis that Nimrod had built for them (*Gen. 11:9*). The Lord had been trying to regain control over them, but they escaped and were given sanctuary in the land of Canaan. Canaan did much damage to the World of the Lord.

Terah and his son Abram were the next to attempt to escape, from the Lord to Canaan (*Gen. 11:30*). Terah died, and the Lord forced Abram to bring him from Nod, down into the land of Canaan (*Gen. 12:1*). The Lord caused famines in Canaan because of his presence there. The Israelis escaped away from the Lord, and his famine in the land of Canaan (*Gen. 42:5, Gen. 47:4, Deut. 26:5*). The Israelis fled down into the land of Egypt and did not have a thought of ever seeing or returning to the Lord again. The Lord and his Host were in hibernation in Mount Horeb for four hundred years, waiting for the Israelis to call him. Before this the Lord had expected a call from Cain's pale children, who had been given sanctuary in the cities of Sodom and Gomorrah.

Notes

# Places
# Sodom and Gomorrah

*Canaan — Grain Cities — Asylum — Cain's Tubal (תֻבַל) — Confounding Sodom and Gomorrah — Lot's mother's people — Egypt (Narrow Gate)*

Sodom and Gomorrah were twin grain cities built deep inside of the land of Canaan (*Genesis 10:19*). The wooly headed brown Canaanite people of the region built these adjacent cities for the **"processing (Sodom)," and "storage" (Gomorrah)**, of their harvested grain, such as corn, wheat, barley, rice, etc. Some of these grains were "scorched" (toasted), or baked into breads. See **Sodom** (סרם) Strong's # 5476 "Scorch," "Burn," "Roast," "Bake," and see **Gomorrah** (עמרדה) Strong's # 6014-17 "Storage," "Stack," "Stock," "Stockades." Grain was the only population that Sodom and Gomorrah ever had. Sodom and Gomorrah were located in the southwestern portion of Canaan, near Gaza, the entrance to Egypt. The wooly headed brown Canaanites had built Sodom, and Gomorrah along with all of their other cities, after the flood.

Sodom and Gomorrah only began to be associated with homosexual behavior, when Cain's pale children from the confounded metropolis of Ur/Babel (*Gen. 11:9*), asked for and were given asylum there. The pale ones brought homosexuality down into Sodom and Gomorrah. The twin cities were converted from grain processing and storage, to a place of habitation and quarantine. Quarantined in Sodom and Gomorrah, Cain's pale children from the north, became the first and only Sodomite citizens.

The mother of Sarah and Lot in the north, was kin to the Sodomites in Canaan. Their mother was born in the north, a descendant from the Chaldeans remnant, who did not flee the north, when the Lord Confounded Ur/Babel (*Gen. 11:9*). Sodom and Gomorrah were occupied for four hundred years, by the refugees who fled from Ur of the Chaldeans in the north. Ur/Babel was the nativity of Abram, Lot, and Sarah (*Gen. 11:28*). Abram migrated from Ur on the plains of Shinar in the side of the north (*Jos. 24:3 14*), down to Sodom on the plains of Mamre in Canaan (*Gen. 18:1*). From there the Lord and Abram took Sarah, to play the whore in Egypt (*Gen. 12:14, 16*).

After they returned from prostituting Sarah in Egypt (*Gen. 13:12, 13*), Lot went to Sodom to live with his mother's people. Lot became a permanent Sodomite (*Gen. 13:12*).

The Lord overthrew Sodom and Gomorrah (*Gen. 19:24*), as he had overthrown Ur/Babel hundreds of years before (*Gen. 11:9, Isaiah 23:13*). Hundreds of years still later after the Israelis were in Egypt, the Lord brought the Israelis back, to destroy the remnants of these Caucasians who had escaped the Lord's overthrow of Sodom and Gomorrah before (*Gen. 19:29*). These pale ones were the "Nations or Goyim, that the Lord accused of committing Incest, sodomy, Lesbianism, Bestiality etc. (*Lev, 18:7-29*). The Lord called them "Nations" (Gentiles / Goyim). The wooly headed brown Canaanites were never Nations or Gentiles, or Sodomites.

When the Lord came to destroy Sodom and Gomorrah, it was not because the pale ones there were Lesbians, and Homosexuals. The Lord had made their ancestors lesbians, and homosexuals.

Their ancestors had escaped from him, when the Lord overthrewn Ur/Babel. Next the Lord destroyed these pale ones in Sodom, because none of them had ever called him down to Canaan. Part of the Lord's revenge on Canaan was because they had given Cain's pale children sanctuary. Sodom and Gomorrah were near Egypt, the Narrow Gate the final protection for Eden. (Africa).

Observation

# Places
# Egypt the Narrow Gate

*Sodom/Gomorrah — Strait Gate — Eden*

The twin grain cities of Sodom and Gomorrah had become a place of quarantine, in the land of Canaan near Egypt. Egypt is Ham's second son Mizraim (*Gen. 10:6*). The word Mizraim (מצרים) roots from the word Zer (צר), which means Strait, Narrow, or Restricted, as when something is squeezed, pressed, or transformed, from a raw state, into a finished state. Israel would be transformed here, from being murder/rape tribes, to being like the peaceable people of Ham.

Egypt (Mizraim) was a Strait and Narrow Gate, the only land entrance into Eden (Africa). Africa (Eden) must be defended from the Lord, and Egypt was the last defence for Eden, from the Lord. Therefore Ham establish his chief strength with his son Egypt, in that Narrow Gate of land (*Ps. 78:51*). Egypt is the Strait and Narrow Gate, that Jesus talked about that leads into the Eternal Life (*Matt. 7:13, 14*), of Eden (Africa) which is the Paradise, of Jesus (*Luke 24:43*).

Ham's defense strategy for the Narrow Gate was peace, not aggression, for Ham and his children were peaceable from old (*I Chron. 4:40*). Rather the defense strategy was to defuse, the Lord being able to send anyone to attack Egypt.

Ham's Egypt in the Narrow gate was brilliant, in cities, sciences, architecture, roads, ship building, canals, etc. This model of civil centers was repeated in the Land of Canaan, and in Cush's Mesopotamia.

Nimrod was sent from his father Cush's land in Mesopotamia, across the Tigris. He was sent to the north of Nod to build an entire civilizing system, cities and all, for the pale leper children of Cain. This was the Ur/Babel Metropolis, it was a paradise, and garden, to keep the pale ones in Nod. This would defuse any possibility of the Lord using them, to invade, down into the Narrow Gate.

Nimrod raised Cain his pale leper children, and the Lord wanted to use them to invade down into the Land of Ham, but they wanted to stay in their cities, and refused to leave Nod. That is when the Lord confounded their cities and scattered them down into the land of Ham (*Gen. 11:9*), but they would not bring the Lord with them. The Lord had lost his invasion troops. They were given asylum from the Lord, by Ham's children, in the land of Canaan.

The Lord would force Abram to bring him down across the Tigris, to where the Lord could take his revenge on those pale ones, who had fled from him.

The Israelis were the Lord's next attempt at having a military force, but they fled from him and his famine, and sought asylum from the Lord also, in Egypt. The Lord had wanted to make the Israelis an army to invade Eden also. The eyes of the Lord were always upon the peaceable land of Ham (*Deut. 11:12*). It would take the Lord four hundred years to get Israel out of Egypt, to take his revenge on them in the wilderness, outside of Egypt.

The Lord had failed to invade, but was persistent, that hundreds of years later he would bring pale ones the pale Romans, and pale Greeks, from the west to destroy all of the lands of the children of Ham, including the Narrow Gate of Egypt, then what protection would Eden have?

Notes

# Places
# Eden

*Narrow Gate — Eden the Keystone — Eternal Life — Eden the Old South Pole — Eden the last place that Man was himself (God) — Eden the Garden of Gods (Ezek. 28:13) — Trees of Eden (Best)(Ezek. 31:16, 18) — Did not move)*

Egypt the Strait and Narrow strip of land (*Matt. 7:13, 14*), was the last land defense for Eden (Africa). The rest of the entire coast line around Eden (Africa) was protected by water. Eden (Africa) is the old south polar region, of Assiah, while the moon is the old north polar region of Assiah. The planet was altogether different, before the Lord Hallel (Lucifer) exploded Assiah, into being Ertz (Earth) or "continents" (*Isa. 24:1, 3-6*). The Lord had meant to destroy the entire planet, including Eden.

The word Eden (עדן) means "pleasant," and it roots from the base word Ed (עד), which means "Perpetual Witnessing." Perpetual Witnessing means All Seeing, All Knowing, and All Understanding. These three qualities describe Gods, who are the wooly headed original inhabitants of the entire planet. Thus Eden (עדן) is/was the "Pleasant (עד) Place (ן)," of those who could still "observe (עד)," because their bodies were still full of **Light**, because their **Single Eye** was still active, and **All Seeing**. They also had the **Single Ear**, that is **all hearing**, and an **All Understanding Heart/Mind** (*Matt. 13:16*). This is what Yeshua (Jesus) meant when he said an Eye, that see, an Ear that hear, and a heart/mind that understands (*Matt. 13:15*).

Eden is/was the last place that original man was himself, which is God. Eden it's self was/is the Garden (Guarded Place) of the Gods (*Ezekiel 28:13*). But Eden's Garden (Guarding Place) was east of Eden. Because the People of Eden (Africa) were Gods, with open eyes, ears, and minds, they have always had solutions for all that has ever occurred, on the planet.

One can imagine that Eden was the most pleasant of all the landmasses, for it had been the least effected, when the Lord exploded the planet. Eden did not move away from it's place, but all other land masses (continents) broke away from it, and moved away from the four sides of Eden.

Anyone who looks at a model of the planet will see the continents scattered out around the globe like giant pieces of a jig saw puzzle. When modern scientists became sufficient to measuring the land distribution on the planet they discovered that the continent now called Africa (Eden) was at the geographical center of all the land mass distribution of the planet. The exact center of that land distribution is now down through the center of the great pyramid in Egypt. The center had been in the center of Africa (Eden), before the planet had been exploded, but when the land shifted, from being exploded, it made Egypt (Zero / צרו) the center! Central (Equatorial) Africa is this planet's old south polar axis. Before the experiment can be completely over, all land masses (Continents) must be rapped back around Eden (Africa) again. Then the planet's spin must be reorientated, to central Eden (Africa) again. Then the moon must be brought back to it's place as the planet's old north polar region in the Pacific Ocean again. Then the planet must be made to rotate through the old south polar/ north polar axis. Then the other planets can be brought back into this planet, and the intact planet can be carried back into the sun again.

To counteract the planet coming back together again the Lord have caused his agents to do all that they can, to break into, and destroy Eden (Africa). The first necessity was to attack and to break down the Narrow land Gate of Egypt, which was the last defense for the whole of Eden.

Observation

# Places
# Eden

*Eden — In the Narrow Gate (Geology) — Goshen*

The Lord's first action was when he brought Abram down from the north to Egypt, and brought Sarah with them to prostitute her to the Pharaoh. The Lord had dropped vials of disease and plagues on the entire planet (***Rev. 15:6; Rev. 16:1-17***). Now he caused disease and plague in Egypt, so that he Abram, and Sarai, could leave Egypt with the goods they had gotten from Pharaoh (***Gen. 12:17***).

The next time the Lord would bring biological warfare into Egypt, was when he came to bring the Israelis out of Egypt against their will. The Lord's Host poured out vials of plague and disease, over the entire country, as he had poured them out on the whole planet before (***Exodus 15:26, Deut. 7:15, Rev. 16:1-17***). Egypt the Narrow Gate into Eden, was being battered down.

Next came the Pale Greeks through Alexander, and his generals, who captured the Narrow Gate of Egypt, and neutralized it.

Then came the Roman who not only entrenched in Egypt, but had broke through into all of northern Eden (Africa). this was all before they had murdered Jesus (Yeshua). The Romans would be the cause of the beginning of the Sahara Desert, by poor land management, while farming north west Africa (Eden).

All of the time that the Lord was sending his agents against Eden, Eden was sending saviors to those who were being imposed upon by the Lord, and his Darkness. The wooly headed Black Moors from North Africa (Eden) spent eight hundred years in Europe, civilizing the wild pale tribes up out of the Lord's Dark Ages there. These pale ones that the Moors had saved and given countries in Europe, turned on Eden (Africa) the homeland of those who had saved them.

The Portuguese, Spanish, Dutch, French, English, Germans, Israelis, and Arabs, all attacked Eden, and the Children of Eden who had been responsible for all of their salvations. Over time the Pale Ones came by sea in ships, to attack Eden from every side, and on land, through the now broken Narrow Gate Egypt, that had been Eden's final protection.

Finally came the Lord's pale leper American agents. The British Press (London Times, 1972), accused that the Americans developed the Aides virus in the Army's biological warfares laboratory, at Ft Detrick, Maryland. The London Times said they poured out their vials of Aids on Eden (Africa), through the World Health Organization, who gave shots for smallpox, in Central Africa. The first aids virus appeared in Central Africa (Eden), in the exact same pattern as the smallpox vaccination that had been given there. In these modern times was the Lord's agents pouring out the final vials of plague on Eden, to finally destroy it?

This was full circle for the Lord had poured out disease in Egypt, to force the Egyptians to drive the Israelis out (***Ex. 6:1, Ex. 12:33***). The Egyptians had saved the Israelis from the Lord's famine and plagues and diseases, in the land of Canaan. The Egyptians had allowed the Israelis to come to to live in Goshen, the best land in Egypt, to save them.

But even though the Egyptians allowed the Israelis to live on the very best land in Egypt, that land began to be known as Goshen (Place of Filth), after the Israelis practiced their corrupt lifestyle there.

Notes

# Place
# Goshen

*Eden — Best land in Egypt (**Gen. 47:6, 11**) — Shepards an abomination to Egyptian (**Gen. 46:34**) — Preservation of Corruption — Lying, Prostitution, Incest, Rape, Murder — Jacob the Syrian (מצרי) (Egyptian / מצרי) ready to Die — Saved by the Egyptians (**Deut. 26:4**) — Invaded Eden*

The district of Egypt, that would be called Goshen was the very best land in Egypt (**Gen. 47:4, 6**). It was not called Goshen until the Israelis lived their lifestyle there (**Gen. 45:10; 46:28**). Goshen (גושן) is the old language word for the English phrase, "**Place** (en / ן) of **Filth** (Gosh / גוש)." The term Goshen "(Place of Filth)," was not applied to the land, as much as it was applied to the way of life of the Israelis living there, who turned it into a Goshen (Place of Filth).

Noah had sacrificed all cleanness and preserved filth (Gosh / גוש)(**Gen. 8:20**). Preservation of Gosh (Filth) eludes to the lifestyle of the Israelis, even before they lived in Egypt! Thus the Egyptians in saving Jacob and the Israelis, were unknowingly preserving the continuation of the filthiness that Noah had knowingly preserved for the Lord, when he sacrificed all that was clean (**Gen. 8:20**). The Israelis were ready to perish in Canaan from the Lord's famine (**Deut. 26:5**), but they were allowed to became fruitful and multiplied into a multitude in Egypt (**Ex. 1:7**).

Egypt saved Israel, from the Lord's plague. Jacob on his death bed made the statement that his little group had been about to perish, from the Lord's famine, in the Land of Canaan, but the Egyptians sent wagons, to bring Israel to Egypt to save their lives (**Gen. 45:19, Deut. 26:5**). Yet the Egyptians did not want Israel to practice any element of their lifestyle on Egyptian soil: **Incest** from Abraham to Jacob. **Prostitution** of Sarah there in Egypt (**Gen. 12:16**). **Prostitution** of Dinah, in the Land of Canaan (**Gen. 34:1, 2**). Israelis had **Murdered** the men and boys of the city of Shechem, and then **raped** themselves into tribal existence with the women and girls, of that city, in the land of Canaan (**Gen. 34:25 - 29**).

Israel was in Egypt for seventeen years, before Jacob passed away. The Israelis took his body back to Canaan, to bury him. The Canaanites were grounding flour, and there was no famine, so the Israelis could have stayed in the land of Canaan, but they rushed back to Goshen in Egypt. The Israelis had left their children and herds in Egypt, to guarantee that they would be allowed to return (**Gen. 50:6-14**). The Israelis had no plans of ever leaving Egypt to serve the Lord again. After all Jacob declared himself to be Syrian (צרי), which is the root for the word Egyptian (מצרי). The Syrians were a colony of Egyptians who had gone north in the time of Nimrod, to assist in the building of Ur/Babel. They lived with Aram in northern Canaan, before and after the project in Nod. Rebecca the mother of Jacob (Israel) was Syrian or Egyptian through her mother an Egypto/Syrian woman. The Israelis were staying in Egypt, as Syrians (Egyptians), and Goshen (filth / גושן) could have eventually been changed into Tehorah (Cleanness / שהורה).

By all indications Israel was at home in Egypt, and would not have ever come out of Egypt again, and would have eventually became Children of Eden (Africa), like the Egyptians.

The Lord knew he could not use Israel to break into Eden, so he came to Egypt with his Darkness, to reclaim them from the Light. The Lord only brought Israel out of Egypt, to take revenge for them not serving him. He would send agents back in the future to break Egypt down, so as to invade Eden (Africa) the place of Eternal Life.

Observation

# Place
# Invaded Eden

*Goshen — Europe, Israel, Arabia — England, France, United States — Western Eden*

The Lord attacked Egypt, and did as much damage as he could, to bring Israel out of Goshen. This was the beginning of his invasion of Eden (Africa). The Israelis in Goshen, were only a state of mind away from qualifying to enter Eden (Africa), from Egypt the Strait Gate (*Matt. 7:13*). That was when the Lord came and invaded Egypt to bring Israel out by force. The Lord knew that Israel would not leave Egypt on their own, with him. The Egyptians had even tried to persuade Israel to leave their land (*Ex. 1:10*). The Israelis had stayed in Egypt for four hundred years, so that they would not have to go back, into bondage to the Lord!

The Egyptians always worked for themselves, and had even built all of the housing for the Israelis, for the four hundred years that Israel had been in Egypt. But when it was time to leave and Israel refused, the Egyptians forced the Israelis to start making bricks, and were going to teach, them how to build their own housing. If the Israelis could have tolerated getting use to working for themselves, and had not cried out, the Lord could not have come to Egypt to get them. Even then the Lord knew that he could not get Israel out, because they did not want to leave. But with Egypt destroyed, the Israelis would have to leave. The Lord and his Host battered down Egypt, the Narrow Gate before Eden, to retrieve the Israelis from the Great Light in Egypt. The Lord brought Israel back into his Thick Darkness, a Darkness that can be felt (*Ex. 10:22, Amos 5:18, 20*).

From the time of the resuscitation of the planet the Lord have designed to end the experiment by subplanting and enslaving the original inhabitants of Eden (Africa). The irony is that the Lord did not even have agents to invade Eden, until the people of Eden raised the Gentiles, Israelis, and Arabians. The people of Eden (Africa) raised these three groups and gave them the choice to be civil rather than savage, but they chose to be, and still are savage. These three groups eventually attacked Eden from every side. These very ones who had been saved by the people of Eden, now attempted to destroy their saviors, as their ancestors had crucified Nimrod and Jesus. These invaders, the Gentiles (Pale Romans, and Pale Greeks), the Pale Israelis, and Pale Arabs attackers of Eden (Africa), were and still are agents of the Lord, the Prince of Darkness.

None of these three groups or their lands existed, when the planet was whole. When the experiment is finished, Europe of the Gentiles, Israel of the Israelis, and Arabia of the Arabs will all disappear, along with all other continents, and nationalities, and the planet will be made whole again. Europe will disappear into the top of Eden (Africa), and Israel and Arabia will disappear into the east side of Eden (Africa). That will be the end of the World of the Lord. As it was in the beginning, so it shall be in the end. The wooly headed brown meek shall reinherit their planet. That is why the Lord had his agents to invade Eden (Africa) to stop the processes that are still in motion, to bring his World to an end. Then Assiah will be reamalgamated with Shemesh (The Sun), to bring the experiment to a satisfied conclusion. Without Eden there would be no keystone, to set all back to order. Eden had to be guarded at all cost. The wooly headed people of Western Eden took 800 years to prepare Cain's pale leper children now in Europe, for the finalizing of the experiment, in the western hemisphere, of the planet.

Notes

# Place
# Western Eden (Moors)

*Invaded Eden — Moors (Mowers/Shavers / מור) #4171, 77 — Amorites/America*

The Moors from Western Eden (Africa) went up into what is now called Europe. But Europe was not, until the Moors founded it for those who dwelled in the wilderness there (*Isa. 23:13*).

Moor (מור) is an old language word used by the later Pale Europeans, to describe the the Blacks of Western Eden, who "mowered," or "shaved" their beards. The Europeans were making the distinction, that they themselves did not shave, or groom their faces. *See Strong's Concordance #4171 - #4177 (all carry the root idea of "cutting down," or "shaving off." In northern Africa the Moors (shavers) were also called Barbers/Berbers.*

The Moors (Mowers) occupied northern and western Eden (Africa), but had descended from the Carthaginians, who descended from the Phoenician, who were the children of Canaan, the son of Ham. Thus the Moors of west Africa were descendants of Ham. The Moors called Eden (Africa) El Cabulan (אל כבולון) or "The Civil Place." Thus the Cabalah (Kabalah) book is a book, or manual on "Civilness." Africa (Eden / El Cabulan), is the Great Light (*Isa. 9:2*), the Civilizer of the Europeans. It took the Moors of Western Eden several hundred years to raise the Caucasians to a point, where they could establish countries for them (*Isa. 23:13*).

The reason that the Moors went to civilize the Caucasians again, for perhaps the fifth time, was to prepare them to go through the remainder of the experiment, to it's termination. The wooly headed brown Moors of West Eden (Africa), established Spain, Portugal, and France, and spread out from that base, up into the rest of what would be called Europe, to established the foundations for all of the countries that would be Europe. Other Moors had entered protoEurope from the eastern end, to develope countries westward. This included Russia, Finland, Germany, Holland, Norway, Denmark, Sweden, etc. The wooly headed Eutruscans had developed the Romans, and the Romans had murdered all of the true wooly headed Israelis in Palestine, except for a remnant, who escaped back into Egypt. A portion of that remnant left Egypt, and came to Europe with the Moors, and were assimilated by Caucasians in Spain. These Pale Ones took on the lifestyle, and identity of the wooly headed brown Israelis.

Western Europe became a staging area, for a final training of the Gentile (Caucasian) Race. These pale children of Cain had been brought into existence by the Lord (Lucifer), to subplant the original inhabitants of the entire planet. Yet they can not even self sustain, even into modern times. The whole of the reason the Caucasians were allowed to leave Europe was to allow the experiment to play it's self out, to an end termination. Transported away from Europe, and Isolated in the western hemisphere, away from the influences of Europe, these pale ones would have only their true nature to guide them, in all of their actions. The pale leper children of the Lord have always been in exodus away from him. They always escaped from him, to the place of the children of Adam. The crossing of the Atlantic was another exodus away from the Lord.

In **"Amori" (America)** the wooly headed brown children of Western Eden would play cut the role that the Lord told AbramHam that his children would play to the **Amorites** (*Gen. 15:13-16*).

The Caucasians were brought across the Atlantic for the final portion of an experiment that began in the sun. The wooly headed brown children of Adam have always given the pale leper children of Cain asylum, from the Lord. America would be the last place that the wooly headed brown children of Adam would build a society for the pale children, of the Lord's son Cain.

Observation

# Place
# Amorites/America

*Western Eden — Washington in Pattern of crucifixed Nimrod — Heaven*

Behold, North America was not until it was founded by Aboriginals, and people from Western Eden (Africa)(*Isa. 23:13*). The English Europeans first used the east coast of what would become North America, as 13 penal colonies. The thirteen colonies were thirteen prisons. Blacks who had built the 13 penal colonies, turned the thirteen penal colonies into thirteen civilized states. In that transition from colonies to states, there were seven presidents before George Washington. Those seven presided over the **ununited** states. The first two presidents were Black before, and when the states first became united States. The first Black president of the united States was named John Hanson. The second president of the states was Black also, and his name was Elias Boudinot. *See the Journals of the Continental Congress.*

Black skilled tradesmen allowed American Caucasians to join their gilds, and the Blacks taught them to become skilled trades journeymen. English Ships were removing these American skill tradesmen from American ships on the high seas, and carried them to England. England had not allowed any skilled trades to leave England, to come into America. The English reasoned that these Caucasian tradesmen had left England illegally, and came to America. The American journeymen would not admit that they had been trained in America by Black skilled tradesmen.

The taking of these American Caucasian skilled tradesmen from American ships by the British, was the true cause of the war of 1812 between the American states and England.

Benjamin Banniker and hundreds of Black skilled tradesmen had originally built Washington. before the English burned it. From Nimrod to Benjamin Banniker, wooly headed brown men had built of all of the capitals, and civil societies of the Caucasian Race.

After the British burned Washington down, hundreds of other Black skilled tradesmen rebuilt it. They rebuilt Washington, as Banniker had first built it. Banniker laid out Washington in the basic X form, of the cross that Nimrod had been crucified on, after he had saved the the ancestors of these Americans (*Isa. 53:10*).

Benjamin Banniker built Washington in the X shape, to demonstrate what the Caucasian society do to each group of Blacks who save them, from the time of Nimrod to Benjamin Banniker and beyond. The Caucasian Race murdered all of their wooly headed, brown saviors, using the statement that their saviors died that they might live. America took it's name from the Amorites (*Gen. 15:16*). Actually Amori was one of the sons of Canaan (*Gen. 10:16*). The Lord told Abram that "his seed (זרע)," would be afflicted by Amorites (Americans) in a land "not their own," and they shall serve them, and be afflicted by them, for four hundred years (*Gen. 15:4*). The Lord then told Abram that he would judge the Amorites (Americans), that they served, and the afflicted would come out with great substance (*Gen. 15:14*).

The people who served for four hundred years, are the wooly headed brown people of western Eden (Africa), enslaved in North America. The ones that were to be served were Americans. The **great substance** brought out is the knowledge that the corrupt nature of the Caucasian Race shall never change, under any circumstance. Trodden down, meted out, scattered, and peeled by their Lord, the Caucasians are a people terrible from their beginning (*Isa. 18:2*). North America is the end of an experiment that began in the inner heavens.

Notes

# Thing
# Heaven

America (Amori) — Eve (הוה) = Havah = Heaven — Seek first the kingdom — Sunday

America is the end of a process that began in the inner heaven. Scripture have Jesus saying that God's kingdom of Heaven is within (*Luke 17:21*). This would seem incredible until you find out what **Heaven** means, and what **God** means. Heaven (הון) means "Place of Life," and God (Elohim / אלוהים) means "Invisible One." Thus the "**Living Place**"(heaven) of the "**Invisible One**" (God) is within the body, of each original inhabitant of the planet. Thus it becomes reasonable that Gods (Invisible Ones), and Heaven (Life Place), can both be inside the body.

Before the Gods (Original Man) put on Coats of Skins (bodies)(*Gen. 3:21*), they existed in the invisible Electromagnetic Field. The Invisible Electric Field was the first **Living Place** or **Heaven**. It is the place of Eternal Life, with no beginning or end (*Luke 17:21*). Heaven and the sun seem to be on the outside, but in actuality all including the outer heaven is being projected from inside of original men (*Luke 17:21, Matt. 7:21*). Scripture say that whatever is in heaven (שמים) (outside/above), is also in the earth (inside/below)(*Matt.16:19, 18:18*). Thus the earth (physical) is an illusion, that is actually being projected from the heaven (space) within. Jesus say seek first the kingdom of heaven within, and all else shall be added unto you (*Luke 17:21; Matt. 6:33*). Phonetically "Heaven (הון)" and Eve (הוה) are synonymous, for Eve means "Life," and Heaven means "Living Place." This becomes intriguing when we realize that heaven is within the Original Man (Adam), as Eve was within Adam. Thus perhaps the separation of Eve out of Adam was the projecting of the heaven within, out into the physically manifested realm.

Jesus speak of the children of the inner kingdom having been cast out to the Outer Darkness of the outer heaven and earth (*Matt. 8:12*). The Outer Darkness is the World of the Lord (*Amos 5:18, 20*). Jesus speak of the outer heavens and earth passing away (*Matt. 24:35; Mark 13:31*). This imply that the outer heaven and earth are temporary with a beginning and a ending, while the inner is Eternal .

Seeking the Eternal inner heaven is seeking the Eternal Life of the inner kingdom. This sets one in a place to go through the process of making ones' self whole and perfect, as the father in the inner heaven again (*Matt. 5:48*).

Yeshua told the Israelis that the scribes and Pharisees had cast them out, of their inner kingdoms. Then he called the scribes and Pharisees (Rabbis) hypocrites, accusing them of having shut up the inner kingdoms of heaven, for all, including even their own selves (*Matt. 23:13*)! Caught in the Outer Darkness of the Lord, the Israelis were full of Darkness. The Lord instructed the Scribes and Pharisees (Rabbis) to keep the congregations hearts fat, their ears heavy, and their eyes shut; lest they see, hear, and understand. Then they could convert and heal themselves, from him, and reenter their inner heavens (*Isa. 6:9, 10*).

Jesus taught that to reenter, Israel must be like the little children they were, before they were cast out of their kingdoms of heaven, by the Rabbis (*Matt. 18:3*). Jesus told them in effect they had to be born again inward (*John 3:3*). That they must raise the Christ substance to it's throne (*Acts 2:30*). In the process the Single Eye opens, to fill the entire bodies with Light (*Matt. 6:22*). The glow around Jesus's head demonstrates the complete act of being in the inner heaven. Those who reenter, from the Darkness of the World of the Lord, shine like the sun ( *Matt. 5:16, 45, 48*).

Observation

# Thing
# Sunday

*Heaven — Only One Day — Law*

"Sun" "day" (Yom Shemesh / יום שמש) is the "day" of the "sun," and the sun rules in it (*Psalms 136:8*). All that has ever occurred has occurred in the one great day of the sun. The day of the sun is it's very existence. Shemesh (the sun) is the most perfect representation of Original Selves in physical manifestation. The sun in it's nakedness (invisible state) is an electromagnetic entity, that pours life from the Electromagnetic Field out into the physical illusion. The garment that the sun wears in the physical is the Ultraviolet purpleness of Black Light. This is even though the sun appear to be yellow from inside the atmosphere of Assiah the mother planet. The mother planet which is Assiah (Fireness / אישה) was separated from the sun, to continue the experiment, down into the particular (Physical) state. The Sun (Shemesh/שמש) is the father of us the Ca-Shemeshu (כשמשו)(666) or "those who are like the Sun" (*Rev. 13:17, 18*). The sun is the father (Ab / אב) simply because we brought ourselves out of it. Yet we are the source of the very sun that we manifested from. We designated the sun as the Most High / עליון.

It is all one day, because the sun does not rise or set. It is only the planet turning that makes it appear that there are days. Originating from the sun we are all Sols (Souls) or Solar Beings. Original Men (איש) are Invisible (אלוהים), and are firey beings inside of the physical form. We designated the sun as the Most High / עליון.

The sun and it's day radiates to maintain a life energy environment for those on the planet. The sun is also a reference place for the planet to orbit to generate seasons within it's cycles. Proverbs speak of there being seasons (Four in total), for all things (*Proverbs 3:1-8*).

Also as man descend deeper into the Darkness of the particular state the sun is mental and physical Light to see by.

The entire solar realm was intact before it was ever made manifest. All of the designs that exist in the manifested universe, are described in the patterns in the woolliness of the hair of the original inhabitants of the planet. Their hair and brown/Black complexions are totally conducive, to the solar state that they would be operating in. Nothing had to be changed, no evolution, no creation, no need for civilizing. The physical was brought into existence as a laboratory by Gods (Invisible Ones), to investigate the very nature of themselves, as individual particle Beings.

The sum total of the purpose for the Day of the Sun (Sunday) is to experiment to understand Self in the particular. All that has ever taken place has taken place, in the one great Day the day of the sun. As there was the beginning of the experiment, in the sun, there must be an ending of the experiment, in the sun.

As much as the word day implies light, it also imply darkness, for day (Dia / diameter) describes a circle being divided in two. The apparent day (circle) is divided into twelve of light and twelve of darkness. As such if one has the light of self they can still accomplish all even in Darkness.

When all have been satisfied in the experiment, all that left the sun shall return, and Sunday shall come to an end, that is the Law.

Notes

# Thing
# Law

*Sunday — Law (תרה) #8451 Outlaws and Inlaws — Iota/Alpha/Omega — Dot (דוח) = death — Light (Mental and Physical)*

All law (Torah) concerning the physical began in the day of the sun. Law pertains to all that exists in the particular realm. All that exists in the physical is held together by laws. A law or set of laws is a peaceable code of conduct. This is peaceable conduct between solar systems, between planets and their suns, between planets and their moons, between people on a planet, and between the very atomic components that hold together all substances of the physical illusion. Without this peaceable conduct (Law), all would fall apart and bring the experiment to an unsatisfied end. Law must prevails at every level. This is universal law.

It is universal Law that Jesus spoke about, not the Lord's commandments handed down through Moses. The Law that Jesus was speaking of (*Matt. 5:17, 18*), supersedes the Lord's commandments to Noah, Abraham, and Moses etc.

In actuality the term LAW (Ιαω) are the three Greek alphabets: Iota, Alpha, and Omega. These three letters generate a **circle (Alpha/Omega)**, with a **dot (Iota)** in the center of it. This symbolizes the continuous nature of the make up of the universe, which has no beginning or ending. This is also the Eternal nature of Self.

Any violation or breaking of this pattern is an outlaw act. The Lord and his Host broke the Law, and became Outlaws. It was the Lord and his Host as outlaws that caused the solar war (*Rev. 12:7*). All of the Lord's "Great Wonders" (נפלא) are "crimes"(נפלא), which are the breaking of the law. When the Lord boast that he had performed, Wonders (נפלא) in Egypt, he was admitting that he had done Felonies (נפלא) or violations of the Law. *See Strong's Concordance #5307-5309).* The whole purpose of Nimrod, Jesus and all of the others before and after them, was to fulfill, or repair the breaks, that the Lord made in the Law. As the Day of the sun is for experiment, the Law is a description of conduct to fulfill that experiment. This symbolizes the complete nature that make up the physical universe. The Law encompasses all that have been made manifest. This nature of the Law is the exact same as the nature of Self.

Adverse to the Universal Law of Self is the Outlaw nature of the Lord of Abraham. Where as the law of the universe unites, the lawlessness of the Lord breaks apart the same that would be united.

The law is broken when God/Man can no longer see to make legitimate choices. The Lord's whole purpose is to take away the Law, so that the Gentiles, Israelis and all others under his influence will do exactly what he commands, without weighing the harm they might be doing to others.

Those under the influence of the Lord are absent from themselves, in the Outer Darkness with the Lord (*II Cor. 5:6; Matt. 8:12; Amos 5:18, 20*). The true fulfillment of the Law is when original man is back inside, at the center of their being. In that place all are Self again. In that place the Law is no longer broken as Jesus say, for man is his true self again, which is God (*Psalms 82:6; John 10:34, 35*). The law is active when original man (God), occupies his inner kingdom again (*Luke 17:21*). Then man's Single Eye is active, and his body shall be full of Light (*Matt. 6:22, 23*).

Observations

# Thing
# Light

*Law — Single Eye full of Light — Choice*

Fulfillment of the Law (*Matt. 5:17*), is to be cast from the Outer Darkness of the Lord (*Matt. 8:12*), back into the True Light, at the center of the Self. Light is the illuminated state, that allow one to see hears, and understand. The Light of the body is the open Single Eye: if therefore the Single Eye be opened, then the entire body shall be full of Light (*Matt. 6:22*). But if your Single Eye be shut (Evil), then your whole body shall be full of Darkness. It is a Great Darkness (*Matt. 6:23*). Light was inside all of the original inhabitants of the planet. Light (אור) is necessary to accomplish the experiment in the physical realm.

All of the original inhabitants of the planet were full of Light. Among these Illuminated Ones, there were two Great Lights. Michael/Melchezedek, and Hallel (The Lord) are the two Great Lights (*Gen. 1:16*). Melchezedek is the Greater, and rule the Day and Light (*Gen. 1:16*). The Lord is the Lesser Light, the Prince of Darkness, The Lord rule the Night, and Darkness (*Gen. 1:16*). The Lord's Day is Darkness (*Amos 5:18, 20*).

Nimrod had attempted to bring a Great Light to the pale leper children of Cain who walked in the Darkness of the Lord (*Isa. 9:2*). But it pleased the Lord the Prince of Darkness to bruise him, for attempting to bring Light to those he held in bondage in his Darkness (*Isa 53:10*)!

Jesus (Yeshua) attempted to bring Light to the Lost Sheep of Israel, and was crucified like Nimrod had been crucified.

The Moor of North Africa brought the same Great light from Africa (Eden), to the pale leper European descendants of those that Nimrod had brought Light to, in the ancient times. Many of the wooly headed Moors suffered the same fate as wooly headed Nimrod and Jesus (Yeshua).

Jesus (Yeshua) said that Light is associated with the Single Eye (open). He said that if your Eye be single that your whole body shall be full of Light (*Matt. 6:22*). But then Jesus said that if your Eye be evil (closed), that your whole body shall be full of Darkness. Therefore if the light in you is Darkness, how great is that Darkness (*Matt. 6:23*). It is the Outer Darkness of the Lord, who rules Night and Darkness, not Day and Light (*Gen. 1:16*).

Light is inside, and is evidence that one is still within their inner kingdoms. The whole of the purpose of the Lord was to kill the inner Light, by casting those who serve him out of their inner kingdoms, to his Outer Darkness (*Matt. 8:12*), as he the Lord Lucifer as the Prince of Darkness (*Amos 5:18, 20*), had been cast out (*Rev. 12:9*), and fell (*Isa. 14:12*).

The Lord had the Rabbis (Scribes, and Pharisees) to cast the Israelis out, by shutting the Israeli's eyes, ears, and minds, and having cast them out to his Darkness, to shut up their inner heavens of Light (*Isa, 6:9; Matt. 23:13*), so that they could not ever convert, be healed and reenter (*Isa. 6:10*).

But Jesus was sent to make the Lost Sheep of Israel free from bondage to the Darkness of the Lord (*Matt. 10:6*). Jesus attempted to cause them to be converted, and healed, and for their eyes, ears, and minds to be opened again (*Matt. 13:15*). You can not serve two Masters, for either you will hate the one (Light), and love the other (Darkness); or else you will hold to the one (Light), and you will despise the other (Darkness). Jesus said you can not serve God inside, and Man (Lord) outside (*II Cor. 5:6*). esus came to give the Israelis a **choice**.

Notes

# Thing
# Choice

*Light — True Choice — Creation/Evolution (Opposite Sides Same Coin) — Meekness*

Without Light there is no true choice. True choice is the ability to choose between two distinctly different things. The Judeo/Gentile masses have only been given the "choice," between two sides of the same thing. They have been given the seeming choice between creation and evolution. But creation and evolution are only the opposite sides, of the same counterfeit coin. The one side of the coin is religious faith, and the other side is scientific theory. Both **creation** and **evolution** speak to the physical state, coming into existence from nothing. It is not a choice between one or the other, but is seeing the same thing from two distorted directions. The fact is that the entire physical realm is a manifested or dissatisfied state of atoms that are normally invisible.

Understanding that **Manifestation** is the source of physical existence, is the beginning of the ability for true choice. True choice is to see pass what someone else offer you as "choices." Neither of the two concepts of **creation** and **evolution** existed before the seventh century A. D., when the Moors went north from Africa up into what would be Europe. The Moors went to lay the foundation for the civilizing of the wild tribes of Caucasians there. Those among the Caucasians who had the ability to be taught were taught, and became the clerical (clerks) community, and the clerical community became the foundation for first the religious community, and then later for the scientific community in Europe.

Early European clerics (clerks) called **priest** invented the **creation theory**, to correspond to their crafting of the Bible/Torah, while later clerics called **scientists** became the source for Darwin, who invented the **evolution theory**. Clerics for creation, and clerics for evolution. Not two choices, but one choice divided in such a way as to trick, all European minds into "choosing" either creation or evolution.

On choice, scripture have Jesus (Yeshua) saying that no man can serve two masters: for either he will hate the one and love the other; or else he will hold to the one and despise the other. You can not serve God and mammon (*Matt. 6:24*). The Lord is mammon (Man)(*Ex. 15:3*).

All of the masses of Judaism, and Christianity think that the Lord (Yeweh/Jehovah/Hashem) is God. Plus they do not know that in childhood they were cast out of their inner kingdoms, out into the Outer Darkness of the World of the Lord (*Matt. 8:12*). They also do not know that the Lord used his Darkness to close their eyes, ears, and minds (*Deut. 29:4*). The Lord then instructed the Rabbis (Scribes and Pharisees), Priest, and ministers to keep the congregations deaf, dumb, blind, and mentally cripple, less they convert, and "chose" to be healed from the Lord's Darkness (*Isa. 6:9, 10; Amos 5:18, 20*).

Throughout the ages Nimrod, Jesus (Yeshua), and thousands of other wooly headed brown men have attempted to bring choice to the the pale leper masses that the Lord and his agents have kept in the Darkness. Even into the modern times the masses do not to have a true choice. To have true choice is to have complete information, and also have open eyes, open ears, and an open mind/ heart (*Matt. 13:15*).

Nimrod, Jesus (Yeshua), and thousands of other wooly headed, brown men are the meek who attempted to give back a choice, to everyone.

Observations

# Thing
# Meekness

*Choice — Survival of the fittest — Ability to Withstand All — Planetary Reinheritors — Life*

Meekness is an inate choice. Meek (ענוה) *Anvah* does not mean weak or submissive, as it is defined but means something altogether different. The word Meek is directly associated with the word "Answer" (ענה), and the word "Afflicted (ענה)." In the Strong's Concordance Meekness is #6037-6043, and the word for "Answer" is #6030-6034, and the word for "Afflicted," is #6031.

It is all the same between the three words. Thus to be **meek** is not to be weak, but is to have the ability to withstand being **afflicted**, and to still come up with an **answer**, or solution to what ever the situation is, that is at hand. To be meek is to be softer than soft when necessary, and to be harder than hard when necessary. It is the ability to change from ice, to water, to steam, to gas, to solve for whatever is necessary at the moment.

The Bible/Torah have Jesus saying that the meek (afflicted) shall reinherit the earth (*Psalms 37:11; Matt. 5:5*). It seems that in the ancient times, that most of the original inhabitants of the planet fled away from being meek (afflicted).

A verse is translated to say that the Egyptians afflicted (ענה) the Israelis (*Ex. 1:12*), and another verse is translated to say that the Lord afflicted (ענה) the Israelis (*II Kings 17:20*). But the Egyptians never afflicted the Israelis (*John 8:33*), but were an **answer** (solution / ענה) for the Israelis. The Lord was never an **answer** (ענה) for Israel, but brought them out of Egypt with a mighty hand and "**afflicted** (ענה)" Israel, by letting the Israelis and their children die in the wilderness, after wandering around for forty years!

The Israelis were never the children of Abraham, but they afflicted the children of Abraham out of existence. The Lord's Roman agents, would afflict (ענה) the Israelis out of existence.

The meek are afflicted, but the afflicted may not be meek, for the truly meek survive having been afflicted. The Egyptians were meek, because they recovered from the Lord afflicting them. But the Israelis were not meek, for they were exterminated when the Lord's Roman agents finally afflicted them out of existence, seventy years after the death of Jesus. Only the Israelis who did not leave Egypt in the exodus survived. These Israelis went out of Egypt, with Egyptians escaping affliction, to western Eden, and became known as Moors.

Eventually even most of the afflicted Egyptians who remained in Egypt were destroyed by the combined might of the pale leper Greeks and Romans children, of the Lord's son Cain. Yet no one had experienced being afflicted for four hundred years (*Gen. 15:13*), and survived to be designated as "**the meek who would reinherit the earth.**"

The meek would not be apparent until the wooly headed brown people of western Eden were carried into enslavement in North America, and survived four hundred years of the most brutal affliction ever experienced on this planet (*Gen. 15:13*). They are still being afflicted, for the iniquity of the Amori/American is not yet fulfilled (*Gen. 15:16*). The Great Substance that the Blacks obtain (*Gen. 15:14*), is the knowledge that the pale are not redeemable from their negative nature. The truly meek do not try to find (preserve) their lives in the physical realm, for physical life is only an illusion anyway (*Matt. 7:14*). But the meek seek first the narrow gate, that leads back to the kingdom inside of their being, where Life is Eternal (*Matt. 7:14*).

Notes

# Thing
# Life

*Meekness-Hi (חי) = "Life" (#2416, 18), Him (הים) = "Invisible Living Ones," Host (חות) - Dream*

The Meek are of the Eternal Life in Eden (Africa), beyond the Strait and Narrow Gate of Egypt (*Matt. 7:13, 14*). They do not find life, in the physical realm (*Matt. 19:39*). By definition Life (חי) pronounced "Hi (חהים, חי, חות) is Existence or Being, in all of it's states, whether it be inside physical forms or not. Scripture say that ....the breath of "life" was breathed into the nostrils of the man (the form), and the form became alive (*Gen. 2:7*). Life is the breath, that was breathed into the form. The form has no life of it's own. Life reduced to it's element, is an invisible entity sufficient to self. Life as that invisible entity is electric male, and magnetic female, combined. This is a description of Gods, who are invisible Male/Female beings (*Gen. 1:27*).

The first garment that Life put on was not a physical form, but was a garment made of invisible Light. It was the first garment that Adam (Atom) wore. In that light body original Man has a Single Eye, a Single Ear, and a Heart/Mind that Understands all (*Matt. 6:22*). In his naked (invisible) body, Original Man is All Seeing, All Hearing, and All Knowing.

God (Elohim / אלוהים) is the invisible state of Man, and Man is the manifest state of God. These are the two states of Life: Adam (Atom), can be unmanifested (invisible) wave, or manifest particle. Beyond the physical particle state, life is without beginning or ending. This is Heim (חים), or non physical Life. This life state is the source of the physical, and Heim (Invisible Life) existed, before there was ever the physical illusion.

The physical as an illusion, is a dream state. All of the Gods including Adam were originally awake in the dream state. All of the Gods including Adam were male/female, until he was put to sleep, and split (Altered/created) into separated male and female (*Gen. 1:27; 2:22, 23*). Adam was never reawakened afterwards, and is therefore asleep in the physical or dream realm.

Life has infinite steps, from existence in the invisible Electromagnetic Field, down to existence in the lowest form, which is the Human or Caucasian Race. It was from the nonphysical Life (**Heim**)(חים)(Male/Female combined) state, that original Man put on flesh bodies or Coats of Skins (*Gen. 3:21*). Life in this first physical state was also **Heim** (Male/Female combined), or HermsAphrodite. The first physical separations of male life, from female life, was the Lord, and his Host (Hoth (חות). **Host** or **Hoth** means "Lives," in the sense of a male/female being who can shift to being a male, or a female, then shifting back to male/female.

Then Adam was put to sleep in this dream (*Gen. 2:21*), and was split, into separate life forms that were not Heim (חים), or Hoth (חות), but were a third form of life for the male called **Hi** (הי), and a fourth form of Life, for the female, called **Havah** (הוה / Eve). It was a permanent unshiftable separation.

Cain was born from the beguilement of the female Lifeforce Eve (הוה) who was far removed from **Heim**, the Eternal Life state. But even worst Cain was then mutated into a pale leper, and lost his soul or solar association. Cain and his pale children were then isolated in Nod to fall into an even lower form of Life, a by-product of Adam's sleep called **Necro** (Negro / Νεκρω), or mental death. The entire Caucasian Race are Negroes (Necro / Νεκρω), which means "mental death." Mental death or sleep is the lowest state, of life in the physical Dream realm.

Observation

# Thing
# Dream

*Life — Adam — Nod — Noah — Abram — Jacob — Love*

Dream is the sum total of physical Life existence. The original inhabitants of the planet are the source of the dream (physical) state. The term "Dream (חלם)" is pronounced Halam in the Old Language. Halam the word for "dream" describes the nature of the dream substance, which is the microscopic makeup of physical. "Halam (dream substance) describes "Spiraling," Swirling," Rotating," energy, that accumulates into apparent "firmness." This describes atoms rotating on axises, and merging together into "particles," to form all forms, that make up all substances, of physical existence. Thus the physical realm is dream substance. *See Strong's Concordance #2492* (חלם) — *#2495* חלמות *Plural), and #2342* (חול) — *2344* חולים *plural)*. As hard (solid) as any physical substance appear to be, it is only swirls or spirals, of rotating energy. As dream substance, the entire physical realm is only an illusion.

The purpose for the dream, is to allow for the playing out to a full understanding of Self, in the particular realm. Particular understanding, can only be obtained in the particular (dream) state.

Once there was only one group of entities operating inside the dream. They were all awake in the dream, at the center of their beings. But there are now two elements, operating inside the physical or dream state: There are the few who are still awake, and the masses, who have since fallen asleep, in the dream (physical).

The highest form of existence in the dream (physical) state is to be mentally awake in it. To be awake in the dream realm, is to have activated the invisible inner body. Then the Single Eye (Peniel / פניאל) will be open, and the entire body will be full of the Inner Light, which illuminate all who are at the center of their being (*Matt. 6:22*). Those who are mentally awake in the dream (physical), have the ability to manipulate the substance here, to accomplish any purpose that becomes necessary.

Those who are asleep can not accomplish anything, and the very reason that the illusion of the physical dream was brought into being, can not be fulfilled.

In those who are asleep the inner body is not activated, there is no Inner Light, the Single Eye is closed (Evil), and the sleeping one is in a Great Darkness (*Matt. 6:22*). The Great Darkness, is the Day of the Lord (*Amos 5:18, 20*). All of the servants of the Lord are in the Lord's Darkness, asleep in the dream.

Noah was not physically asleep, but was mentally asleep, by his actions in his tent, with his grandson Canaan (*Gen. 9:21*). Mental sleep is a requirement for all who serve the Lord. Noah helped the Lord, to save his World by being mentally asleep. Abraham also became a savior to the Human, Caucasian, or Gentile World when he decided to serve the Lord, who caused him to fall into the deep sleep, of the Lord's Great Darkness (*Gen. 15:12*). Isaac and Jacob (Subplanter), along with all of the other sons of the Lord also fell asleep in his service. All who serve the Lord, Jew and Gentile alike, have their eyes, ears, and heart/minds shut by the commandments of the Lord (*Isa. 6:10*). Thus by design the Lord has put those to sleep, who would have been awake in this dream. By the acts commanded by the Lord, of those who serve him, they have no love of Self. Love (Understand) of Self is the prime operative for all of the original inhabitant of the planet, who manifested the dream (physical) into being.

# Thing
# Love

*Dream —"Attracted (לו)" — "Lust After (אהב)" — "Understand (בינה)" — Exodus*

True Love (Binah / בינה) is Understanding, but there is little or no true Love (understanding), among those who are asleep in the physical dream. Love (Understanding) is Universal Law, and is the whole reason for the existence of the physical universe.

Phonetically "Love" (לב) means to be "Attracted." In the English translation of the Bible/Torah the word "Love" is translated from the word **Ahav** (אהב), which means **"To Lust after."** Yet a third more appropriate word for "love" is **Binah** (בינה), which in translation means "To **Distinguish Between**," one thing and another, which **"Builds up"** to **"Understanding."**

Further the word Love has been made to mean "to be affectionate," while there does not have to be any affection in understanding (Love).

To **love** (לב) one's Self phonetically is to be focused (attracted) to "understand" ones Self. Surely when Jesus said to "love" (be attracted to) the Lord he did not mean be "attracted" to the Lord to "lust"(Ahav/אהב) after him. Jesus (Yeshua) meant to "be attracted to" the Lord to "understand" (Binah/בנה) what the Lord truly represents, then one can tell the Lord, like Jesus did "get thee hence Satan (*Matt. 4:10*)." The Lord is Satan who represents Outer Darkness (*Matt. 8:12*), not Inner Light! The Light serves the purpose of allowing one to see (mental/physical). Thus they can Love (understand) Self, and fulfill the whole purpose of the physical experiment.

Man in his original being was never created. Man in truth is an invisible being who manifested, bringing the entire physical state into being, in the same instance.

Love (Understanding) require Light, to see by. The lack of Light (Mental/Physical), is the Darkness that cancels Understanding. Lack of Light (Darkness), is the source of all Creating. The Darkness of Creating is actually a negative mental process, that manifests over into the physical.

Creation is the **Sin** (Hate / חטא), that the Lord the Man brought into his own World on his planet, to cancel out Understanding (Love)(*Romans 5:12; Ex. 15:3*). *See pages 240, 241 "Creation."*

Love (understanding) implies wisdom, and knowledge. With wisdom and knowledge properly applied, Understanding (love) comes. Understanding (Love) stops the creative process. As understanding (Love) comes, less and less creative force is manifested into the physical realm. As such Darkness began to vanishing. Satisfaction (understanding) ends the creation process. As creating stops solutions come, and all is simple, thus no more mysteries, for everyone will see everything for what it is. There will be no more exploiting, or victimizing. Lying cease for men will be themselves again, and that trait (Lying), will be a useless activity.

To Love the Self is to understand Self. To Love ones brother is to understand ones brother. To Love the Lord is to understand the Lord. To Love ones enemy is to understand ones enemy. Finally to Love God (Self) is to understand God, which is full circle back to the beginning of the experiment.

Understanding (Love) comes with knowing. Perfect Love is perfect understanding. With perfect understanding comes satisfaction. In this experiment, satisfaction is the end of the experiment. Everyone who truly Love (Understand) the Darkness of the Lord make an Exodus from it!

# Thing
# Exodus

*Love — Voting with the feet — Exoduses: Ham, Chaldeans (Caucasians/Gentile) — Lord's Exodus with Abram — Israeli from Canaan to Egypt — Yeshua's families Exodus — Peace*

Anyone who Love (Understand) the Lord, flee from him. People tend to vote with their feet. Exodus (שמות) means "To Relocate," as in relocating away from an undesirable location. None of the people impose upon by the Lord in the north of Nod, ever willingly chose to stay with the Lord. Ham and his entire family exodused (relocated) from Nod/Ararat to be away from the Lord, and his corrupt influences. The Pale Leper children of Cain were "located" in Nod, with the Lord, and were imposed on by him without a choice. These Mutant children of Cain could not leave the presence of the Lord, in the shadows of Nod (*Isa. 18:1; 9:2*). They could not survive coming out into the sun. Nimrod the Great Light grafted them back out into the sunlight (*Isa. 9:2*). The Lord confounded the Ur/Babel Metropolis that Nimrod built for them. It was then that the pale ones made exodus away from the Lord, and were given asylum in Sodom and Gomorrah, in the Garden land of Canaan. Next Terah the father of Abram began an exodus, away from the Lord in Nod. Terah was trying to escape from the Lord's plagues, and famine, that had killed his son Haran (*Gen. 11:28*). But in his exodus away from the Lord, Terah died in the city of his son Haran (*Gen. 11:32*). The Lord caught up with them in the city of Haran, and forced Abram to continue the exodus, but now bringing the Lord with him, down into the Land of Canaan (*Gen. 12:1*). The Lord was exodusing away from his own famished condition in Nod! Now the Lord was safe like everyone else who had exodused away from the him in Nod. The Lord's Darkness and famine that had been in Nod was now exodused (relocated) to the land of Canaan. The Israelis even had to make an exodus, away from the Lord and his famine, from the land of Canaan. Israel exodused down into the land of Egypt to save themselves from the Lord.(*Deut. 26:5,* ).

The so-called exodus of the Israelis from Egypt was actually the Lord removing Israel from Egypt by brute force, for the Israelis did not want to leave to go with him! Even though the Lord had destroyed Egypt, none of the Israelis wanted to leave, and the Egyptians had to drive them out, to save Egypt from the Lord (*Ex. 6:1*), while the Lord pulled them out with a mighty hand, at the same time! Many Israelis hid in Egypt, and never left in the Exodus. In the wilderness, many Israelis wanted to exodus back to Egypt even though it had been destroyed (*Numbers 11:5*).

Many of Cain's Caucasian children who escaped from being murdered by the Lord in Sodom and Gomorrah, went westward in another exodus away from the Lord. The Archaic Greek a wooly headed brown aboriginal people saved the pale ones, by allowing them to live in their cities. The Aboriginal Italians the Etruscans a wooly headed brown people, also save them as they continue to move westward in a perpetual exodus from the Lord, the Prince of Darkness.

The Lord was always a step behind the pale ones, but he eventually caught up with them in what would become Europe. The Lord imposed his Darkness on them in a Great Dark Age that enveloped all of Europe, as he had imposed Darkness on their ancestors, in the land of Nod. The wooly headed Moors from North Africa spent eight hundred years in Europe, preparing the Caucasians to escape from the Lord on one last exodus across the Atlantic ocean. America would be the final exodus to **peace** for the pale ones, away from the Lord, and his Dark Ages, in Europe!

The Peace living children of Ham continued to be saviors to the Caucasian Race.

Notes

# Thing
# Peace

*Exodus — Peaceful Nature, Peaceful Life (I Chron. 4:40) — Islam*

A true exodus is a migration from confusion to peace. Peace (שלום) is defined as "Perfect," "Balanced," "Complete," "Sufficient," "Secure," "Righteousness," etc. These descriptions, describe the people, and the land of Ham which was peaceful (*I Chron. 4:40*). That is why all of the servants of the Lord including Israel, fled from him, and came to the land of Ham, where there was peace. No one ever left the land of the children of Ham, to go to the Lord!

The land of Ham and his children was from Egypt, eastward to the Tigris River. The eyes of the Lord of the North, cared for the land of Ham (*Deut. 11:11, 12*). It was Abram, who brought the Lord a Man of War (*Ex. 15:3*), across the Tigris River, down into the peace of the land of Ham.

The entire theme of peace in the Bible/Torah is centered around Ham, his children, and their peaceable way of life. There was no need for war, killing, stealing, or any of the other activities, that the Israelis did to the children of Ham, when the Lord brought them out of Egypt, back to the land of Canaan (*I Chron. 4:40*).

The entire land of Ham and his children, had been a land of milk and honey, from of old, until the Lord brought the first famine to the land of Canaan (*Gen.12:10*). The Lord causing famine in the land of Canaan gave him the excuse, to take Abram and Sarai from there, down to the land of Ham's second born son Mitzraim (Egypt)(*Psalms 78:51*), to disturb the peace there.

But long before the Lord had come to disturb the peace, Ham, had sent his children to give peace to those who were under the corrupt influence of the Lord: **Nimrod** and thousands went north, into the land of Nod to take a Great Light (*Isa. 9:2, Matt. 4:16*), to give peace to the Gentiles, or Pale Leper children, of Cain. Next the children of Ham in Egypt sent **Yeshua (Jesus)** back to Israel as a Prince of Egypt, a Prince of Peace, to the the Lost Sheep (wool headed) of Israel, to teach them the peace that would give them freedom from the Lord (*Isa. 9:7*). Finally **Muhammad** was given Peace, from the children of Ham, to teach to the Arabians.

Yebus the son of Canaan and his children, had the privilege of building Jerusalem a "City of Peace (*II Sam. 5:6; Judge 19:10*)," for themselves and Michael/Melchezedek the King of Peace (*Heb. 7:2, 3*). Jesus entered the City of Peace (Jerusalem), as a Egyptian Prince of Peace (*Isa. 9:6*), after the **Order of Melchezedek** (*Heb. 5:6*), the King of Peace (*Heb. 7:2*), not after the **Chaos of the Lord** a Man of war (*Ex. 15:3*).

The three groups, the Caucasians, Israelis, and Arabs, came to make war, against those who had given them peace. They warred against and defeated Ham's children. Then they made Jerusalem a shrine, for the three religions that they had invented, out of the peace that had been taught to them. First came wooly headed Black David and the other Israelis in ancient times to conquer (*II Sam. 5:6*). Then came the wooly headed Black Arabs, to conquer Jerusalem, and then in Medieval times the pale lepers from Europeans came to defeat the Arabs, and mix with them to make them pale. All three have come to co-exist in Jerusalem, and have collaborated to enslave the peaceful children of Eden (Africa).

The peace (שלום) that the Caucasians, Israelis and Arabs were given is called Islam (אשלום). The word Islam in Arabic translates to the word Peace (Salem) in English.

Observations

# Thing
# Islam

*Islam — Jerusalem (City of Peace) — (Nimrod, Jesus, Muhammad) — Mutainy*

The western world has gone to great length, and have successfully convinced the people of the planet, that Islam is a religion, and that it was began in Arabia, by a man named Muhammad. Those who are devout to the Muhammad faith will admit that the Muhammadan Faith began within the lifetime of Muhammad. But when they are asked when Islam began, the Muhammadans will say that Islam has no birthday, but has existed forever. Thus the Muhammadan Faith practice by a billion people, is not Islam at all! Islam has existed forever, even before Muhammad was ever born, and it did not have Korans, Mosques, Shrines, Imams etc. None of these existed in the teachings of Muhammad! What would be the purpose of any of it, if Islam had existed without Korans, Mosques, and Imams forever before? What does Islam mean in the etymology of the Arabic language? **Islam** in Arabic literally means "**I Peace**." "Peace" is pronounced "Islam," also in the languages of the English, and Israelis: In English it is "**I Salem** (I Peace)," and in Israeli it is "**Ishalom** (אשלום)." Islam (Peace) is not a religion, but was the comprehensive way of life in Africa, and around the planet, before there was an Arabian subcontinent! Peace (Islam) and life is not lived in Korans, Bibles, Talmuds, Torahs, or in Temples, by Imams, Priest, Rabbis, Ministers, or in Shrines, Masjids, or Mosques.

The wooly headed Moors who went up into Europe did not go there to convert the pale ones there, to or from any religion. There was no religion in Europe, nor did the Moors bring religion there, for Islam (Peace) is not a religion. The Moors stayed in Europe for eight hundred years, teaching civilness to the uncivil pale people in Europe. It would stand to reason that if Islam (Peace) is a religion, then the Moors would have enveloped all of Europe with religion under the name of Islam. It was the Gentiles of Europe who took the teachings that the Moors gave them and invented, what is now called the Christian Church. The remnant of the last wooly headed brown Israelis (Judeans) from Egypt, and Palestine, came from north Africa (Eden) up into Europe along with the Moors. The Moors had gone to shine light into the World of Darkness, that the Lord imposed on the pale leper children of Cain. Some Gentiles in Europe who did not make themselves churches, but took on the lifestyle of the wooly headed brown Judeans, or Israelis. These Gentiles did not call themselves Judeans but called themselves Jews. They mixed with, and assimilated the original wooly brown Israelis. The original Wooly headed brown Arabians (Mohammedans) also came into Europe with the Moors, and were also assimilated by mixing with the pale Europeans. They did not have a Koran, because it did not exist yet!

The Caucasians, and now pale Mohammedans, and pale Jewish cooperated to enslave the very Africans (Edenites) who had civilized them. All three were directly involved, and profited from the enslavement of the very ones who gave them peace (Islam) as a civilizer.

The pale Jewish, the Christians, and Mohammedans all descended on Jerusalem the City of Islam (Peace) to turn it into a shrine for their invented religions, and pretended that they had a claim to the city. But Jerusalem had been built by, and was the city of the wooly headed Peaceable children of Ham. Ham's children gave the Arabs, Christians, and Jewish peace (Islam), but they have practiced nothing but war, on a planet that was once peace (Islam).

These three **mutant** pale leper groups committed **mutiny**, against their wooly brown saviors.

Notes

# World Element Mutiny

*Islam — Cain Mutainy (Mutation) — Apostasy — World*

This planet Assiah was always in Peace (Islam), until some inhabitants of Assiah mutinied (מות). To mutiny is to mutate, or overwhelm order, and curve away to abnormality. The root of the word mutiny/mutate is the old language word Mute (מות), which means "To be dead." Death in this sense is to cease to be normal, by curving away, mentally, physically, or genetically.

The first mutants or mutineer were those who took planets out of Assiah, and went out to set up orbits around the sun, other then the orbit of the mother planet Assiah.

Hallel who would become the Lord of Abram, was one of the mutants. Mutants (Mutineers) can not sustain themselves, so they must take substance from others. It was the Lord in mutiny, and taking from others, that caused the solar war, that he was defeated in (*Rev. 12:7-9; Isa. 14:12*).

The Lord is that Old Fallen Serpent (*Rev. 12:9*), who beguiled Eve (*Gen. 3:1, 13*), and became the father of Cain (*Gen. 4:1*). The Lord wanted Cain to allow his effeminate twin brother Abel to desire him, and for Cain to rule over him (*Gen. 4:7*), as Eve would desire Adam, and Adam would rule over her (*Gen. 3:16*). Cain was to be Abel's husband (keeper)(*Gen. 4:9*). Cain killed his effeminate brother in the field (*Gen. 4:8*). The Lord marked (mutated) Cain (*Gen. 4:15*), to warn those who Cain feared, would kill him, that Cain's death would be avenged (*Gen. 4:14*). The mark on Cain was to warn all around him, not to harm him (*Gen. 4:15*). Cain did not have a choice, but was caused to be a permanent genetic Pale (fair) Leper. The mutation of Cain is the Cain Mutiny. Now the Mutant Lord, had a mutant son, the father of a line of mutants.

Thus Cain became a permanent Genetic Albino (*Leviticus 13:12, 17*). This albinism at the genetic level, could not correct it's self, in the next generation, as normally happens. Cain's pale complexion along with blond hair (*Lev. 13:30*) and blue eyes, made Cain stand out from all of the wooly headed, brown eyed, brown complexioned, multitudes, that were around him. Cain had been wooly and brown, before he was "marked" (*Gen. 4:15*). Cain's children are the Caucasian or Human Race a created or mutated Being. The "fairness" of the daughters of the man Cain was their pale complexion (*Gen. 6:2*).

The Lord mutated Moses' hand, with paleness to show Moses his power (*Exodus 4:6*). Then the Lord turned it back brown again (*Exodus 4:7*). Later the Lord mutated Moses' sister Miriam into a totally pale leper when she spoke with disrespect to Moses, about his Ethiopian wife (*Nu. 12:1*). Then later he turned Miriam back to the brown woman she was when she was born.

The Lord and his Host mated with the females, of the children of the children of the Egyptian Israelis tribes, to bring the pale Israeli mutants into existence. This was how the Lord began to mutate them into Pale Lepers (*Exodus 13th Chptr.*). The Lord's intent seemed to be to turn as many of the Israelis into Pale Lepers, as he could, as he had had "mutated" Cain and his children (*Gen. 4:15*). Many of the Israelis mutated into, or were born as permanent albinos lepers, without incident. Only those that the Rabbis checked that had yellow hair, and pale complexions, but did not have open wounds, or running sores, were declared "Clean Lepers" (*Lev.13:13, 32, 36*). Many who were put through the process developed open wounds, were infectious, and were called "Unclean" (Tamia / תמיא) contaminated lepers. Mutiny had been the beginning of the Lord's World

Observations

# World Element
# World

*Mutainy — Tubal (Universal Crime) — Christianity*

The beginning of the Lord's World (TBL), was his Mutiny, of taking his planet Crypton, out of this, the mother planet Assiah. The World is not the planet, nor is the planet the World.

Originally the Lord with his World did not exist on this planet. When the Lord was defeated, and his planet Crypton (Corrupt Place) was destroyed, he was cast back down to this planet. The end of Crypton was the end of the Lord's World in space. But when the Lord fell (*Nu. 24:4, 16*) he brought his World, the infection of Crypton with him.

A distinction is made between World and Earth several times throughout the Bible/Torah. (*1Sam. 2:8, I Chron.16:30, Job 34:13, Job 37:12, Psalms 19:4, Psalms 24:1, Psalms 33:8, Psalms 77:18, Psalms 89:11, Psalms 90:2, Psalms 96:10, Isaiah 18:3, etc.*). The last distinction between World and Earth is made at (*Revelation 16:14*). The word "World" in the Old Language, is pronounced Tubal (תבל). *See Strong's Concordance (תבל) #8397 for the definition for World, which speak to a total state of Chaos, or Confusion.* Tubal #8397 describes that which is "Unnatural," or "Against Natural Law: Tubal (תבל) or "World" is a totally depraved state of existence. Some of the main components of the depraved state called World are: **Mutation** (*Pg. 236*), **Bestiality** (Sex with Animals)(*Gen.1:28*)(*Pg. 254*), **Homosexuality** (Sodomy / Lesbianism)(*Pg. 263*), **Rape** (*Pg. 261*), **Genocide/Murder, Incest** (*Pg. 264*), **Prostitution** (*Pg. 260*), **Famine** (*Pg. 258*), **Pediphilia** (Child Molestation), etc. *See also Gesenius Hebrew/Chaldee Lexicon (תבל) pages 855b (bottom),and page 856a (top).* The end of the World (TBL), is the end of all of this corruption!

Once there was no World on this planet at all. Then the Lord establish his World here, that had existed on Crypton. Originally the existence of the Lord's World on this planet was only a spot on the eastern side of the Tigris River, at it's northern extreme. This was the northern extreme of the Land of Nod, where the Lord God (Melchezedek) drove the Lord (the Man), away from the Garden (*Gen. 3:23, 24*). The Lord's World (Chaos) was designed, to eventually infect the entire planet, so that he could take his existence, out of the energy of the confusion .

The World (תבל) by it's negative nature can not and has never sustained it's self. The only justification for the World is that it contains the experimental species called Mankind, the Caucasian Race. Even though much has been done to preserve the World, The World is a very fragile situation. All that it would take for the World to come to an end is for the original inhabitants of the globe to wake up in this dream, the sleep of Adam (*Gen. 2:21*), which contains the World. The World (TBL) has never been a solution to anything, but has been the source of all of the problems on the planet. None of the problems existing now, existed on this planet before the World was brought here from Crypton. The end of the World is the end of all the problems for the original people on the planet.

Yet the World nature is a perfecting agent in a cosmic experiment. The Word nature is a percolator, a sieve, a strainer. The whole of the experiment has been to find out about Self in the particular. Self is put to the ultimate test having the World imposed upon it. Percolating up out and sifted, through it, the Self will have extracted all of the information that original man came into the physical to find. Since the World's inception on the planet Crypton, Christi<u>anity</u> (AntiChrist) has been the garment that the World has worn, to protect it's self.

# World Element Christianity (AntiChrist)

*World (TBL) (Planetary Domination) — Judaism, Church, Mohammadism — Church has never taught or obeyed the commandments of Jesus — Church: Religious garment (Roman Sword)(Hang Jesus from a tree and cursed him) Deut. 21:23, Galatians 3:13 — Greek Mythology, Roman Law, Christian Faith — Religion a controlled substance — Judeo/Christian system teaches it's congregations out of themselves into negative vernacular: belief, hope, faith, praise, bowing — Deception a source of mischoice — Once the confessional was a boast of how corrupt one could be — Whole purpose is to destroy teachings of Jesus*

As the World is not the earth, Christianity is not a religion but is the preservation system for the World (TBL) of the Lord. As such Christianity is as old as the World system that it defends. Yet the Church/Synagogue element of Christianity is only as old as it's invention by the Caucasian or European agents of the World. Christianity is the sum total of all bondages imposed on people by the World System. Christ<u>ianity</u> is the <u>Anti</u>Christ. The Christ has been anyone, crucified/murdered by Christianity (AntiChrist), for being a threat to the World System. Nimrod and Yeshua (Jesus) were both Christ (Crucified Ones)(*Isa. 53rd Chptr.*). Both were threats to the World. Nimrod, Jesus and others were the source of the knowledge, that would bring the World of the Lord to an end.

The whole of the purpose of the Church/Synagogue System is not to restore souls, but to destroy the possibility of people being restored. In the church system "winning souls" cancel out some of the damage that was done when Jesus (Yeshua) returned to Israel, from Egypt to teach the Israeli masses Peace (Islam). This was 600 years before the birth of Muhammad. The religious element of Christ<u>ianity</u> (AntiChrist) is composed of Judaism, the Christian Church, and the Mohammedan Faith.

The World system existed before the Roman Empire founded the church. In fact the Roman Empire came into existence as a garment of disguise for the World System. In an on going process The Roman Empire is the core of Christianity which far exceeds the Christian Church.

One can imagine the threat that the teachings that Jesus brought from Eden (Egypt), would be to the leadership of the Roman and Israeli Gentiles. Thus the joint leadership of these two groups conspired to murder the man who would have brought their collective Judeo/Gentile World to an end. The World is not the people or planet, but the corrupt mental system imposed first on the Israeli, and other Gentile masses, and then on the people of the planet.

Had Jesus' (Yeshua's) teaching of peace (Islam), from Egypt been successful, Judaism would have come to an end. Judaism is the source of the Christian church. Judaism and the Christian Church are the two religious elements of Christianity. Without Judaism there would not have been a Christian Religion. As such without Judaism, and the Christian church, the World of the Lord would have come to an end. Christ<u>ianity</u> means <u>Anti</u>Christ or <u>Anti</u> the ones they (Jews / Gentiles) Crucify.

Jesus never founded or commanded anyone to found a religion (Church), but told his disciples not to establish anything (*Matt.10:9-14*). Yeshua (Jesus) also instructed his twelve not to go in the Way (Darkness / הדרכ) of the Gentiles (Goyim)(*Matt. 10:5*).

Long after the Romans had murdered Jesus (Yeshua) they were having trouble throughout their empire. The Romans taxed the people subject to them, to the limits of their endurance. As such

# World Element
# Christianity (AntiChrist)

*Christianity — Christianity is not so much a religion as it is a garment of the World — Suffering keeps religions going. People bow down in distress, but soon set religion aside when there is peace and prosperity. Eccles. 5:1 says keep your feet, Yeshua says "all of you are Gods ( John 10:34) — Which direction do Gods bow and for what purpose?— Creation*

the people ceased to have fear of death, and rebelled against the Romans. They ceased to have fear for the Roman sword. In effect they symbolically broke off the tip of the Roman sword. This was the seed origin of the religious arm of the Roman Empire. The Romans turned the sword with the broken tip over, and turned it into a Roman cross. With this cross the Romans in effect told those enslaved to them that if they did not fear for their physical lives, that they should fear for their immortal souls, for one (Jesus) had come to give his life to save their immortal souls, by dying on this cross (Sword) for their salvation.

In modern times Christianity (Antichrist) count it's years by how long ago they crucified Jesus, and therefore how long they have extended the existence of their World, that Yeshua (Jesus) came to destroy. The Caucasian Race (Christianity) recently celebrated the second millennium (Year 2000) that their World has been extended because they killed Yeshua (Jesus) to save their World, from him destroying it.

The church states that Yeshua (Jesus) was born as a lamb without spot or blemish to be offered up as a sacrifice for the sins of their World. If in deed Jesus was supposed to be sacrificed, he was to be sacrificed by the Levitican priesthood on an altar. The ritual is not for a lamb as they claimed Jesus was, but for a male kid goat, a scapegoat. Jesus as a sacrificial goat would not have been crucified, but chopped up into pieces. Some of his blood would have been placed on the horns of the altar, and the rest of Jesus' blood would have been poured out at the base of the altar. All of the fat inside of Jesus' body would have been burnt on the altar (*Leviticus 4:23 - 25*). Jesus would have then been a scapegoat for the Israelis, not the Gentile or Caucasian Race!

Furthermore Christianity in general and the Christian church in particular is not obeying the commandments of Jesus (Yeshua), of whom they claim to follow. Jesus made the statement: "If you loved me you would obey my commandment (*John14:15*). Judeo/Christianity does not Love Jesus, but hate him (*John 7:7*), like Jesus taught his followers to hate the Judeo/Christian World (*I John 2:15*), the World that the Lord still so love (*John 3:16*)! Jesus told his followers that if they did not hate the World of the Lord that the love of the father within was not in them (*I John 2:15*).

If the Gentiles as they claim, truly discovered that they had made a mistake by killing Jesus (Yeshua), they would not be celebrating having killed him, and calling it a "Good Friday!" They would not have established a religion, with the basis that by his shed blood their World is saved!

Christianity would not display that horrible cross with Jesus' murdered impaled corpse on it. The cross would be banished, not worn as a talisman. The doctrine of salvation by the shedding of his blood would be banished as an insult to the man, that they had murdered. Finally if they were truly sincere they would preach his doctrine 110% rather than cancelling it out as much as they possibly can, with the preachings of Paul. The World of the Lord, and it's shield Christianity was Created in Adam's sleep.

Notes

# World Element Creation

*Christianity — The Original Sin is Creation — Can a creation exceed the corruption of it's Creator? — Can a creation be better than when it was created? — How can a creator blame it's creation? — Creation is artificial and Manmade (All that comes from creating is temporary)(Moon, Continents, Mankind [Human Beings], Nationalities — Hallel the Lord of Abraham is the Creator (Alterer) of a portion of what is Eternal*

Christianity gives the false impression, that nothing existed before creation. But before the alleged "creation (*Gen. 1:1*), there were star systems, including the sun, and the planets. All of the planets including Assiah (Earth), had life on them. At the start of Genesis (*Gen. 1:1*), there had been a war in the solar system (*Rev. 12:7*). A planet Crypton, between Mars and Jupiter had been destroyed (*Rev. 12:8*). Hallel the Lord, the Almighty of Crypton, had been defeated, and was cast out, to fall down to the earth (*Rev. 12:9; Nu. 24:4, 16*). There was rejoicing on the planets in the solar heavens, but woe to the inhabitants on the earth, for El Shaddai (God Almighty) the Devil God had come down (*Rev. 12:12, Ex. 6:3, Nu. 24:4, 16*). When the Lord could not get co-operation from the inhabitants of the planet, he destroyed Assiah (Earth) (*Isa. 24:1, 3-6*).

A Solar War (*Rev. 12:7*), and the destruction of Crypton, and the Earth (*Rev. 12:8; Isa. 24:1, 3-6*), all occurred before the alleged creation of Genesis 1:1! The planet was not being created (Carat / כרת), it was being **found** (Bara / ברא)(*Gen. 1:1*), after it had been knocked out of it's course (*Psalms 82:5*). To **find** the Earth, in this case implies that Earth already existed, and someone was searching for it, because it had been knocked out of it's normal course around the sun (*Ps. 82:5*).

There are two words to define *"true creation:"* The phonetic word is Carat, and the translation word Bara. Carat means "To Break Off," and Bara means "To See." Both words Bara (See), and Carat (Break Off), imply that something already exists to be "Seen," and have a part "Broken Off," from it! Phonetically to "Create" (Carat/כרת) is to "cutoff," "craft," or "corrupt," a portion of something that already exists, into something other than it's self. The original is viable and sufficient to it's self, such as a living growing tree. The only "creating" that a tree has ever had, has been for someone to "Cut Off" a branch from the tree, and then "alter" or "create" the branch into a wooden statue, or some other object. The life that was in the branch, will soon leave the wood. The tree continue to live, bearing seed and fruit. The created (corrupted) wooden object will not bare a next generation, and will eventually fall apart, and cease to exist. All creation has beginning and end, but that which exists before creation is eternal. No one can say when or if there was ever a first tree, but every carved wooden object has a date when it was shaped (created) into existence. The same created object also have a date and when it shall cease to be. Yet trees continue on Eternally through their seeds and fruit.

Original Man, and the sun existed before there was any creating. Original Man is Alpha/Omega, having no beginning or ending (*Revelation 1:8*). Original Man existed without the aid of a mother or father, or beginning, or ending of days (*Heb. 7:3*). Original man separated the sun into two. The one part continued to be the sun. The duplicate became Assiah (Fireness), the mother planet. The first creating (Carat / כרת) began when apostates "broke off," or (created) planets from this the original, or mother planet and carried them out into their own individual

Observations

# World Element Creation

*Evolution is a theory, and Creation as defined by the western world is also a theory. Both are the opposite sides of the same coin. Neither of these theories existed before the Caucasian Race had been made civil, and were taught to read and write, by the original inhabitants of the planet. That is when the two theories were invented, to hide the fact that everyone on the planet were already in existence, and civil, before the Caucasian Race ever existed! — Solar Wars*

orbits around the sun. Life energy began to leave those planets as soon as they were remove from Assiah. The next creating (Altering) may have taken place on the created planet named Crypton.

Original Man the Alpha and Omega is/was an HermesAphrodite, or intact male/female being (*Gen. 1:27*). The creating (altering) process separate the male portion from the female. Phonetically Crypton (Krypton) means "Creating Place," "Crafting Place," or "Corrupting Place." The first creating (altering) of this planet Assiah was when the other planets were removed from it. The next creating or altering of this the mother planet was when Hallel (Lucifer) and his Host destroyed it (*Isaiah 24:1, 3-6*). The effects of the exploding, Altering or creating of Assiah could only be seen after the water had been drained back up off of the planet surface (*Gen. 1:9*). With the water removed from the surface of Assiah, it was no longer Assiah, but was now called Ertz (Earth), or "Broken" because the once solid land mass had been "fragmented into "Continents", which is what "Ertz" means (*Gen. 1:10*).

After the planet and it's lifeforces had been restored, the next creating or altering began. Adam was put to sleep and separated into separate male and female (*Gen. 2:21-24*). It was the female side called Eve that the Lord impregnated, to make her the mother of his son Cain (*Gen. 4:1; I Chron. 1:1*). The birth of Cain (*Gen. 4:1, 2*) and his mutation (Marking) into a Pale Leper was the beginning of the creating of Mankind the Human Being (*Gen. 4:15*), a branch cutoff from the tree of Man. Cain and his line, the Human or Caucasian Race, was the **man** that the Lord repented, that he had **created**/made (*Gen. 6:6, 7*). The Cain Mutiny was a permanent genetic mutation.

As the wooden object was "created" from a branch, from a living tree, the Human or Caucasian Race was created from the Tree (Original Man). Original Men is Alpha and Omega with no beginning or end (*Rev. 1:8*). The Original man has the birth certificate for the creating of Mankind. Original Man had cities all over the entire planet before the Creation of the Human Race took place. Created Mankind the Human Race have a beginning, and humanity shall come to an end. Only original Man can attain to Eternity.

The Original Man has no beginning or end, and was never created, into existence. The Lord (Hallel) himself is one of the Original Uncreated Men of this planet (*Ex. 15:3*).

The Lord Hallel created or altered himself on the planet Crypton long before he created the Caucasians on the earth. Hallel attempted to export creation (corruption) from Crypton (Corrupt Place) out onto the other planets in the solar (Soul) system. None of the rest of those in the solar system wanted to be created further than they had been, by taking planets out of the mother planet. Their planets were already dying, since they had been removed from Assiah, as branches die that are removed from a tree. When the souls on the other planets resisted being further created (corrupted/altered) by the Lord, that was the start of the Solar Wars.

Notes

# World Elements
# Solar War

*Creation (Crypton) — War for Souls — Alienation — Host /Friends(רע)(חור) — See Krypton (World War) — Outcast — Tribunal*

Hallel the Lord of Crypton caused the Solar (Soul) War. He and his Host attempted to Create (corrupt / alter) the entire solar (Soul) system away from it's original state, including the sun.

And there was war in the heavens, Michael and his angels fought against the Dragon; and the Dragon fought and his angels, and prevailed not; neither was "their place (Planet)" found anymore in heaven (*Rev. 12:7, 8*). And the Great Dragon was cast out, that Old Serpent, called the Devil, and Satan, which deceiveth his whole **World**, was cast out **into the earth**, and his angels were cast out with him (*Rev. 12:9*). The Most High (Sun/God) saw the Almighty fall (*Nu. 24:4, 16*).

Therefore rejoice, ye heavens, and ye that dwell in them. But woe to the **inhabiter of Assiah (earth)** and of the sea, for the Devil God (El Shaddai / God Almighty) is come down to you, having great wrath, because he know that he has but a short time (*Rev. 12:13*).

Behold the Lord maketh the planet empty, and maketh it waste and turneth it upside down, and scattereth abroad the inhabitants thereof (*Isaiah 24:1*). The land shall be utterly empty, and spoiled, **because the Lord spoke it** (*Isa. 24:3*). Therefore has the curse devoured the planet, and they that dwell therein are desolate: therefore the **inhabitants of the planet** are burned and few men are left alive (*Isaiah 24:6*). And all the host of the sky were dissolved, and the sky rolled together as a scroll: and all their host fell down, as the leaf fall off from the vine...(*Isa. 34:4*). ....and the atmosphere passed away with a great noise, and the elements melted with a fervent heat, the planet also and the works therein were burnt up (*II Peter 3:10*).

The Lord beheld and lo there was no man, and all of the birds of the air were fled (*Jer. 4:25*). He beheld and lo the fruitful place was a wilderness, and all the **cities** thereof were broken down at the presence of the Lord, and by his fierce anger. For thus has the Lord said, the whole land shall be desolate; yet will I not make a full end (*Isa. 13:19*). For this shall the planet mourn, and the skies above be black: because He have spoken it, he had purposed it, and did not repent, neither did he turn back from it (*Jeremiah 4:23-28*). .... there was a great land quake and the sun became black as sackcloth of hair... and the stars of space (pieces of Crypton) fell upon the earth... and the heaven departed as a scroll when it is rolled together and every mountain and island was moved out of it's place..., except Eden (Africa), for the great day of the Lord's wrath is come, and who shall be able to stand it (*Rev. 6:12, 13, 17*)? The atmosphere rolled up with a great noise, and sack cloth was over the sun (*Rev. 6:13*).

I beheld the planet and the heavens, and lo they were without form and void, and they had no light (*Jeremiah 4:23, Gen. 1st Chapter*).

Afterwards the Gods **found** (bara / ברא) the planet and it's heaven (*Gen. 1:1*). The planet Assiah (Ertz /Earth) had been knocked out of it's course, and it was without form and was void; and Darkness was on the face of the deep.... (*Gen. 1:1, 2; Psalms 82:5*).

A Tribunal against the Lord was the aftermath of the Solar War. Michael/Melchezedek (Ancient of Days) tried Hallel (Lucifer) for his crimes in space, and on this planet. Hallel (Lucifer) became the Lord of Abraham. The Lord's trial was held in the midst of the Garden.

Observations

# World elements
# Tribunal (Process)

*The elements of a tribunal are scattered out into several books of the Bible/Torah: Genesis, Daniel, Psalms, Ezekiel, etc.*

*Solar War — Genesis — Psalms — Daniel — Ezekiel — Dark Ages*

Hallel and his Host were being tried for his war crimes, in the solar system, and his destroying Crypton, and Assiah the planet now called Ertz (Earth). Hallel the future Lord of Abraham and his Host were being tried, as the defeated rulers of their destroyed planet Crypton, that they also destroyed (*82nd Psalms verses 1-7*).

*82 Psalms*

1) Hallel (Hallelujah) the Almighty the future Lord of Abraham, and his Host are gods. They are standing in the midst of other Gods who defeated them, in the solar war. They are being judged (*Ps. 82:1-8, Numbers 24:4, 16, Daniel*)

2) The Ancient of Days asked the Lord (Hallel) how long will he be in favor of wicked ones.

3) Hallel was commanded to give restitution, to those he and his Host have made destitute.

4) Hallel was instructed to deliver them out of the control of his Wicked ones.

5) Hallel was accused of having knocked the planet out of it's course (*Isa. 13:13; Ps. 82:5*), and keeping people unknowingly walking in his Darkness (*Isa. 5:20*).

6) Hallel's Host are reminded that they are Gods (*Ps. 82:6*) in their own right, like Hallel, and that they are children and inheritors from the Most High, like Hallel is (*Deut. 32:8, 9*).

7) The Lord (Hallel's) Host are finally warned that if they continue to follow him that they will be caused to die like him (a Man), and fall like Hallel fell, as the Prince of his World of Darkness (*Amos 5:18, 20; John 12:31*).

8) Melchezedek give the Host of the Lord as Gods the option, of inheriting and judging the Nations or Gentiles children of Cain (*Ps. 82:7*).

These verses in Psalms mirror similar verses in the book of Daniel that speak of the same Tribunal :

## Daniel 7

7:9) Thrones of judgment are cast down and the wooly headed **Ancient of Days** sat to officiate with others to judge (*Daniel 7:9*).

7:10) Millions come down with the Ancient one to attend the trial of the accused ones. The books are opened, and judgment is set.

7:11) The Lord is the Beast in *Dan. 7:10* is the beast in *Revelations 13:18*, who is the Beast of *Gen. 3:1*, who is Hallel the Man of War *Exodus 15:3*. Hallel's body was slain and casted in to the flames.

7:12) The other Beasts the Host of Hallel are given a reprieve for a short season to make themselves right. They lost the dominion that had been given to them (*Gen. 1:28*).

The **Lord** is the Man **casted out** (Shaddai), of the East Gate *Gen. 3:24* of the Garden over into the Land of Nod. It was the **Lord God Michael/Melchezedek** who casted the Lord and his Host out of the Garden, eastward across the Tigris, over into Mount Ararat, in the north of Nod. Nod is where the Lord (Man) had been taken from (*Gen. 3:24*). Nod was the continuation of the Dark Ages.

Notes

# World Elements
# Dark Ages

*Tribunal — Dracula — Prince of Darkness — Dark (חשך) #2820-2825 (Ezek. 8:12) — Nimrod, Jesus (Yeshua), (Great Lights / אור גדל)(Gen. 1:16, Isa. 9:2)(Isa. 13:10, Matt. 4:16)*

The Dark ages began even before the solar war, and the Tribunal against the Lord. Dark Ages are the periods that the Lord impose on those who are under his control. The Lord declared that his Day is Darkness (חשך), which is not the opposite of Light, but is to be away from the "Light of Self. The Dark Ages, is the Thick Outer Darkness (Awful/Apple / אפל), of the Lord. Outer Darkness is the core of the Lord's World, and his Day (*Amos 5:18:20*), that he want his followers to be glad in *Psalms 118:24*).

Phonetically Darkness (דרכה) pronounced "Dracah (Dracula)" means "Wayward," or having a "Direction," away from the Central Light that radiates from Self. Thus to be absent from the body is to be with the Lord "in" Outer Darkness (*II Corin. 5:6-8*).

In translation Darkness (חשך) "Hoshack" means to be "weak," or "debilitated," which is the effect of being "away from" mental or optical light. An example would be like when Cain and his descendants lived in the darkness, of his subterranean cave city of Enoch. The Lord speaks of his day which is total Darkness, that has no brightness in it. The Lord's Darkness is as much a mental Darkness as it may be an optical Darkness.

The Lord gave an explicit commandment to his servants, the Rabbis, Priests, and Ministers. The Lord's commandment was for them to keep the eyes of their congregations closed, the ears of their congregation closed, and the hearts (minds) of their congregations closed, so that these billions of deceived Jews, Gentiles, and others could not convert, away from church and synagogue, and be healed (*Isa. 6:9, 10*). The loss of eyes to see, ears to hear, and a mind to understand, is the total Darkness of the day of the Lord (*Amos 5:18, 20*).

### 1st Dark Age (Solar)

The First Dark Age was before Genesis when the Lord (Hallel) the Prince of Darkness was defeated in the heavens and was Casted Down, in chains of Darkness (*II Pet. 2:4*), to the vicinity of this the mother planet Assiah (*Rev. 12:9*). Darkness fell with Hallel (Lucifer), the future Lord of Abram. The Lord is the Casted Down God (El Shaddai), who covered the planet with his gross (Thick) Darkness (*Isa. 60:2, Deut. 10:22; Ex. 20:21*). The Lord and his Host were full of wrath, because they knew they only had a short time, to impose their Darkness upon the inhabitants of the planet, before Michael/Melchezedek the Ancient of Days would come down, to judge him (*Rev. 12:12*).

### Dark Age (Planetary/Garden)

The Lord is the **Serpent** (beast)(*Rev. 12:9; Gen. 3:1*), and his Host are the **Beasts of the Field** above (*Gen. 2:19, 20; 3:1*). They were cast down and became the **Beast of the Earth** below (*Gen. 1:24, 25*), after they were defeated in the war in the heavens (*Rev. 12:9*). The Lord and his Host are the "Tree," that the Lord God Michael/Melchezedek "planted" in the midst of the Garden (Guarded Place)(*Gen. 2:8, 9*).

The fruit that Adam and Eve consummated was the Mandrake (Man Of Darkness) Fruit, from

Observations

# World Elements
# Dark Ages (Apple)

*Thick Darkness (Apple)(Awful)(I Fall) #651-653 (Ex. 10:22) — Mandrake (Man of Darkness) Fruit— Sleeping Beauties — Mandrake (Man of Darkness) Fruit (Fruit of the "fall") — Sleeping Beauty*

the Lord's tree (*Gen. 30:14 - 16; Solomon 7:13*). The Mandrake Fruit, produces the Thick Darkness (אפל) pronounced "Apple," or "Awful" which was on the tree of the Lord, in the midst of the Garden (*Gen. 3:3*). The Apple (Thick Darkness / אפל) is the core of the World of the Lord.

### Dark Age (Nod)

The next Dark age was after the Tribunal. It was then that Darkness in the form of the Lord and his Host were casted (Shaddai) out of the Garden, They were cast eastward into the North of the Land of Nod. The Lord had been casted out, back to the "ground" that he the Lord/Man had been "taken (Formed) from." (*Gen. 2:7, 8, Gen.3:19, 23 Isaiah 43:10*). The Lord was the Man of Darkness, or Mandrake.

The Darkness in Cain's daughters the **Daughters of Chaldea** was from consuming the Lord's fruit, and it's root (*Isa. 47:1-6*). There are obvious sexual connotations in these passages, when the Lord tell the young Chaldean girls that he is going to take away their virginity (*Isa. 47:1*). He tells them to prepare themselves for him, by setting in the dirt, letting down their hair, and baring their legs and their vaginas (*Isa. 47:3, 4*). He tell them that he will come to them, as a man comes to a woman (*Isa. 47:3*). He tells them to recline and be still, and let the Darkness take them over (*Isa. 47:5*)." He then tell them that they will no longer be ladies because he will pollute them (*Isa. 47:6*). Yet in a narcotic fog these young Chaldean girls did not even know, that they were being raped (*Isa. 47:7*). Having been temporarily poisoned by eating the Lord's Mandrake fruit or Love Apple, the daughters of Cain became "Sleeping Beauties." It must have been a requirement of the Lord of the North, and his Host, who are the Sons of the Gods, who mated with the Chaldean Daughters of the Man Cain (*Gen. 6:2-4*). Cain's pale leper children were and still are in the Darkness of the Lord (*Isa. 9:2, Isa. 18:1*).

Nimrod and thousands from the south went north into the Land of Nod, to bring a Great Light into the shadows, and Thick Darkness of the Lord (*Isa. 9:2*). Nimrod's Light was for the resurrection or Raising of Cain (*Gen. 1:15, Matt. 4:16*). Nimrod had almost set the Gentiles/Chaldean Children of Cain free from bondage to the Prince of Darkness, the Lord of the North. That was when the Lord and his Host came down from Ararat, to confound the Great Light with his Thick Darkness (*Gen. 11:5, Amos 5:18, 20*).

Those Gentiles (Chaldeans) who could, fled from the Prince of Darkness. They fled westward across the Tigris down into the Light of the Gardenlands of Ham and his children. The Chaldeans were given asylum from their Lord. The children of Ham quarantined Cain's pale leper children, in the twin grain cities of Sodom and Gomorrah.

Four hundred years later, Terah the father of Abram was escaping from the Lord, his famine, and Darkness there in the land of Nod. Terah was fleeing Nod, for the Life and Light of the land of Canaan (*Gen. 11:31*). The Lord caught up with them in the city of Haran, where Terah had died while escaping to the land of Canaan. It was from the city of Haran in the land of Nod that the

Notes

# World Elements
# Dark Ages

*Apple — Darkness of Nod to overshadow Light of Canaan — Darkness is not the opposite of Light, but is being absence from Light II Chron.5:6 Amos 5:18, 20 — Light chase Darkness, but Darkness fills in when light leaves. Gen. 15:12 (Deep Sleep/Great Darkness) — That which is in the Darkness shall come to the Light (Self Motivation)(other than Self dies in the Light) — Sleep*

Lord made Abram "hebrew" the the Tigris, and Euphrates rivers, the rivers of Cush (Ethiopia)(*Gen.2:13; Isa. 18:1, Zephoniah 3:10*). The Lord forced Abram to bring him, and his Darkness, down into the land of Canaan (*Gen. 12:1*).

### Dark Age (Canaan)

The next Dark Age, was when Abram made it possible for the Lord to bring his Darkness, down into Canaan. The Darkness of the Lord was now spread from Ararat, and Nod, to the Garden, from whence he and his Host had been casted out (*Gen. 3:22-24*). The Lord the Prince of Darkness, is the Man who became the Lord, or God of Abraham, Isaac, Jacob, the Israelis, and the rest of the Western World. It was in the land of Canaan that Abram in his time of choosing willingly fell asleep, into the Great Darkness of the Lord (*Gen. 15:12*).

Jacob had to escape the Lord's famine and Darkness, in Canaan, as Terah had attempted to escape the Lord's famine and Darkness in Nod. Jacob was successful in escaping from the Darkness now in Canaan, into the Light of Egypt. The Egyptians sent wagons to Canaan to save Israel, by bringing them to Egypt (*Gen. 45:19, 21, 27, Gen. 46:5*). Israel (Jacob) had fled from the Darkness, famine and bondage to the Lord, and his Host in the Land of Canaan. Jacob went down into Egypt, to the source of the Great Light, that Nimrod had taken to the north in Nod (*Isaiah 9:2, Isaiah 18:1*).

### Dark Age (Egypt)

Four hundred years later it was Moses that made it possible for the Lord to bring his Thick Darkness (Apple / אפל) down into Egypt, to kill the Light there. Moses and the Lord brought Thick Darkness from Mount Horeb (Horrible) in Canaan, down into Egypt. It was a Darkness that could be felt (*Ex. 10:22, Ex. 20:21*). The Prince of Darkness (Lord) wanted to reclaim the Israelis, from the Great Light of Egypt (*Exodus 10:21, 22; 20:21*). The Lord brought them back into bondage to himself (*Gen. 1:15, Isaiah 9:2, Matt 4:16*). Later the Israelis declared to Jesus (Yeshua), that they had never been in bondage to any man, including the Egyptians (*John 8:33*), but they were in bondage to the Lord, a Superman of War (*Ex. 15:3*). The Dark Age included Joshua who led the Israelis in the final holocaust against the children of Canaan. Now the Darkness and sleep of Nod had been imposed on all who lived in the Garden.

Thick Darkness is the fruit of the **Man of Darkness**, it is called the Mandrake (Man of Darkness) Fruit. Mandrake is the name of the fruit that Reuben found and gave to his mother Leah (*Gen. 30:14*). The properties of this plant, it's roots and it's fruit are narcotic, and aphrodisiac. In other words when the fruit is consumed, the consumer (a female) is put into a drugged (narcotic) state, and at the same time that person becomes highly sexually aroused (*Desire*)(*Gen. 3:16*). The sexually aroused state draws the Lord, and or his male Host to the one who is to be

Observations

# World Elements
# Dark Ages

*Dark Ages — Moorish Light, To The European Darkness — European Darkness Given as Light — Sleep*

ravished.

The thirty-two little Ishmael/Midianite "Women Children" given to the Lord, were probably forced to consume the mandrake fruit to put them in the Darkness to prepare them, for the Lord to come to them, as a man comes to a woman (*Nu. 31:40; Isa. 47:3*).

### Dark Age (Europe)

Dark ages are the sum total of the entire existence of the species called the Human or Caucasians Race. What is now called Europe and it's pale leper inhabitants were in the Lord's Dark Age, until the wooly headed brown Moors came north from Eden (Africa), to Raised Cain (his children), from the Dark Age that their Lord was imposing on them. The Moors brought the Great Light of Eden (Africa/Egypt), up into what would be called Europe. The pale leper children of Cain had migrated there, with the wooly headed brown children of Japheth. The Lord and his Host had followed them there to hold them in his bondage. All of Europe was in the total Darkness of the Lord and his Host, as Nod had been.

The Moors arrive around 711 A.D. When the Moors came up from Eden (Africa) the land was not called Europe. There was not a Spain, Portugal, Germany, France, England, Italy, Russia, Denmark, or any other Caucasian country in existence. There were no towns, villages, or cities. This was the same as Nod, when Nimrod went there to enlighten the pale leper ancestors of these pale lepers that the Moors had come north to enlighten.

Ham's wooly headed brown Phoenician children had given an alphabet, to Japheth,s wooly brown Etruscans, and wooly headed brown Archaic Greek children. The Archaic (Brown) Greeks and Etruscans gave the same alphabet to the Pale leper Romans. Yet almost a thousand years later in 711 A.D. none of the pale inhabitants of what is now called Europe had even retained the alphabet!

### Dark Ages (Americas)

All Dark Ages are within the negative. The negative state is the Outer Darkness of the physical realm. In the negative all that seem to be Light is actually Darkness, as in a film negative. And thus the inhabitants of the Earth and the World also are all deceived into bowing down, to the Prince of Darkness, thinking he is the source of Light. The entire physical realm is a cosmic experiment, that was contrived by the aboriginal inhabitants of this the mother planet. As with any experiment this experiment has been allowed to run it's true course. The only intervention was when Hallel (The Lord) attempted to take the solar (Soul) system by storm. That was the cause of the solar war, in which the Lord and his Host were defeated and cast down. But even after having been defeated, the Lord was allowed to continue in what ever direction he would go, he is only prevented from destroying the experiment. The whole of the experiment since the war and the Tribunal has in fact been the preservation of the Lord's World, which is Darkness. The Lord's World could not have come into existence on this planet, nor could it have survived and

Notes

# World Elements
# Dark Ages

*Dark Ages — Mental Darkness leads to sleep.— Sleep (שלף) phonically means to be pulled out from the center of ones Self.— (שלף, יסן) — Mounds (נד) — Adam's Sleep (Entire Experiment) — Nod (sleep / שלף) — Nod (Fall to sleep/נוד)(Pulled Out/Carried Away) — Sleep*

flourished, without the continued assistance of the original inhabitants of the planet.

The entire Pale Leper species called Mankind, Human Being, or the Caucasian Race had it's origin from Cain, who was originally wooly and Black, until he was "marked," by his father the Lord to become an albino, a permanent pale leper (*Gen. 4:15*).

**"From Nimrod to Benjamin Banniker,"** is a phrase that describes the wooly headed Black to Brown aboriginal man, who has built and maintained civilizing societies for the Caucasian Race from their pale genetic beginning in the land of Nod (Babel), to their ending in North America. Nimrod built the first civilizing capital Ur/Babel, and Benjamin Banniker built the Last civilizing capital Washington D.C. Every capital between these two: Jerusalem, Athens, Rome, London, and every original capital in Europe, were founded by wooly headed Black men. The Moors built the European capitals as masters, not slaves. Beyond building cities for them, the Moors gave the European Caucasians Light, in the form of all of the arts crafts and skills, that finally allowed them to build those old sailing ships, that they sailed across the Atlantic, to the western hemisphere.

In North America millions of wooly headed brown men built the thirteen penal colonies, and finally Benjamin Banniker and thousands of others built Washington D. C., the final capital for Cain's pale leper children. In all of the previously described cases, the Caucasian race had been offered Light, but have always turned to the Darkness of the Lord. As Jesus (Yeshua) said you can not serve two, for you will Love Light, and despised the Darkness, or you will love the Darkness, and despise the Light (*Matt. 6:24*). The entire deceived population has been deceived into loving the Darkness, and despising light (*Matt.6:24*). Woe to them who call Evil Good, and Good Evil, who put Darkness for Light, and call Light Darkness...(*Isa. 5:20*). The Light of the body is in the Single Eye. Therefore if the Single Eye be active the whole body shall be full of Light (*Matt. 6:22*). But if the Single Eye be shut (Evil), then the whole body shall be full of the Lord's Darkness. If therefore the body be in Darkness, how great is that Darkness? Woe to those who desire the day of the Lord, it is Darkness and not Light, even very Dark, with no brightness in it (*Amos 5:18, 20*). Yeshua asked "what does it profit a man if he should gain the whole World, but lose his own soul in the process (*Mark 8:36*).

The whole of the Lord's purpose, for his Dark Ages, is to take his continuance from the confusion generated in a state where all eyes, ears, and minds are shutdown.

To keep the experiment going to it's finish, the wooly headed Blacks fell asleep on their own in the Americas. In the western hemisphere Blacks have even allowed themselves to be infected by the Mentally dead (Necro / Negro) Caucasians, and have become Necroes, or Negroes, just like the Caucasian masses. The entire Human or Caucasian Race exists inside of the sleep of Adam Necro (Adam/ Negro), the mentally dead Blacks.

Observations

# World Elements
# Sleep

*Dark Ages — Carried Away — Adam's Sleep — Faith*

In the Dream State of physical existence, here are several forms of sleep down into the Dark Ages. Phonetically "sleep (שלך)" *Strong's #8025* means to be "Carried Away," or "Casted Out" (from absolute), into physical existence. Phonetically Sleep (שלך) and Self (Sleeper / שלך) are the same. Sleep is the Self, existing in the Dream Realm, that composes the Physical state. The highest form of sleep in the dream, is to be mentally awake in it. To be awake in the dream, is to be conscious, alert, and aware of having been ejected out of the absolute, into physical.

It was in this first stage of sleep that the sun and the planets were made manifest, and that the solar war occurred. It was also the time when Krypton, and Assiah were destroyed, and Assiah was revived (*Gen. 2:1*). The wooly headed brown aboriginal inhabitants of the planets were still themselves. They were Gods, when they built the Great Pyramid as a land mark.

The next sleep stage is described by the word in translation for sleep *Strong's #3462* (יש׳) "Yesen," which means to "languish" as between Life and death, this is the sleep of Adam (*Gen. 2:21*). **Adam** was put to **sleep** (יסן) by the Lord God Michael/Melchezedek, and separated into separate male and female. Before that time Adam was in the image and likeness of the rest of the Gods, who existed without the aid of mother or father, thus having no navel, and existing without beginning or end (*Hebrews 7:3*). Adam was never awakened, and the entire physical experiment is taking place inside of Adam's Sleep (*Gen. 2:21*). It was in this state of sleep (Adam's sleep), that the Human Being or Caucasian Race came into existence. They are the pale leper children of pale leper Cain who was born out of the Lord beguiling Eve the female of Adam.

There are other forms of Sleep also in physical existence: First there is Shenah (שנה), or the regular night "Sleep Cycle" (שנה) of Jacob (*Gen. 28:16*).

Next there is Radam (רדם), or being "stunned," or "stupefies," as Abraham was when he fell into a **deep sleep** #7290 (רדם), and a **great darkness** (*Gen. 15:12*).

**Noah** was not physically asleep, but was **mentally asleep**, when he brought his grandson Canaan into his tent . Noah was never physically asleep (*Gen. 9:24*).

The Lord imposed a final form of sleep on his son Cain's children, in the land of Nod. The final form is **Mental Death** (Necro / Negro). The land of Nod (nodding) is synonymous with sleep. Darkness is associated with Nod, and Nod is associated with death (Νεκρω). Isaac, Jacob, and the Israelis are all a continuation of the sleep/death of Nod. The Lord instructed the leaders of the Israelis, to close their eyes, ears, and minds (*Isa. 6:10*), that is the same sleep that was imposed on Cain's pale leper children in Nod. One "Nods," as they are falling into sleep.

The World can not survive without the sleep of those who think that they have to depend on the World for their existence. Without the sleep state of the billions, the World would come to an end. Christianity in all of it's elements, Judaism, Catholicism, Protestation, Mohammadism, and all of the governments around the planet keep their masses asleep for the preservation of the World system. The wooly headed children of Eden, are in mental chains in the wilderness of the western hemisphere. North America represent the sum total of the sleeping Adam, who is the keystone. The faithful (אמן) are asleep, their eyes and ears are full of the Darkness of the Lord.

Notes

# World Elements
# Faith

*Sleep — Amen (Study) — Be Informed/Know — Repent (rethink) — Holy*

In modern times Faith (אמן) is the action of closing ones eyes and falling mentally asleep. Faith is pronounced *Amen* in the old language. The word Amen (faith) means "To Know," by "Studying, Training," and Drilling." Amen (Ammon) is therefore also the Egyptian God of knowledge from **disciplined thought**.

In the modern times the word faith is a very damaged word, which have come to mean, excepting something as true, without having knowledge. "Amen" (אמן) the Old Language word for Faith, was brought into the English, and placed at the end Christian prayers, without a meaning."

But in truth to have "faith" (Amen / Ammon) is/was to have "information," or "knowledge." When Jesus (Yeshua) spoke of a mustard seed having faith, he meant a mustard seed having information or knowledge. He was saying, if you had the information or knowledge contained inside of a mustard seed, you would know how to cause a mountain to move (*Matt. 17:20*). This is the whole of what Jesus meant when he spoke to having "eyes that see, and ears that hear." Eyes and ears are the main tools for taking in information or knowledge. Once you see and know know you don't have to see every time, because you have seen before, and know it! That is what faith really was until it was corrupted, into excepting as true something that you don't know.

The whole of the use by Jesus of the word "Faith" was with the original definition, as his teachings all spoke to doing for your self, without outside intervention. Self action not sitting on your hands waiting for something to happen! For Jesus (Yeshua), the word **"Faith"** meant **"knowledge,"** along with the word **"repent"** which means to **"Rethink."**

With Jesus' use of the true meaning of the words "faith" and "repentance," Judaism would have come to an end, and there would not have been a Western Civilization (Christianity), for the World of the Lord would have come to an end with the ending of Judaism! For Jesus was telling the "Lost Sheep of Israel," not to except the teachings of their mothers and fathers, which was Holy (Corrupt). He told them to Rethink (Repent), and have Faith (Information/Knowledge) about the life style that had been handed down to them. Have eyes that see, ears that hear, and a mind/heart that understand (*Deut. 29:4; Matt. 13:14, 15*). The Lord did not want the Israeli masses to think, or know anything (*Isa. 6:9, 10*). Jesus' teaching to the Israelis of rethinking (Repenting), and having knowledge (Faith), was information sent from Egypt, to make them free from the Lord (*John 8:32*).

The Lord did not want the Israelis to repent at all, but he did want them to have faith, but not the faith that Jesus was teaching. The Lord wanted for them to have faith (Blind and deaf), to follow whatsoever their leaders told them. They must maintain their old corrupt lifestyle.

The life style that the Israelis were living is written throughout the old Testament. Incubi, Sodomy, Incest, Rape, Pediphilia, Murder, Theft, Lying etc. These were all major ingredients in their lifestyle, that Jesus was asking his people to repent (rethink), and have knowledge (faith) about.

Holiness (קדש) is religious ritual sodomy (קדש), that was performed on the first born son of every family in Israel. The Lord's faith (Lack of Knowledge) is the beginning of Holiness.

Observations

# World Elements
# Holy(ness)

*Faith — Corrupt (חלל) — Religious Sodomy (קדש) — Male/Female Prostitution — Bondage*

Faith has become the act of closing one's eyes and allowing one's Self to be made Holy or Corrupt. Phonetically "Holy" (חלל) means "Corrupt," or "Profane." The word "Holy" translates back to the word pronounced Kadesh (קָדֵשׁ) which means "to prostate" or "Prostitute." This word for Holy (קָדֵשׁ) is describing a male prostitute (Sodomite)(קָדֵשׁ), and a female prostitute (whore)(קְדֵשָׁה)(*Deut.23:17*). Yet the scripture for this verse (*Deut. 23:17*) says: "There shall be no whore (**Kadesh**ah) of the daughters of Israel, nor a sodomite (Kadesh) of the sons of Israel.

"Hebrew" is a language in which you can not lie, for each word sets back to a root. The root idea for the word Kadesh (קָדֵשׁ) which means to "Be Holy" is "to be prostrate" (Prostituted). This certainly describes a male or female prostitute but this word also speak to the idea of being Sanctified, and or Holy (קָדֵשׁ). Thus this male and female prostitution is strictly a religious act!

To show that Holiness is temple (religious) prostitution/sodomy there is a secular form of sodomy under the Hebrew word root Shakav (שכב). The root idea of this word is "to lie down" for whatever purpose. Under this root are words such as "bed," "sleep," "recline," and "copulate." In each case the basic idea is "to lie down." To copulate in general is Shikev (שִׁכֵב)(*Lev. 15:18*).

To show how articulate this language is, each of the following words are generated by using the same three root consonants שכב, with different vowel combinations. The "Hebrew" can distinguish whether a female is being copulated with vaginally (שָׁכַב)(*Lev. 15:18*) or **she is being sodomized (שָׁכַב)(*Num.31:17*). A man sodomizing a man is** (שָׁכַב)(*Lev. 18:22*). A woman being penetrated by an animal is denoted by the combination (שָׁכַב)(*Lev. 20:15*). Bestiality or sex between a man and animal can also be noted. (שָׁכַב)(*Lev. 18:23*).

To firmly establish that Kedesh (קָדֵשׁ) or Religious Sodomy is an official act the Lord commanded that the Israelis bring their firstborn (Future leaders) sons before him to be sanctified (Sodomized)(קָדֵשׁ). This happened to the firstborn male animals also (*Ex.13:2, Ex.13:13*)! Then they were to bring back the firstborn three time each year, to repeat the process (*Ex. 34:23*). The Israelis had to "Sanctify" (קדש) their first born sons to the Lord, which was to perform Ritual Religious Sodomy (קדש) on them. None were to appear before the Lord, with empty hands (*Ex. 34:20*). *See Strong's Concordance # 6942, #6944, #6945* these are the numbers for the words **Sanctify, Sodomy,** and **Holy** in that order.

Thus the basis of the entire Judeo/Christian Religion is the act of being made Holy or being ritually sodomized. Once religious sodomy (קדש) is excepted in a community, there is nothing to stop secular sodomy (שכב) from being imposed on women and men, of the same community.

A people deep enough in Darkness to sodomize (קדש) it's male children is capable of doing any degree of horrible deeds to themselves and others. Atrocities are the history of the ancient Israelis

In bondage the people are so corrupt that they demand the very rituals that keep them in corruption! The bondage of Holiness becomes perpetual.

Notes

# World Elements
# Bondage

*Holy(ness) — Service (עבד) #5656 Bondage (Exodus 6:5) (To who and for what) — Servant (Jer. 2:14) — Truth makes free, lies captivate (Bound) — Bond #632 (אסר) Obligation, Vow, Bondage #5656 (אבדה), Bound #6125 (עקה) Constraint, Oppression — Service (Bondage) to the Lord (Keeping someone against their will, (Exodus 4:23) — Evil*

Holiness (קדש)(חללי) or "corruption" is the source of Israeli bondage to the Lord. The word for "Bondage" (עבד) #5656 and the word for "Service" (עבד) #5656 are the same word (*Exodus. 6:5, Exodus 4:23*). After four hundred years in Egypt, the Israelis refused to leave, so the Egyptians forced the Israelis to learn how to make bricks, and to build homes for themselves. They had not ever worked for the four hundred years they had been in Egypt. This was not "bondage," but was the Israelis being forced to "serve" themselves. The Israelis confirmed this by saying that they had never been in bondage to the Egyptians or any man (*John 8:33*). To be forced to "serve" yourself is not "bondage."

To be forced to "serve" someone else is "bondage." The Israelis were forced to "serve" the Lord, before and after being in Egypt. They were always in bondage to the Lord.

Jesus was sent by the Egyptians to the "Lost Sheep" of Israel, to make them free from "bondage to the Lord. Jesus told the Israelis that the truth shall make them free (*John 8:33*). The fact that Jesus was sent **from Egypt to Israel** to make the lost Sheep free, meant that they were in bondage in Israel, not Egypt! The Israelis in the time of Jesus were Black, and denied being in bondage in Egypt. "Egyptian bondage" is an invention of the modern Pale Israelis. The only Bondage that the Israelis were ever in was to the Lord, a Super Man (*Ex. 15:3*).

Service is a superior place, for the servant is providing services to the served, that he can not provide for himself. The perfect example for this is parents serving their children.

In the case of Jesus (Yeshua), and his disciples, Jesus stooped to wash their feet. This was not because they could not wash their own feet, but to show the humility that exists in true superiority.

Noah said that Canaan would be a servant to servants. This was true, for the children of Canaan served the Israelis who were in service to the Lord. This made the children of Canaan superior to Israel, and the the Israelis superior to the Lord that they served. The Canaanites and Egyptians originally served the Israelis willingly, and saved them. The Israelis' association to the Lord was always service by force, which is bondage.

The Blacks who were brought into service (Bondage/enslavement) in the Americas were never inferior. They were always superior to those who put chains on them. The Caucasians had to chain the Blacks to themselves, because other wise the the Blacks would have walked away from them! The enslaver could not serve themselves, and still can not. Those who have to force someone to serve them have always been inferior, including Caucasians, and their Lord, the God of Abraham! The Lord of Abraham bound as many agents as he could, to himself. The whole end agenda of Abraham's Lord Hallel was to bring Evil upon all flesh. (*Jer. 45:5*). Bondage is the ultimate Evil.

Observations

# World Elements
# Evil (רע)

*Bondage — Creation (HLL) — Incompleteness — The Lord of Evil (Jer. 45:5) — Bestiality*

Evil (Ra / רע) is the ultimate tool of the Lord, to hold those who are in bondage to him. The Old Language word for Evil is pronounced Ra (רע) which means Incomplete," or needing a "Friend." Thus in translation Evil (רע) means "incompleteness," in the sense of being "Broken," with pieces missing. Thus evil carries the idea of needing a patch, or needing a crutch to lean on. In the case of the Lord it is to need a **host**, or "**friend (רע)**," or "**companions**" to make him artificially complete. *See Lexicon "Evil."* Evilness or incompleteness is a **breaking** of the circuit of Universal Law, which is normally complete. The Lord was a breaker of the Law or Felon (Fallen One).

The Lord announced that eventually he would bring Evil or incompleteness upon all flesh (*Jer. 45:5*).

The Lord and his Host were the tree of good and **evil** in the Garden (*Gen. 2:9, 17, Matt. 7:17*). The Lord is the origin of **evil** (*II Kings 6:33*). There is no **evil** without the Lord creating it (*Isaiah 45:7*).

The Lord brought **Evil** from the north (*Jeremiah 4:6, Gen. 12:1, Job 42:11*). Evil spirits come from the Lord (*I Sam. 16:14,* ). The Lord imposed Evil on Israel (*II Sam. 12:11, I Kings 9:9*). The Lord made the wicked for his day of **evil** (*Proverbs 16:4, Jeremiah 17:18*). The souls of the Lord's wicked ones desire his **evil** (*Proverbs 21:10*). The Lord sends **evil angels** (*Psalms 78:49*).

The Lord of Abraham has the Israelis in deep bondage when he is told them that [eventually] he intended to bring Evil on all flesh (*Jer. 45:5*). Creation is **Evil**, for it is and was the process of altering to incompleteness, what was perfect and complete.

The Lord and his Host brought evil to this planet, from their planet Crypton. The Lord and his Host had been defeated in the solar (Soul) war, against Michael and his angels (*Rev. 12:8*). The purpose of the Lord's evil is to bring people to a state of low self esteem, so that they do not feel complete or worthy of any form of good treatment from the Lord. The Lord never treated well, any who served him.

The state of evilness has it's best effect when it is imposed those who are totally innocent. That is why the Lord beguiled Eve to get children from her (*Gen. 4:1*). It was an evil act when the Lord had his son Cain to become the husband, or keeper of his effeminate brother Abel (*Gen. 4:7*). It was evil when the Lord sent his son Cain down into the ground to marry and get offspring with the females of his Host. Cain's children are the Gentiles, the Evil Ones that the Lord eventually brought from the north (*Jeremiah 4:6, Gen. 12:1, Job 42:11*).

It was an **evil** act when the Lord "visited" (פקד) young Sarah and all of the other young Chaldean girl to rob them of their virginity (*Isa. 47:1-6*). It was evil when the Lord turn them into Horites (Whores). It was **evil** when the Lord sponsored incest, rape, incubi, theft murder and bestiality, to bring his World (TBL), including Israel, into existence on this planet.

Arphaxad (Isaiah) warns that Evil should not be called Good, and Good should not be called Evil (*Isaiah 5:20*). People who are just do not fear, the evil of the Lord (*Proverbs 12:21*).

The Evil of Bestiality (TBL) or sex with animals is the core of the World (TBL) of the Lord.

Notes

# World Elements
# Bestiality (TBL)

*Evil — Tubal — Dominion Cabash (כבשר) Gen. 1:28 means the same as Tubal (תובל) both which mean "bestiality" or sexual contact with animals. Gesenius "Hebrew"- Chaldee Lexicon Pg. 383b Betrayal*

Bestiality (TBL), or sex with animals is a core of the Lord's World's (TBL), foundation on this planet. The old Language word for World (TBL), and Bestiality (TBL), are the same, and mean the same. The Man of *Gen. 1:26, 27* is the Lord who instructed his Host, to "go down into" (רד) the animal of the planet first of all to subdue (כבש / Subdue sexually) them, and to have dominion over or in them (*Gen. 1:28*). These acts by the Lord and his Host were past on to the children of the Lord's son Cain: **Jubal** Cain, **Jabal** Cain, and **Tubal** Cain. Bestiality was epidemic in the land of Nod where Cain and his descendants dwelt.

Their bestial lifestyle was the source of a secret cargo, that the Lord had Noah to store on the third story of his ark (*Gen. 7:2*). The designation for all of the various kinds that made up this strange cargo was: "Beast (בהמה) a man (איש) and his wife (אשתו)(*Genesis 7:2*)." *See the word "כבש" Page 383b Gesenius' Hebrew/Chaldee Lexicon* This word pronounced "Cabash" translated as the English word "subdue" really means to have sex with animals to get an offspring.

European museums are full of sculptures depicting the fruit of the mixing between "Human Beings," and animals: Menataurs (cattle mix), Centaurs (horse mix), and Satyrs (sheep and goat mix), are only four of these mixes between man and animal. **Leda and the swan** is a piece of sculpture showing a pale Greek woman having sex with a male swan. The Greco/Roman mythology for this sculpture says that Leda was made pregnant, by the goose, and gave birth.

The commandments given to the Israelis to not lie down with animals indicate that they had committed bestiality with their herds, the cattle, horses, sheep, goats, and dogs. You do not have to tell an entire mass of people not to do, unless they are doing it! (*Leviticus 18:23*)! In fact the Lord had demanded that the Israelis sanctify (sodomize) the firstborn male animals, along with their firstborn sons (*Ex.13:2, Ex.13:13*)!

The Israelis were shepherds, and male and female shepards are very familiar with bestiality (*Leviticus 20:15, 16, 25*). In the United States until recent times on paper bestiality was a crime against nature. The act of having sex with sheep and goats were especially noted since these two animals can easily be made pregnant by a man and give birth to an offspring (Tubal / תבל)! The male animal can make a woman pregnant with a resulting birth also (Tubal).

Thus the word Tubal (תֵבֵל) denotes not only Bestiality, but also impregnation and birth from bestiality. If these words exist someone must be doing it! The third story of the arc of Noah must have been full of hybrid beings who were the results of bestiality (*Gen. 7:2*).

In modern times the World (TBL) have been doing experiments to see if sheep and cows can carry fertilized human eggs to a full term birth. Also experiment have been done where the wombs of sheep, goats, cattle and many kinds of animals have been used to "store" and preserve human eggs. The obvious purpose for bestiality (TBL) from primitive times to the modern times have been to preserve the World or Tubal (TBL) of the Lord, and the Human Race at all cost. To cause someone to be corrupt enough to casually perform acts of bestiality is an act of betrayal.

Observations

# World Elements
# Betrayal

*Bestiality— Jeremiah ("He (Lord) Shall Betray") — Cross*

Even though the Children of Cain performed Bestiality (TBL), at the commandment of the Lord, the Lord would betray them. The word "Jeremiah" (ירמיה) literally means "The Lord Shall Betray You." *See Strong's # 7411(Rama), and # 7423(Ramyah).* The Lord's betrayal is not deception, for those who are betrayed already know the nature of the Lord.

Noah, Shem, Japheth, Abraham, Isaac, Jacob, the Israeli Rabbis, Moses, Joshua, and the entire Judeo/Christian World leadership, knew and still know that Hallel the Lord of Abraham is El Shaddai, (אל שדי) or the Devil God, a Jeremiah (Betrayer Jah)!

All who are in service to the Lord. know that they shall be personally betrayed by the Lord, before they pass away. They have scripture that proves this: The Lord betrayed many of **Cain's Pale Leper children** and allowed them to drown in the flood (*Gen. 7:21, 22*). **Noah** sacrificed all cleanness, and preserved filth for the Lord, but when he failed to Sanctify (Sodomize) Canaan to make him Holy, the Lord betrayed Noah, and left him to to die alone on Mt. Ararat (*Gen. 8:20, 9:28, 29*).

After the flood the Lord betrayed the pale leper children of his son Cain again, by confounding their city Ur/Babel (*Gen. 11:9*). Years later Abram brought the Lord down from Nod, to Sodom and Gomorrah in the land of Canaan. A remnant of Cain's children from Ur/Babel had survived there. The Lord removed the incestuous homosexual Lot (*Gen. 19:30-36*), and his corrupt family, and then destroyed Sodom and Gomorrah *(Gen. 19:24)*.

The Lord betrayed the **Egyptians** who saved the Israelis from his famine in the land of Canaan (*Deut. 26:5*). The Egyptians had sent wagons to bring Jacob and his little band from the Lord's famine in the land of Canaan. The Egyptians allowed Israel to live on the very best land in their country, for four hundred years. Then the Lord came and destroyed Egypt in an act of betrayal.

The Lord then betrayed all of the **Egyptian Israelis** in the wilderness. He had forced them to come out of Egypt, and then took revenge on them by causing them to wander around in the wilderness, for forty year until they and all of their children had died. This was betrayal. Only the pale leper children of the Lord and his Host with the Israeli females left the wilderness.

The Lord betrayed his promise to Abraham, that Abraham's children Ishmael/Midian would inherit Canaan. The Lord took the pale leper Israelis to the East Country to murder Abraham's children, Ishmael/Midian (*Numbers 31th Chptr*). Afterwards the Lord betrayed **Moses** the Israeli leader. The Lord murdered Moses on Mt. Nebo, while he was still in good health (*Deut. 34:5, 7*). The Lord was betraying Moses, as a final reward, for the atrocities he helped the Lord commit against the children of Abraham.

The Lord betray all of his servants as a matter of course of business. This was from one individual, to the entire population on his planet Crypton. The Lord and his Host betrayed the population of Crypton by destroying them along with his planet, in his pending defeat (*Rev. 12:8*). Just as the Lord betrayed or crossed those who served him in the ancient times, he betray or cross those who serve him in the modern times. All who wear the cross thinking that they are being protected, are being deceived. But all of those who know that the cross represents betrayal, shall eventually be crossed by the Lord, themselves.

Notes

# World Elements
# Cross (Noun/Verb)

*Betrayal — Crossing (Betrayal) — Unkindness — Crossovers (Defections) — Infiltration — The cross is the salvation of the World (Not Yeshua) — Bless*

As a verb " to cross" can be an act of betrayal, or deception. As a noun a cross is a physical object that defines it's self by it's shape. A cross as the Romans used it has no redeeming value at all, and is a most repulsive device. The Romans used the cross to exact the greatest pain and torture. The purpose of the cross and the act of crucifixion, was also designed to strike fear and dread in the hearts of the people, where the crucifixion was taking place. The Pale Leper Gentile children of Cain murdered innocent Nimrod on a cross two thousand years before the birth of Yeshua (Jesus)(*Isaiah 53rd Chptr*). The descendants of these same Gentiles as Romans murdered Yeshua (Jesus) on a crucifix (Cross) also. The purpose of the cross was the same in both cases. Jesus the one who was impelled on the cross was tortured to the point, that he defecated on himself. The blood and gore pouring from his wounds drew flies. The people of his community, and his family were forced to watch this lynching, and were struck with fear and terrorized.

The torture and murder of Jesus was was never a Good Friday for any one on the planet, except those ancient Roman clansmen who lynched him.

Many walk about wearing crosses around their necks. Those who wear crosses have been taught in church that the cross represent the sacrifice that Jesus (Yeshua) made for them. They are told the lie that Yeshua (Jesus) had been born to die, on the cross for their sins. As such on some level in the minds of some who wear this instrument, it becomes an amulet, or talisman, to protect one from evil and misfortune. The irony is that those who program the masses to wear the cross are the source of the Evil, and misfortune that the cross wearer is trying to avoid.

To "be cross" is to be unkind, to "be crossed" is to be betrayed. To "cross another" is to betray them. To "cross over" in many circumstances is to desert the one side to become a part of the other side. But in some cases to cross over is an act of infiltration for the purpose of undermining and or corrupting, as when Abram and the Lord crossed (Hebrewed) over the Tigris, down into the land of the children of Ham. Ham "crossed" over (Hebrewed) from Nod/Ararat back to the Garden westward to remove his family from the Lord's corruption in Nod/Ararat. The Chaldeans or Caucasians (Gentiles) fled Ur/Babel in Nod, when the Lord and his Host confounded their city (*Gen. 11:7*). They **"crossed"** the Tigris River as Ham had done, to get away from the Lord. Hundreds of years later Abram and the Lord himself left Nod to **cross** (hebrew) the Tigris into the Garden. Ham **crossed** the Tigris to escape corruption in Nod. The Caucasian/Chaldean children of Cain **crossed** to escape the Corrupting Lord of the North also. But when Abram and the Lord **crossed** the Tigris it was to **infiltrate** the Garden.

The church system teach that the crossing/crucifixion (betrayal) of Jesus on a Friday was a Good Friday. Jesus a wooly headed brown man (*Rev. 1:14*), being crucified by a pale mob is a lynching. The Romans, and Rabbis crossed Jesus, for the Lord, to stop him from teaching the Israelis free from the Lord. They killed Yeshua (Jesus), and set up a religion to celebrate his death, not because they loved him, but because they hated him (). Millions think that to be blessed (Bara/ברך) is a good thing, but being blessed is the end of all self respect.

Observations

# World Elements
# Bless

*Cross — Domesticate (Break/ברך) #1288 — Beat down, Castrate, Tame — Famine*

To be blessed (ברך) is to be crossed or betrayed. The western World system has made it's masses think, that being blessed is opposite to being cursed. But to be blessed (ברך) is to be cursed (ארד), and to be cursed is to be blessed (*Gen. 12:2*)! This misunderstanding originate with the statement made by the Lord to Abraham: "I shall bless those who bless you, and curse those who curse you (*Gen. 12:3*)." Blessed and cursed are the same thing from two directions.

The word Bless is the translation of the old word **Barak** (ברך), which was brought phonetically into the English language as the word "**break**" or "**broke**." This is in the sense of "breaking" or "domesticating." a horse, or house pet  For a man or woman to be blessed (Broken / ברך), is for that person to have been treated very badly, in such a way that they have absolutely lost any self respect. This is the "battered wife syndrome." There is no goodness in being broken (blessed / ברך).

Enslavement is the closest description of being blessed. A Man who is in his right mind would fight to the death to defend his wife and child. The same man having been successfully "blessed," or "broken" will in this mentally enslaved condition hurt his wife and child, if commanded to do so by his enslaver. Thus it was the case when the Lord commanded Abraham to send Hagar and and his son Ishmael, off to die, in the wilderness with a piece of bread and a bottle of water (*Gen. 21:14*). Abraham was truly blessed (cursed), to send his child and the child's mother to their death!

The Lord blessed (cursed) Cain and his children, with pale leprosy, and imposed much corruption upon them, long before the birth of Abraham. This was the conditions that the Gentiles lived under, with the Lord in the Land of Nod, on Mt. Ararat and it's plains. The Israelis lived under a blessed (cursed) conditions in the Land of Canaan with the Lord (*Nu. 6:23, 24*).  It was the Lord of the North Abraham's Lord, who imposed "blessing" on both the Israelis and the other Gentiles. The Israelis under Jacob finally had to flee from the Lord, and his blessing (curse) of famine, in the land of Canaan (*Deut. 26:5*).  The Chaldean children of Cain had fled from the blessing (cursing) of the Lord, who confounded their city Ur in the north of the land of Nod. This was hundreds of years before the time of Abram. Cain's Gentile children had fled down into the land of Canaan before the Lord had arrived there with Abraham, to bless (curse) the land with famine (*Gen. 12:10*). Abram and the Lord went down into Egypt, and the Lord eventually blessed (cursed) the Pharoah's house with a plague of diseases (*Gen. 12:17*).

When Jesus used the term "blessed" it was a different term #3107 Greek, Μεκαρ, which means "fortunate." Yet this term is over ridden by the fact that the ones described by Jesus are "fortunate" (blessed / Μεκαρ) to have escaped from the "blessing (curse)," of the Lord of Abraham.

In modern times these two groups the Jewish and other Gentiles have exported the corrupt living condition called "blessing" around the entire planet. They have imposed it on the very ones who gave them the options to be set free from the Lord, who "blessed," or enslaved them. Land can also be blessed. When land is blessed, it is called a famine.

Notes

# World Elements (Things) Famine

*Bless — Famine — Jealousy*

Blessed (Barak / ברך) land is land that is famished (רעב). Famine is a condition where all mineral, animal, and vegetable life is greatly depleted. Famine (#7458 / רעב) is pronounced "Rob," in the original language. The word Rob (רעב) in the old language means "to hunger." In famine the ground is "in hunger," is "robbed," or "famished."

Nod was a land in perpetual famine (cursed), because the Lord's presence there drained away all life (*Gen. 3:17*). The Lord stated that Life is in the blood (fluid) of plants, animals, and people (*Lev. 17:11*). The Lord needed all of the life he could get, so that he could stay associated with the physical realm. The Lord's body had been slain, by the Lord God Melchezedek, in the Tribunal (*Dan. 7:11; Ezek. 28:18*). Stripped of his body, the Lord wanted to touch the Tree of Life and live again forever (*Gen. 3:22*), but the Lord God cast the disembodied Lord out of the Garden, back into Nod, where he had been taken from (*Gen. 23:24*). Michael/Melchezedek had said that the ground would be cursed, for the Lord's sake, anywhere that the Lord went (*Gen. 3:17*).

The entire land of Nod was a dead lunar landscape. Any place that the Lord went became cursed (famished) for his sake, or because he was there (*Gen. 3:17*). The first famine in the land of Ham ever, came when Abram and the Lord hebrewed the Tigris River. The Lord brought his famine with him, from Nod down into the Garden (*Gen. 12:10, Gen. 26:1*).

The Lord could also cause famines to occur, by his own will (*II Kings 8:1, Psalms 105:16, Isa. 14:30*). As such the Lord (Satan) became angry at David, for not properly counting the Israeli population, as he the Lord (Satan) had commanded (*I Chron. 21:1, II Samuel 24:1*). One of the Lord's choices of punishment, to David was for Israel to suffer three to seven years of famine (*I Chron. 21:12, II Sam. 24:13*).

Before this famine against the Israelis, the Lord had caused a seven year famine in Egypt (*Gen. 41:27*). Egypt had produced corn and other grain for it's self, and for others including Jacob's tribe in the land of Canaan (*Gen. 41:57, 42:1*). Egypt had once produced an abundance of food, but the Lord brought famine to Egypt. When Egypt recovered from the Lord's famine, the land was so poor that the Egyptians had to water their sparse crops with water running down the tip of their big toes (*Deut. 11:10*).

The famine was wherever the Lord was, and when the the Lord left the famine went with him! The Lord and his famine went from Nod, to Canaan, and from Canaan to Egypt, and from Egypt back to Canaan. Then the famine ceased everywhere, because the Lord went into hibernation in Mt. Horeb for the four hundred years, that Israel stayed in Egypt. The Lord is the source of all of the famines that ever occurred as written in the Bible (*Gen. 12:10, 26:1, Gen. 41:27, 30, 31, 36, 50, 56,57 etc.*). The Lord was also the source of all of his diseases, and plagues that he had carried about from Nod to Canaan, and then to Egypt. After Four hundred years the Lord would awake and bring his diseases and plagues back down into Egypt again (*Ex. 15:26, Deut. 7:15; 2Kings 8:1, 1Chron. 21:12, Ps. 105:16, Amos 8:11, Zephoniah 2:11, Deut. 32:8, 9*) The Lord's famines are states of lacking and incompleteness, which is why the Lord was Jealous (קין).

Observations

# World Elements (Things) Jealousy (Evil)

*Famine — Lack — Jealousy — Service/Bondage — Prostitution*

In famine there is lacking, and in lacking there is jealousy (Cain / קין). The Lord of Abraham is a Jealous God. There is no good quality in jealousy, nor can there be any good quality, in any form of jealousy. The Lord is the Gardener, or Serpent in the Garden that beguiled Eve and "got" (קין) Cain with her (*Gen. 3:1, 1 Chron. 1:1*). Jealous (קין) in the old language is pronounced "Cain," which means to be "Possessive," and "Incomplete."

These shortcomings were characteristics of Cain. The source of all these short comings in Cain were from Cain's father, the Cain or Jealous God (*Ex. 20:5*). The cause of the jealousy in the Lord was that he had lost his soul (solar association). He and his Host had been defeated in the solar war (*Rev. 12:8*), and had been casted down in Chains of Darkness (*2Peter 2:4*). Michael/Melchezedek the Ancient of Days then tried the Lord, and found this Great Beast guilty, and sentenced him to have his body slain, and to be cast into the flames (*Daniel 7:11*). Michael brought a flame from the Lord's midst to consume him (*Ezekiel 28:18*). The Lord's form was brought to ashes before the millions, who had come to see him executed (*Dan. 7:10; Ezekiel 28:18*).

Thus having no body in which to be a solar entity, the Lord declared that his name would be Jealousy (*Ex.34:14*). The Lord's jealousy implies insatiable need, and the sensation of never being satisfied. Jealousy as a nature can not be made an honorable trait in any Man or any God. Jealousy is a sign of low self esteem, and Self hatred. Those who bow down to please the jealous entity can never please this one, who has no Self esteem or Self love. The jealousy state is a hole that can never be filled, by any amount of worship, bowing down, sacrifice, or praise. Yet the Lord in his jealousy, demanded that all who served him, bow down, worship and praise him.

Any one who is complete have self esteem, and self love, and can not be jealous, nor are they in need of worship, bowing down, sacrifice, or praise, for they are sufficient to themselves. Those who are in the house of God (body) keep their feet, and do not bow down, sacrifice, or praise, it is all foolishness (*Eccles. 5:1*).

The sufficient man, or God is in "service" to his children to "praise" them, to "sacrifice" for them, and he will "bow down" to their level, to bring them up to his level. Jesus bowed down, to wash the feet of those who followed him (*John 13:5*).

For a Jealous God to survive he needs what a child requires to survive! The jealous one enslaves his own people (his children), and force them, to "bow down" to whatever level is needed to sustain him! Once he have them prostrate he never allow them to rise again.

In trying times a parent will do almost anything to preserve their next generation, their children. In reverse the Jealous God always have trying times and require that his worshippers do anything to preserve him, by whatever means necessary. As a mother may become a prostitute to obtain food for her child to sustain it, a jealous God is capable of prostituting those who bow to him, that he be sustained by their prostitution. Abraham and Sarah worked along with the Lord to commit prostitution in Egypt.

Notes

# World Elements
# Prostitution

*Jealousy —Sarah/Iscah (Sister/Wife/Niece/Prostitute) — Dinah — Tamar — Rahab (Israeli National Heroine)* **Deut. 23:17**— *Prostitution fills in when other talents (Intelligence) for survival cease — Rape*

Out of his Jealousy the Lord made prostitutes of those who serve him. The core of prostitution is to **prostrate** one's self to give sexual favor, or other service for a promise of reward. Prostitution (חלל) #2486-90 is the act of Corrupting, or Profaning (חלל). Prostitution is a major element in the origin of the Israeli Tribes. The people from which the Israelis truly originated were **prostitutes,** and **whores, or "mountaineers."** These people are called Gentiles, and they originally lived north of Mesopotamia, on mount Ararat, and on it's plains southward down to the Tigris River. The Gentiles there **prostituted** or **prostrated** themselves before the Lord of the Mound of Ararat in Nod. All of the males and female Gentiles there in Nod prostrated upon their faces before the Lord. They were the Lord's Whores, or Horites, or Mountaineers

The Gentiles or Chaldeans are the children of Cain. Nimrod built Ur/Babel for these pale ones to raise them, from the conditions that the Lord of the mound had caused them to fall. Ur is the Babel that the Lord confounded and sent the Caucasians fleeing down across the Tigris into the land of Ham (*Gen. 11:9*). The children of Ham in the Garden subdued them, and rounded them up into the twin grain cities, of Sodom and Gomorrah. These male and female prostitutes (*Deut. 23:17*), were quarantine in Sodom and Gomorrah, to insulate the people of the land from these corrupt ones from the Land of Nod/Chaldea.

Abram's nativity four hundred years later, was Ur of the Chaldeans where these Sodomites had fled from (*Gen. 11:28*). The Lord brought Abram his sister/wife/niece Sarah/Iscah, and Lot down the same route the first male and female prostitutes from Ur, had fled to come to Sodom.

Abram and Sarah were destitute when they entered the Land of Ham. All that they had brought with them from the north was the famine of the Lord, which consumed the Land of Canaan. They left Canaan to go to Egypt, where they **prostituted** Sarah/Iscah for very much wealth, in herds, gold, silver, and enslaved people (*Gen. 12:16*).

Leaving Egypt they returned to the Land of Canaan, where they prostituted Sarah, to Abimeleck, and extorted him for as much as they had gotten from the Pharaoh (*Gen. 20:2, 14*)!

Dinah the daughter of Jacob played the whore with Shechem the Prince of Salem (*Gen. 34:2, 3*). The Judeans as a tribe came into existence, from an act of prostitution between Judah and his daughter-in-law Tamar, a Canaanite/Hamite woman (*Gen. 38:15-17; 26-30*). Rahab a Canaanite prostitute is an Israeli and Gentile heroine because she betrayed the people of her Canaanite city, to help the Israelis (*Joshua 2:1, Joshua 6:17*). This woman Rahab and her family sacrificed their city, to preserve the corrupt Israelis (*Joshua 2:1-3; 17- 25*). Hosea was commanded by the Lord to marry a whore (Prostitute), with children from her trade (*Hosea 1:2*). How can the Lord say no prostitution when prostitution is a major element in the very existence of his people?

Beyond prostitution was the "taking" of girls and women of the city of Shechem. Rape was the prime methods that the Israelis used to come into existence.

Observations

# World Elements
# Rape

*Prostitution — Rape Tribes (Israel): Shechem, Ishmael/Midian, Canaan — Sacrifice*

In the land of Nod and in their youth the Lord and his Host made Cain's daughters the young Chaldean (Gentile) girls prostitutes, after taking their virginity by raping them (*Gen. 6:4, Isaiah 47:1-8*). Rape (חזק) #2388 is the act of forced sexual penetration of a girl, woman or anyone else against their will. No self respecting man would rape a woman, little girl, or little boy.

The Lord forced Cain to be Abel's husband, because Effeminate Abel desired him (*Gen. 4:7*). But Cain was killed by his descendant Lamech, because Cain took part, when a young man raped (חברתי) Lamech (*Gen. 4:23, 24*).

The Lord told Cain's little Chaldean girls to sat in the dirt, and to expose their vaginas, so that he could see their nakedness. The Lord told them that he was going to take his vengeance on them, as as a man does with a woman. The Lord made them consume his mandrake (Man of Darkness) fruit, to get them into his Darkness, same as Eve had consumed to get into the Lord's Darkness (*Gen. 3:3, 4; Isa. 47:5*). The Lord then told them that he was going to pollute (rape) them, and that they would no longer be ladies, but for them to take it to heart that, they would not remember what he did to them, except they would have pleasure (*Isa. 47:1-7*)

If a man lie with a woman without her consent, and penetrates her, he has committed rape. Abraham committed rape on Hagar (Shari Mizraim), and became the father of Ishmael (*Gen. 16:3, 4*). Jacob committed rape on Bilhah, and Zilpah, and impregnated them with six of his twelve sons. These twelve sons in their turn raped themselves into tribal existence with the girls and women of the murdered city of Salem/Shechem in the land of Canaan. Shechem did not "defile" or rape Dinah, for she prostituted herself. But Dinah's brothers did commit rape, after they murdered all the males of Shechem (*Gen. 34:25*). They took all of the girls and women of Shechem and used these females to rape themselves into tribal existence (*Gen. 34:29*)!

After the exodus from Egypt the Lord commanded that the young firstborn Israeli males be sanctified (rape/sodomized)(*Ex. 13:2*). The young female Israelis did not want the Lord and his Host to rape them to get the pale lepers, who came forth from the wilderness (*Lev. 13th Chptr*).

The pale fruit of this raping, in the wilderness were taken to the east country, to rape the little "Women Children" of Ishmael/Midian the "Children of Abraham (*Nu. 31:18*)." As such the "Children of Israel" raped themselves into being the "Seed of Abraham." (*Numbers 31:9, 18*). The Lord,s portion was thirty two little girl women (souls) (*Numbers 31:40*). The Levite priest got fifty of these little girls to rape (*Num. 31:47*). The Lord and his Host would rape these little Ishmael/Midianite girl children, as he and his Host had raped the young Cainite/Chaldean girls in the Darkness of the north in the land of Nod (*Isaiah 47:1- 6*). And as the Lord had raped the daughters of Zion (*Isa. 3:17*). The Israelis would complete a circuit, that began in the Land of Canaan, by returning there. There in the land of Canaan, they raped the girls and women of Canaan again (*Deut. 21:11, 13*).

The Lord of Abraham was with them throughout this entire circuit, defending Israel from any possible harm and commanding them through Moses to do their raping. In all cases the Lord and the Israelis had preserve the filth of their own World (TBL) existence, by sacrifice of the innocent and clean.

# World Elements
# Sacrifice

*Rape — Preserve the World — Pouring Blood into the Ground — Good Friday — Sodomy*

Noah's sacrificed all that was clean, when he attempt to rape his own grand son Canaan. Sacrifice (Zebah / זבח) is the act of "Killing, to offer up a victim to the Lord." The killing may not only be a physical act, but may also be mental. Jesus (Yeshua) warned: "Fear not them who can only kill the body, but fear him (Lord) who is able to kill both body and soul (*Matt. 10:28*). The Lord had already taken Noah's soul, but Noah still had to get drunk to attempt to sacrifice Canaan, by sodomizing him (*Gen.9:21*). This was the same sacrifice that the Lord had commanded Cain to do, to his effeminate (האבל) brother Abel (האבל)(*Gen. 4:7*). Jesus said that Abel had been clean or righteous, before the Lord sacrificed him (*Matt. 23:25*).

To sacrifice only all that is clean, is also to preserve all that is filth (*Gen. 8:20*). Noah did that when he sacrificed all that was clean, including animals to the Lord, and continued to preserve the unclean. Christianity from it's very beginning embraced this theme of sacrificing the clean to preserve the filth, when they murdered Jesus (The Clean), to save their Lord's World.

Sacrifice can not be justified, for it is the act of murdering, or corrupting the innocent to preserve the corrupt. The Lord commanded sacrifice from all that served him from Cain through the Israelis, down to the present time. What is sacrifice and what is it's basic purpose?

The Lord of Abraham instructed the Israelis that the life of the sacrifice is in the blood (*Gen. 9:4, Lev. 17:13*). He told them therefore not to eat the flesh with the blood in it. They were to first pour the blood into the ground (where the Lord is)(*Deut. 15:23*). Cursively he was telling them that he wanted, and perhaps needed the life in the blood, to sustain himself. There can be no other purpose for shedding blood and pouring it into the ground, where the Lord is (*Ex. 8:22*).

With the Roman soldiers having just murdered (sacrificed) Jesus imagine them standing beneath Jesus' crucified corpse with his blood dripping down upon them. They recite a series of phrases that are very familiar in these modern time: "washed in the blood of Jesus,"..."by his shed blood are we saved," .... "he died that we may live," .... "he died to save our World," etc.

These are all phrases uttered by members of the church system that says it love Jesus. Add to this that the Romans are pale, and that Jesus as the Son of Man is wooly headed brown Man, with feet (and body) like burnt brass (*Rev. 1:14*). A Black Man tortured and murdered by Caucasians

No one has ever been born to be lynched! The Friday that Jesus was murdered, was not a Good Friday for himself, his family, or his community. It was a good Friday for the ancient Roman clansmen who lynched him. It was also a good Friday for their World, that saved itself by murdering him!. All sacrifice is a sacrificing of the innocent, and clean for the preservation of the corrupt and unclean. There is no other explanation for any kind of sacrifice. All sacrificing is to or for the preservation of the Lord, and his World. To remove the last essence of life blood from the flesh the Israelis were instructed to cut up the flesh, and set it on fire, to burn the last life out of the flesh. Thus for the Life/Blood to be absent from the body, was for it to be with the Lord (*IICor. 5:6*). The life from the blood of the sacrifice was the preservation, of the Being of the Lord.

This would include Jesus' blood, and the blood of millions of others who have been sacrificed. Another form of sacrifice commanded by the Lord to preserve his World is Sodomy.

# World Elements
# Sodomy

*Sacrifice — Abel (Effeminate) — Three Tubals — Cain's Holy People — Incest*

The sacrifice that the Lord demanded from Cain and Abel was not so much the sacrifice of grain or flesh on an altar, but was the sacrifice of flesh through sodomy (*Gen. 4:7*). The word Sodom comes from the Canaanite city, that was not associated with sex at all, just grain. But the Lord in effect pushed Cain's offer of grain off the altar. The sacrifice that the Lord wanted on the altar was Abel's flesh, meaning for Cain to be the husband or keeper of his effeminate brother Abel (הבל)(*Gen.4:7, 9*). Abel (הבל) means "effeminate," and implies that the Lord wanted Cain to commit sodomy on his brother. The meaning of the base of the word Abel (הבל) is the word Bal (בל) which is the base for the word "World" (Tubal / תבל), which literally means "Thou Degeneracy." The three descendants of Cain who survived the flood were Ju**bal** Cain, Ja**bal** Cain, and Tu**bal** Cain. All three were "**Bals**," Cain's of the World (TBL) of the Lord.

Grain was pushed aside, in the grain city of Sodom, as the Lord had pushed aside Cain's grain (*Gen. 4:5*). Then Sodom became an altar, to sacrifice flesh to the Lord, like Abel did (*Gen. 4:4*).

Sodomy (Kedesh/Shekav) as defined in the modern dictionary is the act of penetrating the anus with a penus. The one being sodomized may be a male or female. In the ancient language of the Bible /Torah, there are two basic words for the act of sodomy. The first word for sodomy "Shekav" (שכב) is secular or non religious. This word is concealed under the word "lying" (reclining) in the book of Numbers, at *Numbers 31:17, 18, 35,* This scripture pertains to the Israeli males sodomizing (שכב) young Midianite girls. The Israelis murdered all of the men, women and boys of Ishmael/Midian. They had kept the little pubelescent Midianite girls for themselves. The scripture says: "..those who have not known man by being sodomisized (שכב)(*Nu. 31:17*). The Israeli males had sodomized many of the little girls of Ishmael/Midian (*Num. 30:16, 17*). The Israeli males were commanded to murder all of the little girls they had sodomized (שכב).

The other form of sodomy is religious, and is pronounced Kedesh (קדש). Kedesh means to be "prostrate"(Prostitute) before the Lord. Kedesh is the Old Language word under the Englisized word "Holy." Therefore in the true term to be Holy is to be religiously sodomized. *See Strong's Concordance #6944 (Holy), and #6945 (Sodomy)*. To be Holy/Sanctified (religiously sodomized) was a commandment to the Israelis from the Lord their God (*Lev. 20:6, 7, 8, 9*).

This shows that the Lord and his Host did not murder the Sodomites because they were homosexuals. Also the Israelis had a Sodomite city on the same plains, where Sodom and Gomorrah had been. That city was called Kedesh (Sodomy), a "Holy City," like Sodom and Gomorrah (*Genesis 14:7*). The purpose of the Lord making the Israelis Holy was because the Lord himself was Holy. The Lord had made Cain's Caucasian children Sodomites in Ur, before they ever came down into the land of Ham to dwell in the old grain cities of Sodom and Gomorrah.

When the Lord told the Israelis that he would no longer tolerate a Sodomite (קדש) or Prostitute (קדשה), in Israel (*Deut. 23:17*) it was simply a ploy of the Bible/Torah writers to carry the readers of the book away from the fact that sodomy (קדש) and prostitution (קדשה) is the core of the Holiness (קדש) that the Lord command religiously from Judeo/Christianity. Holy (חולי) also include all World Elements including incest and adultery.

Notes

# World Elements
# Incest

*Sodomy — Keep it in the Family — Lot Did Not Know? — Adultery*

The act of sodomy between Cain and Abel (*Gen. 4:7*), and between Cain and Lamech (*Gen. 4:23*), is also incest under the definition for incest, because it is defined as "a sexual act between close relatives." The word incest does not appear in the Bible/Torah, even though incest was rampant among the Israelis, and those they descended from, in the land of Nod. The term "**uncover nakedness of close relatives** (*Lev. 18:6 - 18*)" is the same as saying committing "incest" with close relatives.

**Terah** said "**Haran's Widow** is my daughter-in-law", and **Haran's widow** said "**Terah** is my father-in-law." They had **Milcah** and **Sarah** (Iscah) together! *Terah (Abram's father), and his son Haran's widow (Gen. 11:29; Lev. 18:15)(Terah's dead son Haran's wife).*

**Abraham** said "**Sarah** is my sister", and **Sarah/Iscah** said "**Abraham** is my brother" (*Gen. 20:5*). *Sarah was Abraham's sister/wife/niece, they had sex together (Lev. 18:9)(Abram's sister/ niece).*

**Milcah** said "**Nahor** is my brother," and **Nahor** said "**Milcah** is my sister." They had three children together! *Milcah and her brother Nahor (Gen. 11:29, Gen. 22:21)(Lev. 18:9)(Nahor's sister).*

**Kemuel** said "**Milcah** is my mother", and **Milcah** said "**Kemuel** is my son". They had five children together! *Milcah and her son Kemuel (Gen. 22:21-22)(Lev. 18:7, 8)(his father's wife, his mother).*

**Lot**, his **sons, son's in law**, said "**Sodomites** are our close kin, from the north, in Ur," and the **Sodomites** said Lot is our brother, from the remnants of our descendants, that stayed north in Ur (*Lev. 18:22*)(*Lot, his son, and sons-in-law were all Sodomites*).

**Lot** said "These are my two daughters," and they said "Lot is our father." Each of his daughters had a son by him. (**Ammon and Moab**) *Lot and his two daughters (Gen. 19:32-38)(Lev. 18:7).*

**Isaac** said **Rebecca** is my first cousin, and **Rebecca** said **Isaac** is my first cousin. They were married and had sex (*Gen. 25:20*)(*Lev. 18:17*)(*Isaac's near kinswoman*).

**Jacob** said **Leah** and **Rachael** are my first cousins, and **Leah** and **Rachael** said **Jacob** is our first cousin. *Jacob was married to and had sex with both and had children with Leah (Gen. 30:17-21)*

**Amram** said: "**Jochebed** is my aunt", and **Jochebed** said "**Amram** is my nephew". They are the parents of Miriam, Aaron, and Moses! *Amram and Jochebed (Ex. 6:20)(Lev. 18:12)(Amram's aunt)*

Imagine Moses congregating the Israelis in the wilderness to tell them that they can no longer have sex with their close relatives. Incest and Adultery were two of the main methods used to bring the Israelis into existence!

Observations

# World Elements
# Adultery

*Incest — Adultery (נאף אף) #5003 Corrupting (מהל) #4107, Mixing (ערב) #6151-6 — Flood*

The Israelis as with the other Gentiles went from incest, to adultery/rape. Adultery is to adulterate. The old language word for adultery (Mahal / מהל) Strong's #4107 means "To Mix" or "To Pollute." As such adultery is the act of "mixing "or "corrupting," between two different kinds of people, or beings.

Forced into isolation in Nod the Lord mutated (Marked) his originally wooly brown son Cain, with permanent pale leprosy (*Gen. 4:15*). Not only would the descendants of Cain be pale, but the Lord would make them as corrupt as he could possibly make them. Then the Lord wanted to eventually subplant the wooly brown people of the Garden, with the Cain Mutainy. There would eventually be adultery between the pale leper children of Marked Cain in Nod, and the wooly headed brown descendants of Adam, in the Garden. The Lord would do his best to adulterate, as many Blacks into pale lepers, as he could, starting with the Blacks in the Garden.

First the Lord married Cain to his effeminate twin brother Abel (*Gen. 4:7*). Cain killed him (*Gen. 4:8*). Next the Lord married Cain to one of his Liliths, or female Host (*Gen. 4:17*). They had sons and daughters, who carried the genetic pale leprosy that had been put permanently in the genetics of Cain (*Gen. 4:15*). Cain's sons from the Lilah that he married, married the Lord's Liliths, or Female Hosts. The first son of Cain was Enoch (*Gen. 4:17*), then Irad, Mehujael, Methuselah, and Lamech. They all married the females of the Lord's Hosts (*Gen. 4:17-19*). All of Cain's daughters married the Lord's Lilim or Male Hosts (*Gen. 6:2*).

These "marriages" were not marriages in the sense of one man to one woman, but was endless mixing between couples, both male and female, and male with male, and female with female. It was a corrupt adulterous soup.

Children had sex with their parents (*Lev. 18:9*). Sisters and brothers had sex together (*Lev. 18:9, 11*). Grandparents were having sex with their grandchildren (*Lev. 18:10*). Aunts and uncles had sex with their nephews, and nieces (*Lev. 18:12-14*). Mothers and fathers were having sex with their son's and daughter's mates (*Lev. 18:15*).

The Lord made the adultery worst when he raped the little pale (fair) Chaldean daughters of his son Cain in Nod (*Isa. 47:1, 3*). In an attempt to eventually break out of Nod, the Lord sent these corrupted little girls wading across the Tigris, with their vaginas exposed (*Isa. 47:2*), down into the Garden to commit adultery, with the wooly headed inhabitants there. Noah and his two younger sons Shem and Japheth, may have been involved with these little girls, and became servants, of the Lord of the North because of them.

Ham the elder son of Noah never participated in any of this adultery, before or after the flood. The Lord had corrupted all of the pale lepers in Nod, causing them to perform all kinds of corrupt acts. Some of these acts were: **incest, child molestation, and sodomy**. Now through adultery orchestrated by the Lord, between Noah and the girls from Nod, these corruptions and more survived and spread down through the line of Shem (and Japheth) through Terah, And his three sons, Haran, Nahor, and Abraham. Haran fathered Lot by committing Adultery by marrying and impregnating one of the pale (fair) leper women of the line of Cain.

Before Haran even passed away his father Terah committed Adultery, and incest with his pale

Notes

# World Elements
# Adultery

*Incest — Mixing two kinds into one — Adultery Tribes — Adulterous Seed — Flood*

(fair) daughter in law (*Gen. 11:28, 29*). Abraham, and Lot made "very fair" (pale) Sarah commit adultery in Egypt (*Gen. 12:11*). Sarah's first adultery was prostitution with the sons of the Pharaoh. They penetrated (commended / חלל) her in front of Pharaoh (*Gen.12:15*). Then she was taken into pharaohs house as a prostitute (*Gen. 12:15*). Abraham was paid very well for her services (*Gen. 12:16*). Abraham also committed adultery, when he raped Hagar and impregnated her with a son Ishmael (*Gen. 16:3*).

This goes to show that there can also be adultery if both groups are wooly and brown. Abraham was wooly and brown, the Egyptians were wooly and brown, and the Israelis were wooly and brown, like all of the peaceable children of Adam. But Abraham, Jacob (Israel), and the twelve were not peaceable, but had the nature and mentality, of the pale leper children of Cain. The Israelis murdered all of the boys and men of Shechem, and then committed adultery against the girls and women of that peaceable Canaanite city. Israel used them to rape themselves into tribal existence (*Gen. 34:26-29*). The offspring of this violence and rape were the continuation of Israel, who would commit adultery again, by raping other Canaanite girls and women, including Tamar (*Gen. 38:2-11*). Judah himself committed incest, adultery, and prostitution with Tamar his Canaanite "daughter in law." Jacob impregnated this Canaanite girl and she became the prostitute mother of all Judeans (*Gen. 38:15-30*).

The Lord's World (TBL) was saved, because all of those under his influence committed adultery. From Cain to Noah to Jacob (Israel), the Lord made his way out of Nod, down into the land of Ham, who would not commit adultery, or serve the Lord.

Not only did the Israeli males commit adultery, the Israeli female committed adultery too, as Sarah and Dinah had! The adultery continued down into Egypt again, where this time many of the young Israeli girls and women made their living by being prostitutes, or whores for the young Egyptians, who ejaculated like horses (*Ezek. 23:3, 20*). The Israeli girls and women also committed adultery, with the wooly headed Assyrians, and had their breasts bruised by them (*Ezek. 23:5*). The Israelis females even became whores for, and mixed (Adulterated) back with the Heathens (Gentiles / Goyims), the pale leper children of Cain, who cheated them and left them naked (*Ezek. 23:29, 30*)!

The Israelis came out of the wilderness, and committed the ultimate acts of adultery, when they kept over thirty two thousand of the little Ishmael/Midianite girls, to rape themselves into being the "Seed of Abraham" (*Num. 31:17, 35*).

The Lord got thirty two of the little girls, to do with as he pleased (*Lev. 31:40*), and the Levitican priesthood got fifty of the little girls also, to do with as they please (*Lev. 31:47*). Full circuit the Israelis came back to the land of Canaan, and after murdering all of the boys and men, they again committed adultery rape with the little Canaanite girls, that they had kept alive (*Deut. 21:11-14*).

The Lord had failed in his attempt to adulterate the inhabitants of the Garden into pale lepers, so in the end he had the Israelis to commit holocaust against them, to take their place. If the pale lepers Gentiles of Nod had been destroyed in the flood there would not have been anyone around to spread adultery across the Tigris River, after the flood.

Observations

# World Elements
# Flood

*Adultery — A local event — Flood (#3999 [מבול], #5104 [נהר]) with sides — Many survive flood (Children of Seth, Giants, Cain, etc. — Land in and out of the Water 2Peter 3:5 — Lord's World under water (not planet) 2Peter 2:5 — Exodus*

The first phase of Adultery (מהל) was ended when the entire Tigris/Euphrates plains became flooded. The flood of Noah had "sides," and was the flooding of the Tigris/Euphrates, which flooded the land from the Nile River to the mountains in the east of Nod (*Joshua 24:3*). Those mountains were in and out of the water (*II Peter 3:5*). The whole World of the Lord in Nod was under water.

The word in translation for flood "Mubal" (מבול) #3999 carries the idea of "Flowing," "Washed Out," or "Washed Away." The names Tubal, Jabal, and Jubal (Children of Cain) carry the same root as Mubal. These "Bal" words along with the word Tubal for "World (not planet)," imply that Cain's children (3Balls) are the World (TBL) of the Lord. Theses words: Jubal, Jabal, Tubal, and Mubal, all have the word "bal" as a common root word. Bal (בל) is also the root for the word Babel (בבל), which means "confusion." The root idea common to all of the word that radiate from the word "Bal" is "Chaos." Thus the flood" was to "wash away" the World of the Lord, which is "Chaos," or "Confusion."

The second word in translation for "flood" is the word "Nahar" (נהר) #5104. The word Nahar (Nahor) implies a flowing river, and the word can be contracted to become the word Har (הר) which means to "mount up," or to "swell up." Thus a river (Nahar) swollen (Har) = a flood. Abram's grand father and his brother were both named Nahor or "Flood (*Gen. 11:22, 24,26*)."

The northern extremes of Nod, the mounds, and plains of Shinar were the last portion of Nod to be flooded. Cain's Gentile/Chaldean, children survived the flood sealed in his subterranean cave city, in mound Ararat, at the northern extremes of Nod. Nimrod would build the Ur Complex, on the northern portion of the Tigris River, and the Shinar plains. The Ur city complex would be used to raise Cain's children after the flood.

The flood of Noah was a flood with geographical "sides" (*Joshua 24:2, 3, 14, 15*). Abram Came from the northern "side" of the flood, from Ur where his father Terah and grand father Nahor had lived. The flood, was the flooding of the Tigris, and Euphrates, the rivers of Ethiopia or Cush (*Isaiah 18:1, 2, Zephoniah 3:10*). (*Zephoniah* (צפוניה) *means "Lord of the North"*)".

When Joshua was talking to the Israelis about the "other side" of the flood, they were in the land of Canaan, west of the Tigris/Euphrates. That was the side of the flood they were on. Since the flooding was of the flooding of the entire region between the Tigris and Euphrates, then the other side of the flood (away from Israel), would be east of the Tigris in the land of Nod. Thus Abram came from the city complex of Ur in the land of Nod, on the side of the north, not from southern Mesopotamia. Abram's father Terah was bringing his entire family away from the **wilderness** of Ur, across the Tigris River down into the **civil** land of Canaan (*Gen. 11:31*).

Notes

# World Elements
# Civilizing I (Temporary)

### Flood —Ur/Babel was not...— Kabalah — Civilization

After the flood Nimrod went east of Eden to Nod, to civilize the Gentile/Chaldean children of Cain (*Isa. 18:2*). The word "Civil" comes from the phonetic root CBL (קבל) or (כבל)(Cable), both of which mean "to be responsive," or "receptive," and therefore having "conscience" and being "conscious" in one's conduct, around others. Civilness is natural to the original inhabitants of the entire planet, they have never had to be made civil. Eden (אדן) is now called Africa, but the Moors of North and Western Africa called it, El Cabulan (אל כבולן), or "The Civil Place." The Kabalah (Cabalah) takes it's name from the the word El Cabulan. As Cabulan means "Civil Place," Cabalah or Kabalah means "Civilness." Africa (Eden / El Cabulan), is the "Civil Place." the Civilizer of the Europeans. "Marked Cain's" pale leper children were never civil from their origins, and had to be made artificially civil (*Gen. 4:15*). It is not a complement to have to be made civil. From their inception the Lord made Cain's children mentally deaf, dumb, blind and cripple (*Isa. 6:9, 10*). These Gentiles were terrible from their beginning, for the Lord had trodden them down, and scattered and peeled them (*Isa. 18:2*), The Lord wanted to control (strive with) them (*Gen. 6:3*).

It was Nimrod who brought the Caucasian Race up out of the caves, to convert and heal them, from the lifestyle that the Lord had imposed on them (*Matt. 13:15*). Thus Cain's Caucasian children, did not "evolve" up to civilizing themselves. The first Civilizing Station for the Caucasians was the city complex of Ur. Ur was built by Nimrod and thousands of other wooly headed Brown people, from the Garden. Ur was built to Raise (Civilize) Cain, his fallen Caucasian children. This was the very first civilizing that they ever had. Civilizing was supposed to be a temporary measure. Civilizing was a crutch to hold the Caucasians up, while what was genetically broken inside them could be healed. Then the crutch (civilizing/civilization) must be cast aside, as the healed ones walked away holding themselves civil, without a civilizing crutch. If the crutch of civilization was not sat aside, the civilized would be permanent cripples

Nimrod had brought the Caucased ones close to the state where they could have chose, to set themselves free from the civilizing crutch. They could also be made free from the criminal, crippling influences of the the Lord, and his World of the North. As such the Caucasians could have told the Lord of Nod to get thee hence Satan (*Matt. 4:10*). Thus without bowing down to the Lord, they could have stayed there in the northern paradise that Nimrod had built for them, forever. The paradise that Nimrod built for Cain's children, was the six city Ur Metropolis (*Gen. 10:10-12, Gen. 11:1-9*). Nimrod was in the process of grafting them back, but before he could completely convert (graft) them back, the Lord and his Host, came down from Ararat to the plains of Shinar in Nod, and ruined the Ur/ Babel City Complex (*Isaiah 23:13; Gen. 11:9*). Hallel the Lord of the North made the observation that his son Cain's children had become of one mind, and were setting about to rule themselves (*Gen.11:6*). The Lord did not mean to allow Cain's children the Caucasian (Chaldean) Race to be brought to a state that they could set aside his World, and the crutch of civilizing. The Lord had not brought Nimrod into his World (TBL), to condemn it, but to save it just as corrupt as it still was (*John 3:17*).

The Lord overthrew Ur/Babel, confounding it and brought this civilizing station to ruins (*Gen.*

Observations

# World Elements
# Civilizing II (Permanent)

Civil is inside, civilized is outside — The Civil do not need Civilizing — Salvation *11:9; Isa. 23:13*). Many scattered away, but the Lord incited those who stayed to crucify (Lynch) their savior Nimrod (*Isa. 53rd Chptr.*). It pleased the Lord for the Gentiles to bruise Nimrod's wooly head (*Isa. 53:10*), as it would please the Lord to bruise Jesus' wooly head, two thousand years later, when he came to civilize the Lost Sheep of Israel, free from bondage to the Lord. The Lord would be pleased a third time fifteen hundred years after Jesus, when the Europeans bruised the wooly heads of the Moors, who had spent eight hundred years, pouring a civilizing Light into the Lord's Dark Ages, in Europe.

Upon Nimrod's death the Lord instituted permanent civilization. Permanent civilizing, is a permanent crutch, for a society designed to be permanently cripple. In civilization no one can ever become truly civil. The entire civilizing system that Nimrod had establish, was converted into a system designed to prevent the pale leper from ever being made civil. Nimrod's system had been designed to make the people free from bondage to the Lord. But it was now used to hold them in perpetual bondage to the Lord. Nimrod's civil system was composed of four elements: **Government** for temporary leadership, **Commerce** for the transaction of business, **Military** for self defense, from those pale ones that Nimrod did not retrieve from the caves of Ararat, and **Labor** to organize them into co operative work groups, so that they could build on a constructive basis. With permanent civilizing, the Lord's World was to be made up of permanent Leaders, Church, and State, Commercial, Military, Labor, Judges, Lawyers, Police, Jails, Prisons, Legalities, Courts, Regulations, etc.

Nimrod's entire principle was founded on the basis that once someone is taught away from incorrect behavior, and are held strict away from that behavior for a few generation, they will cease doing negative acts. Also when the old die off with their old bad habit, then the new are born into a World, where these old behaviors no longer existed. This is the end of a need for the civilizing elements, thus the end of a need for being governed, being policed, being schooled etc.

Throughout the generations the Lord has been very concerned that the children of his son Cain, and his other agents never be made Civil, for that would be the end of his World.

In the history of this planet, only three groups have ever had to be made civil: The pale leper Gentile children of Cain, the ancient wooly headed Israelis, and the Arabians. The peaceable children of Ham gave all three of these groups an alternative to be civil, but they stayed savage.

Uncivil (civilized) people live in misery at every level, misery is the source of religion. Once civil nature arrives misery and religion go away. The end of misery is the end of religion.

When people cease to throw paper on the ground, the trash man losses his job. Thousands of jobs are lost when criminal activity cease. Court houses, hospitals, mortuaries, casket factories, churches, cinder block factories, Gun factories, uniform factories, etc. are all shut down.

The Lord and his agents used the need for Caucasians being civilized as the justification for the permanent installation of government and all of it's negative elements, which is the World of the Lord. Civilizing went from being a Temporary Crutch, to being a permanent crutch producing institutions, or permanent cripples. By design, no one would ever be healed. Thus Civilization became permanent for the continuation, and salvation of the World of the Lord.

Notes

# World Elements
# Salvation

*Civilizing — Salvation (ישע) #3442 - #3444 — Free (שע) #7768, #7771 — Commentary*

Civilizing was the salvation of the World (TBL) of the Lord. Salvation (ישע) #3442-44 is the root for the words Jesus (Yeshua), and Joshua (Yoshua). Both words means exactly the same. The root of the word Yeshua/Yoshua is the word Shua (שע) #7768-7771 which mean "Freedom." Thus true salvation is "freedom." The distinction between the two is that Joshua saved (freed) the World of the Lord, to impose itself on people. Yeshua (Jesus) came to destroy the World of the Lord, to save (Free) the people away from the Lord's World imposed on them.

The first salvation of the Lord's world was when Adam was put to sleep. Next Nimrod attempted to save (Make Free) Cain's pale leper descendants from bondage to the Lord. The Lord incited them to crucify Nimrod, and the Lord's World was saved again (*Isaiah 53:1-12*). The next salvation of the World was when Noah defected by exalting the Lord, who is Lucifer, the Lord of the North (*Isaiah 14:12*). The next salvation was when the children of Canaan gave the Gentile/Caucasian/Chaldeans asylum when they fled from the Lord who confounded their city, that Nimrod the Assyrian had built for them. The next salvation was when the Egyptians saved the Israelis from the famine of the Lord by bringing them down to Egypt from the land of Canaan (*Gen. 45:19, Deut. 26:5*). Then came the greatest threat to the World, when Yeshua (Jesus) returned from Egypt to save (Make free), the Israelis from the World of the Lord, in Israel. His parents had fled with him to Egypt, which gave them asylum, and saved Yeshua (Jesus) from his people the Israelis, some of whom were agents of the Lord, and his World.

The Egyptian children of Peaceful Ham had raised Yeshua (Jesus) and sent him back home to Israel to "make free" (Shua), the Lost Sheep of Israel from bondage to the Lord (*John 8:32, 33*). But the Lord so loved his World that he allowed his World agents to crucify Yeshua (Jesus)(*John 3:16*). The Lord did not want Jesus to condemn his World as he did, so he let his agents kill his son, to save his World, that was imposed on the Israelis (*John 3:17*). The World extended it's existence for two thousand extra years, with Jesus' death. With the end of the Lord's World all would have been **made free** from the Lord, not **saved** back into his world!

The Moors of north Africa further made free the pale Europeans from the Lord's World of Darkness, by bringing a great Light up into Europe from Eden (Africa) in 700A.D. Using Spain, Portugal, and southern France as a platform, the Moors spread out into every part of what is now Europe, and took 800 years to established Moorish principalities, that would be the foundation for every country that now exist there. This was the final recivilizing and reraising of the pale leper children of Cain in Europe.

The final salvation of the World has been the enslavement and mental crucifixion of the West African children of Eden, in the Americas. These ones from West Africa are the end of the long and continuous line of Adam, who the Lord purposed to subplant. The question becomes what is being saved from what? The Christian masses think that Jesus (Yeshua) came to save the World. But Jesus came to destroy the World, to save the people! Jesus was murdered to save the World he came to destroy. The question becomes can the World that Jesus (Yeshua) came to destroy, save the people that it is imposed upon?

Observations

# Comentary

*Salvation (Save what) — Truth makes Free — Prince of Egypt — Get thee hence Satan*

Jesus' (Yeshua's) family had to flee with him as a little child, from Israel to Egypt to save his life, from those who wanted to murder him (*Matt. 2:13*).

This commentary is about the deception, being perpetrated against the masses of this planet. Scripture say that the Devil (Lord) would deceive his whole World. The Lord installed his World, on this planet, after he was defeated and cast down (*Rev. 12:9*). The betrayal began in Nod where the Lord first established his World. Nod is the first place that the Lord shut the eyes, ear, and minds of Cain's pale leper children (*Isa. 6:10*). The Lord and Abram spreaded Deception/Betrayal from Nod across the Tigris, down into the land of Ham. Abram (אברם) means I Betray (אברמ). The Lord's deception that Abram represented, extended down to the Israeli Rabbis, who deceived the Israelis masses (*Isa. 6:10*). Woe to them that call Evil Good, and that call Good Evil: They put the Darkness of the Lord for Light, and Light they put as Darkness... (*Isa. 5:20*). No man can serve Light and Darkness for either he will hate the one (Light), and love the other (Darkness); or else he will hold to the one (Light), and despise the other (Darkness)(*Matt. 6:24*). The masses have been tricked into loving the Darkness of the Lord without even knowing it (*Matt. 6:23*)! At the end of each year Christianized masses all over the planet, watch a ball of light fall, and unknowingly celebrate another year of the killing of the Light (Jesus), that could have made them free from the Lord.

Jesus told the Israelis that truth shall make them free, from bondage to the Lord (*John 8:32*). The Israelis had never been in bondage to any man, but were in bondage to the Lord, a super man (*John 8:33; Ex. 15:3*).

When Jesus returned to Israel from Egypt as a young man, he did not return to represent the Lord or the Lord's World. In fact Jesus had been sent to abolish Judaism, in the process of making the Lost Sheep of Israel free, from the Lord and his World.

Without Judaism the World of the Lord of Abraham would have come to an end. Without Judaism, the church of ChristiAnity (Anti Christ) would not have had a way to come into existence. The shedding of Jesus' blood was the salvation of the very World that Jesus came to destroy. The killing of Jesus was the killing of the Light.

It is written that the God of Abraham is the father of Jesus. Abraham's God Jehovah told Moses that he is El Shaddai, which means Devil God (*Ex. 6:3*). Thus the Bible/Torah is saying that the God who "overshadowed" Yeshua's mother was the Devil! As such Yeshua (Jesus) was denying his father when he said "get thee hence Satan (*Matt. 4:10*)." Jesus was after the Order of Melchezedek, not the Chaos of the World of his father, the Lord (*Hebrews 5:6*).

When Yeshua (Jesus) refused to serve his father, who is Abraham's God Jehovah, Jehovah activated a contract against Yeshua's (Jesus') life (*Deut. 13th Chptr*). Thus when the Israelis (Jews) handed Yeshua over to the Gentiles (Romans) to have him killed, it was by the commandment of Jesus' father, the Lord. The Israelis must kill anyone who would carry them away from their God, even the son of of their God! It pleased the Lord to bruise him (*Isa. 53:10*).

When the Gentiles (Romans) finished torturing Jesus, he was dead on their instrument of torture. They made an icon of him being tortured on their Roman cross, to mock him. They also

Notes

# Commentary Statements

*Kill the Light — World Salvation — Outer darkness — Holy Roman Empire*

invented the motto: "he died that we might live," by which they meant "We killed him to save our World from him." The entire theme of Judeo/Christianity is the sacrifice of the innocent to preserve the guilty.

Judeo/ChristiAnity (Anti Christ) have been exported around the planet to instill in the minds of the innocent that it is ok to be sacrificed, to save the World of the Lord. Thus the whole mission of Judeo/Christianity is to seduce the very people who would have been safe, if the Israelis and other Gentiles had not assassinated the man called Jesus (Yeshua). Jesus' teachings would have brought the Judeo/Gentile World, the World of the Lord to an end, and the planet and it's people would be safe, and free.

In the western World at the end of each year, a ball of Light is dropped, and the light is extinguished, to symbolize the successful killing of the Light (Jesus), for another year, and then it is the beginning of a new year for the World! Since the Lord's World system murdered Jesus it has extended itself, for two thousand years! The World is not the planet, nor is the World the people on the planet. But the World (TBL) of the Lord is the Chaos (TBL) imposed on the planet, and it's people. When the World (TBL) of the Lord comes to an end, the planet and it's people will be free of it's negative effects again!

People assume that salvation speak to them being saved, but salvation is the World being saved. Why is the church preaching, and teaching salvation to their congregations, when Jesus taught against salvation? Jesus taught: "Do not find your life in the physical, for you will eventually lose it anyway, but rather be ready to give your life for me (truth), and you shall find it (*Matt. 10:39; 16:25*)." Jesus commanded for his followers to hate the Lord's World, that the Lord so loved (*John 3:16*). Jesus told them "do not love the Lord's World, for if any man love the Lord's World, that the love of the inner father is not in them (*I John 2:15*). Jesus asked the question of what would it profit anyone to gain the entire World of the Lord, and in the process to lose their own soul (*Matt. 16:26*). The Lord has lost his soul to gain his World (*Judges 10:16*)!

The Church/Synagogue system was brought into existence to serve the chief commandment of the Lord. The Lord had already instructed the Rabbis (Scribes and Pharisees) to cast the Israelis out of their inner kingdoms, out to his Outer Darkness (*Matt. 8:12*). The Lord said that being in his Darkness was why the Israelis masses could not see, hear, or understand, even though their eyes, ears, and minds still worked (*Isa. 6:9*). Deaf, dumb, blind, and mentally cripple was the way that the Lord wanted the scribes and Pharisees to keep the Israeli masses (*Isa. 6:10*), in the Darkness of his day (*Amos 5:18, 20*). Mental Darkness is the Day the Lord, want all to be glad in (*Psalms 118:24*)!

Jesus (Yeshua) was killed for attempting to bring Light into the Outer Darkness of the Lord (*John 8:12*). The Light was for the Israelis, as Nimrod had been killed for attempting to bring a Great Light, to the pale leper Gentile children of Cain, who also walked in the Darkness of the Lord (*Isa. 9:2*). The church system was founded by the Roman murders of Jesus (Yeshua), to hold the Gentile masses along with the Israeli (Jewish) masses, in the Thick Darkness of the Lord (*Exodus 10:22*).

Observations

# Commentary Questions

*Wooly Headed Jesus — Cursed be Canaan — Two Lines  (Cain Mutainy)*

Why do the masses in the church think that their religious leaders are teaching what Jesus taught?  Why don't the congregation know that the founders of the very first Christian church (Romans) were those who tortured and then murdered Jesus. The Roman Impire, Holy Roman Impire, Holy Roman Church, Roman Catholic Church, Greek Orthodox, Protestant, Anglican, Baptist, etc., it is all the same. They all root from the Roman Imps, and all celebrate that Jesus' murder was the salvation of their and the Lord's World (TBL), that Jesus came to destroy.

Woe to those who make the masses think that Jesus' Light represent the Darkness of the Lord (*Isa. 5:20*)!

Why are the Christian congregations not taught the scripture that say that Jesus was a wooly headed brown man (*Rev.1:14*)? Why don't the religious scenes show the wooly headed brown Jesus (Son of Man) being tortured and lynched by the pale leper Romans (*Rev. 1:14*)?

Wooly headed brown Cain was the origin of the Caucasian Race. The Lord "marked" Cain with a permanent paleness to distinguish him from the multitude of others around him. In the more modern times the killers of the Light have done all that they can do, to suppress the fact that Blacks are the parents of all people on the planet, including the entire Caucasian Race. Also Black men not as slaves, but as Masters and Builders, have built every civilization that Caucasians have ever had, from Nimrod to Benjamin Banniker. From Ur/Babel to Washington D. C.

### Curse on Ham/Canaan

To suppress all of the above information in their secret teachings to their own, the modern pale Israelis, and pale Europeans (include Americans) teach that being Black (like Jesus)(*Rev. 1:14*) is a curse. Pale Rabbis, Priest, and Ministers twist the Noah story to say that Ham and Canaan were cursed into being Black, for sodomizing Noah. When the story as told straight and truthfully it is Ham and Canaan exposing Noah who was attempting to sodomize his grandson Canaan! The pale religious leaders further tell their congregations that Ham and Canaan represent the Africans. Their twisted story is/was the basis for the enslavement of hundreds of millions of Blacks from the continent of Africa.

But the fact is that Noah and all of his descendants were Black, like the rest of the original population of the entire planet, that was never flooded. Knowing that this is true, the question becomes, if all of the original people of the planet are Black, and normal then where did the unusual pale Caucasians come from?

### Two Lines

In this book you have discovered that Cain and Abel were not the sons of Adam, but are the sons of the Lord with Eve (*Gen. 4:1; I Chron. 1:1*). You have also discovered that originally Cain was wooly headed and brown (Black), until he was marked with a permanent pale leprosy to distinguish him and his line, from the still wooly brown people around him (*Gen. 4:15*). Cain not being the son of wooly brown Adam, and being altered, made Cain and his line distinct from Adam and his line. Man (Adam) existed before creation. Creation is only the process of

Notes

# Commentary

*Asians and Caucasians — Missing Link — Wooly Black Israelis (Amos 9:7)*

"altering" what already exists. The creation of man was the altering of the Original man (Adam), to get Eve (*Gen. 2:21-23*). Next Eve was beguiled and impregnated by the Lord, and gave birth to Cain. Cain's father the Lord "Marked" him with a permanent pale leprosy (*Gen., 4:15*), to turn Cain into the first "created (Altered) man (*Gen. 4:15*).

Thus there are only two kinds of people on this planet, the Original Man, and the "Created" man. Assians are original, and CaucAsians are from the created man Marked Cain. When it is further discovered that CaucAsians were "brought into existence" (Created), out of Assians it become even more simple. Finally it can be discovered that the Aboriginal Assian is the wooly headed Black to brown man, his home is all over the earth, and he is the father of all the inhabitants on this planet.

The next step in countering the fact that Blacks are the actual parents of all of the people on the planet, they used Charles Darwin (1809-1882), to invent the theory of evolution. This was less than 150 years ago. This "theory" state that of course the Black man is the ancestor of all who lives on the planet, but that was only true (they say), because the Black man was the beginning of an evolutionary process, they say! The evolution theory infer that the Original or Black man is in fact a "missing link" between the animal and human (Caucasian) realm. In this theory at best the Original (Black) man (they say) "evolved up from being a gorilla, chimpanzee, or orangutan. Was this a **Planet of the Apes**? The problem with this "theory" of evolution is the fact that the ancient Blacks had cities all over the planet, before there were ever any Caucasians in existence. When the Caucasians were brought into existence it was not from evolution, but was from the "creating" (altering) of Cain a Black man who already existed, into a permanent albino, or genetic pale leper!

**Missing Link**

In this book we have put together information from the Bible/Torah that wooly headed brown (Black) men built an entire first civilizing station made up of several cities, to Raise Cain's pale leper or Caucasian children, from a state of savagery to a civil state. That information in the Bible/Torah is also historical fact. The evolution "theory" fall on this fact alone, because evolution speaks to a progressive advancement from hairy crude Blacks to an advanced Caucasian Civilness. Yet truth is that it was hairy crude Caucasians who were made civil and refined, by advanced nonhairy Black societies (*Isa. 23:13*).

If the Black man was an evolutionary "missing link" he could not have given the Caucasian all of the arts craft, and skills, that Blacks continue to give, to raise them from the barbarous state that they continue to be in. From Nimrod and Ur Babel to Benjamin Banniker and Washington D.C., and all civilizings in between, Black have preserved the pale children of Marked Cain, from the first breath they ever took in existence. Ancient and modern Black cultures have raised Caucasians several times, to only have them fall back into another Dark Age.

Blacks are the Great Light that have always come, to illuminate the pale ones again (*Isa. 9:2*). The World system in modern times have gone to great length to suppress this fact!

For a time the modern pale Israelis had been successful at covering over most of the

# Comentary

*Black Israelis — Pale Abnormal — Marked Cain — Nimrod and Benjamin Banniker*

contradictions, that are now exposing them as being a fraudulent people, perpetrating the identity of the ancient Black Israelis. The ancient Black Israelis themselves were not Shemites, nor were they the children of Abraham, or even the children of Isaac. The Lord was the father of Isaac, and Jacob (Israel)(*Gen. 21:1; Gen. 25:21; Josh. 24:3, 4*). This cut the line between Shem/Abraham, and the Israeli tribes.

Finally even though these ancient Blacks were titled "Israelis," five of the sons of Jacob's twelve were not even the children of Jacob (Israel). Reuben, Simeon, Levi, and Judah were the sons of the Lord, with Leah (*Gen. 29:31-35*). Why would modern pale men take the identity of ancient Black men (Israelis), who were the children of the Lord, who called himself the Devil (El Shaddai / אל שדי)(*Ex. 6:3*)? This book has shown the scripture several times, that speaks to the horrible origins of the true original wooly headed Black Israelis.

There is a consequence to identifying Nimrod and Jesus (Yeshua) as Blacks as they truly were. When you look at the pale Gentiles who crucified them both, you have scenes of two ancient lynchings, to save the Gentile or Caucasian World. This is no less than what the Klu Klux Klan does when they "crucify" Black men in the modern times. They claim that they do it to save their World!

The western society invented the assumptions that it is unusual to be Black, and normal to be White. But the Bible/Torah says just the opposite, it says that paleness is not normal. Moses hand was made pale, and then return to it normal browness (*Ex. 4:6, 7*). The Lord made Mariam pale all over for seven days, and then turned her back to being brown again (*Numbers 12:10*). The complexion of Cain's daughters was denoted as being fair (pale)(*Gen. 6:2*), the same pale "mark" that had been put on Cain, and passed down to his children (*Gen. 4: 15*). The Lord put this same pale leprosy on the tribes of Israelis in the wilderness (*Leviticus 13th Chptr.*). In all of these examples Black/ brown is normal, and paleness is made note of as being unusual. Thus if there was a curse it was paleness. As such, if Noah could have cursed Canaan, then Canaan would have turned from Black into a pale leper. But Noah as a drunkard and child molester could not curse anyone, so Canaan would have remained Black like Noah. The Brown or Black complexion, is still the normal. Thus when we go back to Noah. we know that he was a normal brown, or even Black, because there is no note, that he had paleness imposed on him. Also as Ham is denoted as being the father of the wooly headed Black Africans, he had to be unmixed with any paleness. Thus Ham's father Noah and his one wife had to be unmixed Blacks like Adam and Eve, who had wooly hair like Ham!

No Pale Egyptians (Ham), no Pale Greeks (Japheth), no Pale Israelis (Shem), equal no pale Noah, or Adam. Then comes the dreaded question, that the Pale World has never wanted to be asked: That question is "if Noah and all of his children were Black and wooly, then where did White people come from?" Cain was mutated from wooly and brown into a permanent pale leper.

From Nimrod to Benjamin Banniker, and from Ur/Babel to Palestine, to Greece, to Italy, to England, to Washington D. C., wooly headed Blacks have attempted to Raise Cain, his pale children, and to graft them back, to normal Black.

# Nimrod

*Perhaps five thousand years ago Nimrod and thousands of others Blacks, built the six city Ur/Babel Complex in Northern Nod, to Raise Cain his pale leper children, to civilize them into appearing civil, for the first time.*

Summation

# Benjamin Banniker

*Thousands of Blacks built the Thirteen Penal Colonies, and then fought to turn them into Thirteen Civil States. Then Benjamin Banniker, and thousands of other Blacks built Washington D. C., as a capital to these states. The British burned Washington, and thousands of other Blacks rebuilt the city in a final attempt to Raise Cain, his pale leper children.*

Observation

Lexicon

# Summations
# Reconcilliation

*Commentaries "Church"— Discrepancies, Inconsistencies, Contradictions, it must all be made reconciled — Without reconcilliation much in the Bible/Torah is a contradiction.*

The Church/Synagogue system only exist to close, and keep closed the eyes, ears, and minds of their Judeo/Christian congregations. This is by the commandments of the Lord (*Isa. 6:10*). The Judeo/Christian congregation shall never convert and be healed, away from bondage to the Lord!

**"Summations"** a summing up of all the information in the book down to the Summations. Summations is composed of **four elements**: **Reconciliations, Lexicon, Appeals**, and **Revelations** — This book uses the four components of Summation to finalize all of the book's accumulated information:

(1) **Reconcil(iation)(Versus)** Exposes the contradictions that exist between Jesus (Yeshua), and the church/state system that claim to represent his teachings. 2) Exposes the contradictions between Jesus and Paul. 3), exposes the contradiction between Jesus and the Lord, and 4) exposes the contradiction between Jesus and Jesus!

(2) **Lexicon** along with it's components "Trans/Phone," and "Old Language" explores the ancient language that the moderns translated from. Lexicon is designed to give the, Jewish, Gentile etc. masses, direct access to the root information of the Bible/Torah. This will allow them to make their own decisions on much information in the Bible/Torah.

(3) **Appeals** compel all who have been influenced by the World System to rethink (repent) what they have been taught. Appeals then allow the reader to make a decision based upon what they now know from having read some of the true contents of the Bible/Torah.

(4) **Revelation** (Apocalypse) **reveal** to the readers of this book, that there is a Narrow Gate and a Broad Gate. These gates are a choice between Self (Narrow Gate) and Other (Broad Gate), between Light and Darkness. The end of the World System is eminent. All have a choice to end it with Light (Self), or Darkness (Other) *Amos 5:18, 20* To be with the Lord is to be absent from one's Self and Light (*II Chron. 5:6*)(*Amos 5:18, 20*).

**Revelations** (Revolution) is also a continuation or bridge that allows for a complete circle fusing the end back to the beginning. This is the Alpha and Omega of Adam (Self). This full circle is the true Chronicle and Book of God, a second Revelation, which with full circle becomes the **Chronicles** unaltered again, that Adam represents. The coming together of the Chronicles as a circular document is the beginning of all coming back together of all that has been torn apart, since the beginning of the physical experimenting with Self.

The first situation that must be made reconcile is the contradiction between the purposes of Yeshua (Jesus) and the Lord.

Lexicon

# Reconcile Versus

Bring your firstborn sons, three times in the year, do not come empty handed (*Deut. 16:16*).

| Yeshua (Jesus) | Lord |
|---|---|
| I am the Light of the World (*John 8:12*). | I am the Prince of Darkness — Woe unto those who seek my Day it is Darkness not Light. A Darkness with no brightness in it (*Amos 5:18, 20*). |
| Prince Of Light (Nimrod also)Light of the World ( *Isaiah 18:1*). | |
| Prince of Peace (*Isaiah 9:6*). | **Man of War** — *Exodus 15:3* |
| Order of Melchezedek, the King of Peace (*Hebrews 7:2, Hebrews 5:6*) | Book of the wars of the Lord (*Nu. 21:14*).... |
| Seek first the kingdom of God (inside), and his Righteousness (*Matt.6:33*).... | To be absent (outside) of the body (Self) is to be with the Lord (*II Chron. 5:6*). |
| Only as a little child can you enter in (*Matt. 18:20*). | Sanctify (Sodomize / קדש) your firstborn sons to me ... (*Ex. 13:2*). #6944, #6945 |
| Kingdom at hand (*Matt. 3:2*). Kingdom is within you (*Luke 17:21*). You (the body) are the temple of God, and God (you) is therein (*I Chron. 6:15, 19*). | To be absent from the body is to be with the Lord (*I Cor. 5:6*). |
| All of you are Gods (*Gen. 1:26, John 10:34, 35, Psalms 82:6*) | All of you are Gods (*Psalms 82:6*), but you shall have no God (Yourself) before me (*Ex. 20:3*). |
| I am the Light in the World (Darkness) of the Lord (*John 8:12*). | My day is Darkness, with no brightness in it (*Amos 5:18, 20*). This is the Day that the Lord has made, be glad in it (*Psalms 118:24*). |
| Hate the World.....(*John 15:18:18*). | God (Lord) so loved the (his) World....(*John 3:16*). |
| Go not in the way (Darkness) of the Gentiles (Nations)(*Matt. 10:5*). | ...bear my name before the Gentiles (*Acts 9:15*). |
| Our father in the heavens (*Matt. 6:1*). | I am the Lord in the ground (*Ex. 8:21*). |

Summations

Lexicon

# Reconcile Versus

*Jesus (Yeshua): "Get thee hence Satan (Lord)*

| Yeshua (Jesus) | Lord |
|---|---|
| The people's hearts wax gross, and their ears are dull of hearing, and their eyes have been closed; lest at any time they should see with their eyes, and hear with their ears, and then they would understand, and be healed (*Matt. 13:15*). | Make the hearts of the people fat, and make their ears heavy and shut their eyes; lest they see with their eyes, and hear with their ears, and understand with their hearts (minds), and convert and be healed (from me)(*Isa. 6:10*). |
| Seeing they see not, hearing they hear not, and neither do they understand (because of the Lord)(*Matt. 13:13, 14*). | |
| The Light of the body is The Eye; if therefore your Eye be Single, your whole body shall be full of Light (*Matt. 6:22*). But if your Eye be Evil (closed), then your whole body shall be full of Darkness (*Matt. 6:23, Luke 11:34-36*). | Woe to you that desire the day of the Lord! To what end is it for you? The day of the Lord is Darkness, and not Light. Shall not the day of the Lord be Darkness and not Light? Even very dark, and no brightness in it (*Amos 5:18, 20*)? |
| ....Prince of Peace (*Isa. 9:6*). | The Lord is a Man of War (*Exodus 15:3*). |
| All of you are Gods, children of the Most High (*Psalms 82:6; John 10:34, 35*). | I am a jealous God, have no other God (yourself) before me (*Ex. 34:14*). |
| God and kingdom is within self (*Luke 17:21*). He who is in you (God), is greater than he (the Lord), who is out in his World (*I John 4:4*). | ...to be absent from the Self is to be with me the Lord (*Cor. 5:6*). |
| He who finds his life shall lose it, but he who loses his life for me shall find it (*Matt. 10:39*). | If a prophet, or dreamer rise among you, and attempts to lead you away kill him (*Deut. 13:1*). |
| ...there is none good but God... (*Matt. 19:17*). | The Lord is an Alone (Bad/בד) God (*Luke 5:21*). *See Strong's Concordance "alone"# 905 (Bad/בד). See also Gesenius 102b (Bad/בד).* |

Summations

# Reconcile Versus

*You can not serve two masters : Jesus and the Lord ().*

*Jesus did not found a church or instruct his disciples to found one either. Rather Jesus (Yeshua) instructed those who followed him not to establish or found any institution, including a church (**Matt.10:9, 13**). Yet a church exists, that claim that it follow the commandments of Jesus (Yeshua). The church have never taught or held to the teachings of Jesus (Yeshua). But Jesus said that if you love me obey my commandments, or I do not know you (**John 14:14**).*

| Jesus (Yeshua) | Church |
|---|---|
| Wherefore by one Man (Lord) sin entered his World....(***Romans 5:12***). (Both Adam and the Lord are men (Ex. 15:3). | Wherefore by one Man (Adam) sin entered into the World....(***Romans 5:12***). (The Lord's World [TBL] is sin) |
| He who find (save) your life (in the physical) shall lose it anyway, but he who loses his life for my sake shall find it (***Matt. 10:39***). | ....Jesus....a Prince and a Savior... (***Acts 5:31***). |
| Do not love the **World**, if any man loves the World, the love of the father is not in him (***IJohn 2:15***). What does it profit a man to gain the World and lose his own soul (***Mark 8:36***). | God (Lord) so loved his **World** that he gave his only begotten son (Jesus) ..... (John 3:16). |
| No man can serve two masters: God inside (***Luke 17:21***), and the the Lord outside (***II Cor. 5:6***), for either he will hate the one, and love the other; or he will hold to the one and despise the other (***Matt. 6:24***). | You should worship no other God: for I the Lord your God is a Jealous God (***Ex. 34:15***). |
| Go not in the way of the Gentiles | Paul is the apostle of the Gentiles (***Romans 11:13***). |
| They who are whole have no need of a physician, but they who are sick: I came not to call the righteous, but sinners (Lord's people), to repentance (***Mark 2:17***). | All have sinned and come short of the glory of God (***Romans 3:23***). |
| All of you are Gods (***Psalms 82:6; John 8:***). | The Lord our God is one ..... (***Deut. 6:4***). |

Versus

# Reconcile Versus

*The only way that we can know if Paul represented Yeshua (Jesus) is if Paul taught exactly what Yeshua taught and that Paul did not say anything to cancel out what Yeshua taught!*

| Yeshua (Jesus) | Paul (Outlaw) |
|---|---|
| Do unto others as you would have them do unto you. This is the Law and the Prophets (Matt. 7:12). | I am dead to the Law. *Galatians 2:19* <br> A man is justified by faith, without the deed of the Law. *Romans 3:20* |
| Think not that I come to destroy the Law. I come not to destroy, but to fulfill (Matt. 5:17). | Where there is no Law there is no transgression. *Romans 4:15* |
| For verily I say to you, till the heaven and earth pass away, not one jot or one tittle shall pass from the Law, until all be fulfilled. (Matt. 5:18). | Sin through the Law, deceive me and destroy me (*Romans 7:11*). |
| Whoever shall break one of these least commandments and shall teach men so, he shall be called the least in the kingdom of heaven; but who ever shall do and teach them, the same shall be called great in the kingdom of heaven (Matt. 5:19). | Those who do the Law are cursed. *Galatians 3:13* <br><br> As concerning the Gospels (Commandments), they are an enemies to you .... (*Romans 11:28*). |
| Blessed are those who thirst for Righteousness, for they shall be filled (Matt. 5:6). | If Righteousness came by the Law then Jesus died in vain. (*Galatians 2:21*) *(Jesus did die in vain, for he was murdered. Righteousness is the Law!)* |
| He who say I know him and don't obey his commandments is a liar and the truth is not in him (1 John 2:3, 4). | No man is justified by the Law, in the sight of God (Lord) (*Galatians 2:16, 3:11*). |
| Repent the kingdom of heaven is at hand (Matt. 3:2, Matt 4:17). | ....for the gifts and callings of God are without repentance (*Romans 11:29*). |

Summations

# Reconcile
# Versus

*Preaching of Jesus (Romans 16:25)*     *My doctrine (Rom. 16:25)*

## Yeshua (Jesus) | Paul (Outlaw)

**Yeshua (Jesus)**

If you would enter Life, obey my commandments (*Matt. 19:17*). Keep my commandments (*I John 2:3*).

Go not to the Gentiles, or Samaritans, go only to the Lost Sheep of Israel. (*Matt. 10:5, 6*)

Beware of false prophets who come to you in sheep's clothing, but inwardly are raven wolves (*Matt. 7:1*)

... for those who have eyes to see and ears to hear. *Matt. 13:16* Blind leading the blind all fall in the ditch (*Matt. 5:14*)

Except as a little child you can not re-enter the kingdom of heaven *Matt. 18:2, 3*

### Agreement
Ye are Gods; and all of you are the children of the Most High. (*Psalms 82:6, John 10:34, 35*)

Greater is he who is in you (God/Self) than he who is in the World (Lord) (*1 John 4:4*)

If any man love the World, the love of the inner father is not in him (*I John 2:15*)

---

**Paul (Outlaw)**

Sin through the commandments cause me to be cursed. Without the Law sin was dead (*Roman 7:8*)

I am the Apostle of the Gentiles (*Romans 11:13*)

...my gospel (Paul)...my gospel (Paul) and [or] the preaching of Jesus. (*Romans 2:16, Romans 16:25*)

Walk by faith, not by sight (*II Corinthian. 5:7*)

When a child I acted as a child, as a man I put aside childish things (*I Corinth. 13:11*).

### Agreement
Know you not that you (body) are the temple of God, and that God (You) dwell therein (*IChron. 3:16*)?

...whilst we are at **home** in the body, we are absent from the Lord. *II Corinthian. 5:6*

...the Lord so loved his World .... (not his son)(*John 3:16*).

Lexicon

# Reconcile Versus

The writers of the Bible/Torah have Yeshua/Jesus divided, and this must be made reconcile. The Judeo/Christian System use Jesus so that they can devide, and deceive, and carry both Church and Synogogue congregations into the Darkness of the Lord.

| Yeshua | Jesus |
|---|---|
| Go not in the Way (Darkness) of the Gentiles. *Matt. 10:5* | ...he (Paul) is a chosen vessel unto me to bear my name before the Gentiles... *Acts 9:15* |
| | And the Gospel must first be published among the Nations (Gentiles)(*Mark 13:10*). |
| Do not love the World, if any man loves the World, the love of the father is not in him (*I John 2:15*). | I came to save the World (*John 12:47*) |
| If you were of the World, the World would Love you, but **I have chosen you out** of the World, so the World hates you (*John 15:19*). | God (Lord) did not send his son into his World to condemn the World as he did, but that the World through him might be saved (*John 3:17*). |
| Call none good, but God (*Matt. 19:17*). All of you are God, children of the Most High (*Psalms 82:6; John 10:34*). | ... have no God but me (*Ex. 20:2*) ... I the Lord thy God am a jealous god ...(*Ex. 20:5*). |
| ...and the Devils told Yeshua "send us into the swine,"... and Yeshua cast the unclean spirits (Devils) out of the man, back into the hogs (*Mark 5:13, 14*). | It does not matter what you eat, for it comes out as waste (*Matt. 15:17*). |

Summations

# Reconcile
# Versus
## Self (Inner and Outer)

| Inner Light<br>God (s) | Outer Darkness<br>Lord<br>Amos 5:18, 20, II Corin. 5:6 |
|---|---|
| Kingdom | World (Kingdom) |
| Self (שלח) | Other |
| God (אלוהים) | Lord |
| Peace | War (Numbers 21:14) |
| Love | Hate (sin) (Romans 5:12) |
| Life | Death |
| Law (*Matt. 5:17*) | Outlaw () |
| Inside (Light) | Outer Darkness (*Amos 5:18, 20*) |
| Truth (Free)(*John 8:32*). | Lie (Bondage)(John 8:44). |
| Little Children (*Matt. 18:3*). | Adult(erated) |
| Narrow Gate (Life)(*Matt. 7:13*). | Broad Gate (Destruction)(Matt. 7:13) |
| Whole/Perfection (*Matt. 5:48*). | Evil (Incomplete)(*Jeremiah 45:5*) |
| Garden | Famine () |
| Greater (*I John 4:4*). | Lesser (I John 4:4) |
| Eyes and Ears (*Isa. 6:10*) | Deaf and Blind (Isa. 6:10) |

Lexicon

# Reconcile Versus

## *The splitting of Adam*

*True Man is an hermesaphrodite or male/female being inside of one form (Gen. 1:27). Before Adam was put to sleep he was in the male/female image and likeness of all of the other Gods (Gen. 1:26,27). Original Man was never created, but Adam, same as the Lord, and Melchezedek existed without the aide of mother or father, without descent, without beginning of days, or end of Life... (Heb. 7:3). Therefore original man do not (did not) have a navel, even in the first coats of skin (Gen. 3:21).*

*Original Man was put to sleep and divided into separate male and female. That which was taken out of man was the womb, and the womb was made into a Wombman. It is the Wombman (male and female separate), who is dressed in coats of skins or physical bodies, with navels.*

| Man | Woman (Wombman) | |
| --- | --- | --- |
|  | **Male** | **Female** |
| Male/Female (HermesAphrodite) | | |
| Birth Tract (Womb) | Testicles | Uterus/Womb |
| Urine Tube | Penis | Vagina/Clitoris |
| Sperm/Egg (Seed) | Sperm | Egg |
| No Navel | Navel | Navel |
| Breast (Active In Season) | Dormant Breast | Active Breast |
| Estrogen/Testosterone | Testosterone | Estrogen |
| Birth: Continuation (Herms) | Birth: Child Son | Birth: Child Daughter |

Summations

# Lexicon Introduction

*Man/Woman — Adam (אדמ) = "I am Blood — Holy (הולי) = Corrupt — Bless (ברכ) = Break — Devil (דבל) = Divide — North (נורוח) = "Lamps" — Mandrake (מן דרך) = Man of Darkness — Apple (Awful/אפל) = Thick Darkness — Truth (אמת) = Emit — Multiply (מלח) = Replenish/Fill — Visit (פקד)(Gen. 21:1) = Sexual Intercourse — Lexicon*

Before Man (Adam) was separated into separate male and female (woman) there was no need for outward language, for communication was within. Outward language is the instrument for communication, with others. The Universal language (*Gen. 11:1*), is mental communication between men, between animals, and between all other lifeforces. On this level all has it's own sound or name, that radiates from it. All that exists in the physical radiates it's own unique sound, which is it's name. These sounds are mental, and above what ears hear, and what mouths speak.

The animals, and children still communicate on this speechless level, but Original Man fell down to a lesser level, to vocal communication, because that is where the experiment carried him. When original man began to speak with his mouth, it was a break away from the true speechless Old Language.

Before little children began to speak, they still have a remnant of the old speechless language. It does not matter where they are born, it is the same for all. In the short time before they began to speak, and become Arabs, Chinese, etc., all young eyes see, and young ears hear universally the same. When the child began to have verbal speech the mental is altered, and they began to lose the unspoken communication.

The spoken Old Language came with mental deafness, and mental blindness. With mental blindness man lost the ability to see what is, and only saw through his biases. That is what brought about the different languages of the planet. Anyone who can bring themselves back up through the mental distortion can reattain to the unspoken. There was a split and mental confusion, as to names, for man could no longer hear the sounds coming from all that exists. Mental confusion is the cause of different languages, and then different names for the same entity.

The next confusion was communications by way of writing. As the ability to communicate on the higher level, began to go away, speech and writing to communicate becomes necessary. Writing, and verbal speech, is a falling down, not an advancement.

And yet no one lied in the written **Old Language.** The old writers wrote down exactly what they meant, and did not hide anything. Also the design of the old language is such that no one can mistranslate the words from it, unless they openly intend to lie.

The following Lexicon is an etymology or "word study" of some of the written Old language. The lexicon allows the study of a word at the level, of what the word originally meant. The western world have intentionally mistranslated many old language words to suppress the word's original meanings. The old language is not "Hebrew," Arabic, Syrian, Assyrian, Babylonian, etc., but is the root language, to all of these languages. Each word in the entire language roots back to it's own particular group of consonants, that is common to all other words, that carry the same root idea: Breast, Devil, and Field, carry the same root idea of being "cast out (ShD / שר)."

The following Lexicon will show that many of the old language words are incorporated, in the

# Summation
# Lexicon Introduction

*Almighty is Devil — Language Accurate — Holy is Sodomy*

English in two forms:

The first form is **phonics** or **sound**, meaning that the old language word is brought into the English still sounding basically how the word sounds in the old language. For example the words Shadow, Shade, Shed, Shod etc., were brought into the English from the old language root ShD, which carries the idea of being "*casted out*," "*casted off*," or being "*away from.*"

The second form that old language words are brought into the English, is by *translation*. This means that the old language word is changed into the equivalent English word. Thus the old language word root ShD is translated into the English words common to it: **Breast, Devil,** and **Field**. Translations, and Phonics (Trans./Phones) will be easier to understand in the following lexicon.

The old language is very accurate and is not clumsy at all. For example *Phonetically* "Holy" (חולי) means "Corrupt." In *translation* "Holy" is Kadesh (קדש) which describe what the *corruption* is: In translation Holy (קָדֵשׁ) means "prostrated" or "Prostituted (קָדֵשׁ)." Holy (קדש) is the same old language word that describes a female, or male whore (קדש) or prostitute (*Deut.23:17*). A male can not normally be a prostitute, except by being sodomized!

Thus Holiness is the "corruptness" of "Religious Sodomy," for the male, and possibly for the female also, a strictly religious act! To show that Holiness is male and female religious prostitution/sodomy there is also a secular form of prostitution/sodomy under the Hebrew word root Shakav (שכב). The root idea of this word Shakav is "to lie down" for whatever purpose. Under this root are words such as "bed," "sleep," "recline," and "copulate." In each case the basic idea is "to lie down." To copulate in general is Shikev (שִׁכֵב)(*Lev. 15:18*). Different vowel sets are applied to these same three consonants (שכב), to generate the different words.

To show how articulate this language is, each of the following words are generated by using the same three root consonants, שכב with different vowel combinations. The "Hebrew" can distinguish whether a female is being copulated with vaginally (שָׁכַב)(*Lev. 15:18*), or is being sodomized (שָׁכַב)(*Num.31:17*). A man sodomizing a man is (שָׁכַב)(*Lev. 18:22*). A woman being penetrated by an animal is denoted by the combination (שָׁכַב)(*Lev. 20:15*). Bestiality or sex between a man and animal can also be noted. (שָׁכַב)(*Lev. 18:23*).

To firmly establish that Holiness (קָדֵשׁ) or Religious Sodomy is an official act the Lord commanded that the Israelis bring their firstborn (Future leaders) sons before him, to be **sanctified** (Sodomized)(קדש). The vowel combination for Holy (קָדֵשׁ) and Sodomy (קָדֵשׁ) are exactly the same. Scripture say that the act of sodomy was imposed upon the firstborn male herd animals also, this is Bestiality (*Ex.13:2, Ex.13:13*)! The Israelis were to bring their firstborn sons back before the Lord three time each year, to repeat the process (*Ex. 34:23*). The Israelis had to "Sanctify" (קדש) their first born sons to the Lord, which was to perform Ritual Religious Sodomy (קדש) on them. None were to appear before the Lord, with empty hands (*Ex. 34:20*). *See Strong's Concordance # 6942, #6944, #6945* these are the numbers for the words **Sanctify, Sodomy,** and **Holy** in that order.

# Summation
# Lexicon Introduction

### *Beast is not man or animal but Both — Language does not Lie — Lexicon*

Thus the basis of the entire Judeo/Christian Religion is the act of being made Holy or being ritually sodomized!

In modern times, the meanings of old language words have been skillfully crafted, in translation to sway the minds of the masses, in any direction that the word crafter desire to take them. The Bible/Torah in it's present form is a perfect example of this kind of crafting.

Yet the following Lexicon is for the Old Language that the Bible/Torah was translated from, and it is designed to allow the reader to see many important words, carried from the English back into the Old Language, and retranslated into their true original meanings.

Language at every level is communication, even beyond speech and writing. The Beast (בהמת) or "Mute Ones, (*Gen. 7:2*)," that Noah brought onto the ark were not man or animal, These "Beast" were titled: ... "beast, a man and his wife," not ...beast a male and his female. These beast were the bestial fruit from Cain's children mating with the animals in their midst, it was required by the Lord, for bestiality (TBL) is a portion of the core of the World (TBL) of the Lord.

**Verbal speech** began with the falling away from the old **speechless language**, but the "beast" (בהמת) or "mute ones" could not communicate, on either level. This same fate fell to most of the "normal" children of Cain. They were as mute as the beast, even though they had the mechanics to speak. Nimrod killed all of the "mute ones (beast)," and taught Cain's pale leper children to speak, read and write.

The first vocal speech is designated "Old Language," because it is older than, and is the root of the Israeli, Arabic, Assyrian, Aramaic, etc. This old language in it's pure and ancient form, did not have capital letters, vowels, prefixes, suffixes, or any other form of markings such as periods, commas, and accent marks. All of these are modern inventions of pale Europeans who were only recently given the ability to read and write. They did not have an alphabet, or written languages.

Before the planet was destroyed, the original inhabitants did not have solid physical bodies. Nor did the original inhabitants of the planet have to speak or write down anything. There was no written or spoken languages, nor was there a need for them. Long before the Caucasian Race came into existence communications were at a level above and beyond outward speech, and writing. There are Old Language words beneath each word in the English. The true translation of the Old Language word into English creates, a doorway down inside Judeo/Christianity, that one may see the true purpose that it serve. Judeo/Christianity does not serve it's masses, and congregations at all (*Isa. 6:10*)!

The Lord commanded that the Rabbis, Priest, and Ministers keep the eyes, ears, and minds of their congregations firmly closed, so that they could never convert themselves, and be healed away from being in bondage to the Lord (*Isa. 6:10*).

Jesus' mission was to tell the Lost Sheep of Israel the truth, to make themselves free (*John 8:32*). With opened eyes, ears, and minds, the Israelis could convert, and be healed from bondage to the Lord (*Matt. 13:15*).

When Jesus (Yeshua) told the wooly headed brown Rabbis of his time, that they would know

# Summation
# Lexicon Introduction

### *Lord is Associated with the wrong Words — Truth make Free — Lexicon*

the truth and the truth would make them free (*John 8:32*). Jesus was exposing that the Rabbis did not know the truth, but the Rabbis did know that they were lying. The Rabbis were lying for the Lord the Liar, the father of Israel (*Ex. 4:22*). The Israeli masses were held in bondage to the Lord and his World (*John 8:44*). But Jesus brought the Light of knowledge into the World of the Darkness of the Lord (*Matt. 5:14*).

Jesus represent Light (*John 8:12, John 12:46*), and the Lord represent Darkness (*Amos 5:18*), Jesus represent Truth (*John 14:6*), and the Lord represent Lying (*John 8:44*), Jesus represent Life (*John 14:6*), and the Lord represent Death (Murder)(*John 8:44*). Jesus represent Peace (*Isa. 9:6*), and the Lord represent War (*Ex. 15:3*).

Jesus said that you can not serve two Masters: the Master of Lies, and the Master of Truth (*Matt. 6:24*). Woe to those murderers of Jesus, who make it seem that the Light that Jesus represents, represents the Darkness of the Lord (*Isa. 5:20*). The Jewish Rabbis, the Catholic Priests, and the Protestant Ministers have chose to serve the Lord's commandment, to keep the Judeo/Christian masses in his Darkness, deaf, dumb, blind, and mentally cripple (*Isa. 6:10*). With the truth, from Jesus they could have made themselves and their Judeo/Christian congregations free, from the Lord, and his World. But these "Holy Men" refused to teach their congregations, the true meaning of several words in the Bible/Torah. The scribes (mistranslator), and Pharisees (Preachers), have taught the masses to love the Darkness of the Lord (*John 3:19*).

But everyone in the Judeo/Christian congregations are responsible for themselves, not Rabbis, not Priests, and not Ministers. Every person was born into the physical, by themselves, and shall pass away from the physical, by themselves. Once they are no longer in the body they shall be with the Lord unless they free themselves from the Lord, by saying get thee hence (*Matt. 4:10*).

Everyone must know the truth, and the truth will make them free if they chose to be (*John 8:33*). No one will be excused for not knowing what all should know at this late date. All of the information necessary for all to be made free, is locked up inside of the words of the scriptures, of the Bible/Torah. The masses of the entire western World have been taught away from knowing their inner selves. But the following Lexicon can be used as a tool to allow the masses to convert themselves away from the Darkness of the Lord, and be healed (*Isa. 6:10*).

Knowledge of the old Language through the Lexicon places one in the position to discover the truth about all of the elements of the Bible/Torah. The spoken and written Old Language is a degeneration away from the unspoken. Yet it is a language in which one can not lie, or make a mistake, unless one intend to do so. The main purpose of the following **Lexicons** is to open up the true meaning of many of the key words of the Bible/Torah so that the masses can see and know basically what the Rabbis, Priests, and Ministers that rule them have always known. All that has been in the Darkness shall come into the Light (*I Corin. 4:5*).

# Summations Lexicon

*April 8, 2003 (From MSPub)(Abel)*

*Abel* — הבל - "Effeminate," "Airy," "Faint"- Cain's twin brother Abel was "her Seed." Abel desired his brother Cain, and their father the Lord forced Cain to be his husband (*Gen. 4:7-9*).

*Adam (Phones)* -- אדם -- *"I am Blood (Red),"* *"Earthling"* -- Man (Adam) is a firey being, and progeny of the sun. The redness is not a complexion, but the actual original fervent appearance of Man (Adam), and the Earth (Adamah). To know the present complexion of Adam is to know who can stand on the equator in the sun all day without harm.

*Adultery* -- מהל -- *"From Corrupting," "Alter," "Mix"* -- Adultery is exactly the act of "mixing" two kinds. Genetically this would be the mixing of the two populations on the planet, **Asians** and **CaucAsians**.

*Afflict(able)* -- ענה -- "Answer," "Solution, Having the ability to withstand all situations" -- "Answer" "Solution" to any circumstance.

*Almighty* -- שדי -- "Casted out" (Devil) Shaddai (שדי) is the source of the word "Shadow." The Almighty fell' when he was casted out in defeat (*Rev. 12:9*)

*Alien (Phones.)* -- עליון -- *"One Who Goes Up."* This is the sun, the Most High God, Shemesh (שמש).

*Almighty God* -- אל שדי -- "The God Casted Out" (*Nu. 24:4, 16*) The **"Devil God,"** This is Hallel (Lucifer), the God of Abraham (*Isa. 14:12*).

*Amori (Phones.)* -- אמורי -- These were the Amorites that Abraham temporarily lived among, and who Abraham sent his children to live among in the East Country. They were never afflicted by the Amorites.

*Ancient of Days* -- עתיק יומים -- "Setter free of Days." This is Michael/ Melchezedek the Greater of the two great Luminaries. He rules the day and Light, and therefore is the "Setter Free" of those in bondage to Hallel (Lucifer) the Prince of Darkness (*Amos 5:18, 20*). Jesus (Son of Man) was after the "Order of Melchezedek" to "Set Free," the captive Israelis in bondage to the Lord (Hallel).

*Apostle (Apostate)* -- Αποστωσσ -- *Apostrophe," "Curved," "Perverted"* -- Paul the Apostle, perverted the teachings of Jesus (Yeshua), into what the church is now teaching.

*Apple (Phones.)* -- אפל (*I Fall / Awful*) -- *"Thick Darkness"* -- Thick Darkness is the "Apple," or Fruit of the Fall. This is the fruit of the Serpent or Lord, the Mandrake or Man of Darkness fruit (*Amos 5:18, 19*).

*Ararat* -- אררת -- "I am Cursed." This cursed mount is the northern residence of Hallel the God of Abraham (*Ps. 48:2*).

*Arphaxad* (Arpha Ca-Shaddai) -- ארפא כשדי -- "Border of the Ca-Shaddai (Chaldeans)" *See* "Almighty" above for the term "Shaddai" Arphaxad is the son of Shem who was born two years after the flooding of the Tigris River. *See Chaldea(n)*

*"Awoke"* — קיץ — *"Finish," "Terminate," "End"* This word (קיץ) lie below the word "Awoke," when it said: "...and Noah "awoke." This is an intentional mistranslation. The true translation is ... and Noah "finished" his wine (*Gen.9:24*), he was never asleep!

*Armageddon* -- ערם אגדון -- *"Place of Trading," "Business District"(in Canaan)* -- Armageddon (Megiddo) was a group of Canaanite towns by the sea (*Joshua 12:21, 17:11; Jgs. 1:27*), a business district that is only associated with warfare and killing, because the Lord was jealous of all of the people there including Israel getting along together in business, and trade (*Ezekiel 27Chptr.*). *See Strong's #4023 (Megiddo) "Meeting Place," and #1413, 9 (Gad) = "Prosperous Crowded Stores."*

*Assiah (Asia)* -- אשה -- *"Fire," "Man," "Foundation"* -- This was the first name of this orb which is now called "planet," and "Earth." The words Man, fire, and Adamah (Earth) speak to the true appearance of the original Man and the planet when Man brought it forth from the sun. See Lexicon *"Adam"*

*Asshur* --אששר -- "I encompass." The second son of Shem. Nimrod (Asshur's nephew) inherited childless Asshur's household. Nimrod is the "Assyrian" at Genesis 10:11, and throughout the "book" of Isaiah.

# Summations
# Lexicon

*Baal Zebub* -- בעל זבב -- *"Lord of the Flies," "Inheritor of Flies"* -- This is a title given to Hallel the Lord of Abraham, because he boasted that he could cause flies to be anywhere he wanted them to go in Egypt, while keeping them away from his people, the Israelis in Goshen (*Ex 8:21, 22*) Flies would be all over the blood of sacrificial altars.

*Babel* -- בבל -- "Gate of God" (Confusion), One of the six cities that made up Nimrod's Ur Metropolis. Babel was the phallic or flood tower city used to breed (Graft) Cain's children from the Shadows back into the Light. (*Isa. 9:2*)

*Bad (Phones)* -- בד -- *"Alone," "Part," "Separated," "Incomplete," "Evil"* -- Hallel is a Bad or "Alone" God (*Isa. 43:10*).

*Beast* -- הים -- **"Living Ones,"** "Beast" in this case are not animals, but are Man the "animators," the "Life Forces" dwelling inside of all physical forms, from microbes to plants to animals, to the "manform." **Beast of the Field**, and **Beast of the Earth** are both Man.

> *Hallel and his Host became* Beast of the Field *when they were defeated and Cast Down to the vicinity of the planet. The atmosphere around the planet is the "Field."*
>
> *When they came down, fell down (Nephalim) to the planet they became* Beast of the earth. *They are the Children of the Gods, who mated with (Had Dominion over) the Fair/pale daughters of Cain (Gen. 6:2).*

*Beget* -- לד *(Lad)* -- *"Continuation"* -- The Begotten or continuation of a family are the first born males.

*Beguile* -- נשא -- "To tax," "To Pressure," "To Drive." The Serpent (Lord) "Begged/Beguiled' Eve to **consume/consummate** sex with him (**Gen. 3:13**).

*Believe (Be Live)* -- אם -- *"Study," "Investigate," Discipline* -- "Believe" is a damaged word, by being misdefined into meaning one excepting something without seeing. The true meaning of the word "believe" is to have Eyes to see and Ears to Hear, thus to be able to "Study," and to "investigate" and to "Belive" (believe)," or "Live" what you know.

*Being* -- הים -- *"Life," "Existence"* -- Being is Man. In the physical state Man, the invisible being dwells inside of physical forms.

*Belly (Numbers 25.8)* -- נקבה -- *"Vagina," "Vulva"* -- At *Num.25:8* Cozbi a Midianite woman is having intercourse with an Israeli man. Both are killed because another Israelis man drives a spear down apparently through the man's anus into Cozbi's vagina (not belly).

*Bitter* - מרי *(Mary)* -- Mary (מרי / bitter) is not the name of Jesus' mother, but is a description of what she felt when the Lord who had overshadowed her and impregnated her, had Jesus his son murdered for telling him to "get thee hence Satan (*Matt. 4:10*)!"

*Blessed* -- ברכה -- "Broken," "Domesticated," "Beat Down," "Subdued," "Chastised," "Folded over," "Bent to the will of another." "Castrated," "Spaved" or "Neutered."

*Blood* -- דום -- *"Sameness," "Likeness"* -- Blood is the medium through which a link is made, between the physical form that the blood is in, and the nonphysical beings who makes the body be alive by being the life in the blood. The Lord agrees by saying to those who sacrifice to him that the life (Soul) that he needs is within the blood of the sacrificed (*Leviticus 17:16, 13*). Banishment from the tribe was the Lord's punishment for those who ate blood (*Lev. 7:26, 27*).

*Breast* -- שר *(Sade)* -- Sade (שר) is the old language word for "Lady" pertaining to her breasts being "Casted Out" and producing shade. The whole root idea is "Casted Out." Strong's Concordance #7705. <u>This is next to #7706 which is Shaddai (Breasted One) who is the Lord of Abraham, who was "Casted Out" from the heavens in defeat.</u> (Breasted God).

*Bright (ness)* --הגן -- "Shine," "Illuminate," "Glow," "Absence of Darkness." The Day of the Lord is Darkness with no "Brightness" in it. (Amos 5:18,20) Brightness implies ability to see and know. (Eyes to see, and ears to hear).

*Brother (Phones.)* הים *(Breather/Brother) -- Live(r)"* -- ... and God "breathed" the breath of life into the Man (form) and Man (form) became a "living" Soul (*Gen. 2:7*).

*Brother (Trans.)* -- אהי -- *"I Live"* --- All of the original

# Summations Lexicon

inhabitants of the planet are brothers /breathers or "Living Ones"

*Cain* -- קין -- "Jealous" -- First Begotten son of the Lord with Eve (*Gen. 4:1*). "I have Gotten a man with (את) the Lord." Cain meaning "jealous" making Cain a jealous junior to a jealous God.

*Calah* --כלה-- "Complete," "Mature" The sixth of Nimrod's six city Ur Metropolis.

*Canaan* --כנען -- "Excavator," "Depression" Son of Ham involved in the Tent Incident.

*Chaldea(n)* --כשדי --Ca-Shaddai "Like the Devil(s)," "Like the Almighty." The marked children of Cain. The Horite or whores of Mou<u>n</u>d Ararat. Caucasian Race

*Cherubs* -- כרב -- *"Blockers," "Adversaries"* Guarders of the Tree of Life, and the east gate of Eden.

*Circumcise* -- מול - *(Mule)* -- *"take away"* -- Carried away from normal, as in malcontent,. etc.

*Civilize (Phones.)* -- כבל *(Cable)* -- *"Cable Towed," "Bondage," "Fettered," "Held"* -- To be bounded by force, into doing what is social and proper. To be domesticated as an animal from the wilds. To have to be civilized is not a complement. Only three groups on the entire planet had to have this process. This was the Caucasian Race, the Israelis, and the Arabs. כבל The World wears civility as a false garment. Ladies, Gentlemen, Manners, Taste etc., is all artificial.

*Civil (Phones.)* -- קבל *(Cable)* -- *"To Receive" "Be in Contact"* -- This is the second part of being civil. To be receptive, having conscience, and conscious of ones actions. For the original population of this planet it is a natural state. For those who had to be forced, to be civil it is an artificial state.

*City (Fort/Stockade)* -- (עיר / *Ur*) -- *"Light." "Traffic," "Activity," "Conduit"*

*Confound/Confuse* --בבל *(Babel)* -- "Gate of God" a place of confusion like "Jacob's Ladder (*Gen. 28:12*)"
*Consort (Hurt)* --תבר "Sodomize/Rape." Cain's descendant Lamech is telling his wives that he has been raped (*Gen. 5:23*)!

*Continent(s)* -- ארץ -- *"Fragmented," "Cracked," "Broken"* -- This is the true meaning of the word "Ertz," or "Earth" (*Gen. 1:10*) given by the ones who took the water off the land to see what it looked like after the Lord and his Host had destroyed the planet (*Isa. 24:1-6*).

*Corrupt (Phone)* -- ברפת *(Craft)* -- "To Create" or "craft," or "Alter" something away from it's original state, into something Other than it's self.

*Corrupt (Trans.)* -- הולי -- *"Holy"* -- To be Holy is to be corrupt, in a special way.

*Coven(ant)* -- ברית *(Rite)* -- "Cutting" -- This was the pact made between Abraham and the Lord. Abraham and his descendants would circumcise (cut) the flesh from the head of the penis, as a symbolic gesture of sacrifice of flesh to the Lord. "Sacrifice of penus flesh to the Lord," is a veiled hint as to what "Holy" really means.

*Cozbi* -- כזבי *(Ca--Zebob)* -- "Like a bee" This implies one who walks/dances lightly almost floating, "like a bee (*Nu. 25:15*) ."

*Create (Phones)* -- כרת -- "Break Off' or "Face off." This implies that there is something already existing that is being altered.

*Create (Trans.)* -- ברא -- **"In seeing,"** "Found" To see or find is to imply that something is there to be "seen," or "found!" Therefore to give the impression that something was brought into being from nothing is beyond the full scope of this word!

*Creator (Phones.)* (*Ecclus. 12:1*) -- ברה -- *"See," "Cut Down ," "Break off"* -- A Creator is one who alters what already exists, as when a man cuts down a tree and "Creates" (corrupts) it into an art piece. The "creating" of the Caucasian race was the beguiling (Corrupting) of Eve the female side of Man (Adam) who had been put to sleep, and altered (**Isa. 48:2**).

**Curse** — ארר (Arra) - This is the root to the word Ararat (Thou are Cursed). Cursed (Ararat) is Zion the mound of the Lord in the Side of the North in Nod (*Psalms 48:2*).

*Cush (Ethiopia)* -- כוש - - **"Manly"** One of the sons of

# Summations Lexicon

Ham. **Cash** and **Cushion**, two words derived from the word Cush give a hint at the wealth and luxury of Cush's empire that stretched north from Arabia to the Tigris River, and from the Anti Lebanon mountains eastward to the Indian continent which is Hindu Cush, the land of Sind. (Northwestern India)

*Darkness (Phone)* -- דרכה -- "Wayward" Being away (Absent) from Self is to be with the Lord, or in Darkness (*IICorinthian 5:6 , Amos 5:18, 20*).

*Darkness (Trans.)* -- חושך (Hoshack) -- *"Wayward," "Debilitated,"* "Lacking," "Insufficient," " Obscure." This is the Lord's Day (**Ps.118:24; Amos 5:18, 20**)

*Day* -- יום -- *"Warmth," "Day," "Sea"* -- "Day," and "Sea" are tied together through the root idea of *Yom* (יום) which implies "temperature" (warmth), of the day and the sea, rather than the light.

*Dead (Trans.)* -- מות -- *"Mute," "Canceled out."*

*Dedan* -- דדן -- *"Circler"* -- Dedan and Sheba, are the two sons of Raamah. These three descendants of Cush the founders of Sind or Hindu Cush.

*Defile?* -- ענה -- *"Commend," "Applaud," "Praise"* This word Anna is translated into the English as the word "answer, when the Lord "answered" Job (*Job 38:1*). If shechem "defiled" Dinah, then the Lord "Defiled Job, for the same word is used in the two separate cases.

*Desolation* -- שד -- Isa. 51:19, Hos. 12:1 -- "Devil"

*Destruction* -- שד -- *"Devil"* Broad is the Way (דרכה / Darkness), that leads to the Devil/Lord (שד / Destroyer) (*Job 5:21, 22 Prov. 24:22 Isa. 13:6 Hos. 7:13 -9:6 Joel 1:15*). Joel and Isaiah carry the exact same phrase.

*Devil* - שד - (*Job 5:21, 22 Prov. 24:22 Isa. 13:6 Hos. 7:13 -9:6 Joel 1:15*). Joel and Isaiah carry the exact same phrase, The Lord shall come as a Devil from the Devils (*Job 5:21, 22 Prov. 24:22 Isa. 13:6 Hos. 7:13 -9:6 Joel 1:15*).

*Disciple*(*Isa. 8:16*)—למוד—"Disciplined," "Instructed."

*Diklah* -- דקלה -- "Palm Tree" A descendant of Arphaxad, named after the Tigris River (Haddekel) -- (הדקלה) The Tigris was called the River of Palms, because of the many and varied Palm trees that grew along most of it's length. Diklah is of course named by this being the region that was allocated to him along a northern portion of the Tigris River.

*Dinah* — דנה — "Mistress," "Madame" -- Daughter of Leah with Jacob. She was not "defiled," but was the "Answer" for Shechem the Prince of the city.

*Earth (Phones.)* -- ארץ -- *"Fragments," "Broken," "Continent."* -- This is a description of what **Assiah** looked like when the water had been drained from it's surface. The land had not been broken, before the Lord and his Host came down, to destroy (שד) the planet (Isa. 24:1, 3-6)!

*Earth (Trans.)* — אדמה -- *"Redness," "Fire," "Fervent"* -- This is the original condition and appearance of the planet. **Adamah (Earth)**, corresponds to **Adam (Earthling)**

*East* -- קדם (Cadem) -- *"First"— "Forward," "Front," Forward."* This is the source of the word Accad (Academy) pertaining to Nimrod bringing some of the children of Cain from his city Accad (Academy) to build **Nineveh, Resen, and Calah.**

*Eden* -- עדן -- *"Pleasure"*-- By Biblical description Eden is west of it's Garden (**Gen. 2:8, 10**). The entire land mass between Egypt, and the Tigris River has been declared as the Garden. Therefore Eden (Africa) is west of it's Garden

*Egypt (Misraim)* -- מצרים -- *"Transformers"* -- Egypt is the chief tabernacle of Ham, who would not bow down to Hallel the Corrupter, who is the Lord of Abraham! Egypt and all of the rest of the lands of the children of Ham were places for the Corrupt ones from the north to Transform, Reform, or Repent, if they chose to be whole again.

*Erech* (Iraq) -- ארך -- *"Expanded," "Elongated," "Chained"* --The second city of the six city Ur Complex built east of the Tigris, by Nimrod for the Chaldean, or Caucasian Race, in the north of Nod.

# Summation Lexicon

*Esau* -- עשו -- *"Red"* Hairy and Red Esau is one of the two sons, of the Lord with Rebecca (*Gen. 25:25*).

*Eternity* -- עלם -- *"Elemental," or "Universal."* The entire idea here is "Source." The Universe or "Eternity is the source of all Life, the source of Being, and the source of Time and Space. All pour forth from Eternity, and all pour back into it. *Life Everlasting* pertains to physical existence, but has it's roots in *Eternity*.

*Euphrates (Phones)* -- פרת -- *"Frats"* "Frats," is the source of the name "Fruits." The Frats or Euphrates is the southern river of Mesopotamia, Ethiopia, or Cush.

*Eve* -- הוה *(Havah) "Life," "Breath"* -- This is the Wombman (Woman/Life) taken out of the Earthling Adam. Adam died, and Eve (Life) was a widow.

*Evil* -- רע -- *"State of Eve,"* The whole idea here is "Incompleteness," "broken," "Separated," as Eve was Separated from Adam. Thus needing a "Host," "Friend," or "Companion" to be complete. This is the state that the Lord of Abraham is in, and therefore he needs a Host to make himself artificially complete. This is the condition that the Lord wants everyone to be in when he has finished his agenda (*Jeremiah 45:5*).

*Fall (Phones)* -- נפל פל -- To be "separated," to be "Casted Out." *Lucifer (Hallel),* and his Host became *Nephalim, Giants,* or *Felons (Fallen Ones),* when they were defeated and "Casted" down" to the planet. As Fallen Ones (fellows) they were Giants (גנות) or Gardeners (גנות) made to tend Eden's Garden (גן).

*Fellow (Phones)* — *"Fallow"* -- *"Fell Low"* to "fall low" as in the case of Hallel the Lord of Abraham who fell (*Num. 24:4, 16*). To be yellow or Fallow (Pale).

*Fill* — מלח -- *Multiply (Phones)* -- To increase by dividing (Doubling/Deviling). The commandment at *Gen. 1:28* was given to the Devils or Doublers to Divide the one (Adam) into two. *Garden (Phones)* -- גרדן -- *"Place of Grading," "Sorting," or "Judging" (Tribunal)* -- The Lord of Abraham was tried in the garden for war crimes on earth and in the heavens.

*Garden (Trans.)* — גן -- *"Guarded Place," "Compound," "Shielded" (Magan)*

*Gate* -- בב -- *"Opening"* -- Bab as in Babel (Gate of God) -- A "Gate" is a port in or out. The East gate of the Garden was the entire length of the Tigris River. The land east and north of the Tigris was the land of Nod.

*Gentiles (Phones)* -- גנתל -- *"Rubbish from the Garden."* These ones are descendant from Cain whose father the Lord Hallel was casted forth from the Garden (*Gen. 3:24*).

*Gentiles (Trans.)* -- גוים (Goyim) "Gangs," "Hoards," "Mobs", These are the children of Cain who were confined northward, in the Land of "Nod", which is the land of "Mounds" above the Tigris River in Mound Ararat.

*Gomorrah* -- עמוררה -- *"Storage," "Stack," "Stock" "Stockade"* One of the twin prison cities of Sodom and Gomorrah. These two cities were originally built to store corn, wheat and other grains, after harvest. There were no people living there in either city!

The twin cities were converted into a quarantine, to hold the people of Ur/Babel, after the Lord of the North confounded the Children of Cain, and scattered them down into the fertile land of Ham. These are the "Gentiles" or "Confined Ones" (*Gen. 11:9*).

*Goshen* -- גושן -- *"Place of Filth"* (Corruption) -- Originally the best land, Goshen was the region in Egypt, that the Israelis were "confined" to, like the other Gentiles had been "confined" to Sodom and Gomorrah. Being bound to the vicinity of the "Region of Filth" (Goshen), was the only bondage that the Israelis had in Egypt. The Israelis were forced to stay there in quarantine, so as not to infect the Egyptians with their corrupt lifestyle.

*Hagar* -- הגר -- *"The Stranger," "The Outsider," The Alien"* Hagar is the name given to the mother of Ishmael by Abraham, and his Sister/Wife/Niece Sarah. It shows that there was animosity from these two toward Ishmael mother from the very beginning.

*Hallel* — חלל — *"Lucifer," "Night God"* It was from this name that the term Hallelujah was formed. Hallelujah means "Hallel our Jah," "Lucifer our Jah," or "Lucifer our Jehovah."

Lexicons

# Summations Lexicon

*Ham* -- חם — *"Associated," "Joined," "Confederated"* --Thus "Consolidated", "Prosperous", and "Wealthy." This is in fact the nature of the entire lands of Ham, and all of his children.

*Haran* -- הרן -- *"Mountaineer"* -- Haran (Mountaineer) is the elder brother of Abraham. Nahor (Our Mountain), is the other brother of Abraham. These two names describe that Abraham's entire family lived in the mountains north of Mesopotamia.

*Harlot (Phones.)* -- הרלוט -- *"Veiled Mountaineer"* -- A disguised Prostitute, or Whore (הור) or Mountain Dweller. *Tamar* Judah's daughter-in law mimicked this corrupt habit, imported from the mountains of the north. Sarah was the first to bring prostitution, then Dinah Jacob/Israel's daughter, into the Land of Ham.

*Harlot* -- **(Trans.)** - זנה (Zona) -- This is the old spelling for the word "Zion." This word came into the English as the word "Zone," which implies that someone or some place has been designated for a certain purpose!

*Havilah* -- החוילה (*Gen.2:11*) -- *"Orbit," "Tumble," "Spiral," "Spin" (Gyro)* The idea here is to hold stability by oscillation around a circuit, or track.

*Heaven(s)* -- שמים -- *"Space(s)," "Skies,"* This pertains to the atmosphere (Field) around the planet. This is the "Heavens that the Lord threatened to destroy at *Pet.3:10*

*Heaven* — הוהן — *"Place of Life"* Jesus said that the Place of Life (Heaven) is within (*Luke 7:21*).

*Heber (Eber/Over)* -- עבר -- *"Cross Over," "Pass Over"* This is the source of the word "Hebrew" (הבר), which simply means "To Cross Over."

*Hebrew (Verb)* -- עבברי -- *"Cross Over"* -- Genesis 14:13 Abraham the "Hebrewer," left the famine ridden land of his nativity Ur of the Chaldeans, north of the Tigris River. He "hebrewed (Crossed) the Tigris down into Ham's Land of Milk and Honey.

**Hell (Hills)** — שאול This is not the grave as inferred by some translators, but is the subterranean city that Cain built in the "hills" of Ararat. *Strong's Concordance #7585*

*Hiel* -- היאל -- *"God Lives"* Hiel is descendant from Canaan. Hiel built the city of Jericho (ירהוה) "Lunar."

*Holy (Phones)* -- חולי -- *"Corrupt," "Hollow," "Profane."* Holy (חולי) or corrupt is the sounding or the phonics of the Old Language word behind the word "Formed" (*Deut. 32:18*). See "Profane"

*Holy (Trans.)* — קדש -- *"Prostrated" (flat), "Prostituted," "Sodomized." Deut. 23:17* Use Strong's Concordance, and compare the words *"whore"* #6947, and *"Holy"* #6944. In between the two word and having the same root is *"Sodomite" at #6945.*

*Horn(s)* -- קרן -- *Ex. 34:29 30, 35* -- ... "and the skin of Moses face (forehead) was "horned" not "shone," when he come down from talking with the Lord!

*Horeb* -- הרבה *(Horebah)* -- *"Famine Mountain," Dried Up"* -- Horeb (Horrible) is the mountain of the God of Abraham, Isaac, and Jacob, in the land of Canaan. It was famished because the Lord was there. Jacob (Israel and the twelve had to leave Canaan, to go to Egypt to survive the Lord,s famine (*Deut. 26:5*). When the Lord followed them he brought the famine with him. For the Israelis to survive and multiply the Lord (and his Host), had to return to Horeb to go into hibernation up side down, for approx., 400 years, while the Israelis multiplied in Egypt!

*Horite (Phones.)* -- הורי -- *"Troglodyte," "Cave Dweller" "Whore"*-- Horites are cave dweller in the Horim (Mountains) הורים north of the Tigris River. Seir (Sear) the "hairy one" is the father of the Horites (*Gen. 36:21*). These are the Gentiles, they are the descendants of Cain.

*Horn(s)* -- קרן -- (*Ex. 34:29 30, 35*) -- ...and the skin of Moses face (forehead) was "horned" (when he had come down from talking with the Lord!)

*Host (Phones.)* -- חות -- *"Living Ones" (Manifested)* -- These are the "Companions" of the Lord. They are the

# Summations Lexicon

*Host (Phones.)* -- *"Hostility," "Hostage"* -- The Host of the Lord committed "hostilities" against the Egyptians, and help him to hold the Israelis Hostage (Bondage).

*Host (Trans.)* -- צבאם -- *"Mass," "Mob"* (as are Gentiles or Goyim) -- The Host of the Lord are his friend (רע), and make him complete. "Evil" (רע) On the behalf of the Lord shall be on all flesh. *Jer.45:5*

*Hurt* -- חברת -- *"Consort," Mate," "Rape," "Sodomize"* -- In translation Lamech is made to use the word "hurt" (*Gen. 4:23*), but he is telling his two wives that one man was raping him, while another cut him when he resisted. Lamech caught up with them later and killed them both! Lamech identifies the older man as Cain himself when he makes the statement, "if Cain be avenged seven times (because I killed him), then will I being in Cain's line be avenged seventy times (because he helped my being raped)(*Gen.4:24*)?

*Husband* -- שמר -- *"Keeper"* -- *Gen. 4:9* In the context of the relationship between Cain, Abel, and the Lord. The Lord had ask Cain to allow his effeminate brother to "desire" him, and for Cain to "rule" (Husband) over him, as Adam ruled Eve (*Gen. 3:16, Gen. 4:7*).

Thus the Lord is Asking Cain where the effeminate (Abel) one is. Cain is askng the Lord if he (Cain) is Abel's husband (Keeper), to know where he is!

*Iscah (Sarah)* -- יסכה -- *"Seeress," "Priestess" "Burst out Laughing."* Born in the house of Haran (Abram's dead brother), Iscah is Sarah disguised. Sarah mother is the widow of Haran, and Sarah's father is Terah, Abraham's father. Terah is also Sarah's grandfather, and father-in-law, and Sarah is Abraham's cousin/ wife/niece!

*Ishmael* -- ישמעאל -- *"God Hears"* (*Gen. 16:11*) -- Abraham's first son from the rape of Hagar. (Shari Misraim).

*Islam* -- אשלום -- *"I am Peace"* -- The Order (Peace) of Michael/Melchezedek. Ham and all of his children followed this order of Adam, that Ishmael/Midian, and later Jesus (Yeshua) would also follow.

*Isle(s)* -- אי -- *"Helter Skelter," "Lamentation," "Confusion," "Occident"* -- These isles synonymous with confusion, are the isles of the Gentiles (*Gen. 10:1*). Gentiles or Goyim are the descendants of Cain.

*Israel* -- ישראל -- Means *"He Wrestled God."* The Lord told Jacob to build an altar to the Man/God (the Lord himself)(*Gen. 32:24*), who Jacob "wrestled" in the wilderness (*Gen. 35:1*). The Lord is the man who named Jacob "Wrestled with God" (Israel)(*Gen. 32:28*).

*Jabal Cain* - יבל קין --
*Jubal Cain* - יבול קין --
*Tubal Cain* -- תבל קין -- *"World Cain"* All three sons of Cain's descendant Lamech, fall under this name. -- Jabal, Jubal, are derivations of what the third name Tubal means. Tubal (World), does not mean planet, but means "Total Corruption".

*Jacob* -- יעקב -- *"Heel," "Overtake," "Supplant"* -- One of the Lord,s twin sons with Rebecca, Jacob is actually the third Jacob (Subplanter), with his father the Lord being the first, Cain being the second, and Jacob himself being the third. The twelve representing him would exterminate all the males of Abraham's true children (Ishmael /Midian), and supplant or take their identity, by the rape of the pubelescent little Ishmael/Midianite girls that they had kept for that purpose (*Nu. 31:18*).

*Jah* -- יה -- *"He is"* -- The abbreviation of the word Yeweh, or Jehovah, Abraham's God.

*Japheth* -- יפת *"extended," "Opened," "Gaped"* -- The youngest of the three sons of Noah. Japheth along with Shem "covered up" what Noah was attempting to do with his grandson Canaan in his tent!

It is excepted that wooly headed brown Japheth is the father, or the source of the aboriginal people of Europe. Their chief goddess is/was Europa.

*Javan* -- יון *(Ionia)* -- *"Jovial," "Effervescent"* -- Bubbly like wine. A son of Japheth, perhaps the origin of the Archaic Greeks.

*Jebus* -- יבס -- *"Bridge," "Link"* -- A Son of Canaan. Jebus and his children had the privilege to build

# Summations Lexicon

Jerusalem for themselves and Michael /Melchezedek the Overseer of the Most High (*Gen. 14:18*).

**Jehovah** -- יהוה -- *"He is"* -- Jehovah (Living One) said that life is in the blood (*Gen. 9:4*). Yet the Lord loss blood to exist in, when his body was slain, and cast into the flames (*Dan. 7:10*). Thus the Lord's only continuation has been the Sacrificial Life blood, pourd down into the ground, where he told Moses he dwell (*Ex. 8:22*).

**JeruSalem** — ירושלם — *"City of Peace"* -- Jews, Gentiles and "Mohammedans" see Jerusalem the city of Melchezedek, as a common shrine. Yet the city was built by the children of Canaan. The reason that these three hold reverence for Jerusalem is that this city represents the source of the "peace" that was offered to each group at three individual times by three individuals representing the Universal Order of Melchezedek. These three were **Nimrod** to the **Gentiles**, **Jesus** to the **Jews**, and **Mohammed** to the **Arabians**. None of these three groups have ever lived in peace (Salem / Islam) by their own choice.

**Jericho** -- יריחו — *"Lunar," "Cycles,", "Phases."* -- Perhaps an astronomical center, in the land of Canaan. A place where times and seasonal accuracy can be maintained. City of palm trees.

**Jeremiah** -- ירמיה -- *"He (Jehovah) shall betray you."* -- This compound word, and the Book of Jeremiah (Book of Jehovah Betraying), describe the bondage that the Lord imposed upon the Israelis.

**Jesus (Yeshua)** -- ישוע -- *"He Saves"* -- This is not a saving of life, but is to be "made free (ישע)," from bondage to the Lord. Jesus said the truth shall make you "free (ישע)(*John 8:32*)," and he said do not **find** life in the physical (*Matt. 10:39*), but be willing to die, up through the Narrow Gate, to **find** Eternal (Real) Life (*Matt. 7:14*). See Strong's Concordances #3442, 3443 (Yeshua / Jesus), and #3468 (free) to see that the words for Jesus, and freedom, are the same word.

**Jethro** -- יתרו -- *"Abundant," "Fruitful"* -- A descendant of Ishmael. Jethro is the instructor, and the father-in-Law of Moses.

**Jochebed** -- יוכבד -- *"She (it) is Heavy"* (כבד) -- When Jochebed's husband died she married her nephew Amram! Jochebed and her nephew Amram are the mother and father of Moses, and Aaron (*Ex. 6:20*). Miriam was her step father Amram's cousin!

**Joktan** -- יובטן -- *"He is Small," "Lesser"* -- The second (Lesser) of the two sons of Eber in the line of Arphaxad, before Abraham was born.

**Jonah** -- יונה -- *"Dove," "Effervescence"* -- Jonah was sent by the Lord to the inhabitants of Nineveh to warn them to change their ways. Actually this was the Ur Metropolis, which was composed of **Babel, Erech, Accad, Nineveh, Resen, and Calah.** This same was a great city, taking three days or approximately 60 miles to cross.

**Joseph** -- יוסף -- *"Addition," "Increase"* -- Rachael the mother of Joseph, "wrestled" with the Lord (Great Wrestling), demanding that he give her a child. The end results of this was that the Lord "opened" her womb, and impregnated her with Joseph (*Gen. 30:8*).

**Judah** -- יהודה -- *"Praise the Lord"* -- This is the Lord's fourth son with Leah (*Gen. 29:35*).

**Kadesh** -- קדש -- *"Prostrate," "Holy"* -- Satellite town to Sodom and Gomorrah. Kadesh was a town of religious Sodomites, or "Holy Ones"

**Keturah** — קטורה — *"Perfume," "Incense," "Fragrance"* -- The mother of the several of Abraham's sons after Ishmael. These all eventually fell up under the name "Midian." Their children came into confederation with the children of Ishmael.

**Kingdom** — מלכות — *"Principality," "Council"* -- *Gen. 10:10, Gen. 11:1-9, Dan. 1:2, Isaiah 23:13* These passages speak to the first, civilizing station ever built for the Caucasian Race. It was built by Nimrod and thousand of the wooly headed children of Ham who went north of the Tigris into the land of Nod to save those there.

**Lamech** — למך — *"Bruised," "To Gather Together"* -- Descendant of Cain's line. He killed Cain, and an

# Summations Lexicon

unidentified young man, who had raped him (*Gen. 4:23*)!

***Lemech*** — למך — *"Gather Together"* -- Adam's line, the father of Noah.

***Leah*** — לאה — *"Wearied," "Worked in Vain"* -- The mother of the first four sons of Jacob, with the Lord.

***Leper/Leprous/Leprosy*** — צרוע — *"Smitten of the Lord"* —— This is a condition first accounted for at Ex.4:6, and Lev.13:2, 45, among the Israelis while they were in the wilderness with the Lord.

***Levi*** — לוי — *"Attraction," "Join Closely"* -- This is Leah's third son with the Lord. Leah thought that her husband Jacob would surely be "attracted" to her after she had a third child for the Lord!

***Life*** — חי — *"Breath," "Animation"* -- This word חי (Life) is under the term "Beast," yet life is not an "animal," but an "animator."

***Light*** — אור — *Intelligence," "Illumination"* - *"Brightness"* -- *"Enlightenment," Revelation."* This (light) is opposite to the Lord's Day, which has no brightness (intelligence) at all (*Amos 5:18, 20*).

***Lot*** -- לוט -- *"Veiled," "Covered up"*-- Abraham's nephew, and Sarah's brother. Lot became a permanent citizen of Sodom, and was therefore a Sodomite, as were Lot's sons and sons - in - Law (*Gen. 19:12*).

Lot committed incest with his two daughters and became the father of a son from each. Their names were Ammon (*Gen. 19:38*), and Moab (*Gen. 19:37*).

***Lotan*** -- לוטן -- *"Veiled One," "Hidden"* -- A son of Seir (Sear) the Horite.

***Love*** (trans.) — אהב — *"To Lust After."* This is the love that the Lord demanded from the Israelis (*Ex. 20:6*), to **"lust after"** him!

***Love*** (Phone.) — לו — *"***To be Attracted (Joined), "To be Drawn"*** This is the Love that Leah wanted from Jacob (*Gen. 29:34*)

***Love*** (Trans.) — בנה — **"Understand"** To understand is for the mental to come to a balance, and thought to a minimum. This is wisdom (Binah).

***Lucifer*** (Phones.) -- לוספר -- *"To Number (Count/Counter)"* -- The Prince of Darkness, God of Darkness (DarkEl/Dracula), Man of Darkness (ManDrake)(*Amos 5:18, 20*).

***Lucifer*** (Trans.) — חילל, חלל — *"Hallel (Hallelujah)," "The Night God," "The Prince of Darkness"* -- Hallel the Lord of the North (Siphonijah), the God of Abraham.

***Machpelah*** — מכפלה — *"For Coupling," "Copulation"* -- *Gen. 23:9* -- Machpelah was a cave where people went to have sex. Abraham purchased this cave so that he could bury Sarah there (*Gen. 23:19*).

***Made*** — (Trans.) — עש — *"Ush(er)," "Brought Together", "Pooled"* — All brought to one place

***Make*** (Phones.) — מק (Mecca) -- *"Gather Together"* Bring all to one place.

***Make*** (Trans.) — עש — *"Ush(er)," "Bring Together," "Pooled"* (As in a theater, or church).

***Male*** — זכר — *(Re)Member (Penis)* -- The source of the continuation of kind.

***(Fe)Male*** — נקבה — *"Cavity," "Hole," "Vagina"* -- Not closed up underneath as Adam was after being altered (*Gen. 2:21*).

***Man*** (Phones.) — מן — *"Progeny," "Offspring (Of the Sun)"* -- Man is a "soul" or "solar" Being.

***Man*** (Trans.) — איש — *"Fire"* -- Man the progeny of the sun, is a firey solar Being, wrapped in flesh.

***Man*** (Trans.)— אדם — *"Earthling," "Red /Brown"*
This is Adam, representing those who stayed with the planet.

Lexicons

# Summations Lexicon

*Mandrake (Phones.)* — מן דרך — *"Man of Darkness"* -- The Lord (Hallel), is the Prince of Darkness. *Amos 5:18,20* The Mandrake fruit (Apple/Awful) is Thick Darkness *(*אפל*)*(*Ex.20:21*)

*Mary* -- מרי -- *"Bitter"* -- This expresses the "bitterness" of the mother of Jesus (Yeshua), when the Lord had Jesus (His son) killed for telling him (the Lord) "get thee hence Satan!

*Marvel* (Wonder) — נפלא — "Felonies (Crimes)" The Lord told Moses that he would use the Israelis against the people of Canaan, to commit crimes (Marvels) that had never been seen, ever on this planet (*Ex. 34:10*).

*Megiddon* — מגדון — *"place of crowds," "Place of Exchange"* — All of the land of Canaan was prosperous and this prosperity was expressed ideally in Megiddon, a trade center.

*Melchezedek* — מלכי צדך — *"King of Righteous," "King of Salem"* — This is Michael the overseer for the Most High God (Sun)(*Gen. 14:18; Heb. 6:20*).

*Meek* — ענה — *"Solution," "Answer," "Tenacious"* -- Those who have the ability to adapt to any situation. The meek are the hardest of hard when necessary, or the softest of soft if necessary. The meek have the ability to take any form, be of any consistency, for the purpose of solving for what ever the case may be. Thus it is the meek who shall "reinherit" the entire earth (**Ps. 37:11**).

*Mesopotamia* --Μεσοποταμια -- *"Between the Rivers"* --- This is the land between the Tigris and Euphrates rivers, the Rivers of Ethiopia or Cush. This place is the core of the "Fertile Crescent"of the land of peaceable Ham, which is the heart of the land of Cush (Ethiopia)(*Gen. 2:13*).

*Michael* -- מיבאל -- *"From the likeness of God"* -- Michael/Melchezedek is planetary overseer for the Most High God (Sun)(*Gen. 14:18*).

*Midian* — מדין — *"Place of Decision,""Government," "Seat of Power"* — Son of Abraham This name and title was bestowed upon Ishmael, by his brothers, the other sons of Abraham. Ishmael presided over his brothers the Ishmael/Midian Confederation (*Gen. 16:12*).

*Milcah* — מלכה — Milcah is the first daughter of Terah. She is therefore the sister of Abraham, Sarah/Iscah, and Nahor. Nahor is Milcah's brother, to whom she was married and had three children! She had five children with her third son Kemuel (*Gen. 22:20, 21*)!

*Misraim (Egyptians)* — מצרים — *"Reform," "Transform," "Found"* — Misraim (Egypt), is Ham's oldest son. Ham ruled from Egypt. Ham and his descendants never bowed, sacrificed, or praised the Lord. To praise, bow down or sacrifice to the Lord violates Universal Law. (*Eccles. 5:1*). On the north side of the Tigris River there was praise, bowing, sacrifice, famine, warfare, and all else that made up the World of the Lord there. On the south side of the Tigris River there was self respect, peace, prosperity, and all that goes with being inside of the law. The fruitful south became a place of rescue and "reform," and repentance, for the Famished people of the north.

*Moon (Phones)* — מון — *"Progeny"* — The moon is the offspring or progeny of this planet. The moon was exploded out of this planet into existence by Hallel (The Lord), and his Host (*Isa. 24:1, 3-6*). The moon was originally the northern included polar region of this planet.

*Moon (Trans.)* — יריחו (*Jericho*) — *"Lunar"* — Keeper of cycles, and seasons. Once there were no seasons on the planet, and there was no moon, it was always summer, before the Lord destroyed it. *Isaiah 24:1-6* In restitution the moon now existing became a setter of times and seasons.

*Moriah* — מוריה — *"Bitter Jah," or "Bitter Jahova"* -- The Lord (Jehovah/Hallel), was bitter when Abraham brought Isaac, instead of Ishmael to be sacrificed! The Lord wanted Ishmael (Abraham's son) dead, so that Abraham could raise Isaac (The Lord's son).

*Moses* — משה — *"Withdrawal," "Deficit," "Lessening," "Apostasy"* -- Moses knew better as did Abraham, Isaac, Jacob, and the twelve who all chose to

Summations

# Summations Lexicon

bow down, sacrifice, and to praise El Shaddai the Devil Prince of the Darkness of the north.

*Most High* — עליון — *(Alien)* — *"One who goes up" (Sun)*. This is the sun who is the father (עבה/Origin) of us all. We all inherit from the sun, including the Lord of Abraham (*Deut. 32:8,9*)

*Mountain* — הור — *(Hor)* — The word Hor (Hore) for mountain, is the source of the word "whore," which speaks to the fact that the people who lived on the mountains north of the Tigris River "whored," or prostituted themselves before the Lord of the North. (Siphonijah)(*Psalms 48:2*).

*Multiply (Phones.)* — מלאת — *"Fill," or "Double" (Devil)*. In the case multiplying is done by first dividing the one into two (Adam and Eve). Once the one has been made two (multiplied), then the female side can have "multiple" births from the male side.

*Nahor* — נהור — *"We Mountaineers"* — Named after his grandfather, this is one of the brothers of Abraham whose father Terah married Nahor to his sister Milcah (*Gen. 11:29*)! Nahor's name along with his other brother Haran's name, places this family and the city of Ur in the mountains north of The Tigris River.

*Naked* — עירם — (ארם) -- *"Exposed," "Seen," "Manifest"* This speaks both to the serpent of Gen. 3:1, and Adam and Eve becoming manifest in the concrete physical. Subtle (ערמ), mean exposed (Naked).

*Named* — שם — *(Shem)* — *"Located," "Set"* — "To be identified." "Named," or "Shem" is the name of Noah's second son. All of the children of Noah are named and located. Thus the people at Gen. 11:4 who want a name or identity are not the children of Noah, but are the Chaldean children of Cain (**Isa. 23:13**).

*Nation(s) (Phones.)* — נתן — *"Nathan"* — *"Gift," "Given"* — This pertains to the Lord impregnating women, and then "giving" the children to someone else to raise. Some of the women that the Lord impregnated are Eve, Cain's daughters, Sarah, Rebecca, Leah, Rachael, etc. The Lord "beguiled" and "overshadowed" everyone of these women.

When they gave birth to the Lord's children, he relegated the responsibility for their being raised to the women he had impregnated! These are the "Nations," "Nathan," or "Gifts" from the Lord.

I *"gave"* Isaac to Abraham to raise, *and I "gave"* Isaac Esau and Jacob to Isaac to raise (*Joshua 24:4*).

*Nation (s)(Trans.)*— גוים (Goyim)(Gen. 10:5) Nations are the Gentiles, Heathens, or Caucasian Race. They are not the children of Noah (Ham, Shem, Japheth), but are an "Island'" or remnant of Caucasians, who survived the flood.

*Nativity* — מולד — *"Continuation," "Begetting"* -- Nativity is in reference to Abraham's place of origin (Nativity), which was the city complex of Ur. of the Chaldeans. The true Chaldeans are exclusively the Human, or Caucasian Race. Hallel the Lord of the North "gave" the Gentiles (Caucasians) to Abraham, to be their wooly headed step father. **See Lexicon "Nations"**

*Night* — הליל — *"Serpentine," "Vibrating," "Helix"* -- This speaks more to patterns (Oscillations) lying in the Darkness, rather then the Darkness it's self. Hallel (Hellix) the Lord of Abraham have a Serpent(ine) nature.

*Nimrod* — *Strong's #4174* — נמרוד — *"We Came Down."* — The name Nimrod means "We Came Down." This proves that Nimrod did not hold his family hostage to a religion, he was in his mother's stomach when Ham "brought them down" from Ararat. Ham and his children "Came Down" to repopulate the land that had been flooded! Noah and the Lord were holding Noah's family hostage on Mound Ararat, sacrificing the animals to the Lord, that Noah was suppose to set free (**Gen. 8:20**).

*Nineveh* — נינוה — *"Offspring," "Sprout"* -- The fourth of the six cities composing the Ur Metropolis, of Nimrod (*Gen. 10:11*). It's ruins are in Iraq.

*Noah* — נח — *"comforter"* Son of Lamech in the line of Adam. Noah chose to follow Hallel the Felon.

*Nod (Mou)nd* — נד. מנד — *"Mound(s)," Mountain(s)*. Mou<u>nd</u>s are a place to *"Nod."* The mountains north of

# Summations Lexicon

land of Cain. Nodding, falling asleep. Dwelling in caves, living in the ground. The Lord closed the eyes, ears, and minds of the pale leper children of Cain, in the land of Nod נוד *(Nude)* -- *"Fugitive," "Felon"*

*North (Phones.)* — נורות — *"Torches," "Lamps," "Wicked"* (Having a Wick) -- The north is the home of the Prince of Darkness, and it has no Light except the false light of torches, lamps, or wicks (*Amos 5:18, 20*)

*North (Trans.)* — צפון *(Siphon)* -- A place of sucking. There was famine in the north forever, for the ground was cursed for Hallel (Hallelujah), for he sucked away all of the life there.

*Nothing* — אין *(Ain)* -- *"Absolute," "Perfection"* -- The absence of "things." The state of satisfaction. End of all vibration, planes, dimensions, and at the same time the source of them all.

*Oath (Phones.)* — אות — *"Mark," "Sign"* -- Pale Leprosy, was placed upon Cain to keep Abel's friends the Lord's host from harming him (*Gen. 4:15*).

*Oath (Trans.)* — שבת — *(Sabbath)* -- *"Seventh"* (Day), *"Complete"* — A "swearing" of complete devotion to the Lord.

*Oil* — שמן — *(Semen)* — *"Anointing," "Anointed"* —This is sperm (Semen).

*Paran* — פראן — *"Place of Fruit," "Growing Profusely"* (Wild) — Paran as the homeland of Ishmael was as Ishmael was "fruitful," not "wild!" *Gen. 17:20 Gen. 16:12* Ishmael a "Fruitful" man, his hard in the hand of all men in co-operation. (Ishmael/Midian).

*Profane* — חל — *"Form," "Pierce," "Corrupt"* — The Lord profaned (Formed) Israel (*Deut. 32:18*). See Concordance # 2342 "formed" (חיל), 2490-92 "Profaned" (חלל).

*Rahab* — רהב — *"Broadway," "Expanse"* -- A prostitute of Jericho who betrayed her city, except for her own family, to the Israelis. She helped them kill every man woman and child, in Jericho. Whore Rahab, is a heroine of Judeo/Christianity (**Jos. 2nd Chptr**).

*Rehoboth* — רהבות — *"Streets," "Spaces"* -- Rehoboth is not a city but are the "city Streets" of Nineveh, one of the six lesser cities that made up the Ur Metropolis of Nimrod (*Gen. 10:11*).

*Rebecca (Rebekah)* — רבקה — Rebekah was married to her own cousin, Isaac who attempted to make her pregnant for over twenty years. When Isaac could not he entreated his father the Lord to "rub" against Rebecca, to make her pregnant (*Gen. 25:21*).

*Red (Phones.)* — רד — *"Go, or Come Down"* -- The "RD" consonant combination is the root to the word "Lord", which means "To Go or Come Down." Those who "came down" willingly are the "Redim" (Redeem), But those who refused, and were "Casted down" are called the Nephalim (נפלים①), which means Felons, or Fallers Down. The Lord is chief of the Reds (Fallen Ones).

*Red (Trans.)* — אדמון — *(Edmon)* -- This pertains to Esau (עשו) one of the two twins that the Lord impregnated Rebekah with then gave to his son Isaac to raise.

*Reed* — סוף — This word is intentionally mistranslated into the word "Red," to make it "Red Sea," instead of "Reed Sea." See Strong's "Red Sea."

*Repent* — שוב — *"Rethink," "Reform," "Reevaluate"* — When Jesus (Yeshua) told the Israelis that they must repent he was telling them that the only way that they could "set" themselves "free" from the Lord was to totally rethink all of their actions, customs, habits, and way of life. In so doing they would be set free from the Lord their God, and his World.

*Report* — שמע — *"Hear," "Announce"* — Isaiah 53rd chptr. These are the accounts of the Gentiles who crucified Nimrod, their savior who had raised them from the corrupt life style that they had been living. They are saying that they murdered him because it pleased the Lord that they bruise him (*Isa. 53:10*).

*Resen* — רסן — *"Curb," "Bridle," "control," Restrain"* -- Resen is between Nineveh, and Calah. It is the 5th of the six city Ur Metropolis that Nimrod built.

# Summations Lexicon

Each of the cities held some specialized purpose in the overall raising of Cain's descendants. Resen was a place of Cains reformed children pledging to "resign" (Resen) from their old ways, and dedicating themselves to the way of life (Peace), that Nimrod had raised these Gentiles to. The ruins are in Iraq.

*Reuel --* רעואל *-- "Friend Of God" --* A son of Jacob's brother Esau. Reuel's proper name is Jethro. He was the priest (Overseer) of Midian. Moses married his daughter Zipporah. Ruel (Jethro), instructed Moses how to set the Israelis into order. Reuel did not know that Moses would murder his daughter Zipporah (A Midianite woman), and their sons Gershom, and Eliezer. Moses also instructed the Israelis to kill all Midianite men, women, and male children. He told the Israeli men to keep the little Midianite girls for themselves. *Numbers 31:9, 18 Num. 31:40, Num. 31:47*

*Revelations (Phones.) --* גלים  *— (Gleam) --* The old name of the book of Revelations, was Apocalypse, a Greek word, which have come to mean disaster, but actually means "Apo -" (off) and "Kalyptein" (cover). An Apocalypse is therefore "The taking off of a cover," or "Revelation". What is revealed is a Holocaust in the past that shall repeat in the future, if nothing changes from the way it is now.

*Righteous --* צדיק *-- "Correct," "Balanced," "Perfect," "Standard," "Order" --* Physical manifestation is an experiment. Righteousness is the standard that it all rotates around. *Salem --* שלום *-- "Completeness", "Peace," "Self" --* This is the Order of Melchezedek, that Jesus (Yeshua), and others were "after."

*Sanctuary —* קדש *—* The place to go through the process of being made "Holy." A place of Sodomizing. *See Strong's: "Holy,""Sanctified," and "Sodomy" #6942, 6945*

*Sarah --* שרה *-- "Princess," "Free Woman," "Self Restrained" --* Sarah is Iscah (יסכה) (*Gen. 11:29*). Sarah as Iscah is the sister of Lot, they have the same mother. Sarah as Sarah is the sister of Abraham, they have the same father, incestuous Terah who is also Sarah's father - in - law, and her grandfather!

*Satan --* שטן *-- "Counter (Opposite)," "Adversary," "Census Taker"* *1Chron. 21:1, 2Sam. 24:1* This is Jehovah (Hallel), who inherited Israel from the Most High (*Deut. 32:8, 9*) Being in authority "over" (על) Israel Satan appointed (יסת) David to number (count/census) Israel to see how many he owned! When David did not count them properly Satan (Jehovah) in his anger murdered them on a wholesale level!

*Seduce --* נשא *-- "Obligate," "Lead Astray," "Delude" --* This word seduce does not exist in the old testament, but carries the same meaning as "beguile." Eve was beguiled or seduced.

*Shinar --*שנער *-- "Adolescence" Shinar* are the plains at the northern extreme of Nod. This place is the flat land at the base of the mounds of Ararat. Three of the cities of Nimrod's kingdom were built on this plain, and the other three cities of his kingdom were built adjacent to the Shinar plains, along the Tigris River.

*Sin —* חטא (hate) — The Lord is the "Man (*Ex. 15:3*)," who brought Sin (Hate) into his own World (*Romans 5:6*). By the Lord, it would have been a sin (hateful) against the Lord, for the Israelis not to murder the little Midianite boys, women, and little Midianite girls they had sodomized (שכב) (*Nu 31:17, 18*).

*Siphon (Phones.) —* צפון *— "North" --* The word "North" is pronounced Siphon (צפון) in the old language. North implies north of the Tigris River, a place of Darkness, and sucking (Siphoning).

*Sleep (Trans.) --* יסן *--*To "Languish between life and death." This is the sleep of Adam (*Gen. 2:21*). Adam has never awakened, and the entire physical experiment is taking place inside of his collective sleep. The Human or Caucasian Race only exists inside of Adam's sleep.

*Sleep (Phones.) --* שלף  *— (Slap) -- "Knocked Out," "Pulled Out," "Moved Around" --* To be unconscious

*Seer —* כוהן *— "Beholder," "Priest" —* Priest as communicators between the seen and unseen, must have the ability to "see," and hear beyond the ordinary.

*Seir (Sear) —* שער *—* Devil, Goat, Hairy, Rough, Satyr

# Summations
# Lexicons

(Lev. 17:7). *See Strong's pages 204 and 205*

***Souls (Phones.)*** — ***Sol/Solar*** -- All who originally separated away from the sun are "Solar (Soul) Beings," including Hallel the Lord of Abraham. Judges 10:16, Adam (Earthling) *Gen., 2:7*, and Michael/Melchezedek. *Hebrews 7:3* None of these had mothers or fathers nor did they have navels, for they were never born but exist without beginnings or ends.

***Soul (Trans.)*** — נפש — *"We Separate Away,"* *"spread out" (נפש)* — As when the "Soul" came forth from the sun.

***Supreme (Male plural)*** — ספרים — The plural male nature of the original inhabitants of the planet. This includes Adam (earthling), Hallel (Lucifer), Melchezedek (Michael), Gabriel etc.

***Separate (Plural female)*** — ספרות — The plural female nature of the same Beings. These are the female sides of the same original inhabitants of the planet. This would include Adam, Hallel (Lucifer), Melchezedek (Michael), Gabriel etc. *

*\*Note  The Supreme and the Separate are the two sides male and female respectfully, of the same Being in physical Manifestation that is integrated into one complete male/female Being in the invisible realm beyond the physical. (Electric Male, and Magnetic Female). The word translated as "God" (אלוהים) is a word describing an invisible male/female (HermesAphrodite) Being. This is what Adam was before he was put to sleep and "Separated" permanently into male and female!*

***Truth (Phones.)*** — תרות — *"Thou (ת) Friend (רות)"* -- Loving one's Self, a commandment of Jesus (Yeshua).

***Truth (Trans)*** -- אמת — *(Emit)* -- *"Radiate Out," "Centralized"* -- This speaks to being at the center of ones own being. This is universal Law. The "true" experiment takes place from the center of ones own Being.

***Visited*** -- פקד — *(FKD)* -- *"Rub against," "Penetrate," "Discharge (deposit)" Strong's #* — The Lord of Abraham "visited (פקד)" Sarah and impregnated her with Isaac (*Gen. 21:1; Gen. 17:16*).

***Whore*** *(Phon.)* — הור — "Horites," "Mountain Dwellers" These mountains were east of the Tigris River which is the land of Nod.

***Whore*** *(Trans.)* — זונה — (Zion) "**Mountaineer**"

***Wild*** — פרא — Wild is the word used to describe Ishmael the son of Abraham "from his own loins" (*Gen. 16:12*). This word "wild" in the context that it is used gives the impression that Ishmael was insane. Yet the true meaning of the word Para (פרא) is "Fruitful" (*Gen. 17:20*). Ishmael was "Fruitful," not "wild."

***World*** -- תבל *(Tubal)* -- *"Thou Chaos"* (בל), **"Helter Skelter"** -- The "World" is not the planet, but is a thoroughly "corrupt" nature, or state of being. This is what the Lord loved, but Jesus came to destroy.

# Summations
# Appeal Gentiles

*Lexicon "World"(TBL) — Ur to Washington D.C. (Nimrod to Benjamin Banniker) —
Shielded and Sheltered — Jewish*

You Gentiles, pale children of Marked Cain, are the beginning of the Lord's World on this planet. The Lord impregnated Eve with Cain (***Gen. 4:1, I Chron. 1:1***). You as Caucasians or Gentiles carry the mark of paleness, that was placed upon Cain by his father the Lord (***Gen. 4:15***). The Lord the father of your father Cain, brought you into existence as a line, to subplant Adam's line. Adam's line is the continuation of Adam, the wooly headed brown original population of this entire planet (***Revelations 1:14; Dan. 7:9***).

Even though the Lord's purpose was for you to subplant, you have not been able to even sustain your selves. The wooly headed brown people, of whom you were suppose to subplant have preserved your existence on the planet. They preserve you, because of their compassionate nature.

You have never been left alone, but have been shielded and sheltered away from harm, for most of the time that you have been in existence. You have been given an endless number of civilizings, from Ur/Babel to Washington D.C., from Nimrod to Benjamin Banniker.

Nimrod and thousand from the Garden south of the Tigris came north of the Tigris to upper Nod east of the Tigris River, where your Caucasian ancestors lived. The Gardeners from the south came north to save you Gentiles, by giving you your first civilizing (***Isa. 23:13***). They built the Ur/Babel Metropolis for you. It was a great cities, made of six lesser cities. This was to save you, from the effects of your Lord Hallel, who stripped you of any ability to do anything respectful, for yourselves (***Isa. 18:2***). The Lord came down from Mound Ararat, to see that Nimrod had healed your strips (***Isaiah 53rd Chptr.***). It pleased the Lord to bruise Nimrod (***Isa. 53:10***), because Nimrod had unified you into a positive co-operative community (***Gen. 11:6***). Nimrod was on the verge of bringing you out of bondage to the Lord. But the Lord incite your Gentile ancestors to crucify Nimrod their savior (***Isa. 53:10***). Then the Lord and his Host confounded your six city Ur/Babel Metropolis, bringing it to ruin (***Isa. 23:13, Gen. 11:9***). Those amongst your ancestors who had not been meted out and trodden down, scattered down from the land of Nod (***Isa. 18:2, 7***). Your Chaldean ancestors hebrewed (crossed) the Tigris River down into the gardenlands of the peaceable children of Ham (***I Chron. 4:40***). There in the land of Canaan, your ancestors were given asylum from Hallel the Lord of the North. The Canaanites quarantined your ancestors, to the grain cities, of Sodom and Gomorrah. No people ever occupied these cities, before your ancestors were brought there to dwell. These cities were only grain process/storage facilities.

The test for you as Caucasians (Gentiles) has been to see what your nature is, and to see what you will do under different circumstances. From the time of Ur/Babel to Washington D.C., your leaders have misled you, to harm the very ones who have preserved you. Blacks from Nimrod, to Jesus, to Benjamin Banniker, and beyond represent all of your wooly headed brown saviors.

The **Jewish** declare themselves as the **Chief Gentiles** by displaying the three pawn balls, that represent the Gentile children of Cain: Ju**bal** Cain, Ja**bal** Cain, and Tu**bal** Cain, the "three balls" (Bals) of Cain (***Gen. 4:20-22***). It was your ancestors, the Roman descendants of the three Bals, who conspired with the wooly headed Israelis and killed Jesus (***Gal. 3:13, 14***)

Appeals

# Summations
# Appeal Jewish (Israelis)

*Gentiles - Appeal to the Pale Israelis in this Summations is addressed strictly to the Fake Judeans in the modern times who claim to descend from the Ancient Israelis, who were depicted as wooly and brown by the Assyrians and Egyptians — Animosity against what you are suppose to be (Black) — Taking someone else's identity (How long before you are exposed?) — (Best of the worst, worst of the best) — Association with Aram to Shem — Christianity (Antichrists)*

You the modern Israelis are Gentiles who took on the culture, and lifestyle of the remnants of the true wooly headed brown Israelis, in 8th through 10th century Spain. Those wooly headed Brown Israelis in Spain were assimilated by you, and you pale ones, took on their identity. If you are pretending to be someone you should be proficient at it! You should be wooly headed and brown like the Bible/Torah say (*Rev. 1:14, 15*). You should look like the Ethiopians (*Amos 9:7*).

"Are you not as the children of the Ethiopians unto me oh children of Israel" (*Amos 9:7*)? The Lord ask the Ancient wooly headed brown Israelis this question. This question in your own Jewish Torah, indict you the modern Pale Israelis as not being who you claim to be, for the Ethiopians even to these modern times are wooly headed and brown! You are those who say you are Israelis, but do lie (*Rev. 3:9*).

No one will deny that you who call yourselves Jewish (Judeans?) are superior to any of the other Caucasians. Yet the ancient Israelis that you pretend to be were wooly headed and Black, without exception. Yet the ancient Israelis from their inception were the most corrupt Blacks in all existence. Yet you the best of Caucasians chose to take the identity of the worst Black who ever existed!

Could it be that Blacks are the best, and that the Ancient Black original Israelis were the worst of the best? Could it be that Caucasians are worst, and that you in the modern times are only the best of the worst who are Caucasians? Is it better to pretend to be the worst of the best who are Black, then it is to truly only be the best of the worst who are Caucasians? Only the best of the Human Beings could take on the identity of the worst of the Original Blacks. The best of the best would never choose to be the worst of the worst!

The Bible/Torah describe that the ancient Black Israelis came into existence through Incest, incubi, rape, murder, and prostitution: Five of the twelve sons of Jacob were actually the sons of the Lord, who committed incubi with Leah, and Rachael (*Gen. 29:31-35*). Jacob's other seven sons came from Jacob raping Bilhah, and Zilpah, and Jacob committing incest with Leah, and Rachael. These twelve "sons" murdered the entire male population of the Canaanite city of Shechem (*Gen. 34:25*). They kept all of the girls and women of that city, and used them to rape themselves into tribal existence (*Gen.34:29*).

Judah even "took" another Canaanite woman, and had three sons with her. Then Judah "took" even another Canaanite woman and gave her to two of his sons in turn, trying to get his next generation. Both sons failed to rape Tamar into pregnancy. This is the Canaanite woman Tamar who Judah committed prostitution and incest with, and made her pregnant with twin boys. These two boys from prostitution are the source of all Judeans (*Gen. 38:13-30*). Thus Tamar and a multitude of other wooly headed brown Hamite/Canaanite women were the mothers of all of the

Summations

# Summations
## Appeal Jewish (Israelis)

**Gentiles** — *In the time of Jesus (**no enslavement doctrine**) The Israelis told Jesus that they had never been in bondage to any man (**John 8:33**). The Egyptians wanted Israel to leave Egypt, but they refused to go (**Ex. 1:10**). The Torah affirms that they were never enslaved to Egyptians, but were in bondage to the Lord — Chased to Egypt by the Lord's famine the Israelis had no intention of ever being associated with the Lord again, they forgot him, and Moses had to tell them who he was!* — All of Israel was exterminated in ancient times — Christianity (Antichrists)

children of the twelve tribes (*Gen. 34:29*). This was on top of everyone in the line of Shem including Shem being Black, all the way down to the twelve "sons.

There are consequences if Jews (Judeans/Israelis) are allowed to be seen as Blacks like the Torah say that they were (*Amos 9:7*). Imagine the effect of all of the Bible/Torah characters being depicted as Blacks like they actually were: Adam, Noah, Ham, Shem, Japheth, Egyptians, Canaanites, Ethiopians, Archaic Greeks, Etruscans, Abraham, Sarah, etc. were all Black. At the same time the Caucasian children of Marked Cain were Pale Lepers (*Gen. 4:15*). Cain's pale leper children were an **Isle of Gentiles** in a sea of Black people (*Gen. 10:5*). Caucasians now show Greeks, Egyptians, Israelis etc. as pale people. This is even on the ground of them having excavated images, and statues from city ruins of these ancient Bibleland people, who were brown, to Black, with wooly hair.

In the relatively modern time you the modern or Pale Jewish have invented an Egyptian Bondage that do not exist in the Bible/Torah (*John 8:33*). The Lord brought the Israelis out of Egypt by force, they did not want to leave Egypt! In the wilderness the Israelis even wanted to return to Egypt, while it still lay in ruins (*Numbers 14:4*)! The Lord took his revenge on the Egyptian Israelis, letting them and their children die, in the wilderness over a forty year period (*Nu. 14:32, 33*). In that forty year period **all of the Israelis from Egypt, and their children died in the wilderness**, except Caleb, Joshua, and Moses (*Nu. 26:63-65*). In the same forty year period six hundred thousand new Israelis were born in the wilderness (*Nu. 26:51*).

The Lord never protected Israel, and even commanded them to kill anyone, who would come to take them away from his bondage (*Deut. 13th Chptr.*). These children of the children of those Israelis who had come from Egypt, came out of the wilderness as pale lepers (*Leviticus 13th Chptr.*). The Lord used these pale lepers to murdered all of his servant **Abraham's** true wooly headed children, except the little girls, whom they used to rape themselves into being the "Seed of Abraham." The Lord always reward those who serve him: The Lord allowed **Noah** to die, alone as an exposed child molester on Ararat (*Gen. 9:29*). The Lord rewarded **Moses** by putting horns on his forehead (*Ex. 34:29*), and as a final reward, he murdered Moses and buried him on a mountain (*Deut. 34:5, 6*). Finally the Lord used and abused the wooly headed Ancient Israelis out of existence: The Assyrians murdered them (*II Kings 15:29*). The Babylonians murdered them (*II Kings 24:15, 16*). And finally The Romans murdered them out of existence, except for those who escaped back into the safety, of the land of Egypt (*Matt. 24:2 - 3*). They all in their turn reduced the Israelis to nothing [Yet in the more modern times], "There are those of you who say you are Judeans (Israelis) but do lie" .... (*Revelation 3:9*).

# Summations
# Appeal Judeo/Christianity (AntiChrist)

*Jewish/Israelis — Defender of the World — Outer Darkness — Rabbis, Priest, Ministers*

Judeo/Christianity is not the Jewish Synagogue, or the Christian Church. Judeo/Christianity, preexists both synagogue and church. Christianity or AntiChrist is the defense system of the World of the Lord.

For all of you Israelis (Jewish) and other Gentiles alike, consider whether churches and synagogue can be justified, as having a positive purpose for you as congregations. Yeshua (Jesus) with the Red Letter of the King James claim that you and your children should be in your kingdoms, which are inside, but you all have been pulled out of your inner kingdoms, out into the Outer Darkness of the Lord (*Matt. 8:12, Amos 5:18, 20*). Jesus states that to reenter your kingdoms you have to convert yourselves back to being like you were, as little children before you were pulled out (*Matt. 18:3*). God and the kingdom of heaven are inside (*Luke 17:21*). The Lord and his World is outside (*II Chron. 5:6*). He who is inside (God) is greater, than the Lord who is without in his Outer World of Darkness (*I John 4:4*).

Nimrod and Jesus both taught this information, to stop people from being pulled out to the Darkness of the World of the Lord. Nimrod taught it to the Pale Leper children of Cain. Yeshua (Jesus) taught it to the Lost Sheep of Israel. Both Jesus (Yeshua) and Nimrod were crucified for trying to make the captive Israelis and other Gentiles free from the Lord.

The first Christ or "Crucified One" was Nimrod (*Isaiah 53:10*). The Lord incited the Gentile children of Cain (Three Balls), to crucify their savior Nimrod (*Isa. 53rd Chptr.*). The next Christ or crucified one was Yeshua (Jesus), who Christianity crucified two thousand years after Nimrod.

After murdering Jesus the Roman Empire became Holy Roman Empire, became the Holy Roman Church. Christianity (AntiChrist), now wearing the garment of religion, pretended to represent Yeshua (Jesus) who it had murdered. Judeo/Christianity (AntiChrist) composed of church, and synagogue, is still the guardian of the World of the Lord, that Jesus came to destroyed.

Church and synagogue are still pulling the children out with Bar Mitzvahs, Beth Mitzvahs, Baptism, Sanctification, and Holiness. All of you who call yourselves Christians, and who identify with Christianity, think that Christianity represents the teachings of Jesus. Yet Christianity teach the sacrifice of innocence (clean) for the preservation of the guilty (unclean). Judeo/Christian congregations, Adam did not commit an original sin, nor were your children born in sin. There is no justification for church or synagogue. Leave your children alone. Yeshua (Jesus) warn you that if you tamper with your children, you are tampering with perfect beings. He said that if you offend your children by altering them, you may as well have a millstone tied around your neck, and be cast into a lake to be drowned (*Matt. 18:16; Mark 9:42*). To be perfect you must be like your little children, before you baptize them into the Church/Synagogue system. Protect them until they are viable, for they have come to bring the World of the Lord to an end.

Woe to the Rabbis, Priests, and Ministers of Judeo/Christianity (AntiChrist), who cast their Judeo/Christian congregations out, and then shut up their inner heavens, so they can not reenter (*Matt. 23:13*).

# Summations
# Appeal Rabbis, Priest, Ministers

*Outcasters — Rabbis — Priests — Ministers (Black, Brown, Red, Yellow)*

Scribes, Pharisees, Rabbis, Priests, and Ministers, all of you pull the children of the congregations out of their inner kingdoms, where God dwell (*I John 4:4*). You cast them out to the World of Outer Darkness, where the Lord dwell (*II Cor. 5:6; Matt. 8:12*). Then all of you Rabbis, Priests, and Ministers, through your teachings, and misteachings, shut up their inner kingdoms, so that none can reenter, and you refuse to reenter your own kingdoms also (*Matt. 23:13*)!

**Yeshua say that all of you are damned** (*Matt. 23:14*). He say that all of you are the blind leading the blind, and that if the blind lead the blind, then all of you shall fall into a ditch (*Matt. 15:14*)! Jesus say that he has overcome the World (TBL)(*John 16:33*). Jesus say do not love the World (*I John 2:15*). Jesus (Yeshua) say hate the World of the Lord (*I John 2:15*), that hate him (*John 7:7*).

The fact is that the Lord's World is not the planet. Nor is the World the people on the planet. But the World of the Lord is the Chaos that the Lord impose on the people of the planet that cause them to commit Murder, Rape, Incest, Incubi, Theft, War, Child Molestation, Bestiality, etc.

### Rabbis

Some of you pale Rabbis are proficient in the Old Language, but what have you done with that proficiency? Was it your group who conspired to mistranslating what the old wooly headed brown Israelis scribes wrote down clearly? The old scribes wrote clearly identifying the Devil by quoting his own words. At *Exodus 6:3* the old wooly headed scribes quoted Hallel the God of Abraham as saying to Moses "I appeared unto Abraham, Isaac, and Jacob as El Shaddai, or the Devil (Outcast) God…" וארא אל אברהם ואל צחק ואל עקב באל שרי (*Exodus 6:3*). The modern pale Rabbis have gone out of their way to supress the fact that in the scriptures, the Lord called himself the Devil!

### Priest

Pharisees (Priest) How do you reconcile the fact that the Rabbis have passed on to you the same corruption that they gave to their own people. Did you know that the Holy water that you sprinkle represent ejaculation? Do you know that the pope in his miter (Hat) represent a sperm cell? The "fish" of Friday are sperm. The "seminary" represent a place of "semen", and the "rectory" represent the rectum. St. "Peter" represents the penus. The sanctuary (the sanctifying place) is a place to be sanctified (קדש)(Sodomized), to be made Holy (חלל)(Corrupt).

### Ministers (Black, Brown, Red, and Yellow)

Caucasian Christian missionaries came to every part of the planet, as representative of the Lord, and his World. They took you who are the weakest, and groomed you into being Christian ministers, imposed over your people. The purpose was to have you infect you own people, with the theme of Holiness. You have been very successful, winning souls for the Lord. Yet what does it gain you to have gained the inhabitants of the entire planet, while you have all lost your own souls (*Matt. 16:26*)? You can not have the excuse that you did not know. After all Scribes, Rabbis, Priests and Ministers were the first clerics, clerks, or writers/record keepers.

# Summations
# Appeal Scientist, Intellectuals

*Rabbis, Priest, Ministers —First Clerks (Clerics) — Advance to where? — What Evolving, to where or what? — Batteries, Crystals, Astronomy, Astrology, Architecture, Cities, Electronics, Chemistry, Metallurgy all existed before you — Baalbek, Ponape Island, Rapa Nui, Huge Mexican Stone Heads, Great Walls, Great Pyramids*

There were no scientist in Europe, before the clerks/clerics (record keepers), who were Rabbis, Priests, and Ministers. Some Clerics became the first scientist, or intellects in Europe. Intellect is the stupid step child of intelligence. Once in what is now called Europe there was no alphabet, or written language. You have been taught that science in Europe developed out of an evolving Caucasian intellect. Yet there was no evolvement of intellect in Europe. It was the wooly headed Brown/ Black Moors out of North Africa, who taught reading and writing, and an alphabet to the Europeans.

The very first European scientists/intellectuals were religious, were clerics (clerks) of the church/synagogue system. Your race did not "evolve" up into civilizing your own selves, but it was given to you. How did you come to divide your religion from your science? In actuality there is no break between them, for evolution and creation are both invention, opposite sides of the same counterfeit coin. Both evolution and creation are inventions, and are not choices at all. Both are theories, and neither existed until you were raised to the place that you could think to invent scientific, and religious theories.

Europe and Europeans have no origin of Scientific, Scholastic, or Intellectual Systems at all. The Peaceful people of Northern Eden (Africa) called Moors went north into Spain at the beginning of the seventh century A.D. to began teaching any and all Pale Ones, that had the capacity to learn. The Moors (North African Blacks) established bases, in what is now called Portugal, Spain, and southern France. They built perhaps 16 universities in this region. Then over an 800 years period of time these Moors spread out into the rest of what is now called Europe, establishing the foundations for what would become every country, that now exist in all of Europe. Moorish principalities, were established in location throughout protoEurope, in each place, that would become the center or capital of a country. This was true from Russia, to England (Brith Ain), and every country in between. The Proto Europeans were taught, all of the necessary arts, crafts, and skills, for them to present themselves as civil beings.

Evolution is an invention, along with I. Q. Tests. You Europeans/Caucasians did not evolve into civilizing yourselves. Civilizing was given to you several times from the Ur City Metropolis to Washington D. C., by the wooly headed original inhabitants of this planet. All of the arts crafts, and skills that you have were taught to you by none Caucasians, original inhabitants of this planet. Those wooly headed brown people who gave you all of your civilizings, have had Batteries, Crystals, Astronomy, Astrology, Architecture, Cities, Agriculture, Electronics, Chemistry, Metallurgy and more, all before your race came into existence

**Playing Catch up**

The word "Research" is a slip in the case of those who put the word together. "Research

# Summations
# Appeal Scientist, Intellectuals

*Research — Intellect and Intelligence — Faith and Theories— Continental*

implies that you are "Re" "searching," or searching again to find information again that never belonged to you. It is not information, that you ever had, so you are searching to obtain information that belonged to the original inhabitants on this planet, before your species ever existed. What you have exposed with this word research, is that you are "searching" for evidence of "**intelligence**" on this planet that exceeds your "**intellect**." The whole of the existence of you scientific community serves the purpose of attempting to catchup to someone else's past.

The past is not inferior to the future, the future is not advanced away from the past. There were superior cities existing on this planet before the first Caucasians ever breathed. But cities are not a sign of advancement, they are a sign of degeneration, down from a more superior state. The quality of the first cities, the cities built by the wooly headed first inhabitants of this planet far exceed any cities that have ever been built since. The Bible/Torah say that there were millions of Beings, on and off the planet with cities, and space crafts, in the prehistoric times (*Daniel 7:9, 10, Isaiah 24:6, Rev.4:10, Rev. 12:7*). There are ruins of cities on top of mountains, and cities on man made islands, in the middle of the Pacific Ocean, massive heads in Mexico, weighing tons. The boulders for these heads had to be transported from the Tuxtula Mountains, hundreds of miles, over roadless land and swamps, to central Mexico.

Next for those in the scientific community who deny that there is a connection between religion and science, consider the Noah flood story, where they say that the entire surface of the planet was suppose to have been under water. When the water receded, the entire planet was suppose to be unpopulated, with only Noah and his family surviving, to repopulate it. There was no way to repopulate the western hemisphere from where the ark came down, nor was it necessary, for Noah's flood was not over the entire planet, it was only the flooding of the Tigris/Euphrates Estuary (*Joshua 24:3, 14*). But the scientist did not know that the flood was local, so they invented the frozen Bearing Strait migratory bridge theory. This is a scientific theory from a religious account. There is no evidence that this hemisphere of the planet was ever uninhabited.

The Bible/Torah say that The flood of Noah had "sides (*Joshua 24:3, 14*)," and was actually only the flooding of the Tigris/Euphrates basin.

But most scientists were raised in church. They receive the "Depopulated Planet" theory as a bleed over from religious teachings in church. The fact becomes that there is not a separation between church and science, nor is there a separation between evolution and creation. Each is the opposite sides of the same invented coin. This include scientific theory, and religious faith. Religiously influenced scientists project that the western hemisphere had to be "re" populated. This "Non Populated western Hemisphere" theme also allowed Europeans to claim an equal ownership to the western hemisphere as it's natives. Thus you scientist have been used to convert religious faith, into scientific "fact," to claim an entire hemisphere. The non Caucasian Continental "Nationalities" are highly influenced by you the Western World science, and Intellect.

# Summations
# Appeal Continentals

*Science, Intellect — Ertz (Earth) — Nationalities — American Invitation*

### Ertz (Earth)

Western scientist admit that this planet was once one solid piece of land, without continents. The Bible/Torah scripture have the Lord boasting of how he destroyed this planet in the ancient past (*Isa. 24:1, 3-6*). The Lord exploded the planet knocking it out of it's course (*Psalms 82:5*). In that explosion the planet was broken into Ertz (ארץ)(Earth), meaning "I am Fragments," or "I am Continents." Your continents came into existence by breaking away from the four sides, of the old south polar region of the planet. That old south polar region came to be known as Eden (Africa). It was almost as if your continents with you on them, were all fleeing away, from Eden (Africa). Eden (Africa) is the only part of the planet that did not move away from it's original place. Eden represent those who held the line, down into the experiment, without curving away.

### Nationalities

You as Continentals are those who live on the continents now scattered all around the planet. What did you look like, and what language did you speak, when your continents were attached to Eden (Africa)? When your continents first broke away from the four sides of Eden (Africa), you were all wooly headed and brown. You were not Chinese, or Japanese, or Koreans, or Indians (India), or Arabians. You had no nationalities, borders, countries, or flags.

You Chinese, you Japanese, you of India, Arabia, and Israel, what has happened to your wooly hair, your physical shapes, and brown complexions? Why has your language changed? Originally your language had to be same as that of Africa (Eden), for it was the land that your continents broke away from. What has happened to the love you once had, for your once wooly haired brown appearance? All people from every continent originally saw, heard and spoke the same as those in Eden (Africa)(*Gen. 11:1*). But as your continents moved away, you mutated away into a changed mentality that caused you to began to see, hear and speak different. You along with your continents have all mutated, away from being yourselves. Yet all of your old Gods and your forefathers are still Black.

### America Invitation

Many of you who went away from Eden (Africa) on continents, have recently been invited to come to North America. You could not have come except that you were invited. Nor would you have come except America appear to be better, than where you came from. No one leaves home to come to another place, if things are right at home. You were invited into North America to fill certain requirements: At the one extreme the United States need more people to do manual or lower level labor tasks. The States also need more business minded people to bring business and trade into the country. This country must maintain it's status quo, there must be a certain level of business, and labor to sustain this society.

Thirdly there is a problem of containment: In every society there are different stratas of people and ethnic groups. Those of the lowest levels in North America are the foundation that holds up all the rest. But cracks have appeared in that foundation, and many if not most of you Continentals

# Summations
# Appeal Continentals

*Crumbling Foundation — A Gathering in America — All have failed you — Self — Aliens*

were imported to act as mortar to fill in the cracks, to keep the foundation from falling apart altogether. It is not so much that you can take the place of those who are no longer there to be the lowest level. But you are being used as a temporary containment, and patch to at least delay the inevitable crumbling, and foundation failure. The wealthy have brought you here and are depending on you to buy them time, by serving them. But you shall fail, and the foundation level of this society shall fall apart. And all that you will have invested as laborers, and/or business persons, shall be lost. Your societies where you came from failed you, and you shall be failed again in North America also.

## A Gathering in America

The God images that you brought with you, Buddha, Krishna, Vishnu, etc., have also failed you. The Jesus image that some of you were converted to, have also failed you.

If any of these God images could have helped you they would have helped you in your home countries. All of the true God Beings including Jesus, are Black and wooly headed like your ancestors were/are (***Rev. 1:14***). All of the original inhabitants of the planet are wooly and Black. Your wooly headed God images are only replicas of your ancestors. Rather than serve the images, or serve the Caucasians, why not serve the living wooly headed brown people of North America, they are your ancestors. When you cease to serve the Caucasians, you can turn to the true purpose that all have come to North America, including the Caucasians.

Caucasians from every European country are here. You Continentals are here from every continent on the planet. There are millions of wooly headed Blacks here from Eden (Africa). And already here were the millions of Aboriginal people of North America who are wooly headed Black/Brown. You Chinese, Japanese, Arabs, Lebanese, and people of India, will you continue to serve those pale ones who invited you here to serve them, or will you began to serve the wooly headed brown people here? To serve these Blacks you will be serving your ancestors, and Gods. As such you will be serving your own selves, and you will have the opportunity to convert, and be healed back into being wooly headed and brown again, if you chose. But you must choose to serve one or the other, for you can not serve the Caucasians, and yourselves too (***Matt. 6:24***). The best service to yourselves would be to take on the wooly hair, and Black/brown complexions that your ancestors wore.

The sun is getting ready to kiss the planet with a tremendous outpouring of Black Light radiation. Who can stand an Ultraviolet kiss from the sun, except those who are proper dressed for the occasion? The solar embrace will be the signal for the continents to start their journey back to their individual places around Eden (Africa). At the present few are fit to return to Eden (Africa).

All who left Eden (on Continents) wore wooly hair and brown complexions. This coming together is for the final playing out of an experiment that began in the sun. North America is a time and place for a decision. Will you Continentals cease to be aliens, and embrace your brothers and sisters? Will you change and be in appearance like your ancestors were? When all else have failed you then why not resort to being yourselves again, and cease to be aliens?

Appeals

# Summations
# Appeal Aliens

*Continentals— Apostasy: Planets, Continents, Races, Nationalities*

Continentals are Aliens (Alienated), because their continents broke away from the four sides of Eden (Africa). But you nonplanetary brothers and sisters are Aliens, because you "Went Up" completely away from the planet, and became alienated. In the old Language Alien (עליון) literally means "Ones Who Go Up." You are aliens to this planet because you left, on planets separated from this the mother planet. Do you really exist? Are there really Beings coming from outerspace? If you do exist and have come to this planet from out there, then can you be anything more then Prodigal Sons, brothers of the original inhabitants of this planet? Did you come to recognize your brothers and sisters, who stayed on this the mother planet and did not run away? If you exist, and have returned, why have you not presented yourselves, to your brothers and sisters? Are you still brown, with wooly hair?

How long did it take for you to come to discover, that there was nothing out there, except the planets you took with you? In these modern times you have been described as having spindly, enemic little bodies, and disproportionately large, misshappened heads. Those who left this planet initially were wooly headed, well proportioned, brown complexioned ones, like the original inhabitants of this planet (*Dan. 7:9*). The Bible/Torah say that there were Millions of you who returned back down to this planet for a tribunal. Scripture describe that you millions still had wooly hair and brown complexions (*Dan. 7:9, 10*). If you have lost your original appearance what has it gain you to gain an entire solar system, and lose your own souls (*Matt. 16:26, Mark 8:36*)?

Are you truly in contact with the Caucasian World? Are you sick, do you need medical assistance? Are you ashamed of your appearance?

It would seem that if you left with a portion of this planet, that you would have returned with what you took with you! You should have brought your planets back with you! But don't be concerned for Hallel left here too with a planet (Crypton). He and those on his planet warred with others out there, and were defeated. Pending defeat they destroyed their planet Crypton. The survivors from **Crypton** no longer had a place (*Revelations 12:9*), so they were brought back here to the mother planet, without a planet just like you!

Did any of you war against and or defeat Hallel and his Host? Did any of you come here to attend Hallel's Tribunal (*Ps.82:1-7, Daniel 7:9,10*). The tens of millions reported to have come here from all over the solar system, came to see Hallel and his Host judged! (*Dan. 7:11, 1, Psalms 82:1-8*).

Beyond being judged for the wars in the heavens, Hallel and his Host were being judged for having destroyed this globe Assiah, the mother. This was after they were casted back down here, after defeat in the solar (Soul) war. Hallel the future Lord of Abraham, boasted about how he and his Host destroyed this the mother planet (*Isaiah 24:1, 3-6*). The planet was knocked out of it's course when they exploded it (*Ps.82.5*). When the planet was "found" again all life on it had been suspended (*Genesis 1:1, 2, 3*). The heavens (sky) around it had collapsed, and there was no light even on the sun side of the planet. The "moon" had once been the northern region of the planet, but was blasted away, when Hallel and his Host caused the planet to explode, and knocked it out of it's course.

Were any of you Aliens, with those who found this planet again (*Gen. K1:1, Psalms 82:5*)? Did

Summations

# Summations
# Appeal Aliens

any of you help to restore the atmosphere (*Gen. 1:7*)? Were you here, when the water was being drained off the ground? Did you see that the planet's land mass was different, than before it had been exploded. The land mass was now broken, into huge fragments, that were scattered around the planet, like giant puzzle pieces. Were any of you among those who renamed Assiah, Ertz (Earth), meaning "Fragments," or "Continents (*Gen. 1:10*)?"

Once the planet was operating again, the original Man who stayed here on the mother planet allowed themselves to be put to sleep, to be divided into separated male and female (*Gen. 1:26*). Were any of you present? Did any of you take part in "creating" or altering of us who had been perfect? We original inhabitants on this planet were altered into the imperfect beings that we are now. In the modern times we the originals are the collective "Adam that was put to sleep. We were never reawakened, and are now still asleep mentally even as I speak.

Much has occurred since we who remained with the planet were altered. An entire experimental species was brought into existence out of us. The Lord Hallel our brother, the defeated one was allowed to beguile our separated female side (*Gen. 4:1, 2*). Hallel fathered Cain, and placed the mark of Pale Leprosy on him, and those who would descend from him. Hallel the Lord brought the Pale Ones into existence to subplant, but they could not, and they have become an experimental specimen instead (*Gen. 4:15*).

### Final Choice

All of you who fled the experiment are now returning. North America is the terminal place for our experiment that began in the sun. North America is also the the central gathering place for all of you who curved away from the experiment, whether it was on planets, on slabs of land or on foot.

This final phase of the cosmic experiment, will be to see what final choice each individual will make. Surpassing right and wrong there is the choice between correct and incorrect. As Jesus (Yeshua) said no man can serve two. You as aliens from beneath the ground, or above the clouds, along with the continental aliens from around the planet can make a choice to either continue the curved course you took thousands of years ago, to curve away, or you can correct your actions to help to bring this experiment to a satisfied finality.

If you can see the Light and chose to be correct, you can convert yourselves, and be healed from your body afflictions. But first you must repent (Rethink), and be born again, inwardly. In that process you shall activate your Single Eye, and your body will be full of Light, and you will be healed and restored to wooly headed brownness. All of the continental aliens can do the same. As to whether the pale leper Gentile children of Cain can be converted, and healed and restored to being wooly and brown again, is a major issue. The attempt to graft them back has been tried for thousand of years, and they have murdered or attempted to destroy all who have tried to save them. That is why Jesus said go not in the way (Darkness / דרכה) of the Gentiles, or Caucasian Race (*Matt. 5:10*). They killed him for saying it. You can not serve your Original Black selves, and the pale ones also (*Matt. 6:24*). As all else have failed you, you aliens as prodical sons must return home, to your true original selves.

# Summations
# Appeal North American Blacks

*Aliens— Blacks — Raising Cain*

**Blacks**: Many became alienated, and left, but you Black men and women have held the line of the experiment, from the sun down through all ages and places, to North America. You have held the line without even knowing that there is a line to be held. Some of you came in enslavement, from across the Atlantic, from Western Eden (Africa), but most of you never crossed the Atlantic, but were already the aboriginal population of this the western hemisphere, from the time that it broke away from the western side of Africa.

You are Black in complexion with wooly hair, but Black also means to be without color or change from your original being and purpose. The wooly hair in your head carry all of the designs in the entire universe, in the form of spheres, spirals, curls, circles, and waves. All of the original inhabitants of this planet were physically Black with wooly hair, like you. The first to change were those who alienated themselves, by leaving the planet, to change away from the original intent of the experiment. With their change of intent, came mutation away from their original Black complexion. Of all the inhabitants in the entire solar system you are the only ones who did not curve away from the straight line of Adam, under any circumstance.

As such Eden (Africa) the homeland of the western hemisphere, and thus your homeland is the last place in the solar (Soul) system, that Original Man was still himself, which is God. You are the children of Eden, (Africa) which is the part of the planet that would not move, even when the Lord attempted to destroy the whole planet (*Isa. 24:1, 3-5*)! Few of you were left after the Lord attempted to destroy the planet (*Isa. 24:6*). Your survival was the continuation of life on the planet.

You Blacks are the Aboriginals who rebuilt all of the societies around the entire planet, including what would become the ancient cities and lands of Aboriginal India, Aboriginal China and Aboriginal Japan.

## Raising Cain

**Blacks**: Parallel to the establishing of aboriginal India, aboriginal China, and aboriginal Japan in the east, you in the form of Nimrod and thousands of others Blacks, went north above Mesopotamia to the land of Nod to Raise Cain, his pale leper children. Blacks went north of the River of Cush (The Tigris), to build the six city Ur/Babel Metropolis for the Raising of the Caucasian Race. These Caucasians were also known as Chaldeans. Caucasians were a society who were not, till Nimrod the Assyrian built it for those who dwelt in the wilderness of Nod (*Isa. 23:13*). Ur/Babel was your first attempt to civilize the pale ones, and then to graft them back into being wooly headed Black men, as their father Cain had originally been.

Look at the faces on the statues and murals pulled up out of the ruins of the cities of Nineveh, and Nimrud (Calah), two of the six ruined cities of the Ur/Babel complex (*Gen. 10:10, 11*). They are the wooly heads and brown faces representing Ethiopians, Egyptians, Syrians, Assyrians, Elamites, etc. They all came to northern Nod with Nimrod, to reclaim Cain, who before being mutated, had been their brother. But before Nimrod could completely convert (graft) them back, the Lord and his Host came down from Ararat, to the plains of Shinar in Nod, and ruined the Ur/Babel City Complex (*Isaiah 23:13; Gen. 11:9*). The Lord confounded Ur/Babel, to prevent the pale ones from being grafted back to Black (*Gen. 11:9*). The Lord then incited the pale ones to crucify

# Summations
# Appeal North American Blacks

*Raising Cain (Nimrod, Phonicians, Archaic Greeks, Etruscans, Moors)*

Nimrod, and thousands of others. It pleased the Lord to bruise Nimrod's head (*Isa. 53:10*). Many of the pale lepers that fled from Ur/Babel (*Gen. 11:9*) fled westward, to Proto Europe to live with wooly headed brown Japheth, who is the father of the Etruscans, and Archaic (First) Greeks. It was the wooly headed brown Phoenician descendents of Canaan who gave the wooly headed brown Archaic Greeks, and Etruscans, an alphabet, glass, ceramics, bricks, metallurgy, etc.

You are the **Archaic (first) Greeks**, the non Caucasian Aboriginal inhabitants of Greece. You are the Ancient builders, of what the Caucasians now claim that they built, in Greece. Look at the faces on the Archaic (first) Greek coins. Look at the faces on the exquisite Archaic Greek sculptures in the Acropolis Museum in Athens, they are all your faces. Look at the faces of the Greek Gods and Goddesses. The Goddess Europa is a Black woman, the source of the name Europe). Look at the faces of the other first Gods, and Goddesses in Greece: Zeus, Poseidon, Athena, Nike etc., they are all Black men and women! Look at the ancient vases, murals, statues, and pottery fragments, to see the Black faces of the builders of Athens, Marathon, Syracuse, Olympia, Corinth, and hundreds of other ancient Greek cities. They are all your faces, male and female. The builders of these cities looked exactly like you, and they were not slaves, but were Masters, of these societies. Pale Greece did not exist until you founded it for the pale ones who dwelled in the wilderness around your cities there in Greece (*Isa. 23:13*).

You are the **Etruscans,** the non Caucasian Aboriginals in Italy, long before there was ever a Rome, or Caucasians there! Rome did not exist until you as wooly headed brown Etruscans built it for the pale ones, who dwelled in the wilderness around your cities (*Isa. 23:13*). You originated all that is now identified with the Romans, or Caucasians. Look at the faces of Europa, Jupiter, Apollo, and all of the other original Roman Gods, they are all Black like your faces. Look at the murals of the smiling faces at the feasts, festivals, and celebrations. You had hundreds of cities in the Italian, and Greek peninsulas, before there was a name Rome, or Italy. Look on the murals at the faces of the farmers, housewives and rulers, they are all your Black faces! It was the same in all of the islands throughout the Mediterranean! Once all inhabitants of Europe were Blacks, as were the entire Greco/Roman pantheon of Gods were Blacks.

You are the **Carthaginian** and **Moorish**, descendant of the **Phoenicians**. They are all three the same in the transition of time. Pale Europe did not exist until you the wooly headed brown Moors from North Africa built it for the pale ones, who had come and subplanted the Blacks who had lived in all of the land, that would become known as Europe (*Isa. 23:13*).

From Ur/Babel above Mesopotamia, to Europe westward, you as Blacks had been attempting to Raise Cain, his pale leper children. In each civilizing of the pale ones you were carrying them through the process of converting, and healing them away from the Darkness imposed on them by their Lord, the God of Abraham (*Isa. 6:10*). This was even before there was a church system! You as wooly headed Blacks have preserved the very existence of the entire Caucasian Race, from the time they came into existence. Could this maintenance of an entire species be anything other than an experiment?

**Europe**

# Summations
# Appeal North American Blacks

*Raising Cain — Europe— North America*

**Blacks**: You as Moors from North Africa based in, Portugal, Spain, and southern France, went up throughout all of what would become Europe, to give the pale ones there the Light of civilizing again, for at least the fifth time. Europe was not until you established it for the pale ones (*Isa. 23:13*). You the Black Nobility once ruled all of Europe. There were no countries there in Europe, until you established Moorish principalities in each place that you would turn into a country: Russia, Germany, Sweden, Holland, etc. Look at the royal family crests of much of the nobility of all of the European countries, including England. The wooly heads on those family crests are masters not slaves! You the Blacks were the Great Light that rescued Europe out of it's Dark Ages (*Isa. 9:2*).

Your influence as Moors on the Europeans can be seen by the order in which Caucasians countries gained the ability to build and sail ships out of Europe. The Portuguese were first, then the Spanish, the French, the Dutch, and lastly the English. Each built ships, and sailed out of Europe in the order that you civilized them: Portuguese, Spanish, French, Dutch, and English.

You as Blacks were the navigators of many if not all of the first ships that sailed out of Europe. Thus in effect you brought the pale lepers from Europe, to every part of the planet, including the western hemisphere. You are the Moors from the east, who put the Europeans into the hands of yourselves the Moors of the western hemisphere. Even after the Moors had spent eight hundred years in Europe, attempting to raise the Caucasians there, Caucasians have refused to be truly raised from the Darkness of the Lord. The western hemisphere would be the last place, and the last time that any Caucasian would have the chance to be raise from that Darkness. These pale ones would have their own choice as to what to do with all of the arts, crafts, and skills that were to be given to them yet again by you, for perhaps the sixth but the last time, in North America.

## North America

**Blacks**: Behold the land of North America, this country did not exist until you the wooly headed Black natives here founded it for the pale leper criminals, dumped in the wilderness along the entire east coast, by five European countries: the Portuguese, the Spanish, the French, the Dutch, and the British (*Isa. 23:13*). You made the bricks, glass, steel, and iron, along with other Blacks who had came across the Atlantic with the five European groups You set up the cites, towns, villages, and farms, for the colonies. You built the streets, roads, fields, and canals (*Isa. 23:13*), of the original five diverse (Penal) colonies.

The British eventually overwhelmed the other four (Portuguese, Spanish, Dutch and French), and turned the five original penal colonies into the thirteen British penal colonies.

Europe including England have always been in the perpetual Dark Ages of the Lord, and the inmates of the prison colonies were in the same Darkness. That Darkness still covers all of Europe, and now the Americas, into the present modern times.

You as Moors on this continent had sympathy for the pale ones brought here, as the Moors had sympathy for the pale ones in Europe. And as the Moors in Europe brought a Great Light

# Summations
# Appeal North American Blacks

*North America — First President*

that could have cancelled out the Darkness there, you Blacks of proto North America gave the same Great Light to the convicts of the thirteen penal colonies to light their Darkness (*Isa. 9:2*).

Most of you Blacks were the free aboriginal inhabitants on and around the land, where these thirteen prison regions were established. Seeing the injustice being imposed on these enslaved pale ones you incited them to rebel against the British. This was the beginning of the war that would convert, and heal the the thirteen prison colonies, into thirteen civil states. That war would be called a "war of revolution" or a "turning" War."

The "revolution" would be the "turning" of the penal colonies into states, and the "turning of the pale one from convict/slaves into citizens, of those individual states. Blacks were the leaders of many of the thirteen groups that went out to fight the British. Most of these Blacks go unnamed, but one was Crispus Attucks in New England. Another was named Oliver Cromwell who was with Washington on most of his major war campaigns. There were many thousands of other Blacks leading Caucasians, and fighting, to bring North America into existence as a country. The thousands of George Washington's troops were mostly all Black men!

### First Presidents (John Hanson)

Wooly headed brown Nimrod built and was president (presided) over Ur/Babel. Wooly headed brown John Hanson was the first president over the thirteen united States. But before there was a country for John to preside over, he had been the president over the congress of the "ununited" colony/States. As the president of the Continental congress John Hanson had designated George Washington as the commander over the continental army that he (John Hanson) had been instrumental in forming. John had organized two riflemen groups who became the core around which the rest of the continental army formed. Every seventh soldier who fought in the colonial army was a Black man. Most of the pale colonial American men deserted to the side of the British, and most of the pale men who fought on the colonial side were Frenchmen!*

John Hanson in his capacity raised and donated funds, to put shoes on the feet, clothes on the backs, and food in the stomachs of the colonial army. John sent his brother Samuel Hanson to George Washington in the field, with over eight hundred pounds of sterling silver to initially provision his Black, and White troops. There were over five thousand Black men in the army that George Washington controlled directly.

John Hanson also commissioned Benjamin Banikker to grow and supply wheat to feed the soldiers. The wealthy Caucasian planters supplied nothing to sustain the very fighters, who would make the wealthy planters free from English servitude. In the end it would be John Hanson who would sustain the Blacks and mostly White French troops, who would give them a country independent of England. After the war was over, most of the White colonial men who had deserted over to fight with the British against America, slide back over into being patriots on the American side!

The first president wooly headed Black John Hanson, is literally the father of this country, for if he had not done what he did, there would not be a country here today!

# Summations
# Appeal North American Blacks

*John Hanson First President — Capital Builders — Rich Slaves*

After the war John Hanson removed all foreign troops from the united States. Further he designed the Great Presidential Seal that is still being used unaltered till the present. He created the very office of president, into the complete form that all presidents after him have stepped into, even into the modern times.

At the end of the conflict, and the founding of the colonies into states, John Hanson signed the bill that caused Thanksgiving Day to come into existence. Also after the war and independence, and the forming of the presidency, there was still no national capital, only state capitals. Before his death John Hanson designated a ten (10) square mile portion of his own land in Maryland, as a future District for the building of a capital for the collective united States. This ten square mile area was called a district because it was an entity unto it's self. The District was Autonomous from all thirteen states, but the District was the tie that bound all of the states, into a united group of States. John Hanson accomplished mostly all of his great deeds, within the one year of his being the first president, and the father of this country, the united States.

*See a picture of this Black man John Hanson on the Library of Congress website: (LCWEB2.LOC.Gov), which the picture will be found under "American Memories," under "Search." Type in "John Hanson," and select #3 (His picture).* This extraordinary man supported by thousands of you other Blacks, was literally the founder and savior of North America. John Hanson is also sitting at the central presidential table, on the back of the American two dollar bill.

### Capital Builders

**Blacks**: From Nimrod to Benjamin Banikker, you Black men have been capital builders for the Caucasian Race from their very inception. Wooly headed Nimrod the Assyrian, the Great Light (*Isa. 9:2; 23:13*) built Ur/Babel a great city, for the pale ancestors of the ones you built North America for. The Moors as a Great Light built all of the capitals in Europe, for the pale ones. Now you as a Great Light, in the form of Benjamin Banniker and hundreds of other Blacks, surveyed and built Washington D. C. as a capital, for the pale ones, on the land that John Hanson had donated. Eight years after Ben Banikker death the British burned Washington down (1814), but hundreds of other Blacks rebuilt Washington D.C., on the same basis as Benjamin Banniker had built the city of Washington before.

### Broken Promise

**Blacks**: After the war but before Washington had even been built for the first time, a Constitution had been written, that abolished Black and White slavery, and included all enslaved as citizens. This abolishment of slavery contract was written into the first constitutional draft, but was later removed by Jefferson. Washington and the other planters refused to set you their captives (prisoners) Black and White free (*Isa. 14:17*). (*Charles Bouvier 1853, Page 205*).

Hanson and thousands of other Blacks had saved the American Caucasians from the British, and all that you Blacks wanted in return was for the slave owners to set their Black, and White slaves free after independence. Washington, Jefferson and most of the others land holding slave owners had promised that they would release those in bondage over a short period of time.

# Summations
# Appeal North American Blacks

*Rich Slaves — Divide and Conquer — Willie Lynch*

### George Washington is a Freed Slave
**Blacks**: Before the war had been won, George Washington, and all of the other slave owners were not citizens. They were British Colonial house slaves. Their Black, and White slaves, set George and the other slave owners free, by defeating the British. Those Black and White slaves that fought and won the revolutionary war now expected to be paid, and set free, also by their owners, who they had made free from the British!

You poor and enslaved Blacks along with Whites were the troops who had defeated the British forces. But after the war the same Black and White troops had to rebel, and threaten to overthrow the new government, of their White masters. The wealthy rulers over the government refused to pay the soldiers the wages that had been promised to them, nor would they set them free, Black or White. But eventually Black and White slave army threatened the lives of the old slave owning senators, and congressmen and forced them to keep their word to pay the Blacks and Whites or die.

But then the old land owners made the Whites slaves think that they were free, because they made them false citizens. But the old planters refused you Blacks citizenship, and kept you prisoners. This was the start of the old White slave owners vow, to set a division between you Black and White slaves. The old slave masters ou Black, and White slaves would never ever get their heads together, to come against the slavers again. The prohibiting against you Blacks being citizens was the first step, in dividing you.

### Divide and Conquer Both
**Blacks**: The prohibition against Blacks being citizens was a double trick, on the White masses to make them think that they were no longer slaves, you Blacks, because they thought they were now "citizens," and no longer slaves. The actuality was that both Black and White masses were still slaves, but now they became a house divided. The only sure thing for slaves is death and taxes. True citizens have never paid taxes.

The only true citizens ever in North America are the hand full of wealthy land owners. They have never paid one single penny in taxation, it is you Black and White slaves that pay even in the most modern time for the upkeep of the hand full, who still rule over the entire masses, Black and White alike. All Tax Payers, are Tribute Payers, are slaves. Citizen are not taxed, but slaves are.

From the earliest time in independence, the privileged have designed it that the two divided slave masses never get their heads together, to figure out that you both have been fooled.

Between independence (1777) and the Uncivil War (1865), many laws, codes, and rules were enacted that forever drove a wedge between the White slave masses, and you Blacks.

The White slaves fellow soldiers that once fought beside you were tricked into keeping themselves, and you Blacks in perpetual slavery. The sadness of it all was that you Blacks had been trying to raise these mentally dead Caucasians, and now these White slave were being used

# Summations
# Appeal North American Blacks

### Negroes — Willie Lynch

to pull you Blacks down, into the Darkness with them! The wealthy who instructed them were the ones you had successfully raised, Washington, Jefferson, and the others, that you had raised to being Masons.

Inspite of all that those old Masons did to suppress you, they were still feeling threatened, on Monday, Jan. 16, 1832, when Senator Henry Berry a delegate of the state of Virginia addressed the Senate, to say that all Light must be shut out from you Blacks, so that Whites (wealthy) will finally be safe (*Isa. 6:10*). All Blacks must be turned into Negroes (Mentally Dead).

### Negroes

**Blacks**: The first and only true Negroes are the entire Caucasian Race! The word Negro is the Greek word Necro (νεκρω), which means "Dead." This "Dead" is a mental death, from the origin of the Caucasian Race. The Lord changed his son Cain from a Black man, to a Negro, when he marked Cain with a permanent pale leprosy, and Cain lost his soul (Solar Association). This all occurred in the land of Nod, the place of mental sleep, or mental death.

The Lord wanted the eyes, ears, and minds of Marked Cain and his pale children closed (*Isa. 6:10*). All in Nod, nodded in mental sleep, and mental death. From Nimrod to Benjamin Banniker, you as Black saviors have not been able to raise Caucasians. Now the Mentally Dead (Necro / Negro) Caucasian masses were being used to infect Blacks into being Necroes, or Negroes, like themselves. The poor White masses were divided against each other, and full of self hatred. You Blacks would have to be infected with self hatred also.

### Willie Lynch

**Blacks**: There is a document called the Willie Lynch Letter. The Willie Lynch letter addresses a scheme to turn you Blacks into self haters. The Willie Lynch letter was instructions to the pale slaves in charge over you Blacks, to set a division between every element of your society. The overseers were instructed to outline the differences between each of you Blacks, and to make them bigger. They were instructed to use **fear**, **distrust**, and **envy**, to control you. They were given a lists of differences that they could use to control you. On the list was Age, Color (Shade), Intelligence, Size, Sex, Plantation Size, Attitude of Owners, the location of where you as slaves lived. Whether you lived in the Valley, or on a Hill, in the North, South, East, or West. Do you have Fine Hair, or Course Hair, are you Tall, or Short? With the overseers having this outline of differences, they were instructed that Distrust was stronger than Trust, and that Envy is stronger than Respect, or Admiration. After receiving this indoctrination for a year Black self hatred would be self refueling, and self regenerating for hundreds of years. The White overseers were instructed to pit the Old Black Male against the Young Black Male, and the Young Males against the Old Males, and the Light Skin slave against the Dark Skin slave, and the Dark against the Light. They were to use the Female against the Male, and the Male against the Female. The White overseers were to distrust all of you Blacks, but you Blacks were to be conditioned to love,

# Summations
## Appeal North American Blacks

Willie Lynch — Pork

you intensely for one year, that you Blacks would refuel your own self hatred, and be mentally damaged permanently!

The poor disenfranchise Caucasians could not hold you down in the ditch, without being down in the ditch with you! But the Caucasians must still be kept separate from Blacks even though they were in the same hole with you! The Jim Crow Laws, compelled lawful separation between the White and Black masses. Your overseers the poor Whites, and you the enslaved Blacks would be separated from each other, even in the same ditch together!

### Pork

**Blacks**: But long before Willie Lynch, and Jim Crow, there was pork. Pork is the flesh of the swine. Many of the Host of the Lord lost their physical bodies, and the Lord told them to go down and have dominion inside of all of the animals, that they could subdue (*Gen. 1:26, 28*). The Lord's Host could only subdue the unclean scavenger animals of the air (buzzards etc.), land (swine etc.), and sea (crabs, lobsters, shrimps, etc.)(*Deut. 14:3-21*).

The process of making you Negroes (mentally dead) actually began on ships, in the middle passage, when some of you Blacks were being brought across the Atlantic, in enslavement. The slavers on the ships attempted to feed you pork (Swine) meat. You knew that the pork was Deviled, and absolutely refused to eat it! Many of you starved to death rather than eat it. Many of you jumped from the ship decks and drowned, so as not to eat pork. The enslavers were so very determined to get pork into your system, that they invented a device, to force feed you a pork soup. This instrument called a **Speculum Orum** (See In The Mouth), was used to break the front teeth out, and force the mouth open. Then they would pinch your nose shut, and pour the pork soup down your throat. You would have to swallow the pork drink, so as not to suffocate.

Why would Pale Christians force you to eat pork? (*Deut. 14:8*)? Why would the masses of the Christian Caucasian Race also eat pork themselves? The Caucasians used Paul, Peter, and Jesus to justify pork consumption: Paul said if you are not weak minded, it won't bother you to eat anything (). Peter said the Lord told him to eat unclean animals (*Acts 10:12-14*). Jesus is made to say that everything thing that you eat comes out of you (*Matt. 15:17*). Yet Jesus had to cast Demons out of a man who became possessed, when he ate pork. The cast out Devils begged, and Jesus allow them, to reenter the hogs of a near by herd (*Matt. 8:30, 31; Mark 15:13*). These Devils in the swine were some of the Host of the Lord, who had become disembodied. The Demon Host of the Lord were Gods (*I Sam. 4:8*). The Lord's commanded that the Israelis not to eat pork (*Deut. 14:7*), and that they have no other Gods before him (*Ex. 20:3*). These two were the same commandment from two directions. For those who were in bondage to the Lord, to eat pork was for them to consume the spirits of some of his Hosts (Devil Gods). The Israelis would then have Gods (Devils) inside themselves before the Lord.

The pale Christian enslavers poured the pork soup down your throats, and you Blacks became Demon possessed, like them. The Demons were in control, inside your bodies, like they control

# Summations
# Appeal North American Blacks

*Pork — Unraisable Cain — Final Betrayal*

Caucasians, and you Blacks took on the nature of the Devils, like the Caucasians.

No one have to break your teeth out to feed you pork now, but you will break someone's teeth out, if they keep you from having pork. It is the Demons inside you eating pork to replenish themselves in you. Pork is a narcotic, and is addictive. The same Demons that Jesus cast out of the man, into the hogs, are the same Demons that are now in you Blacks of North America! When you ate pork you were gradually converted from being a prisoner who wanted to be made free. Now you are willing slaves. The North American Caucasians, you tried to raise have caused you to fall.

## Unraisable Cain

**Blacks**: After thousands of years, from Nimrod to Benjamin Banniker, and beyond, you wooly headed Black men have failed to Raise Cain, his pale leper children. Each time you have attempted to raised the pale ones from a dead horizontal, towards a living perpendicular, the Lord through his agents have cast them back down into his Darkness again.

The final conclusion is that the entire Caucasian Race is unraisable. Be they Masons, or Elks, or Roscrucian. Be they Jewish Rabbis, Catholic Priests, or Protestant and Baptist Ministers.

Jesus had said two thousand years ago, "go not in the Way (Darkness / דרכה) of the Gentiles (*Matt. 10:5*). You gave the Caucasian Race six major civilizings. You brought Light into their World, the World of the Lord's Darkness, but Mankind (Caucasian Race) love the Darkness of the Lord (*John 3:19*).

The entire Human (Caucasian) Race is unrepentant. Each time Blacks have saved them they have murdered or enslaved their saviors. After Nimrod saved them, they crucified him because it pleased the Lord to bruise him (*Isa. 53:10*). The later Pale Greeks murdered the wooly headed brown Archaic (First) Greeks who saved them, and took their identity. The pale Romans murdered the wooly headed brown Etruscans who had saved them, and then claimed that they were the source of what the Etruscans had accomplished. The same pale Romans murdered Jesus, and founded a religion, to celebrated his murder, as being the salvation of their World, that he came to destroy. The pale Europeans murdered most of their wooly headed brown Moorish saviors in Europe, and then the pale ones claimed the accomplishments of the Moors in Europe. Now after you had saved these Caucasians in North America, they are deep in the process of destroying you, and claiming that pale ones are the source of the building of North America.

The Gentiles killed Jesus also, because he said: "go not in the way (Darkness / דרכה) of the Gentiles (Pale Ones)(*Matt. 10:5*)." The Gentile's entire history has been to kill the wooly headed brown people, who save them!

The Caucasian Race as permanently unraisable Necro (Negroes), have infected you Blacks to make you Negroes (Mentally Dead) like themselves.

## Final Betrayal

**Blacks**: Black masses of North America you have no friends on the entire planet, including so called Black leaders. All who pretend to be your friends have failed you. The Christian God that

# Summations
# Appeal North American Blacks

*Final Betrayal — Meek— Revelations*

you serve has never been your friend at any time, from deep chain slavery, to your so called freedom. You are full of pork and are possessed, with Demons that tell you to continue to suffer.

Your Black ministers are Full of the self hatred of the Willie Lynch program, and they teach you to hate your selves, and to love your enemies.

The prime operative of the American government is to protect it's citizens (there are only a few). You Black so-called citizens are at least supposed to be protect by the government! But North America has invited Black, Brown, Red, and Yellow vultures from around the entire planet, to come and share with it's self, to dine upon your flesh. They have come to drink your blood, and to eat your flesh. Chinese, so-called Chaldeans, Arabs, Africans, etc., all set up shop down in your noncommunities, to reap the harvest of your devastated neighborhoods.

The forefather's of all of these diverse people were Black like you. All of the ancient cultures were built by those Blacks who were their ancestors. They all lose face, by coming to participate in your destruction. And as pitiful as they all see you, they are all actually vulnerable to you.

On the day that you decide to raise from the dead, is the day that their prosperity and livelihood comes to an end. You as the Black masses in North America are the foundation for this entire American system, and all that you the Black masses have to do to bring it to a halt, is to raise yourselves from a dead horizontal to a living perpendicular. No people who are depending for their livelihood on you shall survive your mental waking up. The only ones who shall survive will be those who can stop hating you. Hatred of you and therefore hatred of their ancient Black ancestors, will prevent them from the possibility of associating with you, on a positive basis. That is very good. North America has been a final test in an experiment that began in the sun. All have come to North America to take advantage of you Blacks, who do not seem to be able to defend yourselves. In the end they are victims of their own twisted natures. Be they Hindus, Buddhist, or Judeo/Christians. How better to test a nature, then to allow it to think that it can do whatever it please, without any kind of repercussions. Each person here have their own record as to how they have thought, and acted against you Blacks in North America, who are the only ones who have held the line in the experiment, from the sun, all the way down the line of time, to North America. Now that everyone and everything has been tested it is time for you to wake up out of the dream, or death state that you have been in, to allow the experiment to come to a satisfactory conclusion. You must be born again, inwardly. As you Blacks have been brought down from Light to Darkness, from prisoners to slaves, you must now reverse the process, and raise you selves from the dead. You are the meek who shall reinsert your planet, the entire earth. You have all kinds of wealth, but you have lost yourselves. America has shut your eyes, your ears, and your minds (*Isa. 6:10*), less you convert and be healed (*Isa. 6:10*). It has gained you nothing to gain the whole World of the Lord, and lost your own souls (Solar Association). But you can raise your own selves from the dead. you can convert yourself and be healed. Raise yourself from the mentally dead state of being called Necro or Negro. Alpha and Omega, once you have reopened your Single Eye, your whole body will be full of Light again (*Matt. 6:24*). This is the revelation for the ending of the World of the Lord.

# Summations
# Revelations

Alpha/Omega — First and Last — fulfillment — Apocalypse

### Alpha/Omega

The Revelation is: As it was in the beginning, so shall it be in the end. Blacks who are the beginners of the planet, who made themselves last inside the World System, are becoming first again as the World comes to an end. The first made themselves last, and now full circle Blacks are becoming first again (*Matt. 19:30, 20:8, 20:16*). Revelation, Revolution (Circuit) the Alpha and Omega, the beginning and the end, full circle is all within the same great day of the sun. The experiment has come full (fulfilled) circle. And full circle the satisfied experiment is being completely reconciled, without any contradictions.

### Fulfillment

Revelation (Revolution) is the revealing of all that has occurred full circle since the solar origin. Fulfillment (מלא) Strong's #4390 means "full," "complete," "accomplished." Jesus (Yeshua) made the statement that he did not come to destroy the Law, but came to fulfill, or make the Law complete again (*Matt. 5:17*). This statement implied that the Law had been "broken (*John 10:35*). The Lord the Almighty, the Fallen One (Felon / פלא) broke the Law (*Nu. 24:4, 14*). Jesus came to fulfill (fix) the Law that the Lord has broken (*Matt. 5:17*). The Law is universal, which means alpha/omega, without beginning or end, a circle. Thus the broken Law is a broken circle, or circuit. The break causes there to be a began and an end, at the break points. The Lord began his World by breaking the Law, and Jesus came to end the World of the Lord by fixing (fulfilling) the break in the Law. Jesus reminded the Israelis that the circuit of the Law (Torah) must no longer be broken (*John 10:34, 35*).

### Apocalypse

Apocalypse means "Covers Off," which means to Reveal, or expose. Revelation (Exposure) is the new name for the old Bible/Torah book called Apocalypse. The Bible/Torah a "broken," book has a back and front "cover," and has a beginning and an ending.

No one will deny that God has no beginning or end. As such the "word of God" must be Alpha and Omega (Eternal), without beginning or end. The Bible/Torah have a beginning and end, because it is the Book of the Lord, not the Book of God. For the Lord's Book the Bible/Torah to even mimic the Book of God, it must have it's "covers removed." Then the "uncovered" (Revealed) Bible/Torah must be made circular, with no beginning or end. With the covers removed the end of last book (Revelations/Revolutions) must be brought around trailing the rest of the Bible/Torah behind it. The end of Revelations must then be fused to the beginning of Genesis, to form a circular revolving seamless eternal book.

With the Bible/Torah in a circular (Circuit) form, Revelations become the book before Genesis, and Genesis cease to be a beginning. As a complete circuit, the Bible/Torah illuminates, and began to revolve/reveal, on its own axis. As the circular book turns, it automatically began to reorder all the information contained in it's circular form.

That is when Apocalypses (covers off) becomes synonymous with "destruction," for all of the crafting in the Bible/Torah is destroyed, as the circular book automatically reexpose all of the

# Summations
# Revelations

Apocalypse — Rendering to Ceasar — World

information that was hidden, when the chronicles were broken up, mixed up, and formed into the "books" of the Bible/Torah.

With the Bible/Torah being seamless and circular, the war in the heavens in Revelations is now before Genesis (*Rev. 12:7*). The Lord's destruction of the planet is also before Genesis, just after the war when he was cast down to the planet (*Rev. 12:9; Isa.24:1, 3-6*). The destroyed condition of the planet (*Gen. 1:1-5*) cease to be a "creation," and becomes a description of how the planet looked before Geneses, after the Lord had destroy it (*Isa. 24:1, 3-6*)!

Thus the false "Creation" at Gen. 1:26, 27 is exposed in the circular book, for there were millions on this planet, and on other planets in the solar system, before Genesis 1:26, 27. Those on other planets would come down later, on "Fiery Thrones," or Space Crafts, to a tribunal against the Lord, This was around the time of the birth of Cain (*Dan. 7:10*). Thus a **Creation** at the beginning of Genesis and it's companion **Evolution** are the opposite sides of the same counterfeit coin.

### Rendering to Caesar (Fulfillment)

Jesus (Yeshua) looked at that counterfeit coin, and said render to Caesar that which belongs to Caesar, and to God what belongs to God (*Matt. 22:21*). What he really meant was to render to the Lord, what belongs to the Lord, and to God what belongs to God. The Lord and his World is on the outside (*II Chron. 5:6*), and God and his kingdom is on the inside (*Luke 17:21*). He who is within (God) is greater than he who is without, in his World (Lord)(*I John 4:4; II Cor. 5:6*).

What belongs to the Lord is his World, the physical illusion, and all of it's counterfeit contents (nothingness). God is projecting the outer physical illusion. The outer illusion that is being projected, including the Lord, all belong to God. God can reclaim the illusion by ceasing to project it. Then there shall be no more sacrificing of the good and clean, for the preservation of the filth of the World of the Lord. North America is the finality of it all.

### World

America seems to have existed forever. Yet it has a birth certificate. North America did not exist until wooly headed Black men, and women founded it, for those pale ones who were dumped as convicts along the entire eastern seaboard, of what became North America (*Isa. 23:13*). Going back in time America cease to exist

It seems as if Pale Europe has existed for ever. Yet it has a birth certificate. Pale Europe did not exist, until wooly headed Black Moors founded it for those Caucasians who wandered about the wilderness, of Paleo Europe (*Isa. 23:13*). Going back in time Pale Europe also cease to exist, like the Americas.

Eternal Rome seems to have existed forever. Yet Rome has a birth certificate. Rome and all that it ever was did not exist, until wooly headed Black Etruscans founded it for the those pale ones who dwelled in the wilderness around the Etruscan cities (*Isa. 23:13*). Going back in time Rome and all that it ever was cease to exist.

Appeals

# Summations
# Revelations

*World — Resurrection — Races — End of Earth*

Pale Greece seems to have existed forever. Yet it has a birth certificate. Pale Greece did not exist until the wooly headed brown Archaic (First) Greeks invited the pale ones, who had dwelled in the wilderness, to dwell in Archaic Greek cities (*Isa. 23:13*). Going back in time Pale Greece cease to exist.

It would seem that Ur/Babel may have existed before the beginning of time. Yet Ur/Babel has a birth certificate. Behold Nod the land of the pale Chaldean children of Marked Cain; this people were not until wooly headed Nimrod the Assyrian founded it for them, who dwelt in the wilderness of Nod. The Lord brought it to ruins (*Isa. 23:13*). Going back in time Ur/Babel ceased to exist.

## Races

The **Caucasian Race** seems to have existed forever. Yet they have a birth certificate. The Caucasian Race did not exist until the Lord marked his son, wooly headed brown Cain with permanent Pale Leprosy (*Gen. 4:15*), and Cain passed it on to his descendants. Going back in time before Cain was marked, there was no Pale or Caucasian race.

It would seem that there have been other **Races** on this planet forever. Yet races have a birth certificate. Races did not exist on this planet until there were continents

It would seem as if continents have existed on this planet forever. Yet continents have birth certificates. Going back in time there were no continents, until the Lord exploded Assiah, and turned Assiah into Ertz (Earth), or continents (*Isa. 24:1, 3-6; Gen. 1:10*). Before the Lord exploded Assiah there were no Races, or Continents. There were just the Aboriginal wooly headed Gods.

It would seem that the **planets** have existed forever. Yet the entire solar planetary system has a birth date. The planets did not exist until they were brought out of Assiah, the mother planet, and were set into orbit around the solar. Going back before that time there were no planet, except Assiah, for all other planets were inside of Assiah.

## End of Earth

Just as all planets were in Assiah, all the present people (races) were in the original wooly headed Black/Brown inhabitants of this planet. All planets in the solar system had been removed from this planet, Assiah before any people came out of the original inhabitants. Thus all people must return to their mother and father people, the original people of the planet, before the planets can began to return.

That is why people from all over the planet are merging in North America. Without knowing it they are here to make a choice by their nature, to either continue to be like they are here to assist the pale ones, or to return to being like their wooly headed Black mothers and fathers.

The ozone layer is thinning out to allow more of the intensity of the solar Black Light to reach the surface of the planet, to make it more pliable and fervent to start the process of the continents coming back together again.

It does not matter if those who have mutated away to paleness and straight hair resist becoming

Summations

# Summations
# Revelations (Middle)

### *Assiah — One Hundred Forty Four Thousand*

Black and wooly again. The Ultra Violet (Black Light) from the sun will sort it all out. The end of continents is the end of countries and nationalities. There will just be original people on the land, and the radiation from the sun will increase in proportion to how close the continents are back to their place around Eden (Africa). Wooly hair, and brown to black complexions were the original garments of the original inhabitants of the planet. Ultraviolet, or Black light from the sun does not harm the original form. Thus those who are on the continents must resort back to being wooly and brown to correspond to the increased intensity of the sun. The Meek (wooly brown) shall reinherit their planet, in peace (*Matt. 5:5, Psalms 37:11, Rev. 1:14*).

### Assiah

The end of Ertz (Earth) or "continents" is the return of all land masses (continents) to their original place around Eden (Africa), and then the return of the moon to it's origin in the north polar region, the old home of the "Moon (מון)," or "Prodigy (מון)," of the planet. When the moon returns, it shall be the north polar region again, and Eden (Africa) shall be the south polar region again, and the planet shall rotate on that old axis again. The planet will then reseat in it's old orbit, and be back in it's proper course around the sun again (*Psalms 82:5*). Traces of the old magnetic lines of the old equator run north to south through the central United States. With the planet complete again, the old equator shall pass around the planet, through central North America again. This will be approximately the end of Races. For when the continents have touched the four sides of Eden (Africa) again, the intense Black Light or Ultra Violet radiation will have sorted out all, leaving only wooly headed Black people alive on the entire surface of the planet. Only Solar (Soul) Beings can reattain (return) to the solar or sun. All of the original souls from the sun were wooly and brown. Woe to those who have lost their own souls (Solar Associations)(*Mark 8:36*).

### One Hundred Forty Four Thousand (144,000)

There will be remaining perhaps only the original one hundred and forty four thousand beings who brought the planet out of the sun (*Rev. 7:4*). By this time they will have stripped away their "coats of skins (*Gen. 3:21*)," and become Invisible (Gods / אלוהים) again. They will have the seal which is the activated Single Eye in their foreheads (*Rev. 7:3*), and they will be firey beings full of Light (*Matt. 6:12*). These ones will bring each planets back in it's proper sequence, that it went out into the solar system. All the planets shall be brought back, the last planet first, down to the first planet last. Thus the first shall be last and the last shall be first (*Matt. 19:30*).

Thus there shall be a new heaven, and a new Earth, which is Assiah again, firey and ready to be carried back into the sun again. All that have a beginning has an end. Only the unchanged survives, and can attain back to that which is beyond endings. From naked wooly headed brown Adam, to naked wooly headed brown Adam, from beginning to end, Eternity with satisfaction, an experiment completed full circle.

www.ingramcontent.com/pod-product-compliance
Lightning Source LLC
Chambersburg PA
CBHW081758300426
44116CB00014B/2168